Fifth Edition

An Introduction to

MANAGEMENT SCIENCE

Quantitative Approaches to Decision Making

DAVID R. ANDERSON
University of Cincinnati

DENNIS J. SWEENEY
University of Cincinnati

THOMAS A. WILLIAMS
Rochester Institute of Technology

West Publishing Company
St Paul   New York   Los Angeles   San Francisco

A study guide has been developed to assist you in mastering concepts presented in this text. The study guide reinforces concepts by presenting them in condensed concise form. Additional illustrations and examples are also included. The study guide is available from your local bookstore under the title, *Study Guide to Accompany An Introduction to Management Science: Quantitative Approaches to Decision Making*, fifth edition, prepared by John A. Lawrence, Jr., and Barry Alan Pasternack.

COPYRIGHT © 1976, 1979, 1982, 1985, 1988 by WEST PUBLISHING CO.

50 West Kellogg Boulevard
P.O. Box 64526
St. Paul, Minnesota 55164–1003

95 94 93 92 91 90 89   8 7 6 5 4 3

Library of Congress Cataloging in Publication Data

Anderson, David Ray, 1941–
    An introduction to management science: Quantitative
    Approaches to decision making/David R. Anderson, Dennis
    J. Sweeney, Thomas A. Williams.
    p.   cm

    Bibliography: p.
    Includes index.
    ISBN 0-314-62969-6
        1. Management Science Mathematical models.
I. Sweeney, Dennis J.   II. Williams, Thomas Arthur, 1944–
III. Title.
HD30.25.A53   1988   658.4'03—dc19
                           87-269341
                           CIP

To Our Parents

CONTENTS

3

Linear Programming: Sensitivity Analysis and Computer Solution/69

4

Linear Programming Applications/109

5

Linear Programming: The Simplex Method/165

6

Simplex-Based Sensitivity Analysis and Duality/217

7

Transportation, Assignment, and Transshipment Problems/248

⑧

Integer Linear Programming/317

9

Network Models/357

10

Project Management: PERT/CPM/387

11

Inventory Models/443

12

Computer Simulation/499

13

Waiting Line Models/541

14

Decision Analysis/569

15

Utility and Decision Making/611

16

Forecasting/629

Markov Processes/677

Dynamic Programming/701

Calculus-Based Solution Procedures/731

Epilogue

Management Science and Decision Support Systems/771

PREFACE

The purpose of this fifth edition, as with previous editions, is to provide students with a sound conceptual understanding of the role that management science plays in the decision-making process. The focus is on the part of management science referred to as quantitative approaches to decision making. The text describes the many quantitative methods that have been developed over the years, explains how they work, and shows how they can be applied and interpreted by the decision maker.

We have written this book with the needs of the nonmathematician in mind; it is applications oriented. In each chapter a problem is described in conjunction with the quantitative procedure being introduced. The development of the quantitative technique or model includes applying it to the problem in order to generate a solution or recommendation. We have found that this approach helps to motivate the student by demonstrating not only how the procedure works, but also how it can contribute to the decision-making process.

CHANGES IN THE FIFTH EDITION

In preparing the fifth edition we have been careful to maintain the overall format and approach of the previous editions. However, based upon our own classroom experience and suggestions from users of previous editions, a number of significant changes have been made to enhance the content, organization, and readability of the text.

Complete Revision of Linear Programming

Chapters 2–4 now provide an earlier focus on problem formulation, sensitivity analysis, and the use of computer software in solving linear programming problems. Chapter 2 introduces the graphical method for solving linear programming problems; a new Chapter 3 provides a complete integration of modeling, computer solution, sensitivity analysis, and the interpretation of computer output; and Chapter 4 describes how selected decision-making problems can be formulated and solved as linear programs. Chapters 5 and 6 then show how the simplex method is used to solve linear programs and to develop the standard sensitivity analysis. Duality is also covered in Chapter 6. This new organization provides greater flexibility for instructors who do not want to teach the simplex method, since Chapters 2–4 now provide a complete introduction to linear programming without discussing the simplex solution procedure. On the other hand, those who want to include the simplex method have two chapters devoted to this topic.

Linear Programming Illustrations and Applications

In this edition we have made a major effort to further improve on the readability and pedagogy of the text. For example, in Chapter 2 a new problem that involves a mixture of constraint forms has been developed to introduce the minimization problem. In Chapter 3 the material on sensitivity analysis and computer solution has been significantly expanded; in Chapter 4, new applications have been added; and in Chapters 5 and 6 a new problem has been developed in order to minimize the computational (number crunching) details associated with teaching the simplex method.

Transportation, Assignment, and Transshipment Problems

In this edition the material on the transportation, assignment, and transshipment problems has been combined into one chapter. For each problem, the discussion begins by showing how to develop a linear programming model. Special-purpose solution procedures are then presented for the transportation and assignment problems to demonstrate the streamlined solution procedures that are possible because of the special problem structure. Users that only want to treat these problems as special cases of the general linear programming approach can do so by skipping the sections on the special purpose algorithms.

Case Problems

Another significant new feature of this edition is the addition of case problems to twelve of the chapters. These case problems provide the student with the opportunity to attempt a larger-scale problem for which a computer solution is generally required. A managerial report is required, and questions at the end of each of the cases suggest important issues to be addressed in the student's analysis and recommendations.

Decision Analysis and Utility

The chapter on decision theory has been renamed "Decision Analysis" in order to reflect the focus of the chapter on applications. The chapter content has been significantly reworked; for example, computations associated with the expected monetary value approach are now presented directly on the decision tree.

This edition of the text further expands on the importance of decision analysis techniques in the decision making process with the addition of a chapter devoted to utility analysis. The student is introduced to types of decision problems for which the expected monetary value criterion does not lead to the best decision alternative. The chapter includes a discussion of the meaning of utility, shows how to develop utilities for monetary payoffs, and discusses the differences between risk avoiders and risk takers.

Other Major Changes

Many of the other chapters in the text have been carefully revised in order to take advantage of all the input we have had from users of previous editions. Some of the specific changes are:

1. The presentation of computer output has been expanded. LINDO/PC is used to solve linear and integer programming problems. Output from *The Management Scientist*™ is presented in the other chapters.

2. A revised labeling procedure for the shortest-route problem is now presented in Chapter 9 on network models.
3. A new section has been added to Chapter 10 to introduce the student to the critical path procedure without the complication of probabilistic activity times.
4. The section in Chapter 11 involving the single-period inventory model has been reworked to better illustrate the incremental analysis method.
5. Chapter 13 has been revised to explain in more detail the difference between single-channel and multiple-channel waiting lines.
6. Chapter 16 now includes a revised section on forecasting with trend and seasonal components.
7. New problems have been added and existing ones revised; approximately 20 percent of the problems are new to this edition. As was true in the previous editions, the problems are suggestive of the types of situations in which the methods can be applied. Many are scaled-down versions of real-life problems.

PREREQUISITE

The mathematical prerequisite for this text is a course in algebra. An introductory knowledge of probability and statistics would be desirable, but not necessary, for Chapters 10–17. Only Chapter 19, which discusses calculus-based solution procedures and which we consider optional, requires a knowledge of differential calculus.

Throughout the text we have utilized generally accepted notation for the topic being covered. In this regard students who pursue study beyond the level of this text will find the difficulties of reading more advanced material minimized. To assist in further study, a bibliography is included in the backmatter of the book.

COURSE OUTLINE FLEXIBILITY

The text has been designed to enhance the instructor's flexibility in selecting topics to meet specific course needs. The single-quarter and single-semester outlines that follow are a sampling of the many options available.

One-quarter outline stressing linear programming, model development, and applications.

Introduction (Chapter 1)
Introduction to Linear Programming (Chapters 2 and 3)
Linear Programming Applications (selected portions of Chapters 4 and 7)
Forecasting (Chapter 16)
Project Management: PERT/CPM (Chapter 10)
Inventory Models (Chapter 11)
Computer Simulation (Chapter 12)

The instructor in a one-semester course who wants to focus on model development and other applications could either spend more time on the applications in Chapter 4 or cover additional topics. One possible outline, stressing linear programming, model development, and applications, would be

Introduction (Chapter 1)
Introduction to Linear Programming (Chapters 2 and 3)

Linear Programming Applications (Chapter 4)
Simplex Method (Chapters 5 and 6)
Transportation, Assignment, and Transshipment Models (Chapter 7)
Integer Linear Programming (Chapter 8)
Project Management: PERT/CPM (Chapter 10)
Inventory Models (Chapter 11)
Computer Simulation (Chapter 12)
Decision and Utility Analysis (Chapters 14 and 15)

ANCILLARIES

A complete package of support materials accompanies the text: an Instructor's Manual; a Study Guide, coauthored by John A. Lawrence and Barry Alan Pasternack, California State University at Fullerton; a Test Bank, prepared by Constance McLaren, Indiana State University; transparency masters; and *The Management Scientist*™, an IBM-compatible software package, capable of solving a variety of management science problems. This menu-driven software package is new to the fifth edition and has been designed to provide a high degree of user flexibility, including the ability to easily save and modify problems. We believe that the applications orientation of the text, combined with this package of support materials, provides a solid framework for introducing students to quantitative methods.

ACKNOWLEDGMENTS

We owe a debt to many of our colleagues and friends for their helpful comments and suggestions during the development of this and previous editions. Among these are E. Leonard Arnoff, Uttarayan Bagchi, Edward Baker, Norman Baker, James Bartos, Richard Beckwith, Stanley Brooking, Jeffrey Camm, Thomas Case, John Eatman, Ron Ebert, Peter Ellis, Lawrence Ettkin, Jim Evans, Robert Garfinkel, Stephen Goodman, Jack Goodwin, Richard Gunther, David Hott, Raymond Jackson, Bharat Kolluri, Darlene Lanier, John Lawrence, Jr., Phillip Lowery, Prem Mann, Kamlesh Mathur, Joseph Mazzola, Richard McCready, Patrick McKeown, Constance McLaren, Edward Minieka, Alan Neebe, David Pentico, Gary Pickett, B. Madhusudan Rao, Richard Rosenthal, Carol Stamm, Willban Terpening, William Truscott, James Vigen, Ed Winkofsky, Bruce Woodworth, M. Zafer Yakin, and Cathleen Zucco.

Our associates from organizations who supplied the Management Science in Practice applications made a major contribution to the text. These individuals are cited in a credit line on the first page of each application.

We are also indebted to our editor, Mary C. Schiller, and others at West Publishing Company for their editorial counsel and support during the preparation of this text. Finally, we would like to express our appreciation to Lois Creech for her typing and secretarial support.

David R. Anderson
Dennis J. Sweeney
Thomas A. Williams
January 1988

1

Introduction

Management science, an approach to managerial decision making that is based on the scientific method, makes extensive use of quantitative analysis. A variety of names exists for the body of knowledge involving quantitative approaches to decision making; in addition to management science, another widely known and accepted name is *operations research* (OR). Today many use the terms "operations research" and "management science" interchangeably. We shall treat them as synonyms throughout the text.

The foundation for MS/OR was laid during the scientific management revolution of the early 1900s initiated by Frederic W. Taylor. But the origin of modern management science/operations research is generally attributed as occurring during the World War II period, when operations research teams were formed to deal with strategic and tactical problems faced by the military. These teams, which often consisted of people with diverse specialties (e.g., mathematicians, engineers, behavioral scientists, etc.), were joined together to solve a common problem through the utilization of the scientific method. After the war, many of these team members continued their research on quantitative approaches to decision making.

Two developments, which occurred during the post-World War II period, led to the growth and use of management science in nonmilitary organizations. First, continued research on quantitative approaches to decision making resulted in numerous methodological developments. Probably the most significant development was the discovery by George Dantzig, in 1947, of the simplex method for solving linear programming problems. Many more methodological developments followed and, in 1957, the first book on operations research was published by Churchman, Ackoff, and Arnoff.[1]

Concurrently with these methodological developments there was a virtual explosion in computing power made available through digital computers. Computers enabled practitioners to implement the methodological advances successfully to solve a large variety of industrial problems. The computer technology explosion continues; microcomputers are more powerful than the mainframe computers of the 1960s. Today, variants of the

---

[1]Churchman, C.W., R.L. Ackoff, and E.L. Arnoff, *Introduction to Operations Research*. New York, John Wiley & Sons, 1957.

post-World War II methodological developments are being used on microcomputers to solve problems larger than those solved on mainframe computers in 1960.

1.1 DOMINANCE OF THE PROBLEM

A central theme in the quantitative approach to decision making is a problem orientation. A management science problem may be as specific as improving the efficiency of a production line or as broad as establishing a long-range corporate strategy involving a combination of financial, marketing, and manufacturing operations. Nearly all projects begin with the recognition of a problem that does not have an obvious solution. Management scientists may then be asked to assist in identifying the "best" decision or solution for the problem. Reasons why a quantitative approach might be used in the decision-making process include the following:

1. The problem is complex, and the manager cannot develop a good solution without the aid of quantitative specialists.
2. The problem is very important (for example, a great deal of money is involved), and the manager desires a thorough analysis before attempting to make a decision.
3. The problem is new, and the manager has no previous experience to draw upon.
4. The problem is repetitive, and the manager saves time and effort by relying upon quantitative procedures to make the routine decision recommendations.

A survey by Thomas and DaCosta[2] showed the application (problem) areas in Table 1.1 as ones most frequently the subject of management science studies in large corpo-

TABLE 1.1
Application Areas for Management Science Studies

Area of Application	Percentage of Companies Reporting Applications in Area
Forecasting	88
Production scheduling	70
Inventory control	70
Capital budgeting	56
Transportation	51
Plant location	42
Quality control	40
Advertising and sales research	35
Equipment replacement	33
Maintenance and repair	28
Accounting procedures	27
Packaging	9

[2]Thomas, G., and J. DaCosta, "A Sample Survey of Corporate Operations Research," *Interfaces*, vol. 9, no. 4, pp. 102–111, 1979.

rations. As the survey shows, nearly all large corporations (88%) are involved in fore-casting and over 50% are utilizing quantitative approaches to production scheduling, inventory control, capital budgeting, and transportation.

Another survey by Gaither[3] reported a variety of manufacturing-related applications that have utilized quantitative techniques. The three problem areas most frequently cited were production planning and control, project planning and control, and inventory analysis.

The problem areas mentioned in both the Thomas and DaCosta and Gaither surveys by no means comprise a complete list of the applications where managers have found management science to be beneficial. However, they do indicate the wide variety of problems in which quantitative methods have been successfully applied.

1.2 QUANTITATIVE ANALYSIS AND THE DECISION-MAKING PROCESS

The role of quantitative analysis in the managerial decision-making process is perhaps best understood by considering the flowchart in Figure 1.1. Note that the process is initiated by the appearance of a problem. The manager responsible for making a decision

FIGURE 1.1
The Decision-Making Process

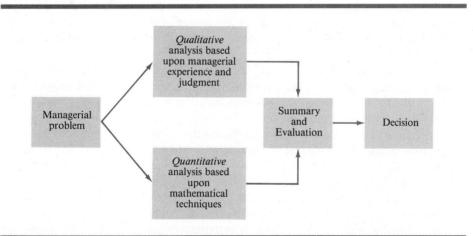

or selecting a course of action will probably make an analysis of the problem, which includes a statement of the specific goals or objectives, an identification of constraints, an evaluation of alternative decisions, and a selection of the apparent "best" decision or solution for the problem.

The analysis process employed by the manager may take two basic forms: qualitative and quantitative. The qualitative analysis is based primarily upon the manager's judgment

[3]Gaither, N., "The Adoption of Operations Research Techniques by Manufacturing Organizations," *Decision Sciences*, vol. 6, no. 4, pp. 797–813, 1975.

and experience. This type of analysis includes the manager's intuitive "feel" for the problem and is more an art than a science. If the manager has had experience with similar problems, or if the problem is relatively simple, heavy emphasis may be placed upon a qualitative analysis. However, if the manager has had little experience with similar problems, or if the problem is sufficiently important and complex, then a quantitative analysis of the problem can be a very important consideration in the manager's final decision. In the quantitative approach to the problem, an analyst will concentrate on the quantitative facts or data associated with the problem and develop mathematical expressions that describe the objectives, constraints, and relationships that exist in the problem. Then, by using one or more quantitative methods, the analyst will provide a recommendation based upon the quantitative aspects of the problem.

Both the qualitative and the quantitative analyses of a problem provide important information for the manager or decision maker. In many cases, a manager will draw upon both sources and, through a comparison and evaluation of the information, make a final decision.

While skills in the qualitative approach are inherent in the manager and usually increase with experience, the skills of the quantitative approach can be learned only by studying the assumptions and methods of management science. A manager can increase decision-making effectiveness by learning more about quantitative methodology and by better understanding its contribution to the decision-making process. The manager who is knowledgeable in quantitative decision-making procedures is in a much better position to compare and evaluate the qualitative and quantitative sources of recommendations and ultimately combine the two sources in order to make the best possible decision.

The section of Figure 1.1 entitled "Quantitative analysis based upon mathematical techniques" encompasses most of the subject matter of this text. We will consider a managerial problem, introduce the appropriate quantitative methodology, and then develop and evaluate the recommended decision.

There are several important tools, or methods, that have been found useful in the quantitative analysis phase of the decision-making process. One of your objectives in studying this book should be to develop an understanding of what these methods are, how they are used, and, most important, how they can assist the manager in making better decisions. The most frequently used quantitative methods as determined in a survey of corporate executives conducted by Forgionne[4] are listed in Table 1.2. The Forgionne findings are consistent with those in the earlier Thomas and DaCosta study. A survey by Ledbetter and Cox[5] lends further support to these findings by ranking regression (statistical analysis), linear programming, simulation, network models (PERT/CPM), queueing, dynamic programming, and game theory in order of usage.

The Gaither study of applications in manufacturing firms also supports the high frequency of utilization for statistical analysis, simulation, and linear programming. However, PERT/CPM is identified as the method most frequently used in the manufacturing firms surveyed. The manufacturing firms also report a higher than average usage of queueing theory, nonlinear programming, and integer programming.

---

[4]Forgionne, G.A., "Corporate Management Science Activities: An Update," *Interfaces*, vol. 13, no. 3, pp. 20–23, 1983.
[5]Ledbetter, W., and J. Cox, "Are OR Techniques Being Used?" *Industrial Engineering*, vol. 9, no. 2, pp. 19–21, 1977.

TABLE 1.2
The Utilization of Management Science and Operations Research Methodologies

| | Frequency of Use (% of respondents) | | |
	Never	Moderate	Frequent
Statistical	1.6	38.7	59.7
Computer simulation	12.9	53.2	33.9
PERT/CPM	25.8	53.2	21.0
Linear programming	25.8	59.7	14.5
Queueing theory	40.3	50.0	9.7
Nonlinear programming	53.2	38.7	8.1
Dynamic programming	61.3	33.9	4.8
Game theory	69.4	27.4	3.2

A survey of practitioners in government, industry, and academia was conducted by Shannon, Long, and Buckles.[6] The authors of this study asked practitioners to indicate whether or not they were familiar with the various quantitative methods and whether or not they had actually used the methods in specific applications. The results of this study are shown in Table 1.3.

Since nearly every student takes a separate course in statistical analysis, we have not included topics from this area in the text. However, we do describe and present

TABLE 1.3
Familiarity with and Use of Various Quantitative Methods by Management Science Practitioners

Method	Familiarity Rank	Usage (%)
Linear programming	1	83.8
Simulation	2	80.3
Network analysis	3	58.1
Queueing theory	4	54.7
Decision trees	5	54.7
Integer programming	6	38.5
Dynamic programming	7	32.5
Nonlinear programming	8	30.7
Markov processes	9	31.6
Replacement analysis	10	38.5
Game theory	11	13.7
Goal programming	12	20.5

[6]Shannon, R.E., S.S. Long, and B.P. Buckles, "Operations Research Methodologies in Industrial Engineering: A Survey," *AIIE Transactions*, vol. 12, no. 4, pp. 364–367, 1980.

applications for the other major quantitative methods most frequently used in decision making.

Before proceeding with the study of the specific quantitative methods, let us look more closely at the general steps that are involved in carrying out the quantitative analysis of a managerial problem.

1.3 THE QUANTITATIVE ANALYSIS PROCESS

We begin our study of quantitative approaches to decision making by considering a five-step procedure: (1) problem definition, (2) model development, (3) data preparation, (4) model solution, and (5) report generation.

Problem Definition

The problem definition step is the most critical phase of the quantitative analysis process. It usually takes imagination, teamwork, and considerable effort to transform a rather general problem description into a well-defined problem that can be approached quantitatively. For example, a broadly described "excessive inventory" problem must be clearly defined in terms of specific objectives and operating constraints before an analyst can proceed to the next step in the quantitative analysis process. User involvement is essential at this step. The management scientist must work closely with the manager or user of the results.

Model Development

Models are representations of real objects or situations. These representations, or models, can be presented in various forms. For example, a scale model of an airplane is a representation of a real airplane. Similarly, a child's toy truck is a model of a real truck. The model airplane and toy truck are examples of models that are physical replicas of real objects. In modeling terminology, physical replicas are referred to as *iconic* models.

A second classification of models includes those that are physical in form but do not have the same physical appearance as the object being modeled. Such models are referred to as *analog* models. The speedometer of an automobile is an analog model; the position of the needle on the dial represents the speed of the automobile. A thermometer is an analog model representing temperature.

A third classification of models—the primary type of model we will be studying—includes those that represent a problem by a system of symbols and mathematical relationships or expressions. Such models are referred to as *mathematical* models and are a critical part of any quantitative approach to decision making. For example, the total profit from the sale of a product can be determined by multiplying the profit per unit by the quantity sold. If we let x represent the number of units sold and P the total profit, then, with a profit of \$10 per unit, the following mathematical model defines the total profit earned by selling x units:

$$P = 10x \qquad (1.1)$$

The purpose, or value, of any model is that it enables us to draw conclusions about the real situation by studying and analyzing the model. For example, an airplane designer might test an iconic model of a new airplane in a wind tunnel in order to learn about the potential flying characteristics of the full-size airplane. Similarly, a mathematical model may be used to draw conclusions about how much profit will be earned if a specified quantity of a particular product is sold. According to the mathematical model of equation (1.1), we would expect to obtain a $30 profit by selling three units of the product.

In general, experimenting with models requires less time and is less expensive than experimenting with the real object or situation. Certainly, a model airplane is quicker and less expensive to build and study than the full-size airplane. Similarly, the above mathematical model allows a quick identification of profit expectations without requiring the manager actually to produce and sell x units. Models also have the advantage of reducing the risk associated with experimenting with the real situation. In particular, bad designs or bad decisions that cause the model airplane to crash or a mathematical model to project a $10,000 loss can be avoided in the real situation.

The accuracy of the conclusions and decisions based on a model are dependent upon how well the model represents the real situation. The more closely the model of the airplane represents the real airplane, the more accurate the conclusions and predictions about the airplane's flight characteristics will be. Similarly, the closer the mathematical model represents the company's true profit–volume relationship, the more accurate the profit projections will be.

Since this text deals with mathematical models, let us look more closely at the mathematical modeling process. When initially considering a managerial problem, we usually find that the problem definition phase leads to a specific objective, such as maximization of profits or minimization of costs, and possibly a set of restrictions or constraints, such as production capacities. The success of the mathematical model and quantitative approach will depend heavily upon how accurately the objective and constraints can be expressed in terms of mathematical equations or relationships.

A mathematical expression that describes the problem's objective is referred to as the *objective function*. For example, the profit equation $P = 10x$ would be an objective function for a firm attempting to maximize profit. A production capacity constraint would be necessary if, for instance, 5 hours are required to produce each unit and there are only 40 hours available per week. Let x indicate the number of units produced each week. The production time constraint is given by

$$5x \leq 40 \tag{1.2}$$

The value of $5x$ is the total time required to produce the x units; the symbol $\leq$ indicates that the production time required must be less than or equal to the 40 hours available.

The question or decision problem is the following: How many units of the product should be scheduled each week in order to maximize profit? A complete mathematical model for this simple production problem is

$$\begin{aligned} \text{maximize} \quad & P = 10x \quad \text{objective function} \\ \text{subject to (s.t.)} \quad & \\ & \left. \begin{array}{r} 5x \leq 40 \\ x \geq 0 \end{array} \right\} \text{constraints} \end{aligned}$$

The $x \geq 0$ constraint requires the production quantity x to be greater than or equal to zero, which simply recognizes the fact that it is not possible to manufacture a negative number of units. The optimal solution to this model can be easily calculated and is given by $x = 8$, with an associated profit of $80. This model is an example of a linear programming model. In subsequent chapters we will discuss more complicated mathematical models and learn how to solve them in situations where the answers are not nearly so obvious.

In the above mathematical model the profit per unit ($10), the production time per unit (5 hours), and the production capacity (40 hours) are environmental factors that are not under the control of the manager or decision maker. Such environmental factors, which can affect both the objective function and the constraints, are referred to as the *uncontrollable inputs* to the model. The inputs that are controlled or determined by the decision maker are referred to as the *controllable inputs* to the model. In the above example, the production quantity x is the controllable input to the model. The controllable inputs are the decision alternatives specified by the manager and thus are also referred to as the *decision variables* of the model.

Once all controllable and uncontrollable inputs are specified, the objective function and constraints can be evaluated and the output of the model determined. In this sense, the output of the model is simply the projection of what would happen if those particular environmental factors and decisions occurred in the real situation. A flowchart of how controllable and uncontrollable inputs are transformed by the mathematical model into output is shown in Figure 1.2. A similar flowchart showing the specific details of the production model is shown in Figure 1.3.

As stated earlier, the uncontrollable inputs are those the decision maker cannot influence. The specific controllable and uncontrollable inputs of a model depend upon the particular problem or decision-making situation. In the production problem the production time available, 40, is an uncontrollable input. However, if it were possible to hire more employees or use overtime, the number of hours of production time would become a controllable input and therefore a decision variable in the model.

Uncontrollable inputs either can be known exactly or can be uncertain and subject to variation. If all uncontrollable inputs to a model are known and cannot vary, the model is referred to as a *deterministic* model. Corporate income tax rates are not under the

FIGURE 1.2
Flowchart of the Process of Transforming Model Inputs Into Output

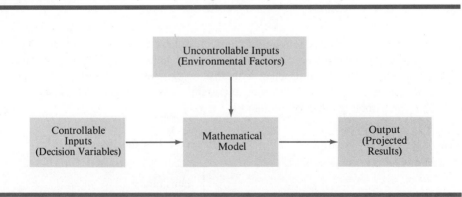

FIGURE 1.3
Flowchart for the Production Model

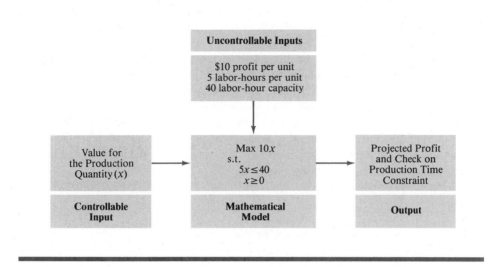

influence of the manager and thus constitute an uncontrollable input in many decision models. Since these rates are known and fixed (at least in the short run), a mathematical model with corporate income tax rates as the only uncontrollable input would be a deterministic model. The distinguishing feature of a deterministic model is that the uncontrollable input values are known in advance.

If any of the uncontrollable inputs are uncertain and subject to variation, the model is referred to as a *stochastic* model. An uncontrollable input to many production planning models is demand for the product. Since future demand may be any of a range of values, a mathematical model that treats demand with uncertainty would be called a stochastic model. In the production model the number of hours of production time required per unit, the total hours available, and the unit profit were all uncontrollable inputs. Since the uncontrollable inputs were all known to take on fixed values, the model is deterministic. If, however, the number of hours of production time per unit could vary from 3 to 6 hours depending upon the quality of the raw material, the model would be stochastic. The distinguishing feature of a stochastic model is that the value of the output cannot be determined even if the value of the controllable input is known because the specific values of the uncontrollable inputs are unknown. In this respect, stochastic models are often more difficult to analyze.

Data Preparation

The third step in the process of quantitative analysis is the preparation of the data required by the model. Data in this sense refer to the values of the uncontrollable inputs to the model. All uncontrollable inputs or data must be specified before we can analyze the model and select a recommended decision or solution for the problem.

In the production model the values of the uncontrollable inputs or data were $10 per unit for profit, 5 hours per unit for production time, and 40 hours for production capacity. In the development of the model these data values were known and were incorporated into the model as it was being developed. If the model is relatively small and the uncontrollable input values or data required are few, the quantitative analyst will probably combine model development and data preparation into one step. That is, in these situations the data values are inserted as the equations of the mathematical model are developed.

However, in many mathematical modeling situations the data, or uncontrollable input values, are not readily available. In these situations the management scientist may know that the model will need profit per unit, production time, and production capacity data, but the values are not known until the accounting, production, and engineering departments can be consulted. Rather than attempting to collect the required data as the model is being developed, the analyst will usually adopt a general notation for the model development step and then perform a separate data preparation step to obtain the uncontrollable input values required by the model.

Using the general notation

$$c = \text{profit per unit}$$
$$a = \text{production time in hours per unit}$$
$$b = \text{production capacity in hours}$$

the model development step of the production problem would have resulted in the following general model:

$$\max cx$$
$$\text{s.t.}$$
$$ax \le b$$
$$x \ge 0$$

Then a separate data preparation step to identify the values for c, a, and b would be necessary in order to complete the model.

Many inexperienced quantitative analysts assume that once the problem has been defined and a general model developed, the problem is essentially solved. These individuals tend to believe that data preparation is a trivial step in the process and can be easily handled by clerical staff. Actually, especially with large-scale models that have numerous data input values, this assumption could not be further from the truth. For example, a moderate-size linear programming model with 50 decision variables and 25 constraints will have over 1300 data elements that must be identified in the data preparation step. The time required to prepare these data and the possibility of data collection errors will make the data preparation step a critical part of the quantitative analysis process. Often a fairly large database is needed to support a mathematical model and information systems specialists become involved in the data preparation step.

Model Solution

Once the model development and data preparation steps have been completed, we can proceed to the model solution step. In this step the analyst will attempt to identify the values of the decision variables that provide the "best" output for the model. The specific decision-variable value or values providing the "best" output will be referred to as the *optimal solution* for the model. For the production problem the model solution step involves finding the value of the production quantity decision variable x that maximizes profit while not causing a violation of the production capacity constraint.

One procedure that might be used in the model solution step involves a trial-and-error approach, where the model is used to test and evaluate various decision alternatives. In the production model this would mean testing and evaluating the model under various production quantities or values of x. Referring to Figure 1.3, note that we could input trial values for x and check the corresponding output for projected profit and satisfaction of the production capacity constraint. If a particular decision alternative does not satisfy one or more of the model constraints, the decision alternative is rejected as being *infeasible*, regardless of the objective function value. If all constraints are satisfied, the decision alternative is *feasible* and is a candidate for the "best" solution or recommended decision. Through this trial-and-error process of evaluating selected decision alternatives, a decision maker can identify a good—and possibly the best—feasible solution to the problem. This solution would then be the recommended decision for the problem.

Table 1.4 shows the results of a trial-and-error approach to solving the production model of Figure 1.3. The recommended decision is a production quantity of 8, since the feasible solution with the highest projected profit occurs at $x = 8$.

TABLE 1.4
Trial-and-Error Solution for the Production Model of Figure 1.3

Decision Alternative (Production Quantity) x	Projected Profit	Total Hours of Production	Feasible Solution? (capacity = 40)
0	0	0	Yes
2	20	10	Yes
4	40	20	Yes
6	60	30	Yes
8	80	40	Yes
10	100	50	No
12	120	60	No

While the trial-and-error solution process is often acceptable and can provide valuable information for the manager, it has the drawbacks of not necessarily providing the best solution, and of being inefficient in terms of requiring numerous calculations if many decision alternatives are tried. Thus quantitative analysts have developed special solution procedures for many models that are much more efficient than the trial-and-error approach. Throughout this text you will be introduced to solution procedures that are applicable to the specific mathematical models that will be formulated. While some relatively small models or problems can be solved by hand computations, most practical applications require the use of a computer.

It is important to realize that the model development and model solution steps are not completely separable. While an analyst will want to develop an accurate model or representation of the actual problem situation, the analyst also wants to be able to find a solution to the model. If we approach the model development step by attempting to find the most accurate and realistic mathematical model, we may find the model so large and complex that it is impossible to obtain a solution. In this case a simpler and perhaps more easily understood model with a readily available solution procedure is preferred, even if the recommended solution is only a rough approximation of the best decision. As you learn more about quantitative solution procedures, you will have a better idea of the types of mathematical models that can be developed and solved.

After a model solution has been obtained, both the management scientist and the manager will be interested in determining how good the solution really is. While the analyst has undoubtedly taken many precautions to develop a realistic model, often the goodness or accuracy of the model cannot be assessed until model solutions are generated. Model testing and validation are frequently conducted with relatively small "test" problems that have known or at least expected solutions. If the model generates the expected solutions, and if other output information appears correct, the go-ahead may be given to the use of the model on the full-scale problem. However, if the model test and validation identifies potential problems or inaccuracies inherent in the model, corrective action such as model modification and/or the collection of more accurate input data may be taken. Whatever the corrective action, the model solution will not be used in practice until the model has satisfactorily passed testing and validation.

Report Generation

The final step in the quantitative analysis process is the preparation of managerial reports based upon the model's solution. Referring to Figure 1.1, we see that the solution based upon the quantitative analysis of a problem is one of the inputs that is considered by the manager before making a final decision. Thus it is essential that the results of the model appear in a managerial report that can be easily understood by the decision maker. The report will include the recommended decision and other pertinent information about the model results that may be helpful to the decision maker. Figure 1.4 summarizes the five-step quantitative analysis process.

1.4 IMPLEMENTATION

Although the generation of a managerial report is the final step in the quantitative analysis process, the implementation of the information contained in the report is a final action that remains to be taken by the manager or decision maker. As discussed in Section 1.2, it is the responsibility of the manager to integrate the quantitative solution with qualitative considerations in order to make the best possible decision. After doing this, the manager must oversee the implementation and follow-up evaluation of the decision. During the implementation and follow-up, the manager should continue to monitor the contribution of the model. At times this process may lead to requests for model expansion or refinement that will cause the management scientist to return to one of the earlier steps of the quantitative analysis process.

Successful implementation of results is of critical importance to the management scientist as well as the manager. If the results of the quantitative analysis process are not implemented, the entire effort may be of no value. It doesn't take too many unsuccessful implementations before the management scientist is out of work. Because implementation often requires people to do things differently (and more effectively, one hopes), it often

FIGURE 1.4
Steps of the Quantitative Analysis Process

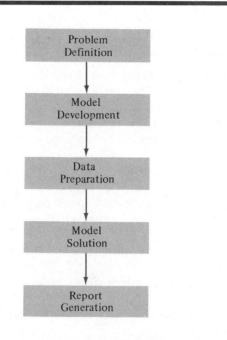

meets with resistance. People want to know, ''What's wrong with the way I've been doing it,'' and so on. One of the most effective ways to ensure a successful implementation is to secure as much user involvement as possible throughout the modelling process. If the user feels he/she has been involved in identifying the problem and developing the solutions, he/she is much more likely to enthusiastically implement the results. The success rate for implementing the results of a management science project is much greater for those projects in which there has been extensive user involvement.

Summary

This is a book about how quantitative approaches to decision problems may be used to help managers make better decisions. The focus of the text is on the decision-making process and on the role of management science in that process. We have discussed the problem orientation of this process and in an overview have shown how mathematical models can be used in this type of analysis.

The difference between the model and the situation or managerial problem it represents is an important point. Mathematical models are abstractions of real-world situations and, as such, cannot capture all the aspects of the real situation. However, if a model can capture the major relevant aspects of the problem and provide a solution recommendation, it can be a valuable aid to decision making.

One of the characteristics of management science that will become increasingly apparent as we proceed through the text is the search for a best solution to the problem.

In carrying out the quantitative analysis, we shall be attempting to develop procedures for finding the "best" or optimal solution.

Glossary

Model Representation of a real object or situation.

Iconic model Physical replica or representation of a real object.

Analog model While physical in form, an analog model does not have a physical appearance similar to the real object or situation it represents.

Mathematical model Mathematical symbols and expressions used to represent a real situation.

Objective function A mathematical expression used to identify the objective of a problem.

Constraints Restrictions or limitations imposed on the problem.

Controllable input The decision alternatives or inputs that can be specified by the decision maker.

Uncontrollable input The environmental factors or inputs that cannot be specified by the decision maker.

Deterministic model A model where all uncontrollable inputs are known and cannot vary.

Stochastic model A model where at least one uncontrollable input is uncertain and subject to variation.

Feasible solution A decision alternative or solution that satisfies all constraints.

Infeasible solution A decision alternative or solution that violates one or more constraints.

Problems

1. Define the terms "management science" and "operations research."
2. Describe the major reasons for the growth in use of management science since World War II.
3. Discuss the different roles played by the qualitative and quantitative approaches to managerial decision making. Why is it important for a manager or decision maker to have a good understanding of both of these approaches to decision making?
4. A firm has just completed a new plant that will produce over 500 different products using over 50 different production lines and machines. The product scheduling decisions are critical in that sales will be lost if customer demands are not met on time. If no individual in the firm has had experience with this production operation, and if new production schedules must be generated each week, why should the firm consider a quantitative approach to the production scheduling problem?
5. List and discuss the five steps of the quantitative analysis process.
6. Give an example of the three types of models discussed in this chapter: iconic, analog, and mathematical.
7. What are the advantages of analyzing and experimenting with a model as opposed to a real object or situation?

8. Recall the production model from Figure 1.3:

$$\max \ 10x$$
$$\text{s.t.}$$
$$5x \leq 40$$
$$x \geq 0$$

Suppose the firm in this example considers a second product that has a unit profit of \$5 and requires 2 hours for each unit produced. Use y as the number of units of product 2 produced.

a. Show the mathematical model when both products are considered simultaneously.

b. Identify the controllable and uncontrollable inputs for this model.

c. Draw the flowchart of the input-output process for this model (see Figure 1.3).

d. What are the optimal solution values of x and y?

9. Is the model developed in problem 8 a deterministic or a stochastic model? Explain.

10. Suppose we modify the model in Figure 1.3 to obtain the following mathematical model:

$$\max \ 10x$$
$$\text{s.t.}$$
$$ax \leq 40$$
$$x \geq 0$$

where a is the number of hours required for each unit produced. With $a = 5$, the optimal solution is $x = 8$. If we have a stochastic model with $a = 3$, $a = 4$, $a = 5$, or $a = 6$ as the possible values for the number of hours required per unit, what is the optimal value for x? What problems does this stochastic model cause?

11. A retail store in Des Moines, Iowa, receives shipments of a particular product from Kansas City and Minneapolis. Let

$$x = \text{units of product received from Kansas City}$$
$$y = \text{units of product received from Minneapolis}$$

a. Write an expression for the total units of product received by the retail store in Des Moines.

b. Shipments from Kansas City cost \$.20 per unit, and shipments from Minneapolis cost \$.25 per unit. Develop an objective function representing the total cost of shipments to Des Moines.

c. Assuming the monthly demand at the retail store is 5000 units, develop a constraint that requires 5000 units to be shipped to Des Moines.

d. No more than 4000 units can be shipped from Kansas City and no more than 3000 units can be shipped from Minneapolis in a month. Develop constraints to model this situation.

e. Of course, negative amounts cannot be shipped. Combine the objective function and constraints developed to state a mathematical model for satisfying the demand at the Des Moines retail store at minimum cost.

12. Suppose you are going on a weekend trip to a city that is d miles away. Develop a model that determines your roundtrip gasoline costs. What assumptions or approximations do you have to make in order to treat this model as a deterministic model? Are these assumptions or approximations acceptable to you?

13. For most products higher prices result in a decreased demand whereas lower product prices result in an increased demand. Let

$$d = \text{annual demand for a product in units}$$
$$p = \text{price per unit}$$

Assume that a firm accepts the following price–demand relationship as being realistic:

$$d = 800 - 10p$$

where the price p must be between $20 and $70.

a. How many units can the firm sell at the $20 per-unit price? At the $70 per-unit price?

b. Show the mathematical model for the total revenue (TR), which is the annual demand multiplied by the unit price.

c. Based on other considerations, the firm's management will only consider price alternatives of $30, $40, and $50. Use your model from part (b) to determine the price alternative that will maximize the total revenue.

d. What are the expected annual demand and total revenue according to your recommended price?

14. Suppose that a manager has a choice between the following two mathematical models of a given situation: (a) a relatively simple model that is a reasonable approximation of the real situation and (b) a thorough and complex model that is the most accurate mathematical representation of the real situation possible. Why might the model described in (a) be preferred by the manager?

15. The O'Neill Shoe Manufacturing Company will produce a special-style shoe if the order size is large enough to provide a reasonable profit. For each special-style order the company incurs a fixed cost of $1000 for the production setup. The variable cost is $30 per pair, and each pair sells for $40.

a. Let x indicate the number of pairs of shoes produced. Develop a mathematical model for the total cost of producing x pairs of shoes.

b. Let P indicate the total profit. Develop a mathematical model for the total profit realized from an order for x pairs of shoes.

c. How large must the shoe order be before O'Neill will break even?

16. Financial Analysts, Inc. is an investment firm that manages stock portfolios for a number of clients. A new client has just requested that the firm handle an $80,000 portfolio. As an initial investment strategy the client would like to restrict the portfolio to a mix of the following two stocks:

Stock	Price/ Share	Estimated Annual Return/Share	Maximum Possible Investment
Oil Alaska	$50	$6	$50,000
Southwest Petroleum	$30	$4	$45,000

Let

$$x = \text{number of shares of Oil Alaska}$$
$$y = \text{number of shares of Southwest Petroleum}$$

a. Develop the objective function, assuming that the client desires to maximize the total annual return.

b. Show the mathematical expression for each of the following three constraints:
1. Total investment funds available is $80,000
2. Maximum Oil Alaska investment is $50,000
3. Maximum Southwest Petroleum investment is $45,000

Note: Adding the $x \geq 0$ and $y \geq 0$ constraints provides a linear programming model for the investment problem. A solution procedure for this model will be discussed in Chapter 2.

17. Models of inventory systems frequently consider the relationship between a beginning inventory, a production quantity, a demand or sales, and an ending inventory. For a given production period j, let

$$s_{j-1} = \text{ending inventory from the previous period}$$
$$\text{(beginning inventory for period } j\text{)}$$
$$x_j = \text{production quantity in period } j$$
$$d_j = \text{demand in period } j$$
$$s_j = \text{ending inventory for period } j$$

a. Write the mathematical relationship or model that describes how the above four variables are related.

b. What constraint should be added if production capacity for period j is given by C_j?

c. What constraint should be added if safety stock requirements for period j require an ending inventory of at least I_j?

Introduction to Chapter Ending ⸺ *Management Science in Practice* ⸺

Management Science in Practice writeups prepared by practitioners are presented at the end of 15 chapters. We feel these provide a meaningful extension to the text material. The purpose of these application writeups is to provide the reader with a better appreciation for the types of companies which use management science and the types of problems these companies are able to solve.

Each Management Science in Practice writeup begins with a description of the company involved and continues with a discussion of the areas where the company has successfully applied quantitative methods. The remainder of the writeup deals with an application that is closely related to the preceding chapter and/or part of the book. An effort has been made to avoid unnecessary technical detail and to focus on the managerial aspects and the value of the results to the company.

Since Chapter 1 is designed to provide an introduction to management science, we have not emphasized any particular solution methodology. Thus, we have placed the Mead Corporation writeup at the end of this first chapter because it provides an overview of several areas in which management science can be used effectively. It is evidence of the impact quantitative approaches to decision making are having at some companies.

Management Science in Practice

MEAD CORPORATION*
Dayton, Ohio

Mead Corporation is basically a forest products company that manufactures paper, pulp, and lumber; converts paperboard into shipping containers and beverage carriers; and distributes paper, school supplies, and stationery. Mead is also a major distributor of pipe, valves, and other industrial materials to refineries, petrochemical and power plants, and oil-well drillers. Mead is the nation's leading independent producer of ductile iron castings for automobiles and construction equipment. The company also makes rubber products for the exploration and production of gas and oil. Mead's Advanced Systems Group develops businesses for the future, including storing, retrieving, printing, and reproducing data through the innovative application of digital technology.

MANAGEMENT SCIENCE AT MEAD CORPORATION

Management science applications at Mead are developed and implemented by the company's Operations Research (OR) Department. The OR department provides timely, efficient internal consulting services to the operating groups and corporate staff in the functional areas of operations, finance, marketing, and human resources. The department assists decision makers by providing them with analytical tools of management science as well as personal analysis and recommendations. Through conversations and observations, the department recognizes needs where management science techniques are applicable and recommends appropriate projects. In addition, the department provides a resource reservoir for information and assistance on quantitative methodology and assumes responsibility for keeping current in management science techniques that could produce efficiencies at Mead. This charter results in a variety of projects and applications that span the corporation. Four examples of management science applications at Mead are described below.

A CORPORATE PLANNING SYSTEM

The OR department built and maintains a corporate planning system. This system allows business units to create and evaluate their 5-year plans in an interactive computer environment.

Once the individual business units have finished their planning, the system consolidates the information at a group level. The assumptions of the units and the

*The authors are indebted to Dr. Edward P. Winkofsky, Mead Corporation, Dayton, Ohio, for providing this application.

group are evaluated and reconciled. The use of this computer model facilitates this process by ensuring uniformity of calculations and reporting by all the planning units. Ultimately, the information is consolidated and evaluated at a corporate level.

A TIMBERLAND FINANCING MODEL

Another example of a management science application involves the development of a timberland financing model. Working directly with financial management, analysts assisted in the creation of a deterministic model that considered the major factors in a timberland financing arrangement. The model was used to examine the liability and profitability of timberland acquisition under various assumptions concerning forest growth rates, the inflation rate, and other financial considerations. By using the model, management was able to examine fully the acquisition and modify the financial arrangement as operating conditions warranted. The model is currently operated and modified by financial management and is considered a major tool in the examination of timberland financing.

INVENTORY ANALYSIS

Inventory analysis is an area in which more sophisticated tools of management science have been used. Simulation models have been used to describe the major factors (e.g., demand or usage rates, lead times, production rates, etc.) in an inventory system. Typical costs included in an inventory model are purchase, storage, ordering, stockout, and degradation costs. The simulation model is used to evaluate reorder points, safety stocks, customer service levels, review periods, and the response time of the inventory system to extraordinary events.

Once developed and in place, the model can be updated as economic and operating conditions change. Thus the model can be used by management to evaluate its inventory system on an ongoing basis and to ensure that it is operating in a cost-efficient manner. These inventory simulation models are user friendly and can be operated and maintained by management with little formal computer training.

A TIMBER-HARVESTING MODEL

Mead has also used models to assist with the long-range management of the company's timberland. Through the use of large-scale linear programs, timber-harvesting plans have been developed to cover a substantial time horizon. These models consider wood market conditions, mill pulpwood requirements, harvesting capacities, and general forest management principles. Within these constraints the model develops an optimal harvesting and purchasing schedule based on discounted cash flow. Alternative schedules are developed to reflect various assumptions concerning forest growth, wood availability, and general economic conditions.

Quantitative methods are also used in the development of the inputs for the linear programming models described above. Timber prices and supplies as well as mill requirements must be forecast over the time horizon. Advanced sampling techniques are used to evaluate land holdings and to project forest growth. The harvest schedule is developed through the use of a number of management science techniques.

SUMMARY

The applications briefly described above—although only a few of the many management science projects at Mead—convey the breadth of the activities currently in use within the company. The management scientist at Mead must be able to work in a number of different environments and be proficient in a wide range of quantitative methods. In addition the analyst must possess exceptional oral and written communication skills. Only with this background will the analyst be able to achieve the major objective of management science at Mead—the development and implementation of user-friendly quantitative models that will support and enhance management decision making throughout the organization.

QUESTIONS

1. Which techniques listed in Table 1.2 are being used in the four management science applications described at the Mead Corporation?
2. Which of the Mead applications used a deterministic model and which used a stochastic model? What were the conditions in the applications that indicated a stochastic model was necessary?
3. Discuss how the five steps of the quantitative analysis process described in Section 1.3 occurred in Mead's inventory analysis application.
4. Discuss the benefits associated with the management science applications at Mead.

2

Linear Programming: The Graphical Method

Linear programming is a problem-solving approach that has been developed to help managers make decisions. Some typical applications where linear programming has been used are described below:

1. A manufacturer wants to develop a production schedule and an inventory policy that will satisfy sales demand in future periods. Ideally the schedule and policy will enable the company to satisfy demand and at the same time *minimize* the total production and inventory costs.
2. A financial analyst must select an investment portfolio from a variety of stock and bond investment alternatives. The analyst would like to establish the portfolio that *maximizes* the return on investment.
3. A marketing manager wants to determine how best to allocate a fixed advertising budget among alternative advertising media such as radio, television, newspaper, and magazine. The manager would like to determine the media mix that *maximizes* the advertising effectiveness.
4. A company has warehouses in a number of locations throughout the United States. Given a set of customer demands for its products, the company would like to determine which warehouse should ship how much product to which customers so that the total transportation costs are *minimized*.

These are only a few examples of situations where linear programming has been used successfully, but the examples illustrate the diversity of linear programming applications. A close scrutiny reveals one basic property that all of these examples have in common. In each example we were concerned with *maximizing* or *minimizing* some quantity. In example 1 we wanted to minimize costs; in example 2 we wanted to maximize return on investment; in example 3 we wanted to maximize advertising effectiveness; and in example 4 we wanted to minimize total transportation costs. *In all linear programming problems the maximization or minimization of some quantity is the objective.*

A second property of all linear programming problems is that there are restrictions or *constraints* that limit the degree to which the objective can be pursued. In example 1 the manufacturer is restricted by constraints requiring product demand to be satisfied and by the constraints limiting production capacity. The financial analyst's portfolio problem is constrained by the total amount of investment funds available and the maximum amounts that can be invested in each stock or bond. The marketing manager's media selection decision is constrained by a fixed advertising budget and the availability of the various media. In the transportation problem the minimum cost shipping schedule is constrained by the supply of product available at each warehouse. *Thus constraints are another general feature of every linear programming problem.*

2.1   A SIMPLE MAXIMIZATION PROBLEM

Par, Inc. is a small manufacturer of golf equipment and supplies whose management has decided to move into the market for medium- and high-priced golf bags. Par's distributor is enthusiastic about the new product line and has agreed to buy all the golf bags Par produces over the next 3 months.

After a thorough investigation of the steps involved in manufacturing a golf bag, management has determined that each golf bag produced will require the following operations:

1. Cutting and dyeing of material
2. Sewing
3. Finishing (such as inserting umbrella holder, club separators, etc.)
4. Inspection and packaging

The director of manufacturing has analyzed each of the operations and concluded that if the company produces a medium-priced, standard model, each bag produced will require $7/10$ hour in the cutting and dyeing department, $1/2$ hour in the sewing department, 1 hour in the finishing department, and $1/10$ hour in the inspection and packaging department. The more expensive deluxe model will require 1 hour of cutting and dyeing time, $5/6$ hour of sewing time, $2/3$ hour of finishing time, and $1/4$ hour of inspection and packaging time. This production information is summarized in Table 2.1

The accounting department has analyzed these production figures, assigned all relevant variable costs, and arrived at prices for both bags that will result in a profit[1] contribution of $10 for every standard bag and $9 for every deluxe bag produced.

TABLE 2.1
Production Operations and Production Requirements per Bag

| | Production Time (hours) | | | |
Product	Cutting and Dyeing	Sewing	Finishing	Inspection and Packaging
Standard bag	$7/10$	$1/2$	1	$1/10$
Deluxe bag	1	$5/6$	$2/3$	$1/4$

[1]From an accounting perspective this is more correctly described as the contribution margin per bag; e.g., overhead has not been allocated.

In addition, after studying departmental workload projections, the director of manufacturing estimates that 630 hours of cutting and dyeing time, 600 hours of sewing time, 708 hours of finishing time, and 135 hours of inspection and packaging time will be available for the production of golf bags during the next 3 months.

Par's problem is to determine how many standard and how many deluxe bags should be produced in order to maximize profit contribution. If you were in charge of production scheduling for Par, Inc., what decision would you make? That is, how many standard bags and how many deluxe bags would you produce in the next 3 months? Write your decision below. Later you can check and see how well you did.

2.2   THE OBJECTIVE FUNCTION

As pointed out earlier, every linear programming problem has a maximization or minimization objective. For the Par problem the objective is to maximize profit. We can write this objective in mathematical form with the introduction of some simple notation. Let

$$x_1 = \text{number of standard bags Par, Inc. produces}$$
$$x_2 = \text{number of deluxe bags Par, Inc. produces}$$

Par's profit contribution will come from two sources: (1) the profit contribution made by producing x_1 standard bags and (2) the profit contribution made by producing x_2 deluxe bags. Since Par makes \$10 for every standard bag produced, the company will make \$10x_1 if x_1 standard bags are produced. Also, since Par makes \$9 for every deluxe bag produced, the company will make \$9x_2 if x_2 deluxe bags are produced. Denoting the total profit contribution by z, we have

$$\text{Total profit contribution} = z = \$10x_1 + \$9x_2$$

From now on we will assume that the profit contribution is measured in dollars and write the total profit contribution expression without the dollar signs. That is,

$$\text{Total profit contribution} = z = 10x_1 + 9x_2 \qquad (2.1)$$

Par's problem can now be stated as one of choosing values for the variables x_1 and x_2 that will yield the highest possible value of z. In linear programming terminology we refer to x_1 and x_2 as the *decision variables*. Since the objective—maximize total profit contribution—is a function of these decision variables, we refer to $10x_1 + 9x_2$ as the *objective function.* Using max as an abbreviation for maximize, Par's objective is written as follows:

$$\max z = \max 10x_1 + 9x_2 \tag{2.2}$$

In the Par, Inc. problem any particular production combination of standard and deluxe bags is referred to as a *solution* to the problem. However, only those solutions that satisfy *all* the constraints are referred to as *feasible solutions*. The particular feasible production combination (feasible solution) that results in the largest profit contribution will be referred to as the *optimal* production combination or, equivalently, the *optimal solution*. At this point, however, we have no idea what the optimal solution will be. Indeed, we have not even developed a procedure for identifying feasible solutions. The procedure for determining feasible solutions requires us first to identify all the constraints of the problem.

2.3   THE CONSTRAINTS

Every standard and deluxe bag produced must go through four manufacturing operations. Since there is a limited amount of production time available for each of these operations, we can expect that four constraints will limit the total number of golf bags Par can produce.

From the production information (see Table 2.1) we know that every standard bag Par manufactures will use $7/10$ hour of cutting and dyeing time. Hence the total number of hours of cutting and dyeing time used in the manufacture of x_1 standard bags will be $7/10 x_1$. On the other hand, every deluxe bag Par produces will use 1 hour of cutting and dyeing time; thus x_2 deluxe bags will use $1x_2$ hours of cutting and dyeing time. The total cutting and dyeing time required for the production of x_1 standard bags and x_2 deluxe bags is given by

Total cutting and dyeing time required = $7/10 x_1 + 1x_2$

Since the director of manufacturing has stated that Par has at most 630 hours of cutting and dyeing time available, it follows that the product combination we select must satisfy the requirement

$$7/10 x_1 + 1x_2 \leq 630 \tag{2.3}$$

where the symbol $\leq$ means *less than or equal to*. Relationship (2.3) is referred to as an inequality and denotes the fact that the total number of hours used for the cutting and dyeing operation in the production of x_1 standard bags and x_2 deluxe bags must be less than or equal to the maximum amount of cutting and dyeing time Par, Inc. has available.

From Table 2.1 we also see that every standard bag manufactured will require $1/2$ hour of sewing time and that every deluxe bag manufactured will require $5/6$ hour of sewing time. Since there are 600 hours of sewing time available, it follows that

$$1/2 x_1 + 5/6 x_2 \leq 600 \tag{2.4}$$

is the mathematical representation of the sewing constraint. Verify for yourself that the constraint for finishing capacity is

$$1x_1 + \tfrac{2}{3}x_2 \le 708 \qquad (2.5)$$

and that the constraint for inspection and packaging capacity is

$$\tfrac{1}{10}x_1 + \tfrac{1}{4}x_2 \le 135 \qquad (2.6)$$

We now have specified the mathematical relationships for the constraints associated with the four production operations. Are there any other constraints we have forgotten? Can Par produce a negative number of standard or deluxe bags? Clearly, the answer is no. Thus in order to prevent the decision variables x_1 and x_2 from having negative values two constraints

$$x_1 \ge 0 \qquad \text{and} \qquad x_2 \ge 0 \qquad (2.7)$$

must be added. The symbol $\ge$ means *greater than or equal to*. These constraints ensure that the solution to the problem will contain nonnegative values for the decision variables and are thus referred to as the *nonnegativity constraints*. Nonnegativity constraints are a general feature of all linear programming problems and will be written in the following abbreviated form:

$$x_1, x_2 \ge 0$$

2.4 THE MATHEMATICAL STATEMENT OF THE PAR, INC. PROBLEM

The mathematical statement or mathematical formulation of the Par, Inc. problem is now complete. We have succeeded in translating the objective and constraints of the "real-world" problem into a set of mathematical relationships referred to as a *mathematical model*. The complete mathematical model for the Par problem is as follows:

$$
\begin{aligned}
\max \quad & 10x_1 + 9x_2 \\
\text{subject to (s.t.)} \quad & \\
& \tfrac{7}{10}x_1 + 1x_2 \le 630 \quad \text{Cutting and dyeing} \\
& \tfrac{1}{2}x_1 + \tfrac{5}{6}x_2 \le 600 \quad \text{Sewing} \\
& 1x_1 + \tfrac{2}{3}x_2 \le 708 \quad \text{Finishing} \\
& \tfrac{1}{10}x_1 + \tfrac{1}{4}x_2 \le 135 \quad \text{Inspection and packaging} \\
& x_1, x_2 \ge 0
\end{aligned}
$$

Our job now is to find the product mix (that is, the combination of x_1 and x_2) that satisfies all the constraints and, at the same time, yields a value for the objective function that is greater than or equal to the value given by any other feasible solution. Once this is done, we will have found the optimal solution to the problem.

The above mathematical model of the Par problem is a *linear program*. The problem has the objective and constraints that we said earlier were common properties of all linear programs. But what is the special feature of this mathematical model that makes it a linear program? The special feature that makes it a linear program is that the objective function and all constraint functions (the left-hand sides of the constraint inequalities) are linear functions of the decision variables.

Mathematical functions in which each variable appears in a separate term and is raised to the first power are called *linear functions*. The objective function $(10x_1 + 9x_2)$ is linear since each decision variable appears in a separate term and has an exponent of 1. If the objective function had appeared as $10x_1^2 + 9\sqrt{x_2}$, it would not have been a linear function and we would not have a linear program. The amount of production time required in the cutting and dyeing department $(\frac{7}{10}x_1 + 1x_2)$ is also a linear function of the decision variables for the same reason. Similarly, the functions of the left-hand side of all the constraint inequalities (the constraint functions) are linear functions. Thus the mathematical formulation of the Par problem is referred to as a linear program.

We can now note that linear programming has nothing to do with computer programming. The use of the word programming here means "choosing a course of action." Linear programming involves choosing a course of action when the mathematical model of the problem contains only linear functions.

2.5   GRAPHICAL SOLUTION

A linear programming problem involving only two decision variables can be solved by a graphical solution procedure. Let us begin the graphical solution procedure by developing a graph that displays the possible solutions (x_1 and x_2 values) for the Par problem. The graph (Figure 2.1) will have values of x_1 on the horizontal axis and values of x_2 on the vertical axis. Any point on the graph can be identified by the x_1 and x_2 values, which indicate the position of the point along the x_1 and x_2 axes, respectively. Since every point (x_1, x_2) corresponds to a possible solution, every point on the graph is called a *solution point*. The solution point where $x_1 = 0$ and $x_2 = 0$ is referred to as the origin.

The next step is to determine which of the solution points correspond to feasible solutions for the linear program. Both x_1 and x_2 are required to be nonnegative, so we need only consider that portion of the graph where $x_1 \geq 0$ and $x_2 \geq 0$. In Figure 2.2 the arrows point to the portion of the solution region where these nonnegativity requirements are satisfied. Since linear programming decision variables are always required to be nonnegative, all future graphs will show only the portion of the solution region corresponding to nonnegative values for the decision variables.

Earlier we saw that the inequality representing the cutting and dyeing constraint is

$$\tfrac{7}{10}x_1 + 1x_2 \leq 630$$

To show all solution points that satisfy this relationship, we start by graphing the solution points satisfying the constraint as an equality. That is, the points where $\frac{7}{10}x_1 + 1x_2 = 630$. Since the graph of this equation is a line, it can be obtained by identifying two points that satisfy the equation and then drawing a line through the points. Setting $x_1 = 0$ and solving for x_2, we see that the point ($x_1 = 0, x_2 = 630$) satisfies the above equation. To find a second point satisfying this equation, we set $x_2 = 0$ and solve for x_1. By doing

FIGURE 2.1
Graph of Solution Points for the Two-Variable Par, Inc. Problem

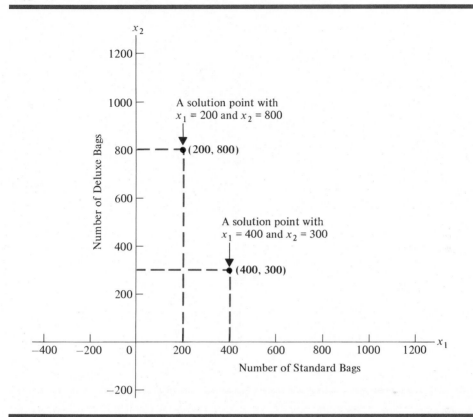

this, we obtain $\frac{7}{10}x_1 + 1(0) = 630$, or $x_1 = 900$. Thus a second point satisfying the equation is $(x_1 = 900, x_2 = 0)$. Given these two points we can now graph the line corresponding to the equation

$$\frac{7}{10}x_1 + 1x_2 = 630$$

This line, which will be called the cutting and dyeing *constraint line*, is shown in Figure 2.3. We label this line "C & D" to indicate that it represents the cutting and dyeing constraint.

Recall that the inequality representing the cutting and dyeing constraint is

$$\frac{7}{10}x_1 + 1x_2 \leq 630$$

Can you identify all of the solution points that satisfy this constraint? Since all points on the line satisfy $\frac{7}{10}x_1 + 1x_2 = 630$, we know any point on this line must satisfy the constraint. But where are the solution points satisfying $\frac{7}{10}x_1 + 1x_2 < 630$? Consider two solution points $(x_1 = 200, x_2 = 200)$ and $(x_1 = 600, x_2 = 500)$. You can see from Figure 2.3 that the first solution point is below the constraint line and the second is above

FIGURE 2.2
The Nonnegativity Constraints

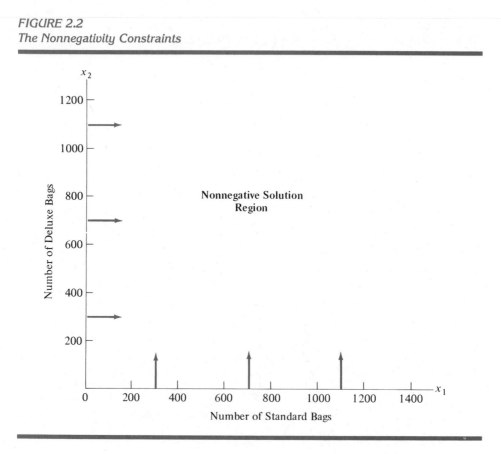

the constraint line. Which of these solutions will satisfy the cutting and dyeing constraint? For the point ($x_1 = 200$, $x_2 = 200$) we see that

$$\tfrac{7}{10}x_1 + 1x_2 = \tfrac{7}{10}(200) + 1(200) = 340$$

Since the 340 hours is less than the 630 hours available, the $x_1 = 200$, $x_2 = 200$ production combination, or solution point, satisfies the constraint. For $x_1 = 600$, $x_2 = 500$ we have

$$\tfrac{7}{10}x_1 + 1x_2 = \tfrac{7}{10}(600) + 1(500) = 920$$

The 920 hours is greater than the 630 hours available, so the $x_1 = 600$, $x_2 = 500$ solution point does not satisfy the constraint and is thus not feasible.

It turns out that if a particular solution point is not feasible, then all other solution points on the same side of the constraint line are not feasible. If a particular solution point is feasible, then all other solution points on the same side of the constraint line are feasible. Thus one needs only to evaluate the constraint function for one solution point to determine which side of a constraint line is in the feasible region. In Figure 2.4, we indicate all points satisfying the cutting and dyeing constraint by the shaded region.

FIGURE 2.3
The Cutting and Dyeing Constraint Line

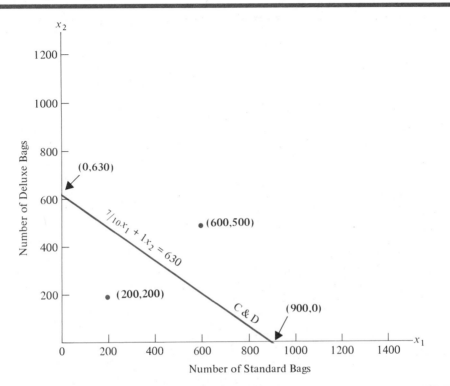

We continue by identifying the solution points satisfying each of the other three constraints. The solutions that are feasible for each of these constraints are shown in Figure 2.5.

We now have four separate graphs showing the feasible solution points for each of the four constraints. In a linear programming problem we need to identify the solution points that satisfy *all* the constraints *simultaneously*. To find these solution points, we can draw all four constraints on one graph and observe the region containing the points that do in fact satisfy all the constraints simultaneously.

The graphs in Figures 2.4 and 2.5 can be superimposed to obtain one graph with all four constraints. This combined-constraint graph is shown in Figure 2.6. The shaded region in this figure includes every solution point that satisfies all the constraints simultaneously. Since solutions that satisfy all the constraints are termed *feasible solutions*, the shaded region is called the feasible solution region, or simply the *feasible region*. Any point on the boundary of the feasible region or within the feasible region is a *feasible solution point*.

Now that we have identified the feasible region we are ready to proceed with the graphical solution method and find the optimal solution to the Par, Inc. problem. Recall that the optimal solution for a linear programming problem is the feasible solution that provides the best possible value of the objective function.

FIGURE 2.4

Feasible Solutions for the Cutting and Dyeing Constraint Are Represented by the Shaded Region

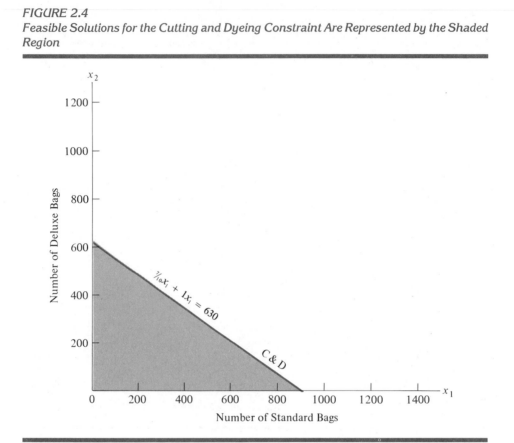

One approach to finding the optimal solution would be to evaluate the objective function for each feasible solution; the optimal solution would then be the one yielding the largest value. The difficulty with this approach is that there are too many feasible solutions (actually an infinite number), and thus it would not be possible to evaluate all feasible solutions. Hence this trial-and-error procedure would not necessarily lead to the optimal solution. We need a better way.

Let us start the optimizing step of the graphical solution procedure by redrawing the feasible region on a separate graph. The graph is shown in Figure 2.7. Rather than trying to compute the profit contribution for each feasible solution, we select an arbitrary value for profit contribution and identify all the feasible solutions (x_1, x_2) that yield the selected value. For example, what feasible solutions provide a profit contribution of $1800? These solutions are given by the values of x_1 and x_2 in the feasible region that will make the objective function

$$10x_1 + 9x_2 = 1800$$

The above expression is simply the equation of a line. Thus all feasible solution points (x_1, x_2) yielding a profit contribution of $1800 must be on the line. We learned earlier in this section how to graph a constraint line. The procedure for graphing the

FIGURE 2.5
Feasible Solutions for the Sewing, Finishing, and Inspection and Packaging Constraints
Are Represented by the Shaded Regions

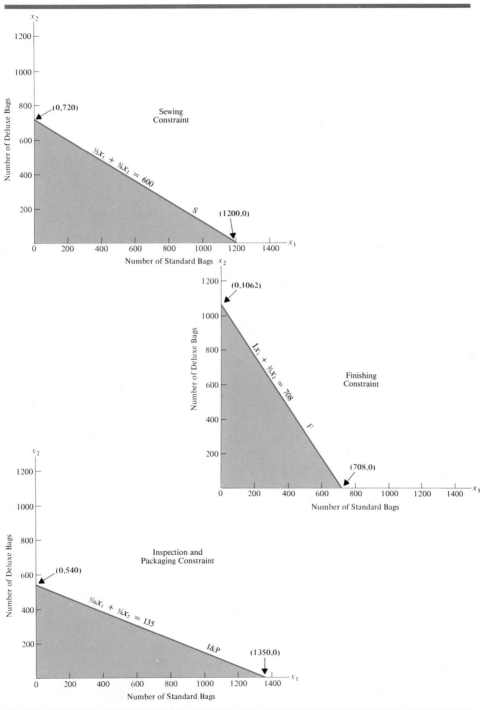

FIGURE 2.6
Combined-Constraint Graph Showing the Feasible Solution Region for the Par, Inc. Problem

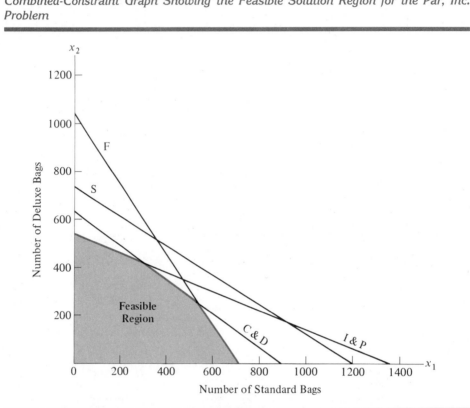

profit or objective function line is the same. Letting $x_1 = 0$, we see that x_2 must be 200; thus the solution point ($x_1 = 0$, $x_2 = 200$) is on the line. Similarly, by letting $x_2 = 0$ we see that the solution point ($x_1 = 180$, $x_2 = 0$) is also on the line. Drawing the line through these two points identifies all the solutions that have a profit contribution of $1800. A graph of this profit line is presented in Figure 2.8.

Since the objective is to find the feasible solution yielding the largest profit contribution, let us proceed by selecting higher profit contributions and finding the solutions yielding the selected values. For instance, let us find all solutions yielding profit contributions of $3600 and $5400. To do so we must find the x_1 and x_2 values that are on the following lines:

$$10x_1 + 9x_2 = 3600$$

and

$$10x_1 + 9x_2 = 5400$$

Using the previous procedure for graphing profit and constraint lines, we have drawn the $3600 and $5400 profit lines on the graph in Figure 2.9. While not all solution points

FIGURE 2.7
Feasible Solution Region for the Par, Inc. Problem

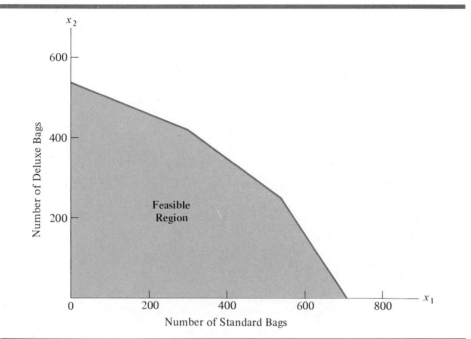

FIGURE 2.8
$1800 Profit Line for the Par, Inc. Problem

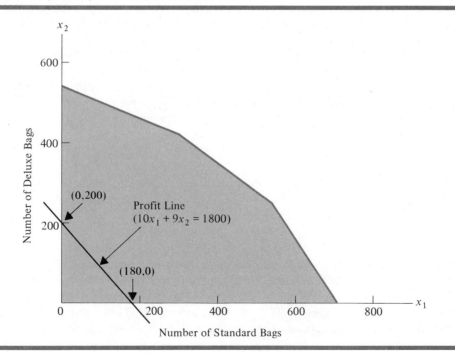

FIGURE 2.9
Selected Profit Lines for the Par, Inc. Problem

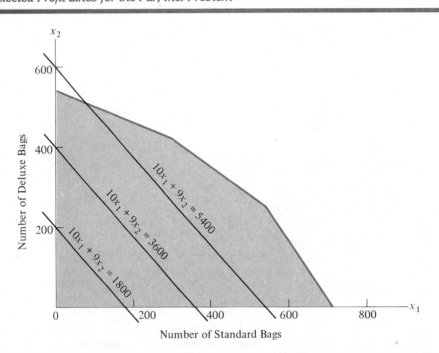

on the $5400 profit line are in the feasible region, at least some points on the line are, and thus it is possible to obtain a feasible solution that provides a $5400 profit contribution.

Can we find a feasible solution yielding even higher profit contribution? Look at Figure 2.9 and see what general observations you can make about the profit lines already drawn. Note the following: (1) the profit lines are *parallel* to each other, and (2) higher profit lines are obtained as we move farther from the origin. This can also be seen algebraically. Let z represent total profit. The objective function is

$$z = 10x_1 + 9x_2$$

Solving for x_2 in terms of x_1 and z, we obtain

$$9x_2 = -10x_1 + z$$
$$x_2 = -\tfrac{10}{9}x_1 + \tfrac{1}{9}z \qquad (2.8)$$

Equation (2.8) is the *slope-intercept form* of the linear equation relating x_1 and x_2. The coefficient of x_1, $-\tfrac{10}{9}$, is the slope of the line, and the term $\tfrac{1}{9}z$ is the x_2 intercept (that is, the value of x_2 where the graph of equation (2.8) crosses the x_2 axis). Substituting the profit contributions of $z = 1800$, $z = 3600$, and $z = 5400$ into equation (2.8) yields the following slope-intercept equations for the profit lines shown in Figure 2.9:

For $z = 1800$,

$$x_2 = -\tfrac{10}{9}x_1 + 200$$

For $z = 3600$,

$$x_2 = -\tfrac{10}{9}x_1 + 400$$

For $z = 5400$,

$$x_2 = -\tfrac{10}{9}x_1 + 600$$

The slope $(-\tfrac{10}{9})$ is the same for each profit line, since the profit lines are parallel. Further, we see that the x_2 intercept increases with larger profit contributions. Thus higher profit lines are farther from the origin.

Because the profit lines are parallel and higher profit lines are farther from the origin, we can obtain solutions that yield increasingly larger values for the objective function by continuing to move the profit line farther from the origin in such a fashion that it remains parallel to the other profit lines. However, at some point we will find that any further outward movement will place the profit line completely outside the feasible region. Since solutions outside the feasible region are unacceptable, the point in the feasible region that lies on the highest profit line is the optimal solution to the linear program.

You should now be able to identify the optimal solution point for the Par, Inc. problem. Use a ruler or the edge of a piece of paper and move the profit line as far from the origin as you can. What is the last point in the feasible region that you reach? This point, which is the optimal solution, is shown graphically in Figure 2.10.

The optimal values of the decision variables are the x_1 and x_2 values at the optimal solution. Depending upon the accuracy of the graph, you may or may not be able to determine the *exact* x_1 and x_2 values. Referring to the graph in Figure 2.10, the best we can do is conclude that the optimal production combination consists of approximately 550 standard bags (x_1) and approximately 250 deluxe bags (x_2).

A closer inspection of Figures 2.6 and 2.10 shows that the optimal solution point is at the intersection of the cutting and dyeing and the finishing constraint lines. That is, the optimal solution point is on both the cutting and dyeing constraint line

$$\tfrac{7}{10}x_1 + 1x_2 = 630 \qquad (2.9)$$

and the finishing constraint line:

$$1x_1 + \tfrac{2}{3}x_2 = 708 \qquad (2.10)$$

Thus the optimal values of the decision variables x_1 and x_2 must satisfy both equations (2.9) and (2.10) simultaneously. Using equation (2.9) and solving for x_1 gives

$$\tfrac{7}{10}x_1 = 630 - 1x_2$$

or

$$x_1 = 900 - \tfrac{10}{7}x_2 \qquad (2.11)$$

FIGURE 2.10
Optimal Solution for the Par, Inc. Problem

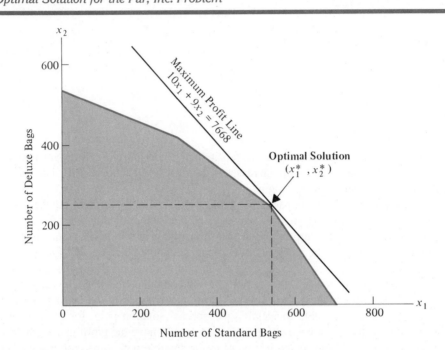

Number of Standard Bags

Substituting this expression for x_1 into equation (2.10) and solving for x_2 provides the following:

$$1(900 - {}^{10}\!/_7 x_2) + {}^2\!/_3\ x_2 = \quad 708$$
$$900 - {}^{10}\!/_7 x_2 + {}^2\!/_3\ x_2 = \quad 708$$
$$900 - {}^{30}\!/_{21} x_2 + {}^{14}\!/_{21} x_2 = \quad 708$$
$$- {}^{16}\!/_{21} x_2 = \ -192$$
$$x_2 = \quad \frac{192}{{}^{16}\!/_{21}} = 252$$

Using $x_2 = 252$ in equation (2.11) and solving for x_1 provides

$$x_1 = 900 - {}^{10}\!/_7(252)$$
$$= 900 - 360 = 540$$

The exact location of the optimal solution point is $x_1 = 540$ and $x_2 = 252$. Hence the optimal production quantities for Par, Inc. are 540 standard bags and 252 deluxe bags with a resulting profit contribution of $10(540) + 9(252) = \$7668$.

In any graphical solution of a two-decision variable linear programming problem the exact values of the decision variables at the optimal solution can be determined by first using the graphical procedure to identify the optimal solution point and then solving the two simultaneous constraint equations associated with this point.

A Note on Graphing Lines

As can be seen from the graphical solution of the Par, Inc. problem, an important aspect of the graphical method is the ability to graph lines showing the constraints and the objective function of the linear program. The procedure we have used for graphing the equation of a line is to find any two points satisfying the equation, and then draw the line through the two points. For the Par, Inc. constraints, the two points were easily found by first setting $x_1 = 0$ and solving the constraint equation for x_2. Then we set $x_2 = 0$ and solved for x_1. For the cutting and dyeing constraint line

$$\tfrac{7}{10}x_1 + 1x_2 = 630$$

this procedure identified the two points $(x_1 = 0, x_2 = 630)$ and $(x_1 = 900, x_2 = 0)$. The cutting and dyeing constraint line was then graphed by drawing a line through these two points.

All constraint and objective function lines in two-variable linear programs can be graphed if two points on the line can be identified. However, finding the two points on the line is not always as easy as shown in the Par, Inc. problem. For example, consider the following constraint:

$$2x_1 - 1x_2 \le 100$$

Using the equality form and setting $x_1 = 0$, we find the point $(x_1 = 0, x_2 = -100)$ is on the constraint line. Setting $x_2 = 0$, we find a second point $(x_1 = 50, x_2 = 0)$ on the constraint line. If we have drawn only the nonnegative $(x_1 \ge 0, x_2 \ge 0)$ portion of the graph, the first point $(x_1 = 0, x_2 = -100)$ cannot be plotted because $x_2 = -100$ is not on the graph. Whenever we have two points on the line but one or both of the points cannot be plotted in the nonnegative portion of the graph, the simplest approach is to enlarge the graph to include the negative x_1 and/or x_2 axes. In this example the point $(x_1 = 0, x_2 = -100)$ can be plotted by extending the graph to include the negative x_2 axis. Once both points satisfying the constraint equation have been located, the line can be drawn. The constraint line and the feasible solutions for the constraint $2x_1 - 1x_2 \le 100$ are shown in Figure 2.11.

As another example, let us consider a constraint of the form

$$1x_1 - 1x_2 \ge 0$$

To find all solutions satisfying the constraint as an equality, we first set $x_1 = 0$ and solve for x_2. This shows that the origin $(x_1 = 0, x_2 = 0)$ is on the constraint line. Setting $x_2 = 0$ and solving for x_1 provides the same point. However, we can obtain a second point on the line by setting x_2 equal to any value other than zero and then solving for x_1. For instance, setting $x_2 = 100$ and solving for x_1, we find that the point $(x_1 = 100, x_2 = 100)$ is on the line. With the two points $(x_1 = 0, x_2 = 0)$ and $(x_1 = 100, x_2 = 100)$, the constraint line $1x_1 - 1x_2 = 0$ and the feasible solutions for $1x_1 - 1x_2 \ge 0$ can be plotted as shown in Figure 2.12.

FIGURE 2.11
Feasible Solutions for the Constraint $2x_1 - 1x_2 \leq 100$

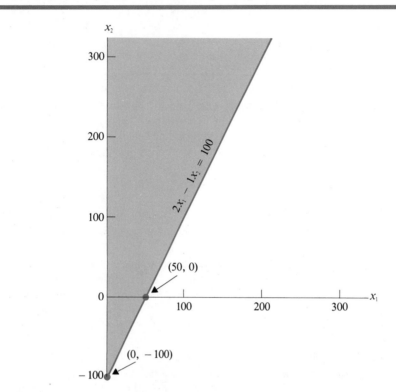

Summary of the Graphical Solution Procedure for Maximization Problems

As we have seen, the graphical solution procedure is a method of solving two-variable linear programming problems such as the Par, Inc. problem. The steps of the graphical solution procedure for a maximization problem are summarized below.

1. Prepare a graph of the feasible solution points for each of the constraints.
2. Determine the feasible region by identifying the solution points that satisfy all the constraints simultaneously.
3. Draw an objective function line showing all values of the x_1 and x_2 variables that yield a specified value of the objective function.
4. Move parallel objective function lines toward larger objective function values until further movement would take the line completely outside the feasible region.
5. A feasible solution point on the objective function line with the largest value is an optimal solution.

Slack Variables

In addition to the optimal solution of $x_1 = 540$ standard bags and $x_2 = 252$ deluxe bags and the expected profit of $7668, management of Par, Inc. will probably want information

FIGURE 2.12
Feasible Solutions for the Constraint $1x_1 - 1x_2 \geq 0$

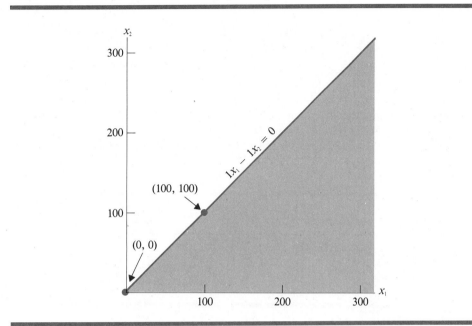

about the production time requirements for each production operation. We can obtain this information by substituting the optimal x_1 and x_2 values into the constraint functions for the linear program. For the Par, Inc. problem the production time requirements are as follows:

$$\tfrac{7}{10}(540) + 1(252) = 630 \text{ hours of cutting and dyeing time}$$
$$\tfrac{1}{2}(540) + \tfrac{5}{6}(252) = 480 \text{ hours of sewing time}$$
$$1(540) + \tfrac{2}{3}(252) = 708 \text{ hours of finishing time}$$
$$\tfrac{1}{10}(540) + \tfrac{1}{4}(252) = 117 \text{ hours of inspection and packaging time}$$

The complete solution tells management that the production of 540 standard bags and 252 deluxe bags will require all available cutting and dyeing time (630 hours) and all available finishing time (708 hours), while 120 hours of sewing time (600 − 480) and 18 hours of inspection and packaging time (135 − 117) will remain idle. The 120 hours of unused sewing time and 18 hours of unused inspection and packaging time are referred to as *slack* for the two departments. In linear programming terminology any unused or idle capacity for a ≤ constraint is referred to as the *slack* associated with the constraint.

Often variables are added to the formulation of a linear programming problem to represent the slack, or idle capacity. Such variables are called *slack variables*, and since the unused capacity makes no contribution to profit, they have coefficients of zero in the objective function. After the addition of slack variables to the mathematical statement of the Par, Inc. problem, the mathematical model appears as follows:

$$\max \quad 10x_1 + 9x_2 + 0s_1 + 0s_2 + 0s_3 + 0s_4$$

s.t.

$$\begin{array}{rcl} \tfrac{7}{10}x_1 + 1x_2 + 1s_1 & = & 630 \\ \tfrac{1}{2}x_1 + \tfrac{5}{6}x_2 \quad\quad + 1s_2 & = & 600 \\ 1x_1 + \tfrac{2}{3}x_2 \quad\quad\quad + 1s_3 & = & 708 \\ \tfrac{1}{10}x_1 + \tfrac{1}{4}x_2 \quad\quad\quad\quad + 1s_4 & = & 135 \\ x_1, x_2, s_1, \ s_2, s_3, s_4 \geq 0 \end{array}$$

Whenever a linear program is written in a form with all constraints expressed as equalities, it is said to be written in *standard form*.

At the optimal solution, $x_1 = 540$ and $x_2 = 252$, the values for the slack variables are as follows:

Constraint	Value of Slack Variable
Cutting and dyeing	$s_1 = 0$
Sewing	$s_2 = 120$
Finishing	$s_3 = 0$
Inspection and packaging	$s_4 = 18$

Could we have used the graphical solution to provide some of this information? The answer is yes. By finding the optimal solution point on Figure 2.6, we can see that the cutting and dyeing and the finishing constraints restrict, or *bind*, the feasible region at this point. Thus this solution requires the use of all available time for these two operations. In other words, the graph shows us that the cutting and dyeing and the finishing departments will have zero slack. On the other hand, since the sewing and the inspection and packaging constraints are not binding the feasible region at the optimal solution, we can expect some unused time or slack for these two operations.

As a final comment on the graphical analysis of the Par, Inc. problem, we call your attention to the sewing capacity constraint as shown in Figure 2.6. Note, in particular, that this constraint did not affect the feasible region. That is, the feasible region would be the same whether the sewing capacity constraint was included or not. This tells us that there is enough sewing time available to accommodate any production level that can be achieved by the other three departments. Since the sewing constraint does not affect the feasible region and thus cannot affect the optimal solution, it is called a *redundant* constraint. Redundant constraints can be dropped from the problem without having any effect upon the optimal solution.[2]

2.6 EXTREME POINTS AND THE OPTIMAL SOLUTION

Suppose that the profit contribution for the Par, Inc. standard bag is reduced from $10 to $5 per bag while the profit contribution for the deluxe bag and all the constraints

---

[2]We point out here that in most linear programming problems redundant constraints are not discarded because these constraints are often not immediately recognizable as being redundant.

remain unchanged. The complete linear programming model of this new problem is identical to the mathematical model in Section 2.4, except for the revised objective function:

$$\max z = 5x_1 + 9x_2$$

How does this change in the objective function affect the optimal solution to the Par, Inc. problem? Figure 2.13 shows the graphical solution of the Par, Inc. problem with the revised objective function. Note that since the constraints have not changed, the feasible region has not changed. However, the profit lines have been altered to reflect the new objective function.

FIGURE 2.13
Optimal Solution for the Par, Inc. Problem with an Objective Function of $5x_1 + 9x_2$

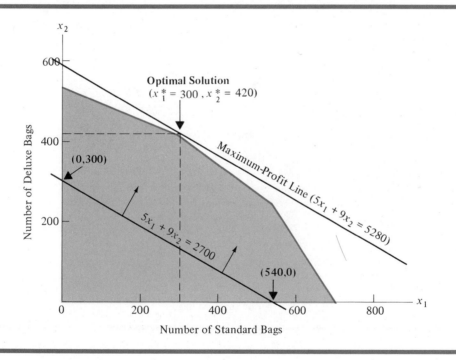

By moving the profit line in a parallel manner toward higher profit values, we find the optimal solution as shown in Figure 2.13. The values of the decision variables at this point are $x_1 = 300$ and $x_2 = 420$. The reduced profit contribution for the standard bag has caused a change in the optimal solution. In fact, as you may have suspected, we are cutting back the production of the lower-profit standard bags and increasing the production of the higher-profit deluxe bags.

What have you noticed about the location of the optimal solutions in the two linear programming problems that we have solved thus far? Look closely at the graphical solutions in Figures 2.10 and 2.13. An important observation that you should be able to make is that the optimal solutions occur at one of the vertices or "corners" of the feasible region. In linear programming terminology these vertices are referred to as the *extreme points* of the feasible region. The Par, Inc. problem has five vertices, or five extreme points, for its feasible region (see Figure 2.14). We can now formally state our observation about the location of optimal solutions as follows[3]:

> An optimal solution to a linear programming problem can be found at an extreme point of the feasible region for the problem.

FIGURE 2.14
The Five Extreme Points of the Feasible Region for the Par, Inc. Problem

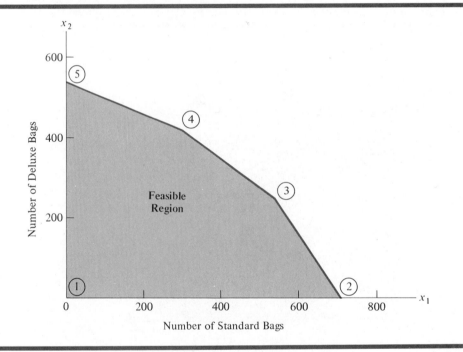

This property means that if you are looking for the optimal solution to a linear programming problem, you do not have to evaluate all feasible solution points. In fact, you have to consider *only* the feasible solutions that occur at the extreme points of the feasible region. Thus for the Par, Inc. problem, instead of computing and comparing the profit contribution for all feasible solutions, we can find the optimal solution by evaluating the five extreme-point solutions and selecting the one that provides the largest profit contribution. Actually the graphical solution procedure is nothing more than a convenient way of identifying an optimal extreme point for two-variable problems.

[3]We will see in section 2.8 that there are two special cases (infeasibility and unboundedness) in linear programming where there is no optimal solution. Thus the above statement does not apply to these cases.

2.7   A SIMPLE MINIMIZATION PROBLEM

The Par, Inc. problem involved maximization; many linear programming problems involve minimization. For example, consider the case of M&D Chemicals. M&D Chemicals produces two products that are sold as raw materials to companies manufacturing bath soaps, laundry detergents, and other soap products.

Based on an analysis of current inventory levels and potential demand for the coming month, M&D's management has specified that the total production for products 1 and 2 combined must be at least 350 gallons. Separately, a major customer's order for 125 gallons of product 1 must also be satisfied. Product 1 requires 2 hours of processing time per gallon while product 2 requires 1 hour of processing time per gallon and, for the coming month, 600 hours of processing time are available. M&D's objective is to satisfy the above requirements at a minimum total production cost. Production costs are $2 per gallon for product 1 and $3 per gallon for product 2.

To find the minimum cost production schedule, let us write the M&D Chemicals problem as a linear program. Following a procedure similar to the one used for the Par, Inc. problem, we first define the decision variables and the objective function for the problem. Let

$$x_1 = \text{number of gallons of product 1 produced}$$
$$x_2 = \text{number of gallons of product 2 produced}$$

Since the production costs are $2 per gallon for product 1 and $3 per gallon for product 2, the minimization of the total cost objective function can be written as

$$\min \quad 2x_1 + 3x_2$$

Next consider the constraints placed on the M&D Chemicals problem. To satisfy the major customer's demand for 125 gallons of product 1, we know x_1 must be at least 125. Thus we write the constraint

$$1x_1 \geq 125$$

Since the total combined production of both products must be at least 350 gallons, we can write the constraint

$$1x_1 + 1x_2 \geq 350$$

Finally, since the limitation on available processing time is 600 hours, we add the constraint

$$2x_1 + 1x_2 \leq 600$$

By adding the nonnegativity constraints ($x_1, x_2 \geq 0$), we have the following linear program for the M&D Chemicals problem:

$$\min \quad 2x_1 + 3x_2$$
$$\text{s.t.}$$

$$
\begin{array}{lll}
1x_1 & \geq 125 & \text{Demand for product 1} \\
1x_1 + 1x_2 & \geq 350 & \text{Total production} \\
2x_1 + 1x_2 & \leq 600 & \text{Processing time} \\
x_1, \ x_2 & \geq 0 &
\end{array}
$$

Since the linear programming model has only two decision variables, the graphical solution procedure can be used to find the optimal production quantities. The graphical method for this problem, just as in the Par problem, requires us first to graph the constraint lines in order to find the feasible region. By graphing each constraint line separately and then checking points on either side of the constraint line, the feasible solutions for each constraint can be identified. By combining the feasible solutions for each constraint on the same graph, we obtain the feasible region shown in Figure 2.15.

To find the minimum cost solution, we now draw the objective function line corresponding to a particular total cost value. For example, we might start by drawing the line $2x_1 + 3x_2 = 1200$. This line is shown in Figure 2.16. Clearly there are points in the feasible region that would provide a total cost of \$1200. To find the values of x_1 and x_2 that provide smaller total cost values, we move the objective function line in a lower

FIGURE 2.15
The Feasible Region for the M&D Chemicals Problem

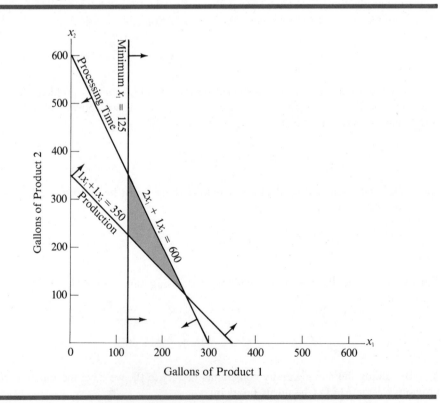

FIGURE 2.16
Graphical Solution for the M&D Chemicals Problem

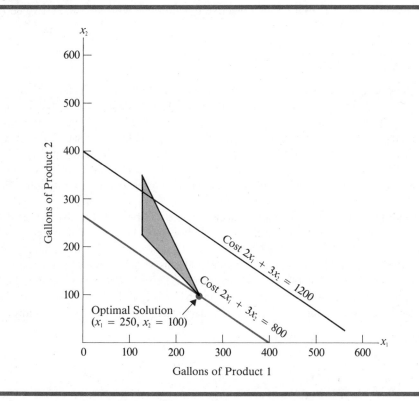

left direction until, if we moved it any further, it would be entirely outside the feasible region. Note that the objective function line $2x_1 + 3x_2 = 800$ intersects the feasible region at the extreme point $x_1 = 250$ and $x_2 = 100$. This extreme point provides the minimum cost solution with an objective function value of 800. From Figures 2.15 and 2.16 we can see that the total production volume constraint and the processing time constraint are binding. Just as in every linear programming problem, the optimal solution occurs at an extreme point of the feasible region.

Summary of the Graphical Solution Procedure for Minimization Problems

The steps of the graphical solution procedure for a minimization problem are summarized below:

1. Prepare a graph of the feasible solution points for each of the constraints.
2. Determine the feasible solution region by identifying the solution points that satisfy all the constraints simultaneously.
3. Draw an objective function line showing all values of the x_1 and x_2 variables that yield a specified value of the objective function.

4. Move parallel objective function lines toward smaller objective function values until further movement would take the line completely outside the feasible region.
5. A feasible solution point on the objective function line with the smallest value is an optimal solution.

Surplus Variables

A complete analysis of the minimum cost solution to the M&D Chemicals problem shows that the desired total production of $1x_1 + 1x_2 = 350$ gallons has been achieved by using all available processing time of $2x_1 + 1x_2 = 2(250) + 1(100) = 600$ hours. In addition, note that the constraint requiring meeting product 1 demand has been satisfied with $x_1 = 250$ gallons. In fact, the production of product 1 exceeds its minimum level by $250 - 125 = 125$ gallons. This excess production for product 1 is referred to as *surplus*. In linear programming terminology any excess quantity corresponding to a $\geq$ constraint is referred to as surplus.

Recall that with a $\leq$ constraint, a slack variable can be added to the left-hand side of the inequality to convert the constraint to equality form. With a $\geq$ constraint a *surplus variable* can be subtracted from the left-hand side of the inequality to convert the constraint to equality form. Just as with slack variables, surplus variables are given a coefficient of zero in the objective function because they have no effect on its value. After including two surplus variables for the $\geq$ constraints and one slack variable for the $\leq$ constraint, the linear programming model of the M&D Chemicals problem appears as follows:

$$
\begin{aligned}
\min \quad & 2x_1 + 3x_2 + 0s_1 + 0s_2 + 0s_3 \\
\text{s.t.} \quad & \\
& 1x_1 \qquad\qquad - 1s_1 \qquad\qquad = 125 \\
& 1x_1 + 1x_2 \qquad\qquad - 1s_2 \qquad = 350 \\
& 2x_1 + 1x_2 \qquad\qquad\qquad + 1s_3 = 600 \\
& x_1, x_2, s_1, s_2, s_3 \geq 0
\end{aligned}
$$

All the constraints are now equalities. Hence the above formulation is the standard form representation of the M&D Chemicals problem. At the optimal solution of $x_1 = 250$ and $x_2 = 100$, the values of the surplus and slack variables are as follows:

Constraint	Value of Surplus or Slack Variables
Demand for product 1	$s_1 = 125$
Total production	$s_2 = 0$
Processing time	$s_3 = 0$

Refer to Figures 2.15 and 2.16. Note that the zero surplus and slack variables are associated with the constraints that are binding at the optimal solution: that is, the constraints total production and processing time. The surplus of 125 units is associated with the nonbinding constraint on the demand for product 1.

Note that in the Par, Inc. problem all the constraints were of the $\leq$ type and that in the M&D Chemicals problem the constraints were a mixture of $\geq$ and $\leq$ types. The number and types of constraints encountered in a particular linear programming problem will depend upon the specific conditions existing in the problem. Linear programming problems may have some $\leq$ constraints, some $\geq$ constraints, and some $=$ constraints. For an equality constraint, feasible solutions must lie directly on the constraint line.

An example of a linear program with all three constraint forms is given below (problem 35 at the end of the chapter will ask you to solve this problem using the graphical procedure):

$$
\begin{aligned}
\min \quad & 2x_1 + 2x_2 \\
\text{s.t.} \quad & \\
& 1x_1 + 3x_2 \leq 12 \\
& 3x_1 + 1x_2 \geq 13 \\
& 1x_1 - 1x_2 = 3 \\
& x_1, x_2 \geq 0
\end{aligned}
$$

The standard form representation of this problem is

$$
\begin{aligned}
\min \quad & 2x_1 + 2x_2 + 0s_1 + 0s_2 \\
\text{s.t.} \quad & \\
& 1x_1 + 3x_2 + 1s_1 \quad\quad = 12 \\
& 3x_1 + 1x_2 \quad\quad - 1s_2 = 13 \\
& 1x_1 - 1x_2 \quad\quad\quad = 3 \\
& x_1, x_2, s_1, s_2 \geq 0
\end{aligned}
$$

This formulation requires a slack variable for the $\leq$ constraint and a surplus variable for the $\geq$ constraint. However, neither a slack nor a surplus variable is required for the third constraint, since it is already in equality form.

The graphical solution method is a convenient way to find optimal extreme point solutions for two-variable linear programming problems. When solving linear programs graphically it is not necessary to write the problem in its standard form. Nevertheless, we should be able to compute the values of the slack and surplus variables and understand what they mean. In Chapter 3, we shall see that the values of slack and surplus variables are included in the computer solution of linear programs. In Chapter 5 we will introduce an algebraic solution procedure, the simplex method, which can be used to find optimal extreme-point solutions for linear programming problems having as many as several thousand decision variables. The mathematical steps of the simplex method involve solving simultaneous equations that represent the constraints of the linear program. Thus in setting up a linear program for solution by the simplex method we must have one linear equation for each constraint in the problem; therefore the problem must be in its standard form.

As a final point, it is important to realize that the standard form of the linear programming problem is equivalent to the original formulation of the problem. That is, the optimal solution to any linear programming problem is the same as the optimal solution to the standard form of the problem. The standard form has not changed the basic problem; it has only changed how we write the constraints for the problem.

2.8   SPECIAL CASES

In this section we discuss three special situations that can arise when we attempt to solve linear programming problems.

Alternate Optimal Solutions

From our discussion of the graphical method, we know that optimal solutions can be found at the extreme points of the feasible region. Now let us consider the special case where the optimal objective function line coincides with one of the constraint lines on the boundary of the feasible region. We will see that this can lead to the case of *alternate optimal solutions*; in such cases more than one solution provides the optimal value for the objective function.

As an example of the case of alternate optimal solutions, let us return to the Par, Inc. problem with the four constraints and feasible region as previously defined. However, let us assume that the profit for the standard bag (x_1) has been decreased to \$6.30. The revised objective function becomes $6.3x_1 + 9x_2$. The graphical solution of this problem is shown in Figure 2.17. Note that the optimal solution still occurs at an extreme point.

FIGURE 2.17
Par, Inc. Problem with an Objective Function of $6.3x_1 + 9x_2$ **(Alternate Optima)**

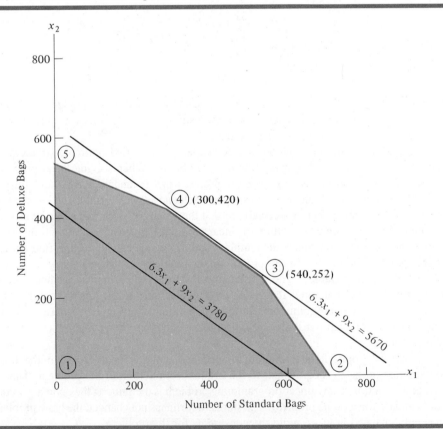

In fact, it occurs at two extreme points: extreme point ④ ($x_1 = 300$, $x_2 = 420$) and extreme point ③ ($x_1 = 540$, $x_2 = 252$).

The objective function values at these two extreme points are identical; that is

$$6.3x_1 + 9x_2 = 6.3(300) + 9(420) = 5670$$

and

$$6.3x_1 + 9x_2 = 6.3(540) + 9(252) = 5670$$

Furthermore, any point on the line connecting the two optimal extreme points also provides an optimal solution. For example, the solution point ($x_1 = 420$, $x_2 = 336$), which is halfway between the two extreme points, also provides the optimal objective function value of

$$6.3x_1 + 9x_2 = 6.3(420) + 9(336) = 5670$$

A linear programming problem with alternate optima is generally a good situation for the manager or decision maker. It means that several combinations of the decision variables are optimal and that the manager can select the specific optimal solution that is the most desirable.

Infeasibility

Infeasibility occurs when there is no solution to the linear programming problem that satisfies all the constraints, including the nonnegativity conditions $x_1, x_2 \geq 0$. Graphically, infeasibility means that a feasible region does not exist; that is, there are no points that satisfy all of the constraints and the nonnegativity conditions simultaneously. To illustrate this situation, let us look again at the problem faced by Par, Inc.

Suppose that management had specified that at least 500 of the standard bags and at least 360 of the deluxe bags must be manufactured. The graph of the solution region may now be constructed to reflect these new requirements (see Figure 2.18). The shaded area in the lower left-hand portion of the graph depicts those points satisfying the departmental constraints on the availability of time. The shaded area in the upper right-hand portion depicts those points satisfying the minimum production requirements of 500 standard and 360 deluxe bags. But there are no points satisfying both sets of constraints. Thus we see that if management imposes these minimum production requirements, there will be no feasible solution to the linear programming model.

How should we interpret infeasibility in terms of this current problem? First we should tell management that given the resources available (that is, cutting and dyeing time, sewing time, finishing time, and inspection and packaging time), it is not possible to make 500 standard bags and 360 deluxe bags. Moreover, we can tell management exactly how much of each resource must be expended in order to make it possible to manufacture 500 standard and 360 deluxe bags. Table 2.2 shows the minimum amounts of resources that must be available, the amounts currently available, and the additional amounts that are required. Thus we need 80 more hours of cutting and dyeing time, 32 more hours of finishing time, and 5 more hours of inspection and packaging time in order to meet management's minimum production requirements.

If, after seeing the above information, management still wants to manufacture 500 standard and 360 deluxe bags, additional resources must be provided. Perhaps this will

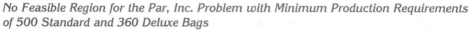

FIGURE 2.18
No Feasible Region for the Par, Inc. Problem with Minimum Production Requirements
of 500 Standard and 360 Deluxe Bags

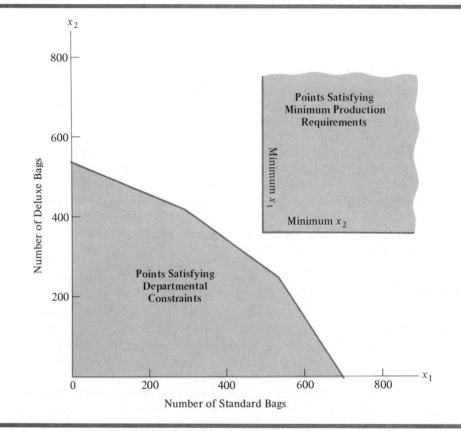

TABLE 2.2
Resources Needed to Manufacture 500 Standard Bags and 360 Deluxe Bags

Operation	Minimum Required Resources (hours)	Available Resources (hours)	Additional Resources Needed (hours)
Cutting and dyeing	$\frac{7}{10}(500) + 1(360) = 710$	630	80
Sewing	$\frac{1}{2}(500) + \frac{5}{6}(360) = 550$	600	none
Finishing	$1(500) + \frac{2}{3}(360) = 740$	708	32
Inspection and packaging	$\frac{1}{10}(500) + \frac{1}{4}(360) = 140$	135	5

mean hiring another person to work in the cutting and dyeing department, transferring a
person from elsewhere in the plant to work part time in the finishing department, or
having the sewing people help out periodically with the inspection and packaging. As
you can see, there are many possibilities for corrective management action, once we
discover that there is no feasible solution. The important thing to realize is that linear
programming analysis can help determine whether or not management's plans are feasible.

By analyzing the problem using linear programming, we are often able to point out infeasible conditions and initiate corrective action.

Unboundedness

A solution to a linear programming problem is *unbounded* if the value of the solution may be made infinitely large without violating any of the constraints. This condition might be termed "managerial utopia." If this condition were to occur in a profit maximization problem, it would be true that the manager could achieve an unlimited profit.

In linear programming models of real-world problems the occurrence of an unbounded solution means that the problem has been improperly formulated. For example, we know that it is not possible to increase profits indefinitely. Therefore we must conclude that if a profit maximization problem results in an unbounded solution, the mathematical model is not a sufficiently accurate representation of the real-world problem. Usually

FIGURE 2.19
Example of an Unbounded Problem

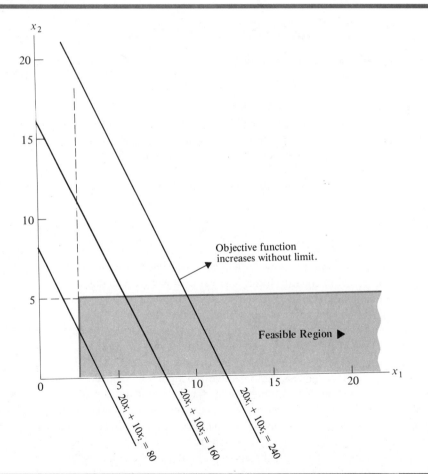

what has happened is that a constraint has been inadvertently omitted in the problem formulation.

As an illustration, consider the simple numerical example:

$$\max \quad 20x_1 + 10x_2$$

s.t.

$$
\begin{aligned}
1x_1 \quad\quad &\geq 2 \\
1x_2 &\leq 5 \\
x_1, \ x_2 &\geq 0
\end{aligned}
$$

In Figure 2.19 we have graphed the feasible region associated with this problem. Note that we can only indicate part of the feasible region, since the feasible region extends indefinitely in the direction of the x_1 axis. Looking at the objective function lines in Figure 2.19, we see that the solution to this problem may be made as large as we desire. That is, no matter what solution we pick, there will always be some feasible solution with a larger value. Thus we say that the solution to this linear program is *unbounded*.

Summary

Two problems, Par, Inc. and M&D Chemicals, were formulated as linear programs and solved by a graphical procedure. In studying the graphical solution procedure we noted that if an optimal solution to a linear programming problem exists, it can be found at an extreme point of the feasible region.

In the process of formulating mathematical models of the problems presented in this chapter the following general definition of a linear program was developed. A linear program is a mathematical model that has the following properties:

1. A linear objective function that is to be maximized or minimized
2. A set of linear constraints
3. Variables that are all restricted to nonnegative values

We have seen how slack variables can be used to write less-than-or-equal-to constraints in equality form and how surplus variables can be used to write greater-than-or-equal-to constraints in equality form. The value of a slack variable can usually be interpreted as the amount of unused resource, while the value of a surplus variable indicates the amount over and above some stated minimum requirement. When all constraints have been written as equalities, the linear program has been written in its standard form. In the special cases of infeasibility and unboundedness we showed that there is no optimal solution to the problem. In the case of infeasibility there are no feasible solutions, while in the case of unboundedness the objective function can be made infinitely large for a maximization problem and infinitely small for a minimization problem. In addition, a third special case, alternate optima, was discussed. In this case we have two optimal extreme points, and all the points on the line segment connecting them are also optimal.

While the graphical solution procedure is not used to solve larger linear programs, the intuition developed in this chapter is helpful in understanding the solution of any linear program.

Glossary

Objective function   All linear programs have a linear objective function that is either to be maximized or minimized. In many linear programming problems the objective function will be used to measure the profit or cost of a particular solution.

Constraint   An equation or inequality that rules our certain combinations of decision variables as feasible solutions.

Constraint function   The left-hand side of a constraint (that is, the portion of the constraint containing the variables).

Solution   Any set of values for the variables.

Optimal solution   A feasible solution that maximizes or minimizes the value of the objective function.

Nonnegativity constraints   A set of constraints that requires all variables to be non-negative.

Mathematical model   A representation of a problem where the objective and all constraint conditions are described by mathematical expressions.

Linear program   A mathematical model with a linear objective function, a set of linear constraints, and nonnegative variables.

Linear equations or functions   Mathematical expressions in which the variables appear in separate terms and are raised to the first power.

Feasible solution   A solution that satisfies all the constraints.

Feasible region   The set of all feasible solutions.

Redundant constraint   A constraint that does not affect the feasible region. If a constraint is redundant, it can be removed from the problem without affecting the feasible region.

Extreme point   Graphically speaking, extreme points are the feasible solution points occurring at the vertices or "corners" of the feasible region. With two variable problems, extreme points are determined by the intersection of the constraint lines.

Slack variable   A variable added to the left-hand side of a less-than-or-equal-to constraint to convert the constraint into an equality. The value of this variable can usually be interpreted as the amount of unused resource.

Surplus variable   A variable subtracted from the left-hand side of a greater-than-or-equal-to constraint to convert the constraint into an equality. The value of this variable can usually be interpreted as the amount over and above some required minimum level.

Standard form   A linear program in which all the constraints are written as equalities. The optimal solution of the standard form of a linear program is the same as the optimal solution of the original formulation of the linear program.

Alternate optima   The situation when a linear program has two or more optimal solutions.

Infeasibility   The situation in which there is no solution to the linear programming problem that satisfies all the constraints.

Unboundedness   A maximization linear programming problem is said to be unbounded if the value of the solution may be made infinitely large without violating any of the constraints. A minimization problem is unbounded if the value of the solution may be made infinitely small.

Problems

1. Which of the following mathematical relationships could be found in a linear programming model and which could not? For the relationships that are unacceptable for linear programs, state your reasons.
    a. $-1x_1 + 2x_2 - 1x_3 \leq 70$
    b. $2x_1 - 2x_3 = 50$
    c. $1x_1 - 2x_2^2 + 4x_3 \leq 10$
    d. $3\sqrt{x_1} + 2x_2 - 1x_3 \geq 15$
    e. $1x_1 + 1x_2 + 1x_3 = 6$
    f. $2x_1 + 5x_2 + 1x_1x_2 \leq 25$

2. Find the feasible solution points for the following constraints:
    a. $4x_1 + 2x_2 \leq 16$
    b. $4x_1 + 2x_2 \geq 16$
    c. $4x_1 + 2x_2 = 16$

3. Graphing constraint lines is an essential step in the graphical method. Show a separate graph of the constraint lines and feasible solutions for each of the following constraints:
    a. $3x_1 + 2x_2 \leq 18$
    b. $12x_1 + 8x_2 \geq 480$
    c. $5x_1 + 10x_2 = 200$

4. Show a separate graph of the constraint lines and feasible solutions for each of the following constraints:
    a. $3x_1 - 4x_2 \geq 60$
    b. $-6x_1 + 5x_2 \leq 60$
    c. $5x_1 - 2x_2 \leq 0$

5. Given below are three objective functions for linear programming problems:

    $$z = 7x_1 + 10x_2$$
    $$z = 6x_1 + 4x_2$$
    $$z = -4x_1 + 7x_2$$

    Determine the slope of each objective function. Show the graph of each of the three objective functions for $z = 420$.

6. Solve the following linear program:

    $$\max \quad 5x_1 + 5x_2$$
    $$\text{s.t.}$$
    $$1x_1 \qquad\quad \leq 100$$
    $$1x_2 \leq 80$$
    $$2x_1 + 4x_2 \leq 400$$
    $$x_1, x_2 \geq 0$$

7. Identify the feasible region for the following set of constraints:

    $$\tfrac{1}{2}x_1 + \tfrac{1}{4}x_2 \geq 30$$
    $$1x_1 + 5x_2 \geq 250$$
    $$\tfrac{1}{4}x_1 + \tfrac{1}{2}x_2 \leq 50$$
    $$x_1, x_2 \geq 0$$

8. Identify the feasible region for the following set of constraints:

$$2x_1 - 1x_2 \le 0$$
$$-1x_1 + 1.5x_2 \le 200$$
$$x_1, x_2 \ge 0$$

9. Identify the feasible region for the following set of constraints:

$$3x_1 - 2x_2 \ge 0$$
$$2x_1 - 1x_2 \le 200$$
$$1x_1 \qquad \le 150$$
$$x_1, x_2 \ge 0$$

10. Consider the following linear programming problem:

$$\max \quad 2x_1 + 3x_2$$
$$\text{s.t}$$
$$1x_1 + 2x_2 \le 6$$
$$5x_1 + 3x_2 \le 15$$
$$x_1, x_2 \ge 0$$

Find the optimal solution. What is the value of the objective function at the optimal solution?

11. Consider the following linear programming problem:

$$\max \quad 3x_1 + 3x_2$$
$$\text{s.t.}$$
$$2x_1 + 4x_2 \le 12$$
$$6x_1 + 4x_2 \le 24$$
$$x_1, x_2 \ge 0$$

a. Find the optimal solution.
b. If the objective function were changed to $2x_1 + 6x_2$, what would the optimal solution be?
c. How many extreme points are there? What are the values of x_1 and x_2 at each extreme point?

12. Consider the following linear programming problem:

$$\max \quad 3x_1 + 2x_2$$
$$\text{s.t.}$$
$$2x_1 + 2x_2 \le 8$$
$$3x_1 + 2x_2 \le 12$$
$$1x_1 + .5x_2 \le 3$$
$$x_1, x_2 \ge 0$$

a. Find the optimal solution. What is the value of the objective function?

b. Does this problem have a redundant constraint? If so, what is it? Does the solution change if the redundant constraint is removed from the problem? Explain.

13. What constraint lines combine to form extreme point ④ of the Par, Inc. problem (see Figure 2.6 and Figure 2.14)? Solve the simultaneous linear equations to show that the exact values of x_1 and x_2 at this extreme point are $x_1 = 300$ and $x_2 = 420$.

14. Suppose that the management of Par, Inc. encounters each of the following situations:

a. The accounting department revises its estimate of profit contribution on the deluxe bag to $18 per bag.

b. A new low-cost material is available for the standard bag, and the profit contribution per standard bag can be increased to $20 per bag. (Assume the profit contribution of the deluxe bag is the original $9 value.)

c. New sewing equipment is available that would increase the sewing operation capacity to 750 hours. (Assume $10x_1 + 9x_2$ is the appropriate objective function.)

If each of the above conditions is encountered separately, what are the optimal solution and profit contribution for each situation?

15. Refer to the feasible region for the Par, Inc. problem in Figure 2.14.

a. Develop an objective function that will make extreme point ⑤ the optimal extreme point.

b. What is the optimal solution using the objective function you selected in part (a)?

c. What are the values of the slack variables associated with this solution?

16. Kelson Sporting Equipment, Inc. makes two different types of baseball gloves: a regular model and a catcher's model. The firm has 900 hours of production time available in its cutting and sewing department, 300 hours of production time available in its finishing department, and 100 hours of production time available in its packaging and shipping department. The production time requirements and the profit per glove are given below:

| | Production Time (hours) | | | |
Model	Cutting and Sewing	Finishing	Packaging and Shipping	Profit/Glove
Regular model	1	$\frac{1}{2}$	$\frac{1}{8}$	$5
Catcher's model	$\frac{3}{2}$	$\frac{1}{3}$	$\frac{1}{4}$	$8

a. Assuming that the company wants to maximize profit, how many gloves of each model should Kelson manufacture?

b. What is the profit Kelson can earn with the above production quantities?

c. How many hours of production time will be scheduled in each department?

d. What is the slack time in each department?

17. The Erlanger Manufacturing Company makes two products. The profit estimates are $25 for each unit of product 1 sold and $30 for each unit of product 2 sold.

The labor-hour requirements for the products in each of three production departments are summarized below:

	Product 1	Product 2
Department *A*	1.50	3.00
Department *B*	2.00	1.00
Department *C*	.25	.25

The production supervisors in the departments have estimated that the following number of labor-hours will be available during the next month: 450 hours in department *A*, 350 hours in department *B*, and 50 hours in department *C*. Assuming that the company is interested in maximizing profits, answer the following:

a. What is the linear programming model for this problem?

b. Find the optimal solution. How much of each product should be produced, and what is the projected profit?

c. What is the scheduled production time and slack time in each department?

18. Yard Care, Inc. manufactures a variety of lawn care products, including two well-known lawn fertilizers. Each fertilizer product is a blend of two raw materials known as K40 and K50. During the current production period, 900 pounds of K40 and 400 pounds of K50 are available. Each pound of the product known as "Green Lawn" uses $3/5$ pound of K40 and $2/5$ pound of K50. Each pound of the product known as "Lawn Care" uses $3/4$ pound of K40 and $1/4$ pound of K50. In addition, a current limit on the availability of packaging materials restricts the production of Lawn Care to a maximum of 500 pounds.

a. If the profit contribution for both products is $3 per pound, how many pounds of each product should the company manufacture?

b. Should it be a concern to the company that the availability of packaging materials is restricting the production of Lawn Care? What would happen to the production quantities and the projected profit if the firm were able to remove the restriction on the amount of Lawn Care that could be produced?

19. Special K Candy Company has a limited supply of a chocolate ingredient that is used in the production of two of its candy bar products. The company's "Chocolate Wonder Bar" uses .5 ounce of the chocolate ingredient per bar. The company's "Big Crunch Bar" uses .3 ounce per bar. During the coming month the company has a maximum of 250 pounds of chocolate available for use in these two products. In addition, the marketing department reports that the maximum quantities that the company can sell are 5000 bars of Chocolate Wonder and 7500 bars of Big Crunch. If the company can make a profit of 12 cents for each Chocolate Wonder Bar and 8 cents for each Big Crunch Bar, what mix of these two products will maximize the firm's profits?

20. Investment Advisors, Inc. is a brokerage firm that manages stock portfolios for a number of clients. A new client has requested that the firm handle an $80,000 investment portfolio. As an initial investment strategy the client would like to restrict the portfolio to a mix of the following stocks:

Stock	Price/Share	Estimated Annual Return/Share	Risk Index/Share
U.S. Oil	$25	$3	.50
Hub Properties	$50	$5	.25

The risk index for the stock is a rating of the relative risk of the two investment alternatives. For the data given, U.S. Oil is judged to be the riskier investment. By constraining the total risk for the portfolio, the investment firm avoids placing excessive amounts of the portfolio in potentially high-return but also high-risk investments. For the current portfolio an upper limit of 700 has been set for the total risk index of all investments. In addition, the firm has set an upper limit of 1000 shares for the more risky U.S. Oil stock. How many shares of each stock should be purchased in order to maximize the total annual return?

21. Consider the following linear program:

$$\min \quad 3x_1 + 4x_2$$
$$\text{s.t.}$$
$$1x_1 + 3x_2 \geq 6$$
$$1x_1 + 1x_2 \geq 4$$
$$x_1, x_2 \geq 0$$

Identify the feasible region and find the optimal solution. What is the value of the objective function?

22. Identify the three extreme point solutions for the M&D Chemicals problem. Identify the value of the objective function and the values of the slack and surplus variables at each extreme point.

23. Greentree Kennels, Inc. provides overnight lodging for a variety of pets. A particular feature at Greentree's is the quality of care the pets receive, including excellent food. The kennel's dog food is made by mixing two brand-name dog food products to obtain what the kennel calls the "well-balanced dog diet." The data for the two dog foods are as follows:

Dog Food	Cost/ Ounce	Protein (%)	Fat (%)
Bark Bits	$.06	30	15
Canine Chow	$.05	20	30

If Greentree wants to be sure that the dogs recieve at least 5 ounces of protein and at least 3 ounces of fat per day, what is the minimum cost mix of the two dog food products?

24. Jack Kammer has been trying to figure out the correct amount of fertilizer that should be applied to his lawn. After getting his soil analyzed at the local agricultural agency, he was advised to put at least 60 pounds of nitrogen, 24 pounds of phos-

phorus compounds, and 40 pounds of potassium compounds on the lawn this season. One-third of the mixture is to be applied in May, one-third in July, and one-third in late September. After checking the local discount stores, Jack finds that one store is currently having a sale on packaged fertilizer. One type on sale is the 20-5-20 mixture containing 20% nitrogen, 5% phosphorus compounds, and 20% potassium compounds, and selling at $4 for a 20-pound bag. The other type on sale is a 10-10-5 mixture selling for $5 for a 40-pound bag. Jack would like to know how many bags of each type he should purchase so he can combine the ingredients to form a mixture that will meet the minimum agricultural agency requirements. Like all homeowners plagued by large lawns, Jack would like to spend as little as possible to keep his lawn healthy. What should Jack do?

25. Car Phones, Inc. sells two models of car telephones: model x and model y. Records show that 3 hours of sales time are used for each model x phone that is sold, and 5 hours of sales time for each model y phone. A total of 600 hours of sales time is available for the next 4-week period. In addition, management planning policies call for minimum sales goals of 25 units for both model x and model y.
   a. Show the feasible region for the Car Phones, Inc. problem.
   b. Assuming the company makes a $40 profit contribution for each model x sold and a $50 profit contribution for each model y sold, what is the optimal sales goal for the company for the next 4-week period?
   c. Develop a constraint and show the feasible region if management adds the restriction that Car Phones must sell at least as many model y phones as model x phones.
   d. What is the new optimal solution if the constraint in part (c) is added to the problem?

26. Kats is a new pet-food product. Each 16-ounce can of Kats consists of a blend, or mixture, of two pet-food ingredients. Let

   x_1 = the number of ounces of ingredient A in a 16-ounce can
   x_2 = the number of ounces of ingredient B in a 16-ounce can

   Each ounce of ingredient A contains $1/2$ ounce of protein and $1/8$ ounce of fat. Each ounce of ingredient B contains $1/10$ ounce of protein and $1/3$ ounce of fat. Restrictions are that a 16-ounce can of Kats must have at least 4 ounces of protein and 2.5 ounces of fat. If ingredient A costs $.04 per ounce and ingredient B costs $.03 per ounce, what is the minimum cost blend of ingredients A and B in each 16-ounce can of Kats? Identify and interpret the values of the surplus variables for the problem.

27. Photo Chemicals produces two types of photograph-developing fluids. Both products cost Photo Chemicals $1 per gallon to produce. Based upon an analysis of current inventory levels and outstanding orders for the next month, Photo Chemicals' management has specified that at leat 30 gallons of product 1 and aţ least 20 gallons of product 2 must be produced during the next two weeks. Management has also stated that an existing inventory of highly perishable raw material required in the production of both fluids must be used within the next 2 weeks. The current inventory of the perishable raw material is 80 pounds. While more of this raw material can be ordered if necessary, any of the current inventory that is not used within the next 2 weeks will spoil; hence the management requirement that at least 80 pounds be used in the next 2 weeks. Furthermore, it is known that product 1 requires 1

pound of this perishable raw material per gallon and product 2 requires 2 pounds of the raw material per gallon. Since Photo Chemicals' objective is to keep its production costs at the minimum possible level, the firm's management is looking for a minimum cost production plan that uses all the 80 pounds of perishable raw material and provides at least 30 gallons of product 1 and at least 20 gallons of product 2. What is the minimum cost solution?

28. Bryant's Pizza, Inc. is a producer of frozen pizza products. The company makes a profit of $1.00 for each regular pizza it produces and $1.50 for each deluxe pizza produced. Each pizza includes a combination of dough mix and topping mix. Currently the firm has 150 pounds of dough mix and 50 pounds of topping mix. Each regular pizza uses 1 pound of dough mix and 4 ounces of topping mix. Each deluxe pizza uses 1 pound of dough mix and 8 ounces of topping mix. Based on past demand Bryant can sell at least 50 regular pizzas and at least 25 deluxe pizzas. How many regular and deluxe pizzas should the company make in order to maximize profits?

    a. Show the above problem in standard form.
    b. What are the values and interpretations of all slack and surplus variables?
    c. Which constraints are binding the optimal solution?

29. Wilkinson Motors, Inc. sells standard automobiles and station wagons. The firm makes $400 profit for each automobile it sells and $500 profit for each station wagon it sells. The company is planning next quarter's order, which the manufacturer says cannot exceed 300 automobiles and 150 station wagons. Dealer preparation time requires 2 hours for each automobile and 3 hours for each station wagon. Next quarter the company has 900 hours of shop time available for new car preparation. How many automobiles and station wagons should be ordered so that profit is maximized?

    a. Show the linear programming model of the above problem.
    b. Show the standard form and identify the slack variables.
    c. Identify the extreme points of the feasible region.
    d. Find the optimal solution.
    e. Which constraints are binding?

30. Ryland Farms in northwestern Indiana grows soybeans and corn on its 500 acres of land. An acre of soybeans brings a $100 profit and an acre of corn brings a $200 profit. Because of a government program no more than 200 acres may be planted in soybeans. During the planting season 1200 hours of planting time will be available. Each acre of soybeans requires 2 hours, while each acre of corn requires 6 hours. How many acres of soybeans and how many acres of corn should be planted in order to maximize profits?

    a. Show the linear programming model of the above problem.
    b. Show the standard form and identify all slack variables.
    c. Find the optimal solution.
    d. Identify all the extreme points of the feasible region.
    e. If the farm could get either more hours of labor for planting or additional land, which should it attempt to obtain? Why?

31. RMC is a small firm that produces a variety of chemical products. In a particular production process, three raw materials are blended (mixed together) to produce two products: a fuel additive and a solvent base. Each ton of fuel additive is a mixture of $2/5$ ton of material 1 and $3/5$ ton of material 3. A ton of solvent base is a

mixture of $\frac{1}{2}$ ton of material 1, $\frac{1}{5}$ ton of material 2, and $\frac{3}{10}$ ton of material 3. After deducting relevant costs, the company makes $40 for every ton of fuel additive produced and $30 for every ton of solvent base produced.

RMC's production is constrained by a limited availability of the three raw materials. For the current production period RMC has available the following quantities of each raw material:

Raw Material	Amount Available for Production
Material 1	20 tons
Material 2	5 tons
Material 3	21 tons

a. Given the limited availability of raw materials, how many tons of each product should RMC produce in order to maximize profits? What is the maximum profit?
b. Is there any unused material? If so, which material is used?
c. Are there any redundant constraints? If so, which ones?

32. Reconsider the RMC situation in problem 31.
   a. Identify all the extreme points of the feasible region.
   b. Suppose RMC discovers a way to increase the profit of solvent base to $60 per ton. Does this change the optimal solution? If so, how?
   c. Suppose the profit for the solvent base is $50 per ton. What is the optimal solution now? Comment on any special characteristics that may exist with this profit for the solvent base.
33. Reconsider the RMC situation in problem 31. Suppose that management adds the requirements that at least 30 tons of fuel additive and at least 15 tons of solvent base must be produced.
   a. Graph the constraints for this revised RMC problem. What happens to the feasible region? Explain.
   b. If there are no feasible solutions, explain what is needed to produce 30 tons of fuel additive and 15 tons of solvent base.
34. Consider the following linear program:

$$\max \quad 1x_1 + 2x_2$$
$$\text{s.t.}$$
$$1x_1 \qquad\qquad \leq 5$$
$$\qquad 1x_2 \leq 4$$
$$2x_1 + 2x_2 = 12$$
$$x_1, x_2 \geq 0$$

a. Show the feasible region.
b. What are the extreme points of the feasible region?
c. Find the optimal solution using the graphical procedure.

35. Consider the following linear program:

$$\min \quad 2x_1 + 2x_2$$
$$\text{s.t.}$$
$$1x_1 + 3x_2 \leq 12$$
$$3x_1 + 1x_2 \geq 13$$
$$1x_1 - 1x_2 = 3$$
$$x_1, x_2 \geq 0$$

a. Show the feasible region.
b. What are the extreme points of the feasible region?
c. Find the optimal solution using the graphical procedure.

36. Write the following linear program in standard form:

$$\max \quad 5x_1 + 2x_2 + 8x_3$$
$$\text{s.t.}$$
$$1x_1 - 2x_2 + \tfrac{1}{2}x_3 \leq 420$$
$$2x_1 + 3x_2 - 1x_3 \leq 610$$
$$6x_1 - 1x_2 + 3x_3 \leq 125$$
$$x_1, x_2, x_3 \geq 0$$

37. For the linear program

$$\max \quad 4x_1 + 1x_2$$
$$\text{s.t.}$$
$$10x_1 + 2x_2 \leq 30$$
$$3x_1 + 2x_2 \leq 12$$
$$2x_1 + 2x_2 \leq 10$$
$$x_1, x_2 \geq 0$$

a. Write this problem in standard form.
b. Solve the problem.
c. What are the values of the three slack variables at the optimal solution?

38. Given the linear program

$$\max \quad 3x_1 + 4x_2$$
$$\text{s.t.}$$
$$-1x_1 + 2x_2 \leq 8$$
$$1x_1 + 2x_2 \leq 12$$
$$2x_1 + 1x_2 \leq 16$$
$$x_1, x_2 \geq 0$$

a. Write the problem in standard form.
b. Solve the problem.
c. What are the values of the three slack variables at the optimal solution?

39. For the linear program

$$\min \quad 6x_1 + 4x_2$$
$$\text{s.t.}$$
$$2x_1 + 1x_2 \geq 12$$
$$1x_1 + 1x_2 \geq 10$$
$$1x_2 \leq 4$$
$$x_1, \ x_2 \geq 0$$

a. Write the problem in standard form.
b. Solve the problem using the graphical solution procedure.
c. What are the values of the slack and surplus variables?

40. Does the following linear program involve infeasibility, unboundedness, and/or alternate optimal solutions? Explain.

$$\max \quad 4x_1 + 8x_2$$
$$\text{s.t}$$
$$2x_1 + 2x_2 \leq 10$$
$$-1x_1 + 1x_2 \geq 8$$
$$x_1, x_2 \geq 0$$

41. Does the following linear program involve infeasibility, unboundedness, and/or alternate optimal solutions? Explain.

$$\max \quad 1x_1 + 1x_2$$
$$\text{s.t.}$$
$$8x_1 + 6x_2 \geq 24$$
$$4x_1 + 6x_2 \geq -12$$
$$2x_2 \geq 4$$
$$x_1, x_2 \geq 0$$

42. Consider the following linear program:

$$\max \quad 1x_1 + 1x_2$$
$$\text{s.t.}$$
$$5x_1 + 3x_2 \leq 15$$
$$3x_1 + 5x_2 \leq 15$$
$$x_1, x_2 \geq 0$$

a. What is the optimal solution for this problem?
b. Suppose that the objective function is changed to $1x_1 + 2x_2$. Find the new optimal solution.
c. By adjusting the coefficient of x_2 in the objective function, develop a new objective function that will make the solutions found in parts (a) and (b) above alternate optimal solutions.

43. Consider the following linear program:

$$\max \quad 1x_1 - 2x_2$$

$$\text{s.t.}$$

$$-4x_1 + 3x_2 \leq 3$$

$$1x_1 - 1x_2 \leq 3$$

$$x_1, \, x_2 \geq 0$$

    a. Graph the feasible region for the problem.

    b. Is the feasible region unbounded? Explain.

    c. Find the optimal solution.

    d. Does an unbounded feasible region imply that the optimal solution to the linear program will be unbounded?

44. Discuss what happens to the M&D Chemicals problem (see Section 2.7) if the cost per gallon for product 1 is increased to $3.00 per gallon. What would you recommend? Explain.

45. For the M&D Chemicals problem in Section 2.7, discuss the effect of management requiring total production of 500 gallons for the two products. List two or three actions M&D should consider to correct the situation you encounter.

46. Reconsider the Kelson Sporting Equipment, Inc. production example (problem 16). Discuss the concepts of infeasibility, unboundedness, and alternate optima as they occur in each of the following situations:

    a. Management has requested that the production of baseball gloves (regular model plus catcher's model) be such that the total number of gloves produced is at least 750. That is, $1x_1 + 1x_2 \geq 750$.

    b. The original problem has to be solved again because the profit for the regular model is adjusted downward to $4 per glove.

    c. What would have to happen for this problem to be unbounded?

47. Management of High Tech Services (HTS) would like to develop a model that will help allocate technician's time between service calls to regular contract customers and new customers. A maximum of 80 hours of technician time is available over the 2-week planning period. In order to satisfy cash flow requirements, at least $800 in revenue (per technician) must be generated during the 2-week period. Technician time for regular customers generates $25 per hour. However, technician time for new customers only generates an average of $8 per hour because in many cases a new customer contact does not provide billable services. To ensure that new customer contacts are being maintained, the time technicians spend on new customer contacts must be at least 60% of the time technicians spend on regular customer contacts. Given the above revenue and policy requirements, HTS would like to determine how to allocate technician's time between regular customers and new customers so that the total number of customers contacted during the 2-week period will be maximized. Technicians require an average of 50 minutes for each regular customer contact and 1 hour for each new customer contact.

    a. Develop a linear programming model that will enable HTS to determine how to allocate technician's time between regular customers and new customers.

    b. Graph the feasible region.

c. Solve the appropriate simultaneous linear equations to determine the values of x_1 and x_2 at each extreme point of the feasible region.
d. Find the optimal solution.

━━━━━ Case Problem: ━━━━━
ADVERTISING STRATEGY

Midtown Motors, Inc. has hired a marketing services firm to develop an advertising strategy for promoting Midtown's used-car sales. The marketing firm has recommended that Midtown use spot announcements on both television and radio as the advertising media for the proposed promotional campaign. Advertising strategy guidelines are expressed as follows:

1. Use at least 30 announcements for combined television and radio coverage.
2. Do not use more than 25 radio announcements.
3. The number of radio announcements cannot be less than the number of television announcements.

The television station has quoted a cost of $1200 per spot announcement and the radio station has quoted a cost of $300 per spot announcement. Midtown's advertising budget has been set at $25,500. The marketing services firm has rated the various advertising media in terms of audience coverage and recall power of the advertisement. For Midtown's media alternatives, the television announcement is rated at 600 and the radio announcement is rated at 200. Midtown's president would like to know how many television and how many radio spot announcements should be used in order to maximize the overall rating of the advertising campaign.

Midtown's president believes the television station will consider running the Midtown spot announcement on its highly rated evening news program (at the same cost) if midtown will consider using additional television announcements.

MANAGERIAL REPORT

Perform an analysis of advertising strategy for Midtown Motors and a report to Midtown's president presenting your findings and recommendations. Include (but do not limit your discussion to) a consideration of the following:

a. The recommended number of television and radio spot announcements.
b. The relative merits of each advertising medium.
c. The rating that would be necessary for the news program before it would make sense to increase the number of television spots.

d. The number of television spots that should be purchased if the news program is rated highly enough to make increasing the number of television spots advisable.

e. The restrictions placed on the advertising strategy that Midtown might want to consider relaxing or altering.

f. The best use of any possible increase in the advertising budget.

g. Any other information that may help Midtown's president make the advertising strategy decision.

Include a copy of your linear programming model and graphical solution in the appendix to your report.

3

Linear Programming: Sensitivity Analysis and Computer Solution

In this chapter we provide an introduction to sensitivity analysis and the use of computers for solving linear programming problems. Sensitivity analysis associated with the optimal solution provides valuable supplementary information for the decision maker. After showing how sensitivity analysis can be conducted using a graphical approach, we demonstrate how LINDO/PC, a software package for solving linear programming problems on a microcomputer, can be used to solve the Par, Inc. and M&D Chemicals problems presented in Chapter 2. In discussing the computer solution for these problems we will focus on the interpretation of the computer output, which includes the optimal solution and sensitivity analysis information. The chapter concludes with a discussion of the formulation, computer solution and sensitivity analysis for a linear programming problem involving more than two decision variables.

3.1 INTRODUCTION TO SENSITIVITY ANALYSIS

Sensitivity analysis is the study of how changes in the coefficients of a linear program affect the optimal solution. Using sensitivity analysis we can answer questions such as the following:

1. How will a *change in a coefficient of the objective function* affect the optimal solution?
2. How will a *change in the right-hand-side value for a constraint* affect the optimal solution?

Since sensitivity analysis is concerned with how the above changes affect the optimal solution, the analysis does not begin until the optimal solution to the original linear programming problem has been obtained. For this reason sensitivity analysis is often referred to as *postoptimality analysis*.

One of the primary reasons that sensitivity analysis is important to decision makers is that real-world problems exist in a dynamic, or changing, environment. Prices of raw materials change, demand for various products shifts, companies purchase new machinery to replace old, stock prices fluctuate, employee turnover occurs, and so on. If a linear programming model has been used in such an environment, we can expect some of the coefficients to change over time. As a result we will want to determine how these changes affect the optimal solution to the original linear programming problem. Sensitivity analysis provides us with the information needed to respond to such changes without requiring the complete solution of a revised linear program.

Recall the Par, Inc. problem introduced in Chapter 2.

$$\begin{aligned}
\max \quad & 10x_1 + 9x_2 \\
\text{subject to (s.t.)} \quad & \\
& \tfrac{7}{10}x_1 + 1x_2 \le 630 \quad \text{Cutting and dyeing} \\
& \tfrac{1}{2}x_1 + \tfrac{5}{6}x_2 \le 600 \quad \text{Sewing} \\
& 1x_1 + \tfrac{2}{3}x_2 \le 708 \quad \text{Finishing} \\
& \tfrac{1}{10}x_1 + \tfrac{1}{4}x_2 \le 135 \quad \text{Inspection and packaging} \\
& x_1, x_2 \ge 0
\end{aligned}$$

The optimal solution, $x_1 = 540$ standard bags and $x_2 = 252$ deluxe bags, is based on profit figures of \$10 per standard bag and \$9 per deluxe bag. However, suppose we later learn that because of a price reduction the profit contribution per standard bag has been reduced to \$7. Sensitivity analysis can be used to determine whether or not the production schedule calling for 540 standard bags and 252 deluxe bags is still the best solution. If it is, there will be no need to solve a modified linear program with $7x_1 + 9x_2$ as the objective function.

Sensitivity analysis can also be used to determine which coefficients in a linear programming model are most critical. For instance, suppose Par, Inc.'s management believes that the \$9 profit contribution per deluxe bag is only a rough estimate of the profit contribution that will actually be obtained. If sensitivity analysis shows that 540 standard bags and 252 deluxe bags will be the optimal solution as long as the profit contribution for the deluxe bag is between \$5 and \$13, management should feel comfortable with the rough estimate of \$9 per bag and the recommended production quantities. However, if sensitivity analysis shows 540 standard bags and 252 deluxe bags will be the optimal solution only if the profit contribution for the deluxe bag is between \$8.90 and \$9.25, management may want to review the accuracy of the \$9-per-bag profit estimate.

Another aspect of sensitivity analysis is concerned with changes in the right-hand sides of the constraints. Recall that in the Par, Inc. problem the optimal solution used all the cutting and dyeing time and all the finishing time. What would happen to the optimal solution, and total profit, if Par, Inc. could obtain additional time for either of these operations? Sensitivity analysis can help determine how much each added hour is worth and how many hours can be added before diminishing returns set in.

3.2   GRAPHICAL SENSITIVITY ANALYSIS

For linear programming problems with two decision variables, graphical solution methods can be used to perform sensitivity analysis on the objective function coefficients and the right-hand side values for the constraints.

Objective Function Coefficients

Let us first consider how changes in the objective function coefficients might affect the optimal solution to the Par, Inc. problem. For instance, what range of values can the profit per standard bag take on without causing Par, Inc. to change from the solution of 540 standard bags and 252 deluxe bags? Such a range of values is called the *range of optimality* for the objective function coefficient.

Figure 3.1 shows the graphical solution to the Par, Inc. problem. A careful inspection of this graph shows that as long as the slope of the objective function is between the slope of line *A* (which coincides with the cutting and dyeing constraint line) and the slope

FIGURE 3.1

Graphical Solution of Par, Inc. Problem with Slope of Objective Function Between Slopes of Line A and Line B. Extreme Point ③ Is Optimal

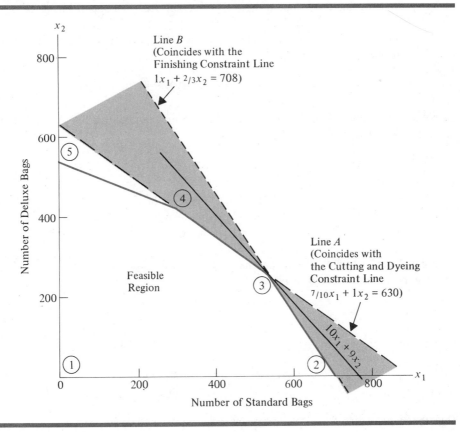

of line B (which coincides with the finishing constraint line), extreme point ③ with $x_1 =$ 540 and $x_2 = 252$ will be optimal. Changing an objective function coefficient for x_1 or x_2 will cause the slope of the objective function to change. In Figure 3.1 we see that such changes cause the objective function line to rotate around extreme point ③. However, as long as the objective function line stays within the shaded region, extreme point ③ will remain optimal.

Rotating the objective function line *counterclockwise* causes the slope to become less negative and hence the slope increases. When the objective function line has been rotated counterclockwise (slope increased) enough to coincide with line A, we obtain alternate optima between extreme points ③ and ④. Any further counterclockwise rotation of the objective function line will cause extreme point ③ to be nonoptimal. Hence the slope of line A provides an upper limit for the slope of the objective function line.

Rotating the objective function line *clockwise* causes the slope to become more negative and hence the slope decreases. When the objective function line has been rotated clockwise (slope decreased) enough to coincide with line B, we obtain alternate optima between extreme points ③ and ②. Any further clockwise rotation of the objective function line will cause extreme point ③ to be nonoptimal. Hence the slope of line B provides a lower limit for the slope of the objective function line.

From the above discussion it should be clear that extreme point ③ will be the optimal solution as long as

Slope of line $B \leq$ slope of objective function line $\leq$ slope of line A

In Figure 3.1 we see that the equation for line A, the cutting and dyeing constraint line, is as follows:

$$\tfrac{7}{10}x_1 + 1x_2 = 630$$

By solving the above equation for x_2, we can write the equation for line A in its slope-intercept form. This yields

$$x_2 = -\tfrac{7}{10}x_1 + 630$$

Slope of line A Intercept of line A on x_2 axis

Thus the slope for line A is $-\tfrac{7}{10}$ and its intercept on the x_2 axis is 630.

The equation for line B in Figure 3.1 is

$$1x_1 + \tfrac{2}{3}x_2 = 708$$

Solving for x_2 provides the slope-intercept form for line B. Doing so yields

$$\tfrac{2}{3}x_2 = -1x_1 + 708$$
$$x_2 = -\tfrac{3}{2}x_1 + 1062$$

Thus the slope of line B is $-\tfrac{3}{2}$ and its intercept on the x_2 axis is 1062.

Now that the slopes of line A and B have been computed, we see that in order for extreme point ③ to remain optimal we must have

$$-\tfrac{3}{2} \leq \text{slope of objective function} \leq -\tfrac{7}{10} \qquad (3.1)$$

Let us now consider the general form of the slope of the objective function. Let c_1 denote the profit of a standard bag, c_2 denote the profit of a deluxe bag, and z denote the value of the objective function. Using this notation, the objective function can be written as

$$z = c_1 x_1 + c_2 x_2$$

Writing this equation in slope-intercept form, we obtain

$$c_2 x_2 = -c_1 x_1 + z$$

and

$$x_2 = -\frac{c_1}{c_2} x_1 + \frac{z}{c_2}$$

Thus we see that the slope of the objective function is given by $-c_1/c_2$. Substituting $-c_1/c_2$ into expression (3.1), we see that extreme point ③ will be optimal as long as the following expression is satisfied:

$$-\tfrac{3}{2} \leq -\frac{c_1}{c_2} \leq -\tfrac{7}{10} \qquad (3.2)$$

To compute the range of optimality for the standard-bag profit contribution, we hold the profit contribution for the deluxe bag fixed at its initial value $c_2 = 9$. Doing so in (3.2), we obtain

$$-\tfrac{3}{2} \leq -\frac{c_1}{9} \leq -\tfrac{7}{10}$$

Using the left-hand inequality, we have

$$-\tfrac{3}{2} \leq -\frac{c_1}{9} \qquad \text{or} \qquad \tfrac{3}{2} \geq \frac{c_1}{9}$$

Thus

$$\tfrac{27}{2} \geq c_1 \qquad \text{or} \qquad c_1 \leq \tfrac{27}{2} = 13.5$$

Using the right-hand inequality, we have

$$-\frac{c_1}{9} \leq -\tfrac{7}{10} \qquad \text{or} \qquad \frac{c_1}{9} \geq \tfrac{7}{10}$$

Thus

$$c_1 \geq {}^{63}\!/_{10} \quad \text{or} \quad c_1 \geq 6.3$$

Combining the above limits for c_1 provides the following range of optimality for the standard-bag profit contribution:

$$6.3 \leq c_1 \leq 13.5$$

In the original Par, Inc. problem the standard bag had a profit contribution of $10. The resulting optimal solution was 540 standard bags and 252 deluxe bags. The range of optimality for c_1 tells Par, Inc.'s management that, with other coefficients unchanged, the profit contribution for the standard bag can be anywhere between $6.30 and $13.50 and the production quantities of 540 standard bags and 252 deluxe bags will remain optimal. Note, however, that while the production quantities will not change, the total profit contribution (value of objective function) will change due to the change in profit contribution per standard bag.

The above computations can be repeated holding the profit contribution for standard bags constant at $c_1 = 10$. In this case the range of optimality for the profit contribution of deluxe bags, c_2, can be determined. Check to see that this range is $6.67 \leq c_2 \leq 14.29$.

In cases where the rotation of the objective function line about an optimal extreme point causes the objective function line to become *vertical*, there will be either no upper limit or no lower limit for the slope as it appears in the form of expression (3.2). To see how this special situation can happen in graphical sensitivity analysis, assume that the objective function for the Par, Inc. problem had been $18x_1 + 9x_2$; in this case extreme point ② in Figure 3.2 provides the optimal solution. Rotating the objective function line counterclockwise around extreme point ② provides an upper limit for the slope when the objective function line coincides with line B. Since we have previously seen that the slope of line B is $-\frac{3}{2}$, the upper limit for the slope of the objective function line must be $-\frac{3}{2}$. However, rotating the objective function line clockwise results in the slope becoming more and more negative, approaching a value of minus infinity as the objective function line becomes vertical; in this case there is no lower limit for the slope of the objective function. Using the upper limit of $-\frac{3}{2}$, we can write

$$-\frac{c_1}{c_2} \leq -\frac{3}{2}$$

Slope of the
objective function line

Following our previous procedure of holding c_2 constant at its original value, $c_2 = 9$, we have

$$-\frac{c_1}{9} \leq -\frac{3}{2} \quad \text{or} \quad \frac{c_1}{9} \geq \frac{3}{2}$$

Solving for c_1 provides the following result:

$$c_1 \geq {}^{27}\!/_{2} = 13.5$$

FIGURE 3.2
Graphical Solution of Par, Inc. Problem with Optimal Solution at Extreme Point ②

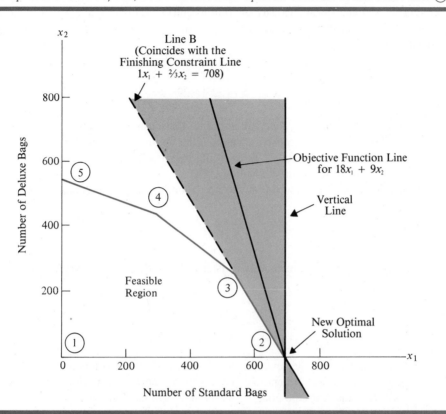

In reviewing Figure 3.2 we note that extreme point ② remains optimal for all values of c_1 above 13.5. Thus we obtain the following range of optimality for c_1 at extreme point ②:

$$13.5 \leq c_1 < \infty$$

Simultaneous Changes. The range of optimality for objective function coefficients is only applicable for changes made to one coefficient at a time. All other coefficients are assumed fixed at their initial values. If two or more objective function coefficients are changed simultaneously, further analysis is necessary to determine whether the optimal solution will change. However, when solving two variable problems graphically, inequality (3.2) suggests an easy way to determine whether simultaneous changes in both objective function coefficients will cause a change in the optimal solution. Simply compute the slope of the objective function ($-c_1/c_2$) for the new coefficient values. If this ratio is greater than or equal to the lower limit on the slope of the objective function and less than or equal to the upper limit, then the changes made will not cause a change in the optimal solution.

Let us illustrate this approach by considering changes in both of the objective function coefficients for the Par, Inc. problem. Suppose the profit contribution per standard bag is increased to $13 and simultaneously the profit contribution per deluxe bag is reduced to $8. Recall that the ranges of optimality for c_1 and c_2 (both computed in a one-at-a-time manner) are

$$6.3 \leq c_1 \leq 13.5 \tag{3.3}$$
$$6.67 \leq c_2 \leq 14.29 \tag{3.4}$$

Given these ranges of optimality, we can conclude that changing either c_1 to $13 or c_2 to $8 (but not both) would not cause a change in the optimal solution of $x_1 = 540$ and $x_2 = 252$. But we cannot conclude that changing both coefficients simultaneously will not result in a change in the optimal solution.

In expression (3.2) we showed that extreme point ③ remains optimal as long as

$$-\tfrac{3}{2} \leq -\frac{c_1}{c_2} \leq -\tfrac{7}{10}$$

If c_1 is changed to 13 and simultaneously c_2 is changed to 8, the new objective function slope will be given by

$$-\frac{c_1}{c_2} = -\frac{13}{8} = -1.625$$

Since this value is less than the lower limit of $-\tfrac{3}{2}$, the current solution of $x_1 = 540$ and $x_2 = 252$ will no longer be optimal. By resolving the problem with $c_1 = 13$ and $c_2 = 8$ we will find that extreme point ② is the new optimal solution.

Looking at the ranges of optimality, we concluded that changing either c_1 to $13 or c_2 to $8 (but not both) would not cause a change in the optimal solution. But in recomputing the slope of the objective function with simultaneous changes for both c_1 and c_2, we saw that the optimal solution did change. This emphasizes the fact that a range of optimality can only be used to draw a conclusion about changes made to one *objective function coefficient at a time*.

Right-Hand Sides

Let us now consider how a change in the right-hand side for a constraint may affect the feasible region and perhaps cause a change in the optimal solution to the problem. For example, let us consider what happens if an additional 10 hours of production time is made available in the cutting and dyeing department. The right-hand side of the cutting and dyeing constraint is changed from 630 to 640, and the constraint is rewritten as

$$\tfrac{7}{10}x_1 + x_2 \leq 640$$

By obtaining an additional 10 hours of cutting and dyeing time, we have expanded the feasible region for the problem, as shown in Figure 3.3. Since the feasible region has been enlarged, we want to determine whether or not one of the new feasible solutions

FIGURE 3.3
Effect of a 10-Unit Change in the Right-Hand Side of the Cutting and Dyeing Constraint

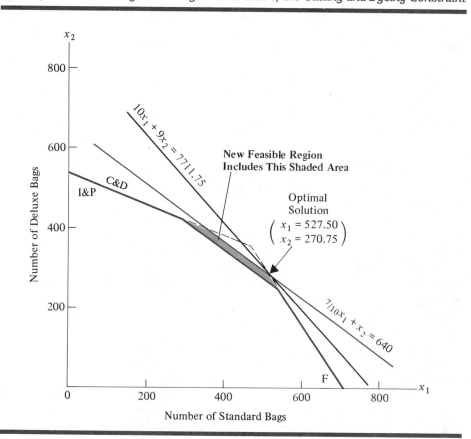

provides an improvement in the value of the objective function. Applying the graphical solution procedure to the problem with the enlarged feasible region shows that the extreme point at $x_1 = 527.5$ and $x_2 = 270.75$ now provides the optimal solution. The new value for the objective function is $10(527.5) + 9(270.75) = \$7711.75$; this provides an increase in profit of $\$7711.75 - 7668.00 = \$43.75$. Thus the increased profit occurs at a rate of $\$43.75/10$ hours $= \$4.375$ per hour added.

The change in the value of the objective function per unit increase in the value of the right-hand side is called the *shadow price*. Thus the shadow price for cutting and dyeing production time is \$4.375 per hour. The shadow price of a particular constraint is considered important because it may be possible to purchase or obtain additional units of the resource. If the cost of cutting and dyeing time has not been deducted in computing the profit coefficients, it can be shown that management should be willing to pay up to \$4.375 per hour for additional hours of this resource.

We caution here that the value of the shadow price may be applicable only for small changes in the right-hand side. As more and more resources are obtained and the right-hand side continues to increase, other constraints will become binding and reduce the rate of change in the value of the objective function. For example, in the Par, Inc. problem at some point enough hours can be added to the cutting and dyeing department so that the constraint will no longer be binding. The optimal solution will then be found at the intersection of the inspection and packaging constraint line and the finishing constraint line. At this point additional hours for the cutting and dyeing department will be of no value. The topic of how much one can change a right-hand side before it is no longer desirable to do so will be discussed further in the next section. Finally, we note that the shadow price for any nonbinding constraint will be zero because a change in the right-hand side of such a constraint will affect only the amount of the slack or surplus variable for that constraint.

Cautionary Note on the Interpretation of Shadow Prices

As stated previously, the shadow price is the change in the value of the objective function per unit increase in the right-hand side of a linear programming constraint. When the constraint right-hand side represents the amount of a resource available, the associated shadow price is often interpreted as the amount one should be willing to pay for one additional unit of the resource. However, such an interpretation is not always correct. To see why, we need to understand the difference between sunk and relevant costs. A sunk cost is one that is not affected by the decision made. It will be incurred no matter what values the decision variables assume. A relevant cost is one that depends on the decision made. The amount of a relevant cost will vary depending on the values of the decision variables.

Let us reconsider the Par, Inc. problem. The amount of cutting and dyeing time available is 630 hours. The cost of the time available is a sunk cost if it must be paid regardless of the number of standard and deluxe golf bags produced. It would be a relevant cost if Par only had to pay for the number of hours of cutting and dyeing time actually used to produce golf bags. All relevant costs should be deducted in the objective function of a linear program. Sunk costs should not be reflected in the objective function. For Par, Inc. we have been assuming that the company must pay its employees for labor time whether or not it is used. Therefore the cost of the labor hours resource for Par, Inc. is a sunk cost and has not been reflected in the objective function.

When the cost of a resource is *sunk*, the shadow price can be interpreted as the value of an additional unit of the resource. It is the amount the company should be willing to pay for one additional unit of the resource. When the cost of a resource used is relevant, the shadow price can be interpreted as the amount by which the value of the resource exceeds its cost. Thus, when the resource cost is relevant the shadow price can be interpreted as the maximum premium over the normal cost that the company should be willing to pay for one unit of the resource.

3.3 COMPUTER SOLUTION USING LINDO/PC: A MICROCOMPUTER SOFTWARE PACKAGE

Computer programs designed to solve linear programming problems are now widely available. Most large companies, as well as most universities, have access to these computer programs. The developmental effort for large-scale "software packages" has come primarily from computer manufacturers and/or software service companies such as IBM, Control Data, and Ketron. Usually after a short period of familiarization with the specific features of the package, users can solve linear programming problems with few difficulties. Problems involving thousands of variables and thousands of constraints can now be solved routinely through the use of computer packages. Most large linear programs can be solved with just a few minutes of computer time; small linear programs usually require only a few seconds.

More recently there has been a virtual explosion of software for microcomputers. A large number of "user-friendly" computer programs that can be used to solve linear programs on microcomputers are now available. These programs, developed by academicians and small software companies, are almost all easy to use.[1] Most of these programs are designed to solve smaller linear programs (a few hundred variables at most). To solve large-scale linear programs involving several thousand variables and constraints, software packages designed for mainframe computers should be used.

LINDO/PC, developed by Linus E. Schrage at the University of Chicago, is a microcomputer version of the popular LINDO computer package that is widely available on mainframe computers. LINDO/PC allows the user to interact with the computer in a conversational mode. By this we mean that once the program has been loaded in the microcomputer, the user inputs the objective function and constraints as requested by the computer program. When satisfied that all data have been entered correctly, the user enters the command "GO" and the LINDO/PC system solves the problem. The optimal solution and its related information are available at the user's computer monitor.

We will use the Par, Inc. problem to demonstrate the use of LINDO/PC. Since computer input must utilize decimal rather than fractional data values, the Par, Inc. problem is restated below with decimal coefficients:

$$\begin{array}{lll}
\max & 10x_1 + & 9x_2 \\
\text{s.t.} & & \\
& 0.7x_1 + & 1x_2 \le 630 & \text{Cutting and dyeing} \\
& 0.5x_1 + & .83333x_2 \le 600 & \text{Sewing} \\
& 1x_1 + & .66667x_2 \le 708 & \text{Finishing} \\
& 0.1x_1 + & 0.25x_2 \le 135 & \text{Inspection and packaging} \\
& x_1, x_2 \ge 0
\end{array}$$

Note that in the above form the coefficient of x_2 in the sewing constraint is written as .83333, which is the closest five-place decimal value to the fraction $5/6$. A similar rounding occurs for the x_2 coefficient in the finishing constraint, where the decimal .66667 is used as the closest five-place decimal value to the fraction $2/3$. When this rounding of the input data is required, we may expect the computer solution to be slightly different than the hand-calculated solution based on the exact fraction values. However, as you will see, the two solutions are extremely close, and the slight rounding of the input data causes no serious problem.

An example of the data input portion of a LINDO/PC computer session on an IBM Personal Computer is shown in Figure 3.4. The Par, Inc. linear programming problem

---

[1] The *Management Scientist* software package that is available free to adopters includes a user-friendly linear programming routine.

FIGURE 3.4
Data Input Session with the LINDO/PC Microcomputer Package. **Note:** *User Input Shown in Color; Computer Response Shown in Black*

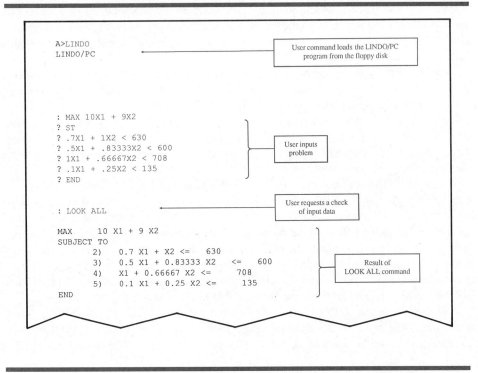

is used as the example in this illustration. The information keyed in by the user is shown in color, and the response from the computer package is shown in black. Note in particular the interactive nature of the system, with the alternating user input and LINDO/PC response. Specific commands and symbols shown in Figure 3.4 are described as follows:

1. The "A>" is the user prompt for the IBM Personal Computer. The user command "LINDO" causes the LINDO/PC program to be loaded.
2. LINDO/PC begins by sending the symbol ":" to indicate that it is waiting for an instruction from the user.
3. The user keys in the objective function as it appears in the mathematical statement of the problem.
4. LINDO/PC then sends the symbol "?" to indicate it is waiting for additional input concerning the linear program being solved.
5. The user input "ST" stands for "subject to" notifying the program that information about the constraints is to follow.
6. After inputting each of the constraints with the symbol <, which is interpreted as ≤ by LINDO/PC, the user inputs "END" to signal that the data input is complete.
7. LINDO/PC again responds with ":" to indicate that it is waiting for an instruction.
8. The user inputs the optional instruction "LOOK ALL," which results in the computer printing the linear programming problem that LINDO/PC is ready to solve. "LOOK

ALL'' is not a required instruction, but using it provides an easy check on the accuracy of the input data. In the computer package the objective function is identified as row 1. Thus under the ''SUBJECT TO'' heading we see the cutting and dyeing constraint identified as row 2, the sewing constraint as row 3, the finishing constraint as row 4, and the inspection and packaging constraint as row 5.

With the input data complete, the LINDO/PC package proceeds to develop the solution of the problem when given the command ''GO.'' The output from LINDO/PC is shown in Figure 3.5.

FIGURE 3.5
Par, Inc. Solution Using the LINDO/PC Microcomputer Package. **Note:** ***User Commands Shown in Color; Computer Response Shown in Black***

```
:GO                                              <-- User requests solution

       OBJECTIVE FUNCTION VALUE                  } Information concerning
                                                 } the
1)         7667.99400                            } optimal solution

VARIABLE        VALUE          REDUCED COST
      X1     539.998400            .000000
      X2     252.001100            .000000

    ROW   SLACK OR SURPLUS     DUAL PRICES
       2)        .000000          4.374956
       3)     120.000700           .000000
       4)        .000000          6.937531
       5)      17.999870           .000000


 DO RANGE (SENSITIVITY) ANALYSIS?
?YES                                             <-- User requests
                                                     sensitivity analysis
    RANGES IN WHICH THE BASIS IS UNCHANGED

                              OBJ COEFFICIENT RANGES          } Sensitivity
VARIABLE         CURRENT        ALLOWABLE         ALLOWABLE   } analysis
                  COEF          INCREASE          DECREASE    } information
      X1       10.000000          3.499932         3.700000
      X2        9.000000          5.285715         2.333000

                              RIGHTHAND SIDE RANGES
    ROW          CURRENT        ALLOWABLE         ALLOWABLE
                   RHS          INCREASE          DECREASE
       2       630.000000        52.363130       134.400000
       3       600.000000       INFINITY         120.000700
       4       708.000000       192.000000       127.998600
       5       135.000000       INFINITY          17.999870

:QUIT                                            <-- User signals completion of session
Stop - Program terminated.
```

Interpretation of Computer Output

Let us look more closely at the LINDO/PC output in Figure 3.5 and interpret the computer solution provided for the Par, Inc. problem. First note the number 7667.99400 which appears under the heading "OBJECTIVE FUNCTION VALUE." Rounding this value, we can conclude that the optimal solution to the Par problem will provide a profit of $7668. Directly below the objective function value we find the values of the decision variables at the optimal solution. Thus after rounding we have $x_1 = 540$ standard bags and $x_2 = 252$ deluxe bags as the optimal production quantities.

The information in the column labeled "REDUCED COST" indicates how much the objective function coefficient of each decision variable would have to improve[2] before it would be possible for that variable to assume a positive value in the optimal solution. Thus if a decision variable is already positive in the optimal solution, its reduced cost is zero. For the Par, Inc. problem the optimal solution is $x_1 = 540$ and $x_2 = 252$. With both variables already having positive values, their corresponding reduced costs are zero. In Section 3.4 we will interpret the reduced cost for a decision variable that does not have a positive value in the optimal solution.

Immediately following the optimal x_1 and x_2 values and the reduced cost information, the computer output provides information about the status of the constraints. Recall that the Par, Inc. problem had four less-than-or-equal-to constraints corresponding to the hours available in each of four production departments. The information shown in the column labeled "SLACK OR SURPLUS" provides the value of the slack variable for each of the departments. This information is summarized below:

Row	Constraint	Slack
2	Cutting and dyeing	0
3	Sewing	120
4	Finishing	0
5	Inspection and packaging	18

From the above information we see that the binding constraints (the cutting and dyeing and finishing constraints) have zero slack at the optimal solution. The sewing department has 120 hours of slack, or unused capacity, and the inspection and packaging department has 18 hours of slack or unused capacity.

The column labeled "DUAL PRICES" contains information about the value of each of the four resources at the optimal solution. For LINDO/PC the dual price is defined as follows:

> The dual price associated with a constraint is the *improvement* in the optimal value of the objective function resulting from a one-unit increase in the right-hand-side value for the constraint.

Thus we see that the nonzero dual prices of 4.374956 for row 2 (cutting and dyeing constraint) and 6.937531 for row 4 (finishing constraint) tell us that an additional hour of cutting and dyeing time improves (increases) the value of the objective function by

[2]For a maximization problem improve means get bigger; for a minimization problem improve means get smaller.

$4.37 and an additional hour of finishing time improves (increases) the value of the objective function by $6.94. Thus if the cutting and dyeing time were increased from 630 to 631 hours, with all other coefficients in the problem remaining the same, Par's profit would be increased by $4.37 from $7668 to $7668 + $4.37 = $7672.37. A similar interpretation for the finishing constraint implies that an increase in available finishing time from 708 to 709 hours, with all other coefficients in the problem remaining the same, would increase Par's profit to $7668 + $6.94 = $7674.94. Since the sewing and the inspection and packaging constraints both have slack or unused capacity available, the dual prices of zero show that additional hours of these two resources will not improve the value of the objective function.

As you may recall from the discussion of shadow prices in Section 3.2, the information in the "DUAL PRICES" column provides the shadow prices for Par's four resources. In fact, in the case of a *maximization* linear program, the LINDO/PC dual price is the *same* as the shadow price. However, as we shall discuss later, in a minimization linear program the dual price provided by the LINDO/PC output is the *negative* of the corresponding shadow price.

Referring again to the computer output in Figure 3.5, we see that after providing the constraint information on slack/surplus variables and dual prices, LINDO/PC asks the user the following question: "DO RANGE (SENSITIVITY) ANALYSIS?" The user response of "YES" requests ranges on the objective function coefficients and the right-hand sides of the constraints.

Considering the information provided under the computer output heading labeled "OBJ COEFFICIENT RANGES," we see that variable x_1, which has a current profit coefficient of 10, has an allowable increase of 3.50 (rounded) and an allowable decrease of 3.70. Adding 3.50 to and subtracting 3.70 from the current coefficient of 10 provides the following range of optimality for c_1:

$$6.30 \le c_1 \le 13.50$$

This tells us that as long as the profit contribution associated with the standard bag is between $6.30 and $13.50, the production of $x_1 = 540$ standard bags and $x_2 = 252$ deluxe bags will remain the optimal solution. Note that this is the range of optimality that we obtained when we performed graphical sensitivity analysis for c_1 in Section 3.2.

Using the objective function coefficient range information for deluxe bags, we can use the allowable increase and allowable decrease values for c_2 to compute the following range of optimality:

$$6.67 \le c_2 \le 14.29$$

This tells us that as long as the profit contribution associated with the deluxe bag is between $6.67 and $14.29, the production of $x_1 = 540$ standard bags and $x_2 = 252$ deluxe bags will remain the optimal solution.

The final section of the computer printout ("RIGHTHAND SIDE RANGES") contains ranging information for the constraint right-hand sides. As long as the constraint right-hand side value stays within this range, the associated dual price gives the improvement in value of the objective function per unit increase in the right-hand side. For example, let us consider the cutting and dyeing constraint with a current right-hand side value of 630 hours. Since the dual price for this constraint is $4.37, we can conclude that additional hours will increase the objective function by \$4.37 per hour. It is also true that a reduction in the hours available will reduce the value of the objective function by \$4.37 per hour. From the range information given we see that the dual price of \$4.37 is valid for increases up to 52.36313 and decreases up to 134.4. A similar interpretation for the finishing constraint right-hand side (row 4) shows that the dual price of \$6.94 is applicable for increases of up to 192 hours and decreases up to 127.9986.

As mentioned, the right-hand-side ranges provide limits within which the dual prices are applicable. For changes outside the range, the problem must be resolved to find the new optimal solution and new dual price. We shall call the range over which the dual price is applicable the *range of feasibility*.

By adding the allowable increase to and subtracting the allowable decrease from the current right-hand-side value of each constraint, we obtain the *ranges of feasibility* for the Par, Inc. problem. These computations provide the following ranges of feasibility for the right-hand-side values:

Constraint	Min RHS	Max RHS
Cutting and dyeing	495.6	682.4
Sewing	480.0	∞
Finishing	580.0	900.0
Inspection and packaging	117.0	∞

As long as the values of the right-hand sides are within the above ranges, the dual prices shown on the computer output will not change. Values of the right-hand sides outside these limits will result in changes in the dual price information.

At this point it is important to note that the sensitivity analysis presented in computer output is based on the assumption that coefficients are changed *one at a time*, with all other coefficients of the problem remaining as stated in the original problem. The sensitivity analysis information provided in computer output does not apply to two or more simultaneous changes in the problem.

Simultaneous Changes.   As stated above, the ranges for objective function coefficients and constraint right-hand sides are only applicable for changes in a single coefficient. However, with the help of the *100 percent rule*,[3] some analysis of simultaneous changes is possible. If simultaneous changes in two or more objective function coefficients are made, the solution will not change as long as the 100 percent rule is satisfied. Similarly, if simultaneous changes are made in two or more right-hand sides, the dual prices will not change as long as the 100 percent rule is satisfied.

To apply the 100 percent rule, for each coefficient changed we must compute the percentage of the allowable increase or decrease represented by the change. *If the sum of the percentages over all changes does not exceed 100%, then we say the simultaneous changes satisfy the 100 percent rule*. Let us illustrate by considering simultaneous changes in the right-hand sides for the Par, Inc. problem.

[3]See *Applied Mathematical Programming*. By S.P. Bradley, Hax, A.C., and Magnanti, T.L., Addison-Wesley, 1977.

Suppose, for instance, that in the Par, Inc. problem we could obtain 20 additional hours of cutting and dyeing time and 100 additional hours of finishing time. The 20 additional hours of cutting and dyeing time are $(20/52.363130)(100) = 38.19\%$ of the allowable increase in the constraint right-hand side. The 100 additional hours of finishing time are $(100/192)(100) = 52.08\%$ of the allowable increase in the finishing time constraint right-hand side. The accumulated percentage of change is $38.19\% + 52.08\% = 90.27\%$. Since the cumulative percentage change does not exceed 100%, we can conclude that the dual prices are applicable and that the objective function will improve by $(20)(4.37) + (100)(6.94) = 781.40$.

Note in Figure 3.5, that at the completion of the sensitivity analysis LINDO/PC sends ":" and waits for another instruction. In this case the user selected "QUIT" to signal the end of the LINDO/PC session. An optional instruction at this point would be "ALT," which would have enabled the user to alter or modify one or more aspects of the problem and seek additional solution information.

Interpretation of Computer Output—A Second Example

As another example of interpreting computer output, let us reconsider the M&D Chemicals minimization problem introduced in Section 2.7. The linear programming model for this problem is restated below, where x_1 = number of gallons of product 1 and x_2 = number of gallons of product 2.

$$
\begin{aligned}
\min \quad & 2x_1 + 3x_2 \\
\text{s.t.} \quad & \\
& 1x_1 \qquad\quad \geq 125 \quad \text{Demand for product 1} \\
& 1x_1 + 1x_2 \geq 350 \quad \text{Total production requirement} \\
& 2x_1 + 1x_2 \leq 600 \quad \text{Processing time limitation} \\
& x_1, x_2 \geq 0
\end{aligned}
$$

The LINDO/PC solution for the M&D Chemicals problem is presented in Figure 3.6. The computer output shows that the minimum cost solution occurs with an objective function value of $800. The values of the decision variables show that 250 gallons of product 1 ($x_1 = 250$) and 100 gallons of product 2 ($x_2 = 100$) provide the minimum-cost solution.

The "SLACK or SURPLUS" information shows that the $\geq$ constraint for the demand of product 1 (see row 2) has a surplus of 125 units. This tells us that production of product 1 in the optimal solution exceeds demand by 125 gallons. The "SLACK or SURPLUS" values are zero for the total production requirement (row 3) and the processing time limitation (row 4); this indicates that these constraints are binding at the optimal solution.

The "DUAL PRICE" column again shows us the *improvement* in the objective function for a one-unit increase in the right-hand side of the constraint. Focusing first on the dual price of 1.00 for the processing time constraint (row 4), we see that if we can increase the processing time from 600 hours to 601 hours, the objective function value will *improve* by $1. Since the objective is to minimize costs, improvement in this case means a lowering of costs. Thus if 601 hours of processing time are available, the value of the optimal solution will improve to $800 − $1 = $799. The "RIGHTHAND SIDE RANGES" section of the output shows that the allowable increase for the processing

FIGURE 3.6
LINDO/PC Output for the M&D Chemicals Problem

```
                    OBJECTIVE FUNCTION VALUE

        1)          800.000000

        VARIABLE         VALUE        REDUCED COST
            X1        250.000000           .000000
            X2        100.000000           .000000


          ROW    SLACK OR SURPLUS    DUAL PRICES
           2)         125.000000          .000000
           3)            .000000        -4.000000
           4)            .000000         1.000000



        DO RANGE (SENSITIVITY) ANALYSIS?
        ? YES


        RANGES IN WHICH THE BASIS IS UNCHANGED:

                                OBJ COEFFICIENT RANGES
        VARIABLE          CURRENT       ALLOWABLE        ALLOWABLE
                          COEF          INCREASE         DECREASE
            X1          2.000000        1.000000         INFINITY
            X2          3.000000        INFINITY         1.000000

                                RIGHTHAND SIDE RANGES
          ROW             CURRENT       ALLOWABLE        ALLOWABLE
                          RHS           INCREASE         DECREASE
            2           125.000000      125.000000       INFINITY
            3           350.000000      125.000000       50.000000
            4           600.000000      100.000000       125.000000
```

time constraint (row 4) is 100 hours. Thus the dual price of $1 per unit would be applicable for every additional hour of processing time up to a total of 600 + 100 = 700 hours.

Let us again return to the "DUAL PRICE" section of the output and consider the dual price for the total production constraint (row 3). The *negative dual price* tells us that the objective function *will not improve* if the value of the right-hand side is increased by one unit. In fact the dual price of −4.00 tells us that if the right-hand side of the total production constraint is increased from 350 to 351 units, the value of the objective function will not improve, but will get worse by the amount of $4. Since becoming worse means an increase in cost, the value of the objective function will become $800 + $4 = $804 if the one-unit increase in the total production requirement is made.

Since the dual price refers to improvement in the value of the objective function for a one-unit increase in the right-hand side, a constraint with a negative dual price should not have its right-hand side increased. In fact if the dual price is negative, efforts should be made to reduce the right-hand side of the constraint. If the right-hand side of the total production constraint were decreased from 350 units to 349 units, the dual price tells us the total cost could be lowered by $4 to $800 − $4 = $796.

The interpretation of the dual price from the LINDO/PC output is the improvement in the value of the objective function from a one-unit increase in the right-hand side of a constraint. However, as we have seen, the interpretation of an *improvement* in the value of an objective function depends upon whether we are solving a maximization or a minimization problem. The following table summarizes the approach to interpreting the value of a dual price:

Problem Type	Interpretation of Dual Price
Maximization	Amount of improvement (*increase*) in the value of the objective function for a one-unit *increase* in the right-hand side of the constraint.
Minimization	Amount of improvement (*decrease*) in the value of the objective function for a one-unit *increase* in the right-hand side of the constraint.

The dual price for a $\leq$ constraint will always be greater than or equal to 0 because increasing the right-hand side cannot make the value of the objective function worse. Similarly, the dual price for a $\geq$ constraint will always be less than or equal to 0 because increasing the right-hand side cannot improve the value of the objective function.

We caution that the interpretation of dual prices here is based upon LINDO/PC's sign convention. Recall that for maximization problems dual prices and shadow prices are the same; for minimization problems they have opposite signs. If you are using a different software package, you should check to see what convention and terminology are being used for this type of sensitivity analysis information.

Finally, consider the right-hand-side ranges provided in Figure 3.6. Adding the allowable increase to and subtracting the allowable decrease from the current right-hand side of each constraint provides the *ranges of feasibility* for the M&D Chemicals problem. These computations provide the following ranges of feasibility for the right-hand sides:

Constraint	Min RHS	Max RHS
Product 1 demand	None	250
Total production requirement	300	475
Processing time limitation	475	700

As long as the right-hand sides are within the above ranges, the dual prices shown on the computer printout are applicable. Let us now consider the computer solution and interpretation of the computer output for a linear program involving more than two decision variables.

3.4 MORE THAN TWO DECISION VARIABLES

The graphical solution procedure is useful only for linear programs involving two decision variables. Computer software packages are designed to handle linear programs involving large numbers of variables and constraints. In this section we discuss the formulation and computer solution of a linear program involving four decision variables. As we shall see, the approach to problem formulation and computer solution is essentially the same as for problems with two decision variables. After obtaining a verbal statement of the problem, we define the decision variables that will enable us to write the objective function and constraints associated with the problem as a linear program. Once the problem has been formulated, we can use a computer software package such as LINDO/PC to obtain the optimal solution.

The Electronic Communications, Inc. Problem

Electronic Communications, Inc. manufactures portable radio systems that can be used for two-way communications. The company's new product, which has a range of up to 25 miles, is particularly suitable for use in a variety of business and personal applications. The distribution channels for the new radio are as follows:

1. Marine equipment distributors
2. Business equipment distributors
3. National retail chain store
4. Mail order

Because of differing distribution and promotional costs, the profitability of the product will vary with the distribution channel. In addition, the advertising cost and the personal sales effort required will also vary with the distribution channels. Table 3.1 summarizes the profit, advertising cost, and personal sales effort data pertaining to the Electronic Communications problem. Additional facts are that the firm has set the advertising budget at $5000 and that there is a maximum of 1800 hours of sales force time available for allocation to the sales effort. Management has also decided to produce exactly 600 units for the current production period. Finally, an ongoing contract with the national chain of retail stores requires that at least 150 units be distributed through this distribution channel.

TABLE 3.1
Profit, Advertising Cost, and Personal Sales Time Data for the Electronic Communications, Inc. Problem

Distribution Channel	Profit per Unit Sold	Advertising Cost per Unit Sold	Personal Sales Effort per Unit Sold
Marine distributor	$90	$10	2 hours
Business distributor	$84	$8	3 hours
National retail stores	$70	$9	3 hours
Mail order	$60	$15	None

Electronic Communications, Inc. is now faced with the problem of establishing a strategy that will provide for the distribution of the radios in such a way that overall profitability of the new radio production will be maximized. Decisions must be made as to how many units should be allocated to each of the four distribution channels, as well as how to allocate the advertising budget and sales force effort to each of the four distribution channels.

Formulation of the Electronic Communications, Inc. Problem

To formulate a linear programming model for the Electronic Communications, Inc. problem, we introduce the following four decision variables:

x_1 = the number of units produced for the marine equipment distribution channel
x_2 = the number of units produced for the business equipment distribution channel
x_3 = the number of units produced for the national retail chain distribution channel
x_4 = the number of units produced for the mail order distribution channel

Using the data in Table 3.1, the objective function for maximizing the profit associated with the radios can be written as follows:

$$\max 90x_1 + 84x_2 + 70x_3 + 60x_4$$

Let us now proceed to formulate the constraints for the problem. Since the advertising budget has been set at $5000, the constraint that limits the amount of advertising expenditure can be written as follows:

$$10x_1 + 8x_2 + 9x_3 + 15x_4 \leq 5000$$

Similarly, since the sales time is limited to 1800 hours, we obtain the constraint

$$2x_1 + 3x_2 + 3x_3 \leq 1800$$

Management's decision to produce exactly 600 units during the current production period is expressed as

$$1x_1 + 1x_2 + 1x_3 + 1x_4 = 600$$

Finally, to account for the fact that the number of units distributed by the national retail chain stores must be at least 150, we add the constraint

$$1x_3 \geq 150$$

Combining all of the constraints with the nonnegativity requirements enables us to write the complete linear programming model for the Electronic Communications, Inc. problem as follows:

$$\max \quad 90x_1 + 84x_2 + 70x_3 + 60x_4$$

s.t.

$$
\begin{array}{ll}
10x_1 + 8x_2 + 9x_3 + 15x_4 \leq 5000 & \text{Advertising budget} \\
2x_1 + 3x_2 + 3x_3 \leq 1800 & \text{Sales force availability} \\
1x_1 + 1x_2 + 1x_3 + 1x_4 = 600 & \text{Production level} \\
1x_3 \geq 150 & \text{Retail stores requirement} \\
x_1, x_2, x_3, x_4 \geq 0 &
\end{array}
$$

Computer Solution and Interpretation for the Electronic Communications, Inc. Problem

A portion of the output from the LINDO/PC computer solution of the Electronic Communications problem is shown in Figure 3.7. The OBJECTIVE FUNCTION VALUE section shows that the optimal solution to the problem will provide a maximum profit of $48,450. The optimal values of the decision variables are given by $x_1 = 25$, $x_2 = 425$, $x_3 = 150$, and $x_4 = 0$. Thus the optimal strategy for Electronic Communications is to concentrate on the business equipment distribution channel with $x_2 = 425$ units. In addition, the firm should allocate 25 units to the marine distribution channel ($x_1 = 25$) and meet its 150-unit commitment to the national retail chain store distribution channel ($x_3 = 150$). With $x_4 = 0$, the optimal solution indicates that the firm should not use the mail order distribution channel.

FIGURE 3.7
A Portion of the Computer Output for the Electronic Communications, Inc. Problem

```
                    OBJECTIVE FUNCTION VALUE

        1)          48450.0000

        VARIABLE         VALUE           REDUCED COST
          X1          25.000000            .000000
          X2         425.000000            .000000
          X3         150.000000            .000000
          X4            .000000          45.000000

        ROW      SLACK OR SURPLUS       DUAL PRICES
         2)            .000000            3.000000
         3)          25.000000             .000000
         4)            .000000           60.000000
         5)            .000000          -17.000000
```

Let us now look at the information contained in the column labeled "REDUCED COST." Recall that the reduced costs indicate how much each objective function coefficient would have to change before the corresponding decision variable could assume a positive value in the optimal solution. As the computer output shows, the first three reduced costs are zero since the corresponding decision variables already have positive values in the optimal solution. However, the reduced cost of 45 for decision variable x_4 tells us that the profit for the new radios distributed via the mail order channel would have to increase from its current value of $60 per unit to at least $60 + $45 = $105 per unit before it would be profitable to begin using the mail order distribution channel.

The computer output information on the slack/surplus variables and the dual prices is restated at the top of page 91.

Row	Constraint	Type of Constraint	Slack or Surplus	Dual Price
2	Advertising budget	≤	0	3
3	Sales force availability	≤	25	0
4	Production level	=	0	60
5	Retail stores requirement	≥	0	−17

We see that the advertising budget constraint has a slack of zero, indicating that the entire budget of $5000 has been used. The corresponding dual price of 3 tells us that an additional dollar added to the advertising budget will improve the objective function (increase the profit) by $3. Thus the possibility of increasing the advertising budget should be seriously considered by the firm. The slack of 25 hours for the sales force availability constraint shows that the allocated 1800 hours of sales time are adequate to distribute the radios produced and that 25 hours of sales force time will remain unused. Since the production level constraint is an equality, the zero slack/surplus shown on the output is expected. However, the dual price of 60 associated with this constraint shows that if the firm will consider increasing the production level for the radios, the value of the objective function, or profit, will improve at the rate of $60 per radio produced. Finally, the surplus of zero associated with the retail store distribution channel commitment is a result of this constraint being binding. The negative dual price indicates that increasing the commitment from 150 to 151 units will actually decrease the profit by $17. Thus Electronic Communications may want to consider reducing its commitment to the retail store distribution channel. A *decrease* in the commitment will actually improve profit at the rate of $17 per unit.

Let us now consider the additional sensitivity analysis information provided by the computer output shown in Figure 3.8. Adding the ALLOWABLE INCREASE and sub-

FIGURE 3.8
Objective Coefficient and Right-Hand Side Ranges for the Electronic Communications, Inc. Problem

```
                        OBJ COEFFICIENT RANGES
   VARIABLE     CURRENT       ALLOWABLE      ALLOWABLE
                COEF          INCREASE       DECREASE
     X1         90.000000     INFINITY        6.000000
     X2         84.000000      6.000000      34.000000
     X3         70.000000     17.000000      INFINITY
     X4         60.000000     45.000000      INFINITY

                    RIGHTHAND SIDE RANGES
    ROW         CURRENT       ALLOWABLE      ALLOWABLE
                RHS           INCREASE       DECREASE
     2          5000.000000    850.000000     50.000000
     3          1800.000000   INFINITY        25.000000
     4          600.000000      3.571429      85.000000
     5          150.000000     50.000000     150.000000
```

tracting the ALLOWABLE DECREASE values from the current objective function coefficients provides the following ranges of optimality for the objective function coefficients:

$$84 \leq c_1 < \infty$$
$$50 \leq c_2 \leq 90$$
$$-\infty < c_3 \leq 87$$
$$-\infty < c_4 \leq 105$$

Thus the current solution, or strategy, remains optimal, provided that the objective function coefficients remain in the above ranges of optimality. Note in particular the range of optimality associated with the mail order distribution channel coefficient c_4. This information is consistent with the earlier observation for the REDUCED COST portion of the output. In both instances we see that the per-unit profit would have to increase to \$105 before the mail order distribution channel could be in the optimal solution with a positive value.

Finally, the sensitivity analysis information on RIGHTHAND SIDE RANGES, as shown in Figure 3.8, can be used to compute the ranges of feasibility for the right-hand-side values. Adding the ALLOWABLE INCREASE and subtracting the ALLOWABLE DECREASE from the current right-hand-side values provides the following ranges of feasibility:

Constraint	Min RHS	Max RHS
Advertising budget	4950	5850
Sales force	1775	∞
Production level	515	603.57
Retail stores requirement	0	200

Several interpretations of the above ranges are possible. In particular, recall that the dual price for advertising budget enabled us to conclude that each \$1 increase in the budget would improve the profit by \$3. The above range for the advertising budget shows that this statement about the value of increasing the budget is appropriate up to an advertising budget of \$5850. Increases above this level would not necessarily be beneficial. Also note that the dual price of -17 for the retail stores requirement suggested the desirability of reducing this commitment. The above range of feasibility for this constraint shows that the commitment could be reduced to zero and the value of the reduction would be at the rate of \$17 per unit.

Let us again point out that the sensitivity analysis or postoptimality analysis provided by computer software packages for linear programming problems considers only *one change at a time*, with all other coefficients of the problem remaining as originally specified. As mentioned earlier, simultaneous changes can sometimes be analyzed without resolving the problem, provided that the cumulative changes are not large enough to violate the 100 percent rule.

Finally, recall that the complete solution to the Electronic Communications problem requested information not only on the number of units to be distributed over each channel but also the allocation of the advertising budget and the sales force effort to each distribution channel. Since the optimal solution is $x_1 = 25$, $x_2 = 425$, $x_3 = 150$, and $x_4 = 0$, we can simply evaluate each term in a given constraint to determine how much of the constraint resource is allocated to each distribution channel. For example, the advertising budget constraint of

$$10x_1 + 8x_2 + 9x_3 + 15x_4 \leq 5000$$

shows $10x_1 = 10(25) = \$250$, $8x_2 = 8(425) = \$3400$, $9x_3 = 9(150) = \$1350$, and $15x_4 = 15(0) = \$0$. Thus the advertising budget allocations are, respectively, \$250, \$3400, \$1350, and \$0 for each of the four distribution channels. Making similar calculations for the sales force constraint enables the managerial summary of the Electronic Communications optimal solution as shown in Table 3.2.

TABLE 3.2
Profit Maximizing Strategy for the Electronic Communications, Inc. Problem

Distribution Channel	Volume	Advertising Allocation	Sales Force Allocation (hours)
Marine distributor	25	$ 250	50
Business distributor	425	$3400	1275
National retail stores	150	$1350	450
Mail order	0	0	0
Totals	600	$5000	1775

Projected total profit = $48,450

Summary

In this chapter we have presented the important concepts of sensitivity analysis and the computer solution of linear programming problems. We first considered graphical sensitivity analysis in order to demonstrate how a change in a coefficient of the objective function or in the right-hand-side value for a constraint can affect the optimal solution to the problem. Methods were introduced for finding the ranges of optimality for the objective function coefficients and the ranges of feasibility for the right-hand sides of the constraints. The concept of a shadow price was introduced as a measure of the change in the value of the objective function for a one-unit increase in the right-hand side of a constraint. In cases where the constraint involves a limit on an available resource, the shadow price provides important information that helps to determine the desirability of obtaining additional units of the resource.

Sensitivity analysis is conducted after the optimal solution to the original linear programming problem has been obtained. For this reason sensitivity analysis is often referred to as postoptimality analysis. The standard sensitivity analysis procedures are based on the assumption that only one of the coefficients of the problem changes; all other coefficients are assumed to be held constant at their initial values. It is possible to do some limited sensitivity analysis on the effect of changing more than one coefficient at a time. For two variable problems the effect of both objective function coefficients changing can be determined by recomputing the slope $(-c_1/c_2)$. For larger problems the effect of simultaneous changes can be determined by using the 100 percent rule.

Since the graphical method and graphical sensitivity analysis are limited to linear programs with two decision variables, a computer solution procedure was presented as a practical method of solving linear programming problems with any number of decision variables. Although many software packages are available for computer solution, we selected the LINDO/PC package to illustrate linear programming solutions on a microcomputer. We demonstrated the ''user-friendly'' aspect of the data input. Then we showed the computer output for three example problems in order to demonstrate the use and interpretation of the results. In addition to the value of the objective function and the optimal values of the decision variables, the computer output provides a variety of additional information concerning slack, surplus, and dual prices, as well as objective function coefficient and right-hand-side ranges.

Glossary

Sensitivity analysis   The evaluation of how changes in the coefficients of a linear programming problem affect the optimal solution to the problem.

Postoptimality analysis   Another name for sensitivity analysis, indicating that the analysis is performed after the optimal solution to the original linear programming problem has been obtained.

Range of optimality   The range of values over which an objective function coefficient may vary without causing any change in the values of the decision variables in the optimal solution.

Shadow price   The change in the value of the objective function resulting from a one-unit increase in the value of the right-hand side associated with a constraint.

Dual price   The improvement in the value of the objective function resulting from a one-unit increase in a constraint right-hand side value. In a maximization problem the dual price is the same as the shadow price. In a minimization problem the dual price is the negative of the shadow price.

Range of feasibility   The range of values over which a right-hand side value may vary without changing the value and interpretation of the dual price.

100 percent rule   A rule indicating when simultaneous changes in two or more objective function coefficients will not cause a change in the optimal values for the decision variables. It can also be applied to indicate when two or more right-hand-side changes will not cause a change in any of the dual prices.

Problems

1.   Recall the RMC problem (Chapter 2, problem 31). Letting

$$x_1 = \text{tons of fuel additive produced}$$
$$x_2 = \text{tons of solvent base produced}$$

leads to the following formulation of the RMC problem:

$$\text{max} \quad 40x_1 + 30x_2$$

s.t.

$$\frac{2}{5}x_1 + \frac{1}{2}x_2 \le 20 \quad \text{Material 1}$$
$$\frac{1}{5}x_2 \le 5 \quad \text{Material 2}$$
$$\frac{3}{5}x_1 + \frac{3}{10}x_2 \le 21 \quad \text{Material 3}$$
$$x_1, x_2 \ge 0$$

Use the graphical sensitivity analysis approach to determine what ranges of values for the profit per ton of the fuel additive and solvent base can exist without causing RMC to change from the current optimal solution of 25 tons of fuel additive and 20 tons of solvent base.

2. For the RMC situation (problem 1) use the graphical sensitivity analysis approach to determine what happens if an additional 3 tons of material 3 becomes available. What is the corresponding shadow price?

3. Consider the linear program given below.

$$\text{max} \quad 2x_1 + 3x_2$$

s.t.

$$x_1 + x_2 \le 10$$
$$2x_1 + x_2 \ge 4$$
$$x_1 + 3x_2 \le 24$$
$$2x_1 + x_2 \le 16$$
$$x_1, x_2 \ge 0$$

a. Solve this problem using the graphical solution procedure.
b. Compute the range of optimality for c_1.
c. Compute the range of optimality for c_2.
d. Suppose c_1 is increased from 2 to 2.5. What is the new optimal solution?
e. Suppose c_2 is decreased from 3 to 1. What is the new optimal solution?

4. Refer again to problem 3.
a. Compute the shadow prices for constraints 1 and 2 and interpret them.
b. What are the dual prices for constraints 1 and 2? Interpret them.

5. Consider the linear program given below.

$$\text{min} \quad x_1 + x_2$$

s.t.

$$x_1 + 2x_2 \ge 7$$
$$2x_1 + x_2 \ge 5$$
$$x_1 + 6x_2 \ge 11$$
$$x_1, x_2 \ge 0$$

a. Solve this problem using the graphical solution procedure.
b. Compute the range of optimality for c_1.
c. Compute the range of optimality for c_2.
d. Suppose c_1 is increased to 1.5. Find the new optimal solution.
e. Suppose c_2 is decreased to $\frac{1}{3}$. Find the new optimal solution.

6. Refer again to problem 5.
   a. Compute and interpret the shadow prices for the constraints.
   b. What are the dual prices? Interpret them.
7. Consider the linear program given below.

$$\max \quad 5x_1 + 7x_2$$

$$\text{s.t.}$$

$$2x_1 + x_2 \geq 3$$
$$-x_1 + 5x_2 \geq 4$$
$$2x_1 - 3x_2 \leq 6$$
$$3x_1 + 2x_2 \leq 35$$
$$\tfrac{3}{7}x_1 + x_2 \leq 10$$
$$x_1, x_2 \geq 0$$

   a. Solve this problem using the graphical solution procedure.
   b. Compute the range of optimality for c_1.
   c. Compute the range of optimality for c_2.
   d. Suppose c_1 is decreased to 2. What is the new optimal solution?
   e. Suppose c_2 is increased to 10. What is the new optimal solution?
8. Refer again to problem 7 and suppose the objective function coefficient for c_2 is reduced to 3.
   a. Resolve using the graphical solution procedure.
   b. Compute the dual prices for constraints 2 and 3.
9. Refer again to problem 3.
   a. Suppose c_1 is increased to 3 and c_2 is increased to 4. Find the new optimal solution.
   b. Suppose c_1 is increased to 3 and c_2 is decreased to 2. Find the new optimal solution.
10. Refer again to problem 7.
    a. Suppose c_1 is decreased to 4 and c_2 is increased to 10. Find the new optimal solution.
    b. Suppose c_1 is decreased to 4 and c_2 is increased to 8. Find the new optimal solution.
11. Recall the Kelson Sporting Equipment problem (Chapter 2, problem 16). Letting

$$x_1 = \text{number of regular gloves}$$
$$x_2 = \text{number of catchers' mitts}$$

leads to the following formulation:

$$\max \quad 5x_1 + 8x_2$$

$$\text{s.t.}$$

$$x_1 + \tfrac{3}{2}x_2 \leq 900 \quad \text{Cutting and sewing}$$
$$\tfrac{1}{2}x_1 + \tfrac{1}{3}x_2 \leq 300 \quad \text{Finishing}$$
$$\tfrac{1}{8}x_1 + \tfrac{1}{4}x_2 \leq 100 \quad \text{Packing and shipping}$$
$$x_1, x_2 \geq 0$$

The LINDO/PC computer solution of this problem is shown in Figure 3.9.

a. What is the optimal solution and what is the value of the profit contribution?

b. Which constraints are binding?

c. What are the dual prices for the resources? Interpret each.

d. If overtime can be scheduled in one of the departments, where would you recommend doing so?

FIGURE 3.9
LINDO/PC Solution of Kelson Sporting Equipment Problem

```
                    OBJECTIVE FUNCTION VALUE

         1)      3700.01500

    VARIABLE          VALUE              REDUCED COST
        X1          500.015000              .000000
        X2          149.992500              .000000


       ROW      SLACK OR SURPLUS       DUAL PRICES
        2)          174.996200             .000000
        3)             .000000            2.999850
        4)             .000000           28.000600



DO RANGE (SENSITIVITY) ANALYSIS?
? YES

RANGES IN WHICH THE BASIS IS UNCHANGED:

                          OBJ COEFFICIENT RANGES
    VARIABLE        CURRENT         ALLOWABLE        ALLOWABLE
                     COEF           INCREASE         DECREASE
        X1         5.000000         7.001200         1.000000
        X2         8.000000         2.000000         4.667000

                          RIGHTHAND SIDE RANGES
       ROW         CURRENT         ALLOWABLE        ALLOWABLE
                     RHS           INCREASE         DECREASE
        2         900.000000        INFINITY       174.996200
        3         300.000000       99.999990       166.680000
        4         100.000000       34.998200        25.000000
```

12. Refer again to the computer solution of the Kelson Sporting Equipment problem in Figure 3.9 (see problem 11 above).

a. Compute the ranges of optimality for the objective function coefficients.

b. Interpret the ranges in part (a) for the Kelson problem.

c. Compute the range of feasibility for the right-hand sides.

d. How much will the value of the optimal solution improve if 20 extra hours of packing and shipping time are made available?

13. Recall the Investment Advisors problem (Chapter 2, problem 20). Letting

$$x_1 = \text{shares of U.S. Oil}$$
$$x_2 = \text{shares of Hub Properties}$$

leads to the following formulation:

$$\begin{array}{ll} \max & 3x_1 + 5x_2 \qquad \text{Maximum annual return} \\ \text{s.t.} & \\ & 25x_1 + 50x_2 \le 80{,}000 \quad \text{Funds available} \\ & 0.50x_1 + 0.25x_2 \le 700 \quad \text{Risk maximum} \\ & 1x_1 \le 1{,}000 \quad \text{U.S. Oil maximum} \\ & x_1, x_2 \ge 0 \end{array}$$

The LINDO/PC computer solution of this problem is shown in Figure 3.10.

a. What is the optimal solution and what is the value of the total estimated annual return?

FIGURE 3.10
LINDO/PC Solution of Investment Advisors Problem

```
              OBJECTIVE FUNCTION VALUE

        1)     8400.00000

   VARIABLE        VALUE          REDUCED COST
       X1        800.000000         .000000
       X2       1200.000000         .000000


     ROW    SLACK OR SURPLUS      DUAL PRICES
      2)        .000000            .093333
      3)        .000000           1.333333
      4)      200.000000           .000000



   DO RANGE (SENSITIVITY) ANALYSIS?
   ? YES

   RANGES IN WHICH THE BASIS IS UNCHANGED:

                        OBJ COEFFICIENT RANGES
   VARIABLE      CURRENT      ALLOWABLE      ALLOWABLE
                  COEF        INCREASE       DECREASE
       X1       3.000000      7.000000        .500000
       X2       5.000000      1.000000       3.500000

                        RIGHTHAND SIDE RANGES
     ROW       CURRENT      ALLOWABLE      ALLOWABLE
                RHS         INCREASE       DECREASE
      2     80000.000000   60000.000000   15000.000000
      3       700.000000      75.000000     300.000000
      4      1000.000000      INFINITY      200.000000
```

b. Which constraints are binding? What is your interpretation of this in terms of the problem?

c. What are the dual prices for the constraints? Interpret each.

d. Would it be beneficial to relax the constraint on the amount invested in U.S. Oil? Why or why not?

14. Refer again to Figure 3.10, which shows the computer solution of problem 13.

a. How much would the estimated per-share return for U.S. Oil have to increase before it would be beneficial to increase the investment in this stock?

b. How much would the estimated per-share return for Hub Properties have to decrease before it would be beneficial to reduce the investment in this stock?

c. How much would the total annual return be reduced if the U.S. Oil maximum were reduced to 900 shares?

15. Recall the Wilkinson Motors problem (Chapter 2, problem 29). Letting

$$x_1 = \text{number of automobiles}$$
$$x_2 = \text{number of station wagons}$$

leads to the following formulation:

$$\max \quad 400x_1 + 500x_2 \qquad \text{Maximum profit contribution}$$

s.t.

$$
\begin{array}{rll}
2x_1 + 3x_2 \le 900 & \text{Dealer preparation time} \\
1x_1 \le 300 & \text{Auto limit} \\
1x_2 \le 150 & \text{Wagon limit} \\
x_1, x_2 \ge 0
\end{array}
$$

The LINDO/PC computer solution of this problem is shown in Figure 3.11.

a. How many regular automobiles and station wagons should Wilkinson order? What will the profit contribution be if all the units ordered are sold?

b. How much would the profit contribution of the regular automobiles have to decrease before Wilkinson would consider modifying its optimal solution?

c. Should Wilkinson consider raising the limit on the number of station wagons ordered beyond 150?

d. If the profit contribution for regular automobiles is reduced by $30 and the profit contribution for station wagons is increased by $50, should Wilkinson consider changing the order? Explain.

16. Recall the Photo Chemicals problem (Chapter 2, problem 27). Letting

$$x_1 = \text{gallons of product 1 produced}$$
$$x_2 = \text{gallons of product 2 produced}$$

leads to the following formulation:

$$\min \quad 1x_1 + 1x_2 \qquad \text{Minimum production cost}$$

s.t.

$$
\begin{array}{rll}
1x_1 + 2x_2 \ge 80 & \text{Raw material} \\
1x_1 \ge 30 & \text{Product 1 minimum} \\
1x_2 \ge 20 & \text{Product 2 minimum} \\
x_1, x_2 \ge 0
\end{array}
$$

FIGURE 3.11
LINDO/PC Solution of Wilkinson Motors Problem

```
              OBJECTIVE FUNCTION VALUE

        1)      170000.000

   VARIABLE          VALUE          REDUCED COST
        X1        300.000000           .000000
        X2        100.000000           .000000


     ROW    SLACK OR SURPLUS      DUAL PRICES
      2)          .000000         166.666700
      3)          .000000          66.666660
      4)        50.000000           .000000



   DO RANGE (SENSITIVITY) ANALYSIS?
   ? YES

   RANGES IN WHICH THE BASIS IS UNCHANGED:

                             OBJ COEFFICIENT RANGES
   VARIABLE         CURRENT        ALLOWABLE       ALLOWABLE
                     COEF          INCREASE        DECREASE
        X1        400.000000       INFINITY        66.666660
        X2        500.000000       99.999980      500.000000

                             RIGHTHAND SIDE RANGES
     ROW          CURRENT         ALLOWABLE       ALLOWABLE
                    RHS           INCREASE        DECREASE
      2          900.000000      150.000000      300.000000
      3          300.000000      150.000000       75.000000
      4          150.000000       INFINITY        50.000000
```

The LINDO/PC solution is shown in Figure 3.12.
a. What is the optimal solution and what is minimum production cost?
b. Compute the range of optimality for the objective function coefficients.
c. What are the dual prices for each constraint? Interpret each.
d. What are the shadow prices for each constraint?
e. If the amount of raw material to be processed were increased from 80 to 85 gallons, how would the optimal solution change?
f. Compute the range of feasibility for each of the right-hand side values.

17. Suppose that in a product-mix problem x_1, x_2, x_3, and x_4 indicate the units of products 1, 2, 3, and 4, respectively, and the linear program is

$$\max \quad 4x_1 + 6x_2 + 3x_3 + 1x_4$$

$$\text{s.t.}$$

$$1.5x_1 + 2x_2 + 4x_3 + 3x_4 \leq 550 \quad \text{Machine } A \text{ hours}$$
$$4x_1 + 1x_2 + 2x_3 + 1x_4 \leq 700 \quad \text{Machine } B \text{ hours}$$
$$2x_1 + 3x_2 + 1x_3 + 2x_4 \leq 200 \quad \text{Machine } C \text{ hours}$$
$$x_1, x_2, x_3, x_4 \geq 0$$

FIGURE 3.12
LINDO/PC Solution of Photo Chemicals Problem

```
              OBJECTIVE FUNCTION VALUE

        1)    55.0000000

    VARIABLE         VALUE        REDUCED COST
        X1         30.000000          .000000
        X2         25.000000          .000000


     ROW    SLACK OR SURPLUS     DUAL PRICES
      2)           .000000         -.500000
      3)           .000000         -.500000
      4)          5.000000          .000000



  DO RANGE (SENSITIVITY) ANALYSIS?
  ? YES

  RANGES IN WHICH THE BASIS IS UNCHANGED:

                          OBJ COEFFICIENT RANGES
  VARIABLE        CURRENT       ALLOWABLE       ALLOWABLE
                   COEF         INCREASE        DECREASE
      X1         1.000000       INFINITY         .500000
      X2         1.000000       1.000000        1.000000

                          RIGHTHAND SIDE RANGES
     ROW         CURRENT       ALLOWABLE       ALLOWABLE
                   RHS         INCREASE        DECREASE
      2          80.000000     INFINITY        10.000000
      3          30.000000     10.000000       30.000000
      4          20.000000      5.000000        INFINITY
```

The computer solution developed using LINDO/PC is shown in Figure 3.13.

a. What is the optimal solution and what is the value of the objective function?

b. Which constraints are binding?

c. Which machines have excess capacity available? How much?

d. If the objective function coefficient of x_1 is increased by 0.50, will the optimal solution change?

18. Refer again to the LINDO/PC solution of problem 17 in Figure 3.13.

a. Compute the range of optimality for each objective function coefficient.

b. Suppose the objective function coefficient for x_1 is decreased by 3, the objective function coefficient of x_2 is increased by 1.5, and the objective function coefficient for x_4 is increased by 1. What will the new optimal solution be?

c. Compute the range of feasibility for the right-hand side values.

d. If the number of hours available on machine A is increased by 300, will the dual price for that constraint change?

19. Consider the following linear program and the LINDO/PC computer solution shown in Figure 3.14.

FIGURE 3.13
LINDO/PC Solution of Problem 17

```
                    OBJECTIVE FUNCTION VALUE

        1)      525.000000

    VARIABLE          VALUE         REDUCED COST
        X1           .000000           .050000
        X2          25.000000          .000000
        X3         125.000000          .000000
        X4           .000000          3.500000


    ROW      SLACK OR SURPLUS      DUAL PRICES
     2)          .000000            .300000
     3)        425.000000           .000000
     4)          .000000           1.800000



    DO RANGE (SENSITIVITY) ANALYSIS?
    ? YES

    RANGES IN WHICH THE BASIS IS UNCHANGED:

                            OBJ COEFFICIENT RANGES
    VARIABLE        CURRENT       ALLOWABLE       ALLOWABLE
                     COEF         INCREASE        DECREASE
        X1         4.000000        .050000        INFINITY
        X2         6.000000       3.000000         .076923
        X3         3.000000       9.000000         .999999
        X4         1.000000       3.500000        INFINITY

                            RIGHTHAND SIDE RANGES
    ROW             CURRENT       ALLOWABLE       ALLOWABLE
                     RHS          INCREASE        DECREASE
     2             550.000000     250.000000     416.666700
     3             700.000000     INFINITY       425.000000
     4             200.000000     625.000000      62.500000
```

$$\min \quad 15x_1 + 15x_2 + 16x_3$$
s.t.
$$1x_1 \qquad\qquad + 1x_3 \le 30$$
$$0.5x_1 - 1x_2 + 6x_3 \ge 15$$
$$3x_1 + 4x_2 - 1x_3 \ge 20$$
$$x_1, x_2, x_3 \ge 0$$

a. What is the optimal solution and what is the optimal value for the objective function?
b. Which constraints are binding?
c. What are the dual prices? Interpret each.
d. What are the shadow prices?
e. If you could change the right-hand side of one constraint by one unit, which one would you choose? What would be the new value of the right-hand side?

FIGURE 3.14
LINDO/PC Solution of Problem 19

```
              OBJECTIVE FUNCTION VALUE

        1)     139.729700

   VARIABLE           VALUE          REDUCED COST
        X1          7.297297           .000000
        X2           .000000           .675674
        X3          1.891892           .000000


        ROW    SLACK OR SURPLUS    DUAL PRICES
        2)        20.810810           .000000
        3)          .000000         -3.405405
        4)          .000000         -4.432433



   DO RANGE (SENSITIVITY) ANALYSIS?
   ? YES

   RANGES IN WHICH THE BASIS IS UNCHANGED:

                           OBJ COEFFICIENT RANGES
   VARIABLE           CURRENT        ALLOWABLE        ALLOWABLE
                       COEF          INCREASE         DECREASE
        X1          15.000000         .543477        13.666670
        X2          15.000000        INFINITY          .675674
        X3          16.000000       164.000000        2.499995

                           RIGHTHAND SIDE RANGES
        ROW        CURRENT         ALLOWABLE        ALLOWABLE
                     RHS           INCREASE         DECREASE
         2         30.000000        INFINITY        20.810810
         3         15.000000        96.249990       11.666670
         4         20.000000        70.000000       22.500000
```

20. Refer again to the LINDO/PC solution of problem 19 in Figure 3.14.
   a. Develop and interpret the ranges of optimality for the objective function coefficients.
   b. Suppose c_1 is increased by 0.25. What is the new optimal solution?
   c. Suppose c_1 is increased by 0.25 and c_2 is decreased by 0.25. What is the new optimal solution?

21. Supersport Footballs, Inc. has the problem of determining the best number of All-Pro (x_1), College (x_2), and High-School (x_3) models of footballs to produce in order to maximize profits. Constraints include production capacity limitations in each of three departments (cutting and dyeing, sewing, and inspection and packaging) as well as a constraint that requires production of at least 1000 All-Pro footballs. The linear programming model of Supersport's problem is shown below:

$$\max \quad 3x_1 + 5x_2 + 4x_3 \qquad \text{Time in minutes}$$

s.t.

$$12x_1 + 10x_2 + 8x_3 \leq 18{,}000 \quad \text{Cutting and dyeing}$$
$$15x_1 + 15x_2 + 12x_3 \leq 18{,}000 \quad \text{Sewing}$$
$$3x_1 + 4x_2 + 2x_3 \leq 9{,}000 \quad \text{Inspection and packaging}$$
$$1x_1 \qquad\qquad\qquad \geq 1{,}000 \quad \text{All-Pro model}$$
$$x_1, x_2, x_3 \geq 0$$

The computer printout of the LINDO/PC solution to the Supersport problem is shown in Figure 3.15.

a. How many footballs of each type should Supersport produce in order to maximize the profit contribution?
b. Which constraints are binding?
c. Interpret the slack and/or surplus in each constraint.
d. Compute and interpret the range of optimality for the profit contribution of the three footballs.

FIGURE 3.15
LINDO/PC Solution of Supersport Footballs Problem

```
              OBJECTIVE FUNCTION VALUE

         1)      4000.00000

    VARIABLE         VALUE         REDUCED COST
        X1        1000.000000          .000000
        X2            .000000          .000000
        X3         250.000000          .000000


        ROW    SLACK OR SURPLUS      DUAL PRICES
         2)       4000.000000           .000000
         3)           .000000           .333333
         4)       5500.000000           .000000
         5)           .000000         -2.000000



    DO RANGE (SENSITIVITY) ANALYSIS?
    ? YES

    RANGES IN WHICH THE BASIS IS UNCHANGED:

                        OBJ COEFFICIENT RANGES
    VARIABLE        CURRENT       ALLOWABLE      ALLOWABLE
                     COEF         INCREASE       DECREASE
        X1        3.000000        2.000000       INFINITY
        X2        5.000000         .000000       INFINITY
        X3        4.000000        INFINITY        .000000

                        RIGHTHAND SIDE RANGES
        ROW         CURRENT       ALLOWABLE      ALLOWABLE
                     RHS          INCREASE       DECREASE
         2      18000.000000      INFINITY     4000.000000
         3      18000.000000    6000.000000    3000.000000
         4       9000.000000      INFINITY     5500.000000
         5       1000.000000     200.000000    1000.000000
```

22. Refer again to the computer solution of problem 21 (see Figure 3.15).

    a. Overtime rates in the sewing department are $12 per hour. Would you recommend that the company consider using overtime in that department? Explain.

    b. What is the shadow price for the fourth constraint? Interpret its value for management.

    c. Note that the reduced cost for x_2 is zero, but x_2 is not in solution at a positive value. What is your interpretation of this?

    d. Suppose that the profit contribution of the College ball is increased by $1. How do you expect the solution to change?

Note: Problems 23 and 24 and the case problem require computer solution and interpretation of the results.

23. A manufacturer makes three components for sale to refrigeration companies. The components are processed on two machines: a shaper and a grinder. The times (in minutes) required on each machine are given below.

Component	Machine	
	Shaper	**Grinder**
1	6	4
2	4	5
3	4	2

The shaper is available for 120 hours and the grinder is available for 110 hours. No more than 200 units of component 3 can be sold, but up to 1000 units of each of the other components can be sold. In fact the company already has orders for 600 units of component 1 that must be satisfied. The profit contribution for components 1, 2, and 3 are $8, $6, and $9, respectively.

    a. Formulate and solve for the recommended production quantities. Use any computer code available.

    b. What is the range of optimality for the profit contributions of the three components? Interpret these ranges for company management.

    c. What is the range of feasibility for the right-hand sides? Interpret these ranges for company management.

    d. If more time could be made available on the grinder, how much would it be worth?

    e. If more units of component 3 can be sold by reducing the sales price by $4, should the company reduce the price?

24. The Pfeiffer Company manages approximately $15 million for clients. For each client Pfeiffer chooses a mix of three investment vehicles: a growth stock fund, an income fund, and a money market fund. Each client has different investment objectives and tolerance for risk. In order to accommodate these differences, Pfeiffer places limits on the percentage of each portfolio that may be invested in the three funds and assigns a portfolio risk index to each client.

    Here's how the system works for Dennis Hartman, one of Pfeiffer's clients. Based on an evaluation of Hartman's risk tolerance, Pfeiffer has assigned Hartman's portfolio a risk index of .05. Furthermore, to maintain diversity, the fraction of Hartman's portfolio invested in the growth and income funds must be at least 10% for each, and at least 20% must be in the money market fund.

The risk ratings for the growth, income, and money market funds are 0.10, 0.05, and 0.01, respectively. A portfolio risk index is computed as a weighted average of the risk ratings for the three funds where the weights are the fraction of the portfolio invested in each of the funds. Hartman has given Pfeiffer $300,000 to manage. Pfeiffer is currently forecasting a yield of 20% on the growth fund, 10% on the income fund, and 6% on the money market fund.

a. Develop a linear programming model to select the best mix of investments for Hartman's portfolio.

b. Use any linear programming computer code to solve the model you developed in part (a).

c. How much may the yields on the three funds vary before it will be necessary for Pfeiffer to modify Hartman's portfolio?

d. If Hartman were more risk tolerant, how much of a yield increase could he expect? For instance, what if his portfolio risk index is increased to 0.06?

e. If Pfeiffer revised his yield estimate for the growth fund downward to 0.10, how would you recommend modifying Hartman's portfolio?

f. What information must Pfeiffer maintain on each client in order to use this system to manage client portfolios?

g. On a weekly basis Pfeiffer revises the yield estimates for the three funds. Suppose Pfeiffer has 50 clients. Describe how you would envision Pfeiffer making weekly modifications in each client's portfolio and deciding how to allocate the total funds managed among the three investment funds.

═══ *Case Problem:* ═══
PRODUCT MIX

TJ's, Inc. makes three nut mixes for sale to grocery chains located in the Southeast. The three mixes, referred to as the Regular Mix, the Deluxe Mix, and the Holiday Mix, are made by mixing together different percentages of five types of nuts.

In preparation for the fall season, TJ's has just purchased the following shipments of nuts at the prices shown:

Type of Nut	Shipment Amount (pounds)	Cost per Shipment
Almonds	6000	$7500
Brazil	7500	$7125
Filberts	7500	$6750
Pecans	6000	$7200
Walnuts	7500	$7875

The Regular Mix consists of 15% almonds, 25% Brazil, 25% filberts, 10% pecans, and 25% walnuts. The Deluxe Mix consists of 20% of each type of nut, and the Holiday Mix consists of 25% almonds, 15% Brazil, 15% filberts, 25% pecans, and 20% walnuts.

TJ's accountant has analyzed the cost of packaging materials, sales price per pound, etc., and determined that the contribution to profit is $1.65 per pound for the Regular Mix, $2.00 per pound for the Deluxe Mix, and $2.25 per pound for the Holiday Mix. These figures do not include the cost of the nuts included in the different mixes because that cost can vary greatly in the commodity markets.

Customer orders already received are summarized below:

Type of Mix	Orders (pounds)
Regular	10,000
Deluxe	3,000
Holiday	5,000

Because demand is running high, it is expected that TJ will receive many more orders than can be satisfied.

TJ's is committed to using the nuts available to maximize profit over the fall season. But even if it is not profitable to do so, TJ's president has indicated that the orders already received must be satisfied.

MANAGERIAL REPORT

Perform an analysis of TJ's product mix problem and prepare a report for TJ's president that summarizes your findings. Be sure to include information and analysis on the following:

1. The cost per pound of the nuts included in the Regular, Deluxe, and Holiday mixes.
2. The optimal product mix and profit contribution.
3. Recommendations regarding how profit contribution can be increased if additional quantities of nuts can be purchased.
4. Suppose that an additional 1000 pounds of almonds is available for $1000 from a supplier who overbought. Should TJ's purchase these almonds?
5. Recommendations regarding how profit contribution could be increased (if at all) if TJ's does not satisfy all existing orders.

4

Linear Programming Applications

Our study thus far has been directed toward understanding linear programming in terms of the graphical solution method, sensitivity analysis, and the interpretation of computer solutions to linear programs. This background is essential for knowing when linear programming is an appropriate problem-solving tool and for interpreting the results of a linear programming solution to a problem. However, the benefits of this study will be realized only by learning how linear programming can be used to solve practical decision-making problems. The purpose of this chapter is to show how a variety of problems can be formulated and solved using linear programming.

There are two ways in which one may develop skills in model building. (In this chapter model building should be taken to mean formulating a linear program that is a "model" of the real-world decision-making problem for which a solution is desired.) The first way is by on-the-job experience. This is essentially a trial-and-error approach and obviously could not be attempted in a textbook. The second way in which one may develop these skills is by studying how others have developed successful models. In this chapter we attempt to help you develop your skills along these lines by presenting several reasonably detailed examples of successful linear programming applications. Relatively small problems will be used in the examples, but the principles being demonstrated are applicable to much larger problems.

In practice, linear programming has proved to be one of the most successful quantitative aids for managerial decision making. Numerous applications have been reported in the chemical, airline, steel, paper, petroleum, and other industries. The specific problems studied have included production scheduling, capital budgeting, plant location, transportation, media selection, among many others.

As the variety of the applications mentioned would suggest, linear programming is a flexible problem-solving tool with applications in many disciplines. In this chapter we present introductory applications from the areas of marketing, finance, and production management, as well as other common linear programming applications. In addition, an application involving goal programming is presented. Goal programming is a clever extension of the modeling capability inherent in linear programming to problems with multiple criteria. Computer solutions, obtained using LINDO/PC, are presented and interpreted for most of the problems.

4.1 MARKETING APPLICATIONS

Media Selection

Media selection applications of linear programming are designed to help marketing managers allocate a fixed advertising budget across various advertising media. Potential media include newspaper, magazine, radio, television, and direct mail. In most of these applications the objective is the maximization of audience exposure. Restrictions on the allowable allocation usually arise through considerations such as company policy, contract requirements, and availability of media. In the application that follows we illustrate how a media selection problem might be formulated and solved using a linear programming model.

Consider the case of the Relax-and-Enjoy Lake Development Corporation. Relax-and-Enjoy is developing a lakeside community at a privately owned lake and is in the business of selling property for vacation and/or retreat cottages. The primary market for these lakeside lots includes all middle- and upper-income families within approximately 100 miles of the development. Relax-and-Enjoy has employed the advertising firm of Boone, Phillips and Jackson to design the promotional campaign for the project.

After considering possible advertising media and the market to be covered, Boone has made the preliminary recommendation to restrict the first month's advertising to five sources. At the end of the month, Boone will then reevaluate its strategy based upon the month's results. Boone has collected data on the number of potential purchase families reached, the cost per advertisement, the maximum number of times each medium is available, and the expected exposure for each of the five media. The expected exposure is measured in terms of an exposure unit, a measure of the relative value of one advertisement in each of the media. These measures, based on Boone's experience in the advertising business, take into account such factors as audience profile (age, income, and education of the audience reached), image presented, and quality of the advertisement. The information collected is presented in Table 4.1.

Relax-and-Enjoy has provided Boone with an advertising budget of $30,000 for the first month's campaign. In addition, Relax-and Enjoy has imposed the following restrictions on how Boone may allocate these funds: At least 10 television commercials must be used, and at least 50,000 potential purchasers must be reached during the month. In addition, no more than $18,000 may be spent on television advertisements. What advertising media selection plan should the advertising firm recommend?

The first step in formulating a linear programming model of this problem is to define the decision variables. We let

$$x_1 = \text{number of times daytime TV is used}$$
$$x_2 = \text{number of times evening TV is used}$$
$$x_3 = \text{number of times daily newspaper is used}$$
$$x_4 = \text{number of times Sunday newspaper is used}$$
$$x_5 = \text{number of times radio is used}$$

With the overall goal of maximizing the expected exposure, the objective function becomes

$$\max 65x_1 + 90x_2 + 40x_3 + 60x_4 + 20x_5$$

TABLE 4.1
Advertising Media Alternatives for the Relax-and-Enjoy Lake Development Corporation

Advertising Media	Number of Potential Purchase Families Reached	Cost per Advertisement	Maximum Times Available per Month*	Expected Exposure Units
1. Daytime TV (1 min), station WKLA	1000	$1500	15	65
2. Evening TV (30 sec), station WKLA	2000	$3000	10	90
3. Daily newspaper (full page), *The Morning Journal*	1500	$400	25	40
4. Sunday newspaper magazine (½ page color), *The Sunday Press*	2500	$1000	4	60
5. Radio, 8:00 A.M. or 5:00 P.M. news (30 sec), station KNOP	300	$100	30	20

*The maximum number of times the medium is available is either the maximum number of times the advertising medium occurs (e.g., four Sundays for medium 4) or the maximum number of times Boone will allow the medium to be used.

The constraints for the model can now be formulated from the information given:

$$
\begin{aligned}
x_1 &\leq 15 \\
x_2 &\leq 10 \\
x_3 &\leq 25 \\
x_4 &\leq 4 \\
x_5 &\leq 30
\end{aligned}
\left.\right\} \text{Availability of media}
$$

$$1500x_1 + 3000x_2 + 400x_3 + 1000x_4 + 100x_5 \leq 30{,}000 \quad \text{Budget}$$

$$
\left.\begin{aligned}
x_1 + x_2 &\geq 10 \\
1500x_1 + 3000x_2 &\leq 18{,}000
\end{aligned}\right\}
\begin{aligned} &\text{Television} \\ &\text{restrictions} \end{aligned}
$$

$$1000x_1 + 2000x_2 + 1500x_3 + 2500x_4 + 300x_5 \geq 50{,}000 \quad \begin{aligned}&\text{Audience}\\&\text{coverage}\end{aligned}$$

$$x_1, x_2, x_3, x_4, x_5 \geq 0$$

The solution to this five-variable, nine-constraint linear programming model is presented in Table 4.2.

We point out that the above media selection model, probably more than most other linear programming models, requires crucial subjective evaluations as input. The most critical of these inputs is the expected exposure rating measure. While marketing managers may have substantial data concerning expected advertising exposure, the final coefficient that includes image and quality considerations is based primarily on managerial judgment. However, judgment input is a very acceptable way of obtaining necessary data for a linear programming model.

TABLE 4.2
Advertising Plan for the Relax-and-Enjoy Lake Development Corporation

Media	Frequency	Budget
Daytime TV	10	$15,000
Daily newspaper	25	10,000
Sunday newspaper	2	2,000
Radio	30	3,000
		$30,000

Total audience contacted = 61,500
Expected exposure = 2370

A possible shortcoming of this model is that even if the expected exposure measure were not subject to error, there is no guarantee that maximization of total expected exposure will lead to a maximization of profit or of sales (a common surrogate for profit). However, this is not a shortcoming of linear programming; rather it is a shortcoming of the use of exposure as a criterion. Certainly if we were able to measure directly the effect of an advertisement on profit, we would use total profit as the objective to be maximized.

In addition, you should be aware that the media selection model as formulated in this section does not include considerations such as the following:

1. Reduced exposure value for repeat media usage
2. Cost discounts for repeat media usage
3. Audience overlap by different media
4. Timing recommendations for the advertisements

A more complex formulation—more variables and constraints—can often be used to overcome some of these limitations, but it will not always be possible to overcome all of them with a linear programming model. However, even in these cases a linear programming model can often be used to arrive at an approximation of the best decision. Management evaluation combined with the linear programming solution should then make possible the selection of an overall effective advertising strategy.

Marketing Research

Marketing research is conducted by a variety of organizations in order to learn about consumer characteristics, attitudes, and preferences toward products and/or services offered by an organization. Often the actual research is performed by a marketing research firm that specializes in providing client organizations with the desired market information. Typical services offered by a marketing research firm include designing the study, conducting market surveys, analyzing the data collected, and providing summary reports and recommendations for the client. In the research design phase targets or quotas may be established for the number and types of respondents to be reached by a survey. With quota guidelines established, the objective of the marketing research firm is to conduct the survey so as to meet the client's needs at a minimum cost.

Market Survey, Inc. (MSI) is a marketing research firm that specializes in evaluating consumer reaction to new products, services, and advertising campaigns. A client firm has requested assistance from MSI in ascertaining consumer reaction to a recently marketed product for household use. During meetings with the client it was agreed that door-to-door, personal interviews would be used to obtain information from both households with children and households without children. In addition, it was agreed that both day and evening interviews would be necessary in order to allow for a variety of household work schedules. Specifically, the client's contract called for MSI to conduct 1000 interviews with the following quota guidelines:

1. At least 400 households with children would be interviewed.
2. At least 400 households without children would be interviewed.
3. The total number of households interviewed during the evening would be at least as great as the number of households interviewed during the day.
4. At least 40% of the interviews for households with children would be conducted during the evening.
5. At least 60% of the interviews for households without children would be conducted during the evening.

Since the interviews of households with children take additional interviewer time, and since evening interviewers are paid more than daytime interviewers, the cost of an interview varies with the type of interview. Based upon previous research studies, estimates of the interview costs are as follows:

	Interview Cost	
Household	Day	Evening
Children	$20	$25
No children	$18	$20

What is the household, time-of-day interview plan that will satisfy the contract requirements at a minimum total interviewing cost?

The formulation of a linear programming model for the Market Survey problem is a good opportunity to introduce the use of double-subscripted decision variables. Using x to represent the decision variables, we will use two subscripts for x, with the first subscript indicating whether the interview involves children or not and the second subscript indicating whether the interview is in the day or evening. Using 1 for children and 2 for no children, and 1 for day and 2 for evening, double subscripts can be used to identify the following four decision variables:

$$x_{11} = \text{the number of interviews for households with children to be conducted during the day}$$
$$x_{12} = \text{the number of interviews for households with children to be conducted during the evening}$$
$$x_{21} = \text{the number of interviews for households without children to be conducted during the day}$$
$$x_{22} = \text{the number of interviews for households without children to be conducted during the evening}$$

We begin the linear programming model formulation by using the cost-per-interview data to develp the following objective function:

$$\min 20x_{11} + 25x_{12} + 18x_{21} + 20x_{22}$$

The constraint requiring a total of 1000 interviews is written:

$$x_{11} + x_{12} + x_{21} + x_{22} = 1000$$

The five specifications concerning the types of interviews are as follows:

1. Households with children:

$$x_{11} + x_{12} \geq 400$$

2. Households without children:

$$x_{21} + x_{22} \geq 400$$

3. At least as many evening interviews as day interviews:

$$x_{12} + x_{22} \geq x_{11} + x_{21}$$

The usual format for linear programming model formulation and computer input places all decision variables on the left-hand side of the inequality and a constant (possibly zero) on the right-hand side. Thus, we will rewrite this constraint as

$$-x_{11} + x_{12} - x_{21} + x_{22} \geq 0$$

4. At least 40% of interviews for households with children during the evening:

$$x_{12} \geq .4(x_{11} + x_{12})$$

or

$$-.4x_{11} + .6x_{12} \geq 0$$

5. At least 60% of interviews for households without children during the evening:

$$x_{22} \geq .6(x_{21} + x_{22})$$

or

$$-.6x_{21} + .4x_{22} \geq 0$$

By adding the nonnegativity requirements, the four-variable, six-constraint linear programming model becomes

min $\quad 20x_{11} + 25x_{12} + 18x_{21} + 20x_{22}$

s.t.

$$
\begin{array}{llll}
x_{11} + & x_{12} + & x_{21} + & x_{22} = 1000 \quad \text{Total interviews} \\
x_{11} + & x_{12} & & \geq \ \ 400 \quad \text{Households with children}
\end{array}
$$

$$x_{21} + \quad x_{22} \geq 400 \quad \text{Households without children}$$
$$-x_{11} + \quad x_{12} - \quad x_{21} + \quad x_{22} \geq \quad 0 \quad \text{More evening interviews}$$
$$-.4x_{11} + \quad .6x_{12} \qquad\qquad \geq \quad 0 \quad \text{Evening households with children}$$
$$-.6x_{21} + .4x_{22} \geq \quad 0 \quad \text{Evening households without children}$$
$$x_{11}, x_{12}, x_{21}, x_{22} \geq 0$$

The computer solution to the above linear program is shown in Figure 4.1. Using the results of the computer solution, we see that the minimum cost of \$20,320 occurs with the following interview schedule:

| | Number of Interviews | | |
Household	Day	Evening	Totals
Children	240	160	400
No children	240	360	600
Totals	480	520	1000

As can be seen, 480 interviews will be scheduled during the day and 520 during the evening. Households with children will be covered by 400 interviews and households without children will be covered by 600 interviews.

FIGURE 4.1
Computer Solution of the Marketing Research Problem Using LINDO/PC

```
                    OBJECTIVE FUNCTION VALUE

        1)          20320.0000

        VARIABLE            VALUE          REDUCED COST
            X11          240.000000           .000000
            X12          160.000000           .000000
            X21          240.000000           .000000
            X22          360.000000           .000000



          ROW      SLACK OR SURPLUS        DUAL PRICES
           2)             .000000         -19.200000
           3)             .000000          -2.799999
           4)          200.000000           .000000
           5)           40.000000           .000000
           6)             .000000          -5.000000
           7)             .000000          -2.000000
```

As mentioned in Chapter 3, when using LINDO/PC, row 1 refers to the objective function, row 2 refers to constraint 1, row 3 refers to constraint 2, and so on. Dual price information for each constraint is provided in the column labeled DUAL PRICES.

Selected sensitivity analysis information from Figure 4.1 shows a dual price of -19.2 for row 2. This tells us that the objective function will get worse (cost increase) by $19.20 if the number of interviews is increased from 1000 to 1001. Thus $19.20 is the incremental cost of obtaining additional interviews. It is also the savings that could be realized by reducing the number of interviews from 1000 to 999. The dual price for the requirement of 400 households with children (row 3) is -2.799999. This dual price indicates that requesting additional interviews of households with children will not improve the objective function. In fact, additional interviews of households with children will add to the total cost at a rate of approximately $2.80 per additional interview.

The surplus variable with a value of 200 for row 4 shows that 200 more households without children will be interviewed than required. Similarly, the surplus variable with a value of 40 for row 5 shows that the number of evening interviews exceeds the number of daytime interviews by 40. The zero values for the surplus variables in rows 6 and 7 indicate that the more expensive evening interviews are being held at a minimum.

4.2 FINANCIAL APPLICATIONS

Portfolio Selection

Portfolio selection problems involve situations in which a financial manager must select specific investments—for example, stocks, bonds—from a variety of investment alternatives. This type of problem is frequently encountered by managers of mutual funds, credit unions, insurance companies, and banks. The objective function for portfolio selection problems is usually maximization of expected return or minimization of risk. The constraints usually take the form of restrictions on the type of permissible investments, state laws, company policy, maximum permissible risk, and so on.

Problems of this type have been formulated and solved using a variety of mathematical programming techniques. However, if in a particular portfolio selection problem it is possible to formulate a linear objective function and linear constraints, then linear programming can be used to solve the problem. In this section we show how a portfolio selection problem can be formulated and solved as a linear program.

Consider the case of Welte Mutual Funds, Inc., located in New York City. Welte has just obtained $100,000 by converting industrial bonds to cash and is now looking for other investment opportunities for these funds. Considering Welte's current investments, the firm's top financial analyst recommends that all new investments should be made in the oil industry, steel industry, or government bonds. Specifically, the analyst has identified five investment opportunities and projected their annual rates of return. The investments and rates of return are shown in Table 4.3.

Management of Welte has imposed the following investment guidelines:

1. Neither industry (oil or steel) should receive more than 50% of the total new investment.
2. Government bonds should be at least 25% of the steel industry investments.
3. The investment in Pacific Oil, the high-return but high-risk investment, cannot be more than 60% of the total oil industry investment.

TABLE 4.3
Investment Opportunities for Welte Mutual Funds

Investment	Projected Rate of Return (%)
Atlantic Oil	7.3
Pacific Oil	10.3
Midwest Steel	6.4
Huber Steel	7.5
Government bonds	4.5

What portfolio recommendations—investments and amounts—should be made for the available $100,000? Given the objective of maximizing projected return subject to the budgetary and managerially imposed constraints, we can answer this question by formulating a linear programming model of the problem. The solution to this linear programming model will then provide investment recommendations for the management of Welte Mutual Funds.

Let

$$x_1 = \text{dollars invested in Atlantic Oil}$$
$$x_2 = \text{dollars invested in Pacific Oil}$$
$$x_3 = \text{dollars invested in Midwest Steel}$$
$$x_4 = \text{dollars invested in Huber Steel}$$
$$x_5 = \text{dollars invested in Government bonds}$$

Using the projected rates of return shown in Table 4.3, the objective function for maximizing the total rate of return for the portfolio can be written as

$$\max 0.073x_1 + 0.103x_2 + 0.064x_3 + 0.075x_4 + 0.045x_5$$

The constraint specifying the investment of $100,000 is written as

$$x_1 + x_2 + x_3 + x_4 + x_5 = 100,000$$

The requirements that neither the oil nor the steel industry should receive more than 50% of the $100,000 investment are as follows:

$$x_1 + x_2 \leq 50,000 \quad \text{Oil industry}$$
$$x_3 + x_4 \leq 50,000 \quad \text{Steel industry}$$

The requirement that government bonds be at least 25% of the steel industry investment is expressed as follows:

$$x_5 \geq 0.25 (x_3 + x_4)$$

or

$$-0.25x_3 - 0.25x_4 + x_5 \geq 0$$

Finally, the constraint that Pacific Oil cannot be more than 60% of the total oil industry investment becomes

$$x_2 \le 0.60(x_1 + x_2)$$

or

$$-0.60x_1 + 0.40x_2 \le 0$$

By adding the nonnegativity restrictions, the complete linear programming model for the Welte Mutual Fund investment problem is as follows:

max $0.073x_1 + 0.103x_2 + 0.064x_3 + 0.075x_4 + 0.045x_5$
s.t.

$x_1 +$	$x_2 +$	$x_3 +$	$x_4 +$	$x_5 = 100,000$	Available funds
$x_1 +$	x_2			$\le 50,000$	Oil industry maximum
		$x_3 +$	x_4	$\le 50,000$	Steel industry maximum
		$- 0.25x_3 -$	$0.25x_4 +$	$x_5 \ge 0$	Government bonds minimum
$-0.6x_1 +$	$0.4x_2$			≤ 0	Pacific Oil restriction

$$x_1, x_2, x_3, x_4, x_5 \ge 0$$

This problem was solved using LINDO/PC. The output is shown in Figure 4.2. In Table 4.4 we show how the funds are divided among the securities. Note that the optimal

FIGURE 4.2
Computer Solution of Welte Mutual Funds Problem Using LINDO/PC

```
                   OBJECTIVE FUNCTION VALUE

         1)        8000.00000

         VARIABLE          VALUE         REDUCED COST
            X1        20000.000000          .000000
            X2        30000.000000          .000000
            X3            .000000           .011000
            X4        40000.000000          .000000
            X5        10000.000000          .000000


         ROW       SLACK OR SURPLUS     DUAL PRICES
            2)          .000000            .069000
            3)          .000000            .022000
            4)        10000.000000         .000000
            5)          .000000           -.024000
            6)          .000000            .030000
```

TABLE 4.4
Optimal Portfolio Selection for Welte Mutual Funds

Investment	Amount	Expected Annual Return
Atlantic Oil	$ 20,000	$1460
Pacific Oil	30,000	3090
Huber Steel	40,000	3000
Government bonds	10,000	450
	$100,000	$8000

Expected annual return of $8000 = 8%

solution indicates that the portfolio should be diversified among all the investment opportunities except Midwest Steel. The projected annual return for this portfolio is $8,000, which is an overall return rate of 8%.

Using the computer printout for the Welte investment problem as shown in Figure 4.2, we see that the dual price for row 4 is zero. This is because constraint 3 (steel industry maximum) is not a binding constraint; increases in the steel industry limit of $50,000 will not improve the value of the objective function. Indeed, the slack variable for this constraint shows that the current steel industry investment is $10,000 below its limit of $50,000. The dual prices for the other constraints are nonzero, indicating that they are binding constraints at the optimal solution.

The dual price of 0.069 for row 2 (constraint 1) shows that the objective function can be increased by 0.069 if one more dollar can be made available for the portfolio investment. If more funds can be obtained at a cost of less than 6.9%, management should consider obtaining them. On the other hand, if a return in excess of 6.9% can be obtained by investing funds elsewhere (other than in these five securities), management should question the wisdom of investing the entire $100,000 in this portfolio.

Similar interpretations can be given to the other dual prices. Note, however, that the dual price for row 5 (constraint 4) is negative; its value is -0.024. This indicates that increasing the value on the right-hand side of the constraint by one unit can be expected to cause a change in the objective function of -0.024. In terms of the optimal portfolio, this means that if Welte invests one more dollar in government bonds, the total return will decrease by 2.4 cents. To see why this is so, note again from the dual price for constraint 1 that the marginal return on the funds invested in the portfolio is 6.9% (the average return is 8%). The rate of return on government bonds is 4.5%. Thus the cost of investing one more dollar in government bonds is the difference between the marginal return on the portfolio and the marginal return on government bonds: 6.9% $-$ 4.5% = 2.4%.

Note that the optimal solution with $x_3 = 0$ shows that Midwest Steel should not be included in the portfolio. The associated REDUCED COST for x_3 of .011 tells us that the objective function coefficient for Midwest Steel would have to increase by .011 before it would be desirable to consider the Midwest Steel investment alternative. With this increase the Midwest Steel return would be 0.064 + 0.011 = 0.075, making this investment just as desirable as the currently used Huber Steel investment alternative.

Two other points concerning this problem are worth mentioning. First, a simple modification of this model permits determining the fraction of available funds invested in each security. That is, we divide each of the right-hand-side values by 100,000. Then the optimal values for the variables will give the fraction of funds that should be invested in each security for a portfolio of any size. Second, a shortcoming of the linear programming approach to the portfolio selection problem is that we may not be able to invest the exact amount specified in each of the securities. For example, if Atlantic Oil sold for $75 a share, we would have to purchase exactly $266\frac{2}{3}$ shares in order to spend exactly the recommended $20,000. The approach usually taken to avoid this difficulty is to purchase the largest possible whole number of shares with the amount of funds recommended (for example, 266 shares of Atlantic Oil). Hence we guarantee that our budget constraint will not be violated. This, of course, introduces the possibility that our solution will no longer be optimal, but the danger is slight if large numbers of securities are involved.

Financial-Mix Strategy

Financial-mix strategies involve the selection of means for financing company projects, inventories, production operations, and various other activities. In this section we illustrate how linear porgramming can be used to solve problems of this type by formulating and solving a problem involving the financing of production operations. In this particular application a financial decision must be made with regard to how much production is to be supported by internally generated funds and how much is to be supported by external funds.

The Jefferson Adding Machine Company will begin production of two new models of electronic calculators during the next 3 months. Since these models require an expansion of the current production operation, the company will need operating funds to cover material, labor, and other expenses during the initial production period. Revenue from this initial production period will not be available until after the end of the period. Thus the company must arrange financing for these operating expenses before production can begin.

Jefferson has set aside $3000 in internal funds to cover expenses of this operation. If additional funds are needed, they will have to be generated externally. A local bank has offered a line of short-term credit in an amount not to exceed $10,000. The interest rate over the life of the loan will be 12% per year on the average amount borrowed. One stipulation set by the bank requires that the remainder of the company cash set aside for this operation plus the accounts receivable for this product line be at least twice as great as the outstanding loan plus interest at the end of the initial production period.

In addition to the financial restrictions placed on this operation, labor capacity is also a factor for Jefferson to consider. Only 2500 hours of assembly time and 150 hours of packaging and shipping time are available for the new product line during the initial 3-month production period. Relevant cost, price, and production time requirements for the two models, referred to as models Y and Z, are shown in Table 4.5.

Additional restrictions have been imposed by company management in order to guarantee that the market reaction to both products can be tested; that is, at least 50 units of model Y and at least 25 units of model Z must be produced in this first production period.

Since the cost of the units produced using borrowed funds will in effect experience an interest charge, the profit contributions for the units of models Y and Z produced on

TABLE 4.5
Cost, Price, and Labor Data for the Jefferson Adding Machine Company

Model	Unit Cost (Materials and Other Variable Expenses)	Selling Price	Profit Margin	Labor Hours Required	
				Assembly	Packaging and shipping
Y	$ 50	$ 58	$ 8	12	1
Z	$100	$120	$20	25	2

borrowed funds will be reduced. Hence we adopt the following notation for the decision variables in this problem:

$$x_1 = \text{units of model } Y \text{ produced with company funds}$$
$$x_2 = \text{units of model } Y \text{ produced with borrowed funds}$$
$$x_3 = \text{units of model } Z \text{ produced with company funds}$$
$$x_4 = \text{units of model } Z \text{ produced with borrowed funds}$$

How much will the profit contribution be reduced for units produced on borrowed funds? To answer this question, one must know for how long the loan will be outstanding. We assume that all units of each model are sold as they are produced to independent distributors and that the average rate of turnover of accounts receivable is 3 months. Since company management has specified that the loan is to be repaid by funds generated by the units produced on borrowed funds, the funds borrowed to produce one unit of model Y or Z will be repaid approximately 3 months later. Hence the profit contribution for each unit of model Y produced on borrowed funds is reduced from $8 to $8 − ($50 × 0.12 × ¼ yr) = $6.50, and the profit contribution for each unit of model Z produced on borrowed funds is reduced from $20 to $20 − ($100 × 0.12 × ¼ yr) = $17. With this information we can now formulate the objective function for Jefferson's financial mix problem:

$$\max 8x_1 + 6.5x_2 + 20x_3 + 17x_4$$

We can also specify the following constraints for the model:

$$
\begin{array}{rrrrrll}
12x_1 + & 12x_2 + & 25x_3 + & 25x_4 & \le & 2500 & \text{Assembly capacity} \\
x_1 + & x_2 + & 2x_3 + & 2x_4 & \le & 150 & \text{Packaging and shipping capacity} \\
50x_1 & & + 100x_3 & & \le & 3000 & \text{Internal funds available} \\
& 50x_2 & & + 100x_4 & \le & 10{,}000 & \text{External funds available} \\
x_1 + & x_2 & & & \ge & 50 & \text{Model } Y \text{ requirement} \\
& & x_3 + & x_4 & \ge & 25 & \text{Model } Z \text{ requirement}
\end{array}
$$

In addition, the following constraint must be included to satisfy the bank loan requirement:

$$\text{Cash} + \text{accounts receivable} \ge 2(\text{loan} + \text{interest})$$

This restriction must be satisfied at the end of the period. Recalling that accounts receivable are outstanding for an average of 3 months, the following relationships can be used to derive a mathematical expression for the above inequality at the end of the period:

$$\text{Cash} = 3000 \quad - \quad 50x_1 - 100x_3$$
$$\text{Accounts receivable} = \quad 58x_1 + \quad 58x_2 + 120x_3 + 120x_4$$
$$\text{Loan} = \quad 50x_2 + 100x_4$$
$$\text{Interest} = (0.12 \quad \times \tfrac{1}{4} \text{ yr})(50x_2 + 100x_4) = 1.5x_2 + 3x_4$$

Therefore the constraint resulting from the bank restriction can be written as

$$3000 - 50x_1 - 100x_3 + 58x_1 + 58x_2 + 120x_3 + 120x_4 \geq 2(51.5x_2 + 103x_4)$$

or

$$3000 \geq -8x_2 + 45x_2 - 20x_2$$

which is equivalent to

$$-8x_1 + 45x_2 - 20x_3 + 86x_4 \leq 3000$$

Adding the nonnegativity constraints, the complete linear programming model for the Jefferson Adding Machine Company can now be stated:

$$\max \quad 8x_1 + 6.5x_2 + 20x_3 + 17x_4$$
$$\text{s.t.}$$
$$12x_1 + 12x_2 + 25x_3 + 25x_4 \leq 2500$$
$$x_1 + x_2 + 2x_3 + 2x_4 \leq 150$$
$$50x_1 + 100x_3 \qquad \leq 3000$$
$$50x_2 + 100x_4 \leq 10{,}000$$
$$x_1 + x_2 \qquad \geq 50$$
$$x_3 + x_4 \geq 25$$
$$-8x_1 + 45x_2 - 20x_3 + 86x_4 \leq 3000$$
$$x_1, x_2, x_3, x_4, \geq 0$$

The computer solution to this four-variable, seven-constraint financial-mix problem is shown in Figure 4.3. The profit of $1191.86 is realized with the optimal solution of $x_1 = 50$, $x_2 = 0$, $x_3 = 5$, and $x_4 = 40.7$. Note that the reduced cost of zero for x_2 tells us that the objective function coefficient *does not have to increase* in order to consider bringing x_2 into the optimal solution. This is an indication that alternate optimal solutions exist for the problem. Figure 4.4 shows a computer solution yielding an alternate optimal solution. The profit of $1191.86 is now associated with the solution $x_1 = 0$, $x_2 = 50$, $x_3 = 30$, and $x_4 = 15.7$.

Obviously management could implement either of the solutions shown in the figures and maximize profit. The solution in Figure 4.4 is rounded and summarized in Table 4.6 along with the expected profit and borrowed funds for each model of calculator. This

FIGURE 4.3
Computer Solution of Jefferson Adding Machine Problem Using LINDO/PC

```
                    OBJECTIVE FUNCTION VALUE

        1)        1191.86000

        VARIABLE           VALUE         REDUCED COST
              X1        50.000000           .000000
              X2          .000000           .000000
              X3         5.000000           .000000
              X4        40.697670           .000000

         ROW      SLACK OR SURPLUS      DUAL PRICES
          2)        757.558200            .000000
          3)          8.604652            .000000
          4)           .000000            .239535
          5)       5930.232000            .000000
          6)           .000000          -2.395350
          7)         20.697670            .000000
          8)           .000000            .197674
```

FIGURE 4.4
Alternate Optimal Solution to Jefferson Adding Machine Problem Using LINDO/PC

```
                    OBJECTIVE FUNCTION VALUE

        1)        1191.86000

        VARIABLE           VALUE         REDUCED COST
              X1          .000000           .000000
              X2        50.000000           .000000
              X3        30.000000           .000000
              X4        15.697670           .000000

         ROW      SLACK OR SURPLUS      DUAL PRICES
          2)        757.558100            .000000
          3)          8.604650            .000000
          4)           .000000            .239535
          5)       5930.232000            .000000
          6)           .000000          -2.395349
          7)         20.697670            .000000
          8)           .000000            .197674
          9)           .000000            .000000
```

TABLE 4.6
Optimal Financial Mix for the Production of Jefferson Adding Machines

		Units	Expected Profit	Amount of Borrowed Funds
Model Y				
Borrowed funds (x_2)		50	$ 325	$2500
Model Z				
Company funds (x_3)		30	600	–
Borrowed funds (x_4)		15.7	267	1570
	Totals		$1192	$4070

solution requires the company to use all its internal funds ($3000), but only slightly more than $4000 of the available $10,000 line of credit.

Some additional interpretations from the computer printout in Figure 4.4 show that assembly capacity (row 2, slack = 757.6 hours) and packaging and shipping capacity (row 3, slack = 8.6 hours) are adequate to meet the production requirements. Additional hours of these resources will not improve the value of the optimal solution. The dual price of 0.239535 associated with the internal funds constraint (row 4) shows that a profit improvement of approximately $0.24 can be made from an additional dollar of internal funds. With this high return on the internal funds investment, Jefferson may want to consider seriously allocating additional internal funds to this project. The negative dual price of −2.39535 for row 6 tells us that increases in the model Y production requirement will reduce the profit margin. In fact, the negative dual price shows that reducing the current 50-unit requirement for model Y will actually increase profits at the rate of approximately $2.40 per unit reduction in the requirement.

4.3 PRODUCTION MANAGEMENT APPLICATIONS

Production Scheduling

One of the most important areas of linear programming deals with multiperiod planning applications such as production scheduling. The solution to a production scheduling problem enables the manager to establish an efficient low-cost production schedule for one or more products over several time periods, such as weeks, months, and so on. Essentially, a production scheduling problem can be viewed as a product-mix problem for each of several periods in the future. The manager must determine the production levels that will allow the company to meet product demand requirements, given limitations on production capacity, labor capacity, and storage space. At the same time, it is desired to minimize the total cost of carrying out this task.

One major reason for the widespread application of linear programming to production scheduling problems is that these problems are of a recurring nature. A production schedule must be established for the current month, then again for the next month, the month after that, and so on. When the production manager looks at the problem each month, he/she will find that while demands for the products have changed, production times, production capacities, storage space limitations, and so on, are roughly the same. Thus the production manager is basically resolving the same problem handled in previous months. Hence a general linear programming model of the production scheduling procedure may be frequently applied. Once the model has been formulated, the manager can simply supply the data—demands, capacities, and so on—for the given production period, and the linear programming model can then be used to develop the production schedule. Thus one linear programming formulation may have many repeat applications.

Let us consider the case of the Bollinger Electronics Company, which produces two different electronic components for a major airplane engine manufacturer. The airplane engine manufacturer notifies the Bollinger sales office each quarter as to what the monthly requirements for components will be during each of the next 3 months. The monthly requirements for the components may vary considerably depending upon the type of engine the airplane engine manufacturer is producing. The order shown in Table 4.7 has just been received for the next 3-month period.

TABLE 4.7
Three-Month Demand Schedule for Bollinger Electronics Company

	April	May	June
Component 322A	1000	3000	5000
Component 802B	1000	500	3000

After the order is processed, a demand statement is sent to the production control department. The production control department must then develop a 3-month production plan for the components. Knowing the preference of the production department manager for constant demand levels that result in balanced workloads and constant machine and labor utilization, the production scheduler might consider the alternative of producing at a constant rate for all 3 months. This would set monthly production quotas at 3000 units per month for component 322A and 1500 units per month for component 802B. Why not adopt this schedule?

While this schedule would be quite appealing to the production department, it may be undesirable from a total-cost point of view. In particular, this schedule ignores inventory costs. Consider the projected inventory levels that would result from this schedule calling for constant production (Figure 4.5). We see that this production schedule would lead to high inventory levels. When we consider the cost of tied-up capital and storage space, a schedule that provides lower inventory levels might be economically more desirable.

At the other extreme of the constant rate production schedule is the produce-to-meet-demand approach. While this schedule eliminates the inventory holding cost problem, the wide monthly fluctuations in production levels may cause some serious production problems and costs. For example, production capacity would have to be available to meet the total 8000-unit peak demand in June. Also, unless other components could be scheduled on the same production equipment in April and May, there would be significant unused capacity and thus low machine utilization in those months. These large production variations might also require substantial labor adjustments which in turn could lead to increased employee turnover and training problems. Thus it appears that the best production schedule will be one that is a compromise between the two alternatives.

The production manager will want to identify and consider the following costs:

1. Production costs
2. Storage costs
3. Change-in-production-level costs

FIGURE 4.5
Projected Inventory Levels under a Constant-Rate Production Schedule

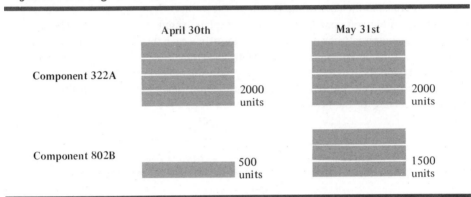

In the remainder of this section we show how a linear programming model of the production and inventory process for Bollinger Electronics can be formulated to account for these costs in such a fashion that the total cost is minimized.

In order to develop the model, we will use a double-subscript notation for the decision variables in the problem. We let the first subscript indicate the product number and the second subscript the month. Thus in general we let x_{im} denote the production volume in units for product i in month m. Here $i = 1, 2$ and $m = 1, 2, 3$; $i = 1$ refers to component 322A, $i = 2$ refers to component 802B, $m = 1$ refers to April, $m = 2$ refers to May, and $m = 3$ refers to June. The purpose of the double subscript is to provide a more descriptive notation. We could simply use x_6 to represent the number of units of product 2 produced in month 3, but x_{23} is more descriptive in that we know directly the product and month the variable represents.

If component 322A costs $20 per unit produced and component 802B costs $10 per unit produced, the production cost part of the objective function becomes

$$\text{Production cost} = 20x_{11} + 20x_{12} + 20x_{13} + 10x_{21} + 10x_{22} + 10x_{23}$$

You should note that in this particular problem the production cost per unit is the same each month, and thus we need not include production costs in the objective function; that is, no matter what production schedule is selected, the total production costs will remain the same. These are not relevant costs for the production scheduling decision under consideration. In cases where the cost per unit is expected to change each month, the variable production costs per unit per month must be included in the objective function. For the Bollinger Electronics problem the solution will be the same whether or not these costs are included. We have elected to include them so that the value of the linear programming objective function will include all the costs associated with the problem.

To incorporate the relevant inventory costs into the model, we introduce the following double-subscripted decision variable to indicate the number of units of inventory for each product for each month. We let s_{im} be the inventory level for product i at the end of month m.

Bollinger has determined that on a monthly basis, inventory holding costs are 1.5% of the cost of the product—that is, $(0.015)(\$20) = \$0.30$ per unit for component 322A and $(0.015)(\$10) = \$0.15$ per unit for component 802B. A common assumption made in linear programming approaches to the production scheduling problem is now invoked. We assume that monthly ending inventories are an acceptable approximation to the average inventory levels throughout the month. Given this assumption, the inventory holding cost portion of the objective function can be written as follows:

$$\text{Inventory holding cost} = 0.30s_{11} + 0.30s_{12} + 0.30s_{13} + 0.15s_{21} + 0.15s_{22} + 0.15s_{23}$$

In order to incorporate the costs due to fluctuations in production levels from month to month, we need to define the following additional decision variables:

$$I_m = \text{increase in the total production level during}$$
$$\text{month } m \text{ compared with month } m - 1$$
$$D_m = \text{decrease in the total production level during}$$
$$\text{month } m \text{ compared with month } m - 1$$

After estimating the effects of employee layoffs, turnovers, reassignment training costs, and other costs associated with fluctuating production levels, Bollinger estimates that the cost associated with increasing the production level for any given month is \$0.50 per unit increase. A similar cost associated with decreasing the production level for any given month is \$0.20 per unit. Thus the third portion of the objective function can be written as follows:

$$\text{Production fluctuation costs} = 0.50I_1 + 0.50I_2 + 0.50I_3 + 0.20D_1 + 0.20D_2 + 020D_3$$

You should note here that Bollinger has elected to measure the cost associated with production fluctuations as a function of the change in the total number of units produced in month m compared with the total number of units produced in month $m - 1$. In other production scheduling applications the production fluctuations might be measured in terms of machine hours or labor hours required rather than in terms of the total number of units produced.

Combining all three costs, the complete objective function becomes

$$\begin{aligned}
\text{Objective function} = \ & 20x_{11} + 20x_{12} + 20x_{13} + 10x_{21} + 10x_{22} \\
& + 10x_{23} + 0.30s_{11} + 0.30s_{12} + 0.30s_{13} + 0.15s_{21} \\
& + 0.15s_{22} + 0.15s_{23} + 0.50I_1 + 0.50I_2 + 0.50I_3 \\
& + 0.20D_1 + 0.20D_2 + 0.20D_3
\end{aligned}$$

Now let us consider the constraints. First we must guarantee that the schedule meets customer demand. Since the units shipped can come from the current month's production or from inventory carried over from previous periods, we have the following basic requirements:

$$\begin{pmatrix} \text{Ending} \\ \text{inventory} \\ \text{from previous} \\ \text{month} \end{pmatrix} + \begin{pmatrix} \text{current} \\ \text{production} \end{pmatrix} \geq \begin{pmatrix} \text{this month's} \\ \text{demand} \end{pmatrix}$$

The difference between the left-hand side and the right-hand side will be the amount of ending inventory at the end of this month. Thus the demand requirement takes the form

$$\begin{pmatrix} \text{Ending} \\ \text{inventory} \\ \text{from previous} \\ \text{month} \end{pmatrix} + \begin{pmatrix} \text{current} \\ \text{production} \end{pmatrix} - \begin{pmatrix} \text{ending} \\ \text{inventory} \\ \text{for this} \\ \text{month} \end{pmatrix} = \begin{pmatrix} \text{this} \\ \text{month's} \\ \text{demand} \end{pmatrix}$$

Suppose that the inventories at the beginning of the 3-month scheduling period were 500 units for component 322A and 200 units for component 802B. Recalling that the demand for both products in the first month (April) was 1000 units, the constraints for meeting demand in the first month become

$$500 + x_{11} - s_{11} = 1000$$
$$200 + x_{21} - s_{21} = 1000$$

Moving the constants to the right-hand side, we have

$$x_{11} - s_{11} = 500$$
$$x_{21} - s_{21} = 800$$

Similarly, we need demand constraints for both products in the second and third months. These can be written as follows:

$$\text{Month 2: } s_{11} + x_{12} - s_{12} = 3000$$
$$s_{21} + x_{22} - s_{22} = 500$$

$$\text{Month 3: } s_{12} + x_{13} - s_{13} = 5000$$
$$s_{22} + x_{23} - s_{23} = 3000$$

If the company specifies a minimum inventory level at the end of the 3-month period of at least 400 units of component 322A and at least 200 units of component 802B, we can add the constraints

$$s_{13} \geq 400$$
$$s_{23} \geq 200$$

Let us suppose that we have the additional information available on production, labor, and storage capacity given in Table 4.8. Machine, labor, and storage space requirements are given in Table 4.9. To reflect these limitations, the following constraints are necessary:

TABLE 4.8
Machine, Labor, and Storage Capacities for Bollinger Electronics

	Machine Capacity (hours)	Labor Capacity (hours)	Storage Capacity (square feet)
April	400	300	10,000
May	500	300	10,000
June	600	300	10,000

TABLE 4.9
Machine, Labor, and Storage Requirements for Components 322A and 802B

	Machine (hours/unit)	Labor (hours/unit)	Storage (sq. ft./unit)
Component 322A	0.10	0.05	2
Component 802B	0.08	0.07	3

Machine capacity:

$$0.10x_{11} + 0.08x_{21} \leq 400 \quad \text{Month 1}$$
$$0.10x_{12} + 0.08x_{22} \leq 500 \quad \text{Month 2}$$
$$0.10x_{13} + 0.08x_{23} \leq 600 \quad \text{Month 3}$$

Labor capacity:

$$0.05x_{11} + 0.07x_{21} \leq 300 \quad \text{Month 1}$$
$$0.05x_{12} + 0.07x_{22} \leq 300 \quad \text{Month 2}$$
$$0.05x_{13} + 0.07x_{23} \leq 300 \quad \text{Month 3}$$

Storage capacity:

$$2s_{11} + 3s_{21} \leq 10,000 \quad \text{Month 1}$$
$$2s_{12} + 3s_{22} \leq 10,000 \quad \text{Month 2}$$
$$2s_{13} + 3s_{23} \leq 10,000 \quad \text{Month 3}$$

One final set of constraints must be added. These are necessary in order to guarantee that I_m and D_m will reflect the increase or decrease in the total production level for month m. Suppose that the production levels for March, the month before the start of the current production scheduling problem, had been 1500 units of component 322A and 1000 units of component 802B for a total production level of $1500 + 1000 = 2500$ units. We can find the amount of the change in production for April from the relationship

$$\text{April production} - \text{March production} = \text{change}$$

Using the April production decision variables, x_{11} and x_{21}, and the March production of 2500 units, the above relationship can be rewritten as

$$x_{11} + x_{21} - 2500 = \text{change}$$

Note that the change can be positive or negative. A positive change reflects an increase in the total production level, and a negative change reflects a decrease in the total production level. Using the above relationship, the increase in production variable for April, I_1, and the decrease in production variable for April, D_1, can be used to specify the following constraint for the change in total production for the month of April:

$$x_{11} + x_{21} - 2500 = I_1 - D_1$$

Of course, we cannot have an increase in production and a decrease in production during the same 1-month period; thus either I_1 or D_1 will be zero. If April requires 3000 units of production, we will have $I_1 = 500$ and $D_1 = 0$. If April requires 2200 units of production, we will have $I_1 = 0$ and $D_1 = 300$. This approach of denoting the change in production level as the difference between two nonnegative variables, I_1 and D_1, permits both positive and negative changes in the total production level. If a single variable, say c_m, had been used to represent the change in production level, then because of the nonnegativity requirement, only positive changes would be permitted.

Using the same approach in May and June (always subtracting the previous month's total production from the current month's total production), we have the following constraints for the second and third months of the production scheduling period:

$$(x_{12} + x_{22}) - (x_{11} + x_{21}) = I_2 - D_2$$
$$(x_{13} + x_{23}) - (x_{12} + x_{22}) = I_3 - D_3$$

Placing the variables on the left-hand side and the constants on the right-hand side, the complete set of what are commonly referred to as production-smoothing constraints can be written as

$$
\begin{aligned}
x_{11} + x_{21} && -I_1 + D_1 &= 2500 \\
-x_{11} - x_{21} + x_{12} + x_{22} && -I_2 + D_2 &= 0 \\
-x_{12} - x_{22} + x_{13} + x_{23} - I_3 + D_3 &= 0
\end{aligned}
$$

The initially rather small, two-product, 3-month scheduling problem has now developed into an 18-variable, 20-constraint linear programming problem. Note that in the problem we were concerned only with one type of machine process, one type of labor, and one type of storage area. In actual production scheduling problems you may encounter several machine types, several labor grades, and/or several storage areas. Thus you are probably beginning to realize how large-scale linear programs of production systems come about. A typical application might involve developing a production schedule for 100 products over a 12-month horizon. Such a problem could have over 1000 variables and constraints.

The computer solution to the Bollinger Electronics production scheduling problem is shown in Figure 4.6. A portion of the managerial report based on the computer solution is shown in Table 4.10.

FIGURE 4.6
Computer Solution of the Bollinger Electronics Production Scheduling Problem Using LINDO/PC

```
                        OBJECTIVE FUNCTION VALUE

        1)          225295.000

        VARIABLE           VALUE            REDUCED COST
            X11        500.000000              .000000
            X12       3200.000000              .000000
            X13       5200.000000              .000000
            X21       2500.000000              .000000
            X22       2000.000000              .000000
            X23           .000000              .060715
            S11           .000000              .192856
            S12        200.000000              .000000
            S13        400.000000              .000000
            S21       1700.000000              .000000
            S22       3200.000000              .000000
            S23        200.000000              .000000
            I1         500.000000              .000000
            I2        2200.000000              .000000
            I3            .000000              .000000
            D1            .000000              .700000
            D2            .000000              .700000
            D3            .000000              .700000


        ROW       SLACK OR SURPLUS        DUAL PRICES
         2)              .000000          -20.000000
         3)              .000000          -10.000000
         4)              .000000          -20.107140
         5)              .000000          -10.150000
         6)              .000000          -20.500000
         7)              .000000          -10.439290
         8)              .000000          -20.800000
         9)              .000000          -10.589280
        10)           150.000000              .000000
        11)            20.000000              .000000
        12)            79.999990              .000000
        13)           100.000000              .000000
        14)              .000000             2.142852
        15)            40.000000              .000000
        16)          4900.000000              .000000
        17)              .000000              .046429
        18)          8600.000000              .000000
        19)              .000000              .500000
        20)              .000000              .500000
        21)              .000000              .500000
```

Let us now consider the monthly variation in the production and inventory schedule shown in Table 4.10. Recall that the inventory cost for component 802B is one-half the inventory cost for component 322A. Therefore, as might be expected, component 802B is produced heavily in the first month (April) and then held in inventory for the demand that will occur in future months. Component 322A tends to be produced when needed. and only small amounts are carried in inventory.

TABLE 4.10
Minimum-Cost Production Schedule Information for Bollinger Electronics

Activity	April	May	June
Production			
Component 322A	500	3200	5200
Component 802B	2500	2000	0
Totals	3000	5200	5200
Ending inventory			
Component 322A	0	200	400
Component 802B	1700	3200	200
Machine usage			
Scheduled hours	250	480	520
Slack capacity hours	150	20	80
Labor usage			
Scheduled hours	200	300	260
Slack capacity hours	100	0	40
Storage usage			
Scheduled storage	5100	10000	1400
Slack capacity	4900	0	8600

Total schedule cost (including production, inventory, and
production smoothing) = $225,295.00

The costs of increasing and decreasing the total production volume tend to smooth (make small) the monthly variations. In fact, the minimum cost schedule calls for a 500-unit increase in total production in April and a 2200-unit increase in total production in May. The May production level of 5200 units is then maintained during June.

The machine usage section of the report shows ample machine capacity available in all 3 months. However, labor and storage capacity both show full utilization (slack = 0 for row 14 and row 17 in Figure 4.6) in the month of May. The dual price of 2.142852 shows that an additional hour of labor capacity in May will improve the objective function (lower cost) by approximately $2.14. This information may help the production manager decide whether to add labor overtime during the month of May. A similar interpretation for the dual price of 0.046429 for row 17 shows that each additional square foot of storage space made available during May will improve the objective function by slightly less than 5 cents per square foot.

We have seen in this illustration that a linear programming model (18 variables and 20 constraints) of a relatively small two-product, 3-month production system has provided some valuable information in terms of identifying a minimum-cost production schedule. In larger production systems, where the number of variables and constraints are too large to track manually, linear programming models can provide a significant advantage in developing cost-saving production schedules.

Labor Planning

Labor planning or scheduling problems frequently occur when managers must make decisions involving departmental staffing requirements for a given period of time. This is particularly true when labor assignments have some flexibility and at least some labor effort can be assigned to more than one department or work center. This is often the case when employees have been cross-trained on two or more jobs. In the following example we show how linear programming can be used to determine not only an optimal product mix but also an optimal labor allocation for the various departments.

McCarthy's Everyday Glass Company is planning to produce two styles of drinking glasses during the next month. The glasses are processed in four separate departments. Excess equipment capacity is available and will not be a constraining factor. However, the company's labor resources are limited and will probably limit the production volume for the two products. The labor requirements per case produced (one dozen glasses) are shown in Table 4.11.

TABLE 4.11
Hours of Labor per Case of Product

Department	Product 1	Product 2
1	0.070	0.100
2	0.050	0.084
3	0.100	0.067
4	0.010	0.025

The company makes a profit of $1.00 per case of product 1 and $0.90 per case of product 2. If the number of hours available in each department is fixed, we can formulate McCarthy's problem as a standard product-mix linear program. We use the usual notation:

x_1 = cases of product 1 manufactured
x_2 = cases of product 2 manufactured
b_i = hours of labor available in department i, i = 1, 2, 3, 4.

The linear program can be written as

$$\max \quad 1.00x_1 + 0.90x_2$$
$$\text{s.t.}$$
$$0.070x_1 + 0.100x_2 \leq b_1$$
$$0.050x_1 + 0.084x_2 \leq b_2$$
$$0.100x_1 + 0.067x_2 \leq b_3$$
$$0.010x_1 + 0.025x_2 \leq b_4$$
$$x_1, x_2 \geq 0$$

To solve the normal product-mix problem, we would ask the production manager to specify the hours available in each department (b_1, b_2, b_3, and b_4); then we could solve for the profit maximizing product mix. However, in this case we assume that the manager has some flexibility in allocating labor resources, and we would like to make a recommendation for this allocation as well as determining the optimal product mix.

Suppose that after consideration of the training and experience qualifications of the workers, we find this additional information:

Possible Labor Assignments	Hours of Labor Available
Department 1 only	430
Department 2 only	400
Department 3 only	500
Department 4 only	135
Departments 1 or 2	570
Departments 3 or 4	300
Total Available	2335

Of the 2335 hours available for the month's production, we see that 870 hours can be allocated with some management discretion. The constraints for the hours available per department are as follows:

$$b_1 \leq 430 + 570 = 1000$$
$$b_2 \leq 400 + 570 = 970$$
$$b_3 \leq 500 + 300 = 800$$
$$b_4 \leq 135 + 300 = 435$$

Since the 570 hours that have a flexible assignment between departments 1 and 2 cannot be assigned to both departments simultaneously, we need the following additional constraint:

$$b_1 + b_2 \leq 430 + 400 + 570 = 1400$$

Similarly, for the 300 hours that can be allocated between departments 3 and 4, we need the constraint

$$b_3 + b_4 \leq 500 + 135 + 300 = 935$$

In this formulation we are now treating the labor assignments to departments as variables. The objective function coefficients for these variables will be zero, since the b_i variables do not directly affect profit. Thus placing all variables on the left-hand side of the constraints, we have the following complete formulation:

$$
\begin{array}{lrcl}
\max & 1.00x_1 + 0.90x_2 + 0b_1 + 0b_2 + 0b_3 + 0b_4 \\
\text{s.t.} \\
& 0.070x_1 + 0.100x_2 - b_1 & \leq & 0 \\
& 0.050x_1 + 0.084x_2 \quad - b_2 & \leq & 0 \\
& 0.100x_1 + 0.067x_2 \quad\quad - b_3 & \leq & 0 \\
& 0.010x_1 + 0.025x_2 \quad\quad\quad - b_4 & \leq & 0 \\
& b_1 & \leq & 1000 \\
& b_2 & \leq & 970 \\
& b_3 & \leq & 800 \\
& b_4 & \leq & 435
\end{array}
$$

$$b_1 + b_2 \leq 1400$$
$$b_3 + b_4 \leq 935$$
$$x_1, x_2, b_1, b_2, b_3, b_4 \geq 0$$

This linear programming model will acutally solve two problems: (1) it will find the optimal product mix for the planning period, and (2) it will allocate the total labor resource to the departments in such a fashion that profits will be maximized. The solution to this six-variable, 10-constraint model is shown in Table 4.12.

TABLE 4.12
Optimal Production Plan and Labor Allocation for McCarthy's Everyday Glass Company

Production plan:
Product 1 = 4700 cases
Product 2 = 4543 cases
Labor allocation:

Department 1	783 hours
Department 2	617 hours
Department 3	774 hours
Department 4	161 hours
Total	2335 hours
Profit =	$8789

Note that the optimal labor plan utilizes all 2335 hours of labor by making the most profitable allocations. In this particular solution there is no idle time in any of the departments. This will not always be the case in problems of this type; however, if the manager does have the freedom to assign certain employees to different departments, the effect will probably be a reduction in the overall idle time. The linear programming model automatically assigns such employees to the departments in the most profitable manner. If the manager had used judgment to allocate the hours to the departments, and we had then solved the product-mix problem with fixed b_i, we would in all probability have found slack in some departments while other departments represented bottlenecks because of insufficient resources.

Variations in the basic formulation of this section might be used in situations such as allocating raw material resources to products, allocating machine time to products, and allocating sales force time to product lines or sales territories.

4.4 BLENDING PROBLEMS

Blending problems arise whenever a manager must decide how to blend two or more resources in order to produce one or more products. In these situations the resources contain one or more essential ingredients that must be blended in such a manner that the final products will contain specific percentages of the essential ingredients. In most of these applications, then, management must decide how much of each resource to purchase in order to satisfy product specifications and product demands at minimum cost.

These types of problems occur frequently in the petroleum industry (such as blending crude oil to produce different-octane gasolines), chemical industry (such as blending chemicals to produce fertilizers, weed killers, and so on), and food industry (such as blending input ingredients to produce soft drinks, soups, and so on). Because of the widespread application of blending problems, the objective in this section is to illustrate how linear programming can be applied to solve these types of problems.

The Grand Strand Oil Company produces regular-grade and premium-grade gasoline products, which are sold to independent service stations in the southeastern United States. The Grand Strand refinery manufactures the gasoline products by blending three petroleum components. The gasolines are sold at different prices and the petroleum components have different costs. The firm would like to determine how to mix or blend the three components into the two gasoline products in such a way as to maximize profits.

Data available show that the regular-grade gasoline can be sold for $0.50 per gallon and the premium-grade gasoline for $0.54 per gallon. For the current production planning period, Grand Strand can obtain the three petroleum components at the cost per gallon and in the quantities shown in Table 4.13.

TABLE 4.13
Petroleum Cost and Supply for the Grand Strand Blending Problem

Petroleum Component	Cost/Gallon	Maximum Available
Component 1	$0.25	5,000 gallons
Component 2	$0.30	10,000 gallons
Component 3	$0.42	10,000 gallons

The product specifications for the regular and premium gasolines restrict the amounts of each component that can be used in each gasoline product. The product specifications are listed in Table 4.14. Current commitments to distributors require Grand Strand to produce at least 10,000 gallons of regular-grade gasoline.

TABLE 4.14
Product Specifications for the Grand Strand Blending Problem

Product	Specifications
Regular gasoline	At most 30% component 1
	At least 40% component 2
	At most 20% component 3
Premium gasoline	At least 25% component 1
	At most 40% component 2
	At least 30% component 3

The Grand Strand blending problem is to determine how many gallons of each component should be used in the regular-grade gasoline blend and how many gallons of each component should be used in the premium-grade gasoline blend. The optimal blending solution should maximize the firm's profit, subject to the constraints on the available petroleum supplies shown in Table 4.13, the product specifications shown in Table 4.14, and the required 10,000 gallons of regular-grade gasoline.

We can use the following double-subscript notation to define the decision variables for the problem:

Let

$$x_{ij} = \text{gallons of component } i \text{ used in gasoline } j,$$
$$\text{where } i = 1, 2, \text{ or } 3 \text{ for components } 1, 2, \text{ or } 3,$$
$$\text{and } j = r \text{ if regular or } j = p \text{ if premium}$$

The six decision variables become

$$x_{1r} = \text{gallons of component 1 in regular gasoline}$$
$$x_{2r} = \text{gallons of component 2 in regular gasoline}$$
$$x_{3r} = \text{gallons of component 3 in regular gasoline}$$
$$x_{1p} = \text{gallons of component 1 in premium gasoline}$$
$$x_{2p} = \text{gallons of component 2 in premium gasoline}$$
$$x_{3p} = \text{gallons of component 3 in premium gasoline}$$

Note that previously we have always used numbers as the subscripts for decision variables. Continuing to use numerical subscripts, we could have let $j = 1$ for regular gasoline and $j = 2$ for premium gasoline. However, the use of the r and p subscripts is descriptive and will enable us easily to identify the gasoline product being referred to by the decision variable. As a general rule, the person developing a linear programming model is free to use the notation that is the most descriptive of the problem under study. In the linear programming formulations presented in this text, we use x to denote a decision variable. Although this is the most common notation, other letters can be used for decision variables based on the preference of the person developing the formulation.

Using the notation for the six decision variables defined above, the total number of gallons of each type of gasoline produced can be expressed by summing the number of gallons in the components blended. That is,

Total Gallons Produced

$$\text{Regular gasoline} = x_{1r} + x_{2r} + x_{3r}$$
$$\text{Premium gasoline} = x_{1p} + x_{2p} + x_{3p}$$

Similarly, the total gallons of each component used can be expressed by the following sums:

Total Petroleum Component Usage

$$\text{Component 1} = x_{1r} + x_{1p}$$
$$\text{Component 2} = x_{2r} + x_{2p}$$
$$\text{Component 3} = x_{3r} + x_{3p}$$

The objective function of maximizing the profit contribution can be developed by identifying the difference between the total revenue from the two types of gasoline and the total cost of the three petroleum components. By multiplying the $0.50 per gallon price by the total gallons of regular gasoline, the $0.54 per gallon price by the total gallons of premium gasoline, and the component cost per gallon figures in Table 4.13 by the total gallons of each component used, the objective function can be written as follows:

$$\text{max} \quad 0.50(x_{1r} + x_{2r} + x_{3r}) + 0.54(x_{1p} + x_{2p} + x_{3p}) \\ -0.25(x_{1r} + x_{1p}) - 0.30(x_{2r} + x_{2p}) - .42(x_{3r} + x_{3p})$$

By combining terms the objective function can be written as

$$\text{max} \quad 0.25x_{1r} + 0.20x_{2r} + 0.08x_{3r} + 0.29x_{1p} + 0.24x_{2p} + 0.12x_{3p}$$

The limitations on the availability of the three petrolum components can be expressed by the following three constraints:

$$
\begin{aligned}
x_{1r} + x_{1p} &\leq 5000 \quad &\text{Component 1} \\
x_{2r} + x_{2p} &\leq 10,000 \quad &\text{Component 2} \\
x_{3r} + x_{3p} &\leq 10,000 \quad &\text{Component 3}
\end{aligned}
$$

Six constraints are now required to meet the product specifications stated in Table 4.14. The first specification states that component 1 can account for at most 30% of the total gallons of regular gasoline produced. That is,

$$\frac{x_{1r}}{x_{1r} + x_{2r} + x_{3r}} \leq 0.30$$

or

$$x_{1r} \leq 0.30(x_{1r} + x_{2r} + x_{3r})$$

Rewriting this constraint with the variables on the left-hand side and a constant on the right-hand side, the first product specification constraint becomes

$$0.70x_{1r} - 0.30x_{2r} - 0.30x_{3r} \leq 0$$

The second product specification listed in Table 4.14 can be written as

$$\frac{x_{2r}}{x_{1r} + x_{2r} + x_{3r}} \geq 0.40$$

or

$$x_{2r} \geq 0.40(x_{1r} + x_{2r} + x_{3r})$$

and thus

$$-0.40x_{1r} + 0.60x_{2r} - 0.40x_{3r} \geq 0$$

Similarly, the four additional blending specifications shown in Table 4.14 can be written as

$$-0.20x_{1r} - 0.20x_{2r} + 0.80x_{3r} \leq 0$$
$$0.75x_{1p} - 0.25x_{2p} - 0.25x_{3p} \geq 0$$
$$-0.40x_{1p} + 0.60x_{2p} - 0.40x_{3p} \leq 0$$
$$-0.30x_{1p} - 0.30x_{2p} + 0.70x_{3p} \geq 0$$

The constraint for at least 10,000 gallons of the regular-grade gasoline is written

$$x_{1r} + x_{2r} + x_{3r} \geq 10,000$$

Thus the complete linear programming model with six decision variables and 10 constraints can be written as follows:

$$\max \quad 0.25x_{1r} + 0.20x_{2r} + 0.08x_{3r} + 0.29x_{1p} + 0.24x_{2p} + 0.12x_{3p}$$

s.t.

$$
\begin{aligned}
x_{1r} \qquad\qquad\qquad\qquad + x_{1p} \qquad\qquad\qquad &\leq 5000 \\
x_{2r} \qquad\qquad\qquad\qquad + x_{2p} \qquad\quad &\leq 10,000 \\
x_{3r} \qquad\qquad\qquad\qquad + x_{3p} &\leq 10,000 \\
0.70x_{1r} - 0.30x_{2r} - 0.30x_{3r} \qquad\qquad\qquad\qquad &\leq 0 \\
-0.40x_{1r} + 0.60x_{2r} - 0.40x_{3r} \qquad\qquad\qquad\qquad &\geq 0 \\
-0.20x_{1r} - 0.20x_{2r} + 0.80x_{3r} \qquad\qquad\qquad\qquad &\leq 0 \\
0.75x_{1p} - 0.25x_{2p} - 0.25x_{3p} &\geq 0 \\
-0.40x_{1p} + 0.60x_{2p} - 0.40x_{3p} &\leq 0 \\
-0.30x_{1p} - 0.30x_{2p} + 0.70x_{3p} &\geq 0 \\
x_{1r} + x_{2r} + x_{3r} \qquad\qquad\qquad\qquad &\geq 10,000 \\
x_{1r}, x_{2r}, x_{3r}, x_{1p}, x_{2p}, x_{3p} &\geq 0
\end{aligned}
$$

The computer solution to the Grand Strand blending problem is shown in Figure 4.7. The blending solution that provides a profit of \$4650 is summarized in Table 4.15. The optimal blending strategy shows that 10,000 gallons of regular gasoline should be produced. Regular gasoline will consist of a blend of component 1 (12.5%) and component 2 (87.5%). The 15,000 gallons of premium gasoline are to be manufactured from a blend of all three petroleum components: 25.0% component 1, 8.3% component 2, and 66.7% component 3.

The interpretation of the slack and surplus variables associated with the product specification constraints (rows 5 to 10) in Figure 4.7 needs some clarification. If the constraint is a $\leq$ constraint, the value of the slack can be interpreted as the gallons of component usage below the maximum amount of the component usage specified by the constraint. For example, the slack of 1750 for row 5 shows that component 1 usage is 1750 gallons below the maximum amount of component 1 that could have been used in the production of 10,000 gallons of regular gasoline. If the product specification constraint is a $\geq$ constraint, a surplus variable shows the gallons of component usage above the minimum amount of component usage specified by the blending constraint. For example, the surplus of 4750 for row 6 shows that component 2 usage is 4750 gallons above the

FIGURE 4.7
Computer Solution of the Grand Strand Blending Problem Using LINDO/PC

```
                    OBJECTIVE FUNCTION VALUE

        1)    46500.00000

        VARIABLE           VALUE         REDUCED COST
            X1R         1250.000000          .000000
            X2R         8750.000000          .000000
            X3R             .000000          .000000
            X1P         3750.000000          .000000
            X2P         1250.000000          .000000
            X3P        10000.000000          .000000


        ROW      SLACK OR SURPLUS        DUAL PRICES
          2)            .000000            .290000
          3)            .000000            .240000
          4)            .000000            .120000
          5)        1750.000000            .000000
          6)        4750.000000            .000000
          7)        2000.000000            .000000
          8)            .000000            .000000
          9)        4750.000000            .000000
         10)        5500.000000            .000000
         11)            .000000           -.040000
```

TABLE 4.15
Grand Strand Gasoline Blending Strategy

| | Gallons of Component (Percentage) | | | |
Gasoline	Component 1	Component 2	Component 3	Total
Regular	1250 (12.5%)	8750 (87.5%)	—	10,000
Premium	3750 (25.0%)	1250 (8.3%)	10,000 (66.7%)	15,000

minimum amount of component 2 that could have to be used in the production of 10,000 gallons of regular gasoline.

4.5 GOAL PROGRAMMING

Linear programming problems are limited to a single objective, such as the maximization of profit or the minimization of cost. However, on occasion, managers or decision makers face problem situations in which more than one objective exists. Goal programming has been developed as a procedure for handling multiple-objective situations within the general framework of linear programming. Each objective is viewed as a "goal." Then, given the usual resource limitations, or constraints, the manager attempts to develop decisions that provide the "best" solution in terms of coming as close as possible to reaching all goals.

The Basic Goal Programming Model

To understand the goal programming approach, let us consider a problem faced by McKenna Office Supplies, Inc.. McKenna's management establishes monthly performance goals for its sales force. While each individual on the sales force has a sales volume quota for the month, McKenna also specifies goals, or quotas, for the types of customers contacted. McKenna's customer contact strategy for next month calls for the sales force to make 200 contacts with customers who have previously purchased supplies from the firm. In addition, the strategy calls for 120 contacts of new customers. The purpose of this latter quota or goal is to ensure that the sales force is continuing to investigate new sources of sales.

Making allowances for travel and waiting time, as well as for demonstration and direct sales time, McKenna has allocated 2 hours of sales force effort to each contact of a previous customer. New customer contacts tend to take longer and require 3 hours per contact. For the upcoming month, McKenna projects a maximum of 640 hours of sales force time available for both previous and new customer contacts.

You might first think of the 200 previous customer contacts and the 120 new customer contacts as constraints, but we will view them as objectives, or goals. The question is, does McKenna have sufficient sales force resources to realize both of these customer contact goals? The goals of 200 previous customer contacts and 120 new customer contacts require a total of $2(200) + 3(120) = 760$ hours, but only 640 hours of sales force time are available. Thus we see that McKenna cannot satisfy both goals simultaneously. This is the type of situation for which the goal programming approach was developed; the goals are in conflict and cannot be achieved simultaneously. An allocation of sales force effort to meet the new customer contact goal completely will reduce the time available, and hence contacts possible, for previous customers. The opposite effect occurs if the firm allocates sales force effort completely to meet the contact goal for previous customers.

Let us proceed with a goal programming formulation to help resolve McKenna's problem. An important first step in goal programming is to state each goal explicitly. For the McKenna Office Supplies problem the goals can be stated as follows:

> **Goal 1:** Reach 200 previous customers.
> **Goal 2:** Reach 120 new customers.

Note that each goal has a stated target value: 200 and 120 in our example. This is a property of all goal programming models. That is, rather than stating objectives in terms of maximizing some quantity, the objectives or goals are expressed in terms of reaching a desired quantity or level for each goal.

Once we have listed the goals with appropriate target values, we can proceed with the model. The next step is the key to a goal programming problem formulation: each goal or objective is written in the form of a constraint. Considering the first goal of reaching 200 previous customers and letting

$$x_1 = \text{number of previous customers contacted}$$

we could write the constraint as

$$1x_1 = 200$$

However, the above constraint form would require meeting the previous customer goal exactly, which we have seen may not be possible. Thus we add deviation variables that reflect the amount the solution deviates from the stated goals. For example, for the previous customer contact goal we would add the following deviation variables:

d_1^+ = number of previous customer contacts over the desired 200
d_1^- = number of previous customer contacts under the desired 200

This notation associates the letter d with the deviation from the goal. A superscript of plus or minus is used to indicate whether the solution exceeds or falls below the stated goal. Including the deviation variables, we write the constraint as

$$1x_1 = 200 + 1d_1^+ - 1d_1^-$$

Thus these deviation variables allow us to miss the goal and still obtain a feasible solution. For example, if $x_1 = 220$ in the final solution, d_1^+ would be 20 to reflect the overachievement of the goal by 20 contacts; d_1^- in this case would be zero. If $x_1 = 175$, then $d_1^- = 25$ and $d_1^+ = 0$ in order to reflect the 25 contacts short of the 200 goal. Rewriting this constraint with all the variables on the left-hand side, the constraint for the 200 previous customer contact goal would be written as

$$1x_1 - 1d_1^+ + 1d_1^- = 200$$

The next step is to develop a similar constraint in order to reflect the second goal of reaching 120 new customers. Letting

x_2 = number of new customers contacted
d_2^+ = number of new customer contacts over the desired 120
d_2^- = number of new customer contacts under the desired 120

the constraint for the new customer goal would be written as follows:

$$1x_2 - 1d_2^+ + 1d_2^- = 120$$

The sales force availability constraint can be handled just as in previous linear programming models. It would be written as

$$2x_1 + 3x_2 \le 640$$

We now have three constraints and six decision variables, which combine to reflect the two goals and the one resource constraint. If we can now develop an objective function, we will have a linear goal programming model with six variables and three constraints. What is the appropriate objective function?

Recall that in the original discussion of the problem we identified two objectives or goals and the deviation variables d_1^+, d_1^-, d_2^+ and d_2^-. If we can make all the deviation variables zero, we have in fact reached the goals exactly with $x_1 = 200$ and $x_2 = 120$. However, even if the deviation variables cannot be reduced to zero, we can at least work to reduce them to their minimum possible values. Small values for the deviation variables are attractive because they imply small deviations from the goals. This is why the objective function in goal programming calls for minimizing the weighted sum of the deviation variables. The deviation variables portion of the objective function for McKenna's problem can be written as follows:

$$\min \quad 0d_1^+ + 1d_1^- + 0d_2^+ + 1d_2^-$$

Note that d_1^+ and d_2^+, which correspond to an overachievement of goals, have been given zero weights or coefficients. The reason for this is that there is no penalty for overachieving the two goals. On the other hand, the d_1^- and d_2^- variables have both been given weights of 1, indicating that management attaches equal importance to deviations from the two goals. Since the firm's overall objective is to minimize the combined underachievement of the two goals, the complete goal programming model can be written as follows:

$$
\begin{aligned}
\min \quad & 0x_1 && + 0x_2 && + 0d_1^+ + 1d_1^- + 0d_2^+ + 1d_2^- \\
\text{s.t.} \quad & \\
& 1x_1 && && - 1d_1^+ + 1d_1^- && = 200 \\
& && 1x_2 && - 1d_2^+ + 1d_2^- && = 120 \\
& 2x_1 && + 3x_2 && && \le 640 \\
& x_1, x_2, d_1^+, d_1^-, d_2^+, d_2^- \ge 0
\end{aligned}
$$

Using LINDO/PC, the optimal solution shown below (see Figure 4.8, where D1MI represents d_1^-, D1PL represents d_1^+, and so on) was obtained:

$$
\begin{aligned}
x_1 &= 200 \\
x_2 &= 80 \\
d_1^+ &= 0 \\
d_1^- &= 0 \\
d_2^+ &= 0 \\
d_2^- &= 40
\end{aligned}
$$

We see the previous customer contact goal is reached while the new customer contact goal is underachieved by $d_2^- = 40$.

With the goal programming approach to the McKenna problem in mind, let us summarize the characteristics common to the basic linear goal programming model:

1. Each goal appears in a separate constraint with the right-hand-side value indicating the target value for the goal.
2. Deviation variables d_i^+ and d_i^- are included for each goal in order to reflect the possible overachievement or underachievement of the goal.
3. Other constraints, reflecting resource capacities or other restrictions, are included just as they would be in any linear programming model.
4. The objective function requires minimizing the weighted sum of the deviation variables. Coefficients (weights) for the deviation variables in the objective function reflect the relative "cost" or "penalty" for each unit deviation from the correspond-

FIGURE 4.8
Solution to McKenna Company Goal Programming Problem Using LINDO/PC

```
              OBJECTIVE FUNCTION VALUE

    1)        40.0000000

      VARIABLE         VALUE        REDUCED COST
         D1MI          .000000          .333333
         D2MI        40.000000          .000000
           X1       200.000000          .000000
         D1PL          .000000          .666667
           X2        80.000000          .000000
         D2PL          .000000         1.000000
```

ing goal's target value. Zero coefficients mean that the corresponding deviations from the target values carry no penalty.

In order to appreciate some of the flexibility offered by the goal programming model, note that in the linear goal programming model of the McKenna problem we assigned a weight (coefficient) of 1 to a one-unit underachievement of each goal (d_1^- and d_2^-). This implied that a one-unit underachievement of one goal was just as undesirable as a one-unit underachievement of the other goal. However, suppose McKenna's management was very much concerned about contacting new customers in order to provide growth in future sales. In fact, suppose that on a per-unit basis management felt the new customer contacts were twice as important as the previous customer contacts. The changed relative importance of the two goals can be reflected by altering the weights or coefficients for the deviation variables in the objective function. This reevaluation of the importance of new customer contacts could be expressed with the following objective function:

$$\min \quad 0x_1 + 0x_2 + 0d_1^+ + 1d_1^- + 0d_2^+ + 2d_2^-$$

Using the same three constraints and the revised objective function, the following goal programming solution is obtained:

$$x_1 = 140$$
$$x_2 = 120$$
$$d_1^+ = 0$$
$$d_1^- = 60$$
$$d_2^+ = 0$$
$$d_2^- = 0$$

The increased importance of goal 2 now leads to reaching the new customer goal while underachieving the previous customer goal by $d_1^- = 60$.

The Bollinger Electronics production scheduling problem in Section 4.3 utilized the goal programming approach to smooth production fluctuations. In that problem the goal was to have no production fluctuations. The increase and decrease variables (I_m and D_m) were the deviation variables; the costs due to fluctuations in production levels were the weights for these deviation variables in the objective function.

Priority Levels for Goals

A further extension of goal programming provides the capability of specifying different priority levels for each of the goals or objectives. This extension is valuable in situations where one goal is so much more important than the others that the decision maker is unwilling to "trade off" satisfaction of the one goal for any amount of deviation from another goal. In the current version of the McKenna problem, while we might select different objective function coefficients, or weights, to reflect the relative importance of the goals, the problem contained only one priority level since the objective function and constraints permitted trading off the satisfaction of one goal for the satisfaction of the other.

In goal programming problems with priority levels, first-priority (P_1) goals are treated in an objective function much like the one used in the McKenna problem. Second-priority (P_2) goals are considered only after the priority level 1 goals are reached. An objective function containing P_2 goals is then used. The solution is revised under the P_2 goal objective function as long as it does not cause a reduction in achievement of the P_1 goals. In this extension of goal programming, P_1 goals are considered first, the P_2 goals second, the P_3 goals third, and so on. At each stage a solution revision can be made as long as it causes no reduction in achievement of the higher priority goals.

—————— *Summary* ——————

In this chapter we have presented a broad range of situations that illustrate how linear programming can be a useful decision-making aid. Using a variety of application situations, we have formulated and solved problems from the areas of marketing, finance, and production management. In addition, we have shown how linear programming can be applied to blending problems. An application involving goal programming showed the flexibility of linear programming as a problem-solving approach when there are multiple criteria.

All the illustrations presented in this chapter were simplified versions of actual situations in which linear programming has been applied. In real-world applications the reader will find that the problem is not as concisely stated, that the data are not as readily available, and that the problem has a larger number of variables and constraints. However, a thorough study of the applications in this chapter is a good place for the reader who eventually hopes to apply linear programming to real-world problems to begin.

In conjunction with most of the applications we have included computer output provided by the LINDO/PC microcomputer software package. This provided us with an opportunity to discuss more fully the interpretation of computer output and to perform sensitivity analysis. In the chapter-ending problems, we present computer output for some of the other applications. The questions asked concerning this computer output are suggestive of the type of information that should be included in a managerial report following a linear programming analysis.

Problems

Note to Student. The problems for this chapter have been designed to give you an understanding and appreciation of the broad range of problems that can be formulated as linear programs. You should be able to formulate the linear programming model for each of the problems. However, you will need access to a linear programming computer package in order to develop the solution and make the requested interpretations.

1. *Product mix.* Better Products, Inc. is a small manufacturer of three products. The products are produced on two machines. In a typical week 40 hours of time are available on each machine. Profit contribution and production time in hours per unit are as follows:

	Product 1	Product 2	Product 3
Profit/unit	$30	$50	$20
Machine 1 time/unit	0.5	2.0	0.75
Machine 2 time/unit	1.0	1.0	0.5

Two operators are required for machine 1. Thus 2 hours of labor must be scheduled for each hour of machine 1 time. Only one operator is required for machine 2. A maximum of 100 labor hours is available for assignment to the machines during the coming week. Other production requirements are that product 1 cannot account for more than 50% of the units produced and that product 3 must account for at least 20% of the units produced.
   a. How many units of each product should be produced in order to maximize the profit contribution? What is the projected weekly profit associated with your solution?
   b. How many hours of production time will be scheduled on each machine?
   c. What is the value of an additional hour of labor?
   d. Assume labor capacity can be increased to 120 hours. Would you be interested in this additional resource? Develop the optimal product mix assuming the extra hours are made available.
2. *Media selection.* The Westchester Chamber of Commerce periodically sponsors public service seminars and programs. Currently, promotional plans are under way for this year's program. Advertising alternatives include television, radio, and newspaper. Audience estimates, costs, and maximum media usage limitations are shown below:

	Television	Radio	Newspaper
Audience per advertisement	100,000	18,000	40,000
Cost per advertisement	$2,000	$300	$600
Maximum media usage limitation	10	20	10

To ensure a balanced usage of advertising media, radio advertisements are not to exceed 50% of the total number of advertisements authorized. In addition, it has been requested that television account for at least 10% of the total number of advertisements authorized.

a. If the promotional budget is limited to $18,200, how many commercial messages should be run on each medium in order to maximize total audience contact? What is the allocation of the budget among the three media, and what is the total audience reached?

b. What is the estimated audience contact that would result from an extra $100 allocated to the advertising budget?

3. *Diet problem.* Bluegrass Farms, Inc. in Lexington, Ky., is experimenting with a special diet for its racehorses. The feed components available for the diet are a standard horse feed product, a vitamin-enriched oat product, and a new vitamin and mineral feed additive. The nutritional values in units per pound and costs for the three feed components are as follows:

	Standard	Enriched Oats	Additive
Ingredient A	0.8	0.2	0
Ingredient B	1.0	1.5	3.0
Ingredient C	0.1	0.6	2.0
Cost per pound	$0.25	$0.50	$3.00

a. Suppose that the horse trainer sets the minimum daily diet requirement at three units of ingredient A, six units of ingredient B, and four units of ingredient C. Also suppose that for weight control the trainer does not want the total daily feed for a horse to exceed 6 pounds. What is the optimal daily mix of the three feed components?

b. What is the cost per pound for the daily mix?

c. Using the shadow price, determine what would happen to the total cost if the total daily feed allowance were increased from 6 to 7 pounds? Explain why this occurs.

4. *Overtime planning.* Hartman Company is trying to determine how much of each of two products should be produced over the coming planning period. The only serious constraints involve labor availability in three departments. Shown below is information concerning labor availability, labor utilization, and product profitability.

	Product 1	Product 2	Labor Available
Profit/unit	$30.00	$15.00	—
Dept. A hours/unit	1.00	0.35	100 hours
Dept. B hours/unit	0.30	0.20	36 hours
Dept. C hours/unit	0.20	0.50	50 hours

a. Develop a linear programming model of the Hartman Company's problem. Solve it to determine the optimal production quantities of products 1 and 2.

b. In computing the per-unit profit Hartman does not deduct labor costs because they are considered fixed for the upcoming planning period. However, suppose overtime can be scheduled in some of the departments. Which departments would you recommend scheduling for overtime? How much would you be willing to pay per hour of overtime in each department?

c. Suppose that 10, 6, and 8 hours of overtime may be scheduled in departments *A, B*, and *C*, respectively. The cost per hour of overtime is $18 in department *A*, $22.50 in department *B*, and $12 in department *C*. Formulate a linear programming model that can be used to determine optimal production quantities if overtime is made available. What are the optimal production quantities, and what is the revised profit? How much overtime do you recommend using in each department? What is the increase in profit if overtime is used?

5. *Investment and loan planning*. The employee credit union at State University is planning the usage of funds for the coming year. The credit union makes four types of loans to its members. In addition, it invests in "risk-free" securities in order to stabilize income. The various revenue-producing investments together with annual rates of return are as follows:

Type of Loan/Investment	Annual Rate of Return (%)
Secured loans	
Automobile	8
Furniture	10
Other secured loans	11
Signature loans	12
"Risk-free" securities	9

State laws and credit union policies impose the following restrictions on the composition of the credit union's loans and investments:

1. "Risk-free" securities may not exceed 30% of the total funds.
2. Signature loans may not exceed 10% of total loans.
3. Furniture loans plus "other secured loans" may not exceed 50% of the total of the three types of secured loans.
4. Signature loans plus "other secured loans" may not exceed the amount invested in "risk-free" securities.

If the firm projects $2 million available for loans and investments during the coming year, how should the funds be allocated to each of the loan investment alternatives in order to maximize total annual return? What is the projected annual dollar return?

6. *Quality assurance*. Hilltop coffee manufactures a coffee product by blending three types of coffee beans. The cost per pound and the available pounds of each bean are as follows:

Bean	Cost/Pound	Available Pounds
1	$0.50	500
2	0.70	600
3	0.45	400

Consumer tests with coffee products were used to provide quality ratings on a 0-to-100 scale, with higher ratings indicating higher quality. Product quality standards for the blended coffee require a consumer rating for aroma to be at least 75 and a consumer rating for taste to be at least 80. The individual ratings of the aroma and taste for coffee made from 100% of each bean are as follows:

Bean	Aroma Rating	Taste Rating
1	75	86
2	85	88
3	60	75

It can be assumed that the aroma and taste attributes of the coffee blend will be a weighted average of the attributes of the beans used in the blend.

a. What is the minimum cost blend of the three beans that will meet the quality standards and provide 1000 pounds of the blended coffee product?
b. What is the bean cost per pound of the coffee blend?
c. Use the surplus variables to determine the aroma and taste ratings for the coffee blend.
d. If additional coffee were to be produced, what would be the expected cost per pound?

7. *Blending problem.* Ajax Fuels, Inc. is developing a new additive for airplane fuels. The additive is a mixture of three liquid ingredients: *A, B,* and *C.* For proper performance, the total amount of additive (amount of A + amount of B + amount of C) must be at least 10 ounces per gallon of fuel. However, because of safety reasons, the amount of additive must not exceed 15 ounces per gallon of fuel. The mix or blend of the three ingredients is critical. At least 1 ounce of ingredient A must be used for every ounce of ingredient B. The amount of ingredient C must be greater than one-half the amount of ingredient A. If the cost per ounce for ingredients $A, B,$ and C is $0.10, $0.03, and $0.09, respectively, find the minimum cost mixture of $A, B,$ and C for each gallon of airplane fuel.

8. *Labor planning.* G. Kunz and Sons, Inc. manufactures two products used in the heavy equipment industry. Both products require manufacturing operations in two departments. Production time in hours and profit figures for the two products are as follows:

	Product 1	Product 2
Profit/unit	$25	$20
Dept. *A* hours	6	8
Dept. *B* hours	12	10

For the coming production period, Kunz has a total of 900 hours of labor available, which can be allocated to either of the two departments. Let b_1 be the hours assigned to department A and b_2 be the hours assigned to department B. Find the production plan and labor allocation (hours assigned in each department) that will maximize profits.

9. *Portfolio selection.* National Insurance Associates carries an investment portfolio on a variety of stocks, bonds, and other investment alternatives. Currently $200,000 of funds has become available and must be considered for new investment opportunities. The four stock options National is considering and the relevant financial data are as follows:

| | Investment Alternative | | | |
	A	B	C	D
Price per share	$100	$50	$80	$40
Annual rate of return	0.12	0.08	0.06	0.10
Risk measure per dollar invested (higher values indicate greater risk)	0.10	0.07	0.05	0.08

The risk measure indicates the relative uncertainty associated with the stock in terms of its realizing the projected annual return. The risk measures are provided by the firm's top financial advisor.

National's top management has stipulated the following investment guidelines:

1. Annual rate of return for the portfolio must be at least 9%.
2. No one stock can account for more than 50% of the total dollar investment.

a. Use linear programming to develop an investment portfolio that minimizes risk.
b. If the firm ignores risk and uses a maximum return-on-investment strategy, what is the investment portfolio?
c. What is the dollar difference between the portfolio recommended in parts (a) and (b)? Why might the company prefer the model development in part (a)?

10. *Production routing.* Lurix Electronics manufactures two products that can be produced on two different production lines. Both products have their lowest production costs when produced on the more modern of the two production lines. However, the modern production line does not have the capacity to handle the total production. As a result, some production will have to be routed to an older production line. Shown below are the data for total production requirements, production line capacities, and production costs:

| | Production Cost/Unit | | Minimum Production |
	Modern Line	Old Line	Requirements
Product 1	$3.00	$5.00	500 units
Product 2	$2.50	$4.00	700 units
Production line capacities	800	600	

Formulate a linear programming model that can be used to make the production routing decision. What are the recommended decision and the total cost? (Use notation of the form x_{11} = units of product 1 produced on line 1.)

11. *Purchasing.* Edwards Manufacturing Company purchases two component parts from three different suppliers. The suppliers have limited capacity, and no one supplier

can meet all of Edwards' needs. In addition, the suppliers differ in the prices charged for the components. Component price data are as follows:

	Supplier 1	Supplier 2	Supplier 3
Price/unit—component 1	$12	$13	$14
Price/unit—component 2	$10	$11	$10

Each supplier has a limited capacity in terms of the total number of components it can supply. However, as long as Edwards provides sufficient advance orders, each supplier can devote its capacity to component 1, component 2, or any combination of the two components, as long as the total number of units ordered is within its capacity. Supplier capacities are as follows:

Supplier	Total Components Capacity
Supplier 1	600
Supplier 2	1000
Supplier 3	800

If the Edwards production plan for the next production period includes 1000 units of component 1 and 800 units of component 2, what purchases do you recommend? That is, how many units of each component should be ordered from each supplier? What is the total purchase cost for the components? (For practice in using double-subscripted decision variables, use notation of the form x_{ij} = number of units of component i purchased from supplier j.)

12. *Make or buy.* The Carson Stapler Manufacturing Company forecasts a 5000-unit demand for its Sure-Hold model during the next quarter. This stapler is assembled from three major components: base, staple cartridge, and handle. Until now Carson has manufactured all three components. However, the forecast of 5000 units is a new high in sales volume, and it is doubtful that the firm will have sufficient production capacity to make all the components. The company is considering contracting a local firm to produce at least some of the components. The production time requirements per unit are as follows:

Departments	Production Time (hours) Base	Production Time (hours) Cartridge	Handle	Total Department Time Available (hours)
A	0.03	0.02	0.05	400
B	0.04	0.02	0.04	400
C	0.02	0.03	0.01	400

After considering the firm's overhead, material, and labor costs, the accounting department has determined the unit manufacturing cost for each component. These data, along with the purchase price quotations by the contracting firm, are as follows:

Component	Manufacturing Cost	Purchase Cost
Base	$0.75	$0.95
Cartridge	$0.40	$0.55
Handle	$1.10	$1.40

a. Determine the make-or-buy decision for Carson that will meet the 5000-unit demand at a minimum total cost. How many units of each component should be made and how many purchased?

b. Which departments are limiting the manufacturing volume? If overtime could be considered at the additional cost of $3 per hour, which department(s) should be allocated the overtime? Explain.

c. Suppose that up to 80 hours of overtime can be scheduled in department A. What do you recommend?

13. *Blending problem.* Seastrand Oil Company produces two grades of gasoline: regular and high octane. Both types of gasoline are produced by blending two types of crude oil. Although both types of crude oil contain the two important ingredients required to produce both gasolines, the percentage of important ingredients in each type of crude oil differs, as well as the cost per gallon. The percentage of ingredients A and B in each type of crude oil, and the cost per gallon, are shown below:

Type of Crude Oil	Cost	Ingredient A	Ingredient B
1	$0.10	20%	60%
2	$0.15	50%	30%

Crude 1 is 60% ingredient B

Each gallon of regular must contain at least 40% of A, whereas each gallon of high octane can contain at most 50% of B. Daily demand for regular octane gasoline is 800,000 gallons, and daily demand for high octane is 500,000 gallons. How many gallons of each type of crude oil should be used in regular and in high octane gasoline in order to satisfy daily demand at a minimum cost? Define the four decision variables as follows:

$$x_{11} = \text{gallons of crude 1 used in regular gasoline}$$
$$x_{12} = \text{gallons of crude 1 used in high octane gasoline}$$
$$x_{21} = \text{gallons of crude 2 used in regular gasoline}$$
$$x_{22} = \text{gallons of crude 2 used in high octane gasoline}$$

14. *Cutting stock.* The Ferguson Paper Company produces rolls of paper for use in adding machines, desk calculators, and cash registers. The rolls, which are 200 feet long, are produced in widths of $1\frac{1}{2}$, $2\frac{1}{2}$, and $3\frac{1}{2}$ inches. The production process provides 200-foot rolls in 10-inch widths only. The firm must therefore cut the rolls to the desired final product sizes. The seven cutting alternatives and the amount of waste generated by each are as follows:

Cutting Alternative	Number of Rolls 1½ in	Number of Rolls 2½ in	Number of Rolls 3½ in	Waste (inches)
1	6	0	0	1
2	0	4	0	0
3	2	0	2	0
4	0	1	2	½
5	1	3	0	1
6	1	2	1	0
7	4	0	1	½

The minimum production requirements for the three products are as follows:

Roll Width (inches)	Units
1½	1000
2½	2000
3½	4000

a. If the company wants to minimize the number of units of the 10-inch rolls that must be manufactured, how many 10-inch rolls will be processed on each cutting alternative? How many rolls are required, and what is the total waste (inches)?

b. If the company wants to minimize the waste generated, how many 10-inch units will be processed on each cutting alternative? How many rolls are required, and what is the total waste (inches)?

c. What are the differences in approaches a and b to this trim problem? In this case which objective do you prefer? Explain. What are the types of situations that would make the other objective the more desirable?

15. *Inspection.* The Get-Well Pill Company inspects capsule medicine products by passing the capsules over a special lighting table where inspectors visually check for cracked or partially filled capsules. Currently any of three inspectors can be assigned to the visual inspection task. The inspectors, however, differ in accuracy and speed abilities and are paid at slightly different wage rates. The differences are as follows:

Inspector	Speed (Units per Hour)	Accuracy (%)	Hourly Wage
Davis	300	98	$5.90
Wilson	200	99	$5.20
Lawson	350	96	$5.50

Operating on a full 8-hour shift, the company needs at least 2000 capsules inspected with no more than 2% of these capsules having inspection errors. In addition, because of the fatigue factor of this inspection process, no one inspector can be assigned this task for more than 4 hours per day. How many hours should each inspector be assigned to the capsule inspection process during an 8-hour day if it is desired to minimize the cost of inspection? What volume will be inspected per day, and what is the daily capsule inspection cost?

16. *Equipment acquisition*. The Two-Rivers Oil Company near Pittsburgh transports gasoline to its distributors by trucks. The company has recently received a contract to begin supplying gasoline distributors in southern Ohio and has $600,000 available to spend on the necessary expansion of its fleet of gasoline tank trucks. Three models of gasoline tank truck are available:

Truck Model	Capacity (gallons)	Purchase Cost	Monthly Operating Costs, Including Depreciation
Super Tanker	5000	$67,000	$550
Regular Line	2500	$55,000	$425
Econo-Tanker	1000	$46,000	$350

The company estimates that the monthly demand for the region will be a total of 550,000 gallons of gasoline. Due to the size and speed differences of the trucks, the different truck models will vary in terms of the number of deliveries or round trips possible per month. Trip capacities are estimated at 15 per month for the Super Tanker, 20 per month for the Regular Line, and 25 per month for the Econo-Tanker. Based on maintenance and driver availability, the firm does not want to add more than 15 new vehicles to its fleet. In addition, the company would like to make sure it purchases at least three of the new Econo-Tankers to use on the short-run low-demand routes. As a final constraint, the company does not want more than half of the new models to be Super Tankers.

a. If the company wishes to satisfy the gasoline demand with a minimum monthly operating expense, how many models of each truck should be purchased?

b. If the company did not require at least three Econo-Tankers and allows as many Super Tankers as needed, what would the company strategy be?

17. *Multiperiod planning*. The Silver Star Bicycle Company will be manufacturing both men's and women's models for their Easy-Pedal 10-speed bicycles during the next 2 months, and the company would like a production schedule indicating how many bicycles of each model should be produced in each month. Current demand forecasts call for 150 men's and 125 women's models to be shipped during the first month and 200 men's and 150 women's models to be shipped during the second month. Additional data are shown below:

Model	Production Costs	Labor Required for Manufacturing (hours)	Labor Required for Assembly (hours)	Current Inventory
Men's	$40	10	3	20
Women's	$30	8	2	30

Last month the company used a total of 4000 hours of labor. The company's labor relations policy will not allow the combined total hours of labor (manufacturing plus assembly) to increase or decrease by more than 500 hours from month to month. In addition, the company charges monthly inventory at the rate of 2% of the production cost based on the inventory levels at the end of the month. The company would like to have at least 25 units of each model in inventory at the end of the 2 months.

a. Establish a production schedule that minimizes production and inventory costs and satisfies the labor-smoothing, demand, and inventory requirements. What inventories will be maintained, and what are the monthly labor requirements?

b. If the company changed the constraints so that monthly labor increases and decreases could not exceed 250 hours, what would happen to the production schedule? How much will the cost increase? What would you recommend?

18. *Labor balancing.* The Williams Calculator Company manufactures two kinds of calculators: the TW100 and the TW200. The assembly process requires three people. The assembly times are as follows:

	Assembler 1	Assembler 2	Assembler 3
TW100	4 min	2 min	$3\frac{1}{2}$ min
TW200	3 min	4 min	3 min
Maximum hours available per day	8	8	8

The company policy is to balance workloads on all assembly jobs. In fact, management wants to schedule work so that no assembler will have more than 30 minutes more work per day than other assemblers. This means that in a regular 8-hour shift, all assemblers will be assigned at least $7\frac{1}{2}$ hours of work. If the firm makes a $2.50 profit for each TW100 and a $3.50 profit for each TW200, how many units of each calculator should be produced per day? How much time will each assembler be assigned per day?

19. *Staff scheduling.* Western Family Steakhouse offers a variety of low-cost meals and quick service. Other than management, the steakhouse operates with two full-time employees who work 8 hours per day. All the rest of the employees are part-time employees who are scheduled for 4-hour shifts during meal times. On Saturdays the steakhouse is open from 11:00 A.M. to 10:00 P.M. Management would like a schedule for part-time employees that will minimize labor costs and still provide excellent customer service. The average wage rate for the part-time employees is $3.60 per hour. The total number of full-time and part-time employees needed varies with the time of the day as follows:

Time	Total Number of Employees
11:00 A.M.–Noon	9
Noon–1:00 P.M.	9
1:00 P.M.–2:00 P.M.	9
2:00 P.M.–3:00 P.M.	3
3:00 P.M.–4:00 P.M.	3
4:00 P.M.–5:00 P.M.	3
5:00 P.M.–6:00 P.M.	6
6:00 P.M.–7:00 P.M.	12
7:00 P.M.–8:00 P.M.	12
8:00 P.M.–9:00 P.M.	7
9:00 P.M.–10:00 P.M.	7

One of the full-time employees comes on duty at 11:00 A.M., works 4 hours, takes an hour off, and returns for another 4 hours. The other full-time employee comes to work at 1:00 P.M. and works the same 4-hour-on, 1-hour-off, 4-hour-on work pattern.

  a. Develop a minimum-cost schedule for the part-time employees.

  b. What is the total payroll for the part-time employees? How many part-time shifts are needed? Use the surplus variables to comment on the desirability of scheduling at least some of the part-time employees for 3-hour shifts.

  c. Assume part-time employees can be assigned either a 4-hour shift or a 3-hour shift. Develop a minimum-cost schedule for the part-time employees. How many part-time shifts are needed and what is the cost savings compared with the previous schedule?

20. *Interpretation of computer output.* Shown below is a portion of the computer output from using LINDO/PC to solve the media selection problem for the Relax-and-Enjoy Lake Development Corporation (see Section 4.1).

```
              OBJECTIVE FUNCTION VALUE

       1)        2370.0000

     VARIABLE        VALUE          REDUCED COST
        X1        10.000000           .000000
        X2          .000000         64.999990
        X3        25.000000           .000000
        X4         2.000000           .000000
        X5        30.000000           .000000

      ROW      SLACK OR SURPLUS      DUAL PRICES
       2)        40.000000            .000000
       3)        10.000000            .000000       Media
       4)          .000000          16.000000       Availability
       5)         2.000000            .000000
       6)          .000000          14.000000       Budget
       7)          .000000            .060000
       8)          .000000         -25.000000       T.V. Restriction
       9)      3000.000000            .000000
      10)     11500.000000            .000000       Audience Coverage
```

  a. How much would the expected exposure increase per dollar added to the budget? Given the current budget, what is the average exposure per advertising dollar? Does the marginal return from enlarging the budget seem to make enlarging the budget a good investment?

  b. From an analysis of the dual prices, comment on whether or not the television commercials are a good idea.

21. *Production smoothing.* The L. Young & Sons Manufacturing Company produces two products, which have the following profit and resource requirement characteristics:

	Product 1	Product 2
Profit/unit	$4	$2
Dept. *A* hours/unit	1	1
Dept. *B* hours/unit	2	5

Last month's production schedule used 350 hours of labor in department *A* and 1000 hours of labor in department *B*.

Young's management has been experiencing work force morale and labor union problems during the past six months because of monthly departmental workload fluctuations. New hirings, layoffs, and interdepartmental transfers have been common because the firm has not attempted to stabilize departmental workload requirements.

Management would like to develop a production schedule for the coming month which will minimize deviations from the goals of maintaining department *A* workload at 350 hours and department *B* workload at 1000 hours.

a. Management has specified that a minimum of $1300 profit must be earned. Formulate and solve a goal programming model that will lead to minimum work force fluctuations subject to satisfying the profit requirement.

b. Suppose the firm ignores the workload fluctuations and considers the 350 hours in department *A* and the 1000 hours in department *B* as the maximum available. Formulate and solve a linear programming problem to maximize profit subject to these constraints.

c. Compare the approaches taken in parts (a) and (b). Discuss which approach you favor and tell why.

22. *Machine location.* Morley Company is attempting to determine the best location for a new machine in an existing layout of three machines. The existing machines are located at the following x_1, x_2 coordinates on the shop floor:

$$\text{Machine 1:} \quad x_1 = 1, x_2 = 7$$
$$\text{Machine 2:} \quad x_1 = 5, x_2 = 9$$
$$\text{Machine 3:} \quad x_1 = 6, x_2 = 2$$

a. Develop a goal programming model that can be solved to minimize the total distance of the new machine from the three existing machines. The distance is to be measured rectangularly. For example (see below), if the location of the new machine is ($x_1 = 3, x_2 = 5$), it is considered to be a distance of four units from machine 1. *Hint*: In the goal programming formulation, let

x_1 = first coordinate of the new machine location
x_2 = second coordinate of the new machine location
d_i^+ = amount by which x_1 coordinate of new machine
    exceeds x_1 coordinate of machine *i*. ($i = 1, 2, 3$)
d_i^- = amount by which x_1 coordinate of machine *i*
    exceeds x_1 coordinate of new machine ($i = 1, 2, 3$)

e_i^+ = amount by which x_2 coordinate of new machine
     exceeds x_2 coordinate of machine i ($i = 1, 2, 3$)

e_i^- = amount by which x_2 coordinate of machine i
     exceeds x_2 coordinate of new machine ($i = 1, 2, 3$)

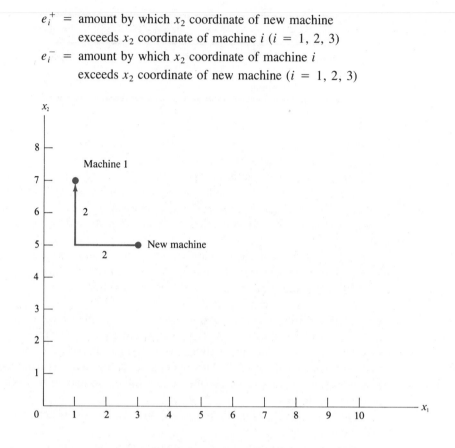

b. What is the optimal location for the new machine?

23. *Store location.* A fast-food chain is attempting to determine the best location for a new outlet. Management would like to determine the best location for drawing customers from three population centers. Letting (x_1, x_2) represent the map coordinates of the three population centers, we can show their locations as follows:

$$\text{Population center 1:} \quad x_1 = 2, x_2 = 8$$
$$\text{Population center 2:} \quad x_1 = 6, x_2 = 6$$
$$\text{Population center 3:} \quad x_1 = 1, x_2 = 1$$

If the new outlet is located at coordinates ($x_1 = 3$, $x_2 = 2$), then it is a distance of $(3 - 1) + (2 - 1) = 3$ miles from population center 3 (distance is measured as the sum of the east–west and north–south differences in coordinates).

a. Formulate and solve a goal programming model to determine what location for the new outlet will minimize the total distance from the three population centers. (*Hint*: Let x_1, x_2 represent the coordinates of the new location.)

b. Population center 1 is four times as large as center 3, and center 2 is twice as large as center 3. The firm feels that the importance of locating near a population center is proportional to its population. Develop and solve a new goal programming model where the weights on the deviations reflect this importance.

—————— *Case Problem* ——————

ENVIRONMENTAL PROTECTION

Skillings Industrial Chemicals, Inc. operates a refinery in southwestern Ohio near the Ohio River. The company's primary product is manufactured from a chemical process that requires the use of two raw materials denoted as material A and material B. The production of 1 pound of the finished product requires the use of 1 pound of material A and 2 pounds of material B. The output of the chemical process is 1 pound of finished product, 1 pound of liquid waste material, and 1 pound of solid waste by-product. The solid waste by-product is given to a local fertilizer plant as payment for picking it up and disposing of it. Since the liquid waste material has no market value, the refinery has been dumping it directly into the Ohio River. Skillings' manufacturing process is shown schematically in Figure 4.9.

Recently imposed governmental pollution guidelines established by the Environmental Protection Agency will not permit disposal of the liquid waste directly into the river. The refinery's research group has developed the following set of alternative uses for the liquid waste material:

1. Produce a secondary product K by adding 1 pound of raw material A to every pound of liquid waste.
2. Produce a secondary product M by adding 1 pound of raw material B to every pound of liquid waste.

FIGURE 4.9
Manufacturing Process at Skillings Industrial Chemicals, Inc.

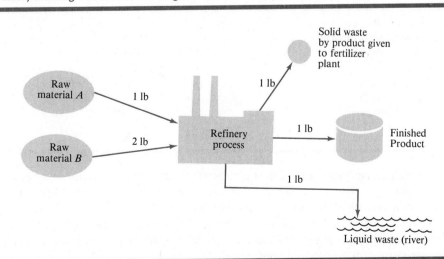

3. Specially treat the liquid waste so that it meets pollution standards before dumping it directly into the river.

FIGURE 4.10
Alternatives for Handling the Refinery Liquid Waste

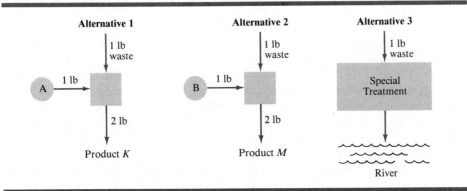

These three alternatives are depicted in Figure 4.10.

The company's management knows that the secondary products will be low in quality and may not be very profitable. However, management is also aware of the fact that the special treatment alternative will be a relatively expensive operation. The company's problem is to determine how to satisfy the pollution regulations and still maintain the highest possible profit. How should the liquid waste material be handled? Should Skillings produce product K, produce product M, use the special treatment, or employ some combination of the three alternatives?

Last month 10,000 pounds of the company's primary product were produced. The accounting department has prepared a cost report showing the breakdown of fixed and variable expenses that were incurred during the month.

Cost Analysis for 10,000 Pounds of Primary Product

Fixed cost allocation	
Administrative expenses	$12,000
Refinery overhead	4,000
Variable costs	
Raw material A	15,000
Raw material B	16,000
Direct labor	5,000
Total	$52,000

In the above cost analysis the fixed cost portion of the expenses is the same every month regardless of production level. Direct labor costs are expected to run $0.20 per pound for product K and $0.10 per pound for product M.

The company's primary product sells for $5.70 per pound. Secondary products K and M sell for $0.85 per pound and $0.65 per pound, respectively. The special treatment of the liquid waste will cost $0.25 per pound.

One of the company's accountants feels that product K is too expensive to manufacture and cannot be sold at a price that recovers its material and labor cost. The accountant's recommendation is to eliminate product K as an alternative.

For the upcoming production period 5000 pounds of raw material A and 7000 pounds of raw material B will be available. Develop a production and waste disposal plan for the production period.

MANAGERIAL REPORT

Develop an approach to the problem that will allow the company to determine how much primary product to produce given the limitations on the amounts of the raw material available. Include recommendations as to how the company should dispose of the liquid waste to satisfy the environmental protection guidelines. How many pounds of product K should be produced? How many pounds of product M should be produced? How many pounds of liquid waste should be specially treated and dumped directly into the river? Include a discussion and analysis of the following in your report.

1. A cost analysis showing the profit contribution per pound for the primary product, product K, and product M.
2. The optimal production quantities and waste disposal plan, including the projected profit.
3. A discussion of the value of additional pounds of each raw material.
4. A discussion of the sensitivity analysis of the objective function coefficients.
5. Comments on the accountant's recommendation to eliminate product K as an alternative. Does the recommendation appear reasonable? What is your reaction to the recommendation? How would the optimal solution change if product K were eliminated?

Management Science in Practice
MARATHON OIL COMPANY*
Findlay, Ohio

Marathon Oil Company was founded in 1887 when 14 oilmen pooled their properties to organize an oil-producing company in the Trenton Rock oil fields of Ohio. In 1924 Marathon entered the refining and marketing phase of the petroleum industry. Today, Marathon is a fully integrated oil company with significant international operations. It employs over 18,000 people, and company activities extend to six continents. In the United States the company markets petroleum products in 21 states, primarily in the Midwest and Southeast.

MANAGEMENT SCIENCE AT MARATHON OIL COMPANY

Most of the management science applications at Marathon Oil involve the firm's Operations Research Department. This department was formed in 1963 in order to aid problem solving and decision making in all areas of the company. Approximately 50% of the applications involve linear programming. Typical problems include refinery models, distribution models, gasoline and fuel oil blending models, and crude oil evaluation studies. Another 30% of the applications involve complex chemical engineering simulation models of process operations. The remainder of the management science applications involves solution techniques using nonlinear programming, network flow algorithms, and statistical techniques such as regression analysis.

A Marketing Planning Model

Marathon Oil Company has four refineries within the United States, operates 50 light products terminals, and has product demand at over 100 locations. The Marketing Operations Division is faced with the problem of determining which refinery should supply which terminal, and at the same time determining which products should be transported via which pipeline, barge, or tanker in order to achieve a minimum cost. Product demand must be satisfied, and the supply capability of each refinery must not be exceeded. To help solve this difficult problem, Marathon's Operations Research Department developed a marketing planning model for the Marketing Operation Division.

*The authors are indebted to Jerry T. Ranney and Keith R. Weiss of Marathon Oil Company, Findlay, Ohio, for providing this application.

The marketing planning model is a large-scale linear programming model that takes into account sales not only at Marathon product terminals but also at all exchange locations. An exchange contract is an agreement with other oil product marketers that involves exchanging or trading Marathon's products for theirs at different locations. Thus some geographic imbalance between supply and demand can be reduced. Both sides of the exchanges are represented, since this not only affects the net requirements at a demand location but in addition has important financial implications. All pipelines, barges, and tankers within Marathon's marketing area are also represented in the linear programming model.

The optimization of gasoline blending for each refinery, based on blendstock availabilities and the gasoline demand structure, is accomplished in the model by the inclusion of gasoline blending submodels. Thus the linear programming model is a combination of a blending model and a transportation model.

The objective of the linear programming model is to minimize the cost of meeting a given demand structure, taking into account sales price, pipeline tariffs, exchange contract costs, product demand, terminal operating costs, refining costs, and product pruchases. The current linear programming matrix size is approximately 1800 rows by 6000 columns. The IBM MPSX/370 system solves the problem in less than 3 minutes using an IBM 3081 computer system.

The marketing planning model is used to solve a wide variety of planning problems. These vary from evaluating gasoline blending economics to analyzing the economics of a new terminal or pipeline. Although the types of problems that can be solved are almost unlimited, the model is most effective in handling the following:

1. Evaluating additional product demand locations, pipelines, refinery units, and exchange contracts.
2. Determining profitability of shifting sales from one product demand location to another.
3. Showing effects on refinery gasoline blending when octane requirements are increased, blendstock availabilities are decreased, or there is a major shift in the demand pattern.
4. Determining the effects on supply and distribution when a pipeline increases its tariff.
5. Optimizing production of the three grades of gasoline at the four refineries.

The linear programming model not only solves these problems, but also gives the financial impact of each solution.

Benefits

With daily sales of about 10 million gallons of refined light product, a saving of even one-thousandth of a cent per gallon can result in significant long-term savings. At the same time, what may appear to be a savings in one area, such as refining or transportation, may actually add to overall costs when the effects are fully realized throughout the system. The marketing planning model allows a simultaneous examination of this total effect.

Questions

1. What is the primary objective of Marathon's marketing planning model?
2. Describe the types of problems the marketing planning model is most effective in handling.
3. If daily savings using the model are one-tenth of a cent per gallon sold, what is the projected daily savings?

5

Linear Programming: The Simplex Method

In Chapter 2 we showed how the graphical solution procedure can be used to solve linear programming problems involving two decision variables. However, most linear programming problems are too large to be solved graphically and thus an algebraic solution procedure must be employed. The most widely used algebraic procedure for solving linear programming problems is called the *simplex method*.[1] Computer programs based on this method can routinely solve linear programming problems having as many as several thousand variables and several thousand constraints.

5.1 AN ALGEBRAIC OVERVIEW OF THE SIMPLEX METHOD

Let us begin our discussion by introducing a problem that will be used to demonstrate the simplex method. HighTech Industries imports electronic components that are used to assemble two different models of personal computers. One model is called the HT Deskpro Computer and the other model is called the HT Portable Computer. HighTech's management is currently interested in developing a weekly production schedule for both of these products.

The Deskpro generates a profit contribution of $50 per unit and the Portable generates a profit contribution of $40 per unit. For the next week's production a maximum of 150 hours of assembly time can be made available. Each unit of the Deskpro requires 3 hours of assembly time and each unit of the Portable requires 5 hours of assembly time. In addition, HighTech currently has in inventory only 20 of the display units used in the Portable; thus no more than 20 units of the Portable may be assembled. Finally, only 300 square feet of warehouse space can be made available for new production of these products. Each unit of the Deskpro requires 8 square feet of warehouse space and each unit of the Portable requires 5 square feet of warehouse space.

[1] Recently N. Karmarkar, at Bell Labs, developed a new linear programming procedure that some say will eventually supersede the simplex method. At this time the simplex method is by far the most widely used.

In order to develop a linear programming model for the HighTech problem, we will use the following decision variables.

$$x_1 = \text{number of units of the Deskpro assembled}$$
$$x_2 = \text{number of units of the Portable assembled}$$

The complete mathematical model for the HighTech Industries problem is presented below.

$$\max 50x_1 + 40x_2$$
s.t.
$$
\begin{aligned}
3x_1 + 5x_2 &\leq 150 && \text{Assembly time} \\
1x_2 &\leq 20 && \text{Portable display} \\
8x_1 + 5x_2 &\leq 300 && \text{Warehouse space} \\
x_1, x_2 &\geq 0
\end{aligned}
$$

Adding a slack variable to each of the constraints permits us to write the problem in standard form.

$$\max 50x_1 + 40x_2 + 0s_1 + 0s_2 + 0s_3 \qquad (5.1)$$
s.t.
$$
\begin{aligned}
3x_1 + 5x_2 + 1s_1 \qquad\qquad\qquad &= 150 && (5.2) \\
1x_2 \qquad + 1s_2 \qquad &= 20 && (5.3) \\
8x_1 + 5x_2 \qquad\qquad + 1s_3 &= 300 && (5.4) \\
x_1, x_2, s_1, s_2, s_3 \geq 0 && (5.5)
\end{aligned}
$$

Algebraic Properties of the Simplex Method

Constraint equations (5.2) to (5.4) form a system of three simultaneous linear equations with five variables. When a set of simultaneous linear equations has more variables than constraints, one can expect an infinite number of solutions. The simplex method is an algebraic procedure that can be used to solve a system of simultaneous linear equations involving more variables than equations. In addition, the simplex method will identify a solution that provides the best possible value for the objective function.

We cannot expect that every solution to equations (5.2)–(5.4) will satisfy the non-negativity conditions $x_1, x_2, s_1, s_2, s_3 \geq 0$. Consequently not every solution to equations (5.2)–(5.4) will be a feasible solution. Thus when solving a set of simultaneous linear equations, the simplex method eliminates from consideration those solutions that do not also satisfy the nonnegativity requirements.

Determining a Basic Solution

Since the HighTech Industries constraint equations have more variables (five) than equations (three), the simplex method finds solutions for these equations by assigning zero values to two of the variables and then solving for the values of the remaining three variables. For example, if we set $x_2 = 0$ and $s_1 = 0$, the system of constraint equations becomes

$$3x_1 \qquad\qquad\qquad = 150 \qquad\qquad\qquad (5.6)$$
$$1s_2 \qquad\quad = 20 \qquad\qquad\qquad (5.7)$$
$$8x_1 \qquad + 1s_3 = 300 \qquad\qquad\qquad (5.8)$$

By setting $x_2 = 0$ and $s_1 = 0$ we have reduced the system of three simultaneous linear equations with five variables to a system of three simultaneous linear equations with three variables (x_1, s_2, and s_3).

Using equation (5.6) to solve for x_1, we have

$$3x_1 = 150$$

and hence $x_1 = 150/3 = 50$. Equation (5.7) provides $s_2 = 20$. Finally, substituting $x_1 = 50$ into equation (5.8) results in

$$8(50) + 1s_3 = 300$$

Solving for s_3 we obtain $s_3 = -100$.

Thus we have obtained the following solution to the three-equation, five-variable set of linear equations determined by the HighTech constraints:

$$x_1 = 50$$
$$x_2 = 0$$
$$s_1 = 0$$
$$s_2 = 20$$
$$s_3 = -100$$

The above solution is referred to as a *basic solution* for the HighTech linear programming problem. In order to provide a general procedure for determining a basic solution, consider a standard-form linear programming problem consisting of n variables (including decision variables, slack variables, and surplus variables) and m linear equations, where n is greater than m.

A Basic Solution.   To determine a basic solution, set $n - m$ of the variables equal to zero and solve the m linear constraint equations for the remaining m variables.[2]

In terms of the HighTech problem, a basic solution can be obtained by setting any two variables equal to zero and then solving the system of three linear equations for the remaining three variables. We shall refer to the $n - m$ variables set equal to zero as the *nonbasic variables* and the remaining m variables (allowed to be nonzero) as the *basic variables*. Thus in the example above, x_2 and s_1 are the nonbasic variables and x_1, s_2, and s_3 are the basic variables.

Basic Feasible Solutions

A basic solution can be either feasible or infeasible. A *basic feasible solution* is a basic solution that also satisfies the nonnegativity conditions. The basic solution found by

---

[2]There are cases where a unique solution cannot be found for the resulting system of m equations in m variables. However, these cases will never be encountered when using the simplex method.

setting x_2 and s_1 equal to 0, and then solving for x_1, s_2, and s_3, is not a feasible solution because $s_3 = -100$. However, suppose that we had chosen to make x_1 and x_2 nonbasic variables (i.e., $x_1 = 0$ and $x_2 = 0$). Solving for the corresponding basic solution is easy, because the three constraint equations reduce to

$$1s_1 \qquad\quad = 150$$
$$1s_2 \quad = 20$$
$$1s_3 = 300$$

The complete solution (including the nonbasic variables) corresponding to $x_1 = 0$ and $x_2 = 0$ is

$$x_1 = 0$$
$$x_2 = 0$$
$$s_1 = 150$$
$$s_2 = 20$$
$$s_3 = 300$$

This solution is a basic solution since it was obtained by setting two of the variables equal to zero and solving for the other three variables. Moreover, it is a basic *feasible* solution since all of the variables are greater than or equal to zero.

In Figure 5.1 we show a graph of the feasible region for the HighTech problem. We see that the basic feasible solution obtained by setting $x_1 = 0$ and $x_2 = 0$ corresponds to extreme point 1 of the feasible region. This is not just a coincidence; all basic feasible solutions correspond to extreme points of the feasible region. Thus for every extreme point of the feasible region of a linear programming problem there is a corresponding basic feasible solution.

In Chapter 2 we showed that the optimal solution to a linear programming problem can be found at an extreme point. Since there is a corresponding basic feasible solution for every extreme point, we can now conclude that there is an optimal basic feasible solution.[3] The simplex method is an iterative procedure for moving from one basic feasible solution (extreme point) to another until the optimal solution is reached.

5.2   TABLEAU FORM

A basic feasible solution to the system of m linear constraint equations and n variables is required as a starting point for the simplex method. From this starting point the simplex method successively generates better basic feasible solutions to the system of linear equations. When the objective function can no longer be improved in this fashion, the optimal solution has been reached. The purpose of tableau form is to provide an initial basic feasible solution that is required to get the simplex method started.

Recall that for the HighTech problem the standard form representation of the problem is

---

[3]We are only considering cases where there is an optimal solution. That is, in the cases of infeasibility and unboundedness there is no optimal solution, so there cannot be an optimal basic feasible solution.

FIGURE 5.1
Feasible Region and Extreme Points for the HighTech Industries Problem

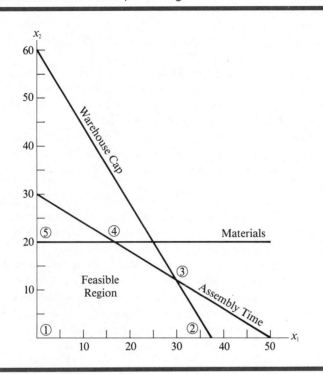

$$\max 50x_1 + 40x_2 + 0s_1 + 0s_2 + 0s_3$$

s.t.

$$
\begin{aligned}
3x_1 + 5x_2 + 1s_1 &= 150 \\
1x_2 + 1s_2 &= 20 \\
8x_1 + 5x_2 + 1s_3 &= 300 \\
x_1, x_2, s_1, s_2, s_3 &\geq 0
\end{aligned}
$$

When a linear programming problem with all less-than-or-equal-to constraints is written in standard form, it is easy to find a basic feasible solution. We simply set the decision variables equal to zero and solve for the values of the slack variables. Note that doing this results in the values of the slack variables being set equal to the right-hand-side values of the constraint equations. For the HighTech problem this yields $x_1 = 0$, $x_2 = 0$, $s_1 = 150$, $s_2 = 20$, and $s_3 = 300$ as the initial basic feasible solution. This solution corresponds to using the origin, extreme point ① in Figure 5.1, as the initial basic feasible solution.

If we study the standard-form representation of the HighTech constraint equations closely, we can identify two properties that make it possible to find an initial basic feasible solution. The first property, which enables us to find a basic solution, requires that the following conditions be satisfied:

a. For each constraint equation the coefficient of one of the *m* basic variables in that equation must be 1, and the coefficients for all the remaining basic variables in that equation must be 0.

b. The coefficient for each basic variable may be 1 in only one constraint equation.

When these conditions are satisfied, there is exactly one basic variable associated with each equation, and for each of the *m* equations it is a different basic variable. Thus if the $n - m$ nonbasic variables are set equal to zero, the values of the basic variables can be read from the right-hand side of the constraint equations.

The second property that enables us to find a basic feasible solution requires that the values on the right-hand sides of the constraint equations be nonnegative. This ensures that the basic solution obtained by setting the basic variables equal to the right-hand-side values is feasible.

If a linear programming problem satisfies the two properties above, it is said to be in tableau form. Thus we see that the standard-form representation of the HighTech problem is already in tableau form. In fact, the standard form and tableau form for linear programs have all less-than-or-equal-to constraints and nonnegative right-hand-side values are the same. Later in this chapter we will show how to set up tableau form for problems involving equality and greater-than-or-equal-to constraints; in these cases the standard-form representation of the problem and the tableau-form representation are not the same.

To summarize, the following three steps are necessary in order to prepare a linear programming problem for solution using the simplex method:

Step 1   Formulate the problem.
Step 2   Set up the standard form representation of the problem by adding slack and/or subtracting surplus variables.
Step 3   Set up the tableau form representation of the problem.

5.3 SETTING UP THE INITIAL SIMPLEX TABLEAU

After a linear programming problem has been converted to tableau form, we have an initial basic feasible solution that can be used to begin the simplex method. To provide a convenient means for performing the calculations required by the simplex solution procedure, we will first develop what is referred to as the initial *simplex tableau*.

Part of the initial simplex tableau is a table containing all the coefficients shown in the tableau-form representation of a linear program. If we adopt the general notation

$$c_j = \text{objective function coefficient for variable } j$$
$$b_i = \text{right-hand-side value for constraint } i$$
$$a_{ij} = \text{coefficient associated with variable } j \text{ in constraint } i$$

we can show this portion of the simplex tableau as follows:

$$
\begin{array}{ccccc|c}
c_1 & c_2 & \cdots & c_n & \\
\hline
a_{11} & a_{12} & \cdots & a_{1n} & b_1 \\
a_{21} & a_{22} & \cdots & a_{2n} & b_2 \\
\cdot & \cdot & \cdots & \cdot & \cdot \\
\cdot & \cdot & \cdots & \cdot & \cdot \\
\cdot & \cdot & \cdots & \cdot & \cdot \\
a_{m1} & a_{m2} & \cdots & a_{mn} & b_m \\
\end{array}
$$

Thus for the HighTech problem we obtain the following partial initial simplex tableau:

$$
\begin{array}{ccccc|c}
50 & 40 & 0 & 0 & 0 & \\
\hline
3 & 5 & 1 & 0 & 0 & 150 \\
0 & 1 & 0 & 1 & 0 & 20 \\
8 & 5 & 0 & 0 & 1 & 300 \\
\end{array}
$$

Note that the row above the first horizontal line contains the coefficients of the objective function in the tableau-form representation of the problem. The elements appearing between the horizontal lines and to the left of the vertical line are the coefficients of the constraint equations, and the elements to the right of the vertical line are the corresponding right-hand-side values.

Later we may want to refer to the objective function coefficients, all the right-hand-side values, or all the coefficients in the constraints as a group. To do this we will find the following general notation helpful:

c row = row of objective function coefficients
b column = column of right-hand-side values of the constraint equations
A matrix = m rows and n columns of coefficients of the variables in the constraint equations

Using this notation we can show the above portion of the initial simplex tableau as follows:

$$
\begin{array}{c|c}
c\text{ row} & \\
\hline
A & b \\
\text{matrix} & \text{column} \\
\end{array}
$$

To help us recall that each of the columns contains the coefficients of one variable, we will write the variable associated with each column directly above the column. Doing this, we obtain

$$
\begin{array}{ccccc|c}
x_1 & x_2 & s_1 & s_2 & s_3 & \\
\hline
50 & 40 & 0 & 0 & 0 & \\
\hline
3 & 5 & 1 & 0 & 0 & 150 \\
0 & 1 & 0 & 1 & 0 & 20 \\
8 & 5 & 0 & 0 & 1 & 300 \\
\end{array}
$$

The initial simplex tableau contains the tableau form of the problem; thus it is easy to identify the initial basic feasible solution. First, we note that for each basic variable there is a corresponding column that has a 1 in the only nonzero position. Such columns are known as unit columns or unit vectors. Second, there is a row of the tableau associated with each basic variable. This row has a 1 in the unit column corresponding to the basic variable. The value of each basic variable is then given by the b_i value in the row associated with the basic variable. For example, in the HighTech problem, row 3 of the simplex tableau is associated with basic variable s_3 since this row has a 1 in the unit column corresponding to s_3; therefore the value of this basic variable is given by $s_3 = b_3 = 300$. Table 5.1 shows the column corresponding to basic variable s_2, the row associated with s_2, and its value, $s_2 = 20$.

TABLE 5.1
Illustration of Procedure for Identifying Values of Basic Variables from the Simplex Tableau

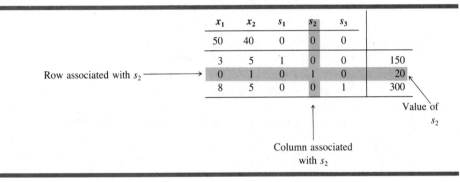

5.4 IMPROVING THE SOLUTION

In order to improve the initial basic feasible solution, the simplex method must generate a new basic feasible solution (extreme point) that yields a better value for the objective function. To do so requires changing the set of basic variables; this is accomplished by selecting one of the current nonbasic variables to make basic and one of the current basic variables to make nonbasic in such a fashion that the new basic feasible solution yields an improved value for the objective function. The simplex method provides an easy way to carry out this change of variables in the basic feasible solution.

For computational convenience we will add two new columns to the present form of the simplex tableau. One column is labeled "Basis" and the other column is labeled "c_B." In the *Basis* column we list the current basic variables, and in the column labeled c_B we list the corresponding objective function coefficient for each of these basic variables. For the HighTech problem this results in the following initial simplex tableau:

Basis	c_B	x_1	x_2	s_1	s_2	s_3	
		50	40	0	0	0	
s_1	0	3	5	1	0	0	150
s_2	0	0	1	0	1	0	20
s_3	0	8	5	0	0	1	300

Note that in the column labeled *Basis*, s_1 is listed as the first basic variable since its value is given by the right-hand-side value for the first equation (that is, $s_1 = b_1 = 150$); s_2 is listed second, since its value is given by $s_2 = b_2 = 20$; and $s_3 = b_3 = 300$ is listed last.

Can we improve the value of the objective function by moving to a new basic feasible solution? To help find out if this is possible, we add two rows to the bottom of the tableau. The first row, labeled z_j, represents the decrease in the value of the objective function that will result if one unit of the variable corresponding to the jth column of the A matrix is brought into the basis; that is, if this variable is made a basic variable with a value of 1. The term basis is used here to refer to the set of basic variables. The second row, labeled $c_j - z_j$, represents the net change in the value of the objective function if one unit of the variable corresponding to the jth column of the A matrix is brought into solution. We refer to $c_j - z_j$ as the *net evaluation row*.

Let us first see how the entries in the z_j row are computed. Suppose that we consider increasing the value of the nonbasic variable x_1 by one unit; that is, from $x_1 = 0$ to $x_1 = 1$. In order to make this change and at the same time continue to satisfy the constraint equations, the values of some of the other variables will have to be changed. As we will show, the simplex method requires that the necessary changes be made to basic variables only. For example, in the first constraint we have

$$3x_1 + 5x_2 + 1s_1 = 150$$

The current basic variable in this constraint equation is s_1. Assuming that x_2 remains a nonbasic variable with a value of 0, if x_1 is increased in value by 1, then s_1 must be decreased by 3 for the constraint to be satisfied. Similarly, if we were to increase the value of x_1 by 1 (and keep $x_2 = 0$), we can see from the second and third equations that although s_2 would not decrease, s_3 would decrease by 8.

From analyzing all the constraint equations, we see that making x_1 a basic variable with a value of 1 will result in a decrease of three units in s_1, a decrease of 0 units in s_2, and a decrease of eight units in s_3. Thus we see that the coefficients in the x_1 column indicate the amount of decrease in the current basic variables when the nonbasic variable x_1 is increased from 0 to 1. In general all the column coefficients can be interpreted this way. For instance, if we make x_2 a basic variable at a value of 1 (while keeping x_1 a nonbasic variable at a value of 0), s_1 will decrease by 5, s_2 will decrease by 1, and s_3 will decrease by 5.

Recall that the values in the c_B column of the simplex tableau are the objective function coefficients for the current basic variables. Hence to compute the values in the z_j row we form the sum of the products obtained by multiplying the elements in the c_B column by the corresponding elements in the jth column of the A matrix. Doing this we obtain

$$z_1 = 0(3) + 0(0) + 0(8) = 0$$
$$z_2 = 0(5) + 0(1) + 0(5) = 0$$
$$z_3 = 0(1) + 0(0) + 0(0) = 0$$
$$z_4 = 0(0) + 0(1) + 0(0) = 0$$
$$z_5 = 0(0) + 0(0) + 0(1) = 0$$

Since the objective function coefficient of x_1 is 50, the value of $c_1 - z_1$ is $50 - 0 = 50$. This indicates that the net result of bringing one unit of x_1 into the current basis will be an increase in profit of \$50. Hence in the net evaluation row corresponding to x_1 we enter 50. In the same manner we can calculate the $c_j - z_j$ values for the remaining variables. The result is the following initial simplex tableau:

Basis	c_B	x_1	x_2	s_1	s_2	s_3	
		50	40	0	0	0	
s_1	0	3	5	1	0	0	150
s_2	0	0	1	0	1	0	20
s_3	0	8	5	0	0	1	300
	z_j	0	0	0	0	0	0
	$c_j - z_j$	50	40	0	0	0	↑
							Profit

In this tableau we also see a 0 in the z_j row in the last column. This zero represents the profit associated with the current basic feasible solution. It was computed by multiplying the values of the basic variables, which are given in the last column of the simplex tableau, by their corresponding contribution to profit as given in the c_B column. That is, profit $= 150(0) + 20(0) + 300(0) = 0$.

From the net evaluation row we see that each unit of the Deskpro (x_1) increases the value of the objective function by 50 and each unit of the Portable (x_2) increases the value of the objective function by 40. Since x_1 causes the largest per-unit increase, we choose it as the variable to bring into the basis. We must next determine which of the current basic variables to make nonbasic. In doing so we first note that since each unit of x_1 that is brought into the solution increases the objective function by \$50, we would like to make x_1 as large as possible.

In discussing how to compute the z_j values, we noted that each of the coefficients in the x_1 column indicates the amount of decrease in the corresponding basic variable that would result from increasing x_1 by one unit. Hence only the positive coefficients need to be considered in determining the current basic variable that will become nonbasic at a value of zero. Considering the first row, we see that every unit of the Deskpro produced will cause us to use 3 hours of assembly time (i.e., reduce s_1 by 3). In the current solution $s_1 = 150$ and $x_1 = 0$. Thus—considering this row only—the maximum possible value of x_1 can be calculated by solving

$$3x_1 = 150$$

which provides

$$x_1 = 50$$

If x_1 is 50 (and x_2 remains a nonbasic variable with a value of 0), s_1 will have to be reduced to zero in order to satisfy the first constraint:

$$3x_1 + 5x_2 + 1s_1 = 150$$

Considering the second row, $0x_1 + 1x_2 + 1s_2 = 20$, we see that the coefficient of x_1 is 0. Thus increasing x_1 will not have any effect on s_2; that is, increasing x_1 cannot drive the basic variable in the second row (s_2) to zero. Indeed, increases in x_1 will leave s_2 unchanged.

Finally, since the coefficient of x_1 is 8 in the third row, every unit that we increase x_1 will cause a decrease of eight units in s_3. Since the value of s_3 is currently $s_3 = 300$, we can solve

$$8x_1 = 300$$

to find the maximum possible increase in x_1 before s_3 will become nonbasic at a value of 0. Solving we see that x_1 cannot be any larger than $300/8 = 37.5$.

Considering the three rows (constraints) simultaneously, we see that row 3 is the most restrictive. That is, producing 37.5 units of the Deskpro will use all of the warehouse space and force the corresponding slack variable to become nonbasic at a value of $s_3 = 0$.

In making the decision to produce as many Deskpro units as possible, we must change the set of variables in the basic feasible solution (i.e., obtain a new basis). The nonbasic variable x_1 will now become a basic variable while the previous basic variable, s_3, will become a nonbasic variable with $s_3 = 0$. This interchange of roles between two variables is the essence of the simplex method. The way the simplex method moves from one basic feasible solution to another is by selecting a nonbasic variable to replace one of the current basic variables. This process of moving from one basic feasible solution to another is called an *iteration*. We now summarize the rules for selecting a nonbasic variable to make basic and selecting a current basic variable to make nonbasic.

Criterion for Entering a New Variable Into the Basis. Look at the net evaluation row ($c_j - z_j$) and select the variable to enter the basis that will cause the largest per-unit improvement in the value of the objective function. In the case of a tie we follow the convention of selecting the variable to enter the basis that corresponds to the leftmost of the columns.

Criterion for Removing a Variable From the Current Basis. Suppose the incoming basic variable corresponds to column j in the A portion of the simplex tableau. For each row i compute the ratio b_i/a_{ij}, for each a_{ij} greater than 0. The basic variable to remove from the basis corresponds to the minimum of these ratios. In case of a tie we follow the convention of selecting the variable to leave the basis that corresponds to the uppermost of the tied rows.

Let us illustrate the above procedure by applying it to the HighTech problem. To illustrate the computations involved, we add an extra column to the right of the tableau showing the b_i/a_{ij} ratios.

Basis	c_B	x_1 x_2 s_1 s_2 s_3 50 40 0 0 0		$\dfrac{b_i}{a_{i1}}$
s_1	0	3 5 1 0 0	150	$\dfrac{150}{3} = 50$
s_2	0	0 1 0 1 0	20	—
s_3	0	⑧ 5 0 0 1	300	$\dfrac{300}{8} = 37.5$
	z_j	0 0 0 0 0	0	
	$c_j - z_j$	50 40 0 0 0		

We see that $c_1 - z_1 = 50$ is the largest positive value in the $c_j - z_j$ row. Hence x_1 is selected to become the new basic variable. Checking the ratios b_i/a_{i1} for values of a_{i1} greater than 0, we see that $b_3/a_{31} = {}^{300}\!/_8 = 37.5$ is the minimum of these ratios. Thus the current basic variable associated with row 3 (s_3) is the variable selected to leave the basis. In the tableau we have circled $a_{31} = 8$ to indicate that the variable corresponding to the first column is to enter the basis and that the basic variable corresponding to the third row is to leave the basis. Adopting the usual linear programming terminology, we refer to this circled element as the *pivot element*. The column and the row containing the pivot element are called the *pivot column* and the *pivot row*, respectively.

To improve the current solution of $x_1 = 0, x_2 = 0, s_1 = 150, s_2 = 20$, and $s_3 = 300$, we should increase x_1 to 37.5. The production of 37.5 units of the Deskpro results in a profit of $50(37.5) = 1875$. In producing 37.5 units of the Deskpro we will use all the available warehouse space and thus s_3 will be reduced to zero. Hence x_1 will become the new basic variable, replacing s_3 in the old basis.

5.5 CALCULATING THE NEXT TABLEAU

In the previous section we concluded that the initial basic feasible solution obtained by setting $x_1 = 0$ and $x_2 = 0$ could be improved by introducing x_1 into the basis to replace s_3. To determine the new basic feasible solution corresponding to making x_1 a basic variable, it will be necessary to update the simplex tableau.

Recall that the initial simplex tableau contains the coefficients of the tableau-form representation of the linear program. Because of the special properties of the tableau form, the initial simplex tableau contains a unit column corresponding to each basic variable.

We now want to update the simplex tableau in such a fashion that the column associated with the new basic variable is a unit column; in this way its value will be given by the right-hand-side value of the corresponding row. Thus we would like the column in the new tableau corresponding to x_1 to look just like the column corresponding to s_3 in the original tableau. Hence our goal is to make the column in the A matrix corresponding to x_1 appear as

$$0$$
$$0$$
$$1$$

The way in which we transform the simplex tableau so that it still represents an equivalent system of constraint equations with the above properties is to use elementary row operations.

Elementary Row Operations

1. Multiply any row (equation) by a nonzero number.
2. Replace any row (equation) by the result of adding or subtracting a multiple of another row (equation) to it.

The application of these elementary row operations to a system of simultaneous linear equations will not change the solution to the system of equations; however, the elementary row operations will change the coefficients of the variables and the values of the right-hand sides.

The objective in performing elementary row operations is to transform the system of constraint equations into a form that makes it easy to identify the new basic feasible solution. Consequently we must perform the elementary row operations in such a manner that we transform the column for the variable entering the basis into a unit column. We emphasize that the feasible solutions to the original constraint equations are the same as the feasible solutions to the modified constraint equations obtained by performing elementary row operations. However, many of the numerical values in the simplex tableau will change as the result of performing these row operations. Thus the present method of referring to elements in the simplex tableau may lead to confusion.

Up to now we have made no distinction between the A matrix and b column coefficients in the tableau-form representation of the problem and the corresponding coefficients in the simplex tableau. Indeed, we showed that the initial simplex tableau is formed by properly placing the a_{ij}, c_j, and b_i elements as given in the tableau-form representation of the problem into the simplex tableau. We will refer to the portion of the simplex tableau that initially contained the a_{ij} values with the symbol $\overline{A}$, and the portion of the tableau that initially contained the b_i values with the symbol $\overline{b}$. In terms of the simplex tableau, elements in $\overline{A}$ will be denoted by $\overline{a}_{ij}$ and elements in $\overline{b}$ will be denoted by $\overline{b}_i$. We recognize that $\overline{A} = A$ and $\overline{b} = b$ in the initial simplex tableau. However, in subsequent simplex tableaus this relationship will not hold. The overbar notation should avoid any confusion when we wish to distinguish between the original constraint coefficient values a_{ij} and right-hand-side values b_i of the tableau form, and the simplex tableau elements $\overline{a}_{ij}$ and $\overline{b}_i$.

Now let us see how elementary row operations are used to create the next simplex tableau for the HighTech problem. Recall that the goal is to transform the column in the $\overline{A}$ portion of the simplex tableau corresponding to x_1 to a unit column; that is,

$$\begin{bmatrix} \overline{a}_{11} \\ \overline{a}_{21} \\ \overline{a}_{31} \end{bmatrix} = \begin{bmatrix} 0 \\ 0 \\ 1 \end{bmatrix}$$

In order to set $\overline{a}_{31} = 1$, we perform the first elementary row operation by multiplying the pivot row (row 3) by $\frac{1}{8}$ to obtain the equivalent equation

$$\tfrac{1}{8}(8x_1 + 5x_2 + 0s_1 + 0s_2 + 1s_3) = \tfrac{1}{8}(300)$$

or

$$1x_1 + \tfrac{5}{8}x_2 + 0s_1 + 0s_2 + \tfrac{1}{8}s_3 = \tfrac{75}{2} \tag{5.9}$$

We refer to (5.9) in the updated simplex tableau as the new pivot row.

In order to set $\overline{a}_{11} = 0$ we perform the second elementary row operation by first multiplying the new pivot row by 3 to obtain the equivalent equation

$$3(1x_1 + \tfrac{5}{8}x_2 + 0s_1 + 0s_2 + \tfrac{1}{8}s_3) = 3(\tfrac{75}{2})$$

or

$$3x_1 + \tfrac{15}{8}x_2 + 0s_1 + 0s_2 + \tfrac{3}{8}s_3 = \tfrac{225}{2} \tag{5.10}$$

Subtracting equation (5.10) from row 1 of the simplex tableau completes the application of the second elementary row operation; thus, after dropping the terms with zero coefficients we obtain

$$(3x_1 + 5x_2 + 1s_1) - (3x_1 + {}^{15}\!/_8 x_2 + {}^3\!/_8 s_3) = 150 - {}^{225}\!/_2$$

or

$$0x_1 + {}^{25}\!/_8 x_2 + 1s_1 - {}^3\!/_8 s_3 = {}^{75}\!/_2 \qquad (5.11)$$

Since $\bar{a}_{21} = 0$, no row operations need be performed on the second row of the simplex tableau. Replacing rows 1 and 3 with the coefficients in equations (5.11) and (5.9), respectively, we obtain the new simplex tableau

		x_1	x_2	s_1	s_2	s_3	
Basis	c_B	50	40	0	0	0	
s_1	0	0	${}^{25}\!/_8$	1	0	$-{}^3\!/_8$	${}^{75}\!/_2$
s_2	0	0	1	0	1	0	20
x_1	50	1	${}^5\!/_8$	0	0	${}^1\!/_8$	${}^{75}\!/_2$
	z						1875
	$c_j - z_j$						

The corresponding system of equations is (terms having zero coefficients are dropped)

$$
\begin{aligned}
{}^{25}\!/_8 x_2 + 1s_1 \quad\quad - {}^3\!/_8 s_3 &= {}^{75}\!/_2 \\
1x_2 \quad\quad + 1s_2 \quad\quad &= 20 \\
1x_1 + {}^5\!/_8 x_2 \quad\quad\quad + {}^1\!/_8 s_3 &= {}^{75}\!/_2
\end{aligned}
$$

Assigning zero values to the nonbasic variables x_2 and s_3 permits us to identify the following new basic feasible solution:

$$
\begin{aligned}
s_1 &= {}^{75}\!/_2 \\
s_2 &= 20 \\
x_1 &= {}^{75}\!/_2
\end{aligned}
$$

This solution is also provided by the last column in the new simplex tableau. The profit associated with this solution is obtained by multiplying the solution values for the basic variables as given in the $\bar{b}$ column by their corresponding objective function coefficients as given in the c_B column; that is,

$$0({}^{75}\!/_2) + 0(20) + 50({}^{75}\!/_2) = 1875$$

Interpreting the Results of an Iteration

Starting with the initial simplex tableau, elementary row operations are used to change the elements in the simplex tableau in such a manner that we are able to identify a new basic feasible solution that improves the value of the objective function. Carrying out the process of determining a new simplex tableau is referred to as an iteration of the simplex method. In our example the initial basic feasible solution was

$$
\begin{aligned}
x_1 &= 0 \\
x_2 &= 0 \\
s_1 &= 150 \\
s_2 &= 20 \\
s_3 &= 300
\end{aligned}
$$

with a corresponding profit of \$0. One iteration of the simplex method moved us to another basic feasible solution with an objective function value of \$1875. This new basic feasible solution is

$$
\begin{aligned}
x_1 &= {}^{75}/_2 \\
x_2 &= 0 \\
s_1 &= {}^{75}/_2 \\
s_2 &= 20 \\
s_3 &= 0
\end{aligned}
$$

In Figure 5.2 we see that the initial basic feasible solution corresponds to extreme point ①. The first iteration moved us in the direction of the greatest increase per unit

FIGURE 5.2
Feasible Region and Extreme Points for the HighTech Industries Problem

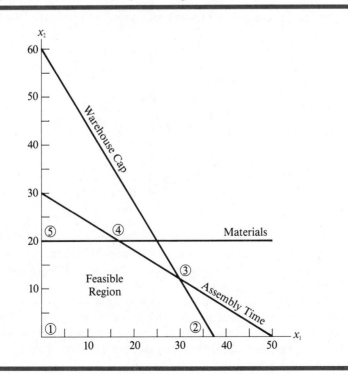

in profit; that is, along the x_1 axis. We moved away from extreme point ① in the x_1 direction until we could not move further without violating one of the constraints. The tableau we calculated after one iteration is the basic feasible solution corresponding to extreme point ②.

We note from Figure 5.2 that at extreme point 2 the warehouse space constraint is binding and that there is slack in the other two constraints. From the simplex tableau we see that the amount of slack for these two constraints is given by $s_1 = {}^{75}\!/_2$ and $s_2 = 20$.

Moving Toward a Better Solution

To see if a new better basic feasible solution can be found, we need to calculate the z_j and $c_j - z_j$ rows for the new simplex tableau. Recall that the elements in the z_j row are the sum of the products obtained by multiplying the elements in the c_B column of the simplex tableau by the corresponding elements in the columns of the $\bar{A}$ matrix. Thus we obtain

$$
\begin{aligned}
z_1 &= 0(0) &+ 0(0) + 50(1) &= 50 \\
z_2 &= 0({}^{25}\!/_8) &+ 0(1) + 50({}^{5}\!/_8) &= {}^{250}\!/_8 \\
z_3 &= 0(1) &+ 0(0) + 50(0) &= 0 \\
z_4 &= 0(0) &+ 0(1) + 50(0) &= 0 \\
z_5 &= 0(-{}^{3}\!/_8) &+ 0(0) + 50({}^{1}\!/_8) &= {}^{50}\!/_8
\end{aligned}
$$

Subtracting z_j from c_j to compute the net evaluation row, we obtain the following simplex tableau:

Basis	c_B	x_1 50	x_2 40	s_1 0	s_2 0	s_3 0	
s_1	0	0	${}^{25}\!/_8$	1	0	$-{}^{3}\!/_8$	${}^{75}\!/_2$
s_2	0	0	1	0	1	0	20
x_1	50	1	${}^{5}\!/_8$	0	0	${}^{1}\!/_8$	${}^{75}\!/_2$
	z_j	50	${}^{250}\!/_8$	0	0	${}^{50}\!/_8$	1875
	$c_j - z_j$	0	${}^{70}\!/_8$	0	0	$-{}^{50}\!/_8$	

Let us now analyze the $c_j - z_j$ row to see if we can introduce a new variable into the basis and continue to improve the objective function. Using the rule for determining which variable should enter the basis next, we select x_2, since it has the highest positive coefficient in the $c_j - z_j$ row.

To determine which variable will be removed from the basis when x_2 enters, we must compute for each row i the ratio $\bar{b}_i / \bar{a}_{i2}$ (remember, though, that we should compute this ratio only if $\bar{a}_{i2}$ is greater than zero); then we select the variable to leave the basis that corresponds to the minimum ratio. As before, we will show these ratios in an extra column of the simplex tableau:

Basis	c_B	x_1	x_2	s_1	s_2	s_3		$\dfrac{\overline{b}_i}{\overline{a}_{ij2}}$
		50	40	0	0	0		
s_1	0	0	$\boxed{25/8}$	1	0	$-3/8$	$75/2$	$\dfrac{75/2}{25/8}=12$
s_2	0	0	1	0	1	0	20	$\dfrac{20}{1}=20$
x_1	50	1	$5/8$	0	0	$1/8$	$75/2$	$\dfrac{75/2}{5/8}=60$
z_j		50	$250/8$	0	0	$50/8$	1875	
$c_j - z_j$		0	$70/8$	0	0	$-50/8$		

Since 12 is the minimum ratio, s_1 will leave the basis. The pivot element is $\overline{a}_{12} = {}^{25}\!/_8$, which is circled in the above tableau. The nonbasic variable x_2 must now be made a basic variable. This means that we must perform the elementary row operations that will convert the x_2 column into a unit column; that is, we will have to transform the second column in the tableau to the form

$$\begin{bmatrix} 1 \\ 0 \\ 0 \end{bmatrix}$$

We can do this by performing the following elementary row operations:

Step 1 Multiply every element in row 1 (the pivot row) by ${}^8\!/_{25}$ in order to make $\overline{a}_{12} = 1$.

Step 2 Subtract the new row 1 (that is, the new pivot row) from row 2 in order to make $\overline{a}_{22} = 0$.

Step 3 Multiply the new pivot row by ${}^5\!/_8$ and subtract the result from row 3 in order to make $\overline{a}_{32} = 0$.

Although the above elementary row operations again change the appearance of the simplex tableau, they do not alter the solutions to the system of equations contained in the tableau. The only difference is that now we have x_2, s_2, and x_1 as the basic variables, and s_1 and s_3 as the nonbasic variables. The new tableau resulting from these row operations is as follows:

Basis	c_B	x_1	x_2	s_1	s_2	s_3	
		50	40	0	0	0	
x_2	40	0	1	$8/25$	0	$-3/25$	12
s_2	0	0	0	$-8/25$	1	$3/25$	8
x_1	50	1	0	$-5/25$	0	$5/25$	30
z_j		50	40	$14/5$	0	$26/5$	1980
$c_j - z_j$		0	0	$-14/5$	0	$-26/5$	

Note that the values of the basic variables are $x_2 = 12$, $s_2 = 8$, and $x_1 = 30$, and the coresponding profit is $40(12) + 0(8) + 50(30) = 1980$.

We must now determine whether or not to bring any other variable into the basis and thereby move to another basic feasible solution. Looking at the net evaluation row, we see that every element is zero or negative. Since $c_j - z_j$ is less than or equal to zero for both of the nonbasic variables s_1 and s_3, any attempt to bring a nonbasic variable into the basis at this point will result in lowering the current value of the objective function. Hence the above tableau represents the optimal solution. In general the simplex method uses the following criterion to determine if the optimal solution has been obtained.

Stopping Criterion.   The optimal solution to a linear programming problem has been reached when all of the entries in the net evaluation row $(c_j - z_j)$ are zero or negative. In such cases the optimal solution is the current basic feasible solution.

Interpreting the Optimal Solution

The optimal solution to the HighTech problem, consisting of the basic variables x_1, x_2 and s_2 and nonbasic variables s_1 and s_3, is written as follows:

$$x_1 = 30$$
$$x_2 = 12$$
$$s_1 = 0$$
$$s_2 = 8$$
$$s_3 = 0$$

The value of the objective function is $1980. Thus if the management of HighTech Industries wants to maximize profit, HighTech should produce 30 units of the Deskpro and 12 units of the Portable. In addition, since $s_2 = 8$, management should note that there will be a slack of eight Portable display units left at the optimal solution. Moreover, since $s_1 = 0$ and $s_3 = 0$, there is no slack associated with the assembly-time constraint and the warehouse-space constraint; in other words, these constraints are both binding. Consequently, if it is possible to obtain additional assembly time and/or additional warehouse space, management should consider doing so.

Referring to Figure 5.2, we can see graphically the process that the simplex method used to determine an optimal solution. The initial basic feasible solution corresponds to the origin ($x_1 = 0$, $x_2 = 0$, $s_1 = 150$, $s_2 = 20$, $s_3 = 300$). The first iteration caused x_1 to enter the basis and s_3 to leave. The new basic feasible solution corresponds to extreme point ② ($x_1 = {}^{75}\!/_2$, $x_2 = 0$, $s_1 = 20$, $s_2 = {}^{75}\!/_2$, $s_3 = 0$). At the next iteration x_2 entered the basis and s_1 left. This brought us to extreme point ③, the optimal solution ($x_1 = 30$, $x_2 = 12$, $s_1 = 0$, $s_2 = 8$, $s_3 = 0$).

For the HighTech problem, with only two decision variables, we had a choice of using the graphical or simplex method. For problems with more than two variables, we shall always use the simplex method.

5.6   SOLUTION OF A SAMPLE PROBLEM

In this section we illustrate the use of the simplex method for a linear programming problem involving four decision variables. To check your understanding of the previous sections, you should attempt to solve the problem before studying the solution presented.

Solve the following linear program using the simplex method:

$$\max\ 4x_1 + 6x_2 + 3x_3 + 1x_4$$

s.t.

$$\frac{3}{2}x_1 + 2x_2 + 4x_3 + 3x_4 \le 550$$
$$4x_1 + 1x_2 + 2x_3 + 1x_4 \le 700$$
$$2x_1 + 3x_2 + 1x_3 + 2x_4 \le 200$$
$$x_1, x_2, x_3, x_4 \ge 0$$

First we add slack variables to convert the problem to standard form:

$$\max\ 4x_1 + 6x_2 + 3x_3 + 1x_4 + 0s_1 + 0s_2 + 0s_3$$

s.t.

$$\frac{3}{2}x_1 + 2x_2 + 4x_3 + 3x_4 + 1s_1 \qquad\qquad = 550$$
$$4x_1 + 1x_2 + 2x_3 + 1x_4 \qquad + 1s_2 \qquad = 700$$
$$2x_1 + 3x_2 + 1x_3 + 2x_4 \qquad\qquad + 1s_3 = 200$$
$$x_1, x_2, x_3, x_4, s_1, s_2, s_3 \ge 0$$

The next step is to write the problem in tableau form. Since all the constraints are less-than-or-equal-to constraints, and since the right-hand-side values for the constraints are all nonnegative, the standard form and tableau form are the same. Thus we can set up the initial simplex tableau and begin the simplex method.

Basis	c_B	x_1	x_2	x_3	x_4	s_1	s_2	s_3		$\dfrac{\bar{b}_i}{\bar{a}_{i2}}$
		4	6	3	1	0	0	0		
s_1	0	$\frac{3}{2}$	2	4	3	1	0	0	550	$550/_2 = 225$
s_2	0	4	1	2	1	0	1	0	700	$700/_1 = 700$
s_3	0	2	③	1	2	0	0	1	200	$200/_3 = 66\frac{2}{3}$
	z_j	0	0	0	0	0	0	0	0	
	$c_j - z_j$	4	6	3	1	0	0	0		

Two iterations of the simplex method are required to reach the optimal solution. Result of iteration 1:

Basis	c_B	x_1	x_2	x_3	x_4	s_1	s_2	s_3		$\dfrac{b_i}{a_{i3}}$
		4	6	3	1	0	0	0		
s_1	0	$\frac{1}{6}$	0	⑩⁄₃	$\frac{5}{3}$	1	0	$-\frac{2}{3}$	$416\frac{2}{3}$	125
s_2	0	$\frac{10}{3}$	0	$\frac{5}{3}$	$\frac{1}{3}$	0	1	$-\frac{1}{3}$	$633\frac{1}{3}$	380
x_2	6	$\frac{2}{3}$	1	$\frac{1}{3}$	$\frac{2}{3}$	0	0	$\frac{1}{3}$	$66\frac{2}{3}$	200
	z_j	4	6	2	4	0	0	2	400	
	$c_j - z_j$	0	0	1	-3	0	0	-2		

Result of iteration 2:

Basis	c_B	x_1 4	x_2 6	x_3 3	x_4 1	s_1 0	s_2 0	s_3 0	
x_3	3	$3/60$	0	1	$15/30$	$3/10$	0	$-6/30$	125
s_2	0	$195/60$	0	0	$-15/30$	$-5/10$	1	0	425
x_2	6	$39/60$	1	0	$15/30$	$-1/10$	0	$12/30$	25
z_j		$81/20$	6	3	$9/2$	$3/10$	0	$54/30$	525
$c_j - z_j$		$-1/20$	0	0	$-7/2$	$-3/10$	0	$-54/30$	

Since the $c_j - z_j$ elements are all less than or equal to zero, there is no nonbasic variable that we can introduce into solution and obtain an increase in the value of the objective function. Therefore the current solution is optimal. The complete optimal solution is given by

$$
\begin{aligned}
x_1 &= 0 \\
x_2 &= 25 \\
x_3 &= 125 \\
x_4 &= 0 \\
s_1 &= 0 \\
s_2 &= 425 \\
s_3 &= 0
\end{aligned}
$$

The value of the objective function is 525.

5.7   TABLEAU FORM: THE GENERAL CASE

When a linear program contains all less-than-or-equal-to constraints with nonnegative right-hand-side values, it is easy to set up a tableau form. In this case, we simply add a slack variable to each constraint. However, obtaining tableau form is somewhat more complex if the linear program contains greater-than-or-equal-to constraints, equality constraints, and/or negative right-hand-side values. In this section we describe how to develop tableau form for each of these situations.

Greater-Than-or-Equal-to Constraints

Suppose that in the HighTech Industries problem, management wanted to ensure that the combined total production for both models would be at least 25 units. This requirement means that the following constraint must be added to the current linear program:

$$1x_1 + 1x_2 \geq 25$$

Adding this constraint results in the following modified HighTech Industries problem

max $50x_1 + 40x_2$

s.t.

$$3x_1 + 5x_2 \leq 150 \quad \text{Assembly time}$$
$$1x_2 \leq 20 \quad \text{Portable display}$$
$$8x_1 + 5x_2 \leq 300 \quad \text{Warehouse space}$$
$$1x_1 + 1x_2 \geq 25 \quad \text{Minimum total production}$$
$$x_1, x_2 \geq 0$$

A graph of the feasible region for this modified problem is shown in Figure 5.3.

FIGURE 5.3
Feasible Region and Extreme Points for Modified HighTech Industries Problem

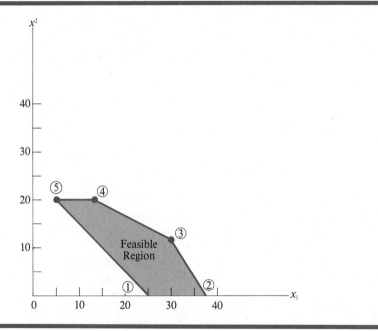

Extreme points ②, ③, and ④ have not changed, but the extreme points we have labeled ① and ⑤ are in different locations than they were in the original problem. The origin ($x_1 = 0$ and $x_2 = 0$) is no longer feasible. We note, however, that extreme point ③ remains feasible. Thus even though part of the original feasible region has been cut off, we should expect to obtain the same optimal solution. To use the simplex method to solve this modified HighTech problem, we need to describe how to set up the tableau form for a linear programming problem that contains greater-than-or-equal-to constraints.

First we use three slack variables and one surplus variable to write the problem in standard form. This provides the following:

$$\text{max } 50x_1 + 40x_2 + 0s_1 + 0s_2 + 0s_3 + 0s_4$$

s.t.

$$3x_1 + 5x_2 + 1s_1 \qquad\qquad = 150 \qquad (5.12)$$

$$1x_2 \qquad + 1s_2 \qquad\qquad\qquad = 20 \qquad (5.13)$$
$$8x_1 + 5x_2 \qquad\qquad + 1s_3 \qquad\qquad = 300 \qquad (5.14)$$
$$1x_1 + 1x_2 \qquad\qquad\qquad - 1s_4 = 25 \qquad (5.15)$$
$$x_1, x_2\ s_1, s_2, s_3, s_4 \geq 0$$

Now let us consider how we obtain an initial basic feasible solution in order to start the simplex method. Previously we set $x_1 = 0$ and $x_2 = 0$, and selected the slack variables as the initial basic variables. The extension of this notion to the modified HighTech problem would suggest setting $x_1 = 0$ and $x_2 = 0$, and selecting the slack and surplus variables as the initial basic variables. However, in looking at the graph in Figure 5.3 we can see that the solution corresponding to $x_1 = 0$ and $x_2 = 0$ which is the origin is no longer a feasible solution. The inclusion of the greater-than-or-equal-to constraint has eliminated the origin from the feasible region.

To see this another way, refer to equation (5.15) in the standard-form representation of the problem. When x_1 and x_2 are set equal to zero, equation (5.15) reduces to $-1s_4 = 25$, and hence $s_4 = -25$. Thus setting x_1 and x_2 to zero results in the basic solution

$$\begin{aligned} x_1 &= & 0 \\ x_2 &= & 0 \\ s_1 &= & 150 \\ s_2 &= & 20 \\ s_3 &= & 300 \\ s_4 &= & -25 \end{aligned}$$

Clearly this is not a basic feasible solution since s_4 violates the nonnegativity requirement. The difficulty is that the standard-form representation of the problem and the tableau-form representation of the problem are not equivalent when the problem contains greater-than-or-equal-to constraints.

In order to set up the tableau form for this problem, we shall resort to a mathematical "trick" that will enable us to find an initial basic feasible solution in terms of the slack variables s_1, s_2, s_3, and a new variable we shall denote a_4. The new variable constitutes the mathematical "trick." Variable a_4 really has nothing to do with the HighTech problem; it merely serves to enable us to set up the tableau form and thus obtain an initial basic feasible solution. Since this new variable has been artificially created in order to start the simplex method, we will refer to it as an *artificial variable*.

The notation for artificial variables is similar to the notation used to refer to the elements of the A matrix. To avoid any confusion between the two, the elements of the A matrix (constraint coefficients) always have two subscripts whereas artificial variables always have only one subscript.

With the addition of an artificial variable, we can convert the standard-form representation of the modified HighTech problem into tableau form. We add artificial variable a_4 to constraint (5.15) to obtain the following representation of the system of equations in tableau form:

$$3x_1 + 5x_2 + 1s_1 \qquad\qquad\qquad = 150$$
$$1x_2 \qquad + 1s_2 \qquad\qquad\qquad = 20$$
$$8x_1 + 5x_2 \qquad\qquad + 1s_3 \qquad\qquad = 300$$
$$1x_1 + 1x_2 \qquad\qquad\qquad - 1s_4 + 1a_4 = 25$$

Note that the subscript on the artificial variable identifies the constraint with which it is associated. This is also the convention we have followed for slack and surplus variables; s_1 is associated with the first constraint, s_2 is associated with the second constraint, and so on. Thus a_4 is the artificial variable associated with the fourth constraint.

Since the variables s_1, s_2, s_3, and a_4 each appear in a different constraint with a coefficient of 1, and since the right-hand sides are nonnegative, both requirements of the tableau form have been satisfied. We can now obtain an initial basic feasible solution by setting $x_1 = x_2 = s_4 = 0$. The complete solution is

$$
\begin{aligned}
x_1 &= 0 \\
x_2 &= 0 \\
s_1 &= 150 \\
s_2 &= 20 \\
s_3 &= 300 \\
s_4 &= 0 \\
a_4 &= 25
\end{aligned}
$$

Is this solution feasible in terms of our real-world problem? No, it is not. It does not satisfy the combined total production requirement of 25 units. We must make an important distinction between a basic feasible solution for the tableau form of our problem and a basic feasible solution for the real-world problem. A basic feasible solution for the tableau form of a linear programming problem is not always a basic feasible solution to the real-world problem.

The reason for creating the tableau form is to obtain an initial basic feasible solution that is required to start the simplex method. Thus we see that whenever it is necessary to introduce artificial variables, the initial simplex solution will not in general be feasible for the real-world problem. This situation is not as difficult as it might seem, however, since the only time we must have a feasible solution for the real-world problem is at the last iteration of the simplex method. Thus if we could devise a way to guarantee that any artificial variable would be eliminated from the basic feasible solution before the optimal solution is reached, there would be no difficulty.

The way in which we guarantee that artificial variables will be eliminated before the optimal solution is reached is to assign each artificial variable a very large cost in the objective function. For example, in the modified HighTech problem we could assign a very large negative number as the profit coefficient for artificial variable a_4. Hence if this variable is in the basis, it will substantially reduce profits. As a result this variable will be eliminated from the basis as soon as possible, and this is precisely what we want to happen.

As an alternative to picking a large negative number like $-100,000$ for the profit coefficient, we will denote the profit coefficient of each artificial variable by $-M$. Here it is assumed that M represents a very large number—in other words, a number of very large magnitude, and hence the letter M. This notation will make it easier to keep track of the elements of the simplex tableau that depend on the profit coefficients of the artificial variables. Using $-M$ as the profit coefficient for artificial variable a_4 for the HighTech problem, we can write the objective function for the tableau form of the problem as follows:

$$\max 50x_1 + 40x_2 + 0s_1 + 0s_2 + 0s_3 + 0s_4 - Ma_4$$

The initial simplex tableau for the modified HighTech Industries problem is shown below.

Basis	c_B	x_1 50	x_2 40	s_1 0	s_2 0	s_3 0	s_4 0	a_4 $-M$	
s_1	0	3	5	1	0	0	0	0	150
s_2	0	0	1	0	1	0	0	0	20
s_3	0	8	5	0	0	1	0	0	300
a_4	$-M$	1	1	0	0	0	-1	1	25
	z_j	$-M$	$-M$	0	0	0	M	$-M$	$-25M$
	$c_j - z_j$	$50+M$	$40+M$	0	0	0	$-M$	0	

The above tableau corresponds to the solution $s_1 = 150$, $s_2 = 20$, $s_3 = 300$, $a_4 = 25$, and $x_1 = x_2 = s_4 = 0$. In terms of the simplex tableau this is a basic feasible solution, since all the variables are greater than or equal to zero and $n - m = 7 - 4 = 3$ of the variables are equal to zero. However, in terms of the modified HighTech problem, $x_1 = x_2 = 0$ is clearly not feasible. This situation is caused by the fact that the artificial variable is in the current basic solution at a positive value. Let us complete the simplex solution to this problem and see if the artificial variable is driven out of solution, as we hope it will be.

Since $c_1 - z_1 = 50 + M$ is the largest value in the net evaluation row, we see that x_1 will become a basic variable during the first iteration of the simplex method. Further calculations with the simplex method shows that x_1 will replace a_4 in the basic solution. The simplex tableau after the first iteration is presented below.

Result of iteration 1:

Basis	c_B	x_1 50	x_2 40	s_1 0	s_2 0	s_3 0	s_4 0	a_4 $-M$	
s_1	0	0	2	1	0	0	3	-3	75
s_2	0	0	1	0	1	0	0	0	20
s_3	0	0	-3	0	0	1	8	-8	100
x_1	50	1	1	0	0	0	-1	1	25
	z_j	50	50	0	0	0	-50	50	1250
	$c_j - z_j$	0	-10	0	0	0	50	$-M-50$	

Graphically, we see in Figure 5.4 that this iteration has moved us from the origin (labeled Ⓐ) to extreme point ①. The current solution is now feasible, since there are no artificial variables in solution. We now have the situation where the basic feasible solution contained in the simplex tableau is also a basic feasible solution to the real-world problem.

Since a_4 is an artificial variable that was added simply to obtain an initial basic feasible solution, we can now drop its associated column from the simplex tableau. Indeed, whenever artificial variables are used, they can be dropped from the simplex tableau as soon as they have been eliminated from the basic feasible solution.

When artificial variables are required to obtain an initial basic feasible solution, the iterations required to eliminate the artificial variables are referred to as *phase I* of the simplex method. When all the artificial variables have been eliminated from the basis,

FIGURE 5.4
Sequence of Simplex Solutions for the Modified HighTech Industries Problem

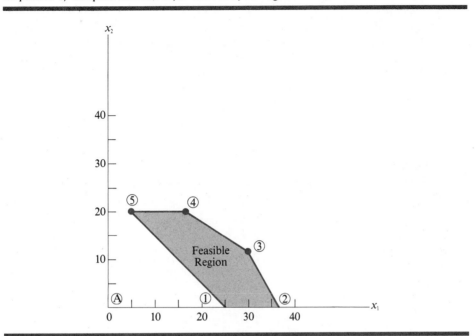

phase I is complete and a basic feasible solution to the real-world problem has been obtained. Thus by dropping the column associated with a_4 from the current tableau, we obtain the following simplex tableau at the end of phase I.

Basis	c_B	x_1 50	x_2 40	s_1 0	s_2 0	s_3 0	s_4 0	
s_1	0	0	2	1	0	0	3	75
s_2	0	0	1	0	1	0	0	20
s_3	0	0	-3	0	0	1	8	100
x_1	50	1	1	0	0	0	-1	25
	z_j	50	50	0	0	0	-50	1250
	$c_j - z_j$	0	-10	0	0	0	50	

We are now ready to begin phase II of the simplex method. This phase simply continues the simplex method computations after all artificial variables have been removed. At the next iteration variable s_4 with $c_j - z_j = 50$ is entered into the solution and variable s_3 is eliminated. The simplex tableau after this iteration is

		x_1	x_2	s_1	s_2	s_3	s_4	
Basis	c_B	50	40	0	0	0	0	
s_1	0	0	$25/8$	1	0	$-3/8$	0	$75/2$
s_2	0	0	1	0	1	0	0	20
s_4	0	0	$-3/8$	0	0	$1/8$	1	$25/2$
x_1	50	1	$5/8$	0	0	$1/8$	0	$75/2$
	z_j	50	$250/8$	0	0	$50/8$	0	1875
	$c_j - z_j$	0	$70/8$	0	0	$-50/8$	0	

In Figure 5.4 we see that this solution corresponds to extreme point ②. One more iteration is required. This time x_2 comes into solution and s_1 is eliminated. After performing this iteration the following simplex tableau shows that the optimal solution has been reached.

		x_1	x_2	s_1	s_2	s_3	s_4	
Basis	c_B	50	40	0	0	0	0	
x_2	40	0	1	$8/25$	0	$-3/25$	0	12
s_2	0	0	0	$-8/25$	1	$3/25$	0	8
s_4	0	0	0	$3/25$	0	$2/25$	1	17
x_1	50	1	0	$-5/25$	0	$5/25$	0	30
	z_j	50	40	$14/5$	0	$26/5$	0	1980
	$c_j - z_j$	0	0	$-14/5$	0	$-26/5$	0	

From Figure 5.4 we see that this optimal solution corresponds to extreme point ③. Thus the optimal solution to the revised problem is the same as the solution for the original problem. However, the simplex method required more iterations to reach this extreme point. This was so because it required an extra iteration to eliminate the artificial variable (a_4), in phase I in order to obtain a basic feasible solution for the real-world problem.

Fortunately, once we obtain an initial simplex tableau using artificial variables, we need not concern ourselves with whether or not the basic solution at a particular iteration is feasible for the real-world problem. We need only follow the rules for the simplex method. If we reach the stopping criterion (that is, all $c_j - z_j \leq 0$) and all the artificial variables have been eliminated from the solution, then we have found the optimal solution. On the other hand, if we reach the stopping criterion and one or more of the artificial variables remains in solution at a positive value, then there is no feasible solution to the problem. This special case will be discussesd further in Section 5.9.

Equality Constraints

When an equality constraint occurs in a linear programming problem, we need to add an artificial variable to obtain tableau form and an initial basic feasible solution. For example, if the equality constraint is

$$6x_1 + 4x_2 - 5x_3 = 30$$

we would simply add an artificial variable, say, a_1, to create a basic feasible solution in the initial simplex tableau. With the artificial variable the above equation becomes

$$6x_1 + 4x_2 - 5x_3 + 1a_1 = 30$$

Once we have created tableau form by adding an artificial variable to each equality constraint, the simplex method proceeds exactly as before.

Eliminating Negative Right-Hand-Side Values

One of the properties of tableau form of a linear program is that the values on the right-hand sides of the constraints have to be nonnegative. In formulating a linear programming problem, we may find one or more of the constraints have negative right-hand-side values. To see how this might happen, suppose that the management of HighTech has specified that the number of units of the Portable model, x_2, has to be less than or equal to the number of units of the Deskpro model, x_1, after setting aside five units of the Deskpro for internal company use. We could formulate this constraint as

$$x_2 \leq x_1 - 5 \qquad (5.16)$$

Subtracting x_1 from both sides of the inequality places both variables on the left-hand side of the inequality. Thus,

$$-x_1 + x_2 \leq -5 \qquad (5.17)$$

Since this is a constraint with a negative right-hand-side value, we can develop an equivalent constraint with a nonnegative right-hand side by multiplying both sides of the constraint by -1. In doing so we recognize that multiplying an inequality constraint by -1 changes the direction of the inequality.

Thus to convert (5.17) to an equivalent constraint with a nonnegative right-hand-side value, we multiply by -1 to obtain

$$x_1 - x_2 \geq 5 \qquad (5.18)$$

We now have an acceptable nonnegative right-hand-side value. Tableau form for this constraint can now be obtained by subtracting a surplus variable and adding an artificial variable.

For a greater-than-or-equal-to constraint, multiplying by -1 creates an equivalent less-than-or-equal-to constraint. For example, suppose we had the following greater-than-or-equal-to constraint

$$6x_1 + 3x_2 - 4x_3 \geq -20$$

Multiplying by -1 to obtain an equivalent constraint with a nonnegative right-hand-side value leads to the following less-than-or-equal-to constraint

$$-6x_1 - 3x_2 + 4x_3 \leq 20$$

Tableau form can be created for this constraint by adding a slack variable.

For an equality constraint with a negative right-hand-side value, we simply multiply by -1 to obtain an equivalent constraint with a nonnegative right-hand-side value. An artificial variable can then be added to create the tableau form.

Summary of the Steps to Create Tableau Form

Step 1. If the original formulation of the linear programming problem contains one or more constraints with negative right-hand-side values, multiply each of these constraints by -1. Doing this will change the direction of the inequalities. This step will provide an equivalent linear program with nonnegative right-hand-side values.

Step 2. For $\leq$ constraints add a slack variable to obtain an equality constraint. The coefficient of the slack variable in the objective function is assigned a value of zero. This provides the tableau form for the constraint and the slack variable becomes one of the basic variables in the initial basic feasible solution.

Step 3. For $\geq$ constraints subtract a surplus variable to obtain an equality constraint, and then add an artificial variable to obtain the tableau form. The coefficient of the surplus variable in the objective function is assigned a value of zero. The coefficient of the artificial variable in the objective function is assigned a value of $-M$. The artificial variable becomes one of the basic variables in the initial basic feasible solution.

Step 4. For equality constraints add an artificial variable to obtain the tableau form. The coefficient of the artificial variable in the objective function is assigned a value of $-M$. The artificial variable becomes one of the basic variables in the initial basic feasible solution.

To obtain some practice in applying the above steps, convert the following example problem into tableau form and then set up the initial simplex tableau:

$$\max \quad 6x_1 + 3x_2 + 4x_3 + 1x_4$$
$$\text{s.t.}$$
$$-2x_1 - \tfrac{1}{2}x_2 + 1x_3 - 6x_4 = -60$$
$$1x_1 \qquad\quad + 1x_3 + \tfrac{2}{3}x_4 \leq 20$$
$$- 1x_2 - 5x_3 \qquad\quad \leq -50$$
$$x_1, x_2, x_3, x_4 \geq 0$$

To eliminate the negative right-hand-side values in constraints 1 and 3, we apply step 1. Multiplying both constraints by -1, we obtain the following equivalent linear program:

$$\max \quad 6x_1 + 3x_2 + 4x_3 + 1x_4$$
$$\text{s.t.}$$
$$2x_1 + \tfrac{1}{2}x_2 - 1x_3 + 6x_4 = 60$$
$$1x_1 \qquad\quad + 1x_3 + \tfrac{2}{3}x_4 \leq 20$$
$$1x_2 + 5x_3 \qquad\quad \geq 50$$
$$x_1, x_2, x_3, x_4 \geq 0$$

Note that the direction of the $\leq$ inequality in constraint 3 has been reversed as a result of multiplying the constraint by -1. By applying step 4 for constraint 1, step 2 for constraint 2, and step 3 for constraint 3, we obtain the following tableau form:

$$\max \quad 6x_1 + 3x_2 + 4x_3 + 1x_4 + 0s_2 + 0s_3 - Ma_1 - Ma_3$$

s.t.

$$
\begin{aligned}
2x_1 + \tfrac{1}{2}x_2 - 1x_3 + 6x_4 \qquad\qquad + 1a_1 \qquad\quad &= 60 \\
1x_1 \qquad + 1x_3 + \tfrac{2}{3}x_4 + 1s_2 \qquad\qquad\quad &= 20 \\
1x_2 + 5x_3 \qquad\qquad - 1s_3 \qquad + 1a_3 &= 50 \\
x_1, x_2, x_3, x_4, s_2, s_3, a_1, a_3 &\geq 0
\end{aligned}
$$

The initial simplex tableau corresponding to this tableau form is

Basis	c_B	x_1 6	x_2 3	x_3 4	x_4 1	s_2 0	s_3 0	a_1 $-M$	a_3 $-M$	
a_1	$-M$	2	1/2	-1	6	0	0	1	0	60
s_2	0	1	0	1	2/3	1	0	0	0	20
a_3	$-M$	0	1	5	0	0	-1	0	1	50
z_j		$-2M$	$-\tfrac{3}{2}M$	$-4M$	$-6M$	0	M	$-M$	$-M$	$-110M$
$c_j - z_j$		$6+2M$	$3+\tfrac{3}{2}M$	$4+4M$	$1+6M$	0	$-M$	0	0	

5.8 SOLVING A MINIMIZATION PROBLEM USING THE SIMPLEX METHOD

There are two ways in which we can use the simplex method to solve a minimization problem. The first approach requires that we change the rule used to introduce a variable into the basis. Recall that in the maximization case we select the variable with the largest positive $c_j - z_j$ as the variable to introduce next into the basis. This is because the value of $c_j - z_j$ tells us the amount the objective function will increase if one unit of the variable in column j is brought into solution. To solve the minimization problem, we can simply reverse this rule. That is, we can select the variable with the most negative $c_j - z_j$ as the one to introduce next. Of course, this approach means the stopping rule for the optimal solution will also have to be changed. Using this approach to solve a minimization problem, we would stop when every value in the net evaluation row is zero or positive.

The second approach to solving the minimization problem is the one we shall employ in this book. It is based on the fact that any minimization problem can be converted to an equivalent maximization problem by multiplying the objective function by -1. Solving the resulting maximization problem will provide the optimal solution to the minimization problem.

Let us illustrate this second approach by using the simplex method to solve the M&D Chemicals problem introduced in Chapter 2. Recall that in this problem management wanted to minimize the cost of producing two products subject to a demand constraint for product 1, a minimum total production quantity requirement, and a constraint on available processing time. The mathematical statement of the M&D Chemicals problem is shown below.

$$\min \quad 2x_1 + 3x_2$$

s.t.

$$
\begin{aligned}
1x_1 \qquad &\geq 125 \quad \text{Demand for product 1} \\
1x_1 + 1x_2 &\geq 350 \quad \text{Total production} \\
2x_1 + 1x_2 &\leq 600 \quad \text{Processing time} \\
x_1, x_2 &\geq 0
\end{aligned}
$$

To solve this problem using the simplex method, we first multiply the objective function by -1 to convert the minimization problem into the following equivalent maximization problem:

$$\max \quad -2x_1 - 3x_2$$

s.t.

$$
\begin{aligned}
1x_1 \qquad &\geq 125 \quad \text{Demand for product 1} \\
1x_1 + 1x_2 &\geq 350 \quad \text{Total production} \\
2x_1 + 1x_2 &\leq 600 \quad \text{Processing time} \\
x_1, x_2 &\geq 0
\end{aligned}
$$

The tableau form for this problem is as follows:

$$\max \quad -2x_1 - 3x_2 + 0s_1 + 0s_2 + 0s_3 - Ma_1 - Ma_2$$

s.t.

$$
\begin{aligned}
1x_1 \qquad - 1s_1 \qquad\qquad\qquad + 1a_1 \qquad &= 125 \\
1x_1 + 1x_2 \qquad - 1s_2 \qquad\qquad\qquad + 1a_2 &= 350 \\
2x_1 + 1x_2 \qquad\qquad + 1s_3 \qquad\qquad &= 600 \\
x_1, x_2, s_1, s_2, s_3, a_1, a_2 &\geq 0
\end{aligned}
$$

The initial simplex tableau is shown below:

Basis	c_B	x_1 -2	x_2 -3	s_1 0	s_2 0	s_3 0	a_1 $-M$	a_2 $-M$	
a_1	$-M$	①	0	-1	0	0	1	0	125
a_2	$-M$	1	1	0	-1	0	0	1	350
s_3	0	2	1	0	0	1	0	0	600
	z_j	$-2M$	$-M$	M	M	0	$-M$	$-M$	$-475M$
	$c_j - z_j$	$-2 + 2M$	$-3 + M$	$-M$	$-M$	0	0	0	

At the first iteration x_1 is brought into the basis and a_1 is eliminated. After dropping the a_1 column from the tableau, the result of the first iteration is shown below.

Basis	c_B	x_1 -2	x_2 -3	s_1 0	s_2 0	s_3 0	a_2 $-M$	
x_1	-2	1	0	-1	0	0	0	125
a_2	$-M$	0	①	1	-1	0	1	225
s_3	0	0	1	2	0	1	0	350
	z_j	-2	$-M$	$2-M$	M	0	$-M$	$-250-225M$
	$c_j - z_j$	0	$-3+M$	$-2+M$	$-M$	0	0	

Continuing with additional iterations of the simplex method provides the final simplex tableau shown below:

Basis	c_B	x_1 -2	x_2 -3	s_1 0	s_2 0	s_3 0	
x_1	-2	1	0	0	1	1	250
x_2	-3	0	1	0	-2	-1	100
s_1	0	0	0	1	1	1	125
	z_j	-2	-3	0	4	1	-800
	$c_j - z_j$	0	0	0	-4	-1	

In Chapter 2 we used the graphical solution procedure to determine the optimal solution to this problem. The feasible region and solution are shown again in Figure 5.5. The simplex method has provided the same optimal solution with $x_1 = 250$, $x_2 = 100$, $s_1 = 125$, $s_2 = 0$, and $s_3 = 0$. Note, however, that the value of the objective function is -800 in the final simplex tableau. We must now multiply this value by -1 to obtain the value of the objective function to the original minimization problem (total cost = 800).

In the next section we shall concentrate on discussing some important special cases that may occur when trying to solve any linear programming problem. We will only consider the case for maximization problems, recognizing that all minimization problems may be placed into this form by multiplying the objective function by -1.

5.9 SPECIAL CASES

In Chapter 2 we discussed how infeasibility, unboundedness, and alternate optima could occur when solving linear programming problems using the graphical solution procedure. These special cases can also arise when using the simplex method. In addition, a special case referred to as *degeneracy* can theoretically cause difficulties for the simplex method. In this section we show how these special cases can be recognized and handled when the simplex method is used.

Infeasibility

Infeasibility occurs whenever there is no solution to the linear program that satisfies all the constraints, including the nonnegativity constraints. From the perspective of the

FIGURE 5.5
Graphical Solution for the M&D Chemicals Problem

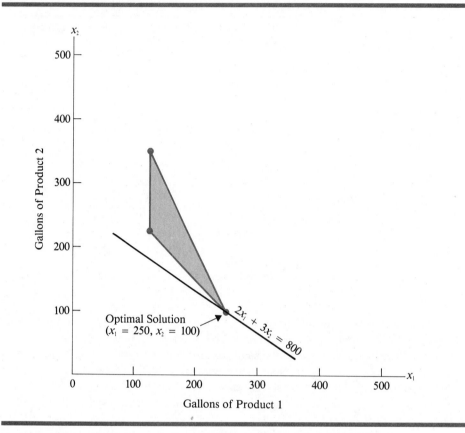

FIGURE 5.5
Graphical Solution for the M&D Chemicals Problem

graphical solution procedure, this means that there is no feasible region. Let us now see how infeasibility is recognized when the simplex method is used.

In Section 5.7, when discussing artificial variables, we mentioned that infeasibility can be recognized when the stopping criterion indicates that an optimal solution has been obtained and one or more of the artificial variables remains in the solution at a positive value. As an illustration of this situation, let us consider another modification of the HighTech Industries problem. Suppose management had imposed a minimum combined total production requirement of 50 units. The revised problem formulation is shown below.

$$\max \quad 50x_1 + 40x_2$$

s.t.

$$
\begin{array}{llll}
3x_1 &+ & 5x_2 \le 150 & \text{Assembly time} \\
& & 1x_2 \le 20 & \text{Portable display} \\
8x_1 &+ & 5x_2 \le 300 & \text{Warehouse space} \\
1x_1 &+ & 1x_2 \ge 50 & \text{Minimum total production} \\
& & x_1, x_2 \ge 0 &
\end{array}
$$

A graph of the feasible region for the problem is shown in Figure 5.6. From the graph we can see that there are no solutions that satisfy both the original HighTech problem constraints and the minimum combined total production constraint ($1x_1 + 1x_2 \geq$ 50). Let us solve this modified HighTech problem using the simplex method. The simplex tableaus are shown below.

FIGURE 5.6
Graph of Solution Region for Modified HighTech Industries Problem

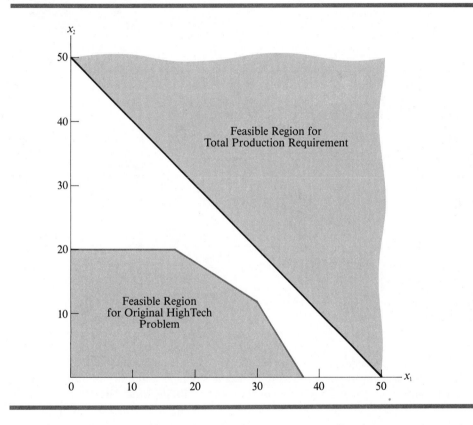

Initial tableau:

Basis	c_B	x_1 50	x_2 40	s_1 0	s_2 0	s_3 0	s_4 0	a_4 $-M$	
s_1	0	3	5	1	0	0	0	0	150
s_2	0	0	1	0	1	0	0	0	20
s_3	0	8	5	0	0	1	0	0	300
a_4	$-M$	1	1	0	0	0	-1	1	50
	z_j	$-M$	$-M$	0	0	0	M	$-M$	$-50M$
	$c_j - z_j$	$50+M$	$40+M$	0	0	0	$-M$	0	

Results of the first iteration:

Basis	c_B	x_1 50	x_2 40	s_1 0	s_2 0	s_3 0	s_4 0	a_4 $-M$	
s_1	0	0	$25/8$	1	0	$-3/8$	0	0	$75/2$
s_2	0	0	1	0	1	0	0	0	20
x_1	50	1	$5/8$	0	0	$1/8$	0	0	$75/2$
a_4	$-M$	0	$3/8$	0	0	$-1/8$	-1	1	$25/2$
z_j		50	$\dfrac{250-3M}{8}$	0	0	$\dfrac{50+M}{8}$	M	$-M$	$1875 - \dfrac{25M}{2}$
$c_j - z_j$		0	$\dfrac{70+3M}{8}$	0	0	$\dfrac{-50-M}{8}$	$-M$	0	

Final tableau:

Basis	c_B	x_1 50	x_2 40	s_1 0	s_2 0	s_3 0	s_4 0	a_4 $-M$	
x_2	40	0	1	$8/25$	0	$-3/25$	0	0	12
s_2	0	0	0	$-8/25$	1	$3/25$	0	0	8
x_1	50	1	0	$-5/25$	0	$5/25$	0	0	30
a_4	$-M$	0	0	$-3/25$	0	$-2/25$	-1	1	8
z_j		50	40	$\dfrac{70+3M}{25}$	0	$\dfrac{130+2M}{25}$	M	$-M$	$1980 - 8M$
$c_j - z_j$		0	0	$\dfrac{-70-3M}{25}$	0	$\dfrac{-130-2M}{25}$	$-M$	0	

In the final tableau, just as you might have suspected, the artificial variable a_4 is in solution at a positive value; thus phase I has not been completed. Note that $c_j - z_j \leq 0$ for all the variables; therefore, according to the stopping criterion, this should be the optimal solution. But this solution is not feasible for the modified HighTech Industries problem since $x_1 = 30$ and $x_2 = 12$ results in a combined total production of 42 units instead of at least 50 units. The fact that the artificial variable is in solution at a value of $a_4 = 8$ tells us that the final solution violates the fourth constraint ($1x_1 + 1x_2 \geq 50$) by eight units.

If management is interested in knowing which of the first three constraints is preventing us from satisfying the total production requirement, a partial answer can be obtained from the final simplex tableau. Note that $s_2 = 8$, but that s_1 and s_3 are nonbasic variables at values of zero. This tells us that the assembly time and warehouse space constraints are binding. Since there are not enough assembly time and warehouse space available, we cannot satisfy the minimum combined total production requirement.

The management implications here are that additional assembly time and/or warehouse space must be made available in order to satisfy the total production requirement. If more time and/or space cannot be made available, management will have to relax the total production requirement by at least eight units.

In summary, a linear program is infeasible if there is no solution that satisfies all the constraints simultaneously. Graphically, we recognize this situation as the case where there is no feasible region. *In terms of the simplex method we recognize infeasibility as the case where one or more of the artificial variables remains in the final solution at a positive value.* In closing, we note that for linear programming problems with all $\leq$ constraints and nonnegative right-hand sides, there will always be a feasible solution. That is, since it is not necessary to introduce artificial variables to set up the initial simplex tableau for these types of problems, there could not possibly be an artificial variable in the final solution.

Unboundedness

For maximization problems we say that a linear program is unbounded if the value of the solution may be made infinitely large without violating any constraints. While discussing unboundedness for graphical method in Section 2.8, we mentioned that unbounded profit maximization problems do not occur in practice. Thus when unboundedness occurs, we can generally look for an error in the formulation of the problem.

The simplex method will automatically identify any unboundedness that exists before the final simplex tableau is reached. What will happen is that the rule for determining the variable to be removed from the basis will not work. Recall that in order to determine which variable to remove from the current basis, we calculate the ratio $\bar{b}_i/\bar{a}_{ij}$ for each $\bar{a}_{ij}$ greater than 0. Then we pick the smallest ratio to tell us which variable to remove from the current basic feasible solution.

The coefficients in a particular column of the $\bar{A}$ matrix indicate how much each of the current basic variables will decrease if one unit of the variable associated with that particular column is brought into solution. Suppose, then, that for a particular linear programming problem we reach a point where the rule for determining which variable to enter the basis results in the decision to enter variable x_2. Assume that for this variable $c_2 - z_2 = 5$, and that all $\bar{a}_{12}$ in column 2 are ≤ 0. Thus each unit of x_2 brought into solution increases the objective function by five units. Furthermore, since $a_{i2} \leq 0$ for all i, this means that none of the current basic variables will be driven to zero, no matter how many units of x_2 we introduce. Thus we can introduce an infinite amount of x_2 into solution and still maintain feasibility. Since each unit of x_2 increases the objective function by 5, we will have an unbounded solution. Hence *the way we recognize the unbounded situation is that all the a_{ij} are less than or equal to 0 in column j, and the simplex method indicates that variable x_j is to be introduced into solution.*

To illustrate this concept, let us consider the example of an unbounded problem we introduced in Section 2.8:

$$
\begin{aligned}
\max \quad & 20x_1 + 10x_2 \\
\text{s.t.} \quad & \\
& 1x_1 \qquad\quad \geq 2 \\
& \qquad\quad 1x_2 \leq 5 \\
& x_1, x_2 \geq 0
\end{aligned}
$$

We subtract a surplus variable, s_1, from the first constraint equation and add a slack variable, s_2, to the second constraint equation to obtain the standard-form representation of the problem. We then add an artificial variable, a_1, to the first constraint equation in order to obtain the tableau form and set up the initial simplex tableau in terms of the basic variables a_1 and s_2. After bringing in x_1 at the first iteration, our simplex tableau is as follows:

Basis	c_B	x_1 20	x_2 10	s_1 0	s_2 0	a_1 $-M$	
x_1	20	1	0	-1	0	1	2
s_2	0	0	1	0	1	0	5
	z_j	20	0	-20	0	20	40
	$c_j - z_j$	0	10	20	0	$-M-20$	

Since s_1 has the largest positive $c_j - z_j$, we know we can increase the value of the objective function most rapidly by bringing s_1 into the basis. But $\bar{a}_{13} = -1$ and $\bar{a}_{23} = 0$; hence we cannot form the ratio $\bar{b}_i/\bar{a}_{i3}$ for all $\bar{a}_{i3} > 0$, since there are no values of $\bar{a}_{i3}$ that are greater than zero. This is our indication that the solution to the linear program is unbounded. The reason the solution is unbounded is that each unit of s_1 that is brought into solution drives zero units of s_2 out of solution (since $\bar{a}_{23} = 0$) and provides one extra unit of x_1 (since $\bar{a}_{13} = -1$). The reason for this is that s_1 is a surplus variable and can be interpreted as the amount of product 1 we produce over the minimum amount required. Since the simplex tableau indicates that we can introduce as much of s_1 as we desire without violating any constraints, this tells us that we can make as much as we want above the minimum amount of x_1 required. Thus there will be no upper bound on the value of the objective function, since the objective function coefficient associated with x_1 is positive.

In summary, a maximization linear program is unbounded if it is possible to make the value of the optimal solution as large as desired without violating any of the constraints. We can recognize this condition graphically as the case where the feasible region extends to infinity in a direction in which the objective function increases. When employing the simplex solution procedure, an unbounded linear program is easy to recognize. *If, at some iteration, the simplex method tells us to introduce variable* j *into the solution and all the* $\bar{a}_{ij}$ *are less than or equal to zero in the* jth *column, the linear program has an unbounded solution.*

We emphasize that the case of an unbounded solution will never occur in real-world cost minimization or profit maximization problems because it is not possible to reduce costs to minus infinity or to increase profits to plus infinity. Thus if we encounter an unbounded solution to a linear programming problem, we should carefully reexamine the formulation of the problem to determine if there has been a formulation error.

Alternate Optimal Solutions

A linear program with two or more optimal solutions is said to have alternate optima. In Section 2.8 we saw that alternate optima is recognized when using the graphical solution procedure when the objective function line is parallel to one of the binding constraint lines. When using the simplex method, we cannot recognize that a linear program has alternate optima until the final simplex tableau is reached. Then if the linear program has alternate optima, $c_j - z_j$ will equal zero for one or more of the *nonbasic* variables.

To illustrate the case of alternate optima when using the simplex method, consider changing the objective function for the HighTech problem from $50x_1 + 40x_2$ to $30x_1 + 50x_2$; in doing so we obtain the revised linear program:

$$\max \quad 30x_1 + 50x_2$$
$$\text{s.t.}$$
$$3x_1 + 5x_2 \leq 150$$
$$1x_2 \leq 20$$
$$8x_1 + 5x_2 \leq 300$$
$$x_1, x_2 \geq 0$$

The graphical solution to this problem is shown in Figure 5.7. Clearly extreme points ③ and ④ are alternate optimal solutions. The final simplex tableau for this problem is shown below.

FIGURE 5.7
Graphical Solution to HighTech Industries Problem with Alternate Optimal Solutions

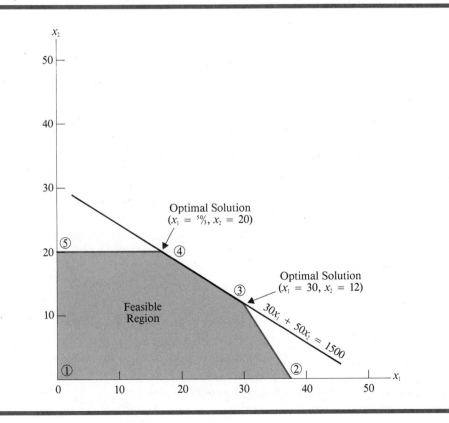

		x_1	x_2	s_1	s_2	s_3	
Basis	c_B	30	50	0	0	0	
x_2	50	0	1	0	1	0	20
s_3	0	0	0	$-8/3$	$25/3$	1	$200/3$
x_1	30	1	0	$1/3$	$-5/3$	0	$50/3$
	z_j	30	50	10	0	0	1500
	$c_j - z_j$	0	0	-10	0	0	

All values in the net evaluation row are less than or equal to zero, indicating that an optimal solution has been found. This solution is given by $x_1 = 50/3$, $x_2 = 20$, $s_1 = 0$, $s_2 = 0$, and $s_3 = 200/3$ and corresponds to extreme point 4 in Figure 5.7. The value of the objective function is 1500.

In looking at the net evaluation row in the optimal simplex tableau, we see that the $c_j - z_j$ value for nonbasic variable s_2 is equal to zero. This indicates that the linear program has alternate optima. In other words, since the net evaluation row entry for s_2 is zero, we can introduce s_2 into the basis without changing the value of the solution. The tableau obtained after introducing s_2 is given below.

		x_1	x_2	s_1	s_2	s_3	
Basis	c_B	30	50	0	0	0	
x_2	50	0	1	$8/25$	0	$-3/25$	12
s_2	0	0	0	$-8/25$	1	$3/25$	8
x_1	30	1	0	$-5/25$	0	$5/25$	30
	z_j	30	50	10	0	0	1500
	$c_j - z_j$	0	0	-10	0	0	

After introducing s_2 we have a different basic feasible solution: $x_1 = 30$, $x_2 = 12$, $s_1 = 0$, $s_2 = 8$, and $s_3 = 0$. However, this new solution is also optimal since $c_j - z_j \leq 0$ for all j. Another way to confirm that this solution is still optimal is to note that the value of the solution has remained equal to 1500. This solution corresponds to extreme point 3 in Figure 5.7.

In summary, we can recognize that a linear programming problem has alternate optima when using the graphical approach by observing that the objective function is parallel to one of the binding constraints. *When using the simplex method, we can recognize alternate optima if* $c_j - z_j$ *equals zero for one or more of the nonbasic variables in the final simplex tableau.*

Degeneracy

A linear program is said to be *degenerate* if one or more of the basic variables has a value of zero. Degeneracy does not cause any particular difficulties for the graphical solution procedure; however, degeneracy can theoretically cause difficulties when the simplex method is used to solve a linear programming problem.

To see how a degenerate linear program could occur, consider a change in the right-hand-side value of the assembly time constraint for the HighTech problem. For example, what if the number of hours available had been 175 instead of 150? The modified linear program is shown below.

$$\max \quad 50x_1 + 40x_2$$

s.t.

$$3x_1 + 5x_2 \leq 175 \quad \text{Assembly time increased to 175 hours}$$
$$1x_2 \leq 20 \quad \text{Portable display}$$
$$8x_1 + 5x_2 \leq 300 \quad \text{Warehouse space}$$
$$x_1, x_2 \geq 0$$

The simplex tableau after one iteration is presented below.

		x_1	x_2	s_1	s_2	s_3	
Basis	c_B	50	40	0	0	0	
s_1	0	0	$25/8$	1	0	$-3/8$	$125/2$
s_2	0	0	1	0	1	0	20
x_1	50	1	$5/8$	0	0	$1/8$	$75/2$
	z_j	50	$250/8$	0	0	$50/8$	1875
	$c_j - z_j$	0	$70/8$	0	0	$-50/8$	

The entries in the net evaluation row indicate that x_2 should enter the basis. By calculating the appropriate ratios to determine the pivot element, we obtain

$$\frac{\bar{b}_1}{\bar{a}_{12}} = \frac{125/2}{25/8} = 20$$

$$\frac{\bar{b}_2}{\bar{a}_{22}} = \frac{20}{1} = 20$$

$$\frac{\bar{b}_3}{\bar{a}_{32}} = \frac{75/2}{5/8} = 60$$

We see that there is a tie between the first and second rows. This is an indication that we will have a degenerate basic feasible solution at the next iteration. Recall that when there is a tie, we follow the convention of selecting the uppermost row as the pivot row. This means that s_1 will leave the basis. But from the tie for the minimum ratio we see that the basic variable in row 2, s_2, will also be driven to zero. Since it does not leave the basis, we will have a basic variable with a value of zero after performing this iteration. The simplex tableau after this iteration is as follows:

		x_1	x_2	s_1	s_2	s_3	
Basis	c_B	50	40	0	0	0	
x_2	40	0	1	$8/25$	0	$-3/25$	20
s_2	0	0	0	$-8/25$	1	$3/25$	0
x_1	50	1	0	$-5/25$	0	$5/25$	25
	z_j	50	40	$70/25$	0	$130/25$	2050
	$c_j - z_j$	0	0	$-70/25$	0	$-130/25$	

As expected, we have a basic feasible solution with one of the basic variables, s_2, equal to zero. Whenever we have a tie in the minimum $\bar{b}_i/\bar{a}_{ij}$ ratio, there will always be a basic variable equal to zero in the next tableau. Since we are at the optimal solution in the above case, we do not care that s_2 is in solution at a zero value. However, if degeneracy occurs at some iteration prior to reaching the optimal solution, it is theoretically possible for the simplex method to cycle; that is, the procedure could possibly alternate between the same set of nonoptimal basic feasible solutions and never reach the optimal solution. Cycling has not proved to be a significant difficulty in practice. Therefore we do not recommend introducing any special steps into the simplex method to eliminate the possibility of degeneracy occurring. If while performing the iterations of the simplex algorithm a tie occurs for the minimum $\bar{b}_i/\bar{a}_{ij}$ ratio, then we recommend simply selecting the upper row as the pivot row.

Summary

In Chapter 2 we showed how linear programming problems with two decision variables can be solved using the graphical method. In this chapter the simplex method was introduced as an algebraic procedure for solving linear programming problems. Although the simplex method can be used to solve small linear programs by hand calculations, as problems get larger, even the simplex method becomes too cumbersome for efficient hand computation. As a result we must utilize a computer if we want to solve large linear programs in any reasonable length of time. In Chapter 3 we showed how computer software packages can be used to solve linear programs. The computational procedures of these software packages are based on the simplex method.

We described how developing the tableau form of a linear program is a necessary step in the simplex solution procedure. This required learning how to convert greater-than-or-equal-to constraints, equality constraints, and constraints with negative right-hand-side values into the form necessary to write a linear program in tableau form.

For linear programs with greater-than-or-equal-to constraints and/or equality constraints, artificial variables are used in order to obtain tableau form. An objective function coefficient of $-M$ where M is a very large number, is assigned to each artificial variable. If there is a feasible solution to the real-world problem, all artificial variables will be driven out of solution before the simplex method reaches its stopping criterion. The iterations required to remove the artificial variables from solution constitute what is called phase I of the simplex method.

Two techniques were mentioned for solving minimization problems. The first approach involved changing the rule for introducing a variable into solution and changing the stopping criterion. The second approach involved multiplying the objective function by -1 to obtain an equivalent maximization problem. With this change any minimization problem can be solved using the steps required for a maximization problem.

As a review of the material in this chapter we now present a detailed step-by-step procedure for solving linear programs using the simplex method.

Step 1   Formulate a linear programming model of the problem.
Step 2   Define an equivalent linear program by performing the following operations.
      a. Multiply each constraint with a negative right-hand side value by -1 and change the direction of the constraint inequality;

b. For a minimization problem convert the problem to an equivalent maximization problem by multiplying the objective function by -1.

Step 3 Set up the standard-form representation of the linear program by adding appropriate slack and surplus variables.

Step 4 Set up the tableau-form representation of the linear program in order to obtain an initial basic feasible solution. All linear programs must be put in this form before the initial simplex tableau can be obtained.

Step 5 Set up the initial simplex tableau to keep track of the calculations required by the simplex method.

Step 6 Choose the nonbasic variable with the largest $c_j - z_j$ to bring into the basis.

Step 7 Choose as the pivot row that row with the smallest ratio of $\bar{b}_i/\bar{a}_{ij}$ for $\bar{a}_{ij} > 0$. This ratio is used to determine which variable will leave the basis when variable j enters the basis. This ratio also indicates how many units of variable j can be introduced into solution before the basic variable in the ith row equals zero.

Step 8 Perform the necessary elementary row operations to convert the column for the incoming variable to a unit column. Once these row operations have been performed, read the values of the basic variables from the $\bar{b}$ column of the tableau.

Step 9 Test for optimality. If $c_j - z_j \leq 0$ for all columns, we have the optimal solution. If not, return to step 6.

In Section 5.9 we discussed how the special cases of infeasibility, unboundedness, alternate optima, and degeneracy can occur when solving linear programming problems with the simplex method.

Glossary

Simplex method An algebraic procedure for solving linear programming problems. The simplex method uses elementary row operations to iterate from one basic feasible solution (extreme point) to another, until the optimal solution is reached.

Basic solution Given a linear program in standard form, with n variables and m constraints, a basic solution is obtained by setting $n - m$ of the variables equal to zero and solving the constraint equations for the values of the other m variables. If a unique solution exists, it is a basic solution.

Basic feasible solution A basic solution that is also feasible; that is, it satisfies the nonnegativity constraints. A basic feasible solution corresponds to an extreme point.

Elementary row operations Operations that may be performed on a system of simultaneous equations without changing the solution to the system of equations.

Tableau form The form in which a linear program must be written before setting up the initial simplex tableau. When a linear program is written in this form, its A matrix contains m unit columns corresponding to the basic variables, and the values of these basic variables are given by the values in the b column. A further requirement is that the entries in the b column be greater than or equal to zero.

Simplex tableau A table used to keep track of the calculations made when the simplex method is employed.

Unit vector or unit column A vector or column of a matrix, which has a zero in every position except one. In the nonzero position there is a 1. There is a unit column in the simplex tableau for each basic variable.

Net evaluation row   The row in the simplex tableau that contains the value of $c_j - z_j$ for every variable (column).

Current solution   When carrying out the simplex method, the current solution refers to the current basic feasible solution (extreme point).

Basis   The set of variables that are not restricted to equal zero in the current basic solution. The variables that make up the basis are termed basic variables, and the remaining variables are called nonbasic variables.

Iteration   An iteration of the simplex method consists of the sequence of steps (row operations) performed in moving from one basic feasible solution to another.

Pivot column   The column in the simplex tableau corresponding to the nonbasic variable that is about to be introduced into solution.

Pivot row   The row in the simplex tableau corresponding to the basic variable that will leave the solution.

Pivot element   The element of the simplex tableau that is in both the pivot row and the pivot column.

Artificial variable   A variable that has no physical meaning in terms of the original linear programming problem, but serves merely to enable a basic feasible solution to be created for starting the simplex method. Artificial variables are assigned an objective function coefficient of $-M$, where M is a very large number.

Phase I   When artificial variables are present in the initial simplex tableau, phase I refers to the iterations of the simplex method that are used to drive the artificial variables out of solution. At the end of phase I the basic feasible solution in the simplex tableau is also feasible for the real-world problem.

Degeneracy   When one or more of the basic variables has a value of zero.

Problems

1. Use elementary row operations to solve the following system of linear equations (that is, what values of x_1 and x_2 satisfy both equations?):

$$6x_1 + 3x_2 = 33$$
$$10x_1 - 2x_2 = 6$$

2. Use elementary row operations to solve the following system of linear equations (that is, what values of x_1, x_2, and x_3 satisfy all three equations?):

$$1x_1 + 3x_2 - 1x_3 = 4$$
$$2x_1 + 4x_2 + 2x_3 = 22$$
$$5x_1 - 2x_2 + 1x_3 = 27$$

3. Consider the following linear program:

$$\max \quad 5x_1 + 9x_2$$

s.t.

$$\tfrac{1}{2}x_1 + 1x_2 \leq 8$$
$$1x_1 + 1x_2 \geq 10$$
$$\tfrac{1}{4}x_1 + \tfrac{3}{2}x_2 \geq 6$$
$$x_1, x_2 \geq 0$$

a. Write the problem in standard form.
b. How many variables will be set equal to zero in a basic solution for this problem? Explain.
c. Use elementary row operations to find the basic solution that corresponds to s_1 and s_2 equal to zero.
d. Use elementary row operations to find the basic solution that corresponds to x_1 and s_3 equal to zero.
e. Are your solutions for part (c) and/or (d) basic feasible solutions? Extreme-point solutions? Explain.
f. Use the graphical approach to determine the solutions found in parts (c) and (d). Do the graphical results agree with your answer to part (e)? Explain.

4. The following partial initial simplex tableau is given:

Basis	c_B	x_1	x_2	x_3	s_1	s_2	s_3	
		5	20	25	0	0	0	
		2	1	0	1	0	0	40
		0	2	1	0	1	0	30
		3	0	$-\frac{1}{2}$	0	0	1	15
z_j								
$c_j - z_j$								

a. Complete the initial tableau.
b. Write the problem in its tableau form.
c. What is the initial basis? Does this correspond to the origin? Explain.
d. What is the value of the objective function at this initial solution?
e. For the next iteration, what variable should enter the basis and what variable should leave the basis?
f. How many units of the entering variable will be in the next solution? Before making this first iteration, what should be the value of the objective function after the first iteration?
g. Find the optimal solution using the simplex method.

5. Solve the following linear program using the graphical approach:

$$\max \quad 4x_1 + 5x_2$$
$$\text{s.t.}$$
$$2x_1 + 2x_2 \leq 20$$
$$3x_1 + 7x_2 \leq 42$$
$$x_1, x_2 \geq 0$$

Put the linear program in tableau form and solve using the simplex method. Show the sequence of extreme points generated by the simplex method.

6. Explain in your own words why the tableau form and the standard form are the same for problems with less-than-or-equal-to constraints and nonnegative b_i's.

7. Solve the Ryland Farm problem (2.30) using the simplex method. Locate the solution found at each iteration on the graph of the feasible region.

8. Recall the Par, Inc. problem introduced in Section 2.1 The complete mathematical model for this problem, originally presented in Section 2.4, is restated below:

$$\begin{array}{llll}
\max & 10x_1 & + 9x_2 \\
\text{s.t.} \\
& \tfrac{7}{10}x_1 & + 1x_2 \leq 630 & \text{Cutting and dyeing} \\
& \tfrac{1}{2}x_1 & + \tfrac{5}{6}x_2 \leq 600 & \text{Sewing} \\
& 1x_1 & + \tfrac{2}{3}x_2 \leq 708 & \text{Finishing} \\
& \tfrac{1}{10}x_1 & + \tfrac{1}{4}x_2 \leq 135 & \text{Inspection and packaging} \\
& x_1, x_2 \geq 0
\end{array}$$

where

$$x_1 = \text{number of standard bags produced}$$
$$x_2 = \text{number of deluxe bags produced}$$

a. Use the simplex method to determine how many bags of each model Par should manufacture?

b. What is the profit Par can earn with the above production quantities?

c. How many hours of production time will be scheduled for each operation?

d. What is the slack time in each operation?

9. Solve the RMC problem (2.31) using the simplex method. At each iteration locate the basic feasible solution found by the simplex method on the graph of the feasible region.

10. Solve the following linear program:

$$\begin{array}{llllll}
\max & 2.5x_1 & + & 5x_2 & + & 1x_3 & + & 1x_4 \\
\text{s.t.} \\
& 1x_1 & + & 1.4x_2 & + & 0.2x_3 & + & 0.8x_4 & \leq 1600 \\
& 2x_1 & + & 2x_2 & + & 1.6x_3 & + & 1x_4 & \leq 1300 \\
& 1.2x_1 & + & 1x_2 & + & 1x_3 & + & 1.2x_4 & \leq 960 \\
& x_1, x_2, x_3, x_4 \geq 0
\end{array}$$

11. Solve the following linear program using both the graphical and the simplex methods:

$$\begin{array}{lll}
\max & 2x_1 & + 8x_2 \\
\text{s.t.} \\
& 3x_1 & + 9x_2 \leq 45 \\
& 2x_1 & + 1x_2 \geq 12 \\
& x_1, x_2 \geq 0
\end{array}$$

Show graphically how the simplex method moves from one basic feasible solution to another. Find the coordinates of all extreme points of the feasible region.

12. How many basic solutions are there to a linear program that has seven variables and four constraints when written in standard form?

13. Explain in your own words why, when we are trying to determine which basic variable to eliminate at a particular iteration, we consider only the $\bar{a}_{ij}$ that are strictly greater than zero.

14. Referring to problem 8, suppose that instead of introducing x_1 into the solution at the first iteration of the simplex method for the Par, Inc. problem, you had mistakenly introduced x_2.

a. Conduct the simplex calculations for the Par, Inc. problem and introduce x_2 into the basis at the first iteration. Then continue with the simplex method until an optimal solution has been reached.

b. Do we always have to introduce the variable into the solution that has the largest $c_j - z_j$ value?

c. Why does the criterion for introducing the variable into the solution use the largest $c_j - z_j$ value?

15. Suppose that we did not remove the basic variable with the smallest ratio of $\bar{b}_i/\bar{a}_{ij}$ at a particular iteration. What effect would this have on the simplex tableau for our next solution?

16. Suppose a company manufactures three products from two raw materials where

	Product A	Product B	Product C
Raw material I	7 lb	6 lb	3 lb
Raw material II	5 lb	4 lb	2 lb

If the company has available 100 pounds of material I and 200 pounds of material II, and if the profits for the three products are $20, $20, and $15, how much of each product should be produced in order to maximize profits?

17. Liva's Lumber, Inc. manufactures three types of plywood. The data below summarize the production hours per unit in each of three production operations and other data for the problem:

Plywood	Operations (hours)			Profit/
	I	II	III	Unit
Grade A	2	2	4	$40
Grade B	5	5	2	$30
Grade X	10	3	2	$20
Maximum time available	900	400	600	

How many units of each grade of lumber should be produced?

18. Ye Olde Cording Winery in Peoria, Ill., makes three kinds of authentic German wine: Heidelberg Sweet, Heidelberg Regular, and Deutschland Extra Dry. The raw materials, labor, and profit for a gallon of each of these wines are summarized below:

Wine	Grapes Grade A (bushels)	Grapes Grade B (bushels)	Sugar (pounds)	Labor (hours)	Profit/ Gallon
Heidelberg Sweet	1	1	2	2	$1.00
Heidelberg Regular	2	0	1	3	$1.20
Deutschland Extra Dry	0	2	0	1	$2.00

If the Winery has 150 bushels of grade A grapes, 150 bushels of grade B grapes, 80 pounds of sugar, and 225 labor-hours available during the next week, what product mix of wines will maximize the company's profit?

a. Solve by the simplex method.

b. Interpret all slack variables.

c. An increase in what resources could improve the company's profit?

19. Set up the tableau form for the following linear program (do not attempt to solve):

$$
\begin{aligned}
\max \quad & 4x_1 + 2x_2 - 3x_3 + 5x_4 \\
\text{s.t.} \quad & \\
& 2x_1 - 1x_2 + 1x_3 + 2x_4 \geq 50 \\
& 3x_1 \qquad\quad - 1x_3 + 2x_4 \leq 80 \\
& 1x_1 + 1x_2 \qquad\quad + 1x_4 = 60 \\
& x_1, x_2, x_3, x_4 \geq 0
\end{aligned}
$$

20. Set up the tableau form for the following linear program (do not attempt to solve):

$$
\begin{aligned}
\min \quad & 4x_1 + 5x_2 + 3x_3 \\
\text{s.t.} \quad & \\
& 4x_1 \qquad\quad + 2x_3 \geq 20 \\
& \qquad 1x_2 - 1x_3 \leq -8 \\
& 1x_1 - 2x_2 \qquad\quad = -5 \\
& 2x_1 + 1x_2 + 1x_3 \leq 12 \\
& x_1, x_2, x_3 \geq 0
\end{aligned}
$$

21. Solve the following linear program:

$$
\begin{aligned}
\min \quad & 3x_1 + 4x_2 + 8x_3 \\
\text{s.t.} \quad & \\
& 4x_1 + 2x_2 \qquad\quad \geq 12 \\
& \qquad 4x_2 + 8x_3 \geq 16 \\
& x_1, x_2, x_3 \geq 0
\end{aligned}
$$

22. Solve the following linear program:

$$
\begin{aligned}
\min \quad & 4x_1 + 2x_2 + 3x_3 \\
\text{s.t.} \quad & \\
& 1x_1 + 3x_2 \qquad\quad \geq 15 \\
& 1x_1 \qquad\quad + 2x_3 \geq 10 \\
& 2x_1 + 1x_2 \qquad\quad \geq 20 \\
& x_1, x_2, x_3 \geq 0
\end{aligned}
$$

23. Captain John's Yachts, Inc., located in Fort Lauderdale, Fla., rents three types of ocean-going boats: sailboats, cabin cruisers, and Captain John's favorite, the luxury yachts. Captain John advertises his boats with his famous "you rent—we pilot" slogan, which means that the company supplies the captain and crew for each rented boat. Each rented boat, of course, has one captain, but the crew sizes (that is, deck hands, galley, and so on) differ. The crew requirements, in addition to a captain, are one for sailboats, two for cabin cruisers, and three for yachts. Ten employees are captains, and an additional 18 employees qualify for the crew positions. Currently Captain John has rental requests for all of his boats: four sailboats, eight cabin cruisers, and three luxury yachts. If Captain John's daily profit is $50 for sailboats, $70 for cruisers, and $100 for luxury yachts, how many boats of each type should he rent?

24. The Our-Bags-Don't-Break (OBDB) plastic bag company manufactures three plastic refuse bags for home use: a 20-gallon garbage bag, a 30-gallon garbage bag, and a 33-gallon leaf and grass bag. Using purchased plastic material, three operations are required to produce each end product: cutting, sealing, and packaging. The production time required to process each type of bag in every operation, as well as the maximum production time available for each operation, are shown below (note that the production time figures in this table are per box of each type of bag):

| | Production Time (seconds/box) | | |
Type of Bag	Cutting	Sealing	Packaging
20 gallons	2	2	3
30 gallons	3	2	4
33 gallons	3	3	5
Time available	2 hours	3 hours	4 hours

If OBDB makes a profit of $0.10 for each box of 20-gallon bags produced, $0.15 for each box of 30-gallon bags, and $0.20 for each box of 33-gallon bags, what is the optimal product mix?

25. Kirkman Brothers ice cream parlors sell three different flavors of Dairy Sweet ice milk: chocolate, vanilla, and banana. Due to extremely hot weather and a high demand for its products, Kirkman has run short of its supply of ingredients: milk, sugar, and cream. Hence Kirkman will not be able to fill all the orders received from its retail outlets, the ice cream parlors. Due to these circumstances, Kirkman has decided to make the best amounts of the three flavors given the constraints on supply of the basic ingredients. The company will then ration the ice milk to the retail outlets.

Kirkman has collected the following data on profitability of the various flavors, availability of supplies, and amounts required for each flavor.

| | | | Usage/Gallon | |
Flavor	Profit/ Gallon	Milk (gallons)	Sugar (pounds)	Cream (gallons)
Chocolate	$1.00	0.45	0.50	0.10
Vanilla	$0.90	0.50	0.40	0.15
Banana	$0.95	0.40	0.40	0.20
Maximum available		200	150	60

Determine the optimal product mix for Kirkman Brothers. What additional resources should be used?

26. Uforia Corporation sells two different brands of perfume: Incentive and Temptation No. 1. Uforia sells exclusively through department stores and employs a three-person sales staff to call on its customers. The amount of sales time necessary for each sales representative to sell one case of each product varies with experience and ability. Data on the average time for each of Uforia's three sales reps is presented below.

Salesperson	Average Sales Time per Case (minutes)	
	Incentive	Temptation No. 1
John	10	15
Brenda	15	10
Red	12	6

Each sales representative spends approximately 80 hours per month in the actual selling of these two products. Cases of Incentive and Temptation No. 1 sell at profits of $30 and $25, respectively. How many cases of each perfume should each person sell during the next month in order to maximize the firm's profits? (*Hint*: Let x_1 = number of cases of Incentive sold by John, x_2 = number of cases of Temptation No. 1 sold by John, x_3 = number of cases of Incentive sold by Brenda, and so on.)

27. Recall the RMC problem (Chapter 2, problem 31). Letting

$$x_1 = \text{tons of fuel additive produced}$$
$$x_2 = \text{tons of solvent base produced}$$

leads to the following formulation of the RMC problem:

$$\max \quad 40x_1 + 30x_2$$
$$\text{s.t.}$$
$$\tfrac{2}{5}x_1 + \tfrac{1}{2}x_2 \leq 20 \quad \text{Material 1}$$
$$\tfrac{1}{5}x_2 \leq 5 \quad \text{Material 2}$$
$$\tfrac{3}{5}x_1 + \tfrac{3}{10}x_2 \leq 21 \quad \text{Material 3}$$
$$x_1, x_2 \geq 0$$

Suppose management required that at least 10 tons of each product be produced. Modify the above formulation, as appropriate, and solve using the simplex method.

28. Catalina Yachts, Inc. is a builder of cruising sailboats. They manufacture three models of sailboats: the C-32, the C-40, and the C-48. The company, because of its excellent reputation, is in the position of being able to sell all the boats it manufactures. Catalina is currently in the process of taking orders for the coming year. How many orders for each model should be accepted in order to maximize profits?

The manufacture of each model requires different amounts of time spent on each of three operations: molding, carpentry, and finishing. The number of days required to perform each of these activities on the three models is given below:

Model	Molding	Production Time (person-days) Carpentry	Finishing
C-32	3	5	4
C-40	5	12	5
C-48	10	18	8

Based on past experience, management expects the profit per boat to be $5000 on the C-32, $10,000 on the C-40, and $20,000 on the C-48.

Catalina currently has 40 people employed in manufacturing these sailboats: 10 in molding, 20 in carpentry, and 10 in finishing. On the average each employee works 240 days per year. The only other constraint is a management-imposed restriction on the number of C-48 models that may be sold. Because Catalina does not want the C-48 to become commonplace, it will not take orders for more than 20 of this model.

Note: In problems 29 to 34, we provide examples of linear programs that result in one or more of the following situations:

1. Optimal solution
2. Infeasible solution
3. Unbounded solution
4. Alternate optimal solution
5. Degenerate solution

For each linear program, determine the solution situation that exists and indicate how you identified each situation using the simplex method. For the problems with alternate optimal solutions, calculate at least two optimal solutions.

29. max $4x_1 + 8x_2$

    s.t.

$$2x_1 + 2x_2 \leq 10$$
$$-1x_1 + 1x_2 \geq 8$$
$$x_1, x_2 \geq 0$$

30. min $3x_1 + 3x_2$

    s.t.

$$2x_1 + 0.5x_2 \geq 10$$
$$2x_1 \geq 4$$
$$4x_1 + 4x_2 \geq 32$$
$$x_1, x_2 \geq 0$$

31. max $1x_1 + 1x_2$

s.t.

$$8x_1 + 6x_2 \geq 24$$
$$4x_1 + 6x_2 \geq -12$$
$$2x_2 \geq 4$$
$$x_1, x_2 \geq 0$$

32. max $2x_1 + 1x_2 + 1x_3$

s.t.

$$4x_1 + 2x_2 + 2x_3 \geq 4$$
$$2x_1 + 4x_2 \leq 20$$
$$4x_1 + 8x_2 + 2x_3 \leq 16$$
$$x_1, x_2, x_3 \geq 0$$

33. max $2x_1 + 4x_2$

s.t.

$$1x_1 + \tfrac{1}{2}x_2 \leq 10$$
$$1x_1 + 1x_2 = 12$$
$$1x_1 + \tfrac{3}{2}x_2 \leq 18$$
$$x_1, x_2 \geq 0$$

34. min $-4x_1 + 5x_2 + 5x_3$

s.t.

$$-1x_2 + 1x_3 \geq 2$$
$$-1x_1 + 1x_2 + 1x_3 \geq 1$$
$$1x_3 \leq -1$$
$$x_1, x_2, x_3 \geq 0$$

35. Supersport Footballs, Inc. manufactures three kinds of football: an All-Pro model, a College model, and a High School model. All three footballs require operations in the following departments: cutting and dyeing, sewing, and inspection and packaging. The production times and maximum production availabilities are shown below:

| | Production Time (minutes) | | |
Model	Cutting and Dyeing	Sewing	Inspection and Packaging
All-Pro	12	15	3
College	10	15	4
High school	8	12	2
Time available	300 hours	200 hours	100 hours

Current orders indicate that at least 1000 all-pro footballs must be manufactured.

a. If Supersport realizes a profit of $3 for each All-Pro model, $5 for each College model, and $4 for each High School model, how many footballs of each type should be produced? What occurs in the solution of this problem? Why?

b. If Supersport can increase sewing time to 300 hours and inspection and packaging time to 150 hours by using overtime, what is your recommendation?

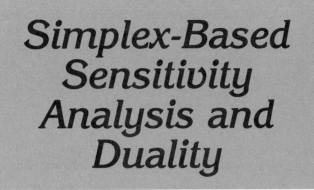

Simplex-Based Sensitivity Analysis and Duality

In Chapter 3 we defined sensitivity analysis as the study of how the optimal solution and the value of the optimal solution to a linear program change, given changes in the various coefficients of the problem. First we showed how graphical sensitivity analysis can be performed for linear programs involving two decision variables; then, as part of the discussion of the computer solution of linear programs, we showed how sensitivity analysis can be performed with the help of computer output. In this chapter we discuss how the sensitivity analysis information contained in the computer solution of linear programs is developed. As we will show, the final simplex tableau contains the information that is used to compute the shadow and/or dual prices, as well as ranges for the objective function coefficients and ranges for the right-hand-side values. The topic of duality is also introduced. We will see that associated with every linear programming problem is a dual problem that has an interesting economic interpretation.

6.1 SENSITIVITY ANALYSIS WITH THE SIMPLEX TABLEAU

The usual sensitivity analysis for linear programs involves computing ranges for the objective function coefficients and the right-side values, as well as shadow and/or dual prices.

Objective Function Coefficients

Sensitivity analysis for an objective function coefficient involves placing a range on the coefficient's value. We call this range the *range of optimality*. As long as the actual value of the objective function coefficient is within the range of optimality, *the current basic feasible solution will remain optimal*. Thus for a nonbasic variable the range of optimality defines the possible objective function coefficient values for which that variable will remain nonbasic. In contrast, the range of optimality for a basic variable defines the objective function coefficient values for which that variable will remain basic, and hence part of the current optimal basic feasible solution.

In computing the range of optimality for an objective function coefficient, all other coefficients in the problem are assumed to remain at their original values; in other words, *only one coefficient is allowed to change at a time*. To illustrate the process of computing ranges for objective function coefficients, recall the HighTech linear programming problem introduced in Chapter 5. The linear program that we developed for this problem is restated below.

$$\max \quad 50x_1 + 40x_2$$

s.t.

$$\begin{array}{rll} 3x_1 + 5x_2 \leq 150 & \text{Assembly time} \\ 1x_2 \leq 20 & \text{Portable display} \\ 8x_1 + 5x_2 \leq 300 & \text{Warehouse space} \\ x_1, x_2 \geq 0 \end{array}$$

where

$$x_1 = \text{number of units of the Deskpro assembled}$$
$$x_2 = \text{number of units of the Portable assembled}$$

The final simplex tableau for the HighTech problem is reproduced below.

Basis	c_B	x_1	x_2	s_1	s_2	s_3	
		50	40	0	0	0	
x_2	40	0	1	$8/25$	0	$-3/25$	12
s_2	0	0	0	$-8/25$	1	$3/25$	8
x_1	50	1	0	$-5/25$	0	$5/25$	30
z_j		50	40	$14/5$	0	$26/5$	1980
$c_j - z_j$		0	0	$-14/5$	0	$-26/5$	

Recall that when the simplex method is used to solve a linear program, an optimal solution is recognized when all entries in the net evaluation row ($c_j - z_j$) are ≤ 0. Since the above simplex tableau satisfies this criterion, the solution shown is optimal. However, if a change in one of the objective function coefficients were to cause one or more of the $c_j - z_j$ values to become positive, then the current solution would no longer be optimal; in such a case one or more additional simplex iterations would be necessary to find the new optimal solution. *Thus we conclude that the range of optimality for an objective function coefficient is determined by those coefficient values that maintain*

$$c_j - z_j \leq 0 \tag{6.1}$$

for all values of j.

To illustrate how the range of optimality is determined, we will compute the range of optimality for c_1, the profit per unit of the Deskpro. Using c_1 (instead of 50) as the objective function coefficient of x_1, the revised final simplex tableau is as follows:

Basis	c_B	x_1 c_1	x_2 40	s_1 0	s_2 0	s_3 0	
x_2	40	0	1	$8/25$	0	$-3/25$	12
s_2	0	0	0	$-8/25$	1	$3/25$	8
x_1	c_1	1	0	$-5/25$	0	$5/25$	30
z_j		c_1	40	$\dfrac{64-c_1}{5}$	0	$\dfrac{c_1-24}{5}$	$480 + 30c_1$
$c_j - z_j$		0	0	$\dfrac{c_1-64}{5}$	0	$\dfrac{24-c_1}{5}$	

Since the $c_j - z_j$ entries for the basic variables are all still zero, the current solution will remain optimal as long as the value of c_1 results in $c_j - z_j \leq 0$ for the two nonbasic variables s_1 and s_3. Hence we must have

$$\frac{c_1 - 64}{5} \leq 0$$

and

$$\frac{24 - c_1}{5} \leq 0$$

Using the first inequality we obtain

$$c_1 - 64 \leq 0$$

or

$$c_1 \leq 64 \tag{6.2}$$

Similarly, from the second inequality we see that

$$24 - c_1 \leq 0$$

or

$$24 \leq c_1 \tag{6.3}$$

Since c_1 must satisfy both (6.2) and (6.3), the range of optimality for c_1 is as given by

$$24 \leq c_1 \leq 64 \tag{6.4}$$

To see how management of HighTech can make use of the above sensitivity analysis information, suppose an increase in material costs reduces the profit contribution per unit for the Deskpro to \$30. The range of optimality indicates that the current solution ($x_1 =$

30, $x_2 = 12$, $s_1 = 0$, $s_2 = 8$, $s_3 = 0$) is still optimal. To verify this, let us recompute the final simplex tableau after reducing the value of c_1 to 30.

Basis	c_B	x_1 x_2 30 40	s_1 0	s_2 0	s_3 0	
x_2	40	0 1	$8/25$	0	$-3/25$	12
s_2	0	0 0	$-8/25$	1	$3/25$	8
x_1	30	1 0	$-5/25$	0	$5/25$	30
z_j		30 40	$34/5$	0	$6/5$	1380
$c_j - z_j$		0 0	$-34/5$	0	$-6/5$	

Since $c_j - z_j \leq 0$ for all variables, the original solution is still optimal. That is, the optimal solution with $c_1 = 30$ is the same as the optimal solution with $c_1 = 50$. Note, however, that the decrease in profit contribution per unit of the Deskpro has caused a reduction in total profit from \$1980 to \$1380.

What if the profit contribution per unit were reduced even further—say to \$20? Referring to the range of optimality for c_1 given by (6.4), we see that $c_1 = 20$ is outside the range; thus we know that a change this large will cause a new basis to be optimal. To verify this, consider modifying the above final simplex tableau by replacing c_1 by 20 (instead of 30).

Basis	c_B	x_1 x_2 20 40	s_1 0	s_2 0	s_3 0	
x_2	40	0 1	$8/25$	0	$-3/25$	12
s_2	0	0 0	$-8/25$	1	$3/25$	8
x_1	20	1 0	$-5/25$	0	$5/25$	30
z_j		20 40	$44/5$	0	$-4/5$	1080
$c_j - z_j$		0 0	$-44/5$	0	$4/5$	

As expected the current solution ($x_1 = 30$, $x_2 = 12$, $s_1 = 0$, $s_2 = 8$, and $s_3 = 0$) is no longer optimal since the entry in the s_3 column of the net evaluation row is greater than zero. This implies that at least one more simplex iteration must be performed to reach the optimal solution. You should continue to perform the simplex iterations (by introducing s_3) on the above tableau to verify that the new optimal solution will require the production of $16\frac{2}{3}$ units of the Deskpro and 20 units of the Portable.

The procedure we used to compute the range of optimality for c_1 is the general procedure used for any basic variable. Compute inequality (6.1) for each nonbasic variable; the smallest upper bound is the upper limit and the largest lower bound is the lower limit of the range. The procedure for computing the range of optimality for nonbasic variables is even easier, since a change in the objective function coefficient for a nonbasic variable causes only one $c_j - z_j$ entry to change in the final simplex tableau. To illustrate the approach we show below the final simplex tableau for the original HighTech problem after replacing 0, the objective function coefficient for s_1, with the coefficient c_{s_1}.

Basis	c_B	x_1	x_2	s_1	s_2	s_3	
		50	40	c_{s_1}	0	0	
x_2	40	0	1	$8/25$	0	$-3/25$	12
s_2	0	0	0	$-8/25$	1	$3/25$	8
x_1	50	1	0	$-5/25$	0	$5/25$	30
	z_j	50	40	$14/5$	0	$26/5$	1980
	$c_j - z_j$	0	0	$c_{s_1} - 14/5$	0	$-26/5$	

Note that the only changes in the tableau are in the s_1 column. In applying inequality (6.1) to compute the range of optimality, we get

$$c_{s_1} - 14/5 \leq 0$$

and hence

$$c_{s_1} \leq 14/5$$

Therefore as long as the objective function coefficient for s_1 is less than or equal to $14/5$, the current solution will be optimal. Since there is no lower bound on how much the coefficient may be decreased, we write the range of optimality for c_{s_1} as

$$-\infty < c_{s_1} \leq 14/5$$

The same approach works for all nonbasic variables. In a maximization problem there is no lower limit on the range of optimality, and the upper limit is given by z_j. Thus the range of optimality for the objective function coefficient of any nonbasic variable is given by

$$-\infty < c_j \leq z_j \tag{6.5}$$

Since s_1 is a slack variable in the HighTech problem, its objective function coefficient is not subject to variability. That is, the objective function coefficient for s_1 will always be zero, and hence s_1 would never be brought into the solution. But, as we will see in the next section, the upper limit on the range for a nonbasic slack variable provides the shadow price for the corresponding constraint.

Let us summarize the steps necessary to compute the range of optimality for objective function coefficients. In stating the steps we assume that it is desired to compute the range of optimality for c_k, the coefficient of x_k, in a maximization problem. Keep in mind that x_k in this context may refer to one of the original decision variables, a slack variable, or a surplus variable.

Steps to Compute the Range of Optimality

Step 1. Replace the numerical value of the objective function coefficient for x_k with c_k everywhere it appears in the final simplex tableau.

Step 2. If variable x_k is a basic variable, recompute $c_j - z_j$ for each nonbasic variable; if x_k is a nonbasic variable, it is only necessary to recompute $c_k - z_k$.

Step 3. Requiring that $c_j - z_j \leq 0$, solve each inequality for any upper or lower bounds on c_k. If there are two or more upper bounds on c_k, the smaller of these is the upper bound on the range of optimality. If there are two or more lower bounds, the largest of these is the lower bound on the range of optimality.

Step 4. If the original problem is a minimization problem that was converted to a maximization problem in order to apply the simplex method, multiply the inequalities obtained in step 3 by -1 and change the direction of the inequalities to obtain the ranges of optimality for the original minimization problem.

By using the range of optimality to determine whether a change in an objective function coefficient is large enough to cause a change in the optimal solution, we can often avoid the process of formulating and solving a modified linear programming problem.

Right-Hand-Side Values

In many linear programming problems we can interpret the right-hand-side values (the b_i's) as the resources available. For instance, in the HighTech Industries problem the right-hand side of constraint 1 represents the available assembly time, the right-hand side of constraint 2 represents the number of Portable display units available, and the right-hand side of constraint 3 represents the available warehouse space. Shadow prices provide information on the value of additional resources; the ranges over which these shadow prices are valid are given by the ranges for the right-hand-side values.

Shadow Prices. In Chapter 3 we stated that the change in value of the objective function resulting from a one-unit increase in a constraint's right-hand-side value is called a *shadow price*.[1] When the simplex method is used to solve a linear programming problem, the values of the shadow prices are easy to obtain. They are found in the z_j row of the final simplex tableau. To illustrate this point, the final simplex tableau for the HighTech problem is again reproduced.

Basis	c_B	x_1 50	x_2 40	s_1 0	s_2 0	s_3 0	
x_2	40	0	1	$8/25$	0	$-3/25$	12
s_2	0	0	0	$-8/25$	1	$3/25$	8
x_1	50	1	0	$-5/25$	0	$5/25$	30
z_j		50	40	$14/5$	0	$26/5$	1980
$c_j - z_j$		0	0	$-14/5$	0	$-26/5$	

[1]The dual prices provided by LINDO are closely related (see Chapter 3). The dual price gives the improvement in the objective function for a one-unit increase in the right-hand side. For maximization problems the shadow and dual prices are the same; for minimization problems the dual price is the negative of the shadow price.

The z_j values for the three slack variables are 14/5, 0, and 26/5, respectively. Thus the shadow price for the assembly time constraint is $14/5 = 2.80$, the shadow price for the Portable display constraint is 0.00, and the shadow price for the warehouse space constraint is $26/5 = 5.20$. We see that obtaining more warehouse space will have the biggest positive impact on HighTech's profit.

To see why the z_j values for the slack variables in the final simplex tableau are the shadow prices, let us first consider the case for slack variables that are part of the optimal basic feasible solution. Each of these slack variables will have a z_j value of zero, implying a shadow price of zero for the corresponding constraint. For example, consider slack variable s_2, a basic variable in the HighTech problem. This variable was added to the constraint $1x_2 \leq 20$ (Portable display) in order to set up the standard-form representation of the problem. With s_2 added to the left-hand side, we obtained

$$1x_2 + 1s_2 = 20$$

Algebraically we see that s_2 is the difference between the number of Portable display units available and the number of those actually used in the optimal solution.

Since $s_2 = 8$ in the optimal solution, HighTech will have eight Portable display units unused. Consequently how much would management of HighTech Industries be willing to pay to obtain additional Portable display units? Clearly the answer is nothing, since at the optimal solution HighTech has an excess of this particular component. Additional amounts of this resource are of no value to the company, and consequently the shadow price for this constraint is zero. In general, if a slack variable is a basic variable in the optimal solution, the value of z_j—and hence the shadow price of the corresponding resource—is zero.

Consider the nonbasic slack variables; for example, s_1. In the previous subsection we determined that the current solution will remain optimal as long as the objective function coefficient for s_1 (denoted c_{s_1}) stays in the following range:

$$-\infty < c_{s_1} \leq \text{14/5}$$

That is, $s_1 = 0$ as long as the objective function coefficient for s_1 is less than or equal to 14/5. Thus HighTech would not allow any slack to occur in the first constraint unless it is worth more than $14/5 = 2.80$ per hour to do so. In other words, HighTech should use all of its assembly time unless it is paid more than \$2.80 per hour not to use it. We can conclude then that \$2.80 is the value to HighTech of 1 hour of assembly time used in the production of Deskpro and Portable computers. Thus if additional time can be obtained, HighTech should be willing to pay up to \$2.80 per hour for it.

A similar interpretation can be given to the z_j value for each of the nonbasic slack variables. That is, z_j is the value of one additional unit of the resource in the row corresponding to that slack variable.

With a greater-than-or-equal-to constraint, the value of the shadow price will be less than or equal to zero because a one-unit increase in the value of the right-hand side cannot be helpful; it makes it more difficult to satisfy the constraint. As a result, for a maximization problem the optimal value of the objective function can be expected to decrease when the right-hand side of a greater-than-or-equal-to constraint is increased. The shadow price gives the amount of the expected change—a negative number, since we expect a decrease. As a result, the shadow price for a greater-than-or-equal-to constraint is given by the negative of the z_j entry for the corresponding surplus variable in the optimal simplex tableau.

Finally, it is possible to compute shadow prices for equality constraints. They are given by the z_j values for the corresponding artificial variables. We will not develop this case in detail here, since we have recommended dropping each artificial variable column from the simplex tableau as soon as the corresponding artificial variable leaves the basis.

To summarize, when the simplex method is used to solve a linear programming problem, the shadow prices for the constraints are contained in the final simplex tableau. The following table summarizes the method for determining the shadow prices for the various constraint types in a maximization problem solved by the simplex method.

Constraint Type	Shadow Price Given by
≤	z_j value for the slack variable associated with the constraint
≥	Negative of the z_j value for the surplus variable associated with the constraint
=	z_j value for the artificial variable associated with the constraint

Recall that we convert a minimization problem to a maximization problem by multiplying the objective function by -1 before using the simplex method. Therefore, for minimization problems we need to multiply the shadow prices computed from the simplex tableau for the equivalent maximization problem by -1 in order to determine the effect of a right-hand-side change on the original minimization problem.

Range of Feasibility.   As we have just seen, the z_j row in the final simplex tableau can be used to determine the shadow price and as a result predict the change in the value of the objective function corresponding to a unit change in a b_i. This interpretation is only valid, however, as long as the change in b_i is not large enough to make the current basic solution infeasible. Thus we will be interested in calculating a range of values over which a particular b_i can vary without any of the current basic variables becoming infeasible (i.e., less than zero). This range of values will be referred to as the *range of feasibility*.

To demonstrate the effect of changing a b_i, consider increasing the amount of assembly time available in the HighTech problem from 150 to 160 hours. Will the current basis still yield a feasible solution? If so, given the shadow price of $2.80 for the assembly time constraint, we can expect an increase in the value of the objective function of $10(2.80) = 28$. Shown below is the final simplex tableau corresponding to an increase in the assembly time of 10 hours.

Basis	c_B	x_1 50	x_2 40	s_1 0	s_2 0	s_3 0	
x_2	40	0	1	$8/25$	0	$-3/25$	15.2
s_2	0	0	0	$-8/25$	1	$3/25$	4.8
x_1	50	1	0	$-5/25$	0	$5/25$	28.0
z_j		50	40	$14/5$	0	$26/5$	2008
$c_j - z_j$		0	0	$-14/5$	0	$-26/5$	

The same basis, consisting of the basic variables x_2, s_2, and x_1, is feasible since all the basic variables are nonnegative. Note also that, just as we predicted, the value of the optimal solution has increased by 28 (from 1980 to 2008).

You may wonder whether we had to resolve the problem completely to find this new solution. The answer is no! The only changes in the final simplex tableau (as compared with the final simplex tableau with $b_1 = 150$) are the differences in the values of the basic variables and the value of the objective function. That is, only the last column of the simplex tableau has changed. The entries in this new last column of the simplex tableau were obtained by merely adding 10 times the first four entries in the s_1 column to the last column in the previous tableau:

$$\text{New solution} = \begin{bmatrix} 12 \\ 8 \\ 30 \\ 1980 \end{bmatrix} + 10 \begin{bmatrix} 8/25 \\ -8/25 \\ -5/25 \\ 14/5 \end{bmatrix} = \begin{bmatrix} 15.2 \\ 4.8 \\ 28.0 \\ 2008 \end{bmatrix}$$

Old solution, Change in b_1, s_1 column, New solution

Let us now consider why this procedure can be used to find the new solution. First recall that each of the coefficients in the s_1 column indicates the amount of decrease in the corresponding basic variable that would result from increasing s_1 by one unit. In other words, these coefficients tell us how many units each of the corresponding current basic variables will be driven out of solution if one unit of variable s_1 is brought into solution. Bringing one unit of s_1 into solution, however, is the same as reducing the availability of assembly time (decreasing b_1) by one unit; increasing b_1, the available assembly time, by one unit has just the opposite effect. Therefore, the entries in the s_1 column can also be interpreted as the changes in the values of the current basic variables corresponding to a one-unit increase in b_1.

The change in the value of the objective function corresponding to a one-unit increase in b_1 is given by the value of z_j in that column (the shadow price). In the foregoing case the availability of assembly time increased by 10 units; thus we multiplied the first four entries in the s_1 column by 10 to obtain the change in value of the solution.

How do we know when a change in b_1 is so large that the current basis will become infeasible? We shall first answer this question specifically for the HighTech Industries problem and then state the general procedure for less-than-or-equal-to constraints. The approach taken with greater-than-or-equal-to and equality constraints will then be discussed.

We begin by showing how to compute upper and lower bounds for the maximum amount that b_1 can be changed before the current optimal basis becomes infeasible. We have seen how to find the new basic feasible solution values given a 10-unit increase in b_1. In general, given a change in b_1 of Δb_1, the new values for the basic variables in the HighTech problem are given by

$$\begin{bmatrix} x_2 \\ s_2 \\ x_1 \end{bmatrix} = \begin{bmatrix} 12 \\ 8 \\ 30 \end{bmatrix} + \Delta b_1 \begin{bmatrix} 8/25 \\ -8/25 \\ -5/25 \end{bmatrix} = \begin{bmatrix} 12 + 8/25\ \Delta b_1 \\ 8 - 8/25\ \Delta b_1 \\ 30 - 5/25\ \Delta b_1 \end{bmatrix} \qquad (6.6)$$

As long as the new value of each basic variable remains nonnegative, the current basis will remain feasible and therefore optimal. We can keep the basic variables nonnegative by limiting the change in b_1 (that is, Δb_1) so that we satisfy each of the following conditions:

$$12 + 8/25\ \Delta b_1 \geq 0 \qquad (6.7)$$
$$8 - 8/25\ \Delta b_1 \geq 0 \qquad (6.8)$$
$$30 - 5/25\ \Delta b_1 \geq 0 \qquad (6.9)$$

Note that the left-hand sides of the above inequalities represent the new values of the basic variables after b_1 has been changed by Δb_1.

Solving for Δb_1 in inequalities (6.7), (6.8), and (6.9), we obtain

$$\Delta b_1 \geq (25/8)(-12) = -37.5$$
$$\Delta b_1 \leq (-25/8)(-8) = 25$$
$$\Delta b_1 \leq (-25/5)(-30) = 150$$

Since all three inequalities must be satisified, the most restrictive limits on b_1 must be satisfied in order for all the current basic variables to remain nonnegative. Therefore, Δb_1, must satisfy

$$-37.5 \leq \Delta b_1 \leq 25 \qquad (6.10)$$

The initial amount of assembly time available was 150 hours. Therefore, $b_1 = 150 + \Delta b_1$, where b_1 is the amount of assembly time available. We add 150 to each of the three terms in expression (6.10) to obtain

$$112.5 \leq 150 + \Delta b_1 \leq 175 \qquad (6.11)$$

Replacing $150 + \Delta b_1$ with b_1, we obtain the range of feasibility for b_1:

$$112.5 \leq b_1 \leq 175$$

This range of feasiblity for b_1 indicates that as long as the available assembly time is between 112.5 and 175 hours, the current optimal basis will remain feasible. This is why we call this range the range of feasibility.

Since the shadow price for b_1 (assembly time) is $^{14}/_5$, we know profit can be increased by \$2.80 by obtaining an additional hour of assembly time. Suppose then that we increase b_1 by 25; that is, we increase b_1 to the upper limit of its range of feasibility, 175. The profit will increase to \$1980 + (\$2.80)25 = \$2050, and the values of the optimal basic variables become

$$x_2 = 12 + 25\,(^8/_{25}) = 20$$
$$s_2 = \ \ 8 + 25\,(-^8/_{25}) = 0$$
$$x_1 = 30 + 25\,(-^5/_{25}) = 25$$

What has happened to the solution? The increased assembly time has caused a revision in the optimal production plan. HighTech should produce more of the Portable and less of the Deskpro. Overall the profit will be increased by (\$2.80)(25) = \$70. Note that although the optimal solution has changed, the basic variables that were optimal before are still optimal.

The procedure for determining the range of feasibility has been illustrated with the assembly time constraint. The procedure for calculating the range of feasibility for the right-hand side of any less-than-or-equal-to constraint is the same. The first step [paralleling equation (6.6)] for a general constraint i is to calculate the range of values for b_i that satisfy the inequalities shown below.

$$\begin{bmatrix} \bar{b}_1 \\ \bar{b}_2 \\ \cdot \\ \cdot \\ \cdot \\ \bar{b}_m \end{bmatrix} + \Delta b_i \begin{bmatrix} \bar{a}_{1j} \\ \bar{a}_{2j} \\ \cdot \\ \cdot \\ \cdot \\ \bar{a}_{mj} \end{bmatrix} \geq \begin{bmatrix} 0 \\ 0 \\ \cdot \\ \cdot \\ \cdot \\ 0 \end{bmatrix} \qquad (6.12)$$

Current solution (last column of the final simplex tableau) Column of the final simplex tableau corresponding to the slack variable associated with constraint i

The inequalities are used to identify lower and upper limits on Δb_i. The range of feasibility can then be established by the maximum of the lower limits and the minimum of the upper limits.

Similar arguments presented can be used to develop a procedure for determining the range of feasibility for the right-hand-side value of a greater-than-or-equal-to constraint. Essentially the procedure is the same, with the column corresponding to the surplus variable associated with the constraint playing the central role. For a general greater-than-or-equal-to constraint i, we first calculate the range of values for Δb_i that satisfy the inequalities shown in equation (6.13).

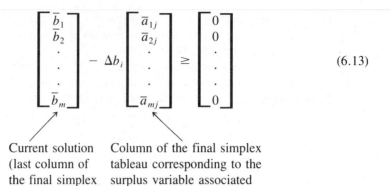

$$
\begin{bmatrix} \bar{b}_1 \\ \bar{b}_2 \\ \cdot \\ \cdot \\ \cdot \\ \bar{b}_m \end{bmatrix} - \Delta b_i \begin{bmatrix} \bar{a}_{1j} \\ \bar{a}_{2j} \\ \cdot \\ \cdot \\ \cdot \\ \bar{a}_{mj} \end{bmatrix} \geq \begin{bmatrix} 0 \\ 0 \\ \cdot \\ \cdot \\ \cdot \\ 0 \end{bmatrix}
\qquad (6.13)
$$

Current solution   Column of the final simplex
(last column of   tableau corresponding to the
the final simplex   surplus variable associated
tableau)   with constraint i

Once again, these inequalities establish lower and upper limits on Δb_i. Given these limits, the range of feasibility is easily determined.

A range of feasibility for the right-hand side of an equality constraint can also be computed. To do so for equality constraint i one could use the column of the final simplex tableau corresponding to the artificial variable associated with constraint i in equation (6.12). Since we have suggested dropping the artificial variable columns from the simplex tableau as soon as the artificial variable becomes nonbasic, these columns will not be available in the final tableau. Thus more involved calculations are required to compute a range of feasibility for equality constraints. Details may be found in more advanced texts.

As long as the change in a right-hand-side value is such that b_i stays within its range of feasibility, the same basis will remain feasible and optimal. Changes that force b_i outside its range of feasibility will force us to perform additional simplex iterations to find the new optimal solution consisting of a different set of basic variables. More advanced linear programming texts show how this can be done without completely re-solving the problem. In any case the calculation of the range of feasibility for each b_i is valuable management information and should be included as part of the management report on any linear programming project. The range of feasibility is typically made available as part of the computer solution to the problem.

Simultaneous Changes

By reviewing the procedures for developing the range of optimality and the range of feasibility, we note that only one coefficient at a time was permitted to vary. That is why our statements concerning changes within these ranges were made with the understanding that no other coefficients are permitted to change. However, sometimes we can make the same statements when either two or more objective function coefficients or two or more right-hand sides are varied simultaneously. When the simultaneous changes satisfy the 100 percent rule, the same statements are applicable. The 100 percent rule was explained in Chapter 3, but we will briefly review it here.

Let us call the amount a coefficient can be increased before reaching the upper limit of its range the allowable increase, and the amount a coefficient can be decreased before reaching the lower limit of its range the allowable decrease. Now suppose simultaneous changes are made in two, or more, objective function coefficients. For each coefficient changed, we compute the percentage of the allowable increase, or decrease, represented by the change. If the sum of the percentages for all changes does not exceed 100%, we say that the 100 percent rule is satisfied and that the simultaneous changes will not cause a change in the optimal solution. However, just as with a single objective function coefficient change, the value of the solution will change because of the change in the coefficients.

Similarly, if two or more changes in constraint right-hand side values are made, we again compute the percentage of allowable increase or decrease represented by each change. If the sum of the percentages for all changes does not exceed 100%, we say that the 100 percent rule is satisfied. The shadow prices are then valid for determining the change in value of the objective function associated with the right-hand-side changes.

6.2 DUALITY

Every linear programming problem has an associated linear programming problem called the *dual*. Referring to the original formulation of the linear programming problem as the *primal*, we will see how the primal can be converted into its corresponding dual. Then we will solve the dual linear programming problem and interpret the results. A fundamental property of the primal–dual relationship is that the optimal solution to either the primal or the dual problem also provides the optimal solution to the other. In cases where the primal and the dual problems differ in terms of computational difficulty, we can choose the easier problem to solve.

Let us return to the HighTech Industries problem. The original formulation—the primal—is as follows:

$$\max \quad 50x_1 + 40x_2$$

s.t.

$$
\begin{aligned}
3x_1 + 5x_2 &\leq 150 \quad \text{Assembly time} \\
1x_2 &\leq 20 \quad \text{Portable display} \\
8x_1 + 5x_2 &\leq 300 \quad \text{Warehouse space} \\
x_1, x_2 &\geq 0
\end{aligned}
$$

A maximization problem with all less-than-or-equal-to constraints and nonnegativity requirements for the decision variables is said to be in *canonical form*. For a maximization problem in canonical form, such as the HighTech Industries problem, the conversion to the associated dual linear program is relatively easy. Let us state the dual of the HighTech problem and then identify the steps taken to make the primal–dual conversion. The HighTech dual problem is as follows:

$$\min \quad 150u_1 + 20u_2 + 300u_3$$

s.t.

$$
\begin{aligned}
3u_1 \quad + \quad 8u_3 &\geq 50 \\
5u_1 + 1u_2 + \quad 5u_3 &\geq 40 \\
u_1, u_2, u_3 &\geq 0
\end{aligned}
$$

The variables u_1, u_2, and u_3 are referred to as dual variables.

With the above example in mind, we make the following general statements about the *dual of a maximization problem in canonical form*.

1. The dual is a minimization problem.
2. The dual has all greater-than-or-equal-to constraints.
3. When the primal has n decision variables ($n = 2$ in the HighTech problem), the dual will have n constraints. The first constraint of the dual is associated with variable x_1 in the primal, the second constraint in the dual is associated with variable x_2 in the primal, and so on.
4. When the primal has m constraints ($m = 3$ in the HighTech problem), the dual will have m decision variables. Dual variable u_1 is associated with the first primal constraint, dual variable u_2 is associated with the second primal constraint, and so on.
5. The right-hand sides of the primal constraints become the objective function coefficients in the dual.
6. The objective function coefficients of the primal become the right-hand sides of the dual constraints.
7. The constraint coefficients of the ith primal variable become the coefficients in the ith constraint of the dual.
8. Both the primal and the dual have nonnegativity restrictions for the variables.

The above eight statements are the general requirements that must be satisfied when converting a maximization problem in canonical form to its associated dual. While these requirements may seem cumbersome at first, practice with a few simple problems will show that the primal–dual conversion process is relatively easy to implement.

Since we have formulated the HighTech dual linear programming problem, let us now proceed to solve it. With three variables in the dual, we will use the simplex method. After subtracting surplus variables s_1 and s_2 to obtain the standard form, adding artificial variables a_1 and a_2 to obtain the tableau form, and multiplying the objective function by -1 in order to convert the dual problem to an equivalent maximization problem, we arrive at the following initial simplex tableau.

		u_1	u_2	u_3	s_1	s_2	a_1	a_2	
Basis	c_B	-150	-20	-300	0	0	$-M$	$-M$	
a_1	$-M$	3	0	8	-1	0	1	0	50
a_2	$-M$	5	1	5	0	-1	0	1	40
	z_j	$-8M$	$-M$	$-13M$	M	M	$-M$	$-M$	$-90M$
	$c_j - z_j$	$-150+8M$	$-20+M$	$-300+13M$	$-M$	$-M$	0	0	

At the first iteration u_3 is brought into the basis and a_1 is removed. The second tableau, with the a_1 column dropped, is shown below.

		u_1	u_2	u_3	s_1	s_2	a_2	
Basis	c_B	-150	-20	-300	0	0	$-M$	
u_3	-300	$3/8$	0	1	$-1/8$	0	0	$50/8$
a_2	$-M$	$25/8$	1	0	$5/8$	-1	1	$70/8$
	z_j	$\dfrac{-900-25M}{8}$	$-M$	-300	$\dfrac{300-5M}{8}$	M	$-M$	$\dfrac{-15{,}000-70M}{8}$
	$c_j - z_j$	$\dfrac{-300+25M}{8}$	$-20+M$	0	$\dfrac{-300+5M}{8}$	$-M$	0	

At the second iteration u_1 is brought into the basis and a_2 is removed. The third tableau, with the a_2 column removed, is:

Basis	c_B	u_1 -150	u_2 -20	u_3 -300	s_1 0	s_2 0	
u_3	-300	0	$-3/25$	1	$-5/25$	$3/25$	$26/5$
u_1	-150	1	$8/25$	0	$5/25$	$-8/25$	$14/5$
	z_j	-150	-12	-300	30	12	-1980
	$c_j - z_j$	0	-8	0	-30	-12	

Note that all of the artificial variables have now been driven out of the basis and that all the entries in the net evaluation row are less than or equal to zero. The optimal solution has been reached; it is $u_1 = 14/5$, $u_2 = 0$, $u_3 = 26/5$, $s_1 = 0$, and $s_2 = 0$. Since we have been maximizing the negative of the dual objective function, the value of the objective function for the optimal dual solution must be $-(-1980) = 1980$.

Shown below is the final simplex tableau for the original HighTech Industries problem.

Basis	c_B	x_1 50	x_2 40	s_1 0	s_2 0	s_3 0	
x_2	40	0	1	$8/25$	0	$-3/25$	12
s_2	0	0	0	$-8/25$	1	$3/25$	8
x_1	50	1	0	$-5/25$	0	$5/25$	30
	z_j	50	40	$14/5$	0	$26/5$	1980
	$c_j - z_j$	0	0	$-14/5$	0	$-26/5$	

The optimal solution to the primal problem is $x_1 = 30$, $x_2 = 12$, $s_1 = 0$, $s_2 = 8$, and $s_3 = 0$. The optimal value of the objective function is 1980.

What observation can we make about the relationship between the optimal value of the objective function in the primal and the optimal value in the dual for the HighTech problem? The optimal value of the objective function is the same (1980) for both. This relationship is true for all primal and dual linear programming problems and is stated as property 1.

Property 1

If the dual problem has an optimal solution, the primal problem has an optimal solution, and vice versa. Furthermore, the values of the optimal solutions to the dual and primal problems are equal.

This property tells us that if we had solved only the dual problem, we would have known that HighTech could make a maximum of $1980.

Economic Interpretation of the Dual Variables

Before making further observations about the relationship between the primal and the dual solutions, let us consider the meaning or interpretation of the dual variables u_1, u_2, and u_3. Remember that in setting up the dual problem, each dual variable is associated with one of the constraints in the primal. Specifically, u_1 is associated with the assembly time constraint, u_2 with the Portable display constraint, and u_3 with the warehouse space constraint.

To understand and interpret these dual variables better let us return to property 1 of the primal–dual relationship, which stated that the objective function values for the primal and dual problems must be equal. At the optimal solution the primal objective function results in

$$50x_1 + 40x_2 = 1980 \qquad (6.14)$$

while the dual objective function is

$$150u_1 + 20u_2 + 300u_3 = 1980 \qquad (6.15)$$

Using equation (6.14), let us restrict our interest to the interpretation of the primal objective function. Since x_1 and x_2 are the number of units of the Deskpro and the Portable that are assembled respectively, we have

$$\begin{pmatrix} \text{dollar value} \\ \text{per unit of} \\ \text{Deskpro} \end{pmatrix} \begin{pmatrix} \text{number of} \\ \text{units of} \\ \text{Deskpro} \end{pmatrix} + \begin{pmatrix} \text{dollar value} \\ \text{per unit of} \\ \text{Portable} \end{pmatrix} \begin{pmatrix} \text{number of} \\ \text{units of} \\ \text{Portable} \end{pmatrix} = \begin{matrix} \text{total dollar} \\ \text{value or} \\ \text{profit} \end{matrix}$$

Performing a similar interpretation of the dual objective function, equation (6.15), we see that the coefficients 150, 20, and 300 can be interpreted as the number of units of resources available. Thus we have

$$\begin{pmatrix} \text{Units of} \\ \text{resource} \\ 1 \end{pmatrix} u_1 + \begin{pmatrix} \text{units of} \\ \text{resource} \\ 2 \end{pmatrix} u_2 + \begin{pmatrix} \text{units of} \\ \text{resource} \\ 3 \end{pmatrix} u_3 = \begin{matrix} \text{total dollar value} \\ \text{or resource} \\ \text{cost} \end{matrix}$$

In order to be consistent in our units, and noting that, at optimality, the values of the primal and dual objective functions are equal, we see that the dual variables must carry the interpretation of being the value per unit of resource. Thus for the HighTech problem,

$$u_1 = \text{dollar value per hour assembly time}$$
$$u_2 = \text{dollar value per unit of the Portable display}$$
$$u_3 = \text{dollar value per square foot of warehouse space}$$

Did we ever attempt to identify the value of these resources previously? Recall that in Section 6.1, when we considered sensitivity analysis of the right-hand sides, we identified the value of an additional unit of each resource. These values were called shadow prices, and are helpful to the decision maker in determining whether additional units of the resources should be made available.

The analysis in Section 6.1 led to the following shadow prices for the resources in the HighTech problem.

Resource	Value per Additional Unit (shadow price)
Assembly time	$2.80
Portable display	$0.00
Warehouse space	$5.20

Let us now return to the optimal solution for the HighTech dual problem. The values of the dual variables at the optimal solution are $u_1 = {}^{14}\!/_5 = 2.80$, $u_2 = 0$, and $u_3 = {}^{26}\!/_5 = 5.20$. This observation leads to the important economic interpretation that the values of the dual variable and the shadow price are one and the same. Thus the optimal values of the dual variables identify the shadow price of each additional resource or input unit at the optimal solution.

In light of the above discussion, the following interpretation of the primal and dual problems can be made.

Primal Problem. Given a value per unit of each product or output unit, determine how much of each output should be produced in order to maximize the value of the total output. Constraints require the amount of each resource used to be less than or equal to the amount available.

Dual Problem. Given the availability of each resource or input, determine the value for each unit of input such that the value of the total input (that is, the resource cost) is minimized. Constraints require the inputed resource value per unit of input to be greater than or equal to the value of each unit of output.

Using the Dual to Identify the Primal Solution

At the beginning of this section we mentioned that an important feature of the primal–dual relationship is that when an optimal solution is reached, the value of the optimal solution for the primal problem is the same as the value of the optimal solution for the dual problem. However, the question remains: If we solve only the dual problem, how can we identify the optimal values for the primal variables?

Recall that in Section 6.1 we showed that when a primal problem is solved by the simplex method, the optimal values of the primal variables appear in the rightmost column of the final tableau and the shadow prices (values of the dual variables) are found in the z_j row. Since the final simplex tableau of the dual problem provides the optimal values of the dual variables, the values of the primal variables should be found in the z_j row of the optimal dual tableau. This is, in fact, the case and is formally stated as property 2.

Property 2

Given the simplex tableau corresponding to the optimal dual solution, the optimal values of the primal decision variables are given by the z_j entries for the surplus variables; furthermore, the optimal values of the primal slack variables are given by the negative of the $c_j - z_j$ entries for the u_j variables.

This property enables us to use the final simplex tableau for the dual of the HighTech problem to determine the optimal primal solution of $x_1 = 30$ units of the Deskpro and $x_2 = 12$ units of the Portable. These optimal values of x_1 and x_2, as well as the values for all primal slack variables, are given in the z_j and $c_j - z_j$ rows of the final simplex tableau of the dual problem, which is shown again below.

Basis	c_B	u_1 -150	u_2 -20	u_3 -300	s_1 0	s_2 0	
u_3	-300	0	$-3/25$	1	$-5/25$	$3/25$	$26/5$
u_1	-150	1	$8/25$	0	$5/25$	$-8/25$	$14/5$
	z_j	-150	-12	-300	30	12	-1980
	$c_j - z_j$	0	-8	0	-30	-12	

Primal solution: $s_1 = 0$ $s_2 = 8$ $s_3 = 0$ $x_1 = 30$ $x_2 = 12$ Profit $= 1980$

Finding the Dual of Any Primal Problem

The HighTech Industries primal problem provided a good introductory problem to illustrate the concept of duality as it was formulated as a maximization problem in canonical form. For this form of primal problem we have seen that conversion to the dual problem is rather easy. However, what if the primal is a minimization problem and/or some of the constraints are not of the $\leq$ form? While we could state a special set of rules for converting each variety of primal problem into its associated dual, we tend to believe it is easier first to convert any primal problem to an equivalent maximization problem in canonical form. Once this has been accomplished, we can find the dual problem by following the procedure used to convert the HighTech Industries primal problem into its dual.

We will show the steps necessary for converting any primal linear program into a maximization problem in canonical form by considering the following primal linear programming problem.

$$\min \quad 2x_1 - 3x_2$$
$$\text{s.t.}$$
$$1x_1 + 2x_2 \leq 12$$
$$4x_1 - 2x_2 \geq 3$$
$$6x_1 - 1x_2 = 10$$
$$x_1, x_2 \geq 0$$

The appropriate steps are stated in general and then are applied to the example problem.

1. If the problem involves a minimization objective function, convert the problem to an equivalent maximization problem by multiplying the objective function by -1.

Thus the objective function for the example becomes

$$\max \quad -2x_1 + 3x_2$$

2. Convert any $\geq$ constraint to an equivalent $\leq$ constraint by multiplying both sides of the constraint by -1.

Thus constraint 2 for the example becomes

$$-4x_1 + 2x_2 \leq -3$$

3. For each equality constraint form two inequality constraints, one with a $\leq$ form and one with a $\geq$ form; then use rule 2 above to convert the $\geq$ constraint to a $\leq$ form.

Thus constraint 3 for the example is rewritten as two inequality constraints:

$$6x_1 - 1x_2 \leq 10$$
$$6x_1 - 1x_2 \geq 10$$

Using rule 2 for the greater-than-or-equal-to constraint, these constraints can be rewritten as

$$6x_1 - 1x_2 \leq 10$$
$$-6x_1 + 1x_2 \leq -10$$

Thus the initial primal problem has been restated in the following equivalent form:

$$
\begin{aligned}
\max \quad & -2x_1 + 3x_2 \\
\text{s.t.} \quad & \\
& 1x_1 + 2x_2 \leq 12 \\
& -4x_1 + 2x_2 \leq -3 \\
& 6x_1 - 1x_2 \leq 10 \\
& -6x_1 + 1x_2 \leq -10 \\
& x_1, \, x_2 \geq 0
\end{aligned}
$$

With the primal problem in canonical form for a maximization problem, we can easily convert to the dual linear programming problem by the primal–dual procedure presented earlier in this section. The dual becomes[2]

---

[2]Note that the right-hand side of the first constraint is negative. Thus we must multiply both sides of the constraint by -1 to obtain a positive value for the right-hand side before attempting to solve the problem with the simplex method.

$$\text{min} \quad 12u_1 \quad - \quad 3u_2 \quad + \quad 10u_3' \quad - \quad 10u_3''$$
s.t.
$$
\begin{aligned}
1u_1 \quad - \quad 4u_2 \quad + \quad 6u_3' \quad - \quad 6u_3'' &\geq -2 \\
2u_1 \quad + \quad 2u_2 \quad - \quad 1u_3' \quad + \quad 1u_3'' &\geq 3 \\
u_1, \, u_2, \, u_3', \, u_3'' &\geq 0
\end{aligned}
$$

Since the equality primal constraint required two $\leq$ constraints, we denoted the dual variables associated with these constraints as u_3' and u_3''. This reminds us that u_3' and u_3'' both refer to the third constraint in the initial primal problem. Since there are two dual variables associated with an equality constraint, the interpretation of the dual variable as the shadow price of the right-hand-side resource must be modified slightly. The shadow price is given by the difference between the two dual variables. Thus the shadow price for the equality constraint $6x_1 - x_2 = 10$ is given by the value of $u_3' - u_3''$ in the optimal solution to the dual. Hence the shadow price for an equality constraint can be negative.

Computational Considerations

We have shown that solving either the primal or the dual problem provides the solution to the other as well. Thus whenever computation time and effort are important considerations in solving linear programs, practitioners have the option of solving either the primal or the dual, depending upon which is easier to solve.

Recall that if the primal problem has m constraints and n variables, the dual problem will have n constraints and m variables. Also recall that the basic solution identified at each iteration of the simplex method contains as many basic variables as constraints in the problem. For most computer implementations of the simplex method, the number of computations performed at each iteration and the total number of iterations are proportional to the number of basic variables in the problem. Thus, in general, we expect linear programs with a larger number of constraints, and therefore a larger number of basic variables, to require greater computational time and effort. As a result, when there is a substantial difference in the number of constraints in the primal and dual problems, practitioners often recommend solving the form of the problem (primal or dual) with fewer constraints.

Summary

In this chapter we showed how sensitivity analysis can be performed using the information in the final simplex tableau. This included computing the range of optimality for objective function coefficients, shadow prices, and the range of feasibility for the right-hand sides. This sensitivity information is routinely made available as part of the solution report provided by most linear programming computer packages.

We stress here that the sensitivity analysis is based on the assumption that only one coefficient is allowed to change at a time; all other coefficients are assumed to remain at their original values. It is possible to do some limited sensitivity analysis on the effect of changing more than one coefficient at a time; the 100 percent rule was mentioned as being useful in this context.

In studying duality we saw how the original linear programming problem, called the primal, can be converted into its associated dual linear programming problem. Solving either the primal or the dual provides the solution to the other. In cases where the primal has relatively few variables but many constraints, the dual often possesses computational advantages. Finally, we learned that the value of the dual variable (shadow price) identifies the economic contribution or value of additional resources in the primal problem.

Glossary

Range of optimality   The range of values over which an objective function coefficient may·vary without causing any change in the optimal solution (that is, the values of all the variables will remain the same, but the value of the objective function will change).
Shadow price   The change in value of the objective function resulting from a one-unit increase in the value of the right-hand side associated with a linear programming constraint.
Range of feasibility   The range of values over which a b_i may vary without causing the current basic solution to become infeasible. The values of the variables in solution will change, but the same variables will remain basic.
Primal problem   The original formulation of a linear programming problem.
Canonical form for a maximization problem   A maximization problem with all less-than-or-equal-to constraints and nonnegativity requirements for the decision variables.
Dual problem   A linear programming problem associated with the primal problem. Solution of the dual also provides the solution to the primal.
Dual variable   The variable in a dual linear programmming problem. Its optimal value is the shadow price for the associated primal resource.

Problems

1. For the HighTech problem we found the range of optimality for c_1, the profit contribution per unit of the Deskpro. Find
   a. The range of optimality for c_2.
   b. The range of optimality for c_{s_2}.
   c. The range of optimality for c_{s_3}.
   d. Suppose the per-unit profit contribution of the Portable (c_2) dropped to $35. How would the optimal solution change? What is the new value for total profit?
2. For the HighTech problem we found the range of feasibility for b_1, the assembly time available. Find
   a. The range of feasibility for b_2.
   b. The range of feasibility for b_3.
   c. How much will HighTech's profit increase if there is a 20-square-foot increase in the amount of warehouse space available (b_3)?
3. Consider the linear program

$$\max \quad 7.5x_1 + 15x_2 + 10x_3$$

s.t.

$$
\begin{aligned}
2x_1 \qquad\quad + 2x_3 &\le 8 \\
\tfrac{1}{2}x_1 + 2x_2 + 1x_3 &\le 3 \\
1x_1 + 1x_2 + 2x_3 &\le 6 \\
x_1, x_2, x_3 &\ge 0
\end{aligned}
$$

a. Find the optimal solution.
b. Calculate the range of optimality for c_1.
c. What would be the effect of a 2.5-unit increase in c_1 (from 7.5 to 10) on the optimal solution and the value of that solution?
d. Calculate the range of optimality for c_3.
e. What would be the effect of a five-unit increase in c_3 (from 10 to 15) on the optimal solution and the value of that solution?

4. Consider again the linear programming problem presented in problem 3.
a. Compute the ranges of feasibility for b_1, b_2, and b_3.
b. How much will the value of the objective function change if b_1 is increased from 8 to 9?
c. How much will the value of the objective function change if b_2 is increased from 3 to 4?
d. How much will the value of the objective function change if b_3 is increased from 6 to 7?

5. Recall the Par, Inc. problem introduced in Chapter 2. The linear program for this problem is

$$\max \quad 10x_1 + 9x_2$$

s.t.

$$
\begin{aligned}
\tfrac{7}{10}x_1 + 1x_2 &\le 630 \quad \text{Cutting and dyeing time} \\
\tfrac{1}{2}x_1 + \tfrac{5}{6}x_2 &\le 600 \quad \text{Sewing time} \\
1x_1 + \tfrac{2}{3}x_2 &\le 708 \quad \text{Finishing time} \\
\tfrac{1}{10}x; + \tfrac{1}{4}x_2 &\le 135 \quad \text{Inspection and packaging time} \\
x_1, x_2 &\ge 0
\end{aligned}
$$

where

$$x_1 = \text{number of standard bags produced}$$
$$x_2 = \text{number of deluxe bags produced}$$

The final simplex tableau is

		x_1	x_2	s_1	s_2	s_3	s_4	
Basis	c_B	10	9	0	0	0	0	
x_2	9	0	1	$30/16$	0	$-21/16$	0	252
s_2	0	0	0	$-15/16$	1	$5/32$	0	120
x_1	10	1	0	$-20/16$	0	$30/16$	0	540
s_4	0	0	0	$-11/32$	0	$9/64$	1	18
	z_j	10	9	$70/16$	0	$111/16$	0	7668
	$c_j - z_j$	0	0	$-70/16$	0	$-111/16$	0	

a. Calculate the range of optimality for the profit contribution, c_1, of the standard bag.
b. Calculate the range of optimality for the profit contribution, c_2, of the deluxe bag.
c. If the profit contribution per deluxe bag drops to $7 per unit, how will the optimal solution be affected?
d. What unit profit contribution would be necessary for the deluxe bag before Par, Inc. would consider changing its current production plan?
e. If the profit contribution of the deluxe bags can be increased to $15 per unit, what is the optimal production plan? State what you think will happen before you compute the new optimal solution.

6. For the Par, Inc. problem (problem 5):
a. Calculate the range of feasibility for b_1 (cutting and dyeing time capacity).
b. Calculate the range of feasibility for b_2 (sewing capacity).
c. Calculate the range of feasibility for b_3 (finishing capacity).
d. Calculate the range of feasibility for b_4 (inspection and packaging capacity).
e. Which of these four departments are you interested in scheduling for overtime? Explain.

7. a. Calculate the final simplex tableau for the Par, Inc. problem (problem 5) after increasing b_1 from 630 to $682\frac{4}{11}$.
b. Would the current basis be optimal if b_1 were increased further? If not, what would be the new optimal basis?

8. Also for the Par, Inc. problem (problem 5):
a. How much would profit increase if an additional 30 hours became available in the cutting and dyeing department (that is, b_1 were increased from 630 to 660)?
b. How much would profit decrease if 40 hours were removed from the sewing department?
c. How much would profit decrease if because of an employee accident there were only 570 hours instead of 630 available in the cutting and dyeing department?

9. Below are additional conditions encountered by Par, Inc. (problem 5).
a. Suppose because of some new machinery Par, Inc. was able to make a small reduction in the amount of time it took to do the cutting and dyeing (constraint 1) for a standard bag. What effect would this have on the objective function?
b. Management believes that by buying a new sewing machine the sewing time for standard bags can be reduced from $\frac{1}{2}$ hour to $\frac{1}{3}$ hour. Do you think this machine would be a good investment? Why?

10. Recall the RMC problem (Chapter 2, problem 31). Letting

$$x_1 = \text{tons of fuel additive produced}$$
$$x_2 = \text{tons of solvent base produced}$$

leads to the following formulation of the RMC problem:

$$\max \quad 40x_1 + 30x_2$$
$$\text{s.t.}$$
$$\tfrac{2}{5}x_1 + \tfrac{1}{2}x_2 \le 20 \quad \text{Material 1}$$
$$\tfrac{1}{5}x_2 \le 5 \quad \text{Material 2}$$

$$\tfrac{3}{5}x_1 + \tfrac{3}{10}x_2 \le 21 \quad \text{Material 3}$$
$$x_1, x_2 \ge 0$$

The final simplex tableau is shown below.

Basis	c_B	x_1	x_2	s_1	s_2	s_3	
		40	30	0	0	0	
x_2	30	0	1	$\tfrac{10}{3}$	0	$-\tfrac{20}{9}$	20
s_2	0	0	0	$-\tfrac{2}{3}$	1	$\tfrac{4}{9}$	1
x_1	40	1	0	$-\tfrac{5}{3}$	0	$\tfrac{25}{9}$	25
z_j		40	30	$\tfrac{100}{3}$	0	$\tfrac{400}{9}$	1600
$c_j - z_j$		0	0	$-\tfrac{100}{3}$	0	$-\tfrac{400}{9}$	

a. Compute the ranges of optimality for c_1 and c_2.
b. Suppose that because of an increase in production costs the profit per ton on the fuel additive is reduced to $30 per ton. What effect will this have on the optimal solution?
c. What is the shadow price for the material 1 constraint? What is the interpretation?
d. If RMC had an opportunity to purchase additional materials, which material would be the most valuable? How much should the company be willing to pay for this material?

11. Refer again to problem 10.
   a. Compute the range of feasibility for b_1 (Material 1 availability).
   b. Compute the range of feasibility for b_2 (Material 2 availability).
   c. Compute the range of feasibility for b_3 (Material 3 availability).
   d. What is the shadow price for material 3? Over what range of values for b_3 is this shadow price valid?

12. Consider the following linear program:

$$\max \quad 3x_1 + 1x_2 + 5x_3 + 3x_4$$
$$\text{s.t.}$$
$$3x_1 + 1x_2 + 2x_3 \qquad\qquad = 30$$
$$2x_1 + 1x_2 + 3x_3 + 1x_4 \ge 15$$
$$2x_2 \qquad\quad + 3x_4 \le 25$$
$$x_1, x_2, x_3, x_4 \ge 0$$

a. Find the optimal solution.
b. Calculate the range of optimality for c_3.
c. What would be the effect of a four-unit decrease in c_3 (from 5 to 1) on the optimal solution and the value of that solution?
d. Calculate the range of optimality for c_2.
e. What would be the effect of a three-unit increase in c_2 (from 1 to 4) on the optimal solution and the value of that solution?

13. Consider the final simplex tableau shown below.

Basis	c_B	x_1	x_2	x_3	x_4	s_1	s_2	s_3	
		4	6	3	1	0	0	0	
x_3	3	$3/60$	0	1	$1/2$	$3/10$	0	$-6/30$	125
s_2	0	$195/60$	0	0	$-1/2$	$-5/10$	1	-1	425
x_2	6	$39/60$	1	0	$1/2$	$-1/10$	0	$12/30$	25
z_j		$81/20$	6	3	$9/2$	$3/10$	0	$54/30$	525
$c_j - z_j$		$-1/20$	0	0	$-7/2$	$-3/10$	0	$-54/30$	

The original right-hand-side values were $b_1 = 550$, $b_2 = 700$, and $b_3 = 200$.
a. Calculate the range of feasibility for b_1.
b. Calculate the range of feasibility for b_2.
c. Calculate the range of feasibility for b_3.

14. Suppose that in a product-mix problem x_1, x_2, x_3, and x_4 indicate the units of products 1, 2, 3, and 4, respectively, and we have

$$\text{max} \quad 4x_1 + 6x_2 + 3x_3 + 1x_4$$
$$\text{s.t.}$$
$$1.5x_1 + 2x_2 + 4x_3 + 3x_4 \le 550 \quad \text{Machine } A \text{ hours}$$
$$4x_1 + 1x_2 + 2x_3 + 1x_4 \le 700 \quad \text{Machine } B \text{ hours}$$
$$2x_1 + 3x_2 + 1x_3 + 2x_4 \le 200 \quad \text{Machine } C \text{ hours.}$$
$$x_1, x_2, x_3, x_4 \ge 0$$

a. Formulate the dual to this problem.
b. Solve the dual. Use the dual solution to show that the profit-maximizing product mix is $x_1 = 0$, $x_2 = 25$, $x_3 = 125$, and $x_4 = 0$.
c. Use the dual variables to identify the machine or machines that are producing at maximum capacity. If the manager can select one machine for additional production capacity, which machine should have priority? Why?

15. Find the dual problem for the linear program given below.

$$\text{max} \quad 10x_1 + 9x_2 + 4x_3 + 6x_4$$
$$\text{s.t.}$$
$$3x_1 + 2x_2 + 4x_3 + 2x_4 \le 70$$
$$5x_1 + 5x_2 + 1x_3 + 3x_4 \le 60$$
$$5x_1 + 6x_2 + 3x_3 + 1x_4 \le 25$$
$$x_1, x_2, x_3, x_4 \ge 0$$

16. Write the following primal linear program in canonical form:

$$\text{max} \quad 5x_1 + 1x_2 + 3x_3$$
$$\text{s.t.}$$
$$1x_1 + 1x_2 \ge 40$$
$$2x_1 + 3x_2 + 1x_3 \le 50$$

$$3x_1 + 2x_2 + 2x_3 \leq 25$$
$$1x_2 + 1x_3 \geq 10$$
$$x_1, x_2, x_3 \geq 0$$

From a computational point of view, would you rather solve the above linear programming problem or its dual?

17. Write the following primal problem in canonical form:

$$\max \quad 3x_1 + 1x_2 + 5x_3 + 3x_4$$

s.t.

$$3x_1 + 1x_2 + 2x_3 \qquad = 30$$
$$2x_1 + 1x_2 + 3x_3 + 1x_4 \geq 15$$
$$2x_2 \qquad + 3x_4 \leq 25$$

$$x_1, x_2, x_3, x_4 \geq 0$$

18. Write the dual of problem 17.

19. Consider the following linear program:

$$\max \quad 2x_1 + 3x_2$$

s.t.

$$1x_1 + 2x_2 \leq 8$$
$$3x_1 + 2x_2 \leq 12$$
$$x_1, x_2 \geq 0$$

a. Write the dual of this problem.
b. Solve both the primal and the dual problems using the graphical procedure.
c. Solve both the primal and the dual problems using the simplex method.
d. Using your results from parts (b) and (c), identify where and how you can observe properties 1 and 2 of the primal–dual relationship.

20. The Photo Chemicals problem (Chapter 2, problem 27) asked you to determine the minimum cost production plan for two of its products. The formulation was as follows:

$$\min \quad 1x_1 + 1x_2$$

s.t.

$$1x_1 \qquad\qquad \geq 30 \quad \text{Minimum product 1}$$
$$1x_2 \geq 20 \quad \text{Minimum product 2}$$
$$1x_1 + 2x_2 \geq 80 \quad \text{Minimum raw material}$$
$$x_1, x_2 \geq 0$$

a. Write this primal linear program in canonical form for a maximization problem.
b. Show the dual problem.
c. Solve the dual problem, and show that the optimal production plan is $x_1 = 30$ and $x_2 = 25$.
d. Recall that the third constraint involved a management request that the current 80 pounds of a perishable raw material be used as soon as possible. However,

after learning that the optimal solution calls for an excess production of five units of product 2, management is reconsidering the raw material requirement. Specifically, you have been asked to identify the cost effect if this constraint were relaxed. Use the dual variable to indicate the change in the cost if only 79 pounds of raw material had to be used.

21. Write the dual problem for the following linear program:

$$\min \quad 3x_1 + 1x_2 + 2x_3$$

s.t.

$$
\begin{aligned}
2x_1 + 1x_2 + 3x_3 &= 5 \\
4x_1 + 1x_2 + 1x_3 &= 4 \\
2x_1 \qquad\quad + 1x_3 &\leq 7 \\
1x_1 + 2x_2 \qquad\quad &\geq 4 \\
x_1, x_2, x_3 &\geq 0
\end{aligned}
$$

22. Find the dual problem for the following linear programming problem:

$$\min \quad 4x_1 + 3x_2 + 6x_3$$

s.t.

$$
\begin{aligned}
1x_1 + 0.5x_2 + 1x_3 &\geq 15 \\
2x_2 + 1x_3 &\geq 30 \\
1x_1 + 1x_2 + 2x_3 &\geq 20 \\
x_1, x_2, x_3 &\geq 0
\end{aligned}
$$

23. A sales representative who sells two products is trying to determine the number of calls that should be made during the next month to promote each product. Based on past experience, there is an average $10 commission for every call for product 1 and a $5 commission for every call for product 2. The company requires at least 20 calls per month for each product and not more than 100 calls per month on any one product. In addition, the sales representative spends about 3 hours for each call for product 1 and 1 hour for each call for product 2. If there are a total of 175 selling hours available next month, how many calls should be made for each of the two products in order to maximize the commission?

   a. Formulate a linear program for this problem.
   b. Formulate and solve the dual problem.
   c. Use the final simplex tableau for the dual to determine the optimal number of calls for the products. What is the maximum commission?
   d. Interpret the values of the dual variables.

24. Consider the linear program

$$\max \quad 3x_1 + 2x_2$$

s.t.

$$
\begin{aligned}
1x_1 + 2x_2 &\leq 8 \\
2x_1 + 1x_2 &\leq 10 \\
x_1, x_2 &\geq 0
\end{aligned}
$$

a. Solve this problem using the simplex method. Keep a record of the value of the objective function at each extreme point.
b. Formulate and solve the dual of this problem using the graphical procedure.
c. Compute the value of the dual objective function for each extreme-point solution of the dual problem.
d. Compare the values of the objective functions for each primal and dual extreme-point solution.
e. Can a dual feasible solution yield a value less than a primal feasible solution? Can you state a result concerning bounds on the value of the primal solution provided by any feasible solution to the dual problem?

25. Consider the following linear program:

$$\max \quad 15x_1 + 30x_2 + 20x_3$$

s.t.

$$
\begin{aligned}
1x_1 \quad\quad\quad + \quad 1x_3 &\leq 4 \\
0.5x_1 + 2x_2 + 1x_3 &\leq 3 \\
1x_1 + 1x_2 + 2x_3 &\leq 6 \\
x_1, x_2, x_3 &\geq 0
\end{aligned}
$$

Solve using the simplex method and answer the following questions:
a. What is the optimal solution?
b. What is the value of the objective function?
c. Which constraints are the binding constraints?
d. How much slack is available in the nonbinding constraints?
e. What are the shadow prices associated with the three constraints? Which right-hand-side value would have the greatest effect on the value of the objective function if it could be changed?
f. Develop the appropriate ranges for the coefficients of the objective function. What is your interpretation of these ranges?
g. Develop and interpret the ranges of feasibility for the right-hand-side values.

Management Science in Practice
PERFORMANCE ANALYSIS CORPORATION*
Chapel Hill, North Carolina

Performance Analysis Corporation, founded in 1979, is a management consulting company that specializes in the use of management science to design more efficient and effective operations for a wide variety of chain stores. Performance Analysis Corporation has evaluated the operation of banks, savings and loans, grocery chains, etc. Recently the company has become involved in evaluating the efficiency of fast-food outlets. In the following application we describe how linear programming methodology has been used to provide an evaluation model for a chain of fast-food restaurants.

FAST-FOOD BUSINESS

The fast-food business for a chain such as McDonalds, Kentucky Fried Chicken, etc., is characterized by hundreds, or even thousands, of individual restaurants, some of which are company owned and some of which are franchised. A typical restaurant may gross close to a million dollars annually; thus the impact of relatively minor improvements at a large proportion of the restaurants can have a substantial effect on a chain's profitability and market share.

Although each individual restaurant in a given chain usually offers the same type of menu (with some minor geographical variations), they often must deal with vastly different environments and competition. In addition, the age of the restaurant, facade used, ease of access and egress, hours of operation, scale of operation, etc., can vary substantially from restaurant to restaurant.

A major objective of company management in the fast-food industry involves the performance evaluations of managers of individual restaurants in the chain. These evaluations are the basis for awarding year-end bonuses and for personal advancement purposes. Unfortunately there is not a single measure of performance such as profit that can be used as the basis for the evaluation, since other measures such as market share and rate of growth are also important.

A LINEAR PROGRAMMING EVALUATION MODEL

One approach to the store evaluation problem utilizes the concept of Pareto optimality. According to this concept, a restaurant in a given chain is *relatively* inef-

*The authors are indebted to Richard C. Morey of Performance Analysis Corp., Chapel Hill, N.C., for providing this application.

ficient if there are other restaurants in the same chain that have the following characteristics:

1. Have the same or worse environment.
2. Produce at least the same levels of *all* outputs.
3. Utilize no more of *any* resource and *less* of at least one of the resources.

The mechanism for discovering which of the restaurants are Pareto inefficient involves the development and solution of a linear programming model. Constraints on the problem involve requirements concerning the minimum acceptable levels of output (e.g., profit, market share, etc.) and conditions imposed by uncontrollable elements in the environment. The objective function calls for the minimization of the resources necessary to produce the output. Solution of the model produces the following output for each restaurant:

1. A score that assesses the level of so-called relative technical efficiency achieved by the particular restaurant over the time period in question.
2. The reduction in controllable resources and/or the augmentation of outputs over the time period in question for an inefficient restaurant to have been rated as efficient.
3. A peer group of other restaurants with which each restaurant can be compared in the future.

Sensitivity analysis, especially that concerning the shadow prices, provides important managerial information. For each constraint concerning a minimum acceptable output level, the shadow price tells the manager how much one more unit of output would increase his/her efficiency measure. Analysis of the ranges for each of the constraint coefficients (the a_{ij}'s) provides information concerning how much outputs could be reduced or inputs increased before the restaurant would become inefficient.

TYPES OF FACTORS UTILIZED

The approach is capable of handling three types of factors: quantitative controllable factors such as salaries paid, local advertising expenditures, etc.; noncontrollable quantitative factors such as the median income in the geographic area served by the restaurant, the unemployment rate, etc.; and qualitative factors such as the degree of competition, appearance of restaurant, etc. The outputs include total sales of various types (e.g., by time of day), profits, market share, rate of growth of sales, etc.

BENEFITS

The analysis typically identifies 40%–50% of the restaurants as underperforming given the previously stated conditions concerning the inputs available and outputs produced. We have found that if all of the relative inefficiencies identified are eliminated simultaneously, the resulting increase in corporate profits is typically in the neighborhood of 5%–10%. This is truly a substantial increase given the large scale of operations involved.

The district manager has an objective score card for each restaurant manager that indicates areas (e.g., overtime salary) where improvements may be in order. The efficient restaurants can be used to generate a set of best practices that can be models for other restaurants. Of primary benefit are the reactions of restaurant managers who appreciate that the evaluation process that they are subject to recognizes the environment they are forced to operate within, deals with noncommensurability of outputs involved, is theory based and nonpolitical, and is defensible, understandable, and equitable.

Questions

1. State in your own words what it means for one restaurant in a chain to be relatively inefficient relative to another restaurant in the same chain.
2. Suppose the evaluation model showed that for a particular restaurant the resource mix necessary to produce a given output mix was 90% of what another restaurant was using to produce that same mix of output. Would you conclude that the restaurant was relatively efficient or inefficient? Why?

7

Transportation, Assignment, and Transshipment Problems

The transportation, assignment, and transshipment problems are special cases of the general linear programming model that we studied in Chapters 2–6; thus these problems can be formulated and solved as linear programs. A separate chapter is devoted to these problems for two reasons. First, because of the wide variety of applications that can be solved as transportation, assignment, or transshipment problems, they are of immense practical importance. Second, these problems have a mathematical structure that has enabled management scientists to develop very efficient specialized solution procedures for solving them.

We will see that a transportation problem involving 12 variables and seven constraints can be solved fairly easily manually if a special-purpose solution procedure is used. However, in order to solve a problem of this size using a standard linear programming approach, a computer code is required if the solution is to be developed in a reasonable amount of time. For very large problems computer programs are also used to carry out the computations for the specialized solution procedures; in such cases the advantage of these specialized solution procedures—as compared with a general linear programming approach—lies primarily in the speed with which the problems can be solved.

The approach we take in this chapter is to introduce each problem with an illustrative application. We then show how a linear programming model can be formulated and solved using LINDO/PC. Next we show how a general linear programming model can be developed to handle problems of any size. Finally, for the transportation and assignment problems, specialized solution procedures are presented after the general linear programming treatment of the problem.

7.1 THE TRANSPORTATION PROBLEM

The transportation problem arises frequently in planning for the distribution of goods and services from several supply locations to several demand locations. Usually the quantity of goods available at each supply location (*origin*) is fixed or limited, and there is a specified amount needed (demand) at each user location (*destination*). With a variety of shipping routes and differing costs for the routes, the objective is to determine how many units should be shipped from each origin to each destination so that all destination demands are satisfied and total transportation costs are minimized.

Let us illustrate the transportation problem by considering the problem faced by Foster Generators, Inc. This problem involves the transportation of a product from three plants to four distribution centers. Foster Generators, Inc. is a firm that has production operations in Cleveland, Ohio; Bedford, Ind.; and York, Pa. Production capacities for these plants over the next 3-month planning period for one particular type of generator are as follows:

Origin	Plant	Three-Month Production Capacity (Units)
1	Cleveland	5000
2	Bedford	6000
3	York	2500
		Total 13,500

Suppose that the firm distributes its generators through four regional distribution centers located in Boston, Chicago, St. Louis, and Lexington (Ky.) and that the 3-month forecast of demand for the distribution centers is as follows:

Destination	Distribution Center	3-Month Demand Forecast (Units)
1	Boston	6000
2	Chicago	4000
3	St. Louis	2000
4	Lexington	1500
		Total 13,500

Management would like to determine how much of its production should be shipped from each plant to each distribution center. Figure 7.1 shows graphically the 12 distribution routes Foster can use.

In Figure 7.1 we refer to the circles as *nodes* and to the lines connecting the circles as *arcs*. The corresponding graph of interconnected nodes and arcs is called a *network*. Thus we see that the transportation problem can be represented graphically as a network; for this reason the problem is often referred to as a *network flow problem*. The goods shipped from the origins to the destination represent the flow in the network.

With identical production costs at the three plants, the only variable costs involved are transportation costs. Thus the problem becomes one of determining the distribution routes to be used and the quantity to be shipped via each route so that all distribution

FIGURE 7.1
The Network Representation of the Foster Generators Transportation Problem

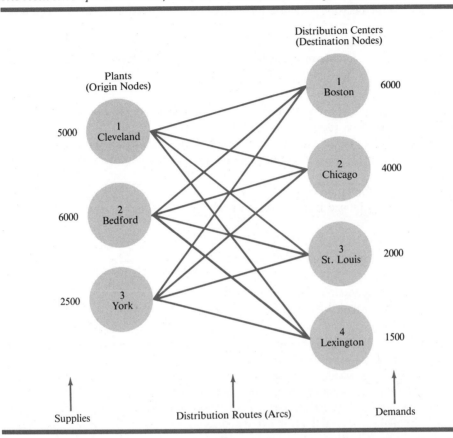

center demands can be met with a minimum total transportation cost. The cost for each unit shipped on each route is given in Table 7.1.

TABLE 7.1
Transportation Cost per Unit for the Foster Generators Transportation Problem

Origin	Destination			
	Boston	**Chicago**	**St. Louis**	**Lexington**
Cleveland	3	2	7	6
Bedford	7	5	2	3
York	2	5	4	5

7.2   THE TRANSPORTATION PROBLEM: A LINEAR PROGRAMMING FORMULATION

A linear programming model can be used to solve the Foster Generators transporation problem. We shall use double-subscripted decision variables, with x_{11} denoting the number of units shipped from origin 1 (Cleveland) to destination 1 (Boston), x_{12} denoting the number of units shipped from origin 1 (Cleveland) to destination 2 (Chicago), and so on. In general the decision variables for a transportation problem having m origins and n destinations are written as follows:

$$x_{ij} = \text{number of units shipped from origin } i \text{ to destination } j,$$
$$\text{where i} = 1, 2, \ldots, m \text{ and } j = 1, 2, \ldots, n$$

Using this notation, $x_{24} = 500$ would correspond to shipping 500 units from Bedford (origin 2) to Lexington (destination 4).

Since the objective of the transportation problem is to minimize the total transportation costs, we can use the cost data in Table 7.1 to develop the following cost expressions:

Transportation costs for
units shipped from Cleveland $= 3x_{11} + 2x_{12} + 7x_{13} + 6x_{14}$

Transportation costs for
units shipped from Bedford $= 7x_{21} + 5x_{22} + 2x_{23} + 3x_{24}$

Transportation costs for
units shipped from York $= 2x_{31} + 5x_{32} + 4x_{33} + 5x_{34}$

The sum of the above expressions provides the objective function showing the total transportation costs for Foster Generators, Inc.

Constraints are needed for a transportation problem because each origin has a limited supply and each destination has a specific demand. Consider the supply constraints first; note that the capacity at the Cleveland plant is 5000 units. With the total number of units shipped from the Cleveland plant expressed as $x_{11} + x_{12} + x_{13} + x_{14}$, the supply constraint for the Cleveland plant can be written as

$$x_{11} + x_{12} + x_{13} + x_{14} \leq 5000 \quad \text{Cleveland supply}$$

With three origins (plants), the Foster Generators transportation problem has three supply constraints. Given the capacity of 6000 units at the Bedford plant and 2500 units at the York plant, the two additional supply constraints are as follows:

$$x_{21} + x_{22} + x_{23} + x_{24} \leq 6000 \quad \text{Bedford supply}$$
$$x_{31} + x_{32} + x_{33} + x_{34} \leq 2500 \quad \text{York supply}$$

With the four distribution centers as the destinations, the following four demand constraints are needed to ensure that destination demands will be satisfied:

$$x_{11} + x_{21} + x_{31} = 6000 \quad \text{Boston demand}$$
$$x_{12} + x_{22} + x_{32} = 4000 \quad \text{Chicago demand}$$
$$x_{13} + x_{23} + x_{33} = 2000 \quad \text{St. Louis demand}$$
$$x_{14} + x_{24} + x_{34} = 1500 \quad \text{Lexington demand}$$

Combining the objective function and constraints into one model provides the following 12-variable, seven-constraint linear programming formulation of the Foster Generators transportation problem:

$$\text{min} \quad 3x_{11} + 2x_{12} + 7x_{13} + 6x_{14} + 7x_{21} + 5x_{22} + 2x_{23} + 3x_{24} + 2x_{31} + 5x_{32} + 4x_{33} + 5x_{34}$$

s.t

$$
\begin{array}{llllllll}
x_{11} + & x_{12} + & x_{13} + & x_{14} & & & & \leq 5000 \\
& & & x_{21} + & x_{22} + & x_{23} + & x_{24} & \leq 6000 \\
& & & & x_{31} + & x_{32} + & x_{33} + & x_{34} \leq 2500 \\
x_{11} & & & + \; x_{21} & & & + \; x_{31} & = 6000 \\
& x_{12} & & & + \; x_{22} & & & + \; x_{32} & = 4000 \\
& & x_{13} & & & + \; x_{23} & & & + \; x_{33} & = 2000 \\
& & & x_{14} & & & + \; x_{24} & & & + \; x_{34} = 1500 \\
\end{array}
$$

$$x_{ij} \geq 0 \quad \text{for } i = 1, 2, 3 \text{ and } j = 1, 2, 3, 4.$$

The LINDO/PC computer solution to the Foster Generators problem (see Figure 7.2) shows that the minimum total transportation cost is $39,500. The values for the decision variables show the optimal amounts to ship over each route. For example, with $x_{11} = 3500$, we see that 3500 units should be shipped over the Cleveland–Boston route and with $x_{12} = 1500$, 1500 units should be shipped from Cleveland to Chicago. Other values of the decision variables indicate the remaining shipping quantities and routes. The minimum cost transportation schedule is shown in Table 7.2. Figure 7.3 provides a graphical summary of the optimal solution.

FIGURE 7.2
Computer Solution of the Foster Generators Problem Using LINDO/PC

```
                    OBJECTIVE FUNCTION VALUE

        1)        39500.0000

        VARIABLE        VALUE          REDUCED COST
           X11       3500.000000          .000000
           X12       1500.000000          .000000
           X13          .000000          8.000000
           X14          .000000          6.000000
           X21          .000000          1.000000
           X22       2500.000000          .000000
           X23       2000.000000          .000000
           X24       1500.000000          .000000
           X31       2500.000000          .000000
           X32          .000000          4.000000
           X33          .000000          6.000000
           X34          .000000          6.000000


        ROW     SLACK OR SURPLUS        DUAL PRICES
         2)          .000000            3.000000
         3)          .000000             .000000
         4)          .000000            4.000000
         5)          .000000           -6.000000
         6)          .000000           -5.000000
         7)          .000000           -2.000000
         8)          .000000           -3.000000
```

TABLE 7.2
Optimal Solution to the Foster Generators Transportation Problem

From	Route To	Units Shipped	Per-Unit Cost	Total Cost
Cleveland	Boston	3500	$3	$10,500
Cleveland	Chicago	1500	$2	3,000
Bedford	Chicago	2500	$5	12,500
Bedford	St. Louis	2000	$2	4,000
Bedford	Lexington	1500	$3	4,500
York	Boston	2500	$2	5,000
				$39,500

FIGURE 7.3
Optimal Solution to the Foster Generators Transportation Problem

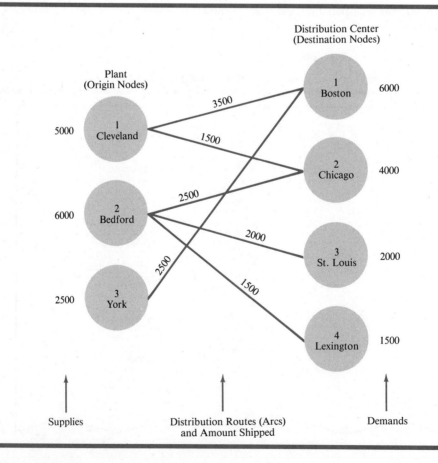

Note that the optimal values for the decision variables in the Foster Generators problem are all integers (e.g., $x_{11} = 3500$, $x_{12} = 1500$, and so on). This result is a property that will hold true under very general conditions when solving any transportation, assignment, or transshipment problem. That is, because of the special structure of the constraints for these problems, it can be shown that the solution values for a transportation, assignment, or transshipment problem will always be integer if the supplies at the origin nodes and the demands at the destination nodes are all integer. Since this will always be the case for the problems we consider in this chapter, the optimal solutions we obtain will always be integer. In the next chapter we present an approach for solving other types of linear programming problems in which the nature of the problem requires some or all of the decision variables to be integer.

Special Considerations

Variations of the basic transportation problem may involve one or more of the following situations:

1. Total supply not equal to total demand
2. Maximization objective function rather than minimization
3. Constraints on specific routes, such as route capacities or route minimums
4. Unacceptable routes

With slight modifications in the linear programming model, these situations can be taken into consideration in arriving at the optimal transportation solution.

A situation that often occurs is the case where the *total supply is not equal to the total demand*. If total supply exceeds total demand, no modification in the linear programming formulation is necessary. Excess supply will appear as slack in the linear programming solution. Slack for any particular origin can be interpreted as the unused supply or amount not shipped from the origin. If total supply is less than total demand, the linear programming model will not have a feasible solution because the demand constraints cannot be satisfied. In this case a modification in the linear programming formulation is necessary to develop the desired transportation problem solution. Specifically we introduce a dummy origin (plant) with supply capacity exactly equal to the excess of total demand over total supply. We assign a zero cost per unit to every route out of the dummy origin so that the value of the optimal solution will still represent total transportation costs for the problem (no shipments will actually be made from the dummy origin). With the inclusion of the dummy plant, total supply is made equal to total demand and a linear programming model can be used to generate a solution. At the optimal solution, destinations showing shipments being received from the dummy plant will be the destinations experiencing a shortfall or unsatisfied demand. Thus with the inclusion of the dummy plant the transportation problem will provide a minimum cost shipping schedule for the available supply and also will indicate which destinations will have unsatisfied demand.

In some problem formulations *it may be desirable to consider profit or revenue per unit shipped rather than cost per unit*. Using the profit or revenue per unit values as coefficients in the objective function, we simply solve a maximization rather than a minimization linear program. The constraints are not affected by this change.

The transportation problem formulation can be further modified to take into account *capacities on one or more of the shipping routes*. For example, suppose the York to Boston route (origin 3 to destination 1) was found to have a capacity of 1000 units because of limited space availability on its normal mode of transportation. This limited route capacity can be taken into consideration by adding a constraint specifying an upper limit on the corresponding decision variable. With x_{31} denoting the amount shipped from York to Boston in the Foster Generators problem, the route capacity constraint for the York to Boston route would appear as

$$x_{31} \leq 1000$$

Similarly, route minimums can be specified. For example

$$x_{22} \geq 2000$$

would guarantee that a previously committed order for a Bedford to Chicago delivery of 2000 units would be maintained in the optimal solution.

As a final special situation, we note that in transportation problems it may not be possible to establish a route from every origin to every destination. That is, *some routes may be unacceptable*. To handle this situation we simply remove the corresponding decision variable from the linear programming formulation of the problem. For example, if the Cleveland to St. Louis route were determined to be unacceptable or unusable, x_{13} could be removed from the linear programming formulation. Solving the resulting 11-variable, seven-constraint model would provide the optimal solution while guaranteeing that the Cleveland to St. Louis route is not used.

A General Linear Programming Formulation of the Transportation Problem

In order to show the general linear programming formulation of the transportation problem, we use the following notation:

$$i = \text{index for origins}, i = 1, 2, \ldots, m$$
$$j = \text{index for destinations}, j = 1, 2, \ldots, n$$
$$x_{ij} = \text{number of units shipped from origin } i \text{ to destination } j$$
$$c_{ij} = \text{cost per unit of shipping from origin } i \text{ to destination } j$$
$$s_i = \text{supply or capacity in units at origin } i$$
$$d_j = \text{demand in units at destination } j$$

The general formulation of the m-origin, n-destination transportation problem is

$$\min \sum_{i=1}^{m} \sum_{j=1}^{n} c_{ij}x_{ij}$$

s.t.

$$\sum_{j=1}^{n} x_{ij} \leq s_i \quad i = 1, 2, \ldots, m \quad \text{Supply}$$
$$\sum_{i=1}^{m} x_{ij} = d_j \quad j = 1, 2, \ldots, n \quad \text{Demand}$$
$$x_{ij} \geq 0 \quad \text{for all } i \text{ and } j$$

If the transportation problem has a total supply (Σs_i) less than total demand (Σd_j), a dummy origin with a supply exactly equal to the difference between the total demand and the total supply must be added. If we let s_{m+1} indicate the fictitious supply, then

$$s_{m+1} = \sum_{j=1}^{n} d_j - \sum_{i=1}^{m} s_i$$

As we indicated previously, to ensure that the value of the optimal solution will still represent total transportation costs for goods actually shipped, all objective function coefficients for the dummy origin will be set equal to zero (no shipments will actually be made from the dummy origin).

In cases where specific routes have capacities, we add constraints of the form $x_{ij} \leq L_{ij}$, where L_{ij} corresponds to an upper limit or capacity for the route from origin i to destination j. Similarly, if specific routes have minimum shipment levels that must be maintained, we add constraints of the form $x_{ij} \geq L_{ij}$. In this case L_{ij} corresponds to the minimum acceptable level for shipments from origin i to destination j.

7.3   THE TRANSPORTATION PROBLEM: A SPECIAL-PURPOSE SOLUTION PROCEDURE

Solving transportation problems using a general-purpose linear programming code, such as LINDO, is fine for small- to medium-sized problems. However, often these problems grow very large (a problem with 100 origins and 1000 destinations would have 100,000 variables), and thus more efficient solution procedures are needed. The special mathematical structure of the transportation problem has enabled management scientists to develop special-purpose solution procedures that greatly simplify the computations.

In the previous section we introduced the Foster Generators, Inc. transportation problem and showed how it could be formulated and solved as a linear program. The linear programming formulation involved 12 variables and seven constraints. It would certainly be time consuming to attempt to solve such a problem by hand using the simplex method; however, in this section we show a special-purpose solution procedure that takes advantage of the special network structure of the transportation problem and makes it possible to solve small transportation problems by hand.

Let us see how the special-purpose solution procedure works by applying it to the Foster Generators problem. The special-purpose solution procedure for the transportation problem involves first finding an initial feasible solution and then proceeding iteratively to make improvements in the solution until an optimal solution is reached. In order to summarize the data conveniently and to keep track of the calculations, a *transportation tableau* is usually employed. The transportation tableau for the Foster Generators problem is presented in Table 7.3.

Note that the 12 *cells* in the tableau correspond to the 12 shipping routes (arcs) shown in Figure 7.1; that is, each cell corresponds to the route from one plant to one

TABLE 7.3
Transportation Tableau for the Foster Generators Transportation Problem

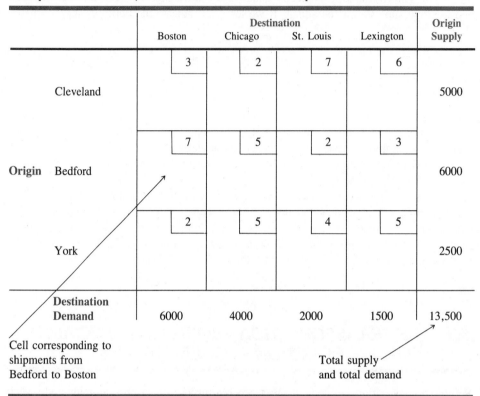

distribution center. The entries at the right-hand border of the tableau represent the supply available at each plant, and the entries at the bottom border represent the demand at each distribution center; note also that total supply equals total demand. The entries in the upper right-hand corner of each cell represent the per-unit cost of shipping over the corresponding route.

Once the transportation tableau is complete, we can proceed with the calculations necessary to determine the minimum cost decision. To begin, let us see how we can obtain an initial feasible solution.

Finding an Initial Feasible Solution: The Minimum Cost Method

The *minimum cost method* for identifying an initial feasible solution requires that we begin by allocating as many units as possible to the minimum cost route. In Table 7.3 we see that the Cleveland–Chicago, Bedford–St. Louis, and the York–Boston routes each qualify as the minimum cost route, since they each have a per-unit transportation cost of 2. When ties such as this occur, we will follow the practice of selecting the route over which we can ship the most units. Since this corresponds to shipping 4000 units from Cleveland to Chicago, we write 4000 in the Cleveland–Chicago cell of our transportation tableau. This reduces the supply at Cleveland from 5000 to 1000; hence we cross out the 5000 supply value and replace it with the revised value of 1000. In addition, since shipping 4000 units on this route satisfies the demand at Chicago, we cross out the 4000 Chicago value and replace it with 0. The Chicago demand is now zero. Thus, we eliminate this column from further consideration by drawing a line through the column. Our transportation tableau now appears as shown in tableau A.

	Boston	Chicago	St. Louis	Lexington	Supply
Cleveland	3	2	7	6	1000 ~~5000~~
		4,000			
Bedford	7	5	2	3	6000
York	2	5	4	5	2500
Demand	6000	~~4000~~ 0	2000	1500	

(A)

Now we look at all unlined cells in order to identify the new minimum cost route. There is a tie between the Bedford–St. Louis and York–Boston routes. But since more units can be shipped over the York–Boston route, we choose it for the next allocation. This results in an allocation of 2500 units over the York–Boston route. Thus the York supply is reduced to zero, and we eliminate this row from further consideration by lining through it. Continuing this process results in an allocation of 2000 units over the Bedford–St. Louis route and results in the elimination of the St. Louis column since its demand goes to zero. The transportation tableau we obtain after carrying out the second and third allocations is shown in tableau B.

We now have two routes which qualify for the minimum cost route with a value of 3: Cleveland–Boston and Bedford–Lexington. Since a maximum of 1000 units can be shipped over the Cleveland–Boston route as compared with 1500 over the Bedford–Lexington route, we will next allocate 1500 units to the Bedford–Lexington route. Doing so results in a demand of zero at Lexington, and hence this column is eliminated. The next minimum cost allocation then becomes 1000 over the Cleveland–Boston route. The transportation tableau now appears as shown in tableau C.

The only remaining unlined cell is now Bedford–Boston. Allocating 2500 units over this route uses up the remaining supply at Bedford and satisfies all the demand at Boston. The resulting tableau is shown in tableau D.

	Boston	Chicago	St. Louis	Lexington	Supply
Cleveland	3	2 / 4000	7	6	1000 / ~~5000~~
Bedford	7	5	2 / 2000	3	4000 / ~~6000~~
~~York~~	2 / 2500	5	4	5	0 / ~~2500~~
Demand	~~6000~~ 3500	~~4000~~ 0	~~2000~~ 0	1500	

(B)

	Boston	Chicago	St. Louis	Lexington	Supply
~~Cleveland~~	3 / 1000	2 / 4000	7	6	0 / ~~1000~~ / ~~5000~~
Bedford	7	5	2 / 2000	3 / 1500	2500 / ~~4000~~ / ~~6000~~
~~York~~	2 / 2500	5	4	5	0 / ~~2500~~
Demand	~~6000~~ ~~3500~~ 2500	~~4000~~ 0	~~2000~~ 0	~~1500~~ 0	

(C)

	Boston	Chicago	St. Louis	Lexington	Supply
Cleveland	3 / 1000	2 / 4000	7	6	0 / ~~1000~~ / ~~5000~~
Bedford	7 / 2500	5	2 / 2000	3 / 1500	0 / ~~2500~~ / ~~4000~~ / ~~6000~~
York	2 / 2500	5	4	5	0 / ~~2500~~
Demand	~~6000~~ / ~~3500~~ / ~~2500~~ / 0	~~4000~~ / 0	~~2000~~ / 0	~~1500~~ / 0	

(D)

This solution is feasible, since all the demand is satisfied and all the supply is used. The total transportation cost resulting from this solution is calculated in Table 7.4.

TABLE 7.4
Total Cost of Initial Feasible Solution Using the Minimum Cost Method

Route From	To	Units Shipped	Per-Unit Cost	Total Cost
Cleveland	Boston	1000	$3	$ 3,000
Cleveland	Chicago	4000	$2	8,000
Bedford	Boston	2500	$7	17,500
Bedford	St. Louis	2000	$2	4,000
Bedford	Lexington	1500	$3	4,500
York	Boston	2500	$2	5,000
			Total	$42,000

The method that we discuss in the next subsection provides an iterative procedure for moving from the initial feasible solution provided by the minimum cost method to an optimal solution. This method can be implemented only if the initial feasible solution of an m-origin, n-destination transportation problem utilizes exactly $m + n - 1$ transportation routes. Hence the Foster Generators transportation problem must have $3 + 4 - 1 = 6$ transportation routes in the initial solution. For the Foster Generators problem, the initial feasible solution just found satisfies this condition. **To guarantee that the minimum cost method will always generate initial feasible solutions with $m + n - 1$ routes being assigned shipments, we must modify it somewhat.**

Note that when we made our last allocation of 2500 units over the Bedford–Boston route, we simultaneously exhausted all the supply at Bedford and the demand at Boston. In developing an initial feasible solution, the last allocation will always reduce both the remaining row supply and column demand to zero. If this situation were to occur at *any prior iteration*, however, we would obtain an initial feasible solution with less than $m + n - 1$ transportation routes in use. To prevent this situation from occurring, whenever we reach an iteration that results in the supply at an origin and the demand at a destination being both reduced to zero simultaneously, we must proceed as follows:

1. Eliminate the row and column in question by drawing a line through each.
2. In addition to the assignment to the cell at the intersection of the lined out row and column we assign a shipment of zero units to any unoccupied cell in either the lined out row or column. We treat this cell the same as all other cells to which shipments are assigned.

To see how the above procedure is applied, consider the following transportation problem consisting of three origins and four destinations; initial transportation tableau E is shown below.

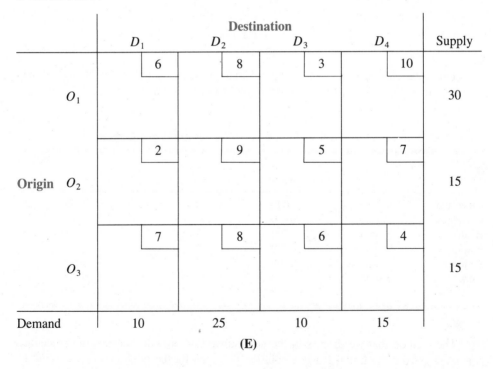

(E)

Carrying out the steps of the minimum cost method we would first allocate 10 units to the O_2-D_1 route followed by an allocation of 10 units to the O_1-D_3 route. The resulting transportation tableau F appears as follows:

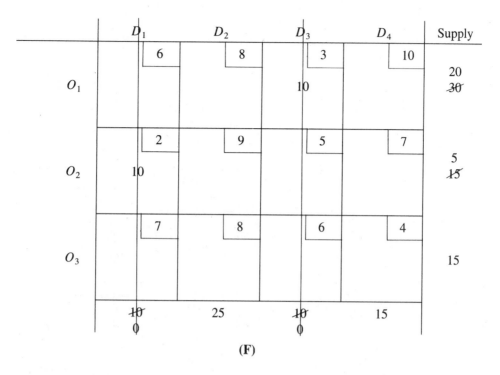

(F)

According to the minimum cost method our next allocation will be 15 units to the O_3-D_4 route. However, we see that making this allocation will simultaneously reduce the O_3 supply and the D_4 demand to zero. When we make this allocation, in order to guarantee that there will be two cell assignments whenever both a row and column are lined out (except when the last cell is assigned), we must also assign a flow of 0 units to one of the unoccupied cells in the O_3 row or the D_4 column. Assigning a flow of 0 units to the O_3-D_1 cell results in the following transportation tableau G.

We leave it as an exercise to the reader to demonstrate that continued application of the minimum cost method will result in an initial feasible solution consisting of $6 = 3 + 4 - 1$ transportation routes, one of which has a flow of 0.

There are many other methods available for finding initial feasible solutions for the transportation problem. Two of the most commonly used approaches are the northwest corner rule and Vogel's approximation method. These two approaches differ in that allocations made using the Vogel's approximation method take into consideration the cost of allocations (as does the minimum cost method we use), whereas the northwest corner rule ignores costs to obtain an initial feasible solution. None of these approaches provide the optimal solution unless a lot of good luck is involved. The minimum cost rule introduced here is easy to apply and takes cost into account to provide good initial feasible solutions. Thus this is the approach we shall use for finding initial feasible solutions.

Summary of the Minimum Cost Method

Before moving on to the second phase of the solution procedure and attempting to improve the initial feasible solution, let us restate the steps of the minimum cost method for obtaining an initial feasible transportation solution.

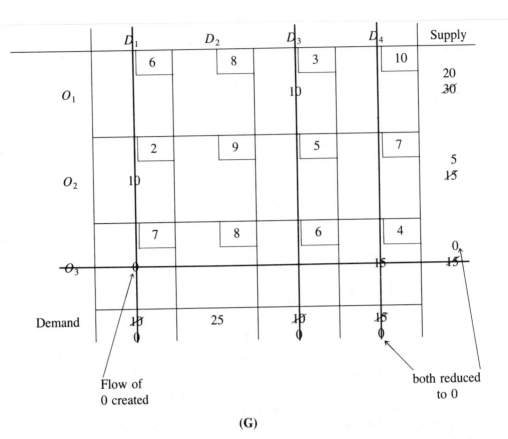

(G)

Step 1 Identify the cell in the transportation tableau with the lowest cost and assign as many units as possible to this transportation route or cell. In case of a tie choose the cell over which the most units can be shipped. If ties still exist, choose any of the tied cells.

Step 2 Reduce the row supply and the column demand by the amount assigned to the cell identified in step 1.

Step 3 If *all* row supplies and column demands have been exhausted, then stop; the allocations made will provide an initial feasible solution. Otherwise continue with step 4.

Step 4 If the row supply is now zero, eliminate the row from further consideration by drawing a line through it. If the column demand is now zero, eliminate the column by drawing a line through it. If both a row and column are lined out, make another allocation of 0 units to any unoccupied cell in the lined out row or column.

Step 5 Continue with step 1 for all unlined rows and columns.

The Stepping-Stone Method

The *stepping-stone method* provides an iterative procedure for moving from the initial feasible solution to an optimal solution. We will use the stepping-stone method to evaluate the economics of shipping via transportation routes that are not currently part of the transportation solution. If we can find cost-reducing routes, the current solution is revised by making shipments via these new routes. By continuing to evaluate the costs associated with routes that are not in the current solution, we will know that we have reached the optimal solution when all routes not in the current solution would increase costs if they were brought into the solution.

To see how the stepping-stone method works, let us return to the initial feasible solution for the Foster Generators problem found by the minimum cost method (H):

	Boston	Chicago	St. Louis	Lexington	Supply
Cleveland	3 1000	2 4000	7	6	5000
Bedford	7 2500	5	2 2000	3 1500	6000
York	2 2500	5	4	5	2500
Demand	6000	4000	2000	1500	

(H)

Suppose we were to allocate 1 unit to the route or cell in row 2 and column 2; that is, ship one unit on the currently unused route from Bedford to Chicago. In order to satisfy the Chicago demand exactly, we would have to reduce the number of units in the Cleveland–Chicago cell to 3999. But then we would have to increase the amount in the Cleveland–Boston cell to 1001 so that the total Cleveland supply of 5000 units could be shipped. Finally, we would reduce the Bedford–Boston cell by 1 in order to exactly satisfy the Boston demand. Tableau I summarizes the series of adjustments just described.

What is the added or reduced cost that will result from allocating one unit to the Bedford–Chicago route? Let us calculate the cost-per-unit change resulting from this change. The cost adjustments are as follows:

	Changes	Effect on Cost
Add 1 unit	Bedford–Chicago	+5
Reduce 1 unit	Cleveland–Chicago	−2
Add 1 unit	Cleveland–Boston	+3
Reduce 1 unit	Bedford–Boston	−7
	Net effect	−1

	Boston	Chicago	St. Louis	Lexington	Supply
Cleveland	3 1001 ~~1000~~	2 3999 ~~4000~~	7	6	5000
Bedford	7 2499 ~~2500~~	5 1	2 2000	3 1500	6000
York	2 2500	5	4	5	2500
Demand	6000	4000	2000	1500	

(I)

This analysis shows that the transportation costs can be reduced by $1 for every unit shipped over the Bedford–Chicago route if corresponding changes are made in other routes as shown.

Before making additions to this new route, let us consider the general procedure for evaluating the costs associated with a new cell or route and then check all currently unused routes to find the best route to add to our current transportation solution.

The method we have just demonstrated for evaluating the Bedford–Chicago route is known as the stepping-stone method. Note that in considering the addition of this new route, we evaluated its effect on other routes *currently in the transportation solution*, referred to as *occupied* cells. In total we considered changes in four cells, the new cell and three *current solution* or *occupied* cells. In effect, we can view these four cells as forming a path, or *stepping-stone path*, in the tableau, where the corners of the path are current solution cells. The idea is to view the tableau as a pond with the current solution cells as stones sticking up in the pond. To identify the stepping-stone path for a new cell, we move in horizontal and vertical directions using current solution cells as the stones at the corners of the path by which we can step from stone to stone and return to the new cell we initially started with. To help focus our attention on which occupied cells are part of the current stepping-stone path, we draw each occupied cell in the stepping-stone path as a cylinder; this should help to reinforce the image of these cells as stones sticking up in the pond. Hence, when evaluating the Bedford–Chicago route using the stepping-stone method, we would depict the solution as in tableau J.

In the above stepping-stone path we depicted the sequence of adjustments as proceeding from the Bedford–Chicago cell to the Cleveland–Chicago cell to the Cleveland–Boston cell to the Bedford–Boston cell and then back to the Bedford–Chicago cell; that is, the adjustments were made moving in a counterclockwise fashion. You should convince yourself that exactly the same adjustments appear if we had proceeded in a clockwise direction. In fact, in our next illustration of how to determine a stepping-stone path we will make the necessary adjustments proceeding in a clockwise manner.

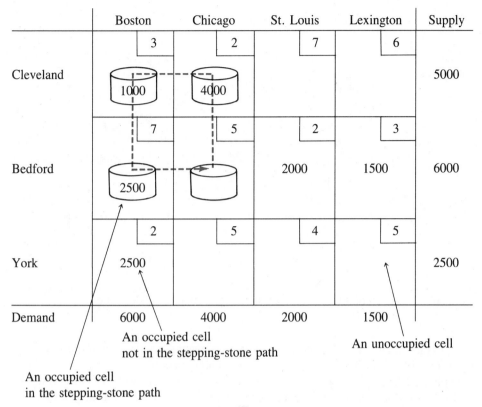

	Boston	Chicago	St. Louis	Lexington	Supply
Cleveland	3 / 1000	2 / 4000	7	6	5000
Bedford	7 / 2500	5	2 / 2000	3 / 1500	6000
York	2 / 2500	5	4	5	2500
Demand	6000	4000	2000	1500	

An occupied cell
not in the stepping-stone path

An unoccupied cell

An occupied cell
in the stepping-stone path

(J)

For example, let us consider how to compute the stepping-stone path if we were to use the Cleveland–St. Louis route. The dotted line in tableau K represents the stepping-stone path for the Cleveland–St. Louis route or cell. In terms of a transportation tableau, the stepping-stone path represents the sequence of adjustments that are necessary to maintain a feasible solution, given that one unit is to be shipped through a new or currently unoccupied cell.

Note that in order to carry out the adjustments necessary to increase the flow on the Cleveland–St. Louis route, the corners of the stepping-stone path are established in such a way that as we "jump" from stone to stone on this path we jump over the occupied Cleveland–Chicago cell. This type of situation frequently arises when we determine a stepping-stone path.

After identifying the stepping-stone path for a new cell, we can evaluate the costs associated with a one-unit addition to the new cell. For example, for the Cleveland–St. Louis cell this would result in the following changes:

Changes		Effect on Cost
Add 1 unit	Cleveland–St. Louis	+7
Reduce 1 unit	Bedford–St. Louis	−2
Add 1 unit	Bedford–Boston	+7
Reduce 1 unit	Cleveland–Boston	−3
	Net effect	+9

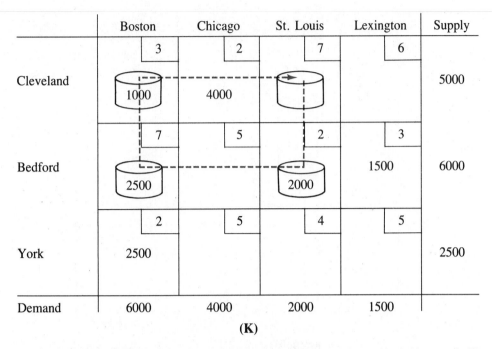

	Boston	Chicago	St. Louis	Lexington	Supply
Cleveland	3 / 1000	2 / 4000	7 /	6 /	5000
Bedford	7 / 2500	5 /	2 / 2000	3 / 1500	6000
York	2 / 2500	5 /	4 /	5 /	2500
Demand	6000	4000	2000	1500	

(K)

Thus we see that the Cleveland–St. Louis route is unattractive; the use of this route will result in a $9 per-unit increase in the total transportation cost.

Finding the stepping-stone path for each possible new cell enables us to identify the cost effect for each new cell or route. Evaluating this cost effect for all possible new cells leads to transportation tableau L. The per-unit cost effect for each possible new cell is circled in the cell.

	Boston	Chicago	St. Louis	Lexington	Supply
Cleveland	3 / 1000	2 / 4000	7 / (+9)	6 / (+7)	5000
Bedford	7 / 2500	5 / (−1)	2 / 2000	3 / 1500	6000
York	2 / 2500	5 / (+4)	4 / (+7)	5 / (+7)	2500
Demand	6000	4000	2000	1500	

(L)

On the basis of the calculated per-unit changes, we see that the best cell in terms of cost reduction is the Bedford–Chicago cell, with a $1 decrease in cost for every unit shipped on this route. The question now is: How much should we ship over this new route? Since the total cost decreases by $1 per unit shipped, we would like to ship the maximum possible number of units. We know from our previous stepping-stone calculation that each unit shipped over the Bedford–Chicago route results in an increase of one unit shipped from Cleveland to Boston and a decrease of one unit in both the amount shipped from Bedford to Boston (currently 2500) and the amount shipped from Cleveland to Chicago (currently 4000). Because of this the maximum we can ship over the Bedford–Chicago route is 2500. This results in a reduction of 2500 units on the Cleveland–Chicago route, an increase of 2500 units on the Cleveland–Boston route, and a decrease of 2500 units on the Bedford–Boston route. Tableau M corresponding to this new solution is presented below.

	Boston		Chicago		St. Louis		Lexington		Supply
		3		2		7		6	
Cleveland	3500		1500						5000
		7		5		2		3	
Bedford			2500		2000		1500		6000
		2		5		4		·5	
York	2500								2500
Demand	6000		4000		2000		1500		

(M)

Note that the only changes from the previous tableau are located on the stepping-stone path originating in the Bedford–Chicago cell. We can now use the stepping-stone method to recalculate the per-unit changes resulting from attempting to add new cells or routes to this new solution. Doing so we get tableau N. Note that the stepping-stone path used to evaluate the York–St. Louis cell is indicated by the dashed line in the tableau.

The per-unit change for every possible new cell is now greater than or equal to zero. Thus since there is no new route which will decrease the total cost, we have reached the optimal solution. The optimal solution, together with its total cost, is summarized in Table 7.5. As expected, this is exactly the same solution as obtained from the linear programming formulation (Table 7.2).

(N)

TABLE 7.5
Optimal Solution to the Foster Generators Transportation Problem

Route		Units	Per-Unit	Total
From	To	Shipped	Cost	Cost
Cleveland	Boston	3500	$3	$10,500
Cleveland	Chicago	1500	$2	3,000
Bedford	Chicago	2500	$5	12,500
Bedford	St. Louis	2000	$2	4,000
Bedford	Lexington	1500	$3	4,500
York	Boston	2500	$2	5,000
				$39,500

Maintaining $m + n - 1$ Transportation Routes Using the Stepping-Stone Method

In the discussion of the minimum cost method we stated that a requirement of the iterative procedure for finding an optimal solution is that the initial feasible solution must utilize $m + n - 1$ transportation routes. This requirement must also be maintained at each iteration of our stepping-stone solution procedure. Although we had no difficulty with the Foster Generators problem, situations can arise where as a result of making an allocation to a new cell the allocation to more than one of the unoccupied cells is reduced to zero. This would cause us to have fewer than $m + n - 1$ transportation routes in the current solution. To provide an illustration of such a situation let us consider the following modification of the Foster Generators transportation problem.

Suppose that the original supply at Cleveland were 3500 (instead of 5000) and that the demand at Chicago were 2500 (instead of 4000). The initial feasible solution we would obtain using the minimum cost method is shown in transportation tableau O:

	Boston	Chicago	St. Louis	Lexington	Supply
Cleveland	3 1000	2 2500	7	6	3500
Bedford	7 2500	5	2 2000	3 1500	6000
York	2 2500	5	4	5	2500
Demand	6000	2500	2000	1500	

(O)

Now if we were to consider shipping 2500 units over the Bedford–Chicago route as we did previously, the flow over the Cleveland–Chicago route would be reduced to zero, the flow over the Cleveland–Boston route would be increased to 3500, and the flow over the Bedford–Boston route would be reduced to zero. Thus two cells would be simultaneously reduced to zero, and hence in our new solution we would have only five transportation routes being utilized instead of the required six. To maintain a solution with six transportation routes, then, we arbitrarily select either the Cleveland–Chicago route or the Bedford–Boston route to receive a flow of zero units. Selecting the Bedford–Boston route to receive this flow results in transportation tableau P.

In further computations the Bedford–Boston cell is treated like any other occupied cell. The assignment of a flow of zero units in cases such as this guarantees that we will always utilize $m + n - 1$ transportation routes at any iteration of the solution procedure.

The most difficult part of the solution procedure we have outlined is the identification of every stepping-stone path so that we can calculate the cost-per-unit change in each new cell. There is an easier way to make these cost-per-unit calculations; it is called the *modified distribution (MODI) method*. Although we will not derive the method, we will demonstrate how it can be used to calculate the per-unit changes for the new or unoccupied cells.

Modified Distribution (MODI) Method

The MODI method provides a simple approach for determining the best unoccupied cell to bring into solution. This method requires that we define an index u_i for each row of

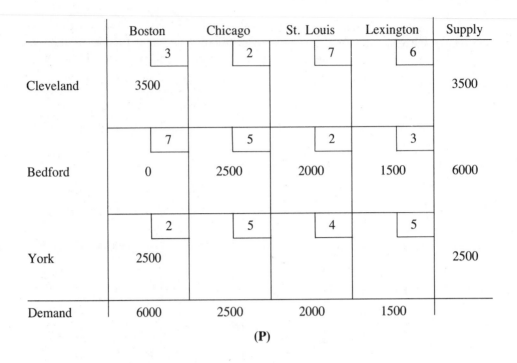

	Boston	Chicago	St. Louis	Lexington	Supply
Cleveland	3 3500	2	7	6	3500
Bedford	7 0	5 2500	2 2000	3 1500	6000
York	2 2500	5	4	5	2500
Demand	6000	2500	2000	1500	

(P)

the tableau and an index v_j for each column of the tableau. The values of these indices are found by requiring that the cost coefficient for each occupied cell equal $u_i + v_j$. If we define c_{ij} to be the per-unit cost of shipping from origin i to destination j, then we require that $u_i + v_j = c_{ij}$ for each occupied cell.

Requiring that $u_i + v_j = c_{ij}$ for all the occupied cells in the final tableau of the Foster Generators problem leads to a system of six equations and seven variables:

Occupied cell:
Cleveland–Boston	$u_1 + v_1 = 3$
Cleveland–Chicago	$u_1 + v_2 = 2$
Bedford–Chicago	$u_2 + v_2 = 5$
Bedford–St. Louis	$u_2 + v_3 = 2$
Bedford–Lexington	$u_2 + v_4 = 3$
York–Boston	$u_3 + v_1 = 2$

Since there is one more variable than equation in the above system, we can freely pick a value for one of the variables and then solve for the others. We shall always choose $u_1 = 0$ and then solve for the values of the other variables. Setting $u_1 = 0$, we get the following system of equations:

$$0 + v_1 = 3$$
$$0 + v_2 = 2$$
$$u_2 + v_2 = 5$$
$$u_2 + v_3 = 2$$

$$u_2 + v_4 = 3$$
$$u_3 + v_1 = 2$$

Solving these equations leads to the following values for u_1, u_2, u_3, v_1, v_2, v_3, and v_4:

$$
\begin{aligned}
u_1 &= 0 & v_1 &= 3 \\
u_2 &= 3 & v_2 &= 2 \\
u_3 &= -1 & v_3 &= -1 \\
& & v_4 &= 0
\end{aligned}
$$

It can be shown that $e_{ij} = c_{ij} - u_i - v_j$ represents the per-unit change in total cost resulting from allocating one unit to the unoccupied cell in row i and column j. Rewriting the final tableau Q for the Foster Generators problem and replacing the previous marginal information with the values of u_i and v_j, we obtain

u_i \ v_j	3	2	−1	0
0	3 — 3500	2 — 1500	7 — ⑧	6 — ⑥
3	7 — ①	5 — 2500	2 — 2000	3 — 1500
−1	2 — 2500	5 — ④	4 — ⑥	5 — ⑥

(Q)

Once again the per-unit cost effect for each new cell (e_{ij}) has been circled.

Note how much easier it is to compute the net changes using the MODI method. For example, $e_{13} = c_{13} - u_1 - v_3 = 7 - 0 - (-1) = 8$ represents the net change in the total cost that would result from allocating one unit to the cell in row 1 and column 3. We also observe that these e_{ij} calculated by the MODI method are exactly the same as the net changes calculated by the stepping-stone method. It is still necessary to search for a stepping-stone path to determine which route to remove from the solution once the best route to bring into the solution has been identified. However, it is not necessary to generate a stepping-stone path for any of the other unoccupied cells. Thus a considerable savings in the work required at each iteration can be obtained by employing the MODI method in the calculation of the e_{ij} for each unoccupied cell.

Summary of the Special-Purpose Solution Procedure for the Transportation Problem

In the preceding discussion we first showed how the minimum cost method can be used to obtain an initial feasible solution to the transportation problem. We then illustrated how the stepping-stone method can be used to determine which route (if any) to bring into the solution, which route to remove from the solution, and the number of units to ship over the new route. Finally, we showed that the MODI method—as compared with the stepping-stone method—provides an easier way to determine which route to bring into the solution.

This discussion suggests that we employ the following approach to solve the transportation problem: (1) use the minimum cost method to determine an initial feasible solution; (2) use the MODI method to determine which new route (if any) to bring into the solution; and (3) use the stepping-stone method to determine which route to remove from the solution and how many units to ship over the new route. Since we have already provided a summary of the steps needed to carry out the minimum cost method, we will not repeat the details of this method in summarizing the following special purpose solution procedure for the transportation problem.

Step 1   Use the minimum cost method to identify an initial feasible solution consisting of $m + n - 1$ occupied cells.

Step 2   Letting $u_1 = 0$, use the occupied cells of the transportation tableau to compute row indices $u_2, u_3, \ldots$ and column indices $v_1, v_2, v_3, \ldots$ such that

$$u_i + v_j = c_{ij}$$

for all occupied cells.

Step 3   Compute the cost e_{ij} of adding one unit to each unoccupied cell by

$$e_{ij} = c_{ij} - u_i - v_j$$

Step 4   In a minimization problem, if the per-unit changes (e_{ij}'s) for all unoccupied cells are nonnegative, the solution is optimal. However, if negative per-unit changes exist, identify the best cell (most negative per-unit change) and continue.

Step 5   For the best cell find the stepping-stone path through the transportation tableau. Label the best cell as cell 1 and number sequentially 2, 3, 4, . . . the occupied cells on the corners of the stepping-stone path. Determine the even-numbered stepping-stone cell over which the smallest quantity is being shipped. Add this quantity to the new cell and all other odd-numbered cells. Subtract this quantity from all even-numbered cells. If more than one of the currently occupied cells on the stepping-stone path is forced to zero, maintain the requirement of $m + n - 1$ occupied cells by entering a flow of zero units on one or more of the cells that were forced to zero. Return to step 2.

Handling Special Situations

Let us see how the following special situations are handled with the special-purpose solution procedure.

1. Total supply not equal to total demand
2. Maximization objective
3. Unacceptable transportation routes

The case where the total supply is not equal to the total demand can be handled easily by the special-purpose solution procedure if we first introduce a dummy origin or dummy destination. If total supply is greater than total demand, we introduce a *dummy destination* with demand exactly equal to the excess of supply over demand. Similarly, if total demand is greater than total supply, we introduce a *dummy origin* with supply exactly equal to the excess of demand over supply. In either the excess demand or excess supply case, we assign cost coefficients of zero to every route into a dummy destination and every route out of a dummy origin. This is because no shipments will actually be made from a dummy origin or to a dummy destination when the solution is implemented.

The special-purpose solution procedure can also be used to solve maximization problems. The only modification necessary involves the selection of an unoccupied cell to allocate units to. Instead of picking the cell with the most negative e_{ij} value, we pick that cell for which e_{ij} is largest. That is, we pick the cell that will cause the largest per-unit increase in the objective function.

To handle unacceptable transportation routes, we require that unacceptable assignments carry an extremely high cost, denoted M, in order to keep them out of solution. Thus if we have a transportation route from an origin to a destination that for some reason cannot be used, we simply assign this route a per-unit cost of M, and thus this route will not enter the solution. Unacceptable routes would be assigned a per-unit cost of $-M$ in a maximization problem.

Let us now consider another example to show how the above difficulties can be resolved. In the process we will also show how production costs can be taken into account in a transportation problem. Suppose we have three plants (origins) with production capacities as follows:

Plants	Production Capacity
P_1	50
P_2	40
P_3	30
Total	120

We also have demand for our product at three retail outlets (destinations). The demand forecasts for the current planning period are presented below:

Retail Outlets	Forecasted Demand
R_1	45
R_2	15
R_3	30
Total	90

The production cost at each plant is different, and the sales prices at the retail outlets vary. Taking prices, production costs, and shipping costs into consideration, the profits for producing one unit at plant i, shipping it to retail outlet j, and selling it at retail outlet j are presented in Table 7.6.

TABLE 7.6
Profit Per Unit for Producing at Plant i and Selling at Retail Outlet j

		Retail Outlets		
		R_1	R_2	R_3
Plants	P_1	2	8	10
	P_2	6	11	6
	P_3	12	7	9

We note first that the total production capacity exceeds the total demand at the retail outlets. Thus we must introduce a dummy retail outlet with demand exactly equal to the excess production capacity. We therefore add retail outlet R_4 with a demand of 30 units. The per-unit profit for shipping from each plant to retail outlet R_4 is set to zero, since these units will not actually be shipped. To obtain an initial feasible solution, we use the minimum cost method. However, since this is a maximization problem, the minimum cost method must be changed to a corresponding maximum profit method. That is, in general we select the shipping route that will maximize profit instead of minimizing cost. The initial feasible solution obtained using this approach is shown in tableau R.

Now let us compute the value of $e_{ij} = c_{ij} - u_i - v_j$, where the value of e_{ij} represents the per-unit change in total profit resulting from allocating one unit to the unoccupied cell in row i and column j. The following tableau S shows the values of u_i, v_j, and e_{ij} that we obtained.

Since this is a maximization problem, we look for the cell with the largest positive e_{ij}. However, since each e_{ij} value is negative, introducing any new allocation will only reduce the profit. Thus, the initial solution is optimal. When implementing this solution, we would ship 30 units from plant P_1 to retail outlet R_3, 15 units from P_2 to R_1, 15 units from P_2 to R_2, and 30 units from P_3 to R_1. Thus we are left with an excess supply of 20 units at P_1 and 10 units at P_2.

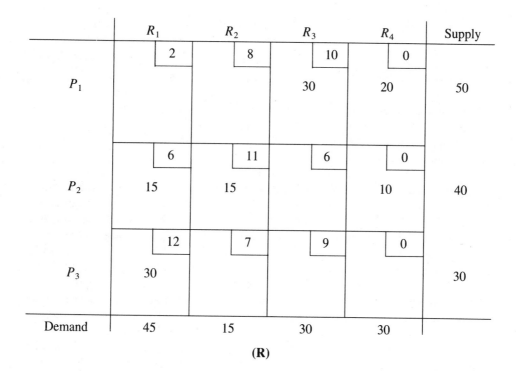

(R)

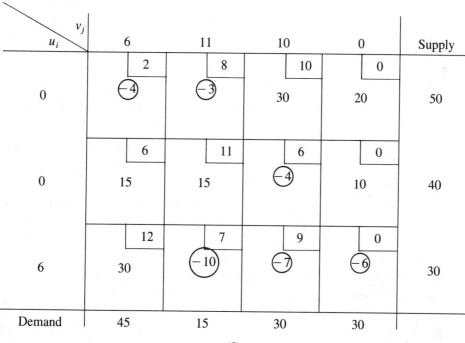

(S)

7.4   THE ASSIGNMENT PROBLEM

The assignment problem arises in a variety of decision-making situations. For example, typical assignment problems involve assigning jobs to machines, assigning workers to tasks or projects, assigning sales personnel to sales territories, assigning contracts to bidders, and so on. A distinguishing feature of the assignment problem is that *one* job, worker, etc., is assigned to *one and only one* machine, project, etc. Specifically, we look for the set of assignments that will optimize a stated objective, such as minimize cost, minimize time, or maximize profits.

As an illustration of the assignment problem, let us consider the case of Fowle Marketing Research, Inc., which has just received requests for market research studies from three new clients. The company is faced with the task of assigning project leaders to each of these three new research studies. Currently three individuals are relatively free from other major commitments and are available for the project leader assignments. Fowle's management realizes, however, that the time required to complete each study will depend upon the experience and ability of the project leader assigned to the study. Since the three projects have been judged to have approximately the same priority, the company would like to assign project leaders such that the total number of days required to complete all three projects is minimized. If a project leader is to be assigned to one and only one client, what assignments should be made?

In order to answer the assignment question, Fowle's management must first consider all possible project leader–client assignments and then estimate the corresponding project completion times. With three project leaders and three clients, there is a total of nine possible assignment alternatives. The alternatives and the estimated project completion times in days are summarized in Table 7.7. Using these data, we see that Terry would require 10 days to complete client 1's project, while Carle would require nine days for the same project. Similar completion time statements can be made about any of the other possible assignments.

TABLE 7.7
Estimated Project Completion Times (Days) for the Fowle, Inc. Assignment Problem

| | Client | | |
Project Leader	1	2	3
1. Terry	10	15	9
2. Carle	9	18	5
3. McClymonds	6	14	3

7.5   THE ASSIGNMENT PROBLEM: A LINEAR PROGRAMMING FORMULATION

Let us develop the linear programming model that can be used to solve Fowle's assignment problem. As in the transportation problem, we shall find it helpful to use double-subscripted decision variables, with x_{11} denoting the assignment of project leader 1 (Terry) to client 1, x_{12} denoting the assignment of project leader 1 (Terry) to client 2, and so on. We will let the decision variable equal 1 if the assignment is made and 0 if the assignment is not made. Thus the decision variables for the Fowle, Inc. assignment problem will be defined as follows:

$$x_{ij} = \begin{cases} 1 \text{ if project leader } i \text{ is assigned to client } j \\ 0 \text{ otherwise} \end{cases}$$

$$\text{where } i = 1, 2, 3, \text{ and } j = 1, 2, 3$$

Using this notation, $x_{21} = 1$ and $x_{31} = 0$ would tell us that project leader 2 (Carle) is assigned to client 1 and project leader 3 (McClymonds) is not assigned to client 1.

Since we are interested in the total number of days required to complete the three client projects, we can use the completion time data in Table 7.7 to develop the following completion time expressions:

$$\text{Days required for Terry's assignment} = 10x_{11} + 15x_{12} + 9x_{13}$$
$$\text{Days required for Carle's assignment} = 9x_{21} + 18x_{22} + 5x_{23}$$
$$\text{Days required for McClymonds' assignment} = 6x_{31} + 14x_{32} + 3x_{33}.$$

The sum of the days required for the three project leaders will provide the total days required to complete the three assignments.

The constraints for the assignment problem reflect the conditions that each project leader can be assigned to at most one client and that each client must have one assigned project leader. These constraints are written as follows:

$$\begin{aligned}
x_{11} + x_{12} + x_{13} &\le 1 \quad \text{Terry's assignment} \\
x_{21} + x_{22} + x_{23} &\le 1 \quad \text{Carle's assignment} \\
x_{31} + x_{32} + x_{33} &\le 1 \quad \text{McClymonds' assignment} \\
x_{11} + x_{21} + x_{31} &= 1 \quad \text{Client 1} \\
x_{12} + x_{22} + x_{32} &= 1 \quad \text{Client 2} \\
x_{13} + x_{23} + x_{33} &= 1 \quad \text{Client 3}
\end{aligned}$$

Combining the objective function and constraints into one model provides the following nine-variable, six-constraint linear programming formulation of the Fowle, Inc. assignment problem:

$$\min \quad 10x_{11} + 15x_{12} + 9x_{13} + 9x_{21} + 18x_{22} + 5x_{23} + 6x_{31} + 14x_{32} + 3x_{33}$$

s.t.

$$\begin{aligned}
x_{11} + x_{12} + x_{13} &\quad\quad\quad\quad\quad\quad\quad\quad\quad \le 1 \\
x_{21} + x_{22} + x_{23} &\quad\quad\quad\quad\quad \le 1 \\
x_{31} + x_{32} + x_{33} &\le 1 \\
x_{11} \quad\quad + x_{21} \quad\quad + x_{31} \quad\quad &= 1 \\
x_{12} \quad\quad + x_{22} \quad\quad + x_{32} &= 1 \\
x_{13} \quad\quad + x_{23} \quad\quad + x_{33} &= 1 \\
x_{ij} \ge 0 \quad \text{for } i = 1, 2, 3 \text{ and } j &= 1, 2, 3.
\end{aligned}$$

At this point have you noticed any similarities between the assignment problem and the transportation problem from the previous section? Viewing the project leaders as origins each with a supply of 1 and the clients as destinations each with a demand of 1, we see that the assignment problem is a special case of the transportation problem. Indeed, the assignment problem can be viewed as a transportation problem where all the supplies and all the demands are equal to 1.

In Figure 7.4 we show the network representation of the assignment problem. In this figure the nodes correspond to project leaders or clients and the arcs represent possible assignments. Note the similarity between the network representation of the assignment problem (Figure 7.4) and the network representation of the transportation problem (Figure 7.1).

FIGURE 7.4
The Assignment Problem Viewed as a Special Case of the Transportation Problem

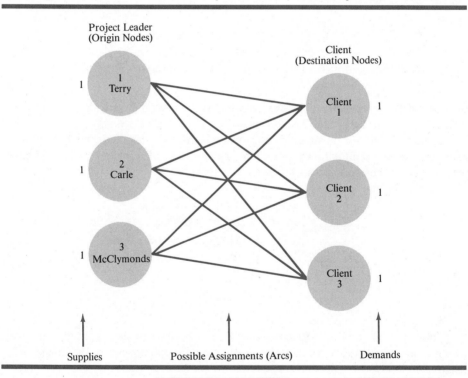

Figure 7.5 shows the LINDO/PC computer solution of the Fowle, Inc. assignment problem. Terry is assigned to client 2 ($x_{12} = 1$), Carle is assigned to client 3 ($x_{23} = 1$), and McClymonds is assigned to client 1 ($x_{31} = 1$). The total completion time required is 26 days. This solution is summarized in Table 7.8.

Handling Special Situations

Since the assignment problem can be viewed as a transportation problem, the special considerations that may arise in an assignment problem parallel those for the transportation

FIGURE 7.5
Computer Solution of Fowle, Inc. Assignment Problem Using LINDO/PC

```
               OBJECTIVE FUNCTION VALUE

       1)        26.0000000

       VARIABLE          VALUE          REDUCED COST
          X11           .000000          2.000000
          X12          1.000000           .000000
          X13           .000000          4.000000
          X21           .000000          1.000000
          X22           .000000          3.000000
          X23          1.000000           .000000
          X31          1.000000           .000000
          X32           .000000          1.000000
          X33           .000000           .000000
```

TABLE 7.8
Optimal Project Leader Assignments for the Fowle, Inc. Problem

Project Leader	Assigned Client	Days
Terry	2	15
Carle	3	5
McClymonds	1	6
Total days		26

problem discussed in Section 7.2. For example, consider the case where the assignment problem's total supply does not equal the total demand. Using the terminology of the Fowle Marketing Research, Inc. assignment problem, supply not equal to demand occurs whenever the total number of project leaders is not equal to the total number of clients. With more project leaders than clients (that is, supply greater than demand), the linear programming model will still provide the optimal solution. Any extra project leaders will simply remain unassigned. However, if total supply is less than total demand, the linear programming model will not generate a feasible solution because the demand constraints cannot be satisfied. Perhaps the easiest way to modify the linear program when demand exceeds supply is to add a dummy origin (project leader) with a fictitious supply equal to the difference between the total demand and the total supply. For example, if the firm had three project leaders and five clients, a dummy origin (project leader) would be added with a capacity for handling two clients. The objective function coefficients for any assignments from the dummy origin would be zero to ensure that the value of the optimal solution will still provide the total number of days required to complete the three assignments (no assignments will actually be made from the dummy origin). In this case the optimal solution provides the best assignment for the available supply of project leaders and also indicates which client demands must remain unassigned.

If the assignment alternatives are evaluated in terms of revenue or profit rather than time or cost, the linear programming formulation can be solved as a maximization rather than a minimization problem. In addition, if one or more assignments are unacceptable, the corresponding decision variable can be removed from the linear programming formulation. This situation would exist, for example, if a project leader did not have the experience necessary for one or more of the client assignments.

A General Linear Programming Formulation of the Assignment Problem

The general assignment problem is one that involves m objects and n tasks. If we let $x_{ij} = 1$ or 0 according to whether object i is assigned to task j or not, and if c_{ij} denotes the cost of assigning object i to task j, then we can write the general assignment model as follows:

$$\min \quad \sum_{i=1}^{m} \sum_{j=1}^{n} c_{ij} x_{ij}$$

$$\text{s.t.}$$

$$\sum_{j=1}^{n} x_{ij} \leq 1 \qquad i = 1, 2, \ldots, m \quad \text{Objects}$$

$$\sum_{i=1}^{m} x_{ij} = 1 \qquad j = 1, 2, \ldots, n \quad \text{Tasks}$$

$$x_{ij} \geq 0 \qquad \text{for all } i \text{ and } j$$

If the number of tasks, n, exceeds the number of objects, m (that is, demand exceeds supply), a dummy object with a capacity of $n - m$ must be included in order for us to obtain a feasible solution.

Handling Multiple Assignments

At the beginning of this section we indicated that a distinguishing feature of the assignment problem is that *one* object is assigned to *one and only one* task. In situations where one object can be assigned to two or more tasks, the linear programming formulation of the problem can be easily modified to account for such cases. For example, let us assume that in the Fowle Marketing Research problem Terry was permitted to be assigned to up to two clients; in this case the constraint representing Terry's assignment would be rewritten as $x_{11} + x_{12} + x_{13} \leq 2$. In general, if a_i denotes the upper limit for the number of tasks to which object i can be assigned, we can write the object constraints as

$$\sum_{j=1}^{n} x_{ij} \leq a_i \qquad i = 1, 2, \ldots, m$$

Thus we see that one advantage of formulating and solving assignment problems as linear programs is that special cases such as the situation involving multiple assignments can be easily handled.

7.6 THE ASSIGNMENT PROBLEM: A SPECIAL-PURPOSE SOLUTION PROCEDURE

As mentioned in the previous section, the assignment problem is a special case of the transportation problem. Thus the special-purpose solution procedure presented for the transportation problem could be used to solve the assignment problem. However, the assignment problem has an even more special structure. Because of this additional special structure, special-purpose solution procedures have been designed specifically to solve the assignment problem; one such procedure is called the *Hungarian method*. In this section we will show how the Hungarian method can be used to solve the Fowle Marketing Research problem.

Recall that the Fowle Marketing Research problem involved assigning project leaders to research projects; there were three project leaders available and three research projects to be completed. Fowle's assignment alternatives and estimated project completion times in days are restated in Table 7.9.

TABLE 7.9
Estimated Project Completion Times (days) for the Fowle, Inc. Assignment Problem

| Project Leader | Client | | |
	1	2	3
Terry	10	15	9
Carle	9	18	5
McClymonds	6	14	3

A table or matrix such as this will be associated with every assignment problem.

The Hungarian method involves what is called matrix reduction. By subtracting and adding appropriate values in the matrix, the method determines an optimal solution to the assignment problem. There are three major steps associated with the procedure. Step 1 provides the initial matrix reduction.

Step 1   Reduce the initial matrix by subtracting the smallest element in each row from every element in that row. Then, using the row-reduced matrix, subtract the smallest element in each column from every element in that column.

Thus we first reduce the matrix in Table 7.9 by subtracting the minimum value in each row from each element in the row. With the minimum values of 9 for row 1, 5 for row 2, and 3 for row 3, our row-reduced matrix becomes

	1	2	3
Terry	1	6	0
Carle	4	13	0
McClymonds	3	11	0

The assignment problem represented by this reduced matrix is equivalent to our original assignment problem in the sense that the same solution will be optimal. To understand why, first note that the row 1 minimum element, 9, has been subtracted from every element in the first row. Since Terry must still be assigned to one of the clients, the only change is that in this revised problem the time for any assignment will be nine days less. Similarly, Carle and McClymonds are shown with completion times requiring five and three fewer days, respectively.

Continuing with step 1 in the matrix reduction process, we now subtract the minimum element in each column of the row-reduced matrix from every element in the column. This also leads to an equivalent assignment problem; that is, the same solution will still be optimal but the times required to complete each project are reduced. With the minimum values of 1 for column 1, 6 for column 2, and 0 for column 3, the reduced matrix becomes

	1	2	3
Terry	0	0	0
Carle	3	7	0
McClymonds	2	5	0

The goal of the Hungarian method is to continue reducing the matrix until the value of one of the solutions is zero, that is, until an assignment of project leaders to clients can be made that, in terms of the reduced matrix, requires a total time expenditure of zero days. Then, as long as there are no negative elements in the matrix, the zero-valued solution will be optimal. The way in which we perform this further reduction and recognize when we have reached an optimal solution is described in the following two steps.

Step 2 Find the minimum number of straight lines that must be drawn through the rows and the columns of the current matrix so that all the zeros in the matrix will be covered. If the minimum number of straight lines is the same as the number of rows (or equivalently, columns) in the matrix, an optimal assignment with value zero can be made. If the minimum number of lines is less than the number of rows, go to step 3.

Applying step 2 as shown below, we see that the minimum number of lines required to cover all the zeros is 2. Thus we must continue to step 3:

	1	2	3	
Terry	0	0	0	Two straight lines will cover
Carle	3	7	0	all the zeros (step 2)
McClymonds	②	5	0	

Step 3 Subtract the value of the smallest unlined element from every unlined element and add this same value to every element at the intersection of two lines. All

other elements remain unchanged. Return to step 2 and continue until the minimum number of lines necessary to cover all the zeros in the matrix is equal to the number of rows.

The minimum unlined element is 2. In the matrix above we have circled this element. Subtracting 2 from all unlined elements and adding 2 to the intersection element for Terry and client 3 produces the new matrix shown below:

	1	2	3
Terry	0	0	2
Carle	1	5	0
McClymonds	0	3	0

Returning to step 2, we find that the minimum number of straight lines required to cover all the zeros in the current matrix is 3. The following matrix illustrates the step 2 calculations:

	1	2	3
Terry	0	0	2
Carle	1	5	0
McClymonds	0	3	0

Three lines must be drawn to cover all zeros; therefore the optimal solution has been reached

According to step 2, then, it must be possible to find an assignment with a value of zero. Such an assignment can be found by first locating any row or column which contains only one zero. We draw a square around the zero, indicating an assignment, and eliminate that row and column from further consideration. Since row 2 has only one zero in the Fowle, Inc. problem, we assign Carle to 3 and eliminate row 2 and column 3 from further consideration. McClymonds must then be assigned to 1 (the only remaining zero in row 3), and finally Terry to 2. The solution to the Fowle, Inc. problem is shown below; in terms of the reduced matrix it requires a time expenditure of zero days.

	1	2	3
Terry	0	[0]	2
Carle	1	5	[0]
McClymonds	[0]	3	0

The value of the optimal assignment can be found by referring to the original assignment problem and summing the solution times associated with the optimal assignment; in this case Terry to 2, Carle to 3, and McClymonds to 1. Thus we obtain the solution time of $15 + 5 + 6 = 26$ days.

Finding the Minimum Number of Lines

Sometimes it is not obvious how the lines should be drawn through rows and columns of the matrix in order to cover all the zeros with the smallest number of lines. In these cases the following heuristic works well. Choose any row or column with a single zero. If it is a row, draw a line through the column the zero is in; if it is a column, draw a line through the row the zero is in. Continue in this fashion until all the zeros are covered.

If you make the mistake of drawing too many lines to cover the zeros in the reduced matrix, and thus conclude an optimal solution has been reached when it has not, you will find you cannot identify a zero-value assignment. Thus if you think you have reached the optimal solution, but the zero-value assignments cannot be found, go back to the previous step and check to see if you have actually determined the minimum number of lines necessary to cover the zero elements.

Handling Special Situations

We now discuss how to handle the following special situations when using the Hungarian method.

1. Number of objects not the same as the number of tasks
2. Maximization objective
3. Unacceptable assignments

The special-purpose solution procedure for the assignment problem requires that the number of rows (people, objects, and so on) equal the number of columns (tasks, clients, and so on). Suppose that in the Fowle, Inc. example four project leaders had been available for assignment to the three new clients. Fowle still faces the same basic problem—namely, which project leaders should be assigned to which clients in order to minimize the total days required. The project completion time estimates with a fourth project leader are shown in Table 7.10.

TABLE 7.10
Estimated Project Completion Time (days) for
the Fowle, Inc. Assignment Problem with Four
Project Leaders

Project Leader	Client 1	2	3
Terry	10	15	9
Carle	9	18	5
McClymonds	6	14	3
Higley	8	16	6

We have seen how to apply the Hungarian method when the number of rows and columns are equal. Therefore, we can apply the same procedure if we can add a new client. Since we do not have another client, we simply add a dummy column, or a dummy client. Since this dummy client is nonexistent, the project leader assigned to the dummy client in the optimal assignment solution will in effect be the unassigned project leader.

What project completion time estimates should we show in this new dummy column? Actually any arbitrary value is acceptable as long as all project leaders are given the same completion time. However, since the dummy client assignment will not take place, a zero project completion time for all project leaders seems logical. The Fowle, Inc. assignment problem with a dummy client, labeled D, is shown in Table 7.11. Problem 15 at the end of the chapter asks you to use the Hungarian method to determine the optimal solution to this problem.

TABLE 7.11
Estimated Project Completion Time (days) for the Fowle,
Inc. Assignment Problem with a Dummy Client

Project Leader	Client 1	2	3	D ← Dummy client
Terry	10	15	9	0
Carle	9	18	5	0
McClymonds	6	14	3	0
Higley	8	16	6	0

Note that if we had considered the case of four new clients and only three project leaders, we would have had to add a dummy row (dummy project leader) in order to apply the Hungarian method. The client receiving the dummy leader would not actually be assigned an immediate project leader and would have to wait until one becomes available. In order to obtain an assignment problem form compatible with the solution algorithm, it may be necessary to add several dummy rows or dummy columns, but never both.

To illustrate how maximization assignment problems can be handled, let us consider the problem facing management of Salsbury Discounts, Inc. Suppose that Salsbury Discounts, Inc. has just leased a new store and is attempting to determine where various departments should be located within the store. The store manager has four locations that have not yet been assigned a department and is considering five departments that might occupy the four locations. The departments under consideration are a shoe, a toy, an auto parts, a housewares, and a record department. The store manager would like to determine the optimal assignment of departments to locations in order to maximize profits. After a careful study of the layout of the remainder of the store, and based on his experience with similar stores, the store manager has made estimates of the expected annual profit for each department in each location. These are presented in Table 7.12.

We now have an assignment problem that requires a maximization objective. However, we have a problem involving more rows than columns. Thus we must first add a dummy column, corresponding to a dummy or fictitious location, in order to apply the Hungarian method. After adding a dummy column, we obtain the 5 × 5 Salsbury Discount, Inc. assignment problem shown in Table 7.13.

We can obtain an equivalent minimization assignment problem by converting all the elements in the matrix to opportunity losses. This conversion is accomplished by subtracting every element in each column from the largest element in the column.

TABLE 7.12
Estimated Annual Profit (thousands of dollars) for Each
Department-Location Combination

Department	Location			
	1	2	3	4
Shoe	10	6	12	8
Toy	15	18	5	11
Auto parts	17	10	13	16
Housewares	14	12	13	10
Record	14	16	6	12

TABLE 7.13
Estimated Annual Profit (thousands of dollars) for Each
Department-Location Combination, Including a Dummy
Location

Department	Location				← Dummy location
	1	2	3	4	5
Shoe	10	6	12	8	0
Toy	15	18	5	11	0
Auto parts	17	10	13	16	0
Housewares	14	12	13	10	0
Record	14	16	6	12	0

It turns out that finding the assignment that minimizes opportunity loss leads to the same solution that maximizes the value of the assignment in the original problem. Thus any maximization assignment problem can be converted to a minimization problem by converting the assignment matrix to one in which the elements represent opportunity losses. Hence we begin our solution to this maximization assignment problem by developing an assignment matrix where each element represents the opportunity loss from not making the "best" assignment. The opportunity losses are presented in Table 7.14.

TABLE 7.14
Opportunity Loss (thousands of dollars) for Each Department-
Location Combination

Department	Location				← Dummy location
	1	2	3	4	5
Shoe	7	12	1	8	0
Toy	2	0	8	5	0
Auto parts	0	8	0	0	0
Housewares	3	6	0	6	0
Record	3	2	7	4	0

The opportunity loss from putting the shoe department in location 1 is $7000. That is, if we put the shoe department, instead of the best department (auto parts), in that location, we forgo the opportunity to make an additional $7000 in profit. The opportunity loss associated with putting the toy department in location 2 is zero, since it yields the highest profit in that location. What about the opportunity losses associated with the dummy column? Well, the assignment of a department to this "dummy" location means that the department will not be assigned a store location in the optimal solution. Since all departments earn the same amount from this dummy location, zero, the opportunity loss for each department is zero.

Following steps 1, 2, and 3 of the Hungarian method, we can proceed to determine the maximum profit assignment. Problem 16(b) at the end of this chapter asks you to use the Hungarian method to determine the optimal solution to this problem.

As an illustration of how we can handle unacceptable assignments, suppose that in the Salsbury Discounts, Inc. assignment problem the store manager believed that the toy department should not be considered for location 2 and the auto parts department should not be considered for location 4. Essentially the store manager is saying that, based on other considerations, such as size of area, adjacent departments, and so on, these two assignments are unacceptable alternatives.

Using the same approach for the assignment problem that we did for the transportation problem, we define a value of M for unacceptable minimization assignments and a value of $-M$ for unacceptable maximization assignments, where M is an arbitrarily large value. In fact, M is assumed so large that M plus or minus any value is still extremely large. Thus an M-valued cell in an assignment matrix retains its M value throughout the matrix reduction calculations. An M-valued cell can never be zero; so it can never be an assignment in the final solution.

The Salsbury Discounts, Inc. assignment problem with the two unacceptable assignments is shown in Table 7.15.

TABLE 7.15
Estimated Profit for the Salsbury Department-Location Combinations

Department	Location				
	1	2	3	4	5
Shoe	10	6	12	8	0
Toy	15	$-M$	5	11	0
Auto parts	17	10	13	$-M$	0
Housewares	14	12	13	10	0
Record	14	16	6	12	0

When this assignment matrix is converted to an opportunity loss matrix, the $-M$ profit value will be changed to M. Problem 17(b) at the end of this chapter asks you to solve this assignment problem.

7.7 THE TRANSSHIPMENT PROBLEM

In the transportation problem shipments were only permitted from origin nodes directly to destination nodes. In the transshipment problem intermediate nodes, referred to as transshipment nodes, are added to account for locations such as warehouses where goods from an origin can be temporarily stored prior to being shipped to the customer destination. In this more general type of distribution problem, shipments are permitted to occur between any pair of the three general types of nodes: origin nodes, transshipment nodes, and destination nodes. For example, the transshipment problem permits shipments of goods from one supply location (origin) to another supply location, from one transshipment location to another, and from one destination location to another.

As was true for the transportation problem the quantity of goods available at each origin is fixed or limited. In addition, the destination demands are known and fixed. Thus the objective in the transshipment problem is to determine how many units should be shipped from one location to another so that all destination demands are satisfied with the minimum possible transportation costs.

In order to illustrate the transshipment problem, let us consider the problem faced by Ryan Electronics. Ryan is an electronics company with production facilities located in Denver and Atlanta. Components produced at either facility may be shipped to either of the firm's regional warehouses which are located in Kansas City and Louisville. From the regional warehouses the firm supplies retail outlets located in Detroit, Miami, Dallas, and New Orleans. The key features of the problem are shown in the transshipment network depicted in Figure 7.6. Note that the supply at each production facility or plant and the demand at each retail outlet are shown in the left and right margins, respectively. Note also that we have numbered the nodes in the network with nodes 1 and 2 the origin nodes, nodes 3 and 4 the transshipment nodes, and nodes 5, 6, 7, and 8 the destination nodes. Table 7.16 shows the transportation cost per unit for each distribution route in the network.

7.8   THE TRANSSHIPMENT PROBLEM: A LINEAR PROGRAMMING FORMULATION

To begin the linear programming formulation of the problem, we let x_{ij} denote the number of units shipped from node i to node j. For example, x_{13} denotes the number of units shipped from the Denver plant to the Kansas City warehouse, x_{14} denotes the number of units shipped from the Denver plant to the Louisville warehouse, and so on. Since the supply at the Denver plant is 600 units, the amount shipped out of the Denver plant must be less than or equal to 600. Mathematically this supply constraint is written

$$x_{13} + x_{14} \le 600$$

Similarly, for the Atlanta plant we have

$$x_{23} + x_{24} \le 400$$

Let us now consider how we must write the constraints corresponding to the two transshipment nodes. For node 3 (the Kansas City warehouse) we must guarantee that the number of units shipped out must equal the number of units shipped into the warehouse. Since

FIGURE 7.6
Network Representation of the Ryan Electronics Transshipment Problem

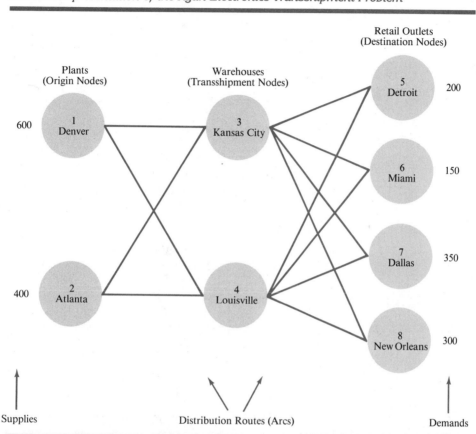

Number of units
shipped out of node 3 $= x_{35} + x_{36} + x_{37} + x_{38}$

and

Number of units
shipped into node 3 $= x_{13} + x_{23}$

then

$$x_{35} + x_{36} + x_{37} + x_{38} = x_{13} + x_{23}$$

Placing all the variables on the left-hand side of the expression enables us to write the constraint corresponding to node 3 as

$$- x_{13} - x_{23} + x_{35} + x_{36} + x_{37} + x_{38} = 0$$

In a similar manner, the constraint corresponding to node 4 is

$$- x_{14} - x_{24} + x_{45} + x_{46} + x_{47} + x_{48} = 0$$

TABLE 7.16
Unit Transportation Costs for the Ryan Electronics Transshipment Problem

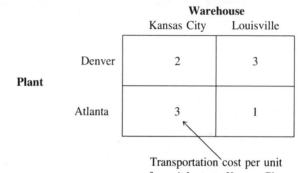

| | | **Warehouse** | |
		Kansas City	Louisville
Plant	Denver	2	3
	Atlanta	3	1

Transportation cost per unit
from Atlanta to Kansas City

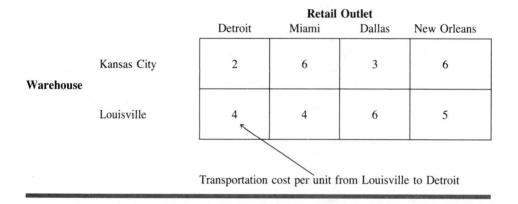

| | | **Retail Outlet** | | | |
		Detroit	Miami	Dallas	New Orleans
Warehouse	Kansas City	2	6	3	6
	Louisville	4	4	6	5

Transportation cost per unit from Louisville to Detroit

In order to develop the constraints associated with the destination nodes, we recognize that for each node the amount shipped to the destination must equal the demand. For example, to satisfy the demand for 200 units at node 5 (the Detroit retail outlet), we can write

$$x_{35} + x_{45} = 200$$

Similarly, for nodes 6, 7, and 8, we have the following constraints:

$$x_{36} + x_{46} = 150$$
$$x_{37} + x_{47} = 350$$
$$x_{38} + x_{48} = 300$$

As usual the objective function reflects the total shipping cost over the 12 shipping routes. Combining the objective function and constraints leads to a 12-variable, eight-constraint linear programming model of the Ryan Electronics transshipment problem (see Figure 7.7).

FIGURE 7.7

Linear Programming Formulation of the Ryan Electronics Transshipment Problem

min $2x_{13} + 3x_{14} + 3x_{23} + 1x_{24} + 2x_{35} + 6x_{36} + 3x_{37} + 6x_{38} + 4x_{45} + 4x_{46} + 6x_{47} + 5x_{48}$

s.t.

$$
\begin{array}{llllllllll}
x_{13} + & x_{14} & & & & & & & & \leq 600 \;\Big\}\; \text{Origin node} \\
& & x_{23} + & x_{24} & & & & & & \leq 400 \;\Big\}\; \text{constraints} \\
-x_{13} & & -\, x_{23} & & + x_{35} + & x_{36} + & x_{37} + & x_{38} & & = \;\;\;0 \;\Big\}\; \text{Transshipment node} \\
& -\, x_{14} & & -\, x_{24} & & & & & + x_{45} + x_{46} + x_{47} + x_{48} = \;\;\;0 \;\Big\}\; \text{constraints} \\
& & & & x_{35} & & & & + x_{45} & = 200 \\
& & & & & x_{36} & & & + x_{46} & = 150 \\
& & & & & & x_{37} & & + x_{47} & = 350 \\
& & & & & & & x_{38} & + x_{48} & = 300 \\
\end{array}
$$

$\quad\quad\quad\quad\quad\quad\quad\quad\quad x_{ij} \geq 0 \text{ for all } i \text{ and } j$

Note that in the linear programming formulation of the transshipment problem we have one variable for each possible shipping route and one constraint for each node.

The optimal solution was obtained using LINDO/PC. Figure 7.8 shows the computer output and Table 7.17 summarizes the optimal solution.

As we mentioned at the beginning of this section, in some transshipment problems it is possible to have shipments between plants, between warehouses, and/or between destinations. All such shipping patterns are possible in a transshipment problem. We still only require one constraint per node, but the constraints may involve more variables. For origin nodes we require that the sum of the shipments out minus the shipments in must be less than or equal to the origin supply. For destination nodes the sum of the shipments

FIGURE 7.8

Computer Solution to Ryan Electronics Transshipment Problem Using LINDO/PC

```
              OBJECTIVE FUNCTION VALUE

       1)        5200.00000

       VARIABLE          VALUE          REDUCED COST
          X13        600.000000             .000000
          X14           .000000             .000000
          X23           .000000            3.000000
          X24        400.000000             .000000
          X35        200.000000             .000000
          X36           .000000            1.000000
          X37        350.000000             .000000
          X38         50.000000             .000000
          X45           .000000            3.000000
          X46        150.000000             .000000
          X47           .000000            4.000000
          X48        250.000000             .000000
```

TABLE 7.17
Optimal Solution to the Ryan Electronics Transshipment Problem

Route		Units	Per-Unit	Total
From	To	Shipped	Cost	Cost
Denver	Kansas City	600	$2	$1200
Atlanta	Louisville	400	$1	400
Kansas City	Detroit	200	$2	400
Kansas City	Dallas	350	$3	1050
Kansas City	New Orleans	50	$6	300
Louisville	Miami	150	$4	600
Louisville	New Orleans	250	$5	1250
				$5200

in minus the sum of the shipments out must equal demand. For transshipment nodes we require that the sum of the shipments out must equal the sum of the shipments in, just as before.

One final case deserves mention. Sometimes there are shipping capacities on routes. In this case we simply add an upper bound constraint on the variable representing the amount shipped over the capacitated route. This is the same way route capacities are handled for the transportation problem. We refer to this more general type of transshipment problem as the *capacitated transshipment problem*.

Special-purpose solution procedures have also been developed for the transshipment problem. One approach makes use of the fact that any transshipment problem can be converted into an equivalent transportation problem; then a special-purpose solution procedure for the transportation problem (such as we introduced in Section 7.3) is used to solve the modified transshipment problem. Details regarding the use of this type of approach, as well as even more efficient procedures, can be found in more advanced books on network models.

Summary

In this chapter we showed how the transportation, assignment, and transshipment problems can be modeled and solved as linear programs. In addition, we also showed how special-purpose solution procedures can be used to solve the transportation and assignment problems. These special-purpose solution procedures are the only practical way to solve small problems by hand, moderate-sized problems on a microcomputer, and very large problems on a mainframe computer.

An important feature to note regarding each of these problems is that under very general conditions, their optimal solutions are integral. That is, when solving any transportation, assignment, or transshipment problem for which the supplies at the origin nodes and the demands at the destination nodes are all intergers, the solution will always consist of integer values.

Glossary

Transportation problem A problem often involving minimizing the cost of shipping goods from a set of origins to a set of destinations. It can be formulated and solved as a linear program.

Assignment problem A problem that often involves the assignment of individuals to tasks. It can be formulated as a linear program and is a special case of the transportation problem.

Transshipment problem An extension of the transportation problem to distribution problems involving transfer points and possible shipments between origins and between destinations. It can be formulated as a linear program.

Network A graphical description of a problem consisting of numbered circles (nodes) interconnected by a series of lines (arcs). The transportation, assignment, and transshipment problem can be shown as networks.

Nodes The intersection or junction points of a network.

Arcs The lines connecting the nodes in the network.

Minimum cost method A simple procedure used to find an initial feasible solution to a transportation problem.

Stepping-stone method A procedure for identifying which routes will receive flow adjustments when a shipment is made over an unused route in the special-purpose solution procedure for the transportation problem.

MODI method A procedure for determining the per-unit cost change associated with shipping over an unused route in the special-purpose solution procedure for a transportation problem.

Dummy origin An origin added to make total supply equal to total demand in a transportation problem. The supply assigned to the dummy origin is the excess of the actual demand over the actual supply.

Dummy destination A destination added to make total supply equal to total demand in a transportation problem. The demand assigned to the dummy destination is the excess of the actual supply over the actual demand.

Hungarian method A special-purpose solution procedure for solving the assignment problem.

Dummy row(s) Extra row(s) added to an assignment problem to provide the equal number of rows and columns required by the Hungarian solution procedure.

Dummy column(s) Extra column(s) added to an assignment problem to provide the equal number of rows and columns required by the Hungarian method.

Opportunity loss For each cell in an assignment matrix the opportunity loss is the difference between the largest value in the column and the value in the cell. The entries in the cells of an assignment matrix must be converted to opportunity losses to solve maximization problems using the Hungarian method.

Problems

1. Consider the following transportation problem:

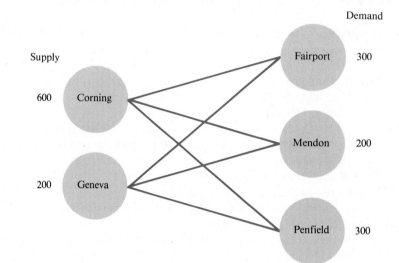

The transportation costs per unit are as follows:

	Fairport	Mendon	Penfield
Corning	16	10	14
Geneva	12	12	20

a. Develop a linear programming model for this problem. Be sure to define all terms. What is the minimum cost solution?
b. Set up the transportation tableau for this problem.
c. Use the minimum cost method to find an initial solution.
d. Use the special-purpose solution procedure to find an optimal solution.

2. A product is produced at three plants and shipped to three warehouses (the transportation costs per unit are shown in the table):

			Warehouse		Plant
		W_1	W_2	W_3	Capacity
	P_1	20	16	24	300
Plant	P_2	10	10	8	500
	P_3	12	18	10	100
Warehouse demands		200	400	300	

a. Develop a linear programming model for minimizing transportation costs; solve this model to determine the minimum cost solution.
b. Suppose the entries in the table above represent profit per unit from producing at plant *i* and selling to warehouse *j*. How does the model formulation change from that in part (a)?
c. Use the special-purpose solution procedure to solve the original problem involving transportation costs.

3. Arnoff Enterprises manufactures the central processing unit (CPU) for a line of personal computers. The CPUs are manufactured in Seattle, Columbus, and New York and shipped to warehouses in Pittsburgh, Mobile, Denver, Los Angeles, and Washington, D.C., for further distribution. The transportation tableau below shows the number of CPUs available at each plant and the number of CPUs required by each warehouse. The shipping costs (dollars per unit) are also shown.
a. Determine the amount that should be shipped from each plant to each warehouse in order to minimize the total shipping cost.
b. The Pittsburgh warehouse has just increased its order by 1000 units and Arnoff has authorized the Columbus plant to increase its production by 1000 units. Do you expect this development to lead to an increase or a decrease in total shipping costs? Solve for the new optimal solution.

| | | Warehouse | | | | | Units |
	Pittsburgh	Mobile	Denver	Los Angeles	Washington		Available
Seattle	10	20	5	9	10		9000
Plant Columbus	2	10	8	30	6		4000
New York	1	20	7	10	4		8000
Units Required	3000	5000	4000	6000	3000		21,000

4. Consider the following transportation problem:

			Destination		
		Boston	Atlanta	Houston	Supply
Origin	Detroit	5	2	3	100
	St. Louis	8	4	3	300
	Denver	9	7	5	300
	Demand	300	200	200	

Cost/unit

a. Develop a linear programming model for this transportation problem.
b. The computer solution to this problem is shown below. What is the minimum cost solution? How many units are shipped over each transportation route?

```
                    OBJECTIVE FUNCTION VALUE

        1)              3900.00000

     VARIABLE            VALUE           REDUCED COST
        X11             .000000            .000000
        X12          100.000000            .000000
        X13             .000000           2.000000
        X21             .000000           1.000000
        X22          100.000000            .000000
        X23          200.000000            .000000
        X31          300.000000            .000000
        X32             .000000           1.000000
        X33             .000000            .000000
```

c. Assume that a requirement is that 100 units must be shipped over the Detroit–Boston route. How would the linear programming model have to be modified to reflect this change?
d. Suppose that a labor dispute temporarily eliminates the Denver–Boston and the St. Louis–Atlanta routes. How would the linear programming model have to be revised to reflect these changes?
e. Solve the transportation problem first with the modification in part (c) and then resolve with the modification in part (d). What effect will each of these changes have on the total transportation costs and the specific transportation schedule?

5. Consider the following minimum cost transportation problem:

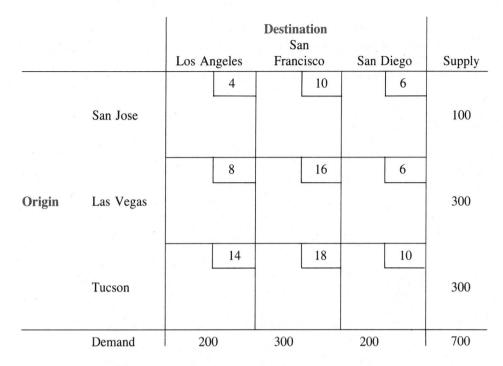

		Los Angeles	San Francisco	San Diego	Supply
		4	10	6	
	San Jose				100
		8	16	6	
Origin	Las Vegas				300
		14	18	10	
	Tucson				300
	Demand	200	300	200	700

a. Use the minimum cost method to find an initial solution.
b. Use the special-purpose solution procedure to find an optimal solution.
c. How would the optimal solution change if we must ship 100 units on the Tucson–San Diego route?
d. Because of road construction, the Las Vegas–San Diego route is now unacceptable. Resolve the initial problem.

6. Consider the minimum cost transportation problem show below:

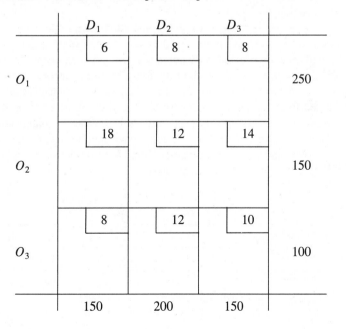

	D_1	D_2	D_3	
	6	8	8	
O_1				250
	18	12	14	
O_2				150
	8	12	10	
O_3				100
	150	200	150	

a. Use the minimum cost method to find an initial feasible solution.
b. Use the special-purpose solution procedure to find an optimal solution.
c. Using your solution to part (b), identify an alternate optimal solution.

7. Solve the following minimum cost transportation problem:

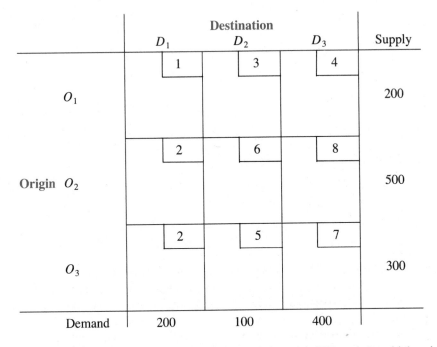

Since total supply (1000 units) exceeds total demand (700 units), which origins may consider alternate uses for their excess supply and still maintain a minimum total transportation cost solution?

8. Klein Chemicals, Inc. produces a special oil-base material that is currently in short supply. Four of Klein's customers have already placed orders which in total exceed the combined capacity of Klein's two plants. Klein's management faces the problem of deciding how many units it should supply to each customer. Since the four customers are in different industries, the pricing structure enables different prices to be charged to different customers. However, slightly different production costs at the two plants and varying transportation costs between the plants and customers make a ''sell to the highest bidder'' strategy unacceptable. After considering price, production costs, and transportation costs, Klein has established the following profit per unit for each plant-customer alternative.

		Customer			
		D_1	D_2	D_3	D_4
Plant	Clifton Springs	$32	$34	$32	$40
	Danville	$34	$30	$28	$38

The plant capacities and customer orders are as follows:

Plant Capacity	Orders	
Clifton Springs: 5000 units	D_1	2000 units
	D_2	5000 units
Danville: 3000 units	D_3	3000 units
	D_4	2000 units

How many units should each plant produce for each customer in order to *maximize* profits? Which customer demands will not be met?

9. Sound Electronics, Inc. produces a battery-operated tape recorder at plants located in Martinsville, N.C.; Plymouth, N.Y.; and Franklin, Mo. The unit transportation cost for shipments from the three plants to distribution centers in Chicago, Dallas, and New York are as follows:

		To	
From	Chicago	Dallas	New York
Martinsville	1.45	1.60	1.40
Plymouth	1.10	2.25	0.60
Franklin	1.20	1.20	1.80

After considering transportation costs, management has decided that under no circumstances will it use the Plymouth–Dallas route. The plant capacities and distributor orders for the next month are as follows:

Plant	Capacity (units)	Distributor	Orders (units)
Martinsville	400	Chicago	400
Plymouth	600	Dallas	400
Franklin	300	New York	400

Because of different wage scales at the three plants, the unit production cost varies from plant to plant. Assuming the costs are $29.50 per unit at Martinsville, $31.20 per unit at Plymouth, and $30.35 per unit at Franklin, find the production and distribution plan that minimizes production and transportation costs.

10. The Ace Manufacturing Company has orders for three similar products:

Product	Orders (units)
A	2000
B	500
C	1200

Three machines are available for the manufacturing operations. All three machines can produce all the products at the same production rate. However, due to varying defect percentages of each product on each machine, the unit costs of the products vary depending upon the machine used. Machine capacities for the next week, and the unit costs, are as follows:

Machine	Capacity (units)
I	1500
II	1500
III	1000

		Product		
		A	B	C
Machine	I	$1.00	$1.20	$0.90
	II	$1.30	$1.40	$1.20
	III	$1.10	$1.00	$1.20

a. Use the transportation model to develop the minimum cost production schedule for the products and machines.

b. Do alternate optimal production schedules exist? If the production manager would like the minimum cost schedule to have the smallest possible number of change-overs of products on machines, which solution would you recommend?

11. Forbelt Corporation has a 1-year contract to supply motors for all refrigerators produced by the Ice Age Corporation. Ice Age manufactures the refrigerators at four locations around the country: Boston, Dallas, Los Angeles, and St. Paul. Plans call for the following number (in thousands) of refrigerators to be produced at each location:

Boston	50
Dallas	70
Los Angeles	60
St. Paul	80

Forbelt has three plants that are capable of producing the motors. The plants and production capacities (in thousands) are as follows:

Denver	100
Atlanta	100
Chicago	150

Because of varying production and transportation costs, the profit Forbelt earns on each lot of 1000 units depends on which plant it was produced at and which destination it was shipped to. The following table gives the accounting department estimates of the profit per unit (shipments will be made in lots of 1000 units):

| Produced At | Shipped To | | | |
	Boston	Dallas	Los Angeles	St. Paul
Denver	7	11	8	13
Atlanta	20	17	12	10
Chicago	8	18	13	16

Given profit maximization as a criterion, Forbelt would like to determine how many motors should be produced at each plant and how many motors should be shipped from each plant to each destination.

12. Scott and Associates, Inc. is an accounting firm that has three new clients. Three project leaders will be assigned to the three clients. Based on the different backgrounds and experiences of the leaders, the various leader–client assignments differ in terms of projected completion times. The possible assignments and the estimated completion times in days are shown below.

| Project Leader | Client | | |
	1	2	3
Jackson	10	16	32
Ellis	14	22	40
Smith	22	24	34

a. Formulate the problem as a linear program and solve. What is the total time required?
b. Use the Hungarian method to obtain the optimal solution to this problem.

13. In problem 12 assume that an additional employee is available for possible assignment. The following table shows the assignment alternatives and the estimated completion times:

| Project Leader | Client | | |
	1	2	3
Jackson	10	16	32
Ellis	14	22	40
Smith	22	24	34
Burton	14	18	36

a. What is the optimal assignment?
b. How did the assignment change compared to the best assignment possible in problem 12? Was there any savings associated with considering Burton as one of the possible project leaders?
c. Which project leader remains unassigned?

14. Wilson Distributors, Inc. is opening two new sales territories in the western states. Three individuals currently selling in the Midwest and the East are being considered

for promotion to regional sales manager positions in the two new sales territories. Management has estimated total annual sales (in thousands of dollars) for the assignment of each individual to each sales territory. The management sales projections are as follows:

	Sales Region	
Regional Managers	Northwest	Southwest
Bostock	$100	$95
McMahon	$85	$80
Miller	$90	$75

a. Formulate and solve a linear programming model to obtain the optimal solution to this problem.
b. Use the Hungarian method to obtain the optimal solution to this problem.

15. Solve the Fowle Marketing Research, Inc. assignment problem (Section 7.6) with four project leaders available for assignment to the three clients. The estimated project completion times in days are as follows:

Project Leader	Client 1	2	3
Terry	10	15	9
Carle	9	18	5
McClymonds	6	14	3
Higley	8	16	6

16. a. Formulate a linear programming model of the Salsbury Discount, Inc. department-location assignment problem using the estimated annual profit data provided in Table 7.12; solve for the department-location assignment that maximizes profit.
    b. Use the Hungarian method to solve the Salsbury Discount, Inc. problem.

17. Consider the Salsbury Discount, Inc. assignment problem with two unacceptable assignments (see Table 7.15).
    a. Formulate and solve a linear programming model for this problem.
    b. Use the Hungarian method to solve this problem.

18. In a job shop operation, four jobs may be performed on any of four machines. The number of hours required for each job on each machine are summarized below. What is the minimum total time job-machine assignment?

Job	Machine A	B	C	D
1	32	18	32	26
2	22	24	12	16
3	24	30	26	24
4	26	30	28	20

19. Mayfax Distributors, Inc. have four sales territories each of which must be assigned a sales representative. From past experience the firm's sales manager has estimated the sales volume for each sales representative in each sales territory. Find the sales representative-territory assignments that will maximize sales (data given in thousands).

Sales Representative	Sales Territory			
	A	B	C	D
Washington	44	80	52	60
Benson	60	56	40	72
Fredricks	36	60	48	48
Hodson	52	76	36	40

20. Each Monday the drivers of the Metor Bus System indicate their preferences for the various bus routes open during the coming week. With 1 indicating a first choice and 5 indicating a last choice, what is the driver-route assignment that minimizes the sum of the choice values?

Driver	Route				
	A	B	C	D	E
1	3	4	2	1	5
2	3	5	2	1	4
3	5	3	2	1	4
4	4	3	2	1	5
5	5	4	1	2	3

21. Four secretaries are available to type any of three company reports. Given the typing times in hours, what is the minimum total time secretary-report assignment?

Secretary	Report		
	A	B	C
Phyllis	24	12	10
Linda	19	11	11
Dave	25	16	16
Marlene	25	14	13

22. Four trucks must be dispatched to each of four customer locations. The assignments and the distances traveled by each truck in making the trips are shown below. What truck–customer assignments minimize the total distance traveled by the four trucks? Note that two unacceptable assignments are indicated because the specific truck involved is not equipped to carry the type of shipment involved. The unacceptable assignments show M as the distance traveled.

Truck	Customer			
	A	B	C	D
1	130	125	120	135
2	120	110	100	120
3	125	120	M	140
4	150	150	140	M

23. A market research firm has three clients who have each requested that the firm conduct a sample survey. Four statisticians are available to assign to these three projects; however, all four statisticians are busy, and therefore each can handle at most one of the clients. The following data show the number of hours it would take for each statistician to complete each job; the differences in time are due to differences in experience and ability among the statisticians.

Statistician	Client A	Client B	Client C
1	150	210	270
2	170	230	220
3	180	230	225
4	160	240	230

a. Formulate and solve a linear programming model for this problem.
b. Specify the range of optimality for the objective function coefficients.
c. Suppose that the time it takes statistician 4 to complete the job for client A is increased from 160 to 165 hours. What effect will this have on the solution?
d. Suppose that the time it takes statistician 4 to complete the job for client A is decreased to 140 hours. What effect will this have on the solution?
e. Suppose that the time it takes statistician 3 to complete the job for client B increases to 250 hours. What effect will this have on the solution?

24. A company has two plants (P_1 and P_2), one regional warehouse (W), and two retail outlets (R_1 and R_2). The plant capacities, retail outlet demands, and the per-unit shipping costs are shown in the following network:

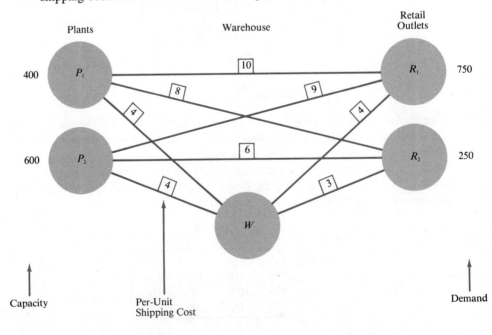

a. Formulate a linear programming model to minimize shipping costs for this problem.

b. If you have access to a linear programming computer code, determine the optimal solution for the model formulated in part (a).

c. What change would have to be made in the linear programming model if the maximum amount of goods that can be shipped from W to R_1 is 500? How would this change the optimal solution?

25. Adirondack Paper Mills, Inc. has paper plants located in Augusta, Me., and Tupper Lake, N.Y. Warehouse facilities are located in Albany, N.Y., and Portsmouth, N.H. Distributors are located in Boston, New York, and Philadelphia. The plant capacities and distributor demands for the next month are as follows:

Plant	Capacity (units)	Distributor	Demand (units)
Augusta	300	Boston	150
Tupper Lake	100	New York	100
		Philadelphia	150

The unit transportation costs for shipments from the two plants to the two warehouses and from the two warehouses to the three distributors are shown below.

		Warehouse	
		Albany	Portsmouth
Plant	Augusta	7	5
	Tupper Lake	3	4

		Distributor		
		Boston	New York	Philadelphia
Warehouse	Albany	8	5	7
	Portsmouth	5	6	10

a. Draw the network representation of the Adirondack Paper Mills problem.

b. Formulate the Adirondack Paper Mills problem as a linear programming problem.

c. If you have access to a linear programming computer code, determine the minimum cost shipping schedule for the problem.

26. Consider a transshipment problem consisting of three origin nodes, two transshipment nodes, and four destination nodes. The supplies at the origin nodes and the demands at the destination nodes are as follows:

Origin	Supply	Destination	Demand
1	400	1	200
2	450	2	500
3	350	3	300
		4	200

The per-unit shipping costs are provided in the following table.

			Transshipment		To Destination			
			1	2	1	2	3	4
From	Origin	1	6	8	–	–	–	–
		2	8	12	–	–	–	–
		3	10	5	–	–	–	–
	Transshipment	1	–	–	9	7	6	10
		2	–	–	7	9	6	8

a. Draw the network representation of this problem.
b. Formulate this as a linear programming problem.
c. Solve for the optimal solution.

27. Moore and Harman Company is in the business of buying and selling grain. An important aspect of the company's business is arranging for the purchased grain to be shipped to customers. If the company can keep freight costs low, profitability will be improved.

Currently the company has purchased three rail cars of corn at Muncie, Ind.; six rail cars at Brazil, Ind.; and five rail cars at Xenia, Ohio. Twelve carloads of grain have been sold. The locations and the amount sold at each location are as follows:

Location	Number of Rail Car Loads
Macon, Ga.	2
Greenwood, S.C.	4
Concord, S.C.	3
Chatham, N.C.	3

All shipments must be routed through either Louisville or Cincinnati. Given below are the shipping costs per bushel (in cents) from the origins to Louisville and Cincinnati as well as the costs per bushel to ship from Louisville and Cincinnati to the destinations.

To From	Louisville	Cincinnati	
Muncie	8	6 ←	─ Cost per bushel
Brazil	3	8	from Muncie to
Xenia	9	3	Cincinnati is 6¢

To From	Macon	Greenwood	Concord	Chatham
Louisville	44	34	34	32
Cincinnati	57	35 ←	28	24

Cost per bushel
from Cincinnati to
Greenwood is 35¢

Determine a shipping schedule that will minimize the freight costs necessary to satisfy demand. Which (if any) rail cars of grain must be held at the origin until buyers can be found?

Case Problem:

ASSIGNING UMPIRE CREWS*

The American Baseball League consists of fourteen professional baseball teams organized into two divisions: the Western Division, with Seattle, Oakland, California, Texas, Kansas City, Minnesota, and Chicago, and the Eastern Division with Milwaukee, Detroit, Cleveland, Toronto, Baltimore, New York, and Boston.

In addition to the schedules for each team, the American League must determine the best way to assign the umpire crews to the various games played throughout the league. Umpire crews are assigned to specific home-team cities for the two-, three-, or four-game series in that city but are not assigned on an individual-game basis. Since there are 14 American League teams, there can be as many as seven "games" (doubleheaders count as one "game" in assigning crews); hence seven umpire crews must be assigned.

Several considerations are important in making the umpire crew assignments. Because of the amount of travel required, airline costs can be substantial. Thus from a cost point of view umpire crew assignments with minimum travel distances are desired. However, a second consideration in the assignment of the umpire crews is that there should be a balance such that each crew works approximately the same number of games with each team and in each city. The considerations of minimizing travel distances and at the same time balancing the crew assignments among the teams and cities are in conflict.

In addition to the above considerations, a number of requirements must be satisfied. The most important of these are:

1. A crew cannot travel from city A to city B if the last game in city A is a night game and the first game in city B is an afternoon game on the next day.
2. A crew cannot travel from a West Coast location (Seattle, Oakland, or California) to Chicago or any Eastern Division city without a day off.
3. Because of flight scheduling difficulties, a crew traveling into or out of Toronto must have a day off unless coming from or going to New York, Boston, Detroit, or Cleveland.
4. Any crew traveling from a night game in Seattle, Oakland, or California cannot be assigned to Kansas City or Texas for a game on the next day.
5. No crew should be assigned to the same team for more than two series in a row.

The umpire crews have already been scheduled for the first four series of the five-series schedule shown in Table 7.18. Table 7.19 summarizes the crew assignments for

---

*The authors are indebted to James R. Evans, consultant to the American League, New York, N.Y., for providing this case problem.

TABLE 7.18
Segment of the American League Schedule Showing Five Series

Series	Date	SEA	OAK	CAL	TEX	KC	MIN	CHI	MKE	DET	CLE	TOR	BAL	NY	BOS
1	Mon.		CAL*		BOS*		SEA		TOR*	NY*			CHI*		
	Tues.		CAL*		BOS*		SEA		TOR*	NY*	KC*		CHI*		
	Wed.		CAL		BOS*		SEA		TOR*	NY	KC*		CHI*		
2	Thurs.	DET*			KC*						CHI*		TOR*		MIN*
	Fri.	DET*	NY*	MKE*	KC*						CHI*		TOR*		MIN*
	Sat.	DET*	NY	MKE*	KC*						CHI		TOR*		MIN*
	Sun.	DET	NY(2)	MKE	KC*						CHI		TOR		MIN*
3	Mon.	MKE*		NY*		BOS*							MIN*		
	Tues.	MKE*	DET*	NY*	CHI*	BOS*						CLE*	MIN*		
	Wed.	MKE*	DET*	NY*	CHI*	BOS*						CLE*	MIN*		
	Thurs.	MKE*	DET	NY*	CHI*							CLE*			
4	Fri.	NY*	MKE*	DET*	BAL*		CLE*	KC*				BOS*			
	Sat.	NY*	MKE	DET*	BAL*		CLE*	KC*				BOS			
	Sun.	NY*	MKE	DET	BAL*		CLE	KC				BOS			
5	Mon.					TEX*		CLE*				BOS*			
	Tues.					TEX*	BOS*	CLE*	CAL*	SEA*			BAL*	OAK*	
	Wed.					TEX*	BOS*	CLE*	CAL*	SEA*			BAL*	OAK*	
	Thurs.					TEX*	BOS		CAL	SEA*			BAL*	OAK*	

*Denotes night game or early-evening start.
(2)Denotes doubleheader (two games in one day).

TABLE 7.19
Umpire Crew Assignment for the First Four Series

Series	SEA	OAK	CAL	TEX	KC	MIN	CHI	MKE	DET	CLE	TOR	BAL	NY	BOS
								Home Team						
1	DET^3	CAL^5		BOS^3		SEA^7		TOR^4	NY^1	KC^6		CHI^2		MIN^1
2	MKE^2	NY^2	MKE^7	KC^5						CHI^6		TOR^4		
3	NY^7	DET^7	NY^3	CHI^6	BOS^5	CLE^5	KC^4				CLE^1	MIN^4		
4		MKE^3	DET^2	BAL^6		BOS	CLE	CAL			BOS^1			
5					TEX	BOS	CLE		SEA		BAL		OAK	

Example: For the fourth series, umpire crew 1 is assigned to the Boston at Toronto series the first four series in the schedule and shows the pairings for the fifth series. The number next to each team identification indicates the umpire crew assigned for that pairing. For example, for the fourth series, crew 1 is assigned to the Boston–Toronto games, crew 2 is assigned to the Detroit–California games, and so on.

Table 7.20 shows the distances from the cities where the fourth series is being played to the cities where the fifth series is being played. There are some other issues league management would like considered in assigning crews to the next series. Over the past nine series, crew 4 has umpired three series with Kansas City and three series with Milwaukee. Also, crew 5 has not been assigned to any games with New York, Toronto, or Detroit over the past month.

TABLE 7.20
A Distance Matrix for Umpire Crew Assignment (Series 5)

Crew From	To						
	KC	MIN	CHI	MKE	DET	TOR	NY
SEA(7)	1825	1399	2007	1694	1939	2124	2421
OAK(3)	1498	1589	2125	1845	2079	2286	2586
CAL(2)	1363	1536	2035	1756	1979	2175	2475
TEX(6)	506	853	798	843	982	1186	1383
MIN(5)	394	0	334	297	528	780	1028
CHI(4)	403	334	0	74	235	430	740
TOR(1)	968	897	497	583	206	0	366

Required

Prepare a written recommendation to league management concerning the assignment of umpire crews to the fifth series. Issues you may want to consider include:

1. What assignment will minimize distance traveled?
2. Where should crew 4 be assigned?
3. Where should crew 5 be assigned?

Management Science in Practice

OPTIMAL DECISION SYSTEMS, INC.*

Cincinnati, Ohio

Optimal Decision Systems, Inc. (ODS) is a management consulting firm that specializes in the development and implementation of decision support systems for manufacturing, transportation, and distribution applications. ODS was formed in 1978 and has a clientele that includes many Fortune 500 companies.

Systems developed by ODS use computerized models to provide managers with a menu of ''good'' alternatives from which the ''best'' alternative can be selected. Several examples of the types of problems for which ODS has developed decision support systems are listed below:

1. Locating manufacturing and distribution facilities
2. Designing sales territories, including how various distribution centers should supply the territories
3. Routing and scheduling of truck fleets
4. Scheduling production systems to minimize inventory costs while maintaining desired service levels
5. Allocating capital to various investment opportunities

The majority of these applications (80%) have involved the development and implementation of large-scale mathematical programming models (linear programming, network, or mixed-integer linear programming models). Probability models and simulation have been the primary quantitative methodologies employed in the remaining applications. In addition, in almost every application, statistical analysis has played a heavy support role, particularly in the estimation of the parameters of the models.

TRUCK FLEET MANAGEMENT

The Fleet Management System (FMS) was developed by ODS for the management of private truck fleets. The heart of this system is a transshipment model that schedules and routes the company fleet over a user-specified time horizon (usually 1 to 7 days) in a way that optimizes one of the following measures of performance:

*The authors are indebted to Richard A. Murphy and Thomas E. Thompson, Optimal Decision Systems, Inc., for providing this application.

1. Savings over the use of common carrier truck fleets
2. Minimum total cost
3. Maximum total net revenue
4. Maximum load ratio (ratio of loaded miles to total miles driven by the fleet)
5. Some weighted combination of the above

In determining the optimal solution, all user-specified constraints on the operation of the truck fleet are simultaneously satisfied. Examples of such constraints are:

1. Specified load movement, pickup and delivery times
2. Minimum or maximum levels of utilization of the fleet
3. Operating hours at pickup points and delivery points
4. Restrictions on driver work hours

The Fleet Management System (FMS) accurately models the operation of a fleet, and thus the results of the optimization are extremely useful input to strategic (long-term), tactical (intermediate-term), and operational (short-term) planning. Some of the strategic issues that can be addressed by FMS are fleet sizing, the location of driver domiciles, equipment selection and mix, alternative operating practices (one-shift versus two-shift operation, use of double teams and/or trailer pools), and location of maintenance and refueling facilities. Tactical issues might include the timing and level of seasonal capacity such as leased drivers and equipment, the determination of which freight should be handled by common carrier and which should be handled by the private fleet, determination of appropriate internal pricing mechanisms, timing the increase or decrease of capacity by driver domicile and/or the determination of scheduling rules and procedures which yield efficient driver tours. The primary issue of operational planning is the determination of an efficient work tour for each driver.

A TRANSSHIPMENT MODEL FOR TRUCK FLEET MANAGEMENT

The primary function of the Fleet Management System is to determine an optimal schedule and route for each driver over the appropriate time horizon. For illustrative purposes, assume that all drivers (each with tractor and trailer) are located at a single domicile and that the objective is to maximize the savings that can be obtained over using common carriers for the same shipments. The system assumes the structure of a transshipment model. Capacity nodes represent the location of a driver at a particular point in time. Demand nodes represent the origin of a load movement which requires a truck to be made available for a load pickup. A driver at a capacity node is assigned to an arc connecting to a demand node. For each unit of flow on this arc (each driver assigned) cost is incurred which is the sum of the cost to travel to the location of the load movement plus any holding or delay costs which will be incurred if the driver experiences idle time. Arcs in the transshipment network are then used to assign the picked-up load to delivery locations. The net contribution on these delivery arcs is a savings the company realizes by using its own fleet of trucks rather than employing common carriers. This savings is the common carrier cost less the fuel, labor, idle time, and any other costs incurred by the company in making its own deliveries. Note that on completion of the delivery, the driver's location is defined as a capacity node and thus the driver becomes available for reassignment at another point in time. Through the use of this transshipment model, the flow of the company's fleet of trucks can be scheduled over the time period of interest.

AN APPLICATION AND RESULTS

The Fleet Management System was used to develop schedules for a Fortune 500 manufacturing company that operates a private fleet of over 100 drivers and tractors. The fleet is used primarily to move raw materials into and out of the company's manufacturing facilities located in over 40 locations throughout the United States and Canada. The fleet is also used to deliver finished goods to high-priority customer accounts where service levels are critical for continued business with the customer. Prior to implementation of the Fleet Management System, the fleet had been dispatched and managed on a purely manual basis, and the company was concerned about the high cost of the truck fleet operation.

The company's objective was to use the Fleet Management System to identify a set of short-range and long-range changes in the operation that could yield significant improvements in cost and efficiency. In this case, an annual saving of $1.9 million was possible through better freight selection and by scheduling the trucks more efficiently (with fewer empty miles). In addition specific recommendations were made to alter the size, location, and equipment mix of the truck fleet.

Questions

1. Draw a network that shows the transshipment model for truck fleet management.
2. What are the units of supply and demand at the nodes in your network? What are the units of flow over the shipping routes?

Integer Linear Programming

In this chapter we turn our attention to a class of problems that are modeled as linear programs with the additional requirement that some or all of the decision variables must be integer. Such problems are called *integer* linear programming problems. The use of integer variables provides additional modeling flexibility. As a result, the number of practical applications that can be addressed with linear programming methodology is enlarged. The cost of the added flexibility is that problems involving integer variables are usually much more difficult to solve. In fact, although linear programming problems involving several thousand continuous variables can be routinely solved with commercial linear programming codes, the solution of integer linear programming problems involving less than 100 variables can cause great difficulty. However, experienced management scientists can usually identify the types of integer linear programs that are easiest to solve; in such cases problems with hundreds (and sometimes thousands) of integer variables can be solved with available computer codes such as IBM's MPSX/370-MIP/370 and LINDO.

The plan of this chapter is to provide an applications-oriented introduction to integer linear programming. After a short section describing the different types of integer linear programming models, we show how a graphical procedure can be used to solve problems involving two-decision variables. We then discuss, in some detail, two common integer linear programming applications: capital budgeting and distribution system design. Next, we have included a section detailing the branch-and-bound solution procedure for integer linear programs with more than two variables. This is the solution procedure employed by almost all commercial integer linear programming computer codes available today and is regarded as the most efficient general purpose solution procedure. The concluding section concerns the computer solution of integer linear programs. A new application involving bank location is introduced, formulated, and solved using LINDO/PC.

8.1 TYPES OF INTEGER LINEAR PROGRAMMING MODELS

The only difference between the problems studied in this chapter and the ones studied in the earlier chapters on linear programming is that some of the variables are required to be integer. If all of the variables are required to be integer, we say we have an *all-integer linear program*. Stated below is a two-variable, all-integer linear programming model:

$$\text{max} \quad 2x_1 + 3x_2$$
$$\text{s.t.}$$
$$3x_1 + 3x_2 \leq 12$$
$$\tfrac{2}{3}x_1 + 1x_2 \leq 4$$
$$1x_1 + 2x_2 \leq 6$$
$$x_1, x_2 \geq 0 \text{ and integer}$$

You will note that if the phrase ''and integer'' is dropped from the above model, we are left with the familiar two-variable linear program. The linear program which results from dropping the integer requirements for the decision variables is referred to as the *LP* (linear programming) *Relaxation* of the integer linear program.

If some, but not all, of the decision variables in a problem are required to be integer, we say we have a *mixed-integer linear program*. The following is a two-variable mixed-integer linear program:

$$\text{max} \quad 3x_1 + 4x_2$$
$$\text{s.t.}$$
$$-1x_1 + 2x_2 \leq 8$$
$$1x_1 + 2x_2 \leq 12$$
$$2x_1 + 1x_2 \leq 16$$
$$x_1, x_2 \geq 0 \text{ and } x_2 \text{ integer}$$

The LP Relaxation of the above mixed-integer linear program is obtained by dropping the requirement that x_2 be integer.

In most practical applications the integer variables are only permitted to assume the values zero or one. In such cases we say we have a *binary* or a *0–1 integer linear program*. Zero–one problems may be either of the all-integer or mixed-integer type. The capital budgeting, distribution system design, and bank location problems discussed in later sections of this chapter all make use of *0–1* variables.

8.2 GRAPHICAL SOLUTION

Security Realty Investors currently has $1,365,000 that is available for new rental property investments. After an initial screening, Security has reduced the investment alternatives to a series of townhouses and a group of apartment buildings in a large apartment complex. The townhouses can be purchased in blocks of three for the price of $195,000 per block, but there are only four blocks of townhouses available for purchase at this time. Each building in the apartment complex contains 12 dwelling units and sells for $273,000. The individual apartment buildings can be purchased separately, and the complex developer has agreed to build as many 12-unit buildings as Security would like to purchase.

Security's property manager is free to devote 140 hours per month to these investments. Each block of townhouses will require 4 hours of the property manager's time each month, while each apartment building will require 40 hours per month. The yearly cash flow (after deducting mortgage payments and operating expenses) is estimated at $2000 per block of townhouses and $3000 per apartment building. Security would like to allocate its investment funds to apartment buildings and townhouses in order to maximize the yearly cash flow.

In order to develop an appropriate mathematical model for this problem, let us introduce the following definitions for the decision variables:

$$x_1 = \text{number of blocks of townhouses purchased}$$
$$x_2 = \text{number of apartment buildings purchased}$$

The objective function, measuring cash flow in thousands of dollars, can be written as

$$\max \quad 2x_1 + 3x_2$$

There are three constraints that must be satisfied:

$$195x_1 + 273x_2 \leq 1365 \quad \text{Funds available in thousands of dollars}$$
$$4x_1 + 40x_2 \leq 140 \quad \text{Manager's time in hours}$$
$$x_1 \qquad\qquad \leq \quad 4 \quad \text{Townhouse availability in blocks}$$

In addition, the variables must be restricted to nonnegative values. Also, since fractional values for the blocks of townhouses and/or number of apartment buildings are unacceptable, the decision variables x_1 and x_2 must be integer. Thus we see that the proper model for the Security Realty problem is the following all-integer linear program:

$$
\begin{aligned}
\max \quad & 2x_1 + 3x_2 \\
\text{s.t.} \quad & \\
& 195x_1 + 273x_2 \leq 1365 \\
& 4x_1 + 40x_2 \leq 140 \\
& x_1 \qquad\qquad \leq \quad 4 \\
& x_1, x_2 \geq 0 \text{ and integer}
\end{aligned}
$$

A first approach to solving such a problem might be to drop the integer requirements and solve the resulting LP Relaxation. You might then round off the decision variables in an attempt to find the optimal solution to the integer linear program. However, as we shall see, such an approach may not yield the optimal solution. In fact, rounding off values of the decision variables can sometimes result in an infeasible solution.

The linear program resulting from dropping the integer requirements for the decision variables (the LP Relaxation) is written as follows:

$$
\begin{aligned}
\max \quad & 2x_1 + 3x_2 \\
\text{s.t.} \quad & \\
& 195x_1 + 273x_2 \leq 1365 \\
& 4x_1 + 40x_2 \leq 140 \\
& x_1 \qquad\qquad \leq \quad 4 \\
& x_1, x_2 \geq 0
\end{aligned}
$$

The optimal solution to the LP Relaxation (see Figure 8.1) is given by $x_1 = 2.44$ and $x_2 = 3.26$. The objective function value for this solution is 14.66, corresponding to a cash flow of $14,660. However, this solution is not feasible for the integer linear programming problem, since the decision variables assume fractional values.

FIGURE 8.1
Graphical Solution to the LP Relaxation of the Security Realty Problem

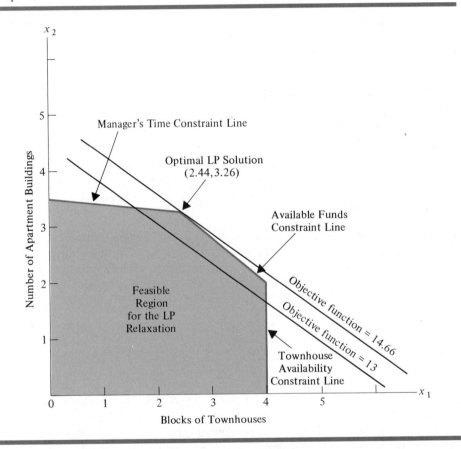

Rounding the decision variables to the nearest integer value yields a solution of $x_1 = 2$ and $x_2 = 3$, for an objective function value of 13, or a $13,000 annual cash flow. In Figure 8.2 we show the feasible solution points that provide integer values for x_1 and x_2. Is the rounded solution of $x_1 = 2$ and $x_2 = 3$ the optimal integer solution? The answer is no! As can be seen in Figure 8.2, the optimal integer solution is $x_1 = 4$ and $x_2 = 2$, with an objective function value of 14.00, or a $14,000 annual cash flow. For Security Realty, the approach of rounding the linear programming solution to the nearest integer solution was not a good strategy. The rounded solution of $x_1 = 2$ and $x_2 = 3$ would have cost Security Realty $1000 a year in cash flow.

As can be seen from the Security Realty problem, the graphical procedure for solving two-variable integer linear programs is quite similar to the graphical procedure for solving linear programs. First a graph of the feasible region for the LP Relaxation is constructed.

FIGURE 8.2
The Integer Solution to the Security Realty Problem

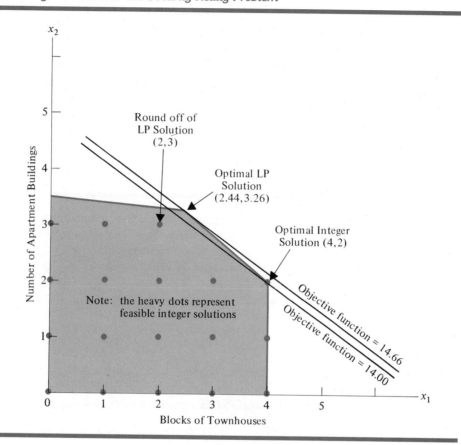

Then the feasible integer points are denoted by heavy dots. The integer solution point on the best objective function line can then be located; this point is the optimal solution to the integer linear programming program.

Also from our analysis of the Security Realty Investors problem, an important observation can be made about the relationship between the value of the optimal integer solution and the value of the optimal LP Relaxation solution. This observation is stated for *maximization problems*[1] as property 1.

Property 1.

The value of the optimal solution to any integer or mixed-integer linear program involving maximization yields a value *less than* or *equal to* the value of the optimal solution to its LP relaxation.

[1]For minimization problems, property 1 would be stated with greater than or equal to substituted for less than or equal to.

The above property means that an *upper bound* on the value of any maximization integer or mixed-integer linear program can be found by solving its associated LP relaxation. This property can be seen in Figure 8.2. The optimal LP solution is on the highest objective function line and has a value of $14.66. The optimal integer solution is on a lower objective function line and has a smaller value, $14.00. As we shall see, property 1 is used in the branch-and-bound solution procedure for solving integer linear programs.

We note in closing this section that mixed-integer linear programs with two-decision variables can be solved by a simple modification of the graphical procedure outlined above. Problem 5 at the end of the chapter requires the graphical solution of a mixed-integer linear program.

8.3 APPLICATIONS OF INTEGER LINEAR PROGRAMMING

In the previous section we saw an illustration of an all-integer linear program: the Security Realty Investors problem. In this section we discuss two applications involving *0–1* or binary integer variables: the capital budgeting and distribution system design problems. We have chosen these applications because they represent two areas in which integer linear programming has been used widely in practice. Through these applications you should begin to develop an appreciation of the flexibility in model development provided by *0–1* variables.

Capital Budgeting

Capital budgeting is an area where the management science approach has often led to considerable savings and/or increased profits. To provide an idea of what is involved in capital budgeting, let us consider the Ice-Cold Refrigerator problem and develop its linear programming formulation.

The Ice-Cold Refrigerator Company can invest capital funds in a variety of company projects that have varying capital requirements over the next 4 years. Faced with limited capital resources, the company must select the most profitable projects and budgets for the capital expenditures. The estimated present values of the projects, the capital requirements, and the available capital projections[2] are shown in Table 8.1.

The following definitions are chosen for the decision variables:

x_1 = 1 if the plant expansion project is accepted; 0 if rejected
x_2 = 1 if the warehouse expansion project is accepted; 0 if rejected
x_3 = 1 if the new machinery project is accepted; 0 if rejected
x_4 = 1 if the new product research project is accepted; 0 if rejected

The linear programming formulation of this capital budgeting problem has a separate constraint for each year's available funds and a separate constraint requiring each variable to be less than or equal to 1. The linear programming formulation is given below (monetary units are expressed in thousands of dollars).

[2]The estimated present value is the net return for the project discounted back to the beginning of year 1.

TABLE 8.1
Project Present Values, Capital Requirements, and Available Capital Projections for the Ice-Cold Refrigerator Company

Project	Estimated Present Value ($)	Capital Requirements ($)			
		Year 1	Year 2	Year 3	Year 4
Plant expansion	90,000	15,000	20,000	20,000	15,000
Warehouse expansion	40,000	10,000	15,000	20,000	5,000
New machinery	10,000	10,000	0	0	4,000
New product research	37,000	15,000	10,000	10,000	10,000
Available capital funds		40,000	50,000	40,000	35,000

$$\begin{aligned}
\max \quad & 90x_1 + 40x_2 + 10x_3 + 37x_4 \\
\text{s.t.} \quad & \\
& 15x_1 + 10x_2 + 10x_3 + 15x_4 \le 40 \\
& 20x_1 + 15x_2 \phantom{{}+ 10x_3} + 10x_4 \le 50 \\
& 20x_1 + 20x_2 \phantom{{}+ 10x_3} + 10x_4 \le 40 \\
& 15x_1 + 5x_2 + 4x_3 + 10x_4 \le 35 \\
& x_1 \le 1 \\
& x_2 \le 1 \\
& x_3 \le 1 \\
& x_4 \le 1 \\
& x_1, x_2, x_3, x_4 \ge 0
\end{aligned}$$

The optimal solution to this linear program is $x_1 = 1$, $x_2 = 0.5$, $x_3 = 0.5$, and $x_4 = 1$, with a total estimated present value of \$152,000. The difficulty with a linear programming approach to the capital budgeting problem is now readily apparent. Unless it is possible to implement the warehouse expansion and new machinery projects in 50% increments, the current solution is not feasible. Thus some adjustment in the linear programming solution, such as rounding x_2 and x_3 (possibly leading to a nonoptimal solution), must be made prior to implementation.

A preferable approach is to reformulate the Ice-Cold Refrigerator Company problem as a *0–1* integer linear program. The *0–1* integer linear programming formulation is shown below:

$$\begin{aligned}
\max \quad & 90x_1 + 40x_2 + 10x_3 + 37x_4 \\
\text{s.t.} \quad & \\
& 15x_1 + 10x_2 + 10x_3 + 15x_4 \le 40 \\
& 20x_1 + 15x_2 \phantom{{}+ 10x_3} + 10x_4 \le 50 \\
& 20x_1 + 20x_2 \phantom{{}+ 10x_3} + 10x_4 \le 40 \\
& 15x_1 + 5x_2 + 4x_3 + 10x_4 \le 35 \\
& x_1, x_2, x_3, x_4 = 0, 1
\end{aligned}$$

The LP Relaxation of the *0–1* integer program is given by the linear programming formulation above.

The optimal integer solution[3] is given by $x_1 = 1$, $x_2 = 1$, $x_3 = 1$, and $x_4 = 0$ with a total estimated present value of \$140,000. We note that this optimal solution could not have been discovered by simply rounding the linear programming solution. In fact, the best feasible solution that can be found by considering all possible roundings of the fractional variables in the linear programming solution is $x_1 = 1$, $x_2 = 0$, $x_3 = 0$, $x_4 = 1$, with a total estimated present value of \$127,000. This is substantially less than the value of the optimal integer solution to the capital budgeting problem.

The ability to avoid fractional values is one of two main reasons that an integer programming formulation is usually preferred for capital budgeting problems. The second reason most management scientists prefer a *0–1* integer programming model for the capital budgeting problem is the flexibility provided in developing certain nonbudgetary constraints. These constraints are often important in capital budgeting problems and can be formulated only through the use of *0–1*—sometimes called logical—variables.

Multiple-Choice and Mutually Exclusive Constraints

Suppose that instead of one warehouse expansion project, the Ice-Cold Refrigerator Company actually has three warehouse expansion projects under consideration. One of the warehouses must be expanded because of increasing product demand, but there is not sufficient new demand to make expansion of more than one warehouse profitable. The following variable definitions and *multiple-choice constraint* could be incorporated into the previous *0–1* integer linear programming model to reflect this situation. Let

$x_2 = 1$ if the original warehouse expansion project is accepted; 0 if rejected

$x_5 = 1$ if the second warehouse expansion project is accepted; 0 if rejected

$x_6 = 1$ if the third warehouse expansion project is accepted; 0 if rejected

The multiple-choice constraint reflecting the requirement that one and only one of these projects must be selected is written as follows:

$$x_2 + x_5 + x_6 = 1$$

It is easy to see why this is called a multiple-choice constraint. Since x_2, x_5, and x_6 are allowed to assume only the values 0 or 1, one and only one of these projects must be selected from among the three choices. Note that if fractional values (as in linear programming) were allowed for the decision variables, we could not enforce the requirement of selecting one and only one project (e.g., $x_2 = \frac{1}{3}$, $x_5 = \frac{1}{3}$, $x_6 = \frac{1}{3}$ would satisfy the constraint).

If it had not been required that one warehouse be expanded, then our multiple-choice constraint could be modified as follows:

$$x_2 + x_5 + x_6 \leq 1$$

This modification allows for the case of no warehouse expansion ($x_2 = x_5 = x_6 = 0$), but does not permit more than one warehouse to be expanded. This type of constraint is often called a *mutually exclusive constraint*.

[3]This solution was found using the branch-and-bound solution procedure presented in Section 8.4. Problem 8 asks you to develop the branch-and-bound solution of this problem.

k Out of n Alternatives Constraint

An extension of the notion of a multiple-choice constraint can be used to model situations in which k out of a set of n projects must be selected. Suppose x_2, x_5, x_6, x_7, and x_8 represent five potential warehouse expansion projects and it is considered necessary to accept two of the five projects. The following constraint ensures satisfaction of this new requirement:

$$x_2 + x_5 + x_6 + x_7 + x_8 = 2$$

If it is required that no more than two of the projects be selected, we would use the following less-than-or-equal-to constraint:

$$x_2 + x_5 + x_6 + x_7 + x_8 \leq 2$$

Once again, each of the above variables must be restricted to *0–1* values.

Conditional and Corequisite Constraints

Sometimes the acceptance of one project is conditional upon the acceptance of another. For example, suppose for the Ice-Cold Refrigerator Company that the warehouse expansion project was conditional on the plant expansion project. That is, the company will not consider expanding the warehouse unless the plant is expanded. With x_1 representing plant expansion and x_2 representing warehouse expansion, the following conditional constraint could be introduced to enforce this requirement:

$$x_2 \leq x_1$$

or

$$x_2 - x_1 \leq 0$$

Since both x_1 and x_2 are required to be 0 or 1, we see that whenever x_1 is 0, x_2 will be forced to 0. When x_1 is 1, x_2 is also allowed to be 1; thus, both the plant and the warehouse can be expanded. However, we note that the above constraint does not force the warehouse expansion project (x_2) to be accepted if the plant expansion project (x_1) is.

If it were required that the warehouse expansion project be accepted whenever the plant expansion project was, and vice versa, then we would say that x_1 and x_2 represented *corequisite* projects. To model such a situation we simply write the above constraint as an equality

$$x_2 = x_1$$

or

$$x_2 - x_1 = 0$$

This constraint forces x_1 and x_2 to take on the same value.

Cautionary Note on Sensitivity Analysis

Sensitivity analysis is often more critical for integer linear programming problems than for linear programming problems. A very small change in one of the coefficients in the constraints can cause a relatively large change in the value of the optimal solution. To see why this is so, consider the following integer programming model of a simple capital budgeting problem involving four projects and a budgetary constraint for a single time period:

$$\max \quad 40x_1 + 60x_2 + 70x_3 + 160x_4$$
$$\text{s.t.}$$
$$16x_1 + 35x_2 + 45x_3 + 85x_4 \le 100$$
$$x_1, x_2, x_3, x_4 = 0, 1$$

The optimal solution to this problem can be quickly found by enumerating the alternatives. It is $x_1 = 1$, $x_2 = 1$, $x_3 = 1$, and $x_4 = 0$, with an objective function value of $170. However, note that if the budget available is increased by $1 (from 100 to 101), the optimal solution changes to $x_1 = 1$, $x_2 = 0$, $x_3 = 0$, and $x_4 = 1$, with an objective function value of $200. That is, one additional dollar in the budget would lead to a $30 increase in the return. Surely management, when faced with such a situation, would increase the budget by $1. Because of the extreme sensitivity of the value of the optimal solution to the constraint coefficients, practitioners usually recommend resolving the integer linear program several times with slight variations in the coefficients before attempting to choose an optimal solution for implementation.

Distribution System Design

In Chapter 7 the following linear programming formulation for the transportation problem was developed:

$$\min \quad \sum_{i=1}^{m} \sum_{j=1}^{n} c_{ij} x_{ij}$$
$$\text{s.t.}$$
$$\sum_{j=1}^{n} x_{ij} \le s_i \quad i = 1, 2, \ldots, m \quad \text{Supply}$$
$$\sum_{i=1}^{m} x_{ij} = d_j \quad j = 1, 2, \ldots, n \quad \text{Demand}$$
$$x_{ij} \ge 0 \quad \text{for all } i \text{ and } j$$

where

i = index for origins, $i = 1, 2, \ldots, m$
j = index for destinations, $j = 1, 2, \ldots, n$
x_{ij} = number of units shipped from origin i to destination j
c_{ij} = cost per unit of shipping from origin i to destination j
s_i = supply or capacity in units at origin i
d_j = demand in units at destination j

In the transportation problem it is assumed that the origins and destinations are fixed. Consequently the problem is to determine how much of the product to ship from each origin to each destination in order to minimize the total transportation cost. However, in more general distribution system design problems, it is necessary to select the best locations for the origins as well as the amounts to ship from each origin to each destination.

Suppose the origins represent m potential locations for plants with capacities s_i and the destinations represent n retail outlets with demand d_j. A more complex distribution system design problem must now be solved. If site i is selected for a plant location, there will be a fixed cost associated with plant construction and then a variable cost associated with the number of units shipped from plant i to the various retail outlets. On the other hand, if site i is not selected, then there is no fixed cost and no units can be shipped from site i. The introduction of one integer $0-1$ variable for each potential plant location allows us to develop a mixed-integer linear programming model for this distribution system design problem. Let

$$y_i = 1 \text{ if a plant is constructed at site } i; 0 \text{ if not}$$
$$f_i = \text{fixed cost of constructing a plant at site } i \text{ with capacity } s_i$$

To represent the constraint that nothing can be shipped from site i if a plant is not constructed, the supply constraints in the transportation model are modified as follows:

$$\sum_{j=1}^{n} x_{ij} \leq s_i y_i \qquad i = 1, 2, \ldots, m$$

or

$$\sum_{j=1}^{n} x_{ij} - s_i y_i \leq 0 \qquad i = 1, 2, \ldots, m$$

Also, another term must be added to the objective function to represent the fixed cost of plant construction at each site selected:

$$\text{Fixed cost of plant construction} = \sum_{i=1}^{m} f_i y_i$$

The complete model for our distribution system design problem can now be written:

$$\min \sum_{i=1}^{m} \sum_{j=1}^{n} c_{ij} x_{ij} + \sum_{i=1}^{m} f_i y_i$$

s.t.

$$\sum_{j=1}^{n} x_{ij} - s_i y_i \leq 0 \quad i = 1, 2, \ldots, m \quad \text{Plant capacities}$$

$$\sum_{i=1}^{m} x_{ij} = d_j \quad j = 1, 2, \ldots, n \quad \text{Demand at retail outlets}$$

$$x_{ij} \geq 0 \text{ for all } i \text{ and } j$$
$$y_i = 0, 1, \quad i = 1, 2, \ldots, m$$

This basic model[4] can be expanded to accommodate distribution systems involving shipments from plants to warehouses to retail outlets, and multiple products.[5] Using the special properties of *0–1* variables, it can also be expanded to accommodate a variety of configuration constraints on the plant locations. For example, suppose site 1 were in Dallas and site 2 in Fort Worth. A company might not want to locate plants in both Dallas and Fort Worth because the cities are so close together. To prevent this, the following constraint can be added to the model:

$$y_1 + y_2 \leq 1$$

This constraint was called a mutually exclusive constraint in the previous subsection. It allows either y_1 or y_2 to equal 1 but not both. If we had written the constraint as an equality, it would be the same as the multiple-choice constraint we encountered in the capital budgeting problem. Other constraints such as the conditional or corequisite constraint can be introduced to satisfy managerially specified requirements on the configuration of plant locations.

8.4 BRANCH-AND-BOUND SOLUTION OF INTEGER LINEAR PROGRAMS

As with linear programs, integer linear programs involving three variables are awkward to solve graphically. Moreover, since larger problems are impossible to solve using a graphical approach, other solution procedures must be employed. Branch and bound is currently the most efficient general-purpose solution procedure for integer linear programs. Almost all commercially available integer programming computer codes employ the branch-and-bound approach.

The branch-and-bound procedure divides the set of all feasible solutions to an integer programming problem into smaller subsets (branching). Then various rules are used to (1) identify the subsets that are most likely to contain the optimal solution and (2) identify the subsets that need not be explored further because they could not possibly contain the optimal solution.

An upper bound on the value of the best solution in each subset is obtained by solving an LP Relaxation. Any time the solution to the LP Relaxation results in an integer solution, the best solution in the subset has been found and a lower bound for the subset is obtained. The best of the integer feasible solutions (considering all the subsets) is the optimal solution.

In this section we show how the branch-and-bound approach can be used to solve integer programming problems by applying it to the all-integer Security Realty Investors problem. We then comment on how it can be extended to mixed-integer linear programs and present a flowchart summarizing the steps in the procedure.

[4]For computational reasons it is usually preferable to replace the m plant capacity constraints with mn shipping route capacity constraints of the form $x_{ij} \leq \min \{s_i, d_j\} y_i$ for $i = 1, \ldots, m$ and $j = 1, \ldots, n$. The coefficient for y_i in each of these constraints is the smaller of the origin capacity or the destination demand. These additional constraints often cause the solution of the LP Relaxation to be integer.

[5]A model of this type was used by a large food chain and resulted in substantial savings in distribution system costs. See Geoffrion and Graves, ''Distribution System Design by Benders Decomposition,'' *Management Science*, January 1974.

The branch-and-bound procedure begins by solving the LP Relaxation of the integer linear program. The LP Relaxation of the Security Realty Investors problem is restated below:

$$
\begin{aligned}
\max \quad & 2x_1 + 3x_2 \\
\text{s.t.} \quad & \\
& 195x_1 + 273x_2 \le 1365 \\
& 4x_1 + 40x_2 \le 140 \\
& x_1 \le 4 \\
& x_1, x_2 \ge 0
\end{aligned}
$$

The solution is $x_1 = 2.44$ and $x_2 = 3.26$, with an objective function value equal to 14.66. Had the optimal solution to the LP Relaxation satisfied the integer requirements, we would have had the optimal solution to the integer linear program. Since this did not occur, we will continue with the branch-and-bound procedure. As a first step, note that property 1 in Section 8.2 indicates that solving the LP Relaxation of an integer linear program provides an upper bound on the value of the solution to the integer linear programming problem. Thus we know that the value of the integer optimal solution to the Security Realty problem cannot exceed 14.66.

Since the coefficients of all the variables in the constraints are nonnegative and since the constraints are all of the $\le$ type, a feasible integer solution can be found by rounding down for each decision variable; that is, rounding down can only reduce the left-hand side of the inequality and hence must always provide a feasible solution. The feasible solution found by rounding down is $x_1 = 2$ and $x_2 = 3$, with an objective function value of 13. The value of this feasible solution provides a lower bound on the value of the optimal solution to the integer linear program, since we know that the value of the optimal solution must yield a value greater than or equal to the value of any feasible solution. Thus a lower bound of 13 can be established. The first node of our branch-and-bound solution tree appears as shown below, where UB refers to upper bound and LB to lower bound.

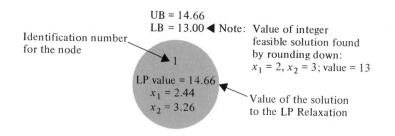

We now know that the value of the optimal solution must be between the upper bound of 14.66 and the lower bound of 13. Although we have already found a feasible solution with a value of 13, we must continue to see if a better solution can be found. This is where the branching part of the branch-and-bound solution procedure comes into play.

The set of feasible solutions to the LP Relaxation is partitioned into two subsets. These subsets are created by choosing the integer variable that is furthest from being integral to branch on; hence x_1 with a value of 2.44 is selected. In the optimal integer solution x_1 must be integer, so we see that either x_1 will be less than or equal to 2 or x_1 will be greater than or equal to 3. Thus two branches and two *descendant nodes* are created for our branch-and-bound solution tree. One descendant node corresponds to the subset of solutions with $x_1 \leq 2$; the other corresponds to the subset of solutions with $x_1 \geq 3$. Since x_1 must be integral, the optimal solution must be contained in one of these two subsets.

The first branch is created by adding the constraint $x_1 \leq 2$ to the Security Realty problem. We will refer to the node created as node 2. Thus at node 2 the LP Relaxation is solved.

LP Relaxation at node 2:

$$
\begin{aligned}
\max \quad & 2x_1 + 3x_2 \\
\text{s.t.} \quad & \\
& 195x_1 + 273x_2 \leq 1365 \\
& 4x_1 + 40x_2 \leq 140 \\
& x_1 \leq 4 \\
& x_1 \leq 2 \\
& x_1, x_2 \geq 0
\end{aligned}
$$

We note that the added constraint ($x_1 \leq 2$) makes the constraint $x_1 \leq 4$ redundant. This is just a coincidence and does not always happen. The solution to this linear program yields $x_1 = 2$ and $x_2 = 3.30$, with value equal to 13.90.

The second branch from node 1 is created by adding the constraint $x_1 \geq 3$ to the LP Relaxation of the Security Realty problem. Thus at node 3 the following LP Relaxation is solved.

LP Relaxation at node 3:

$$
\begin{aligned}
\max \quad & 2x_1 + 3x_2 \\
\text{s.t.} \quad & \\
& 195x_1 + 273x_2 \leq 1365 \\
& 4x_1 + 40x_2 \leq 140 \\
& x_1 \leq 4 \\
& x_1 \geq 3 \\
& x_1, x_2 \geq 0
\end{aligned}
$$

The solution to this linear program yields $x_1 = 3$ and $x_2 = 2.86$, with value equal to 14.58.

From property 1 we know that the value of the LP Relaxation at node 2 is an upper bound on all solutions with $x_1 \leq 2$, and the value of the LP Relaxation at node 3 is an upper bound on all solutions with $x_1 \geq 3$. Since these two subsets include all solutions to the Security Realty problem, we can compute a new upper bound. It is the maximum of the LP Relaxation value for node 2 (13.90) and the LP Relaxation value for node 3 (14.58). Hence our new upper bound on the value of the integer linear programming solution to the Security Realty problem is 14.58. In general, we will recompute the upper bound each time the two branches from a node have been completed.

At this time the lower bound is also recomputed. The new value for the lower bound is the maximum value of all feasible integer solutions found so far. Since the LP Relaxation solutions at nodes 2 and 3 did not yield a feasible integer solution, the lower bound of 13 established at node 1 is not revised. At this point of the branch-and-bound solution procedure we have UB = 14.58 and LB = 13.00. The current partial branch-and-bound solution tree is shown in Figure 8.3.

FIGURE 8.3
Partial Branch-and-Bound Solution Tree for Security Realty Problem

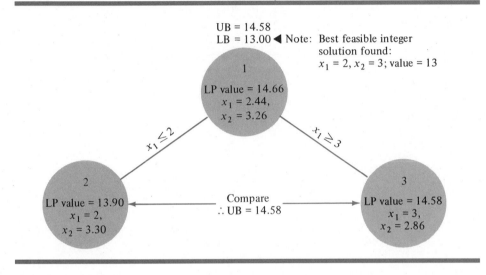

We have established (at node 2) that 13.90 is an upper bound on all solutions with $x_1 \leq 2$ and (at node 3) that 14.58 is an upper bound on all solutions with $x_1 \geq 3$. Property 2 below shows how these results can be used in continuing with the branch-and-bound solution procedure.

Property 2.

The LP Relaxation value at each node of a maximization problem is an upper bound on the LP Relaxation value at any descendant node.

Using this property, we see that if we were to branch from node 2 we could not find any solution with a value greater than 13.90. If we were to branch from node 3 no solution with a value greater than 14.58 could be found. Since node 3 could potentially lead to a better solution we choose to select it (rather than node 2) to branch from. In general we will always select the node with the largest LP Relaxation value to continue branching.

Since x_2 is the only variable with a fractional value at node 3 we choose to branch on it. Thus two branches are created from node 3: one with $x_2 \leq 2$ and another with $x_2 \geq 3$. Two descendant nodes are then created by solving the following LP Relaxations at nodes 4 and 5.

LP Relaxation at node 4:

$$
\begin{aligned}
\max \quad & 2x_1 + 3x_2 \\
\text{s.t.} \quad & \\
& 195x_1 + 273x_2 \leq 1365 \\
& 4x_1 + 40x_2 \leq 140 \\
& x_1 \leq 4 \\
& x_1 \geq 3 \\
& x_2 \leq 2 \\
& x_1, x_2 \geq 0
\end{aligned}
$$

LP Relaxation at node 5:

$$
\begin{aligned}
\max \quad & 2x_1 + 3x_2 \\
\text{s.t.} \quad & \\
& 195x_1 + 273x_2 \leq 1365 \\
& 4x_1 + 40x_2 \leq 140 \\
& x_1 \leq 4 \\
& x_1 \geq 3 \\
& x_2 \geq 3 \\
& x_1, x_2 \geq 0
\end{aligned}
$$

Note that, since we are branching from node 3, we require $x_1 \geq 3$ in both LP Relaxations.

After solving these linear programming problems we can construct the branch-and-bound solution tree shown in Figure 8.4. Note that at node 4, which corresponds to adding the constraint $x_2 \leq 2$, we find a feasible integer solution. At node 5, however, we find that after adding the constraint $x_2 \geq 3$ there is no feasible solution.

At this point we have found a feasible solution ($x_1 = 4$, $x_2 = 2$) with a value of 14.00 (see node 4). From UB = 14.00 we know that the optimal solution cannot yield a value greater than 14.00. Therefore the solution $x_1 = 4$, $x_2 = 2$ with value 14 is optimal for the Security Realty problem. We can now state the stopping rule for the branch-and-bound solution procedure.

Stopping Rule.

When UB = LB, the optimal solution has been found. It is the feasible solution with value equal to LB.

FIGURE 8.4
Complete Branch-and-Bound Solution Tree for Security Realty Problem

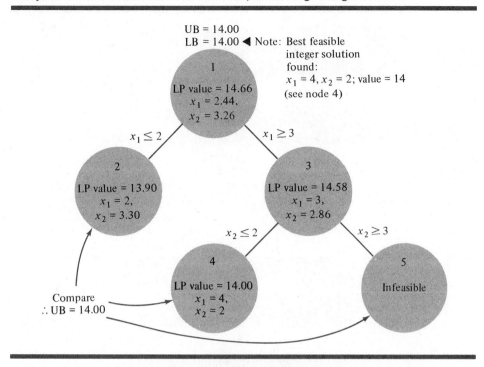

UB = 14.00
LB = 14.00 ◄ Note: Best feasible
integer solution
found:
$x_1 = 4, x_2 = 2$; value = 14
(see node 4)

We have seen how the branch-and-bound solution procedure is applied to solve the all-integer Security Realty Investors problem. A summary of the general procedure for the all-integer linear program is presented in flowchart form in Figure 8.5.

Extension to Mixed-Integer Linear Programs

A big advantage of the branch-and-bound solution procedure for integer programming is that it is applicable to both the all-integer and the mixed-integer linear program. To see how the branch-and-bound approach can be applied to a mixed-integer linear program, let us return to the Security Realty problem and suppose that x_2 was not required to be integer. This would be the case if fractional shares could be purchased in the apartment buildings. In this situation the LP Relaxation solved at node 1 would be exactly the same, yielding a value of 14.66 as an upper bound. But the lower bound would be found by rounding down on x_1 only. Thus the value of the lower bound at node 1 would be 13.78, given by the feasible mixed integer solution $x_1 = 2$, $x_2 = 3.26$. This is shown below.

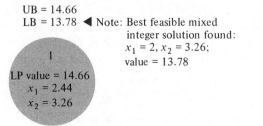

UB = 14.66
LB = 13.78 ◄ Note: Best feasible mixed
integer solution found:
$x_1 = 2, x_2 = 3.26$;
value = 13.78

FIGURE 8.5
Flowchart of Branch-and-Bound Solution Procedure for the All-Integer Linear Program

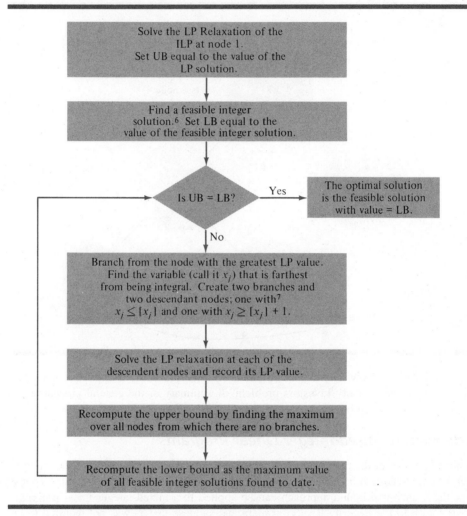

In order to branch, we now restrict consideration to only those variables that are required to be integer. Selecting the integer variable with the largest fractional part leads us to again branch on x_1; we require $x_1 \le 2$ on one branch and $x_1 \ge 3$ on the other. Thus the LP Relaxations solved at nodes 2 and 3 would be the same as before (see Figure 8.6). However, note that a feasible mixed integer solution exists whenever the linear programming solution at a node yields x_1 integer. Thus the solutions at both nodes 2 and 3 are feasible for the mixed-integer linear program. A new lower bound of LB = 14.58 can be established by comparing the values of all the feasible mixed integer solutions

---

[6]In case the constraints are all of the $\le$ type with nonnegative coefficients, the solution found by rounding down will be feasible. Otherwise some knowledge of the particular application may provide a feasible integer solution.

[7]The notation $[x_j]$ means the greatest integer less than or equal to x_j; for example, $[2.86] = 2$.

FIGURE 8.6
Branch-and-Bound Tree for Security Realty Mixed-Integer Linear Program (x_1 Integer, x_2
Not Integer)

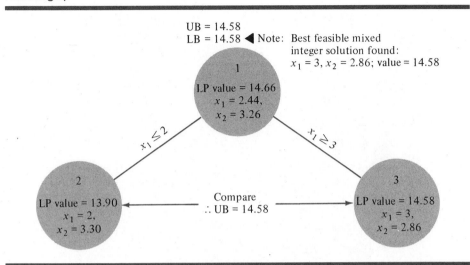

found. A new upper bound of UB = 14.58 can be established by comparing the LP
Relaxation values at nodes 2 and 3. Since the upper and lower bounds are equal, the
optimal solution to the Security Realty problem with only x_1 required to be integer has
been found. It is given by x_1 = 3 and x_2 = 2.86, with an objective function value of
14.58. The branch-and-bound tree for this mixed-integer linear program is shown in
Figure 8.6.

8.5 COMPUTER SOLUTION

As mentioned in the chapter introduction, computer packages for solving integer linear
programs are now widely available. Such codes are generally reliable for problems
involving up to 100 or more integer variables and have often been used to solve specially
structured problems with a few thousand variables.

Most of the general purpose codes use a linear-programming-based branch-and-bound
solution procedure similar to the one described in the previous section. While the branch-
and-bound solution procedure can be used to solve small problems by hand, in practice
a computer code is needed to solve integer linear programs. In this section we will show
how another application of integer programming can be formulated and solved using
LINDO/PC.

A Bank-Location Application

The long-range planning department for the Ohio Trust Company is considering expanding
its operation into a 20-county region in northeastern Ohio (see Figure 8.7). Currently,
Ohio Trust does not have a principal place of business in any of the 20 counties under

FIGURE 8.7
Map of 20-County Area in Northeastern Ohio

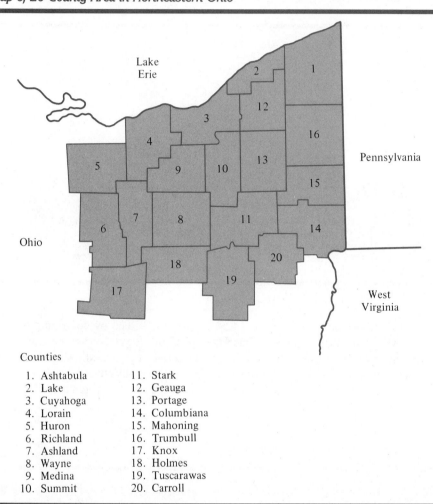

Counties

1. Ashtabula
2. Lake
3. Cuyahoga
4. Lorain
5. Huron
6. Richland
7. Ashland
8. Wayne
9. Medina
10. Summit

11. Stark
12. Geauga
13. Portage
14. Columbiana
15. Mahoning
16. Trumbull
17. Knox
18. Holmes
19. Tuscarawas
20. Carroll

consideration. According to the banking laws in Ohio, if a banking firm establishes a principal place of business (PPB) in any county, then branch banks can be established in that county and in any adjacent county. However, in order to establish a new principal place of business Ohio Trust must either obtain approval for a new bank from the state's superintendent of banks or purchase an existing bank.

Table 8.2 provides a listing of the 20 counties in the region together with the adjacent counties. From the table we see that Ashtabula County is adjacent to Lake, Geauga, and Trumbull counties; Lake County is adjacent to Ashtabula, Cuyahoga, and Geauga counties; and so on.

As an initial step in its planning, Ohio Trust would like to determine the minimum number of PPBs necessary to do business throughout the 20-county region. A *0–1* integer

TABLE 8.2
Counties in Region of Expansion for Ohio Trust

Counties Under Consideration	Adjacent Counties (by Number)
1. Ashtabula	2, 12, 16
2. Lake	1, 3, 12
3. Cuyahoga	2, 4, 9, 10, 12, 13
4. Lorain	3, 5, 7, 9
5. Huron	4, 6, 7
6. Richland	5, 7, 17
7. Ashland	4, 5, 6, 8, 9, 17, 18
8. Wayne	7, 9, 10, 11, 18
9. Medina	3, 4, 7, 8, 10
10. Summit	3, 8, 9, 11, 12, 13
11. Stark	8, 10, 13, 14, 15, 18, 19, 20
12. Geauga	1, 2, 3, 10, 13, 16
13. Portage	3, 10, 11, 12, 15, 16
14. Columbiana	11, 15, 20
15. Mahoning	11, 13, 14, 16
16. Trumbull	1, 12, 13, 15
17. Knox	6, 7, 18
18. Holmes	7, 8, 11, 17, 19
19. Tuscarawas	11, 18, 20
20. Carroll	11, 14, 19

programming model can be used to solve this problem for Ohio Trust. Let us define the following variables:

$$x_i = 1 \text{ if a PPB is established in county } i; 0 \text{ otherwise}$$

With the goal of minimizing the number of PPBs needed, the objective function can be written as

$$\min \quad x_1 + x_2 + \cdots + x_{20}$$

In order to place branch banks in a county, the county must either contain a PPB or be adjacent to another county with a PPB. Thus there will be one constraint for each county. For example, the constraint for Ashtabula County would be written as follows:

$$x_1 + x_2 + x_{12} + x_{16} \geq 1 \quad \text{Ashtabula}$$

Note that satisfaction of this constraint ensures that a PPB will be placed in Ashtabula County *or* in one or more of the adjacent counties. Thus this constraint guarantees that Ohio Trust will be able to place branch banks in Ashtabula County.

The complete statement of the bank location problem is shown below:

$$\min \quad x_1 + x_2 + \quad \cdots \quad + x_{20}$$

s.t.

$$x_1 + x_2 \qquad + x_{12} + x_{16} \qquad \geq 1 \quad \text{Ashtabula}$$
$$x_1 + x_2 + x_3 + x_{12} \qquad \geq 1 \quad \text{Lake}$$

$$\begin{array}{ccc} \cdot & & \cdot \\ \cdot & & \cdot \\ \cdot & & \cdot \end{array}$$

$$x_{11} + x_{14} + x_{19} + x_{20} \geq 1 \quad \text{Carroll}$$

$$x_i = 0, 1 \qquad i = 1, 2, \ldots, 20$$

Given this 20-variable, 20-constraint problem formulation, we can now solve it using LINDO/PC. The input data are entered in the same manner as for a linear program. Then to make LINDO/PC treat each of the 20 decision variables as *0–1* integer variables, we enter the LINDO/PC command "INTEGER 20." When the "GO" command is given, the LINDO/PC program will determine the optimal integer solution.

In Figure 8.8 we show a portion of the computer output. Note that the variable names used correspond to the first four letters in the name of each county. Using the output, we see that the optimal solution calls for principal places of business in Ashland, Stark, and Geauga counties. With PPBs in these three counties, Ohio Trust can place branch banks in all 20 counties (see Figure 8.9). All other decision variables have an optimal value of zero, indicating that a PPB should not be placed in these counties.

FIGURE 8.8
Microcomputer Solution of Bank-Location Problem Using LINDO/PC

```
              OBJECTIVE FUNCTION VALUE

       1)      3.00000000

           VARIABLE        VALUE          REDUCED COST
             ASHT         .000000           .000000
             LAKE         .000000           .000000
             CUYA         .000000           .000000
             LORA         .000000           .000000
             HURO         .000000           .000000
             RICH         .000000          1.000000
             ASHL        1.000000           .000000
             WAYN         .000000           .000000
             MEDI         .000000           .000000
             SUMM         .000000           .000000
             STAR        1.000000           .000000
             GEAU        1.000000           .000000
             PORT         .000000           .000000
             COLU         .000000           .000000
             MAHO         .000000           .000000
             TRUM         .000000           .000000
             KNOX         .000000          1.000000
             HOLM         .000000           .000000
             TUSC         .000000           .000000
             CARR         .000000           .000000
```

FIGURE 8.9
Principal Place of Business Counties for Ohio Trust

Counties

1. Ashtabula	11. Stark
2. Lake	12. Geauga
3. Cuyahoga	13. Portage
4. Lorain	14. Columbia
5. Huron	15. Mahoning
6. Richland	16. Trumbull
7. Ashland	17. Knox
8. Wayne	18. Holmes
9. Medina	19. Tuscarawas
10. Summit	20. Carroll

★ A Principal Place of
Business should be
located in these counties

Clearly the integer programming model could be enlarged to allow for expansion into a larger area or throughout the entire state.[8]

Converting Mixed-Integer Linear Programs to 0–1 Programs

As we mentioned previously, most practical applications of integer linear programming involve only *0–1* integer variables. For this reason a number of mixed-integer programming codes are not designed to handle integer variables that can take on values other than 0 and 1. The LINDO/PC code just discussed was originally designed to only handle

[8]A model of this type allowing for expansion throughout the state and some other variations is presented in Sweeney, D.J., L. Mairose, and R. Martin. "Strategic Planning in Bank Location," *AIDS Proceedings*, November 1979.

0-1 variables. It has recently been revised to handle general integer variables. Nevertheless *0-1* codes can be used to solve general integer programming problems if a clever trick is used to substitute *0-1* variables for the general integer variables. The trick is called *binary expansion* and requires that an upper bound be established for each integer variable. To illustrate how this procedure works, consider the mixed-integer linear program shown below.

$$\max \quad 2x_1 + 3x_2$$
$$\text{s.t.}$$
$$1x_1 + 2x_2 \leq 10.5$$
$$1x_1 \qquad \leq 6$$
$$x_1, x_2 \geq 0 \text{ and } x_1 \text{ integer}$$

For this problem we see that the second constraint provides an upper bound of 6 for the integer variable x_1. Thus, since x_1 can take on the integer values 0, 1, 2, 3, 4, 5, or 6, a *0-1* integer linear programming code cannot be used to solve this problem in its current form. However, consider replacing the variable x_1 with three *0-1* integer variables (y_1, y_2, and y_3) by substituting for x_1 as follows:

$$x_1 = 1y_1 + 2y_2 + 4y_3 \qquad (8.1)$$

With this substitution, x_1 is permitted to assume any value from 0 through 7 depending on the values of y_1, y_2, and y_3. For instance, if $y_1 = 0$, $y_2 = 0$, and $y_3 = 1$, then x_1 would equal 4. If $y_1 = 0$, $y_2 = 1$, and $y_3 = 1$, then x_1 would equal 6. Other combinations of values for y_1, y_2, and y_3 will provide other values for x_1. Thus, using equation (8.1), we can substitute for x_1 in the original problem to obtain an equivalent *0-1* mixed-integer linear program. The substitution results in the following model:

$$\max \quad 2(1y_1 + 2y_2 + 4y_3) + 3x_2$$
$$\text{s.t.}$$
$$(1y_1 + 2y_2 + 4y_3) + 2x_2 \leq 10.5$$
$$(1y_1 + 2y_2 + 4y_3) \qquad \leq 6$$
$$y_1, y_2, y_3, x_2 \geq 0 \text{ and } y_1, y_2, y_3 = 0, 1$$

or

$$\max \quad 2y_1 + 4y_2 + 8y_3 + 3x_2$$
$$\text{s.t.}$$
$$1y_1 + 2y_2 + 4y_3 + 2x_2 \leq 10.5$$
$$1y_1 + 2y_2 + 4y_3 \qquad \leq 6$$
$$y_1, y_2, y_3, x_2 \geq 0 \text{ and } y_1, y_2, y_3 = 0, 1$$

The solution to this problem is $y_1 = 0$, $y_2 = 1$, $y_3 = 1$, and $x_2 = 2.25$. Using equation (8.1) we see that the optimal value for x_1 is $x_1 = 1y_1 + 2y_2 + 4y_3 = 1(0) + 2(1) + 4(1) = 6$. Hence, the value of the optimal solution to the original mixed-integer linear program is $2x_1 + 3x_2 = 2(6) + 3(2.25) = 18.75$.

When using a binary expansion to substitute for a general integer variable, the number of *0-1* variables needed depends on the upper bound for the general integer variable.

Enough terms must be added to allow the binary expansion to take on values that are at least as great as the upper bound for the variable. For example, if we have a mixed-integer linear program with a variable x_1 that can take on integer values from 0 to 15, then four *0–1* integer variables would be required as shown below:

$$x_1 = 1y_1 + 2y_2 + 4y_3 + 8y_4$$

For x_1 to take on a value of 15, we would need to have $y_1 = y_2 = y_3 = y_4 = 1$. If x_1 can take on a value greater than 15, then at least one more 0–1 integer variable would be needed.

Note that each coefficient in the binary expansion is a power of 2; that is, the coefficient for y_1 is $2^0 = 1$, the coefficient for y_2 is $2^1 = 2$, the coefficient for $y_3 = 2^2 = 4$, and so on. A general expression for a binary expansion of a general integer variable x_k, which has an upper bound of μ is given by

$$x_k = \sum_{i=1}^{p} 2^{i-1} y_i$$

where p is the number of 0–1 integer variables required. Specifically, p is the smallest integer such that $2^p - 1 \geq \mu$. Employing a binary expansion of this type enables *0–1* integer programming codes to solve general mixed-integer linear programs.

In closing this section, we comment briefly on the value of general purpose mixed-integer linear programming codes. Such codes can be used for linear programming problems (including the special cases of the transportation, transshipment, and assignment problems), all-integer problems (like the Ohio Trust problem), and problems involving some continuous and some integer variables (mixed-integer linear programs). General-purpose codes are seldom the fastest for solving problems with special structures (such as the transportation, transshipment, and assignment problems); however, unless the problems are very large, speed is usually not a critical issue. As long as a solution can be found in a reasonable amount of time, the practitioner is satisfied. Thus it is probably better for most practitioners to become familiar with one general-purpose computer package that can be used on a variety of problems than to maintain a variety of computer codes that are designed for special problems. If special-purpose codes are needed for particular applications, experts can be consulted.

Summary

We have introduced an important extension of the linear programming model: the integer linear program. The only difference between the integer linear programming problem and the linear programming problem studied in previous chapters is the added restriction on some of the variables. If all of the variables are required to be integer, we have an all-integer linear program; if some but not necessarily all of the variables are required to be integer, we have a mixed-integer linear program. Finally, in case the integer variables are only permitted to assume the values 0 or 1, we have a *0–1* (binary) integer linear program. Binary integer linear programs may be either all integer or mixed integer.

There are two primary reasons for studying integer linear programming. First, in many applications fractional values of the decision variables are not permitted. Since we have seen that rounding the linear programming solution can provide poor results, methods for finding the optimal integer solution are needed. For any two-variable problem a simple extension of the graphical procedure for linear programs can be used to find solutions. The branch-and-bound solution procedure was presented for solving larger integer linear programs. A major advantage of the branch-and-bound solution procedure is its flexibility; it can be used for both the all-integer and the mixed-integer linear programs. Almost all existing commercial computer codes (including LINDO/PC) employ the branch-and-bound approach.

A second reason for studying integer linear programming is that it provides increased modeling flexibility through the use of 0–1 variables. In our discussion of the capital budgeting and distribution system design problems, we saw how a number of important managerial considerations can be incorporated through the use of multiple-choice constraints, conditional constraints, and so on. In addition, the Ohio Trust problem presented in the previous section provided another example of the modeling flexibility available using integer variables.

In recent years, with the availability of commercial integer linear programming computer codes, we have seen a rapid growth in the use of integer linear programming. As researchers develop solution procedures capable of solving integer linear programs with larger numbers of variables, we can expect to see a continuation of this rapid growth and the development of new applications.

Glossary

Integer linear program   A linear program with the additional requirement that some or all of the decision variables must be integer.

All-integer linear program   An integer linear program in which all the decision variables are required to be integer.

LP Relaxation   The linear program that results from dropping the integer requirements for the decision variables. For a maximization problem, the value of the optimal solution to the LP Relaxation is an upper bound on the value of the optimal integer solution.

Mixed-integer linear program   An integer linear program in which some, but not all, of the decision variables are required to be integer.

0–1 integer linear program   An all-integer or mixed-integer linear program in which the integer variables are only permitted to assume the values 0 or 1.

Upper bound   A value that is known to be greater than or equal to the value of any feasible solution. The solution to the LP Relaxation of an integer linear program provides an upper bound for a maximization problem.

Multiple-choice constraint   A constraint requiring that the sum of two or more 0–1 variables equal 1. Thus any feasible solution makes a choice of one of these variables to set equal to 1.

Mutually exclusive constraint   A constraint requiring that the sum of two or more 0–1 variables be less than or equal to 1. Thus if one of the variables equals 1, the others must equal 0. However, all variables could equal 0.

k out of n alternatives constraint   An extension of the multiple-choice constraint. This constraint requires that the sum of n 0–1 variables equal k.

Conditional constraints   Constraints involving *0–1* variables that do not allow certain variables to equal 1 unless certain other variables are equal to 1.

Corequisite constraint   A constraint requiring that two *0–1* variables be equal. Thus they are both in or out of solution together.

Branch and bound   A solution procedure for integer linear programs that sequentially partitions the set of feasible solutions into smaller and smaller subsets until the optimal solution is found.

Lower bound   A value that is less than or equal to the value of the optimal solution. For a maximization problem the value of any feasible integer solution to an integer linear program is a lower bound.

Descendant node   A node created in a branch-and-bound solution tree by branching from another node by adding a constraint to the LP Relaxation solved at the previous node.

Binary expansion   A method used to convert any integer variable into a weighted sum of *0–1* integer variables.

─── *Problems* ───

1. Indicate which of the following are all-integer linear programs, which are mixed-integer linear programs, and which are ordinary linear programs. For each of the all-integer and mixed-integer linear programs write the LP Relaxation. (Do not attempt to solve.)

    a. max $30x_1 + 25x_2$
       s.t.

$$3x_1 + 1.5x_2 \leq 400$$
$$1.5x_1 + 2x_2 \leq 250$$
$$1x_1 + 1x_2 \leq 150$$
$$x_1, x_2 \geq 0 \text{ and } x_2 \text{ integer}$$

    b. min $3x_1 + 4x_2$
       s.t.

$$2x_1 + 4x_2 \geq 8$$
$$2x_1 + 6x_2 \geq 12$$
$$x_1, x_2 \geq 0 \text{ and integer}$$

    c. min $30x_1 + 4x_2$
       s.t.

$$3x_1 + 2x_2 \geq 50$$
$$0.1x_1 + 0.2x_2 \geq 2$$
$$x_1, x_2 \geq 0 \text{ and } x_1 \text{ integer}$$

    d. max $3x_1 + 4x_2$
       s.t.

$$-1x_1 + 2x_2 \leq 8$$
$$1x_1 + 2x_2 \leq 12$$
$$2x_1 + 1x_2 \leq 16$$
$$x_1, x_2 \geq 0 \text{ and integer}$$

e. max $20x_1 + 5x_2$

s.t.

$$5x_1 + 1x_2 \le 15$$
$$6x_1 + 4x_2 \le 24$$
$$1x_1 + 1x_2 \le 5$$
$$x_1, x_2 \ge 0$$

2. Consider the all-integer linear program given below:

max $5x_1 + 8x_2$

s.t.

$$6x_1 + 5x_2 \le 30$$
$$9x_1 + 4x_2 \le 36$$
$$1x_1 + 2x_2 \le 10$$
$$x_1, x_2 \ge 0 \text{ and integer}$$

a. Graph the constraints for this problem. Indicate with heavy dots all the feasible integer solutions.
b. Find the optimal solution to the LP Relaxation. Round down to find a feasible integer solution.
c. Find the optimal integer solution. Is it the same as the solution found in part b above by rounding down?

3. Consider the all-integer linear program given below:

max $1x_1 + 1x_2$

s.t.

$$4x_1 + 6x_2 \le 22$$
$$1x_1 + 5x_2 \le 15$$
$$2x_1 + 1x_2 \le 9$$
$$x_1, x_2 \ge 0 \text{ and integer}$$

a. Graph the constraints for this problem. Indicate with heavy dots all the feasible integer solutions.
b. Solve the LP Relaxation of this problem.
c. Find the optimal integer solution.

4. Consider the integer linear program given below:

max $10x_1 + 3x_2$

s.t.

$$6x_1 + 7x_2 \le 40$$
$$3x_1 + 1x_2 \le 11$$
$$x_1, x_2 \ge 0 \text{ and integer}$$

a. Formulate and solve the LP Relaxation of the problem. Solve it graphically. Round down to find a feasible solution. State upper and lower bounds on the value of the optimal solution.
b. Solve the integer linear program graphically. Compare the value of this solution with the solution found in part a.

c. Suppose the objective function changes to max $3x_1 + 6x_2$. Repeat parts a and b above.

5. Consider the mixed-integer linear program given below:

$$\max \quad 2x_1 + 3x_2$$
$$\text{s.t.}$$
$$4x_1 + 9x_2 \leq 36$$
$$7x_1 + 5x_2 \leq 35$$
$$x_1, x_2 \geq 0 \text{ and } x_1 \text{ integer}$$

a. Graph the constraints for this problem. Indicate on your graph all feasible mixed-integer solutions.
b. Find the optimal solution to the LP Relaxation. Round the value of x_1 down to find a feasible mixed-integer solution. Is this solution optimal? Why or why not?
c. Find the optimal solution for the mixed-integer linear program.

6. Consider the mixed-integer linear program given below.

$$\max \quad 1x_1 + 1x_2$$
$$\text{s.t.}$$
$$7x_1 + 9x_2 \leq 63$$
$$9x_1 + 5x_2 \leq 45$$
$$3x_1 + 1x_2 \leq 12$$
$$x_1, x_2 \geq 0 \text{ and } x_2 \text{ integer}$$

a. Graph the constraints for this problem. Indicate on your graph all feasible mixed-integer solutions.
b. Find the optimal solution to the LP Relaxation. Round the value of x_2 down to find a feasible mixed-integer solution. Specify upper and lower bounds on the value of the optimal solution to the mixed-integer linear program.
c. Find the optimal solution to the mixed-integer linear program.

7. Consider again the all-integer linear program in problem 4. It is restated below.

$$\max \quad 10x_1 + 3x_2$$
$$\text{s.t.}$$
$$6x_1 + 7x_2 \leq 40$$
$$3x_1 + 1x_2 \leq 11$$
$$x_1, x_2 \geq 0 \text{ and integer}$$

Solve this problem using the branch-and-bound procedure.

8. The integer programming formulation of the Ice-Cold Refrigerator Company capital budgeting problem is presented below.

$$\max \quad 90x_1 + 40x_2 + 10x_3 + 37x_4$$
$$\text{s.t.}$$
$$15x_1 + 10x_2 + 10x_3 + 15x_4 \leq 40$$
$$20x_1 + 15x_2 \quad\quad + 10x_4 \leq 50$$
$$20x_1 + 20x_2 \quad\quad + 10x_4 \leq 40$$
$$15x_1 + 5x_2 + 4x_3 + 10x_4 \leq 35$$
$$x_1, x_2, x_3, x_4 = 0, 1$$

Solve this problem using the branch-and-bound procedure. Note that in the case of variables restricted to *0 or 1* each branch corresponds to setting one of the variables equal to *0 or 1*. Thus the branching variable is treated as a constant in the linear programming problem solved at the descendant node.

9. Refer to the Ohio Trust bank location problem introduced in Section 8.5. Table 8.2 shows the counties under consideration and the adjacent counties.

   a. Write the complete integer programming model if Ohio Trust is considering expansion only into the following counties: Lorain, Huron, Richland, Ashland, Wayne, Medina, and Knox.

   b. Solve the problem in part a using trial and error.

10. Consider the mixed-integer linear program given below:

$$\max \quad 1x_1 + 2x_2 + 1x_3$$
$$\text{s.t.}$$
$$7x_1 + 4x_2 + 3x_3 \leq 28$$
$$4x_1 + 7x_2 + 2x_3 \leq 28$$
$$x_1, x_2, x_3 \geq 0 \text{ and } x_1, x_2 \text{ integer}$$

Solve this problem using the branch-and-bound procedure.

11. Grave City is considering the relocation of a number of police substations in order to obtain better enforcement in high-crime areas. The locations being considered together with the areas that can be covered from these locations are given below.

Potential Locations for Substations	Areas Covered
A	1, 5, 7
B	1, 2, 5, 7
C	1, 3, 5
D	2, 4, 5
E	3, 4, 6
F	4, 5, 6
G	1, 5, 6, 7

   a. Formulate an integer programming model that could be solved to find the minimum number of locations necessary to provide coverage to all areas.

   b. Solve the problem in part a using any means at your disposal.

12. The Martin-Beck Company is in the process of planning for new production facilities and developing a more efficient distribution system design. At present they have one plant at St. Louis with a capacity of 30,000 units. But because of increased demand, management is considering four potential new plant sites: Detroit, Denver, Toledo, and Kansas City. The transportation tableau below summarizes the projected plant capacities, the cost per unit of shipping from each plant to each destination (upper right-hand corner of each cell), and the demand forecasts over a 1-year planning horizon.

	Boston	Atlanta	Houston	Capacities
Detroit	5	2	3	10,000
Toledo	4	3	4	20,000
Denver	9	7	5	30,000
Kansas City	10	4	2	40,000
St. Louis	8	4	3	30,000
Demand	30,000	20,000	20,000	

Suppose that the fixed costs of constructing the new plants are

Detroit $175,000
Toledo $300,000
Denver $375,000
Kansas City $500,000

The Martin-Beck Company would like to minimize the total cost of plant construction and distribution of goods.

a. Develop a *0–1* mixed-integer linear programming model of this problem. (Do not attempt to solve.)
b. Modify your formulation in part a to account for the policy restriction that one plant but not both must be located in Detroit or in Toledo. (Do not attempt to solve.)
c. Modify your formulation in part a to account for the policy restriction that at most two plants can be located in Denver, Kansas City, and St. Louis. (Do not attempt to solve.)
d. Suppose that there are two possible sizes for the Denver plant, the one mentioned earlier with a capacity of 30,000 and a cost of 375,000, and another with a capacity of 60,000 and a cost of 550,000. Modify your formulation in part a to account for this consideration. (Do not attempt to solve.)

13. Spencer Enterprises is attempting to choose among a series of new investment alternatives. The potential investment alternatives, the net present value of the future stream of returns, the capital requirements, and the available capital funds over the next 3 years are summarized below:
a. Develop an integer programming model for maximizing the net present value. (Do not solve.)
b. Assume that only one of the warehouse expansion projects can be implemented. Modify your model of part a.
c. Suppose that if the test-marketing of the new product is carried out, then the advertising campaign must also be conducted. Modify your formulation of part b to reflect this new situation.

Alternative	Net Present Value ($)	Capital Requirements ($)		
		Year 1	Year 2	Year 3
Limited warehouse expansion	4000	3000	1000	4000
Extensive warehouse expansion	6000	2500	3500	3500
Test-market new product	10,500	6000	4000	5000
Advertising campaign	4000	2000	1500	1800
Basic research	8000	5000	1000	4000
Purchase new equipment	3000	1000	500	900
Capital funds available		10,500	7000	8750

14. The following questions refer to a capital budgeting problem with six projects represented by $0–1$ variables x_1, x_2, x_3, x_4, x_5, x_6.
   a. Write a constraint modeling a situation in which two of the projects 1, 3, 5, and 6 must be undertaken.
   b. Write a constraint modeling a situation in which projects 3 and 5 must be undertaken simultaneously.
   c. Write a constraint modeling a situation in which project 1 or 4 must be undertaken but not both.
   d. Write constraints modeling a situation where project 4 cannot be undertaken unless projects 1 and 3 are also undertaken.
   e. Revise the requirement in part d to accommodate the case in which, when projects 1 and 3 are undertaken, project 4 must also be undertaken.

15. Consider the following integer linear program:

$$\max \quad 6x_1 + 9x_2 + 11x_3$$
$$\text{s.t.}$$
$$2x_1 + 1x_2 + 1.5x_3 \le 10$$
$$3x_1 + 2x_2 + 8x_3 \le 18$$
$$x_1, x_2, \text{ and } x_3 \ge 0 \text{ and integer}$$

   a. Determine *integer* upper bounds for each variable. *Hint*: From constraint 1 we see that when x_2 and x_3 are 0, $x_1 \le 5$. Similarly, from constraint 2, we see that when x_2 and x_3 are 0, $x_1 \le 6$. Thus, the largest integer value x_1 can take on is 5.
   b. Convert the integer linear program into an equivalent $0–1$ integer programming problem.

16. The Northshore Bank is working to develop an efficient work schedule for full-time and part-time tellers. The schedule must provide for efficient operation of the bank including adequate customer service, employee breaks, and so on. On Fridays the bank is open from 9:00 A.M. to 7:00 P.M. The number of tellers necessary to provide adequate customer service during each hour of operation is summarized below.

Time	9–10	10–11	11–12	12–1	1–2	2–3	3–4	4–5	5–6	6–7
Number of Tellers	6	4	8	10	9	6	4	7	6	6

Each full-time employee starts on the hour and works a 4-hour shift, followed by 1 hour for lunch and then a 3-hour shift. Part-time employees work one 4-hour shift beginning on the hour and extending for 4 consecutive hours. Considering salary and fringe benefits, full-time employees cost the bank $7.50 per hour ($52.50 per day), and part-time employees cost the bank $4 per hour ($16 per day).

a. Formulate an integer programming model that can be used to develop a schedule that will satisfy customer service needs at a minimum employee cost. (*Hint*: Let x_i = number of full-time employees coming on duty at the beginning of hour i and y_i = number of part-time employees coming on duty at the beginning of hour i.)

b. Solve the linear programming relaxation of your model in part a.

c. Solve for the optimal schedule of tellers. Comment on the solution.

d. After reviewing the solution to part c the bank manager has realized that some additional requirements must be specified. Specifically she wants to ensure that one full-time employee is on duty at all times and that there is a staff of at least five full-time employees. Revise your model to incorporate these additional requirements and solve for the optimal solution.

17. CHB, Inc. is a bank holding company that is evaluating the potential for expanding into a 13-county region in the southwestern part of the state. State law permits establishing branches in any county that is adjacent to a county in which a PPB (principal place of business) is located. Below is a map of the 13-county region; the population of each county also is indicated on the map.

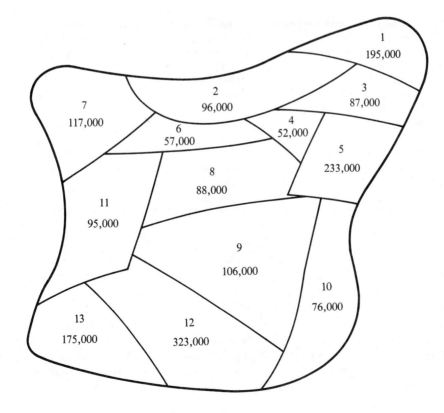

a. Assume that only one PPB can be established in the region. Where should it be located in order to maximize the population served? *Hint*: Review the Ohio Trust formulation in Section 8.5. Consider minimizing the population not served and introduce variable $y_i = 1$ if it is not possible to establish a branch in county i and $y_i = 0$ otherwise.

b. Suppose that two PPBs can be established in the region. Where should they be located to maximize the population served?

c. Management has learned that a bank located in county 5 is considering selling. If CHB, Inc. purchases this bank, it will establish for CHB a PPB in county 5 and provide a base for beginning expansion in the region. What advice would you give the management of CHB?

Case Problem:

TEXTBOOK PUBLISHING

ASW Publishing, Inc., a small publisher of college textbooks, must reach a decision regarding which books to publish next year. The books that the company is considering are listed in the following table, along with the projected sales that are expected from each book over the next 3 years if the book is published.

Book Subject	Type of Book	Projected Sales (units)
Business calculus	New	20,000
Finite mathematics	Revision	30,000
General statistics	New	15,000
Mathematical statistics	New	10,000
Business statistics	Revision	25,000
Finance	New	18,000
Financial accounting	New	25,000
Managerial accounting	Revision	50,000
English literature	New	20,000
German	New	30,000

The books that are listed as revisions are texts that ASW already has under contract; these texts are being considered for publication as new editions. The books that are listed as new have been reviewed by the company but contracts as yet have not been signed.

The company has three individuals who can be assigned to these projects, all of whom have varying amounts of time available; John has 60 days available, Susan has 40 days available, and Monica has 40 days available. The number of days required by each person to complete each project are shown below; in this table an "X" indicates that the person will not be used for the project because of a lack of expertise in the area, a personality conflict with the author(s), or some other reason. At least 2 staff members are capable of being assigned to each project except the finance book.

Book Subject	John	Susan	Monica
Business calculus	30	40	X
Finite mathematics	16	24	X
General statistics	24	X	30
Mathematical statistics	20	X	24
Business statistics	10	X	16
Finance	X	X	14
Financial accounting	X	24	26
Managerial accounting	X	28	30
English literature	40	34	30
German	X	50	36

ASW will not publish more than two statistics books or more than one accounting text in a single year. In addition, management has decided that one of the mathematics books (business calculus or finite math) must be published, but not both.

MANAGERIAL REPORT

Prepare a report for the general manager of ASW that describes your findings and recommendations regarding the best publication strategy for ASW to follow next year. In carrying out your analysis, assume that the fixed costs and the per-unit sales revenues are approximately equal for all books; thus management is primarily interested in maximizing the total sales volume.

The general manager has also asked that you include recommendations regarding the following possible changes:

1. If it would be advantageous to do so, Susan can be moved off another project in order to allow her to work 12 more days.
2. Again, if it would be advantageous to do so, Monica can be made available for another 10 days.
3. If one or more of the revisions could be postponed for another year, should they be? Clearly the company will risk losing market share by postponing a revision.

Include details of your analysis in an appendix to your report.

Management Science in Practice
KETRON*
Arlington, Virginia

Ketron, Inc. is a consulting firm with several branch offices located throughout the United States. An important part of Ketron's business involves national defense and other government applications.

The Management Science Systems division of Ketron is responsible for the maintenance, development, enhancement, and marketing of MPSIII, a proprietary mathematical programming system for use on IBM computers. Members of the Management Science Systems division consult with users of MPSIII and assist them in developing and implementing solutions to their problems. One such mixed-integer programming (MIP) application developed for a major sporting equipment company is outlined below.

A CUSTOMER ORDER ALLOCATION MODEL

A major sporting equipment company satisfies demand for its products by making shipments from its factories and other locations around the country where inventories are maintained. The company markets approximately 300 products and has about 30 sources of supply (factory and warehouse locations). The problem of interest is to determine how best to allocate customer orders to the various sources of supply such that the total manufacturing cost is minimized. Although transportation cost is not directly considered, it can be accounted for indirectly by not including variables corresponding to shipments from distant locations. Figure A8.1 provides a graphical representation of this problem. Note in the figure that each customer can receive shipments from only a few of the various sources of supply. For example, we see that customer 1 may be supplied by sources A or B, customer 2 may be supplied only by source A, and so on.

The customer order allocation problem is solved periodically. In a typical period there are between 30 and 40 customers to be supplied. Since most customers require several products, there are usually between 600 and 800 orders that must be assigned to the sources of supply.

The sporting equipment company classifies each customer order as either a ''guaranteed'' or a ''secondary'' order. Guaranteed orders are single-source orders in that they must be filled by a single supplier to ensure that the complete order will be delivered to the customer at one time. It is this ''single source'' requirement

*The authors are indebted to J. A. Tomlin, Ketron, Inc., San Bruno, Calif., for providing this application.

FIGURE A8.1
Graphical Representation of the Customer Order-Allocation Problem

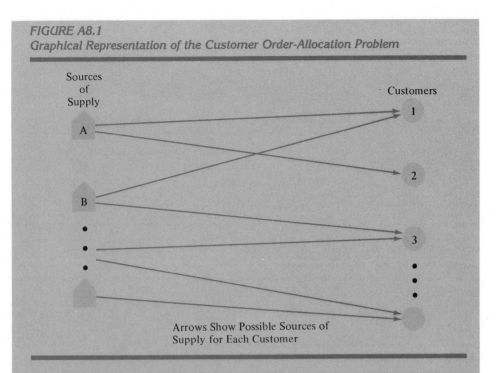

Arrows Show Possible Sources of
Supply for Each Customer

that necessitates the use of integer variables in the model. Approximately 80% of the company's orders are guaranteed orders.

Secondary orders can be split between the various sources of supply. These orders are made by customers restocking inventory, and there is no problem in receiving partial shipments from different sources at different times. The total of all secondary orders for a given product is treated as a goal or target in the model formulation. Deviations below the goal are permitted, but a penalty cost is associated with these deviations in the objective function. When deviations occur in the optimal solution, the secondary orders will not be completely satisfied; the "shortfall" is spread among customers in specified proportions.

Manufacturing considerations are such that raw material availability and the type of process used constrain the amount of production. In addition, groups of items that are similar may belong to a "model group" that must be jointly constrained at some factories. There are also several restrictions on international shipping. For various policy reasons, shipments between sources and customers in certain countries may not be made. This reduces the number of variables in the model but necessitates extensive data checking to ensure that all "guaranteed" orders have a permissible source. If they do not, some means must be found to make the problem feasible before even beginning to solve the mixed-integer programming model.

The primary objective of the model is to minimize the total manufacturing costs, subject to the requirement that the guaranteed orders be met. As indicated previously, the deviations below the secondary demand goals are dealt with by defining "shortfall" variables with an associated cost. This cost represents a penalty for not having the item in inventory when it is required.

A description of the constraints and the objective function for the model is presented below.

CONSTRAINTS

Guaranteed orders: Each customer's order for each product is assigned to a single supplier. (This is a multiple-choice constraint.)

Secondary orders: For each product the total amount of secondary demand assigned plus the shortfall must equal the total demand goal (target).

Raw material capacities: The amount of each type of raw material used at a supply source cannot exceed the amount available.

Manufacturing capacities: At each supply source the capacity for each type of production process cannot be exceeded.

Individual product capacities: The amount of product produced at a site cannot exceed that site's capacity for the product.

Group capacities: The total production for a group of similar products at a site cannot exceed that site's capacity for the group of products.

OBJECTIVE FUNCTION

The objective is to minimize the sum of (1) the manufacturing cost for guaranteed orders, (2) the manufacturing cost for secondary orders, and (3) the penalty cost for unsatisfied secondary demand.

MODEL SOLUTION

It is unreasonable to expect to obtain an optimal solution for a problem of this complexity. Furthermore, the goal programming methodology for handling the secondary demand means that an "optimum" is of questionable interpretation. What is needed is a "good" feasible mixed-integer solution. This is one of the advantages of the branch-and-bound approach. If an integer solution is found whose value is within a few percent of the value of the lower bound, the room for improvement is obviously small.

The solution procedure used is to make a sequence of runs, each beginning where the previous one terminated. Each run allows at most 40 linear programming evaluations (boundings), though many more variables will usually be set to some integer value (branched on). In almost every case the first such run, which includes finding the linear programming relaxation solution, produces a solution satisfactory to the user.

A fairly typical problem has about 800 constraints, 2000 *0–1* assignment variables for the guaranteed orders, and 500 continuous variables associated with the secondary orders. This model is solved using Ketron's MPSIII system. The computer time consumed in producing a solution is approximately 6 minutes on an IBM 3033. Almost half of this time, however, is used to generate the model, optimize the linear programming relaxation, and produce extensive solution reports.

IMPLEMENTATION NOTES

In large-scale applications such as this, considerable systems work is involved in generating the data for the model and the managerial reports. Special data processing languages are often available to ease the programming burden of these phases. The DATAFORM language facility of MPSIII is used to generate the data for this model and to prepare the reports.

In this application it is necessary to make a completely separate preprocessing run to check for internal consistency and errors in the data. Only when the data appear logically error-free is the model generated and solved. Although tedious, this kind of preprocessing effort is critical for mixed-integer models, since the cost of solving the wrong model can be significant. Furthermore, in some cases the data preprocessing step permits the size of the model to be reduced. Such a reduction is possible in this application when a demand for a product has only one legitimate source. The computational benefits of such reductions can be substantial.

Questions

1. Discuss the relationship between the method for handling secondary orders and goal programming. Refer to Chapter 4 for a discussion of goal programming.
2. It is mentioned that an "optimum" is of questionable interpretation. Discuss what is meant by this statement. Does it mean that any feasible solution is acceptable?

9

Network Models

Many managerial problems in areas such as transportation systems design, information systems design, and project scheduling have been successfully solved with the aid of network models and network analysis techniques. In Chapter 7 we showed how *networks* consisting of nodes and arcs can be used to provide graphical representations of transportation, assignment, and transshipment problems. In this chapter we present three additional network problems: the shortest-route problem, the minimal spanning tree problem, and the maximal flow problem. In each case we will show how a network model can be developed and solved in order to provide an optimal solution to the problem.

9.1 THE SHORTEST-ROUTE PROBLEM

In this section we consider the network application of designing a transportation system where the primary interest is determining the *shortest route* or *shortest path* through the network. Let us demonstrate the shortest-route problem by considering the situation faced by the Gorman Construction Company. Gorman operates several construction projects located throughout a three-county area. Construction sites are sometimes located as far as 50 miles from Gorman's main office. With multiple daily trips carrying personnel, equipment, and supplies to and from the construction locations, the costs associated with transportation activities are substantial. For any given construction site, the travel alternatives between the site and the office can be described by a network of roads, streets, and highways. The network shown in Figure 9.1 describes the travel alternatives to and from six of Gorman's newest construction sites. The circles or *nodes* of the network correspond to the site locations. The roads, streets, and highways appear as the *arcs* in the network. The distances between the sites are shown above the corresponding arcs. Note that the length of each arc is not necessarily drawn proportional to the travel distance. If Gorman wishes to minimize the total travel distance from the office to each site, what are the shortest routes or paths for the network?

FIGURE 9.1
Road Network for the Gorman Company Shortest-Route Problem

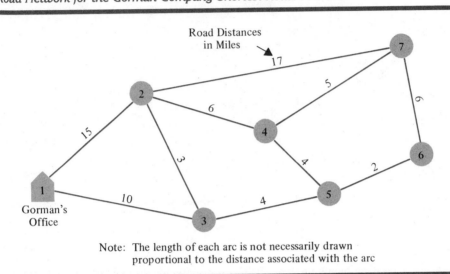

Note: The length of each arc is not necessarily drawn
proportional to the distance associated with the arc

A Shortest-Route Algorithm

In order to solve Gorman's problem, we will need to determine the shortest route from Gorman's office, node 1, to each of the other nodes in the network. The algorithm we present uses a labeling procedure to find the shortest distance from node 1 to each of the other nodes. As we perform the steps of the labeling procedure, we will identify a *label* for each node consisting of two numbers enclosed in brackets. The first number in the label for a particular node indicates the distance from node 1 to that node, while the second number indicates the preceding node on the route from node 1 to that node. We will show the label for each node directly above or below the node in the network. For example, a label for a particular node might appear as shown in Figure 9.2.

At any step of the labeling procedure a node is said to be either labeled or unlabeled. A labeled node is any node for which we have identified a path from node 1 to that node, and an unlabeled node is any node for which no path has yet been identified. For those

FIGURE 9.2
An Example of a Node Label

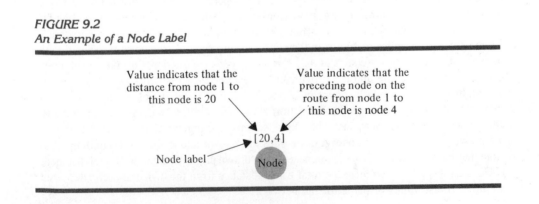

nodes that are labeled, the node is said to be either permanently labeled or tentatively labeled. That is, whenever the algorithm has determined the *shortest* distance from node 1 to a particular node, the node is said to have a *permanent* label. If, however, the shortest distance from node 1 to a particular labeled node has not yet been determined, the node is said to have a *tentative* label. Now that we have an idea of what a label is, let us see how labels are computed and how the labeling process can be used to determine the shortest route from node 1 to each of the other nodes in the network.

We begin the labeling process by associating with node 1 the permanent label [0,S]. The S simply identifies that node 1 is the starting node and the 0 indicates that the distance from node 1 to itself is zero. To distinguish between tentatively and permanently labeled nodes, we follow the practice of shading darkly all permanently labeled nodes in the network. In addition, an arrow will be used to point to the permanently labeled node being investigated at each step of the labeling algorithm. The initial identification of Gorman's network is shown in Figure 9.3. Only node 1 is permanently labeled.

FIGURE 9.3
Initial Network Identification for Gorman's Shortest-Route Problem

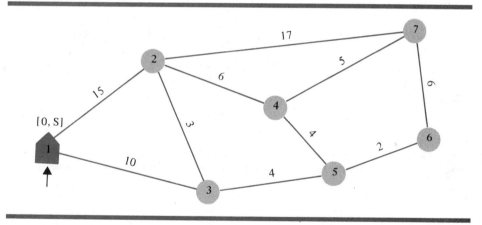

To perform the first step or iteration of the labeling procedure, we must consider every node that can be reached directly from node 1; hence we look at nodes 2 and 3. Consider for the moment node 2. We see that the direct distance from node 1 to node 2 is 15 miles. Thus node 2 can be tentatively labeled [15,1]. The first number in the label indicates that node 2 can be reached in 15 miles and the second number in the label indicates that the preceding node on the route to node 2 is node 1. Next, considering node 3, we find that the direct distance from node 1 to node 3 is 10 miles. Thus the tentative label at node 3 is [10,1]. Figure 9.4 shows the results thus far. Nodes 2 and 3 are tentatively labeled.

Refer to Figure 9.4. We now consider the tentatively labeled nodes and identify the node with the smallest distance value in its label; this is node 3. The tentative label associated with node 3 indicates that we can reach node 3 from node 1 by traveling a distance of 10 miles. Could we get to node 3 following a shorter route? Since any other route to node 3 would require passing through other nodes, and since the distance from node 1 to all other nodes is greater than or equal to 10, there could be no shorter route

FIGURE 9.4
Gorman's Network with Tentative Labels for Nodes 2 and 3

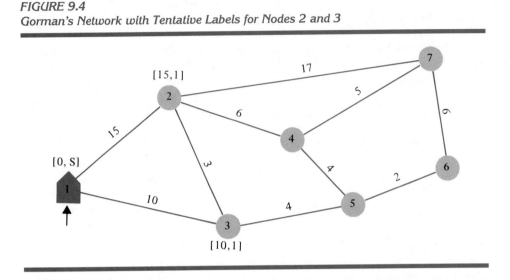

to node 3 found by first going to some other node. Thus we have identified the best, or shortest, route to node 3, and accordingly node 3 is permanently labeled with a distance of 10 miles. Shading node 3 darkly to indicate it is a permanently labeled node and adding an arrow to indicate that node 3 will be used to start the next step of the labeling process provide the network as shown in Figure 9.5.

FIGURE 9.5
Gorman's Network with Node 3 Identified as a Permanently Labeled Node

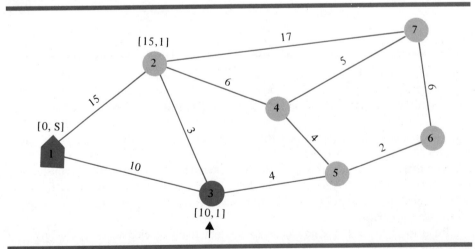

We proceed by considering all nodes that do not have a permanent label and can be reached directly from node 3. Thus we consider nodes 2 and 5. Note that 3 miles is the direct distance from node 3 to node 2 and 4 miles is the direct distance from node 3 to node 5. Since the permanent label for node 3 indicates that the shortest distance to node 3 is 10, we see that we can reach node 2 in 10 + 3 = 13 miles and node 5 in 10 + 4 = 14 miles. Thus the tentative label at node 2 is revised to [13,3] to indicate that we have now found a route from node 1 to node 2 with a distance of 13 miles and that the preceding node on the route to node 2 is node 3. Similarly, the tentative label for node 5 is [14,3]. Figure 9.6 shows the network computations up to this point.

FIGURE 9.6
Gorman's Network with New Tentative Labels for Nodes 2 and 5

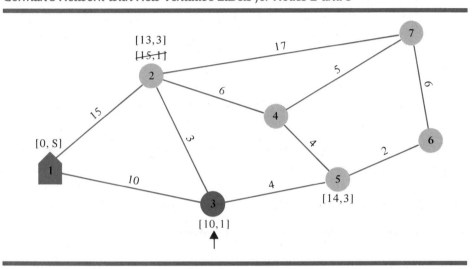

We next consider the tentatively labeled nodes in order to identify the node having the smallest distance value. From Figure 9.6 we see this is node 2 with a distance value of 13 miles. Node 2 is now declared permanently labeled because we can guarantee that node 2 can be reached from node 1 in the shortest possible distance of 13 miles by going through node 3.

The next step or iteration begins at node 2, the most recently permanently labeled node. As before, we consider every nonpermanently labeled node that can be reached directly from node 2; that is, nodes 4 and 7. Starting with the distance value of 13 in the permanent label at node 2, and adding the direct distance from node 2 to each of nodes 4 and 7, shows us that node 4 can be reached in 13 + 6 = 19 miles, while node 7 can be reached in 13 + 17 = 30 miles. Thus the tentative labels at nodes 4 and 7 are as shown in Figure 9.7.

From among the tentatively labeled nodes (nodes 4, 5, and 7), we select the node with the smallest distance value and declare that node permanently labeled. Thus node 5 with a distance of 14 becomes the new permanently labeled node. From node 5, then, we consider all nonpermanently labeled nodes that can be reached directly from node 5. Thus the tentative label on node 4 is revised and node 6 is tentatively labeled. Figure 9.8 depicts these calculations.

Identifying the smallest distance for the remaining tentatively labeled nodes results in node 6 being permanently labeled. From node 6 we can determine a new tentative label for node 7. After this step, the network appears as shown in Figure 9.9.

FIGURE 9.7
Gorman's Network with a Permanent Label at Node 2 and New Tentative Labels for Nodes 4 and 7

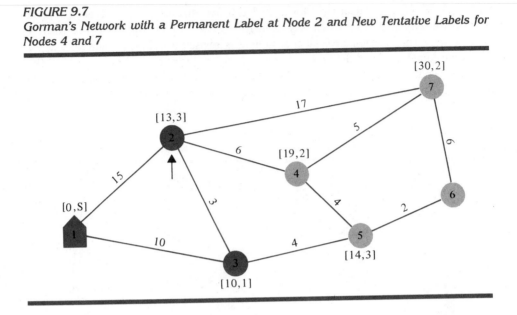

FIGURE 9.8
Gorman's Network with a Permanent Label at Node 5 and New Tentative Labels for Nodes 4 and 6

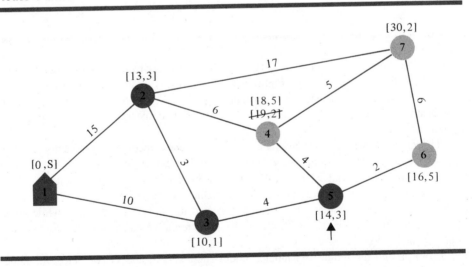

We now have only two remaining nonpermanently labeled nodes. Since the distance portion of the label at node 4 is smaller than the corresponding value at node 7, node 4 becomes the new permanently labeled node. Moreover, since node 7 is the only remaining node that can be reached directly from node 4, we compare the current labeled distance of 22 for node 7 with the sum of the distance in the label on node 4, and the direct distance from node 4 to node 7. Note in this case that the [22,6] tentative label already

FIGURE 9.9
Gorman's Network with a Permanent Label at Node 6 and a New Tentative Label for Node 7.

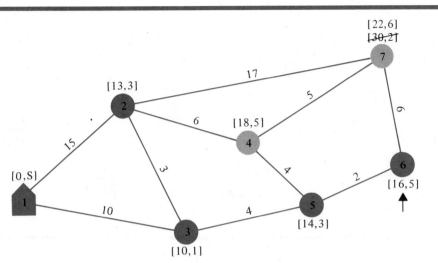

existing at node 7 has the smaller distance value; thus the tentative label at node 7 remains unchanged. Figure 9.10 shows the network at this point in time.

Since node 7 is the only remaining node with a tentative label, it is now permanently labeled. Whenever all nodes have been permanently labeled, we have found the shortest route from node 1 to every node in the network. Figure 9.11 shows the final network with all nodes permanently labeled.

We can now use the information in the permanent labels to find the shortest route from node 1 to each of the nodes in the network. For example, the permanent label at

FIGURE 9.10
Gorman's Network with a Permanent Label at Node 4.

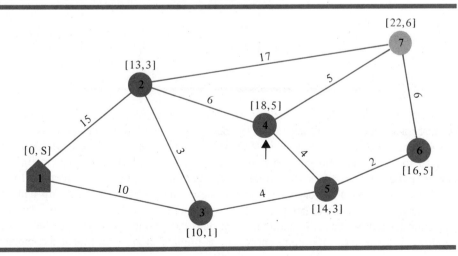

FIGURE 9.11
Gorman's Network with All Nodes Permanently Labeled

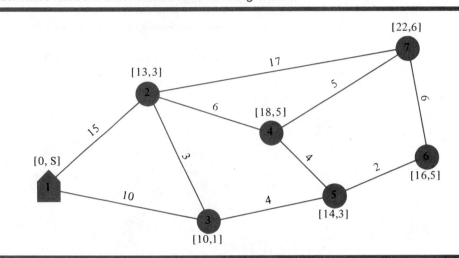

FIGURE 9.11
Gorman's Network with All Nodes Permanently Labeled

node 7 tells us the shortest distance from node 1 to node 7 is 22 miles. To find the particular route that enables us to reach node 7 in 22 miles, we start at node 7 and note that the label tells us that the preceding node on the shortest route from node 1 is node 6. Moving back through the network to node 6, we see from its permanent label that we reach node 6 by coming from node 5. Continuing this process, we note that we reach node 5 from node 3 and finally that we reach node 3 from node 1. Therefore the shortest route from node 1 to node 7 is 1–3–5–6–7. Using this approach, the following shortest routes are identified for the Gorman transportation network:

Node	Shortest Route from Node 1	Distance in Miles
2	1–3–2	13
3	1–3	10
4	1–3–5–4	18
5	1–3–5	14
6	1–3–5–6	16
7	1–3–5–6–7	22

Perhaps for a problem as small as the Gorman problem you could have found the shortest routes just as fast, if not faster, by inspection. The reason is that with only seven nodes there are few alternate routes. However, when we begin to investigate problems with 15 to 20 or more nodes, it becomes very time consuming to attempt to find the shortest routes by inspection. In fact, because of the increased number of alternate routes in a larger network, it is very easy to miss one or more routes and come up with the wrong answer. Thus for larger problems a systematic procedure such as the labeling procedure described above is required. Even with the labeling method, we find that as the networks grow in size it becomes necessary to implement the algorithm on a computer.

In summarizing the shortest-route labeling proedure in general terms, let us think of a network consisting of N nodes. The following procedure can be used to find the shortest route from node 1 to each of the other nodes in the network.

Step 1 Assign node 1 the permanent label [0,S]; the S simply identifies that node 1 is the starting node and the 0 indicates that the distance from node 1 to itself is zero.

Step 2 Compute tentative labels for the nodes that can be reached directly from node 1. The first number in each label is the direct distance from node 1 to the node in question; we refer to this portion of the label as the distance value. The second number in each label, which we refer to as the preceding node value, indicates the preceding node on the route from node 1 to the node in question; thus in this step the preceding node value is 1 since we are only considering nodes that can be directly reached from node 1.

Step 3 Identify the tentatively labeled node with the smallest distance value and declare that node permanently labeled. If all nodes are permanently labeled, go to step 5.

Step 4 Consider all nodes that do not have a permanent label and can be reached directly from the new permanently labeled node identified in step 3. Compute tentative labels for these nodes as follows:

a. If the nonpermanently labeled node in question has a tentative label, compute the sum of the distance value at the new permanently labeled node and the direct distance from the new permanently labeled node to the node in question. If this sum is less than the distance value for the node in question, set the distance value for this node equal to this sum; in addition, set the preceding node value equal to the new permanently labeled node that provided the smaller distance. Go to step 3.

b. If the nonpermanently labeled node in question does not already have a tentative label, a tentative label is created with a distance value equal to the sum of the distance value at the new permanently labeled node and the direct distance from the new permanently labeled node to the node in question. The preceding node value is set equal to the new permanently labeled node. Go to step 3.

Step 5 The permanent labels identify the shortest distance from node 1 to each node and the preceding node on the shortest route. The shortest route to a given node can be found by starting at the given node and moving to its preceding node. Continuing this backward movement through the network will provide the shortest route from node 1 to the node in question.

The above steps will determine the shortest distance from node 1 to each of the other nodes in the network. Note that $N - 1$ iterations of the algorithm are required to find the shortest distance to all other nodes. If the shortest distance is not needed to every node, the algorithm can be stopped when those nodes of interest have been permanently labeled. The algorithm can also be easily modified to find the shortest distance from any node, say node k, to all other nodes in the network. To make such a change, we would merely begin by labeling node k with the permanent label [0,S]. Then by applying the steps of the algorithm, we can find the shortest route from node k to each of the other nodes in the network.

The microcomputer package *The Management Scientist* can be used to solve small shortest-route problems. Input for the program includes the number of nodes, the number of arcs, and the length of each arc. The output shown in Figure 9.12 provides the shortest route to each node in the network, but it requires a separate running of the program for each starting and ending node combination.

FIGURE 9.12
Microcomputer Solution of the Gorman Shortest-Route Problem

NETWORK DESCRIPTION

Number of Nodes 7
Number of Arcs 10

Arc	Start Node	End Node	Distance
1	1	2	15
2	1	3	10
3	2	3	3
4	2	4	6
5	2	7	17
6	3	5	4
7	4	5	4
8	4	7	5
9	5	6	2
10	6	7	6

Results

Node	Shortest Route from Node 1	Distance
2	1–3–2	13
3	1–3	10
4	1–3–5–4	18
5	1–3–5	14
6	1–3–5–6	16
7	1–3–5–6–7	22

One final comment is in order before we close this section. In the Gorman problem we used distance as the measure of primary interest. The same algorithm can be used with other criteria such as travel time, travel cost, and so on. In these situations the labeling algorithm would generate minimum travel time routes, minimum cost routes, and so on. Sometimes, in these cases, the quantitative analyst will encounter networks in which some of the arcs have negative values. This could happen in a cost minimization problem where a negative arc value would indicate a profit for traveling over the associated arc. The labeling algorithm we have presented works only for arc values that are nonnegative. Algorithms have been developed to solve problems with negative arc values, but a discussion of these is beyond the scope of this text.

9.2 THE MINIMAL SPANNING TREE PROBLEM

In network terminology, the minimal spanning tree problem involves using the branches (arcs) of the network to reach *all* nodes of the network in such a fashion that the total length of all branches used to reach the nodes is minimal. To better understand this problem, let us consider the communications system design problem encountered by a regional computer center.

The Southwestern Regional Computer Center must have special computer communications lines installed in order to connect five satellite users with a new central computer. The telephone company will install the new communications network. However, the installation is an expensive operation. In order to reduce costs, the center's management group wants the total length of the new communications lines to be as small as possible. While the central computer could be connected directly to each user, it appears to be more economical to install a direct line to some users and let other users tap into the system by linking with the users that are already connected to the system. The determination of this minimal length communications system design is an example of the *minimal spanning tree* problem. The network for this problem with possible connection alternatives and distances is shown in Figure 9.13. An algorithm that can be used to solve this network model is explained below.

FIGURE 9.13
Communications Network for the Regional Computer System

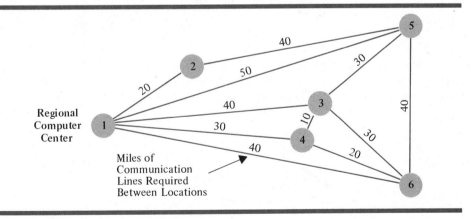

A Minimal Spanning Tree Algorithm

The network algorithm that can be used to solve the minimal spanning tree problem is very simple. It is called a *greedy algorithm* because by making the best possible choice at each step of the algorithm, we obtain the overall optimal solution for the problem. This is one of the few algorithms in management science where being greedy at each step always produces an optimal solution. The steps of the minimal spanning tree algorithm are as follows:

Step 1   Arbitrarily begin at any node and connect it to the closest node. The two nodes are referred to as *connected* nodes, and the remaining nodes are referred to as *unconnected* nodes.

Step 2   Identify the unconnected node that is closest to one of the connected nodes. Break ties arbitrarily if two or more nodes qualify as the closest node. Add this new node to the set of connected nodes. Repeat this step until all nodes have been connected.

This network algorithm is easily implemented by making the connection decisions directly on the graph of the network.

     Referring to the communications network for the regional computer center and arbitrarily beginning at node 1, we find the closest node is node 2 with a distance of 20. Using a bold line to connect nodes 1 and 2, step 1 of the algorithm provides the following result.

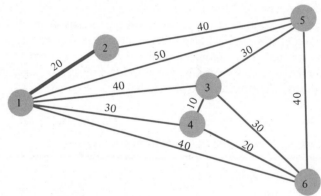

     In step 2 of the algorithm we find the unconnected node closest to one of the connected nodes is node 4 with a distance of 30 miles from node 1. Adding node 4 to the set of connected nodes provides the following result.

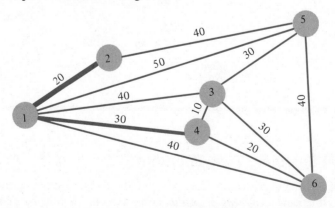

     Repeating the step of always adding the closest unconnected node to the connected segment of the network provides the minimal spanning tree solution shown in Figure

9.14. Follow the steps of the algorithm and see if you obtain this solution. The minimal length of the spanning tree is given by the sum of the distances on the arcs forming the spanning tree. In this case the total distance is 110 miles for the computer center's communications network. Note that while the computer center's network arcs were measured in distance, other network models may measure the arcs in terms of other criteria such as cost, time, and so on. In such cases the minimal spanning tree algorithm will identify the optimal solution (minimal cost, minimal time, and so on) for the criterion being considered.

FIGURE 9.14
Minimal Spanning Tree Communications Network for the Regional Computer Center

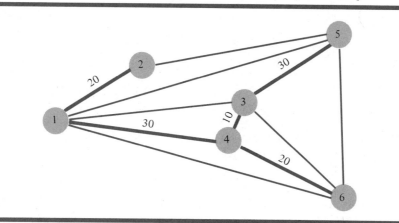

The microcomputer solution to the regional computer center's problem is shown in Figure 9.15. *The Management Scientist* was used to obtain the minimal spanning tree solution of 110 miles.

9.3 THE MAXIMAL FLOW PROBLEM

Consider a network with one input or *source* node and one output or *sink* node. The maximal flow problem asks, What is the maximum amount of flow (that is, vehicles, messages, fluid, and so on) that can enter and exit from the network system in a given period of time? In this problem we attempt to transmit flow through all branches (arcs) of the network as efficiently as possible. The amount of flow is limited due to capacity restrictions on the various branches of the network. For example, highway types limit vehicle flow in a transportation system, while pipe sizes limit oil flow in an oil distribution system. The maximum or upper limit on the flow in a branch is referred to as the *flow capacity* of the branch. While we do not specify capacities for the nodes, we do assume that the flow out of a node is equal to the flow into the node.

As an example of the maximal flow problem, consider the north–south interstate highway system passing through Cincinnati, Ohio. The north–south vehicle flow reaches a level of 15,000 vehicles per hour at peak times. Due to a planned summer highway maintenance program calling for the temporary closing of lanes and lower speed limits,

FIGURE 9.15
Microcomputer Solution of the Regional Computer Center Minimal Spanning Tree
Problem

Network Description

Number of Nodes: 6
Number of Arcs: 11

Arc	Start Node	End Node	Distance
1	1	2	20
2	1	3	40
3	1	4	30
4	1	5	50
5	1	6	40
6	2	5	40
7	3	4	10
8	3	5	30
9	3	6	30
10	4	6	20
11	5	6	40

Results—Minimal Spanning Tree

Start Node	End Node	Distance
1	2	20
1	4	30
4	3	10
4	6	20
3	5	30

Total Length = 110

a network of alternate routes through Cincinnati has been proposed by a transportation planning committee. The alternate routes include other highways as well as city streets. Because of differences in speed limits and traffic patterns, flow capacities vary depending upon the particular streets or roads used. The proposed network with branch flow capacities is shown in Figure 9.16.

The flow capacities are based on the direction of the flow. For example, highway section or branch 1–2 shows a capacity of 5000 vehicles per hour in the 1–2 direction; however, a 0 capacity exists in the 2–1 direction. This means that the highway network planners do not want vehicles flowing from node 2 into node 1. Logically speaking, since node 1 is the input, or source, and a potential traffic jam location, it would be undesirable to permit traffic flow into the node 1 intersection from node 2. The directional capacities on branch 1–2 can also be interpreted as indicating a one-way street leading from the node 1 intersection. In any case, this example shows that the flow capacities of branches can be dependent upon the direction of the flow. Do you believe the highway system network shown in Figure 9.16 can accommodate the north–south maximum flow of 15,000 vehicles per hour? What is the maximal flow in vehicles per hour for the network? How much flow should go over each branch?

FIGURE 9.16
Network of Highway System and Flow Capacities (in 1000s/Hour) for Cincinnati

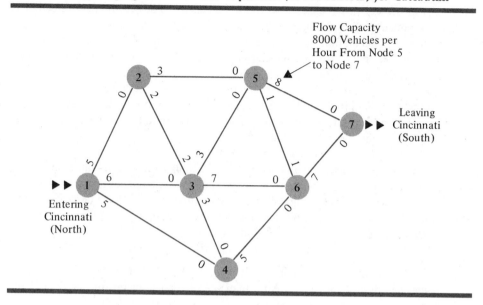

A Maximal Flow Algorithm

As we shall see, the maximal flow algorithm presented in this section uses the following commonsense approach:

1. Find any path from the input (source) node to the output (sink) node that has flow capacities in the direction of the flow greater than zero for all branches on the path.
2. Increase the flow along the path by as much as possible.
3. Continue looking for source-to-sink paths that have remaining flow capacities in the direction of the flow greater than zero for all branches and increase the flow along these paths as much as possible.
4. Stop when it is no longer possible to find a source-to-sink path with flow capacities in the direction of the flow greater than zero for all branches on the path.

Before presenting the details of the maximal flow algorithm, let us briefly discuss a procedure that will ensure that the above intuitive steps result in an optimal solution to the problem of finding the maximal flow from the source to the sink node.

The procedure permits previously assigned flow to take an alternate route by permitting fictional flows in the reverse direction. For example, consider the 3–6 branch:

Here we see that the initial flow capacity in the 3–6 direction is 7000 vehicles per hour, while no flow is permitted in the 6–3 direction.

If we choose to let 6000 vehicles per hour flow in the 3–6 direction, we will revise the flow capacities as follows:

Note that we have decreased the flow capacity in the 3–6 direction by 6000 vehicles per hour and simultaneously increased the flow capacity in the 6–3 direction by the same amount. The revised flow capacity of 1000 vehicles per hour in the 3–6 direction is readily interpreted as the remaining flow capacity in the branch. However, note that the 6–3 direction that had an initial flow capacity of zero now shows a revised flow capacity of 6000 vehicles per hour. This revised capacity in the 6–3 direction is actually indicating that a fictitious flow of up to 6000 vehicles per hour is permitted in this direction. Fictitious flow would not send vehicles in the 6–3 direction, but rather simply decrease the amount of flow originally committed to the 3–6 branch direction. In effect, fictitious flow in the 6–3 direction would result in flow that was originally committed to the 3–6 direction being diverted to other branches in the network.

The above process of tracking flow capacities is an important part of the maximal flow algorithm. For example, in an earlier step of the algorithm we might commit flow along a certain branch. Later, due to flows identified in other branches it may be desirable to decrease the flow along the original branch. The procedure we have described above will identify the extent to which our original decision to commit some flow needs to be revised in order to increase the total flow through the network.

Let us look now at the steps of the maximal flow algorithm.

Step 1   Find any path from the source node to the sink node that has flow capacities in the direction of the flow greater than zero for all branches on the path. If no path is available, the optimal solution has been reached.

Step 2   Find the smallest branch capacity, P_f, on the path selected in step 1. Increase the flow through the network by sending an amount P_f over the path selected in step 1.

Step 3   For the path selected in step 1, reduce all branch flow capacities in the direction of flow by P_f and increase all branch flow capacities in the reverse direction by P_f. Go to step 1.

While the procedure will vary depending upon the analyst's choice of paths in step 1, the algorithm will eventually provide the maximal flow solution. Our calculations for the highway flow network are as follows:

Iteration 1:

The path selected is 1–3–6–7; P_f, determined by branch 1–3, is 6. The revised network is as follows:

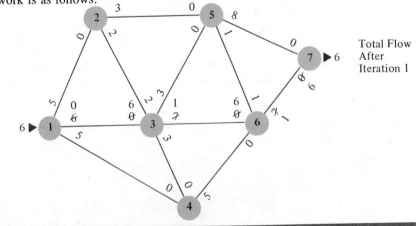

Total Flow After Iteration 1

Iteration 2:

The path selected is 1–2–5–7; P_f, determined by branch 2–5, is 3. The revised network is as follows:

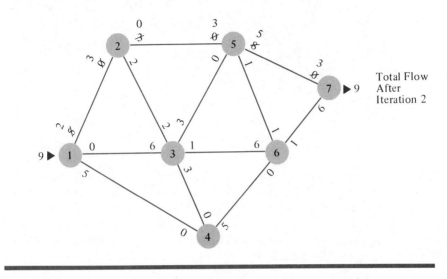

Note that the total flow through the network can be found by summing the P_f values from each iteration.

While we will not show our revised network after each iteration, you should attempt to update the network flow capacities as you follow the discussion. For example, what will this network look like after the following three iterations?

Iteration 3:

The path selected is 1–2–3–5–7; P_f, determined by branch 1–2 (or 2–3), is 2.

Iteration 4:

The path selected is 1–4–6–7; P_f, determined by branch 6–7, is 1.

Iteration 5:

The path selected is 1–4–6–5–7; P_f, determined by branch 6–5, is 1.

At this point we have a total flow of 13,000 vehicles per hour, and the revised network capacities are as follows:

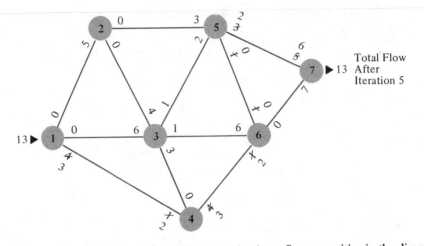

Are there any other paths from node 1 to node 7 that have flow capacities in the direction of the flow greater than 0? Try 1–4–6–3–5–7 with a flow of $P_f = 1$ determined by branch 3–5. This increases the flow to 14,000 vehicles per hour. However, as you can see from the following revised network, there are no more paths from node 1 to node 7 that have flow capacities greater than 0 on all branches of the path; thus 14,000 vehicles per hour is the maximal flow for this network.

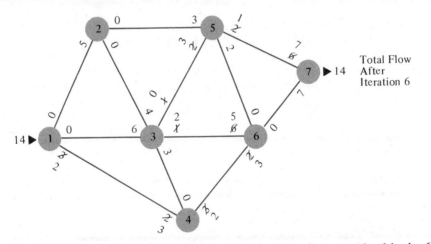

Note that in iteration 6 a flow of 1000 vehicles per hour was permitted in the 6–3 direction. From our initial network, however, we know that the flow capacity in the 6–3 direction is zero; thus the 1000 units of flow in the 6–3 direction represents a fictitious flow. The real effect of this flow is to divert 1000 units of flow originally committed to the 3–6 branch in iteration 1 along the 3–5 branch in order to enable us to get 1000 units more of flow through the network. Let us now determine the amount and direction of flow in each branch so that the total flow of 14,000 vehicles per hour can be attained.

Branch flows for the maximal flow solution can be found by comparing the final branch flow capacities with the initial branch flow capacities. If the final flow capacity is *less* than the initial flow capacity, flow is occurring in the branch with an amount equal to the difference between the initial and final flow capacities. For example, consider the 3–6 branch with initial flow and final flow capacities shown below.

Initial capacities:

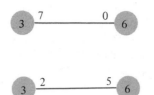

Final capacities:

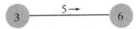

Since the final flow capacity in the 3–6 direction is less than the initial flow capacity, the branch has a flow of $7 - 2 = 5$ in the 3–6 direction. This branch flow is summarized as follows:

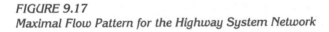

Comparing final and initial branch flow capacities for all branches in the network enables us to determine the final flow pattern as shown in Figure 9.17.

FIGURE 9.17
Maximal Flow Pattern for the Highway System Network

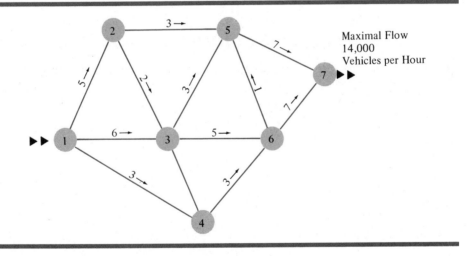

The results of the maximal flow analysis indicate that the planned highway network system will not handle the peak flow of 15,000 vehicles per hour. The transportation planners will have to expand the highway network, increase current branch flow capacities, or be prepared for serious traffic jam problems. If the network is extended or modified, another maximal flow analysis will determine the extent of any improved flow.

Summary

In this chapter we extended the discussion of the use of network models in managerial decision making. We introduced the shortest-route, minimal spanning tree, and maximal flow problems and presented specialized solution algorithms for each. The key to success in network approaches to problem solving is in seeing how the problem can be represented as a network model. While some network formulations are obvious, other problems may require substantial ingenuity to develop the appropriate network representation. In any case, once the network representation has been developed, specialized solution algorithms are readily available to solve the problem.

Glossary

Shortest route   Shortest path between two nodes in a network.
Spanning tree   A set of branches (arcs) that connect every node in the network with all other nodes.
Minimal spanning tree   The spanning tree with the minimum length.
Maximal flow   The maximum amount of flow that can enter into or exit from a network system during a given period of time.
Arc capacity   The maximum flow for an arc of the network. The arc capacity in one direction may not equal that in the reverse direction.
Source   An origin node (that is, no prior nodes exist).
Sink   A destination node (that is, no following nodes exist).

Problems

1. Find the shortest route from node 1 to each of the other nodes in the transportation network shown below.

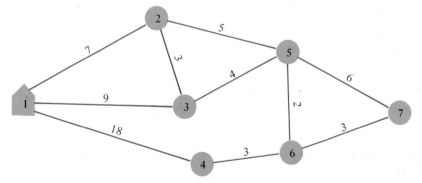

2. For the Gorman Construction Company problem (see Figure 9.1), assume node 7 is the company's warehouse and supply center. Often several daily trips are made from node 7 to the other nodes or construction sites. Using node 7 as the starting node, find the shortest route from this node to each of the other nodes in the network.

3. In the original Gorman Construction Company problem, we found the shortest distance from the office (node 1) to each of the other nodes or construction sites. Because some of the roads are highways and others are city streets, the shortest-distance routes between the office and the construction sites may not necessarily provide the quickest or shortest-time routes. Shown below is the Gorman road

network with travel time values rather than distance values. Find the shortest route from Gorman's office to each of the construction sites if the objective is to minimize travel time rather than distance.

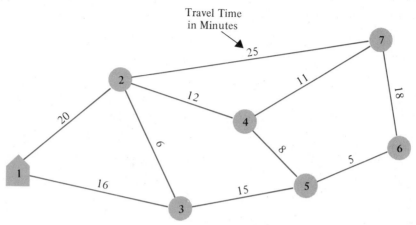

4. Find the shortest route between nodes 1 and 8 in the following network:

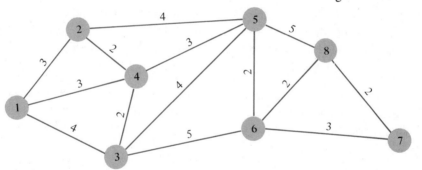

5. Find the shortest route between nodes 1 and 10 in the following network:

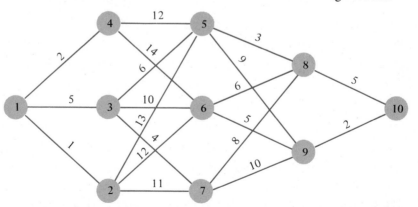

6. Morgan Trucking Company operates a special fast-service pickup and delivery service between Chicago and any of 10 other cities located in a four-state area. When Morgan receives a request for service, it dispatches a truck from Chicago to the city requesting service as soon as possible. Since both fast service and minimum travel costs are objectives for Morgan, it is important that the dispatched truck take the shortest route from Chicago to the specified city. Assume that the following network (not drawn to scale) with distances given in miles represents the highway network for this problem:

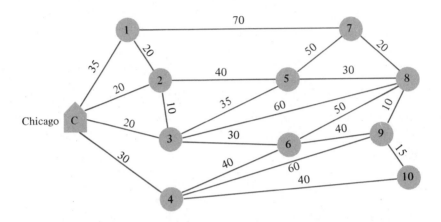

a. Find the shortest-route distances from Chicago to all 10 cities.
b. What is the shortest route to city 7? City 9?

7. City Cab Company has identified 10 primary pickup and drop locations for cab riders in New York City. In an effort to minimize travel time, improve customer service, and improve the utilization of the company's fleet of cabs, management would like the cab drivers to take the shortest route between locations whenever possible. Using the network of roads and streets shown below, what is the route a driver beginning at location 1 should take to reach location 10? The travel times in minutes are shown on the arcs of the network.

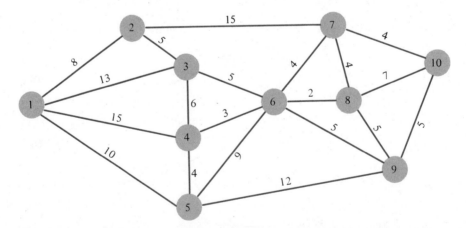

8. The Wisman Candy Company manufactures a variety of candy products. Company trucks are used to deliver local orders directly to retail outlets. When the business was small, the drivers of the trucks were free to take routes of their choice as they made the delivery rounds to the retail outlets. However, as the business has grown,

transportation and delivery costs have become significant. In an effort to improve the efficiency of the delivery operation, Wisman's management would like to determine the shortest delivery routes between retail outlets. For example, the network below shows the roads that may be taken between a retail outlet at node 1 and a retail outlet at node 11. Determine the shortest route for a truck that must make deliveries to both outlets.

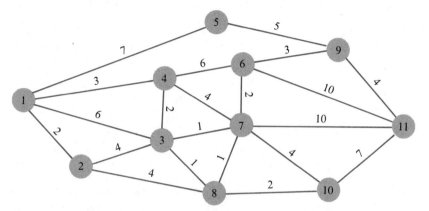

9. The five nodes in the network shown below represent points in time 1 year apart over a four-year period. Each node indicates a time when a decision may be made to keep or to replace computer equipment. If a decision is made to replace the equipment, a decision must also be made as to how long the new equipment will be used. The arc from node 0 to node 1 represents the decision to keep the current equipment 1 year and replace it at the end of the year. The arc from node 0 to node 2 represents the decision to keep the current equipment 2 years and replace it at the end of year 2. The numbers above the arcs indicate the total cost associated with the equipment replacement decisions. These costs include discounted purchase price, trade-in value, operating costs, and maintenance costs. Use the shortest-route algorithm to determine the minimum-cost equipment replacement policy for the four-year period.

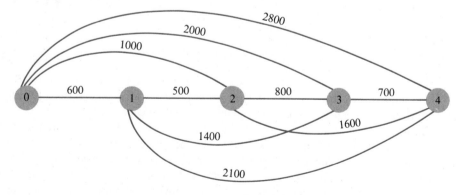

10. Develop the minimal spanning tree solution for the following emergency communications network.

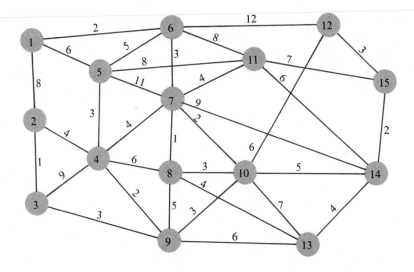

11. The State of Ohio recently purchased land for a new state park. Planners of the park have identified the ideal locations for the lodge, cabins, picnic groves, boat dock, and scenic points of interest. These locations are represented by the nodes of the network below. The branches of the network represent possible road alternatives in the park. If the state park designers want to minimize the total road miles that must be constructed in the park and still permit access to all facilities (nodes), which road alternatives should be constructed? (That is, find the minimal spanning tree for this network.)

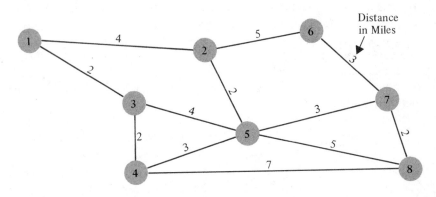

12. In a large soap products plant, quality control inspectors sample various products from the different production areas and then return the samples to the lab for analysis. The inspection process is slow, and the inspectors spend substantial time transporting samples from the production areas to the lab. The company is considering installing a pneumatic tube conveyor system that could be used to transport the samples between the production areas and the lab. The network below shows the locations of the lab and the production areas (nodes) where the samples must be collected. The branches are the alternatives being considered for the conveyor system. What are the minimum total length and layout of the conveyor system that would enable all production areas to send samples to the lab?

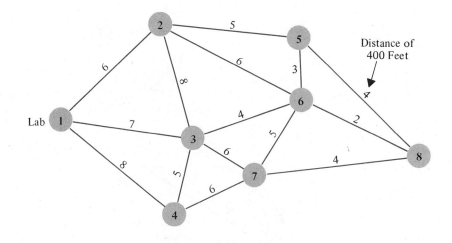

13. Midwest University is installing a computerized electronic mail system that will enable messages to be transmitted instantly among eight college offices. The network with possible electronic connections among the offices is shown below. Distances between offices are shown in thousands of feet. Develop a design for the office communication system that will enable all offices to have access to the electronic mail service. Provide the design that minimizes the total length of connections among the eight offices.

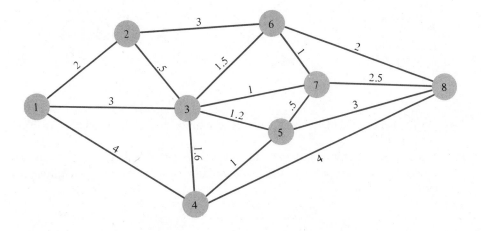

14. The Metrovision Cable Company has just received approval to begin providing cable television service to a suburb of Memphis, Tenn. The nodes of the network below show the distribution points that must be reached by the company's primary cable lines. The arcs of the network show the number of miles between the distribution points. Determine the minimal spanning tree solution that will enable the company to reach all distribution points with the minimum length primary cable line.

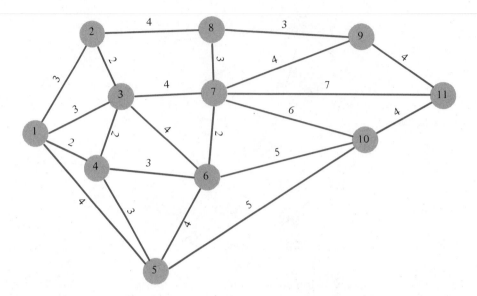

15. The north–south highway system passing through Albany, N.Y., can accommodate the capacities shown in the figure below.

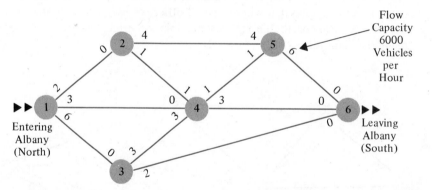

Do you believe the highway system can accommodate a north–south flow of 10,000 vehicles per hour?

16. If the Albany highway system problem has flow capacities revised as shown in the following network, what is the maximal flow in vehicles per hour through the system?

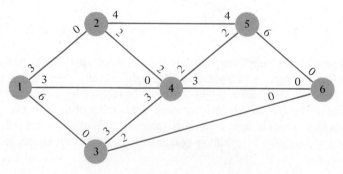

How many vehicles per hour must travel over each road (branch) in order to obtain this maximal flow.

17. A long-distance telephone company uses an underground cable network of communication lines to provide high-quality audio communication between two major cities. Calls are carried through series cable lines and connecting nodes in the network as shown below. Also shown are the number of telephone calls (in thousands) that may occur simultaneously at any point in time. What is the maximum number of telephone calls that can be transmitted simultaneously between the two cities? What are the connecting nodes and cable flows when the system is operating at capacity?

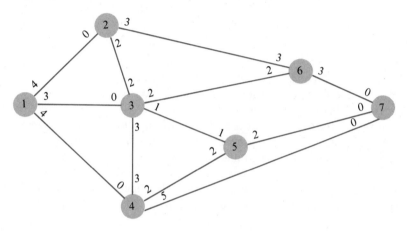

18. The High-Price Oil Company owns a pipeline network that is used to transmit oil from its source to several storage locations. A portion of the network is as follows:

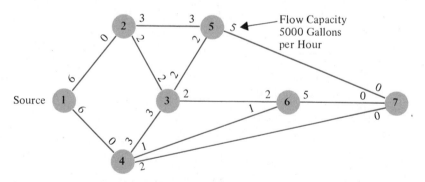

Due to the varying pipe sizes the flow capacities also vary. By selectively opening and closing sections of the pipeline network, the firm can supply any of the storage locations.

a. If the firm wants to supply storage location 7 and fully utilizes the system capacity, how long will it take to satisfy a location 7 demand of 100,000 gallons? What is the maximal flow for this pipeline system?

b. If a break occurs on line 2–3 and it is closed down, what is the maximal flow for the system? How long will it take to transmit 100,000 gallons to location 7?

19. For the highway network system shown below determine the maximal flow in vehicles per hour.

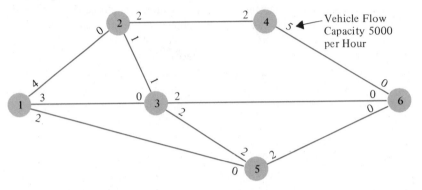

The highway commission is considering expanding highway section 3–4 to permit a flow of 2000 vehicles per hour or, at an additional cost, a flow of 3000 vehicles per hour. What is your recommendation for the 3–4 branch of the network?

20. A chemical processing plant has a network of pipes that are used to transfer liquid chemical products from one part of the plant to another. The pipe network and pipe flow capacities in gallons per minute are shown below. What is the maximum flow capacity for the system if the company wishes to transfer as much liquid chemical as possible from location 1 to location 9? How much of the chemical will flow through the section of pipe from node 3 to node 5?

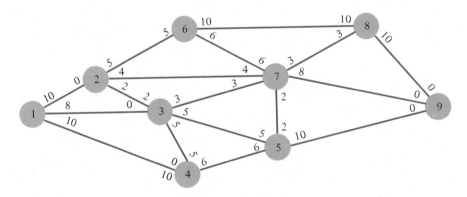

Case Problem:

Ambulance Routing

The city of Binghamton is served by two major hospitals: Western Medical and Binghamton General. Western Medical is located in the southwest part of the city and Binghamton General is in the northeast.

Bob Jones, the hospital administrator at Western Medical, has been discussing the problem of scheduling and routing ambulances with Margaret Johnson, the hospital administrator at Binghamton General. Both administrators feel that some type of system needs to be developed to better coordinate the use of the ambulance services at the two hospitals so that together they can provide the fastest possible emergency service for the city.

A proposal being considered is for all ambulance service calls to be handled through a central dispatcher, who could assign a call to the hospital capable of providing the fastest service. In studying this proposal, a project team consisting of employees from both hospitals met and decided that the best approach would be to divide the city into 20 service zones. In the proposed configuration Western Medical would be located in zone 1 and Binghamton General in zone 20. A map showing the placement of the 20 zones and the travel time (in minutes) between adjacent zones is provided in Figure 9.18.

FIGURE 9.18
Network for Proposed Ambulance Service

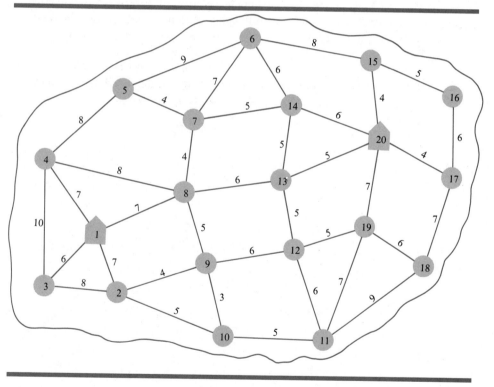

According to the proposed operating procedure incoming emergency calls would be identified by zone number, and an ambulance from the hospital closest to that zone would be assigned the service call. However, if all ambulances from the closest hospital were occupied with other emergencies, the service call would be assigned to the other hospital. Regardless of which hospital responded to the service call, the individual or individuals requiring the emergency service would be taken to the closest hospital.

To make the coordinated service as efficient as possible, the ambulance drivers must know in advance the quickest route to take to each zone, to which hospital the individual or individuals in that zone should be taken, and the quickest route to that hospital.

MANAGERIAL REPORT

Prepare a report for the two hospital administrators describing your analysis of the problem. Include in your report recommendations regarding the following items:

1. A chart for the dispatcher that identifies the primary hospital ambulance service for every zone in the city.
2. A chart for the Western Medical ambulance drivers that provides the minimum-time routes from Western Medical to every zone in the city, including Binghamton General. Include a chart that tells Western Medical drivers which hospital the individuals should be taken to and the route that should be followed.
3. A chart for the Binghamton General ambulance drivers that provides the minimum-time routes from Binghamton General to every zone in the city, including Western Medical. Include a chart that tells Binghamton General drivers which hospital the individuals should be taken to and the route that should be followed.
4. Include recommendations regarding how the system could be modified to take into account varying traffic conditions that occur throughout the day and/or changes in driving conditions resulting from temporary road construction projects.

10

Project Management: PERT/CPM

In many situations managers assume the responsibility for planning, scheduling, and controlling projects that consist of numerous separate jobs or tasks performed by a variety of departments, individuals, etc. Often these projects are so large and/or complex that the manager cannot possibly keep all the information pertaining to the plan, schedule, and progress of the project in his/her head. In these situations the techniques of PERT (Program Evaluation and Review Technique) and CPM (Critical Path Method) have proved to be extremely valuable in assisting managers in carrying out their project management responsibilities.

PERT and CPM have been used to plan, schedule, and control a wide variety of projects, such as

1. Research and development of new products and processes
2. Construction of plants, buildings, highways
3. Maintenance of large and complex equipment
4. Design and installation of new systems

In projects such as these, project managers must schedule and coordinate the various jobs or activities so that the entire project is completed on time. A complicating factor in carrying out this task is the interdependence of the activities; for example, some activities depend upon the completion of other activities before they can be started. When we realize that projects can have as many as several thousand specific activities, we see why project managers look for procedures that will help them answer questions such as the following:

1. What is the total time to complete the project?
2. What are the scheduled start and finish dates for each specific activity?
3. Which activities are "critical" and must be completed *exactly* as scheduled in order to keep the project on schedule?
4. How long can "noncritical" activities be delayed before they cause a delay in the total project?

As you will see, PERT and CPM can be used to help answer the above questions.

387

While PERT and CPM have the same general purpose and utilize much of the same terminology, the techniques were actually developed independently. PERT was introduced in the late 1950s specifically for planning, scheduling, and controlling the Polaris missile project. Since many jobs or activities associated with the Polaris missile project had never been attempted previously, it was difficult to predict the time to complete the various jobs or activities. Consequently, PERT was developed with an objective of being able to handle uncertainties in activity completion times.

On the other hand, CPM was developed primarily for scheduling and controlling industrial projects where job or activity times were considered known. CPM offered the option of reducing activity times by adding more workers and/or resources, usually at an increased cost. Thus a distinguishing feature of CPM was that it enabled time and cost trade-offs for the various activities in the project.

In today's usage the distinction between PERT and CPM as two separate techniques has largely disappeared. Computerized versions of the PERT/CPM approach often contain options for considering uncertainty in activity times as well as activity time–cost trade-offs. In this regard modern project planning, scheduling, and controlling procedures have essentially combined the features of PERT and CPM such that a distinction between the two techniques is no longer necessary.

10.1   PERT/CPM NETWORKS

The first step in the PERT/CPM project scheduling process is to determine the specific jobs, or activities, that make up the project. As a simple illustration involving the process of buying a small business, consider the list of four activities shown in Table 10.1. The development of an accurate list of activities such as this is a key step in any project. Since we will be planning the entire project and estimating the project completion date based on the list of activities, poor planning and omission of activities will be disastrous and lead to inaccurate schedules. We will assume that careful planning has been completed for the example problem and that Table 10.1 lists all activities for the small business project.

TABLE 10.1
Activity List for the Example Project of Buying a Small Business

Activity	Description	Immediate Predecessors
A	Develop a list of sources for financing	—
B	Analyze the financial records of the business	—
C	Develop a business plan (e.g., sales projections, cash flow projections, etc.)	B
D	Submit a proposal to a lending institution	A, C

Note that Table 10.1 contains additional information in the column labeled immediate predecessors. The *immediate predecessors* for a particular activity are the activities that, when completed, enable the start of the activity in question. For example, the information in Table 10.1 tells us we can start work on activities *A* and *B* anytime, since neither of these activities depends upon the completion of prior activities. However, activity *C* cannot be started until activity *B* has been completed, and activity *D* cannot be started until both activities *A* and *C* have been completed. As you will see, immediate predecessor information must be known for each activity in order to describe the interdependencies among the activities in the project.

In Figure 10.1 we have drawn a network that not only depicts the activities listed in Table 10.1 but also portrays the predecessor relationships among the activities. This graphical representation is referred to as the PERT/CPM network for the project. The activities are shown on the branches, or arcs, of the network. The circles, or nodes, of the network correspond to the beginning and ending of the activities. The completion of all the activities that lead into a node is referred to as an *event*. For example, node 2 corresponds to the event that activity *B* has been completed, and node 3 corresponds to the event that both activities *A* and *C* have been completed.

FIGURE 10.1
PERT/CPM Network for the Example Project of Buying a Small Business

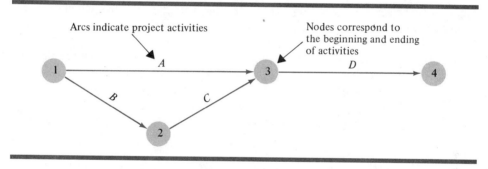

Let us now attempt to develop the network for a project having the following activities and immediate predecessors:

Activity	Immediate Predecessors
A	—
B	—
C	B
D	A, C
E	C
F	C
G	D, E, F

A portion of the PERT/CPM network that could be used for the first four activities is as follows:

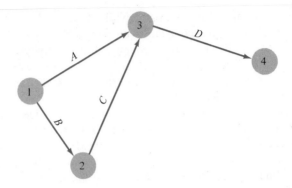

This portion of the network causes no particular problem for activity D, since it shows activities A and C as the correct immediate predecessors. However, when we attempt to add activity E to the network, we encounter a problem. At first we might attempt to show activity E beginning at node 3. However, this indicates that both activities A and C are the immediate predecessors for activity E, which is incorrect. Referring to the original activity schedule for the project, we see that activity E only has activity C as its immediate predecessor.

We can avoid the above problem by inserting a *dummy activity*, which, as the name implies, is not an actual activity but rather a fictitious activity used to ensure that the proper precedence relationships among the activities are depicted in the network. For example, we can add node 5 and insert a dummy activity, indicated by a dashed line, from node 5 to node 3 forming the network shown below.

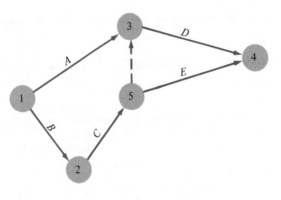

With this change in the network, activity E starting at node 5 has the correct predecessor of only activity C. The dummy activity does not have a time requirement but is merely used to maintain the proper precedence relationships in the network. Note that the insertion of the dummy activity also correctly shows activities A and C as the immediate predecessors for activity D.

Completion of the seven-activity network could be shown as follows:

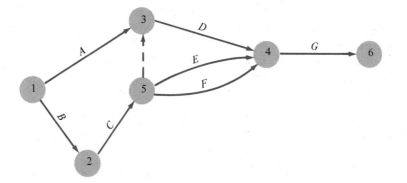

Note how the network correctly identifies activities *D*, *E*, and *F* as the immediate predecessors for activity *G*. However, note that activities *E* and *F* both start at node 5 and end at node 4. This situation causes problems for certain computer programs that use starting and ending nodes to identify the activities in a PERT/CPM network. In these programs the computer procedure would recognize activities *E* and *F* as the same activity since they have the same starting and ending nodes. When this condition occurs, dummy activities can be added to a network to make sure that two or more activities do not have the same starting and ending nodes. The use of node 7 and a dummy activity as shown below eliminates this problem for activities *E* and *F*.

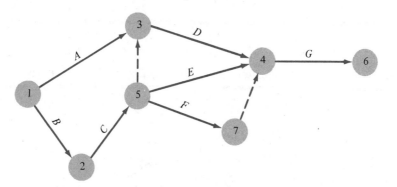

Dummy activities can be used to identify precedence relationships correctly as well as to eliminate the possible confusion of two or more activities having the same starting and ending nodes. Although dummy activities may not be required for all PERT/CPM networks, larger and/or more complex projects may require many dummy activities in order to depict the project network properly.

10.2 PROJECT SCHEDULING WITH PERT/CPM

The owner of the Western Hills Shopping Center is considering modernizing and expanding the current 32-business shopping complex. Financing for the expansion has been arranged through a private investor. If the expansion project is undertaken, the owner hopes to add eight to 10 new businesses or tenants to the shopping complex.

The specific activities that make up the expansion project are listed in Table 10.2. Note that the list includes the immediate predecessor for each activity as well as the number of weeks required to complete the activity. The PERT/CPM network for the project is shown in Figure 10.2. Check for yourself to see that the network does in fact maintain the immediate predecessor relationships shown in Table 10.2.

TABLE 10.2
Activity List for the Western Hills Shopping Center Expansion Project

Activity	Activity Description	Immediate Predecessor	Completion Time (Weeks)
A	Prepare architectural drawings of planned expansion	—	5
B	Identify potential new tenants	—	6
C	Develop prospectus for tenants	A	4
D	Select contractor	A	3
E	Prepare building permits	A	1
F	Obtain approval for building permits	E	4
G	Construction	D, F	14
H	Finalize contracts with tenants	B, C	12
I	Tenants move in	G, H	2
		Total	51

FIGURE 10.2
PERT/CPM Network for the Western Hills Shopping Center Expansion Project

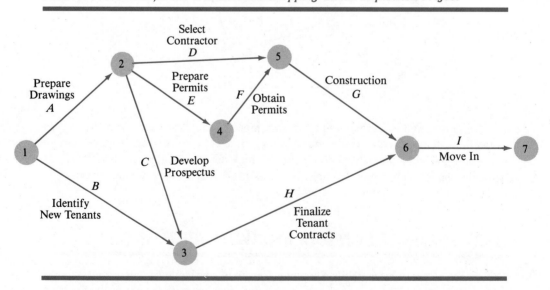

Information in Table 10.2 indicates that the total time required to complete all activities in the shopping center expansion project is 51 weeks. However, we can see from the network (Figure 10.2) that several of the activities can be conducted simultaneously (A and B, for example). Being able to work on two or more activities at the same time will shorten the total project completion time to less than 51 weeks. However, the required project completion time is not directly available from the data in Table 10.2.

In order to facilitate the PERT/CPM computations that we will be making, the project network has been redrawn as shown in Figure 10.3. Note that each activity letter is written above and each activity time is written below the corresponding arc.

FIGURE 10.3
Western Hills Shopping Center Project Network with Activity Times

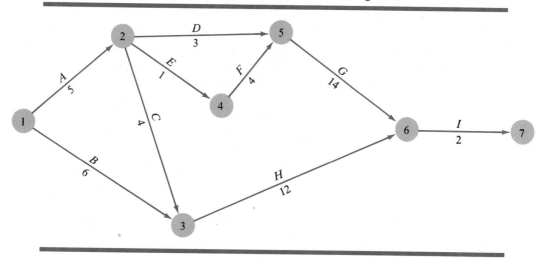

The Critical Path

Once we have the project network and the activity times, we are ready to proceed with the calculations necessary to determine the total time required to complete the project. In addition, we will use the results of the calculations to develop a detailed start and finish schedule for each activity.

In order to determine the project completion time we will have to analyze the network and identify what is called its *critical path*. A *path* is a sequence of connected activities that leads from the starting node (1) to the completion node (7). The connected activities defined by nodes 1–2–3–6–7 form a path consisting of activities A, C, H, and I. Nodes 1–2–5–6–7 define the path associated with activities A, D, G, and I. Since *all* paths must be traversed in order to complete the project, we need to analyze the amount of time the various paths require. In particular, we will be interested in the longest path through the network. Since all other paths are shorter in duration, the longest path determines the total time or duration of the project. If activities on the longest path are delayed, the entire project will be delayed. Thus the longest path activities are the *critical activities* of the project and the longest path is called the *critical path* of the network. If managers wish to reduce the total project time, they will have to reduce the length of the critical path by shortening the duration of the critical activities. The following discussion presents a step-by-step procedure or algorithm for finding the critical path of a project network.

Starting at the network's origin (node 1) and using a starting time of 0, compute an *earliest start* and *earliest finish* time for each activity in the network. Let

ES = earliest start time for a particular activity
EF = earliest finish time for a particular activity
t = expected activity time for the activity

The following expression can be used to find the earliest finish time for a given activity:

$$EF = ES + t \qquad\qquad (10.1)$$

For example, for activity A, ES = 0 and t = 5; thus the earliest finish time for activity A is EF = 0 + 5 = 5.

We will write the earliest start and earliest finish times directly on the network in brackets next to the letter of the activity. Using activity A as an example, we have

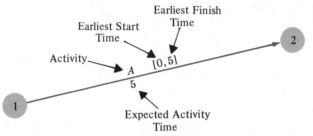

Since activities leaving a node cannot be started until *all* immediately preceding activities have been completed, the following rule can be used to determine the earliest start times for activities:

Earliest Start Time Rule:

The earliest start time for an activity leaving a particular node is equal to the *largest* of the earliest finish times for all activities entering the node.

In applying this rule to a portion of the network involving activities A, B, C, and H, we obtain the following:

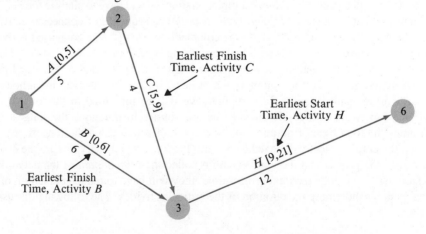

Note that in applying the earliest start time rule for activity C, which leaves node 2, we first recognized that activity A is the only activity entering node 2. Since the earliest finish time for activity A is 5, the earliest start time for activity C is 5. Thus the earliest finish time for activity C must be EF = ES + t = 5 + 4 = 9.

The above diagram also shows that the earliest finish time for activity B is 6. Applying the earliest start time rule for activity H, we see that the earliest start time for this activity must be equal to the largest of the earliest finish times for the two activities that enter node 3, activities B and C. Thus the earliest start time for activity H is 9, and the earliest finish time is EF = ES + t = 9 + 12 = 21.

Proceeding in a *forward pass* through the network, we can establish the earliest start time and then the earliest finish time for each activity. The Western Hills Shopping Center PERT/CPM network, with the ES and EF values for each activity, is shown in Figure 10.4. Note that the earliest finish time for activity I, the last activity, is 26 weeks. Thus the completion time for the entire project is 26 weeks.

FIGURE 10.4
Western Hills Shopping Center Project with Earliest Start Times and Earliest Finish Times Shown Above the Activity Arcs

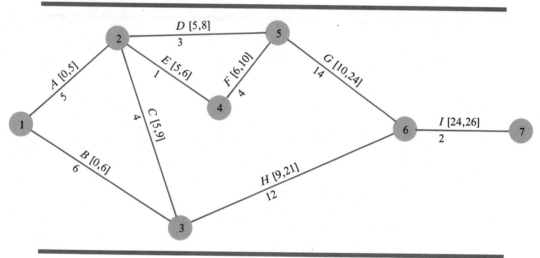

We now continue the algorithm for finding the critical path by making a *backward pass* calculation. Starting at the completion point (node 7) and using a latest finish time of 26 for activity I, we trace back through the network computing a latest start and latest finish time for each activity. Let

LS = latest start time for a particular activity
LF = latest finish time for a particular activity

The following expression can be used to find the latest start time for a given activity:

$$LS = LF - t \qquad (10.2)$$

Given LF = 26 and t = 2 for activity I, the latest start time for this activity can be computed as LS = 26 − 2 = 24.

The following rule is necessary in order to determine the latest finish time for any activity in the network:

> ### Latest Finish Time Rule:
>
> The latest finish time for an activity entering a particular node is equal to the *smallest* of the latest start times for all activities leaving the node.

Logically the above rule states that the latest time an activity can be finished is equal to the earliest (smallest) value for the latest start time of following activities. The complete network with the LS and LF backward pass calculations is shown in Figure 10.5. The latest start and latest finish times for the activities are written in brackets directly under the earliest start and earliest finish times.

FIGURE 10.5
Western Hills Shopping Center Project with Latest Start Times and Latest Finish Times Shown Below the Activity Arcs

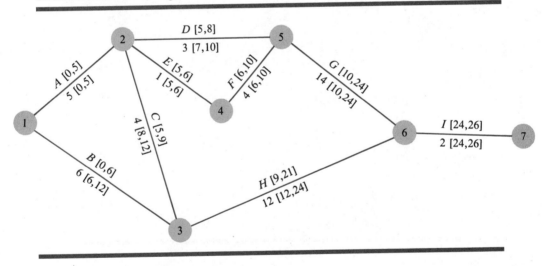

Note the application of the latest finish time rule for activity *A*, which enters node 2. The latest finish time for activity *A* (LF = 5) is the smallest of the latest start times for the activities that leave node 2; that is, the smallest LS value for activities *C* (LS = 8), *E* (LS = 5), and *D* (LS = 7) is 5.

After obtaining the start and finish activity times as summarized in Figure 10.5, we can find the amount of slack or free time associated with each of the activities. *Slack* is defined as the length of time an activity can be delayed without affecting the completion date for the entire project. The amount of slack for each activity is computed as follows:

$$\text{Slack} = \text{LS} - \text{ES} = \text{LF} - \text{EF} \qquad (10.3)$$

For example, we see that the slack associated with activity C is LS − ES = 8 − 5 = 3 weeks. This means that activity C can be delayed up to 3 weeks (start anywhere between weeks 5 and 8) and the entire project can still be completed in 26 weeks. Thus activity C is not a critical activity and is not part of the critical path. Using (10.3), we see that the slack associated with activity E is LS − ES = 5 − 5 = 0. Thus activity E has no slack time and must be held to the 5-week start time schedule. Since activity E cannot be delayed without affecting the entire project, it is a critical activity and is on the critical path. In general, the critical path activities are the activities with zero slack.

The start and finish times shown on the network in Figure 10.5 provide a detailed schedule for all activities. That is, from Figure 10.5 we know the earliest and latest start and finish times for the activities. Putting this information in tabular form provides the activity schedule shown in Table 10.3. Note that by computing the slack associated with each activity, we see that activities A, E, F, G, and I each have zero slack; hence these activities form the critical path in the shopping center expansion network. Note that Table 10.3 also shows the slack or delay that can be tolerated for the noncritical activities before these activities will cause a project delay.

TABLE 10.3
Activity Schedule for the Western Hills Shopping Center Expansion Project

Activity	Earliest Start (ES)	Latest Start (LS)	Earliest Finish (EF)	Latest Finish (LF)	Slack (LS-ES)	Critical Path?
A	0	0	5	5	0	Yes
B	0	6	6	12	6	
C	5	8	9	12	3	
D	5	7	8	10	2	
E	5	5	6	6	0	Yes
F	6	6	10	10	0	Yes
G	10	10	24	24	0	Yes
H	9	12	21	24	3	
I	24	24	26	26	0	Yes

Contributions of PERT/CPM

Previously we stated that project managers look for procedures that will help answer many important questions regarding the planning, scheduling, and controlling of projects. Let us reconsider these questions in light of the information the PERT/CPM network and critical path calculations have provided about the Western Hills Shopping Center expansion project.

1. What is the total time to complete the project?
    Answer: PERT/CPM has shown that the project can be completed in 26 weeks if the individual activities are completed on schedule.

2. What are the scheduled start and completion times for each activity?
    Answer: PERT/CPM has provided the detailed activity schedule that shows the earliest start, latest start, earliest finish, and latest finish times for each activity (Table 10.3).

3. Which activities are "critical" and must be completed *exactly* as scheduled in order to keep the project on schedule?
Answer: PERT/CPM has identified the five activities—*A, E, F, G*, and *I*—as the critical activities for the project.

4. How long can "noncritical" activities be delayed before they cause a delay in the completion time for the project?
Answer: PERT/CPM has identified the slack time available for all activities as shown in Table 10.3.

In the management of any project the above information is important and valuable. While larger projects may substantially increase the time required to draw the PERT/CPM network and to make the necessary calculations, the procedure and contributions of PERT/CPM to larger projects are identical to those observed in the shopping center expansion project. Furthermore, computer packages exist that carry out the steps of the PERT/CPM procedure. Figure 10.6 shows the activity schedule for the shopping center expansion project developed by *The Management Scientist* computer software package. Input to the program included the activities, their immediate predecessors, and the expected activity times. Only a few minutes were required to input the information and generate this critical path and activity schedule information.

FIGURE 10.6
Activity Schedule for the Western Hills Shopping Center Expansion Project Developed using the Management Scientist™

Activity	Earliest Start (ES)	Latest Start (LS)	Earliest Finish (EF)	Latest Finish (LF)	Slack (LS-ES)	Critical Path?
A	0	0	5	5	0	Yes
B	0	6	6	12	6	
C	5	8	9	12	3	
D	5	7	8	10	2	
E	5	5	6	6	0	Yes
F	6	6	10	10	0	Yes
G	10	10	24	24	0	Yes
H	9	12	21	24	3	
I	24	24	26	26	0	Yes

The critical path is *A–E–F–G–I*.
The project completion time is 26.

Summary of the PERT/CPM Critical Path Procedure

Before leaving this section, let us summarize the PERT/CPM critical path procedure that can be used to plan, schedule, and control projects.

Step 1 Develop a list of activities that make up the project.

Step 2 Determine the immediate predecessor activities for each activity in the project.

Step 3 Estimate the completion time for each activity.

Step 4 Draw a network depicting the activities and immediate predecessors listed in steps 1 and 2.

Step 5 Using the network and the activity time estimates, determine the earliest start time and the earliest finish time for each activity by making a forward pass through the network. The earliest finish time for the last activity in the project identifies the completion time for the entire project.

Step 6 Using the project completion time identified in step 5 as the latest finish time for the last activity, make a backward pass through the network to identify the latest start time and latest finish time for each activity.

Step 7 Use the difference between the latest start time and the earliest start time for each activity to identify the slack time available for the activity.

Step 8 The critical path activities are the activities with zero slack.

Step 9 Use the information from steps 5 and 6 to develop a detailed activity schedule for the project.

10.3 PROJECT SCHEDULING WITH UNCERTAIN ACTIVITY TIMES

In this section we consider the details of project scheduling for a problem involving the research and development of a new product. Because many of the activities in this project have never been previously attempted, the project manager wants to identify and account for the uncertainties in the activity times. Let us show how project scheduling can be conducted with uncertain activity times.

The Daugherty Porta-Vac Project

The H. S. Daugherty Company has manufactured industrial vacuum cleaning systems for a number of years. Recently a member of the company's new-product research team submitted a report suggesting the company consider manufacturing a cordless vacuum cleaner that could be powered by a rechargeable battery. The vacuum cleaner, referred to as a Porta-Vac, could contribute to Daugherty's expansion into the household market. Management hopes that the new product can be manufactured at a reasonable cost and that its portability and no-cord convenience will make it extremely attractive.

Daugherty's management would like to initiate a project to study the feasibility of proceeding with the Porta-Vac idea. The end result of the feasibility study will be a report recommending the action to be taken for the new product. In order to complete the feasibility study, information must be obtained from the firm's research and development (R&D), product testing, manufacturing, cost estimating, and market research groups. How long do you think this feasibility study project will take? When should we tell the product testing group to schedule its work? Obviously, we do not have enough information to answer these questions at this time. In the following discussion we will learn how to answer these questions and provide the complete schedule and control information for the project.

Again, the first step in the project scheduling process is to determine all the activities that make up the project as well as the immediate predecessors for each activity. For the Porta-Vac project, these data are shown in Table 10.4.

TABLE 10.4
Activity List for the Daugherty Porta-Vac Project

Activity	Description	Immediate Predecessors
A	R&D product design	—
B	Plan market research	—
C	Routing (manufacturing engineering)	A
D	Build prototype model	A
E	Prepare marketing brochure	A
F	Cost estimates (industrial engineering)	C
G	Preliminary product testing	D
H	Market survey	B, E
I	Pricing and forecast report	H
J	Final report	F, G, I

The PERT/CPM network for the Porta-Vac project is shown in Figure 10.7. Check for yourself to see that the network does in fact maintain the immediate predecessor relationships shown in Table 10.4.

FIGURE 10.7
Network for the Porta-Vac Project

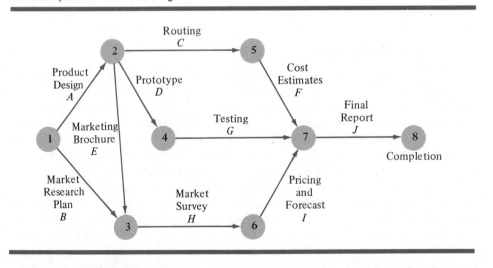

Uncertain Activity Times

Once we have established a network for the project, we will need information on the time required to complete each activity. This information will be used in the calculation of the duration of the entire project and the scheduling of the specific activities. For repeat projects, such as construction and/or maintenance projects, managers may have the experience and historical data necessary to provide accurate activity time estimates. However, for new or unique projects, activity time estimation may be significantly more difficult. In fact, in many cases activity times are uncertain and are perhaps best described by a range of possible values rather than one specific activity time estimate. In these instances the uncertain activity times are treated as random variables with associated probability distributions. As a result, probability statements will be provided about the project meeting specific completion dates.

In order to incorporate uncertain activity times into the network analysis, we will need to obtain three time estimates for each activity. The three estimates are

Optimistic time (a)   The activity time if everything progresses in an *ideal* manner

Most probable time (m)   The most likely activity time under normal conditions

Pessimistic time (b)   The activity time if we encounter significant breakdowns and/or delays

The three estimates enable the manager to develop a best guess of the most likely activity time and then express the uncertainty by providing time estimates ranging from the best possible (optimistic) time to the worst possible (pessimistic) time.

As an illustration of the PERT/CPM procedure with uncertain activity times, let us consider the optimistic, most probable, and pessimistic time estimates for the Porta-Vac activities as presented in Table 10.5.

TABLE 10.5
Optimistic, Most Probable, and Pessimistic Activity Time Estimates (in Weeks) for the Porta-Vac Project

Activity	Optimistic (a)	Most Probable (m)	Pessimistic (b)
A	4	5	12
B	1	1.5	5
C	2	3	4
D	3	4	11
E	2	3	4
F	1.5	2	2.5
G	1.5	3	4.5
H	2.5	3.5	7.5
I	1.5	2	2.5
J	1	2	3

Using activity A as an example, we see that management estimates that this activity will require from 4 weeks (optimistic) to 12 weeks (pessimistic), with the most likely time 5 weeks. If the activity could be repeated a large number of times, what would be the average time for the activity? This average or *expected time* (*t*) can be determined from the following formula:

$$t = \frac{a + 4m + b}{6} \qquad (10.4)$$

For activity *A* we have an estimated average or expected completion time of

$$t_A = \frac{4 + 4(5) + 12}{6} = \frac{36}{6} = 6 \text{ weeks}$$

With uncertain activity times we can use the common statistical measure of the *variance* to describe the dispersion or variation in the activity time values. The variance of the activity time is given by the following formula[1]:

$$\sigma^2 = \left(\frac{b - a}{6}\right)^2 \qquad (10.5)$$

As you can see, the difference between the pessimistic (*b*) and optimistic (*a*) time estimates greatly affects the value of the variance. Large differences in these two values, reflects a high degree of uncertainty in the activity time. Accordingly, the variance given by equation (10.5) will be large. Using (10.5), we see that the measure of uncertainty— that is, the variance—of activity *A*, denoted σ_A^2, is

$$\sigma_A^2 = \left(\frac{12 - 4}{6}\right)^2 = \left(\frac{8}{6}\right)^2 = 1.78$$

Equations (10.4) and (10.5) are based on the assumption that the uncertainty in activity times can be described by a *beta probability distribution*.[2] With this assumption, the probability distribution for the time to complete activity *A* is as shown in Figure 10.8. Using equations (10.4) and (10.5) and the data in Table 10.5, the expected times and variances for all of the Porta-Vac activities are as summarized in Table 10.6.

A network depicting the Porta-Vac project and expected activity times is shown in Figure 10.9. Note that above each arc we write the letter of the corresponding activity, and directly under the arc we write the expected time of the activity.

The Critical Path

Once we have the network and the expected activity times, we are ready to proceed with the critical path calculations necessary to determine the expected project completion time and a detailed activity schedule. In the critical path calculations we will treat the expected

[1]The variance equation is based on the notion that a standard deviation is approximately ⅙ of the difference between the extreme values of the distribution: (*b* − *a*)/6. The variance is simply the square of the standard deviation.
[2]In order for the equations for *t* and σ^2 to be exact, additional assumptions are required about the parameters of the beta probability distribution. However, even when these additional assumptions are not made, the equations still tend to provide very good and useful approximations of *t* and σ^2.

FIGURE 10.8
Activity Time Distribution for Product Design Activity A of the Porta-Vac Project

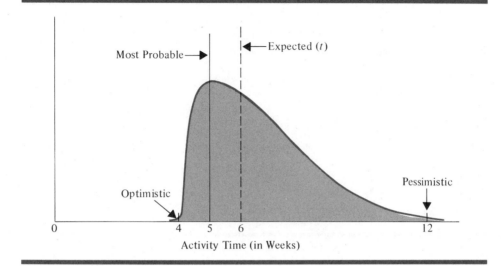

Most Probable → | ← Expected (*t*)

Pessimistic

Optimistic

0   4   5   6   12

Activity Time (in Weeks)

TABLE 10.6
Expected Times and Variances for the Porta-Vac Activities

Activity	Expected Time (in weeks)	Variance
A	6	1.78
B	2	0.44
C	3	0.11
D	5	1.78
E	3	0.11
F	2	0.03
G	3	0.25
H	4	0.69
I	2	0.03
J	2	0.11
Total	32	

activity times (Table 10.6) as the *fixed length* or *known duration* of each activity. As a result, we can use the critical path calculation procedure introduced in Section 10.2 to find the critical path for the Porta-Vac project. After the critical activities and the expected project completion time have been determined, we will analyze the effect of the activity time variability.

Proceeding with a forward pass through the network shown in Figure 10.9, we can establish the earliest start (ES) and earliest finish (EF) times for each activity. The PERT/CPM network with the ES and EF values is shown in Figure 10.10. Note that the earliest finish time for activity *J*, the last activity, is 17 weeks. Thus the expected completion

FIGURE 10.9
Porta-Vac Project Network with Expected Activity Times

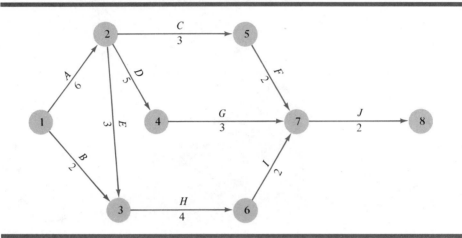

FIGURE 10.10
Porta-Vac Network with Earliest Start and Earliest Finish Times Shown Above Activities

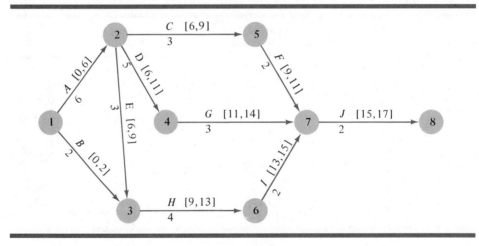

time for the entire project is 17 weeks. Next we continue with the procedure for finding the critical path by making a backward pass through the network. The backward pass provides the latest start (LS) and latest finish (LF) times shown in Figure 10.11.

The start and finish times shown in Figure 10.11 provide the detailed schedule for all activities. Putting this information in tabular form provides the activity schedule shown in Table 10.7. Note that the slack time = (LS − ES) is also shown for each activity. The activities with zero slack show that activities *A, E, H, I,* and *J* form the critical path for the Porta-Vac project network.

FIGURE 10.11
Porta-Vac Network with Latest Start and Latest Finish Times Shown Below Activities

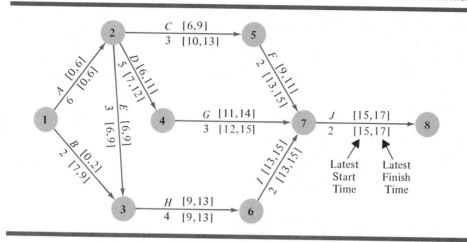

TABLE 10.7
Activity Schedule (in weeks) for the Porta-Vac Project

Activity	Earliest Start (ES)	Latest Start (LS)	Earliest Finish (EF)	Latest Finish (LF)	Slack (LS − ES)	Critical Path?
A	0	0	6	6	0	Yes
B	0	7	2	9	7	
C	6	10	9	13	4	
D	6	7	11	12	1	
E	6	6	9	9	0	Yes
F	9	13	11	15	4	
G	11	12	14	15	1	
H	9	9	13	13	0	Yes
I	13	13	15	15	0	Yes
J	15	15	17	17	0	Yes

Variability in the Project Completion Time

In carrying out the critical path calculations, we treated the activity times as fixed at their expected values; we are now ready to consider the uncertainty in the activity times and determine the effect this uncertainty or variability has on the project completion date. Recall that the critical path determines the duration of the entire project. For the Porta-Vac project the critical path of A–E–H–I–J resulted in an expected project completion time of 17 weeks.

Just as the critical path activities govern the expected project completion date, variation in critical path activities can cause variation in the project completion date. Variation in noncritical path activities will ordinarily have no effect on the project completion date because of the slack time associated with these activities. However, if a noncritical activity were delayed long enough to expend all its slack time, then that activity would become part of a new critical path, and further delays would extend the project completion date. Variability leading to a longer than expected total time for the critical path activities will always extend the project completion date. On the other hand, variability in critical path activities resulting in a shorter critical path will enable an earlier than expected completion date, unless the activity times on the other paths become critical. Let us now use the variance in the critical path activities to determine the variance in the project completion date.

If we let T denote the project duration, then T, which is determined by the critical activities A–E–H–I–J in the Porta-Vac problem, has the expected value of

$$E(T) = t_A + t_E + t_H + t_I + t_J$$
$$= 6 + 3 + 4 + 2 + 2 = 17 \text{ weeks}$$

where t_A, t_E, t_H, t_I, and t_J are the expected completion times for the critical path activities.

Similarly, the variance in the project duration is given by the sum of the variance of the critical path activities. Thus the variance for the Porta-Vac project completion time is given by

$$\text{Var}(T) = \sigma^2 = \sigma_A^2 + \sigma_E^2 + \sigma_H^2 + \sigma_I^2 + \sigma_J^2$$
$$= 1.78 + 0.11 + 0.69 + 0.03 + 0.11 = 2.72$$

where $\sigma_A^2, \sigma_E^2, \sigma_H^2, \sigma_I^2$, and σ_J^2 are the variances of the critical path activities.

This formula is based on the assumption that all the activity times are independent. If two or more activities are dependent, the formula only provides an approximation to the variance of the project completion time. The closer the activities are to being independent, the better is the approximation.

Since we know that the standard deviation is the square root of the variance, we can compute the standard deviation σ for the Porta-Vac project completion time as follows:

$$\sigma = \sqrt{\sigma^2} = \sqrt{2.72} = 1.65$$

A final assumption that the distribution of the project completion time T follows a normal or bell-shaped distribution,[3] allows us to draw the distribution shown in Figure 10.12. With this distribution we can compute the probability of meeting a specified project completion date. For example, suppose that management has allotted 20 weeks for the Porta-Vac project. What is the probability that we will meet the 20-week deadline? Using the normal distribution from Figure 10.12, we are asking for the probability that $T \leq 20$. This is shown graphically as the shaded area in Figure 10.13. The z value for the normal distribution at $T = 20$ is given by

$$z = \frac{20 - 17}{1.65} = 1.82$$

[3]The use of the normal distribution as an approximation is based on the central limit theorem, which indicates that the sum of independent activity times follows a normal distribution as the number of activities becomes large.

FIGURE 10.12
PERT Normal Distribution of the Project Completion Time for the Porta-Vac Project

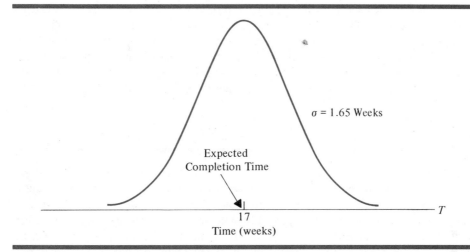

$\sigma = 1.65$ Weeks

Expected
Completion Time

17

Time (weeks)

T

FIGURE 10.13
Probability of a Porta-Vac Project Completion Date Prior to the 20-Week Deadline

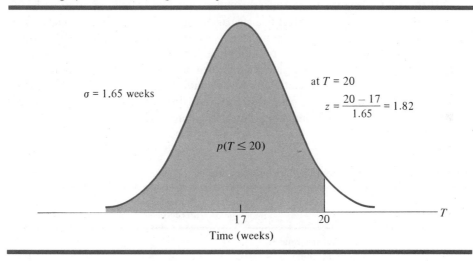

$\sigma = 1.65$ weeks

at $T = 20$

$z = \dfrac{20 - 17}{1.65} = 1.82$

$p(T \leq 20)$

17   20

Time (weeks)

T

Using $z = 1.82$ and the tables for the normal distribution (see Appendix A), we see that the probability of the project meeting the 20-week deadline is $0.4656 + 0.5000 = 0.9656$. Thus while activity time variability may cause the project to exceed the 17-week expected duration, there is an excellent chance that the project will be completed before the 20-week deadline. Similar probability calculations can be made for other project deadline alternatives.

Thus, we see that a PERT/CPM project scheduling procedure can be used to schedule projects with uncertain activity times. A three-time estimate procedure for each activity (optimistic time, most likely time, and pessimistic time) enables the computation of an expected time and a variance for each activity. Using the expected time as the fixed time, the critical activities and critical path for the project can be found using the procedure presented in Section 10.2. The sum of the expected times of critical path activities provides the expected project completion time. The sum of the variances of critical path activities provides the variance in the project completion time. Using the normal probability distribution assumption for the completion time, standard procedures from probability can be used to compute the probability of the project being completed by a specific date.

10.4 CONSIDERING TIME–COST TRADE-OFFS

The original developers of the CPM approach to project scheduling provided the project manager with the capability of adding resources to selected activities in an attempt to reduce activity—and thus project—completion times. Since added resources such as more workers, overtime, and so on generally increase project costs, the decision to reduce activity times must take into consideration the additional cost involved. In effect, the project manager has to make a decision that involves trading off decreased activity time against increased project cost.

In the Porta-Vac project the 17-week scheduled completion time could be reduced if management were willing to add resources to shorten any of the critical path activities: *A, E, H, I*, and *J*. Since the Porta-Vac project has a high probability of meeting the 20-week project deadline, it is doubtful that management would be willing to add costs to reduce activity times for this particular project. Thus let us consider another project where time–cost trade-offs would most likely need to be considered.

Table 10.8 defines a two-machine maintenance project consisting of five activities. Since management has had substantial experience with similar projects, the maintenance activities times are considered known; hence a single time estimate is provided for each activity. The network for this project is shown in Figure 10.14.

TABLE 10.8
Activity List for a Two-Machine Maintenance Project

Activity		Immediate Predecessor	Expected Time (in Days)
A	Overhaul machine I	—	7
B	Adjust machine I	A	3
C	Overhaul machine II	—	6
D	Adjust machine II	C	3
E	Test system	B, D	2

Critical path calculations for the maintenance project network are computed following the procedure we used to find the critical path in both the Western Hills Shopping Center Expansion and the Porta-Vac networks. Making the forward pass and backward pass calculations for the network in Figure 10.14, we can obtain the activity schedule shown in Table 10.9. As you can see, the zero slack times, and thus the critical path, are

FIGURE 10.14
Network of a Two-Machine Maintenance Project

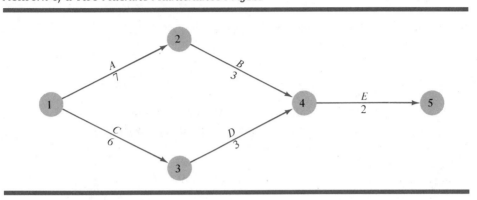

TABLE 10.9
Activity Schedule for the Maintenance Project

Activity	Earliest Start (ES)	Latest Start (LS)	Earliest Finish (EF)	Latest Finish (LF)	Slack (LS − ES)	Critical Path?
A	0	0	7	7	0	Yes
B	7	7	10	10	0	Yes
C	0	1	6	7	1	
D	6	7	9	10	1	
E	10	10	12	12	0	Yes

associated with activities *A–B–E* or nodes 1–2–4–5. The length of the critical path, and thus the project, is 12 days.

Crashing Activity Times

Now suppose that the current production levels make it imperative for the maintenance project to be completed within 2 weeks, or 10 working days. By looking at the length of the critical path of the network (12 days), we realize that it is impossible to meet the project completion date unless we can shorten selected activity times. This shortening of activity times, which usually can be achieved by adding resources such as labor or overtime, is referred to as *crashing* the activity times. However, since the added resources associated with crashing activity times usually result in added project costs, we will want to identify the activities that cost least to crash and then crash those activities only the amount necessary to meet the desired project completion date.

In order to determine just where and how much to crash activity times, we will need information on how much each activity can be crashed and how much the crashing process costs. Possibly the best way to accomplish this is to ask management for the following information on each activity:

1. Estimated activity cost under the normal or expected activity time
2. Activity completion time under maximum crashing (that is, shortest possible activity time)
3. Estimated activity cost under maximum crashing

Let

$$\tau_j = \text{normal time for activity } j$$
$$\tau_j' = \text{time for activity } j \text{ under maximum crashing}$$
$$M_j = \text{maximum possible reduction in time for activity } j \text{ due}$$
$$\text{to maximum crashing}$$

With both τ_j and τ_j' known, we can compute M_j as follows:

$$M_j = \tau_j - \tau_j' \tag{10.6}$$

Next let C_j denote the normal cost for activity j and C_j' denote the cost for activity j under maximum crashing. Thus on a per-unit time basis (for example, per day), the crashing cost K_j for each activity is given by

$$K_j = \frac{C_j' - C_j}{M_j} \tag{10.7}$$

For example, if activity A has a normal activity time of 7 days at a cost of $C_A = \$500$ and a maximum crash activity time of 4 days at a cost of $C_A' = \$800$, equations (10.6) and (10.7) show that activity A can be crashed a maximum of

$$M_A = 7 - 4 = 3 \text{ days}$$

at a crashing cost of

$$K_A = \frac{C_A' - C_A}{M_A} = \frac{800 - 500}{3} = \frac{300}{3} = \$100 \text{ per day}$$

We will make the assumption that any portion or fraction of the activity crash time can be achieved for a corresponding portion of the activity crashing cost. For example, if we decided to crash activity A by only $1\frac{1}{2}$ days, we would assume that this could be accomplished with an added cost of $1\frac{1}{2}(\$100) = \$150$, which results in a total activity cost of $\$500 + \$150 = \$650$. Figure 10.15 shows the graph of the time–cost relationship for activity A.

The complete normal and crash activity data for our example project are given in Table 10.10.

Now the question is: which activities would you crash, and how much should these activities be crashed in order to meet the 10-day project completion deadline at minimum cost? Your first reaction to this question is possibly to consider crashing the critical path activities A, B, or E. Activity A has the lowest crashing costs of the three, and crashing this activity by 2 days will reduce the A–B–E path to the desired 10 days. While this is

FIGURE 10.15
Time–Cost Relationship for Activity A

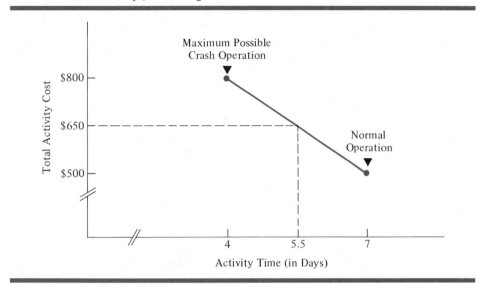

TABLE 10.10
Normal and Crash Activity Data for the Maintenance Project

Activity	Normal Time	Crash Time	Total Normal Cost C_j	Total Crash Cost C_j'	Maximum Crash Days M_j	Crash Cost per Day $K_j = \dfrac{C_j' - C_j}{M_j}$
A	7	4	$500	$800	3	$100
B	3	2	200	350	1	150
C	6	4	500	900	2	200
D	3	1	200	500	2	150
E	2	1	300	550	1	250
			$1700	$3100		

correct, be careful: As you crash the current critical path activities, other paths may become critical. Thus you will need to check the critical path in the revised network and perhaps either identify additional activities to crash or modify your initial crashing decision. While in a small network you may be able to use this trial-and-error approach to making crashing decisions, in larger networks you will need a mathematical procedure in order to arrive at the optimal decision. The following discussion shows how linear programming can be used to solve the network crashing problem.

A Linear Programming Model for Crashing Decisions

While several solution procedures exist for the crashing procedure, the following linear programming model is one approach used to help make crashing decisions. First recall that an event refers to the completion of all the activities that lead into a node. Since we have five nodes or events in the maintenance project example, we need five decision variables to identify the time of occurrence for each event. In addition, we will need five decision variables to represent the amount of crash time used for each of the five activities. Thus we define the following decision variables.

x_i = time of occurrence of event i i = 1, 2, 3, 4, 5
y_j = amount of crash time used for activity j j = A, B, C, D, E

Since the total normal time project cost is fixed at $1700 (see Table 10.10), we can minimize the total project cost (normal cost plus crash cost) simply by minimizing the crashing costs. Thus the linear programming objective function becomes

$$\min \sum_j K_j y_j \tag{10.8}$$

or

$$\min 100y_A + 150y_B + 200y_C + 150y_D + 250y_E \tag{10.9}$$

where K_j is the crash cost for activity j, j = A, B, C, D, E, on a per-unit time basis.[4]

The constraints on the model involve describing the network, limiting the activity crash times, and meeting the project completion date. Of these, the constraints used to describe the network are perhaps the most difficult. These constraints are based on the following conditions:

1. The time of occurrence of event i (x_i) must be greater than or equal to the activity completion time for all activities leading into the node or event.
2. An activity start time is equal to the occurrence time of its preceding node or event.
3. An activity time is equal to its normal time less the length of time it is crashed.

Using an event occurrence time of zero at node 1 (x_1 = 0), we can create the following set of network description constraints:

Event 2:

$$x_2 \geq \underbrace{\tau_A - y_A}_{} + 0$$

  ↑   ←————————Start time
Occurrence   ←——Actual time   for activity A
time for event 2   for activity A   (x_1 = 0)

or

$$x_2 + y_A \geq 7 \tag{10.10}$$

---

[4]Note that the x_i variables indicating event occurrences do not result in costs; thus they have zero coefficients in the objective function.

Event 3:

$$x_3 \geq \tau_C - y_C + 0$$

or

$$x_3 + y_C \geq 6 \qquad (10.11)$$

Since two activities enter event or node 4, we have the following two constraints:

Event 4:

$$x_4 \geq \tau_B - y_B + x_2$$
$$x_4 \geq \tau_D - y_D + x_3$$

or

$$-x_2 + x_4 + y_B \geq 3 \qquad (10.12)$$
$$-x_3 + x_4 + y_D \geq 3 \qquad (10.13)$$

Event 5:

$$x_5 \geq \tau_E - y_E + x_4$$

or

$$-x_4 + x_5 + y_E \geq 2 \qquad (10.14)$$

The five constraints (10.10) to (10.14) are necessary to describe our network.
The maximum allowable crash time constraints are

$$y_A \leq 3 \qquad (10.15)$$
$$y_B \leq 1 \qquad (10.16)$$
$$y_C \leq 2 \qquad (10.17)$$
$$y_D \leq 2 \qquad (10.18)$$
$$y_E \leq 1 \qquad (10.19)$$

and the project completion date provides another constraint:

$$x_5 \leq 10 \qquad (10.20)$$

Adding the nonnegativity restrictions and solving the above nine-variable, 11-constraint (10.10) to (10.20) linear programming model provides the following solution:

$$\begin{array}{ll} x_2 = 5 & y_A = 2 \\ x_3 = 6 & y_B = 0 \\ x_4 = 8 & y_C = 0 \\ x_5 = 10 & y_D = 1 \\ & y_E = 0 \end{array}$$

Objective function = \$350

The solution values of $y_A = 2$ and $y_D = 1$ tell us activity A must be crashed 2 days ($200) and activity D must be crashed 1 day ($150) in order to meet the 10-day project completion deadline. Because of this crashing, the time for activity A will be reduced to $7 - 2 = 5$ days, while the time for activity D will be reduced to $3 - 1 = 2$ days. The total project cost (normal cost plus crashing cost) will be $1700 + $200 + $150 = $2050. To generate the new activity schedule under crashing, we use the crashed activity times and repeat the critical path calculations for the network. Doing this provides the activity schedule shown in Table 10.11. Note that in our final solution all activities are critical. Resolving the linear programming model with alternate project completion dates [constraint (10.20)] will show the project manager the costs associated with crashing the project to meet alternate deadlines.

TABLE 10.11
New Activity Schedule for the Maintenance Project After Crashing Activities A and D

Activity	Time . After Crashing	ES	LS	EF	LF	Slack
A	5	0	0	5	5	0
B	3	5	5	8	8	0
C	6	0	0	6	6	0
D	2	6	6	8	8	0
E	2	8	8	10	10	0

Due to the substantial formulation and computational effort associated with activity crashing, most applications of this technique use specalized computer programs developed to handle crashing and the related network analyses.

10.5 PERT/COST

As you have seen, PERT/CPM concentrates on the *time* aspect of a project and provides information that can be used to schedule and control individual activities so that the entire project is completed on time. While project time and the meeting of a scheduled completion date are primary considerations for almost every project, there are many situations in which the *cost* associated with the project is just as important as time. In this section we show how the technique referred to as PERT/Cost can be used to help plan, schedule, and control project costs. The ultimate objective of a PERT/Cost system is to provide information that can be used to maintain project costs within a specified budget.

Planning and Scheduling Project Costs

The budgeting process for a project usually involves identifying all costs associated with the project and then developing a schedule or forecast of when the costs are expected to occur. Then at various stages of project completion, the actual project costs incurred can be compared to the scheduled or budgeted costs. If actual costs are exceeding budgeted costs, corrective action may be taken to keep costs within the budget.

The first step in a PERT/Cost control system is to divide the entire project into components that are convenient in terms of measuring and controlling costs. While a PERT/CPM network may already show detailed activities for the project, we may find that these activities are too detailed for conveniently controlling project costs. In such cases related activities that are under the control of one department, subcontractor, etc., are often grouped together to form what are referred to as *work packages*. By identifying costs of each work package, a project manager can use a PERT/Cost system to help plan, schedule, and control project costs.

Since the projects we discuss in this chapter have a relatively small number of activities, we will find it convenient to define work packages as having only one activity. Thus in our discussion of the PERT/Cost technique we will be treating each activity as a separate work package. Realize, however, that in large and complex projects we would almost always group related activities so that a cost control system could be developed for a more reasonable number of work packages.

In order to illustrate the PERT/Cost technique, let us consider the research and development project network shown in Figure 10.16. We are assuming that each activity is an acceptable work package and that a detailed cost analysis has been made on an activity basis. The activity cost estimates, along with the expected activity times, are shown in Table 10.12. In using the PERT/Cost technique we will be assuming that activities (work packages) are defined such that costs occur at a constant rate over the duration of the activity. For example, activity B, which shows an estimated cost of $30,000 and an expected 3-month duration, is assumed to have a cost rate of $30,000/3 = $10,000 per month. The cost rates for all activities are provided in Table 10.12. Note that the total estimated or budgeted cost for the project is $87,000.

FIGURE 10.16
A Project Network

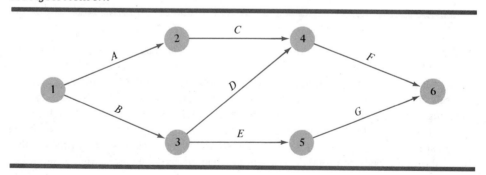

Using the expected activity times, we can compute the critical path for the project. A summary of the critical path calculations and the resulting activity schedule is shown in Table 10.13. Activities B, D, and F determine the critical path and provide an expected project duration of 8 months.

We are now ready to develop a budget for the project that will show when costs should occur during the 8-month project duration. First let us assume that all activities begin at their earliest possible start time. Using the monthly activity cost rates shown in Table 10.12 and the earliest start times, we can prepare the month-by-month cost forecast

TABLE 10.12
Activity Time and Cost Estimates

Activity	Expected Time (months)	Budgeted or Estimated Cost	Budgeted Cost per Month
A	2	$10,000	$ 5,000
B	3	30,000	10,000
C	1	3,000	3,000
D	3	6,000	2,000
E	2	20,000	10,000
F	2	10,000	5,000
G	1	8,000	8,000
	Total project budget =	$87,000	

TABLE 10.13
Activity Schedule

Activity	Earliest Start (ES)	Latest Start (LS)	Earliest Finish (EF)	Latest Finish (LF)	Slack	Critical Path?
A	0	3	2	5	3	
B	0	0	3	3	0	Yes
C	2	5	3	6	3	
D	3	3	6	6	0	Yes
E	3	5	5	7	2	
F	6	6	8	8	0	Yes
G	5	7	6	8	2	

as shown in Table 10.14. For example, using the earliest start date for activity A as 0, we expect activity A, which has a 2-month duration, to show a cost of $5000 in each of the first 2 months of the project. By similarly using the earliest start time and monthly cost rate for each activity, we are able to complete Table 10.14 as shown. Note that by summing the costs in each column we obtain the total cost anticipated for each month of the project. Finally, by accumulating the monthly costs, we can show the budgeted total cost schedule, provided all activities are started at the *earliest* starting times. Table 10.15 shows the budgeted total cost schedule when all activities are started at the *latest* starting times.

Provided the project progresses on its PERT/CPM time schedule, each activity will be started somewhere between its earliest and latest starting times. This implies that the total project costs should occur at levels between the earliest start and latest start costs schedules. For example, using the data in Tables 10.14 and 10.15, we see that by month 3, total project costs should be between $30,000 (latest starting date schedule) and $43,000 (earliest starting date schedule). Thus at month 3 a total project cost between $30,000· and $43,000 would be expected.

In Figure 10.17 we show the forecasted total project costs for both the earliest and latest starting time schedules. The shaded region between the two cost curves shows the

TABLE 10.14
Budgeted Costs for an Earliest Starting Date Schedule ($ $\times$ 10^3)

Activity	Month 1	2	3	4	5	6	7	8
A	5	5						
B	10	10	10					
C			3					
D				2	2	2		
E				10	10			
F							5	5
G						8		
Monthly cost	15	15	13	12	12	10	5	5
Total project cost	15	30	43	55	67	77	82	87

TABLE 10.15
Budgeted Costs for a Latest Starting Date Schedule ($ $\times$ 10^3)

Activity	Month 1	2	3	4	5	6	7	8
A				5	5			
B	10	10	10					
C						3		
D				2	2	2		
E						10	10	
F							5	5
G								8
Monthly cost	10	10	10	7	7	15	15	13
Total project cost	10	20	30	37	44	59	74	87

possible budgets for the project. If the project manager is willing to commit activities to specific starting times, a specific project cost forecast or budget can be prepared. However, based on the above analysis we know that such a budget will have to be in the feasible region shown in Figure 10.17.

Controlling Project Costs

The information that we have developed thus far is helpful in terms of planning and scheduling total project costs. However, if we are going to have an effective cost control system, we will need to identify costs on a much more detailed basis. For example, information that the project's actual total cost is exceeding the budgeted total cost will be of little value unless we can identify the activity or group of activities that are causing the cost overruns.

FIGURE 10.17
Feasible Budgets for Total Project Costs

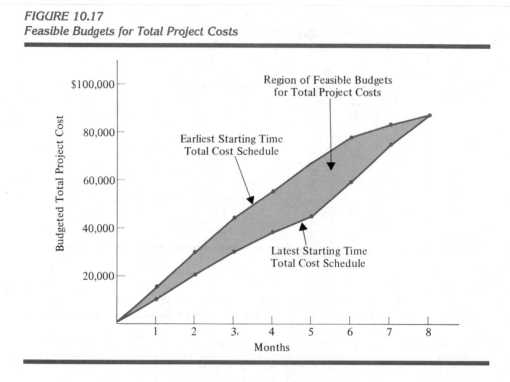

The PERT/Cost system provides the desired cost control by budgeting and then recording actual costs on an activity (i.e., work package) basis. Periodically throughout the project's duration, actual costs for all completed and in-process activities are compared with the appropriate budgeted costs. The project manager is then provided with up-to-date information on the cost status of each activity. If at any point in time actual costs exceed budgeted costs, a cost overrun has occurred. On the other hand, if actual costs are less than the budgeted costs, we have a condition referred to as a cost underrun. By identifying the sources of cost overruns and cost underruns, the manager can take corrective action where necessary. Note that the budgeted or estimated activity costs for the R&D project network of Figure 10.16 are shown in Table 10.16.

TABLE 10.16
Activity Cost Estimates

Activity	Budgeted Cost	Activity	Budgeted Cost
A	$10,000	E	$20,000
B	30,000	F	10,000
C	3,000	G	8,000
D	6,000		

Now at any point during the project's duration the manager can use a PERT/Cost procedure to obtain an activity cost status report by collecting the following information for *each activity*:

1. Actual cost to date
2. Percent completion to date

A PERT/Cost system will require periodic—perhaps biweekly or monthly—collection of the above information. Let us suppose we are at the end of the fourth month of the project and have the actual cost and percent completion data for each activity, as shown in Table 10.17. This current status information shows that activities A and B have been completed, activities C, D, and E are in process, and activities F and G have not yet been started.

TABLE 10.17
Activity Cost and Percent Completion Data at the End of Month 4

Activity	Actual Cost	Percent Completion
A	$12,000	100
B	30,000	100
C	1,000	50
D	2,000	33
E	10,000	25
F	0	0
G	0	0
	Total = $55,000	

In order to prepare a cost status report we will need to compute the value for all work completed to date. Let

V_i = value of work completed for activity i
p_i = percent completion for activity i
B_i = budget for activity i

The following relationship is used to find the value of work completed for each activity:

$$V_i = (p_i/100)B \qquad (10.21)$$

For example, the values of work completed for activities A and C are as follows[5]:

$$V_A = (^{100}/_{100})(\$10,000) = \$10,000$$
$$V_C = (^{50}/_{100})(\$3000) = \$1500$$

Cost overruns and cost underruns can now be found by comparing the actual cost of each activity with its appropriate budget value. Let

---

[5]Equation (10.21) and the succeeding calculations are based on the PERT/Cost assumption that activity costs occur at a constant rate over the duration of the activity.

AC_i = actual cost to date for activity i

D_i = difference in actual cost and budgeted value for activity i

We have

$$D_i = AC_i - V_i \qquad (10.22)$$

A positive D_i indicates the activity has a cost *overrun*, while a negative D_i indicates a cost *underrun*. $D_i = 0$ indicates that actual costs are in agreement with the budgeted costs. For example,

$$D_A = AC_A - V_A = \$12,000 - \$10,000 = \$2000$$

shows that activity A, which has already been completed, has a $2000 cost overrun. However, activity C, with $D_C = \$1000 - \$1500 = -\$500$, is currently showing a cost underrun, or savings, of $500. A complete cost status report such as the one shown in Table 10.18 can now be prepared for the project manager.

TABLE 10.18
Project Cost Status Report at Month 4

Activity	Actual Cost (AC)	Budgeted Value $[V = (p/100)B]$	Differences (D)
A	$12,000	$10,000	$2,000
B	30,000	30,000	0
C	1,000	1,500	−500
D	2,000	2,000	0
E	10,000	5,000	5,000
F	0	0	0
G	0	0	0
Totals	$55,000	$48,500	$6,500

Total project cost overrun to date

This cost report shows the project manager that the costs to date are $6500 over the estimated or budgeted costs. On a percentage basis, we would say the project is experiencing a ($6500/$48,500) × 100 = 13.4% cost overrun, which for most projects is a serious situation. By checking each activity, we see that activities A and E are causing the cost overrun. Since activity A has been completed, its cost overrun cannot be corrected; however, activity E is in process and is only 25% complete. Thus activity E should be reviewed immediately. Corrective action for activity E can help to bring actual costs closer to the budgeted costs. The manager may also want to consider cost reduction possibilities for activities C, D, F, and G in order to keep the total project cost within the budget.

While the PERT/Cost procedure described above can be an effective cost control system, it is not without possible drawbacks and implementation problems. First, the activity-by-activity cost recording system can require significant clerical effort, especially for firms with large and/or numerous projects. Thus the personnel and other costs associated with maintaining a PERT/Cost system may offset some of the advantages. Second, questions can arise as to how costs should be allocated to activities or work packages. Overhead, indirect, and even material costs can cause cost allocations and measurement problems. Third, and perhaps most critical, is the fact that PERT/Cost requires a system of cost recording and control that is significantly different from most cost accounting systems. Firms using departments or other organizational units as cost centers will need a substantially revised accounting system to handle the PERT/Cost activity-oriented system. Problems of modifying accounting procedures and/or carrying dual accounting sytems are not trivial matters.

Summary

In this chapter we have introduced PERT/CPM and PERT/Cost as procedures designed to assist in the project planning, scheduling, and control process. The key to these project management techniques is to develop a network that depicts the activities and their precedence relationships. Given this network and the activity time estimates, the critical path for the network and the associated critical path activities can be identified. In the process an activity schedule showing the earliest start time, the earliest finish time, the latest start time, the latest finish time, and the slack for each activity can be identified.

We showed how we can include capabilities for handling variable or uncertain activity times and how this information can be used to provide a probability statement about the chances the project can be completed in a specified period of time. Crashing was introduced as a procedure for reducing activity times to meet project completion deadlines. A linear programming model can be used to make the crashing decisions that minimize the cost of reducing the project completion time.

In the final section of this chapter we described how the PERT/Cost technique can be used to help plan, schedule, and control project costs. Because of the numerous computations associated with planning, updating, and revising PERT/CPM and PERT/Cost networks, computer programs are frequently used to implement these project management techniques. For modest-sized projects, computerized project managememt procedures are available on microcomputers.

A summary of some of the key steps in any project management task follows:

1. Make a clear statement of the objectives of the project, specifically identifying what is to be accomplished.
2. Make a list of all activities and their immediate predecessors. Provide estimates of the activity times by either specifying the expected time directly or using the optimistic, most likely, and pessimistic time estimates to compute an expected time.
3. Develop the network for the project.
4. Perform the critical path computations to develop an activity schedule for the project, and identify the critical path activities.
5. Make resource allocations and crashing decisions as necessary to achieve the desired project completion date.
6. Be sure someone is responsible for each activity in the project and is working to see that activities are completed as scheduled.
7. Control the project by monitoring actual performance, taking corrective action and replanning where necessary.

Glossary

Program evaluation and review technique (PERT)   A network-based project management procedure.

Critical path method (CPM)   A network-based project management procedure.

Activities   Specific jobs or tasks that are components of a project. These are represented by arcs in a PERT/CPM network.

Immediate predecessors   The activities that must immediately precede another given activity.

Event   An event occurs when *all* the activities leading into a node have been completed.

Dummy activity   A fictitious activity with zero activity time used to create a PERT/CPM network.

Optimistic time   An activity time estimate based on the assumption that the activity will progress in an ideal manner.

Most probable time   An activity time estimate for the most likely activity time.

Pessimistic time   An activity time estimate based on the assumption that the most unfavorable conditions occur.

Expected activity time   The average activity time.

Beta distribution   A probability distribution used to describe PERT activity times.

Path   A sequence of branches (activities) connecting the first node and the last node of a network.

Critical path   The longest path in a project management (PERT/CPM) network. The time it takes to traverse this path is the estimated project duration.

Critical activities   The activities on the critical path.

Earliest start time   The earliest time at which an activity may begin.

Earliest finish time   The earliest time at which an activity may be completed.

Latest start time   The latest time at which an activity may begin without delaying the complete project.

Latest finish time   The latest time at which an activity may be completed without delaying the complete project.

Forward pass   A calculation procedure moving forward through the network that determines the early start and early finish times for each activity.

Backward pass   A calculation procedure moving backward through the network that determines the latest start and latest finish times for each activity.

Slack   The length of time an activity can be delayed without affecting the project completion time.

Crashing   The process of reducing an activity time by adding resources and hence usually cost.

PERT/Cost   A technique designed to assist in the planning, scheduling, and controlling of project costs.

Work package   A natural grouping of interrelated project activities for purposes of cost control. A work package is a unit of cost control in a PERT/Cost system.

Problems

1. The Mohawk Discount Store chain is designing a management training program for individuals at its corporate headquarters. The company would like to design the program so that the trainees can complete it as quickly as possible. There are

important precedence relationships that must be maintained between assignments or activities in the program. For example, a trainee cannot serve as an assistant to the store manager until the trainee has obtained experience in the credit department and at least one sales department. The activities shown below are the assignments that must be completed by each trainee in the program:

Activity	Immediate Predecessor
A	—
B	—
C	A
D	A, B
E	A, B
F	C
G	D, F
H	E, G

Construct a PERT/CPM network for this problem. Do not attempt to perform any further analysis.

2. Consider the PERT/CPM network shown below.

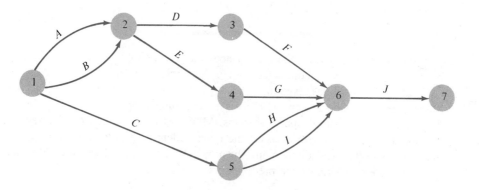

a. Add the dummy activities that will eliminate the problem of activities having the same starting and ending nodes.

b. Add dummy activities that will satisfy the following immediate predecessor requirements:

Activity	Immediate Predecessor
H	B, C
I	B, C
G	D, E

3. Construct a PERT/CPM network for a project having the following activities:

Activity	Immediate Predecessor
A	—
B	—
C	A
D	A
E	C, B
F	C, B
G	D, E

The project is completed when both activities F and G are complete.

4. Assume that the project in problem 3 has the following activity times:

Activity	Time (months)
A	4
B	6
C	2
D	6
E	3
F	3
G	5

a. Find the critical path for the project network.

b. The project must be completed in 1½ years; do you anticipate difficulty in meeting the deadline? Explain.

5. Management Decision Systems (MDS) is a consulting company specializing in the development of decision support systems. MDS has just obtained the contract to develop a computer system to assist the management of a large company in formulating its capital expenditure plan. The project leader has developed the following list of activities and immediate predecessors:

Activity	Immediate Predecessor
A	—
B	—
C	—
D	B
E	A
F	B
G	C, D
H	B, E
I	F, G
J	H

Construct a PERT/CPM network for this problem.

6. Consider the following project network (the times shown are in weeks):

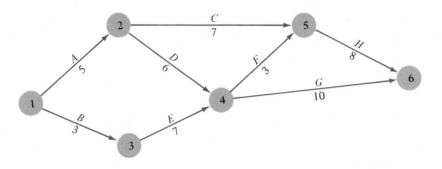

a. Identify the critical path.
b. How long will it take to complete this project?
c. Can activity D be delayed without delaying the entire project? If so, how many weeks?
d. Can activity C be delayed without delaying the entire project? If so, how many weeks?
e. What is the schedule for activity E (that is, start and completion times)?

7. A project involving the installation of a computer system consists of eight activities. The immediate predecessors and activity times in weeks are shown below.

Activity	Immediate Predecessor	Time
A	—	3
B	—	6
C	A	2
D	B, C	5
E	D	4
F	E	3
G	B, C	9
H	F, G	3

a. Draw the PERT/CPM network for this project.
b. What are the critical path activities?
c. What is the expected project completion time?

8. Colonial State College is considering building a new multipurpose athletic complex on campus. The complex would provide a new gymnasium for intercollegiate basketball games. In addition, it would provide expanded office space, classrooms, and intramural facilities. The activities that would have to be undertaken before beginning construction are shown below. Activity times are stated in weeks.

Activity	Description	Immediate Predecessor	Time
A	Survey building site	—	6
B	Develop initial design	—	8
C	Obtain board approval	A, B	12
D	Select architect	C	4
E	Establish budget	C	6
F	Finalize design	D, E	15
G	Obtain financing	E	12
H	Hire contractor	F, G	8

a. Develop a PERT/CPM network for this project.
b. Identify the critical path.
c. Develop a detailed schedule for all activities in the project.
d. Does it appear reasonable that construction of the athletic complex could begin 1 year after the decision to begin the project with the site survey and initial design plans? What is the expected completion time for the project?

9. Hamilton County Parks is planning to develop a new park and recreational area on a recently purchased 100-acre tract. Activities making up the park development project include clearing playground and picnic areas, road construction, shelter house construction, picnic equipment purchases, and so on. The PERT/CPM network shown below is being used to assist in the planning, scheduling, and controlling of this project:

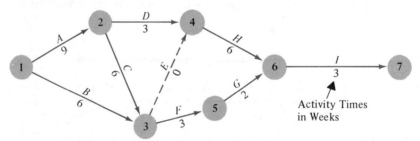

a. What is the critical path for this network?
b. Show the activity schedule and slack for each activity.
c. The park commissioner would like to open the park to the public within 6 months from the time the work on the project is started. Does this opening date appear feasible? Explain.

10. The following estimates of activity times (days) are available for a small project:

Activity	Optimistic	Most Probable	Pessimistic
A	4	5	6
B	8	9	10
C	7	7.5	11
D	7	9	10
E	6	7	9
F	5	6	7

a. Compute the expected activity completion times and the variance for each activity.
b. The management science staff has found that the critical path consists of activities *B–D–F*. Compute the expected project completion time and the variance.

11. The project of building a backyard swimming pool consists of nine major activities. The activities and their immediate predecessors are shown below. Develop the PERT/CPM network for this project.

Activity	Immediate Predecessors
A	—
B	—
C	A, B
D	A, B
E	B
F	C
G	D
H	D, F
I	E, G, H

12. Assume that the activity time estimates in days for the swimming pool construction project from problem 11 are as follows:

Activity	Optimistic	Most Probable	Pessimistic
A	3	5	6
B	2	4	6
C	5	6	7
D	7	9	10
E	2	4	6
F	1	2	3
G	5	8	10
H	6	8	10
I	3	4	5

a. What are the critical path activities?
b. What is the expected time to complete the project?
c. What is the probability that the project can be completed in 25 working days or less?

13. Suppose that the following estimates of activity times (weeks) were provided for the network shown in problem 6:

Activity	Optimistic	Most Probable	Pessimistic
A	4	5	6
B	2.5	3	3.5
C	6	7	8
D	5	5.5	9
E	5	7	9
F	2	3	4
G	8	10	12
H	6	7	14

What is the probability that the project will be completed within
a. 21 weeks?
b. 22 weeks?
c. 25 weeks?

14. Consider the project network given below:

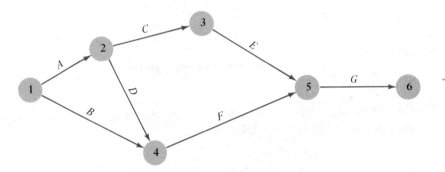

The appropriate managers have made estimates of the optimistic, most probable, and pessimistic times (in days) for completion of the activities. These times are as follows:

Activity	Optimistic	Most Probable	Pessimistic
A	5	6	7
B	5	12	13
C	6	8	10
D	4	10	10
E	5	6	13
F	7	7	10
G	4	7	10

a. Find the critical path.
b. How much slack time, if any, is there in activity C?
c. Determine the expected project completion time and the variance.
d. Find the probability that the project will be completed in 30 days or less.

15. Doug Casey is in charge of planning and coordinating next spring's sales management training program for his company. Doug has listed the following activity information for this project:

Activity	Description	Immediate Predecessors	Times (Weeks)		
			Optimistic	Most Probable	Pessimistic
A	Plan topic	—	1.5	2	2.5
B	Obtain speakers	A	2	2.5	6
C	List meeting locations	—	1	2	3
D	Select location	C	1.5	2	2.5
E	Speaker travel plans	B, D	0.5	1	1.5
F	Final check with speakers	E	1	2	3
G	Prepare and mail brochure	B, D	3	3.5	7
H	Take reservations	G	3	4	5
I	Last-minute details	F, H	1.5	2	2.5

a. Show the PERT/CPM network for this project.
b. What are the critical path activities and the expected project completion time?
c. Prepare the activity schedule for this project.
d. If Doug wants a 0.99 probability of completing the project on time, how far ahead of the scheduled meeting date should he begin working on the project?

16. The Daugherty Porta-Vac project discussed in Section 10.3 had an expected project completion time of 17 weeks. The probability that the project could be completed in 20 weeks or less was found to be 0.9656. Shown below are the noncritical paths in the Porta-Vac project network.

Other Paths in the Porta-Vac Network

A–D–G–J
A–C–F–J
B–H–I–J.

a. Using the information in Table 10.6, compute the expected time and variance for each of the above paths.
b. Compute the probability that each path will be completed in the desired 20-week period.
c. Why is the computation of the probability of completing a project on time based on the analysis of the critical path? In what case, if any, would it be desirable to make the probability computation for a noncritical path?

17. Refer to the Porta-Vac project network shown in Figure 10.7. Suppose Daugherty's management revises the activity time estimates as follows:

Activity	Optimistic	Most Probable	Pessimistic
A	3	7	11
B	2	2.5	6
C	2	3	4
D	6	7	14
E	2	3	4
F	2.5	3	3.5
G	2.5	4	5.5
H	4.5	5.5	9.5
I	1	2	3
J	1	2	3

a. What are the expected times and variances for each activity?
b. What are the critical path activities?
c. What is the expected project completion time?
d. What is the new probability that the project will be completed before the 20-week deadline?
e. Show the new detailed activity schedule.

18. The manager of the Oak Hills Swimming Club is planning the club's swimming team program. The first team practice is scheduled for May 1. The activities, their immediate predecessors, and the activity time estimates in weeks are as follows:

	Activity	Immediate Predecessor	Optimistic Time	Most Probable Time	Pessimistic Time
A.	Meet with board	—	1	1	2
B.	Hire coaches	A	4	6	8
C.	Announce program	B, F	1	2	3
D.	Order team suits	A	1	2	3
E.	Meet with coaches	B	2	3	4
F.	Reserve pool	A	2	4	6
G.	Register swimmers	C	1	2	3
H.	Collect fees	G	1	2	3
I.	Plan first practice	E, H, D	1	1	1

a. Show the PERT/CPM network for this project.
b. Develop an activity schedule for the project.
c. What are the critical path activities and what is the expected project completion time?
d. If the club manager plans to start the project on February 1, what is the probability the swimming program will be ready by the scheduled May 1 date (13 weeks)? Should the manager begin planning the swimming program prior to February 1?

19. The product development group at Landon Corporation has been working on a new computer software product that has the potential to capture a large market share.

Through outside sources, Landon's management has learned that a competitor is working to bring a similar product to the market. As a result Landon's top management has increased its pressure on the product development group. The group's leader has turned to PERT/CPM as an aid to the scheduling of the activities remaining before the new product can be brought to the market. The PERT/CPM network developed is shown below:

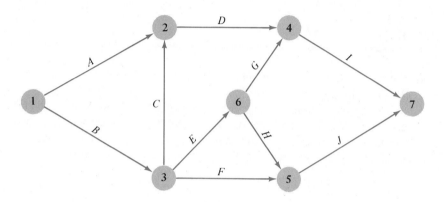

The activity time estimates in weeks are given below:

Activity	Optimistic	Most Probable	Pessimistic
A	3	4	5
B	3	3.5	7
C	4	5	6
D	2	3	4
E	6	10	14
F	7.5	8.5	12.5
G	4.5	6	7.5
H	5	6	13
I	2	2.5	6
J	4	5	6

a. Develop an activity schedule for this project and identify the critical path activities.

b. What is the probability that the project will be completed so that Landon Corporation may introduce the new product within 25 weeks? 30 weeks?

20. Using the computer installation project referred to in problem 7, assume that the project has to be completed in 16 weeks. Crashing of the project is necessary. Relevant information is shown below.

Activity	Normal Time	Crash Time	Normal Cost	Crash Cost
A	3	1	900	1700
B	6	3	2000	4000
C	2	1	500	1000
D	5	3	1800	2400
E	4	3	1500	1850
F	3	1	3000	3900
G	9	4	8000	9800
H	3	2	1000	2000

a. Formulate a linear programming model that can be used to make the crashing decisions for the above network.

b. Solve the linear programming model and make the minimum cost crashing decisions. What is the added cost of meeting the 16-week completion time?

c. Develop a complete activity schedule using the crashed activity times.

21. Consider the following network with activity times shown in days:

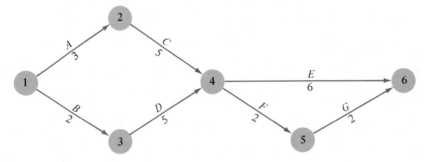

The crash data for this project are as follows:

Activity	Normal Time	Crash Time	Total Normal Cost ($)	Total Crash Cost ($)
A	3	2	800	1400
B	2	1	1200	1900
C	5	3	2000	2800
D	5	3	1500	2300
E	6	4	1800	2800
F	2	1	600	1000
G	2	1	500	1000

a. Find the critical path and the expected project duration.

b. What is the total project cost using the normal times?

22. Refer to problem 21. Assume that management desires a 12-day project completion time. Formulate a linear programming model that can be used to assist with the crashing decisions.

23. Assume that the following crash data are available for the project described in problem 4:

Activity	Normal Time	Crash Time	Total Normal Cost ($ × 10³)	Total Crash Cost ($ × 10³)
A	4	2	50	70
B	6	3	40	55
C	2	1	20	24
D	6	4	100	130
E	3	2	50	60
F	3	3	25	25
G	5	3	60	75

a. Show a linear programming model that could be used to make the crash decisions if the project has to be completed in T months.
b. If $T = 12$ months, what activities should be crashed, what is the crashing cost, and what are the critical activities?

24. Office Automation, Inc. has developed a proposal for introducing a new computerized office system that will improve word processing and interoffice communications for a particular company. Contained in the proposal is a list of activities that must be accomplished in order to complete the new office system project. Information about the activities is shown below. Times are in weeks and costs are in thousands of dollars.

	Activity	Immediate Predecessors	Normal Time	Crash Time	Normal Cost	Crash Cost
A.	Plan needs	—	10	8	30	70
B.	Order equipment	A	8	6	120	150
C.	Install equipment	B	10	7	100	160
D.	Set up training lab	A	7	6	40	50
E.	Training course	D	10	8	50	·75
F.	Testing system	C, E	3	3	60	—

a. Show the network for the project.
b. Develop an activity schedule for the project.
c. What are the critical path activities and what is the expected project completion time?
d. Assume that the company wishes to complete the project in 6 months or 26 weeks. What crashing decisions would be recommended in order to meet the completion date at the least possible cost? Work through the network and attempt to make the crashing decisions by inspection.

e. Develop an activity schedule for the crashed project.

f. What is the added project cost to meet the 6-month completion time?

25. Because Landon Corporation (see problem 19) is being pressured to complete the product development project at the earliest possible date, the project leader has requested an evaluation of the possibility of crashing the project.

   a. Develop a linear programming model that could be used to help in making the crashing decisions.

   b. What information would have to be provided before the linear programming model could be implemented?

26. For the Daugherty Porta-Vac project shown in Figure 10.7, suppose expected activity costs are as follows:

Activity	Expected Cost ($ × 10³)
A	90
B	16
C	3
D	100
E	6
F	2
G	60
H	20
I	4
J	2

Develop a total cost budget based on both an earliest start and a latest start schedule. Show the graph of feasible budgets for the total project cost.

27. Using the Daugherty Porta-Vac project cost data given in problem 26, prepare a PERT/Cost analysis for each of the following three points in time. For each case, show the percent overrun or underrun for the project to date and indicate any corrective action that should be undertaken. *Note:* If an activity is not listed below, assume that it has not been started.

   a. At the end of the fifth week:

Activity	Actual Cost ($ × 10³)	Percent Completion
A	62	80
B	6	50

   b. At the end of the 10th week:

Activity	Actual Cost ($ \times 10^3$)	Percent Completion
A	85	100
B	16	100
C	1	33
D	100	80
E	4	100
H	10	25

c. At the end of the 15th week:

Activity	Actual Cost ($ \times 10^3$)	Percent Completion
A	85	
B	16	
C	3	
D	105	
E	4	100
F	3	
G	55	
H	25	
I	4	

28. The two-machine maintenance project discussed in Section 10.4 is shown below:

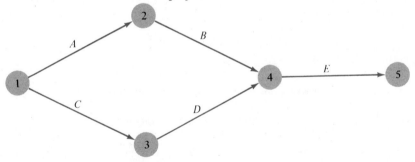

The recommended crashed schedule is shown in Table 10.11. Final times and costs for the project are as follows:

Activity	Expected Time (days)	Cost ($)
A	5	700
B	3	200
C	6	500
D	2	350
E	2	300
	Total	2050

a. Show the graph of feasible budgets for the project's total cost. Does this represent an unusual feasible budget region? Explain.

b. Suppose at the start of day 8 we find the following activity status report:

Activity	Actual Cost ($)	Percent Completion
A	800	100
B	100	67
C	450	100
D	250	50
E	0	0

In terms of both time and cost, is the project on schedule? What action is recommended?

29. A firm is modifying its warehouse operation with the installation of an automated stock handling system. Specific activities include redesigning the warehouse layout, installing the new equipment, testing the new equipment, etc. The project management network is shown below:

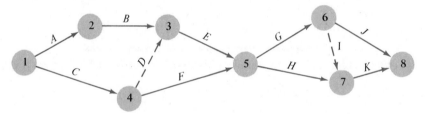

Pertinent time and cost data are as follows:

Activity	Expected Time (weeks)	Variance	Budgeted Cost ($)
A	3	0.3	6,000
B	2	0.5	4,000
C	8	2.0	16,000
D	0	0.0	0
E	6	1.0	18,000
F	4	0.2	20,000
G	5	0.4	15,000
H	1	0.1	2,000
I	0	0.0	0
J	5	1.0	5,000
K	6	0.6	12,000

a. Develop an activity schedule for the project.
   (1) What is the critical path?
   (2) What is the expected completion time?

(3) What is the probability of meeting a desired 6-month (26-week) completion time?
b. Develop a PERT/Cost budget for total project costs over the project's duration. What should the range be for expenditures after 12 weeks of the project?
30. Refer to the network in problem 29. Suppose that after 12 weeks of operation the following data are available on all completed and in-process activities:

Activity	Actual Cost ($)	Percent Completion
A	5,000	100
B	4,000	100
C	18,000	100
E	9,000	50
F	18,000	75

Is the project in control based on both time and cost considerations? What corrective action, if any, is desirable?

Case Problem:

WAREHOUSE EXPANSION

R. C. Coleman distributes a variety of food products sold through grocery store and supermarket outlets. The company receives orders directly from the individual outlets, with a typical order requesting the delivery of several cases of anywhere from 20 to 50 different products. Under the company's current warehouse operation, warehouse clerks dispatch order-picking personnel to fill each order and have the goods moved to the warehouse shipping area. Because of the high labor costs and relatively low productivity of hand order-picking, the company has decided to automate the warehouse operation by installing a computer-controlled order-picking system, along with a conveyor system for moving goods from storage to the warehouse shipping area.

R. C. Coleman's director of material management has been named the project manager in charge of the automated warehouse system. After consulting with members of the engineering staff and warehouse management personnel, the director has compiled a list of activities associated with the project. The optimistic, most probable, and pessimistic times in weeks have also been provided for each activity. This information is as follows:

Activity	Description	Immediate Predecessors
A	Determine equipment needs	—
B	Obtain vendor proposals	—
C	Select vendor	A, B
D	Order system	C
E	Design new warehouse layout	C
F	Layout warehouse	E
G	Design computer interface	C
H	Interface computer	D, F, G
I	Install system	D, F
J	Train system operators	H
K	Test system	I, J

Activity	Optimistic	Activity Times Most Probable	Pessimistic
A	4	6	8
B	6	8	16
C	2	4	6
D	8	10	24
E	7	10	13
F	4	6	8
G	4	6	20
H	4	6	8
I	4	6	14
J	3	4	5
K	2	4	6

MANAGERIAL REPORT

Develop a report that presents the activity schedule and expected project completion time for the warehouse expansion project. Include a PERT/CPM network of the project in the report. In addition, take into consideration the following information and include a discussion of each issue raised in the report.

a. R. C. Coleman's top management has established a required 40-week completion time for the project. Can this completion time be achieved? Include probability information in your discussion. What recommendations do you have if the 40-week completion time is required?

b. Suppose that management requests that activity times be shortened in order to provide an 80% chance of meeting the 40-week completion time. Assuming the variance in the project completion time is the same as you found in part a, how much should the expected project completion time be shortened in order to achieve the goal of providing an 80% chance of completion within 40 weeks?

c. Using the expected activity times as the normal times and the following crashing information, determine the activity crashing decisions and revised activity schedule for the warehouse expansion project.

Activity	Normal Cost	Crashed Activity Time	Crash Cost
A	1,000	4	1,900
B	1,000	7	1,800
C	1,500	2	2,700
D	2,000	8	3,200
E	5,000	7	8,000
F	3,000	4	4,100
G	8,000	5	10,250
H	5,000	4	6,400
I	10,000	4	12,400
J	4,000	3	4,400
K	5,000	3	5,500

Management Science in Practice
Seasongood & Mayer
Cincinnati, Ohio

Seasongood & Mayer, established in 1887, is an investment securities firm that engages in the following areas of municipal finance:

1. Underwriting new issues of municipal bonds
2. Trading—for example, acting as a market maker for the buying and selling of previously issued bonds
3. Investment banking—that is, the process of obtaining money from the capital markets at the lowest possible cost

The major applications of management science at Seasongood & Mayer are in the investment banking area. One particular application involved the use of PERT/CPM in the introduction of a $31 million hospital revenue bond issue.

SCHEDULING THE INTRODUCTION OF A BOND ISSUE

In any major building project there are certain common steps:

1. Defining the project
2. Determining the cost of the project
3. Financing the project

The role of the investment banker in building projects is to develop a method of financing that will result in the owner receiving the necessary funds in a timely manner. In a hospital building project, such as the one we will be discussing, the typical method of financing is tax-free hospital revenue bonds.

The construction cost for the building project is an important factor in determining the best approach to financing. Normally, the construction cost is based on a bid submitted by a contractor or a construction manager. However, this cost is usually guaranteed only for a specified period of time, such as 60 to 90 days. The major function of the hospital's investment banker is to arrange the timing of the financing in such a way that the proceeds of the bond issue can be made available within the time limit of the guaranteed-price construction bid. Since most hospitals must have the proceeds of their permanent long-term financing in hand prior to committing to major construction contracts, the investment banker plays a very significant role.

To arrange for the financing, the investment banker must coordinate the activities of hospital attorneys, the bond counsel, and so on. The cooperation of all parties and the coordination of project activities are best achieved if everyone recognizes the interdependency of the activities and the necessity of completing individual tasks in a timely manner. Seasongood & Mayer has found PERT/CPM to be useful in scheduling and coordinating such a project.

As managing underwriter for a $31,050,000 issue of Hospital Facilities Revenue Bonds for Providence Hospital in Hamilton County, Ohio (December 1980), Seasongood & Mayer utilized a critical path analysis to coordinate and schedule the project financing activities. Descriptions of the activities, times required, and immediate predecessors are given in Table A10.1. The complete network is shown in Figure A10.1. The critical path activities K–L–M–N–P–Q–R–S–U–W resulted in a scheduled project completion time of 29.14 weeks; thus the funds for the project are received approximately 64 days after the receipt of a firm construction price. Specific schedules showing start and finish times for all activities were used to keep the entire project on schedule. The use of PERT/CPM was instrumental in helping Seasongood & Mayer obtain financing for this project within the time specified in the construction bid.

TABLE A10.1
Activities for the Providence Hospital Project

Activity	Time Required (weeks)	Description of Activity	Immediate Predecessor(s)
A	4	Drafting and distribution of legal documents	—
B	3	Preparation and distribution of unaudited financial statements of hospital	—
C	2	Draft and distribution of hospital history, description of services, and existing facilities for Preliminary Official Statement (POS)	—
D	8	Draft and distribution of demand portion of feasibility study	—
E	4	Review (additions/deletions) and approval as to form of legal documents	A
F	1	Review (additions/deletions) and approval of history, etc., for POS	C
G	4	Review (additions/deletions) and approval of demand portion of feasibility study	D
H	2	Draft and distribution of financial portion (as to form) of feasibility study	E, G
I	2	Drafting and distribution of plan of financing and all pertinent facts relevant to the bond transaction for POS	E
J	0.5	Review and approval of unaudited financial statements	B
K	20	Firm price received for cost of project	—
L	1	Review (additions/deletions), approval, and completion of financial portion of feasibility study	H, K

M	1	Draft of POS completed	F, I, J, L
N	0.14	All material sent to bond rating services	M
O	0.28	POS printed and distributed to all interested parties	M
P	1	Presentation to bond rating services (Standard & Poor's, Moody's)	N
Q	1	Bond rating received	P
R	2	Marketing of bonds	O, Q
S	0*	Purchase Contract executed	R
T	0.14	Final Official Statement authorized and completed, legal documents completed	S
U	3	Fulfillment of all terms and conditions of Purchase Contract	S
V	0*	Bond proceeds available to hospital	T, U
W	0*	Hospital's ability to sign construction contract	T, U

*Occurs instantaneously.

FIGURE A10.1
Seasongood & Mayer PERT/CPM Network for Providence Hospital Project

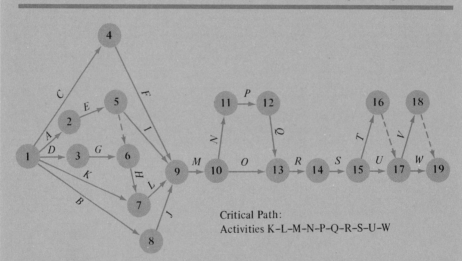

Critical Path:
Activities K–L–M–N–P–Q–R–S–U–W

Questions

1. What is the role of the investment banker in building projects?
2. For the hospital project described, what is the primary objective of the investment banker?
3. Perform the critical path calculations for the network shown in Figure A10.1. Is there more than one critical path? Discuss.

11

Inventory Models

Inventories can be defined as any idle goods or materials that are waiting to be used. For most companies the expenses associated with financing and maintaining inventories are a substantial part of the cost of doing business. In large companies, especially those with many and/or expensive products, the costs associated with raw material, in-process, and finished goods inventories can run into the millions of dollars. To gain an appreciation of how inventory costs arise and what managers can do to control them, let us consider the situation faced by the R & B Beverage Company. R & B Beverage is a distributor of beer, wine, and soft-drink products in central Ohio. From a main warehouse located in Columbus, R & B supplies nearly 1000 retail stores with beverage products.

R & B's beer inventory, which constitutes about 40% of the company's total inventory, averages approximately 50,000 cases. Since the average cost per case is roughly $5, R & B estimates the value of its beer inventory to be $250,000.

There are a number of costs associated with maintaining or carrying a given level of inventory. Taken together, these costs are usually referred to as the *inventory holding costs*. First, there is the cost of financing. If money is borrowed to maintain the inventory investments, an interest charge is incurred. If the firm's own money is used, there is an opportunity cost associated with not being able to use the money for other investments. In either case, a financing charge exists in the form of an interest cost for the capital tied up in inventory. The *cost of capital* is usually expressed as a percentage of the amount invested. Since R & B estimates its cost of capital at an annual rate of 18%, this portion of the inventory cost is 0.18($250,000) = $45,000 per year.

There are a number of other costs such as insurance, taxes, breakage, pilferage,and warehouse overhead that also depend for the most part on the value of the inventory. R & B estimates these other costs at an annual rate of approximately 7% of the value of its inventory. Thus total inventory holding cost for the R & B beer inventory is 25% of its value, or 0.25 ($250,000) = $62,500 per year. When we consider that the beer constitutes only about 40% of R & B's total inventory, we can begin to see that inventory holding cost is a major expense for the R & B Beverage Company.

Managers are faced with the dual problems of maintaining sufficient inventories to meet demand for goods and at the same time incurring the lowest possible inventory

444   CHAPTER ELEVEN

holding cost. Basically, managers attempt to solve these problems by making the best possible decisions with respect to the following:

1. How much should be ordered when the inventory for a given item is replenished?
2. When should the inventory for a given item be replenished?

The purpose of this chapter is to show how quantitative models can assist in making the above decisions. While there are many similarities in all inventory systems, each system also has unique characteristics that prevent the application of one or two general inventory models to all situations. We will first consider *deterministic* inventory models where it is reasonable to assume that the demand for the item occurs at a known and constant rate. Later we will consider *probabilistic* inventory models where the demand for the item fluctuates and can only be described in probabilistic terms. In the final section of the chapter we describe the inventory procedure referred to as *material requirements planning* or MRP. This approach to inventory management is well suited for raw materials, subassemblies and components whose demand is directly dependent upon the demand for final products in the inventory system.

11.1   ECONOMIC ORDER QUANTITY (EOQ) MODEL

The best known and most fundamental inventory model is the *economic order quantity (EOQ) model*. This model is applicable when the demand for the item has a constant, or nearly constant, rate and when the entire quantity ordered arrives in the inventory at one point in time. The *constant demand rate* condition simply means that the same number of units are taken from inventory each period of time, such as five units every day, 25 units every week, 100 units every 4-week period, and so on.

Let us see how the EOQ model can be applied by the R & B Beverage Company. R & B's warehouse manager has conducted a preliminary analysis of overall inventory costs and has decided to do a detailed study of one product for the purpose of establishing the *how-much*-to-order and *when*-to-order decision rules that will result in the lowest possible inventory cost for the product. The manager has selected R & B's number one selling beer, Bub, for this study.

The historical demand data for Bub during the past 10 weeks are as follows:

Week	Demand (cases)
1	2,000
2	2,025
3	1,950
4	2,000
5	2,100
6	2,050
7	2,000
8	1,975
9	1,900
10	2,000
Total cases	20,000
Average cases per week	2,000

Strictly speaking, the above weekly demand figures do not show a constant demand rate. However, given the relatively low variability exhibited by the weekly demands, inventory planning with a constant demand rate of 2000 cases per week appears acceptable.

In practice you will find that the real inventory situation seldom, if ever, satisfies the assumptions of the model exactly. Thus in any particular application it is the job of the manager and the management scientist to determine whether the model assumptions are close enough to reality for the model to be useful. In this situation, since demand varies from a low of 1900 cases to a high of 2100 cases, it appears that the assumption of constant demand of 2000 cases per week is a reasonable approximation.

The how-much-to-order decision involves selecting an order quantity that draws a compromise between (1) keeping small inventories and ordering frequently and (2) keeping large inventories and ordering infrequently. The first alternative would result in undesirably high ordering costs, while the second alternative would result in undesirably high inventory holding costs. In order to find an optimal compromise between these conflicting alternatives, let us develop a mathematical model that will show the total cost[1] as the sum of the inventory holding cost and the ordering cost.

Inventory holding or *inventory carrying costs* are costs that are dependent upon the size of the inventory; that is, larger inventories require larger inventory holding costs. Since R & B estimates its annual inventory holding costs to be 25% of the value of its inventory and since the cost of one case of Bub beer is $5, the cost of holding or carrying one case of Bub beer in inventory for one year is 0.25($5) = $1.25. Note that defining the inventory holding cost as a percentage of value of the product is convenient because it is easily transferable to other products. For example, a case of Carle's Red Ribbon Beer ($4.20/case) would have an annual inventory holding cost of 0.25($4.20) = $1.05 per case.

The next step in our inventory analysis is to determine the cost of placing an order. For R & B the largest portion of this cost involves the salaries of the purchasers. An analysis of the purchasing process showed that a purchaser spends approximately 45 minutes preparing and processing an order for Bub beer. This amount of time is required regardless of the number of cases ordered. With a wage rate and fringe benefit cost for purchasers of $16 per hour, the labor portion of the ordering cost is $12. Making allowances for paper, postage, telephone, transportation, and receiving costs at $8 per order, the manager estimates that the cost of ordering is $20 per order. That is, R & B is paying $20 per order regardless of the quantity requested in the order.

The inventory holding costs, the order costs, and the demand information are the three data items that must be prepared prior to the use of the EOQ model. Since these data have now been developed for the R & B example, let us see how they are used to develop a total cost model. We begin by defining Q to be the order quantity. Thus the *how-much*-to-order decision involves finding the value of Q which will minimize the sum of inventory holding and ordering costs.

The inventory level for Bub will have a maximum value of Q units when the order of size Q is received from the supplier. R & B will then satisfy customer demand from inventory until the inventory is depleted, at which time another shipment of Q units will be received. With the assumption of a constant demand rate of 2000 cases per week or,

---

[1]While management scientists typically refer to "total cost" models for inventory systems, often these models describe only the total *variable* or total *relevant* costs for the decision being considered. Costs that are not affected by the how-much-to-order decision are considered fixed or constant and are not included in the model.

assuming R & B is open five days each week, 400 cases per day, the sketch of the inventory level for Bub beer is shown in Figure 11.1.

FIGURE 11.1
Sketch of the Inventory Level for Bub Beer

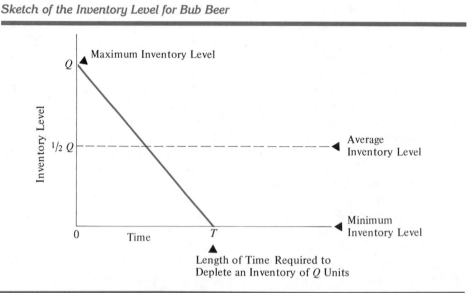

Note that the sketch indicates that the average inventory level for the period in question is ½ Q. This should appear reasonable since the maximum inventory level is Q, the minimum is 0, and the inventory level declines at a constant rate over the period.

Figure 11.1 shows the inventory pattern during one order cycle of length T. As time goes on, this pattern will repeat. The complete inventory pattern is shown in Figure 11.2.

FIGURE 11.2
Inventory Pattern for the EOQ Inventory Decision Model

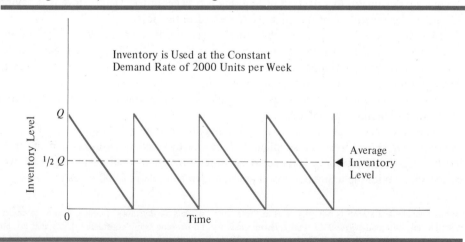

If the average inventory during each cycle is ½ Q, the average inventory level over any number of cycles is also ½ Q. Thus, as long as the time period involved contains an integral number of order cycles, the average inventory for the period will be ½ Q.

The inventory holding cost can be calculated using the average inventory level. That is, we can calculate the inventory holding cost by multiplying the average inventory by the cost of carrying one unit in inventory for the stated period. The period of time selected for the model is up to you; it could be 1 week, 1 month, 1 year, or more. However, since the inventory carrying costs for many industries and businesses are expressed as an *annual* percentage or rate, most inventory models are developed on an *annual cost* basis.

Let

$$I = \text{annual inventory carrying charge (25\% for R \& B)}$$
$$C = \text{unit cost of the inventory item (\$5 for Bub beer).}$$

The cost of storing or holding one unit in inventory for the year, denoted by C_h, is given by $C_h = IC$, which for Bub is $0.25(\$5) = \$1.25$. Thus the general equation for annual inventory holding cost is as follows:

$$\begin{pmatrix} \text{Annual inventory} \\ \text{holding cost} \end{pmatrix} = \begin{pmatrix} \text{average} \\ \text{inventory} \end{pmatrix} \begin{pmatrix} \text{annual holding} \\ \text{cost} \\ \text{per unit} \end{pmatrix}$$

$$= \tfrac{1}{2} Q C_h \qquad (11.1)$$

To complete the total cost model, we must now include the ordering cost. Our goal is to express this cost in terms of the order quantity Q. Since the inventory holding cost was expressed as an annual cost, we need to express ordering costs on an annual basis. The first question is, how many orders will be placed during the year? Let D denote the annual demand for the product [for R & B, $D = (52 \text{ weeks})(2000 \text{ cases per week}) = 104{,}000$ cases per year]. We know that by ordering Q units each time we order, we will have to place D/Q orders per year. If C_0 is the cost of placing one order, the general equation for the annual ordering cost is as follows:

$$\begin{pmatrix} \text{Annual ordering} \\ \text{cost} \end{pmatrix} = \begin{pmatrix} \text{number of} \\ \text{orders} \\ \text{per year} \end{pmatrix} \begin{pmatrix} \text{cost} \\ \text{per} \\ \text{order} \end{pmatrix}$$

$$= \left(\frac{D}{Q}\right) C_0 \qquad (11.2)$$

Thus the total annual cost—inventory holding cost plus ordering cost—can be expressed as follows:

$$\text{TC} = \tfrac{1}{2}QC_h + \frac{D}{Q}C_0 \qquad (11.3)$$

Using the Bub beer data, the total cost model with $C_h = \$1.25$, $C_0 = \$20$, and $D = 104,000$ becomes

$$\text{TC} = \tfrac{1}{2}Q(\$1.25) + \frac{104,000}{Q}(\$20) = 0.625\,Q + \frac{2,080,000}{Q} \qquad (11.4)$$

The development of the above total cost model has gone a long way toward helping solve the inventory problem. We now are able to express the total annual cost as a function of *how much* should be ordered. The development of a realistic total cost model is perhaps the most important part of applying quantitative techniques to inventory decision making. Equation (11.3) is the general total cost equation for inventory situations in which the assumptions of the economic order quantity model are valid.

The How-Much-to-Order Decison

The next step is to find the order quantity Q that does in fact minimize the total cost as stated in equation (11.4). Using a trial-and-error approach we can compute the total cost for several possible order quantities. As a starting point, let us consider $Q = 8000$. The total annual cost is

$$\text{TC} = 0.625\,(8000) + \frac{2,080,000}{8000} = \$5260$$

A trial order quantity of 5000 gives

$$\text{TC} = 0.625\,(5000) + \frac{2,080,000}{5000} = \$3541$$

The results of several other trial order quantities are shown in Table 11.1. As can be seen, the lowest cost solution is around 2000 units. Graphs of the inventory holding, ordering, and total costs are shown in Figure 11.3.

TABLE 11.1
Inventory Holding and Ordering Costs for Various Order Quantities of Bub Beer

Order Quantity	Annual Inventory Holding Cost	Annual Ordering Cost	Annual Total Cost
5000	$3125	$ 416	$3541
4000	2500	520	3020
3000	1875	693	2568
2000	1250	1040	2290
1000	625	2080	2705

FIGURE 11.3
Graph of Annual Inventory Holding, Ordering, and Total Cost for Bub Beer

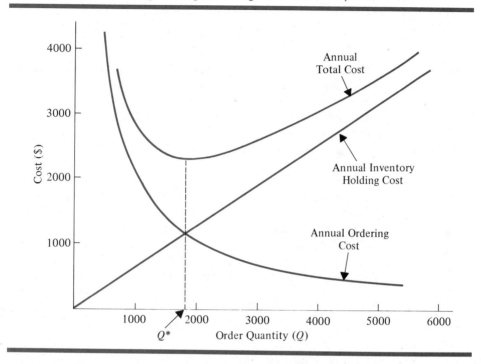

The advantage of the trial-and-error approach is that it is rather easy to do and provides the total cost for a number of possible order quantity decisions. Also, we can see that approximately 2000 units appears to be the minimum cost order quantity. The disadvantage of this approach, however, is that it does not provide the exact minimum cost order quantity.

Refer to Figure 11.3. The minimum total cost order quantity is denoted by an order size of Q^*. By using differential calculus it can be shown (see Appendix 11.1) that the value of Q^* that minimizes the total cost is given by the formula

$$Q^* = \sqrt{\frac{2DC_0}{C_h}} \tag{11.5}$$

This formula is well known to management scientists and is referred to as the *economic order quantity (EOQ) formula*.

Using (11.5), the minimum total cost order quantity for Bub beer is

$$Q^* = \sqrt{\frac{2(104,000)20}{1.25}} = \sqrt{3,328,000} = 1824$$

The use of an order quantity of 1824 in equation (11.4) shows that the minimum cost inventory policy for Bub beer has a total annual cost of $2280. Note that $Q^* = 1824$

has balanced the inventory holding cost and the ordering cost. Check for yourself to see that these costs are equal.[2] Problem 2 at the end of the chapter will ask you to show that equal inventory holding cost and ordering cost are a property of the EOQ model.

The When-to-Buy Decision

Now that we know how much to order, we want to address the question of *when* to order. The when-to-order decision is most often expressed in terms of a *reorder point*—the inventory level at which a new order should be placed. For this purpose, the *inventory level* is considered the amount on hand plus the amount on order.

The manufacturer of Bub beer guarantees a 2-day delivery on any order placed by R & B. Hence, assuming a constant demand rate of 2000 cases per week or 400 cases per day, we expect (2 days) (400 cases/day) = 800 cases of Bub to be sold during the 2 days it takes a new order of Bub to reach the R & B warehouse. In inventory terminology, the 2-day delivery period is referred to as the *lead time* for a new order, and the 800 cases of demand anticipated during this period is referred to as the *lead time demand*. Thus R & B should order a new shipment of Bub beer from the manufacturer when the inventory level reaches a level of 800 cases. For inventory systems using the constant demand rate assumption and a fixed lead time, the reorder point is the same as the lead time demand. The general expression for the reorder point is given as follows:

$$r = dm \tag{11.6}$$

where

r = reorder point
d = demand per day
m = lead time for a new order in days

We note that whenever the lead time demand exceeds Q^* there will be at least one order outstanding when a new order is placed. For instance, if lead time demand for Bub beer were 2000 cases, we would place a new order for 1824 cases of Bub beer whenever inventory on hand plus inventory on order dropped to 2000 cases. Thus, the amount of inventory on hand when a new order is placed would be 176 = 2000 − 1824 cases and the amount on order would be 1824 cases.

The question of how frequently the order will be placed can now be answered. This period between orders is referred to as the *cycle time*.Previously [see equation (11.2)] we defined D/Q as the number of orders that will be placed in a year. Thus D/Q^* = 104,000/1824 = 57 is the number of orders R & B will place for Bub each year. If R & B places 57 orders over 250 working days, they will order approximately every 250/57 = 4.4 working days. Thus the cycle time is computed to be 4.4 working days. The general expression[3] for a cycle time of T days is given by

$$T = \frac{250}{D/Q^*} = \frac{250Q^*}{D} \tag{11.7}$$

[2]Actually, Q^* from equation (11.5) is 1824.28, but since we cannot order fractional cases of beer, a Q^* of 1824 is shown. This value of Q^* may cause a few cents deviation between the two costs. If Q^* is used at its exact value, the inventory holding and ordering costs will be exactly the same.
[3]This general expression for cycle time is based upon 250 working days per year. If the firm operated 300 working days per year and wanted to express cycle time in terms of working days, the cycle time would be given by $T = 300Q^*/D$.

Sensitivity Analysis in the EOQ Model

Even though substantial time may have been spent in arriving at the cost per order ($20) and inventory holding cost (25%), we should realize that these figures are at best good estimates. Thus we may want to consider how much the recommended order quantity would change if the estimated ordering and holding costs had been different. To determine this, we can calculate the recommended order quantity under several different cost conditions; Table 11.2 shows the minimum total cost order quantity for several cost possibilities. As you can see from the table, the value of Q^* appears relatively stable, even with some variations in the cost estimates. Based on these results it appears that the best order quantity for Bub is somewhere around 1700 to 2000 units. If operated properly, the total cost for the Bub inventory system should be close to $2200 to $2300 per year. We also note that there is very little risk associated with implementing the calculated order quantity of 1824. In the worst case (when $c_h = \$1.20$, $c_o = \$21$ and the true optimal order quantity $Q^* = 1908$), there is only a $3 increase in the total annual cost; that is, $2292 - $2289 = $3.

TABLE 11.2
Optimal Order Quantities for Several Cost Possibilities

Possible Inventory Holding Cost (%)	Possible Cost per Order	Optimal Order Quantity (Q^*)	Projected Total Cost	
			Using Q^*	Using $Q = 1824$
24	$19	1815	$2178	$2178
24	$21	1908	$2289	$2292
26	$19	1744	$2267	$2269
26	$21	1833	$2383	$2383

From the above analysis we would say that this EOQ model is insensitive to small variations or errors in the cost estimates. This is a property of EOQ models in general, which indicates that if we have at least reasonable estimates of ordering costs and inventory holding costs, we can expect to obtain a good approximation of the true minimum cost order quantity.

The Manager's Use of the EOQ Model

The EOQ model results in a recommended order quantity of 1824 units. Is this the final decision, or should the manager's judgment enter into the establishment of the final inventory policy? Although the model has provided a good order quantity recommendation, it may not have taken into account all aspects of the inventory situation. As a result, the decision maker may want to modify the final order quantity recommendation to meet the unique circumstances of his or her inventory situation. In this case the warehouse manager felt that it would be desirable to increase the order quantity from 1824 units to 2000 units in order to have an order quantity equal to 5 working days' demand. By doing so, R & B can maintain a weekly order cycle.

The warehouse manager also realized that the EOQ model was based on the constant demand rate assumption of 2000 units per week. While this is a good approximation, we must also recognize that sometimes the demand exceeds 2000 units per week. If a reorder point of 800 units is used, we would be expecting an 800-unit demand during the lead time and the new order to arrive exactly when the inventory level reached zero. Such close timing would leave little room for error, and the scheduling of arrivals would be very critical if stockouts were to be avoided. To protect against shortages due to higher-than-expected demands or slightly delayed incoming orders, the warehouse manager recommended a 1200-unit reorder point. Thus under normal conditions R & B will order 2000 cases of Bub whenever the current inventory reaches 1200 units. During the expected 2-day lead time 800 cases should be demanded, and thus 400 cases should be in inventory when an order arrives. The extra 400 cases serves as a safety precaution against a higher-than-expected demand or a delayed incoming order. In general the amount by which the reorder point exceeds the expected lead time demand is referred to as *safety stock*.

The decisions to adjust the order quantity and reorder point were purely judgment decisions and were not necessarily made with a minimum cost objective in mind. However, they are examples of how managerial judgment might interface with the inventory decision model to arrive at a sound inventory policy. The final decision of $Q = 2000$ with a 400-unit safety stock resulted in a total annual cost of $2790.[4]

How Has the EOQ Decision Model Helped?

The EOQ model has objectively included inventory holding costs and ordering costs and, with the aid of some management judgment, has led to a low-cost inventory policy. In addition, the general optimal order quantity model, equation (11.5), is potentially applicable to other R & B products. For example, Red Ribbon beer ($4.20/case), which has an ordering cost of $20.00, a constant demand rate of 1200 cases per week (62,400 cases/year), and a 2-day lead time period, has a recommended order quantity of

$$Q^* = \sqrt{\frac{2(62,400)(20.00)}{(0.25)(4.20)}} = 1542 \text{ cases}$$

a cycle time of $T = (1542/62,400)250 = 6.18$ days, and a reorder point of $r = (240)(2) = 480$ cases.

We will now investigate additional inventory decision models that are designed to make *how-much-* and *when*-to-order decisions for other types of inventory systems.

11.2 ECONOMIC PRODUCTION LOT SIZE MODEL

The following inventory decision model is similar to the EOQ model in that we are attempting to determine *how much* we should order and *when* the order should be placed. Again we will make the assumption of a constant demand rate. However, instead of the goods arriving at the warehouse in a shipment of size Q^* as assumed in the EOQ model, we will assume that units are supplied to inventory at a constant rate over several days

[4]A Q of 2000 units resulted in a total cost of $2290 (see Table 11.1). The additional safety stock inventory of 400 units increases the average inventory by 400 units, since it is on hand all year long. Thus the inventory carrying charge is increased by 1.25(400) = $500, and the total cost of the revised policy is $2290 + $500 = $2790.

or several weeks. The *constant supply rate* assumption implies that the same number of units is supplied to inventory each period of time (for example, 10 units every day, 50 units every week, and so on). This model is designed for production situations in which, once an order is placed, production begins and a constant number of units is added to inventory each day until the production run has been completed.

If we have a production system that produces 50 units per day and we decide to schedule 10 days of production, we have a $50(10) = 500$-unit *production lot size*. In general, if we let Q indicate the production lot size, the approach to the inventory decisions will be similar to the EOQ model; that is, we will attempt to build an inventory holding and ordering cost model that expresses the total annual cost as a function of the production lot size. Then we will attempt to find the production lot size that minimizes the total cost.

One other condition that should be mentioned at this time is that the model will only apply to situations where the production rate is greater than the demand rate. Stated more simply, the production system must be able to satisfy the demand. For instance, if the constant demand rate is 2000 units per week, the production rate must be at least 2000 units per week in order to satisfy demand.

Since we have assumed that the production rate will exceed the demand rate, each day during a production run we will be producing more units than we ship. Thus we will put the excess production into inventory, resulting in a gradual inventory buildup during the production period. When the production run is completed, the inventory will show a gradual decline until a new production run is started. The inventory pattern for this system is shown in Figure 11.4.

FIGURE 11.4
Inventory Pattern for the Production Lot Size Inventory Model

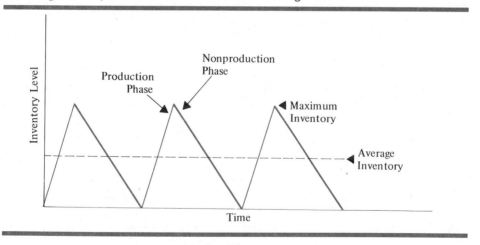

As in the EOQ model, we are now dealing with two costs, the inventory holding cost and the ordering cost. While the inventory holding cost is identical to our definition in the EOQ model, the interpretation of the ordering cost is slightly different. In fact, in a production situation the ordering cost is more correctly referred to as production setup cost. This cost, which includes hours of labor, material, and lost production costs incurred while preparing the production system for operation, is a fixed cost which occurs for every production run, regardless of the production lot size.

The Total Cost Model

Let us begin building the production lot size model by writing the inventory holding cost in terms of the production lot size, Q. Again, the approach will be to develop an expression for average inventory, and then establish the holding costs associated with the average inventory level. We will use a 1-year time period and an annual cost for the model.

We saw in the EOQ model that the average inventory was simply one-half the maximum inventory or $\frac{1}{2} Q$. Since Figure 11.4 shows a constant inventory buildup rate during the production run and a constant inventory depletion rate during the nonproduction period, the average inventory for the production lot size model will also be one-half of the maximum inventory level. However, in this inventory system the production lot size Q does not go into inventory at one point in time, and thus the inventory level never reaches a level of Q units.

Let us see how we can compute the maximum inventory level. First we define the following symbols:

$$d = \text{daily demand rate for the product}$$
$$p = \text{daily production rate for the product}$$
$$t = \text{number of days for a production run}$$

Since we are assuming p will be larger than d, the excess production each day is $p - d$, which is the daily rate of inventory buildup. If we run production for t days and place $p - d$ units in inventory each day, the inventory level at the end of the production run will be $(p - d)t$. From Figure 11.4 we can see that the inventory level at the end of the production run is also the maximum inventory level. Thus

$$\text{Maximum inventory} = (p - d)t \tag{11.8}$$

If we know we are producing a production lot size of Q units at a daily production rate of p units, then $Q = pt$, and the length of the production run t must be

$$t = \frac{Q}{p} \text{ days} \tag{11.9}$$

Thus

$$\text{Maximum inventory} = (p - d)t = (p - d)\left(\frac{Q}{p}\right) \tag{11.10}$$
$$= \left(1 - \frac{d}{p}\right)Q$$

The average inventory, which is one-half of the maximum inventory, is given by

$$\text{Average inventory} = \frac{1}{2}\left(1 - \frac{d}{p}\right)Q \tag{11.11}$$

With an annual inventory holding cost of $C_h = IC$ per unit, the general equation for annual inventory holding cost is as follows:

$$\text{Annual inventory holding cost} = \left(\begin{array}{c}\text{average}\\\text{inventory}\end{array}\right)\left(\begin{array}{c}\text{annual holding}\\\text{cost}\\\text{per unit}\end{array}\right) \quad (11.12)$$

$$= \frac{1}{2}\left(1 - \frac{d}{p}\right)QC_h$$

If D is the annual demand for the product and C_0 is the setup cost for a production run, then the total annual setup cost, which takes the place of the total annual ordering cost in the EOQ model, is as follows:

$$\text{Annual setup cost} = \left(\begin{array}{c}\text{number of production}\\\text{runs per year}\end{array}\right)\left(\begin{array}{c}\text{setup cost}\\\text{per run}\end{array}\right) \quad (11.13)$$

$$= \frac{D}{Q}C_0$$

Thus the total annual cost (TC) model is

$$\text{TC} = \frac{1}{2}\left(1 - \frac{d}{p}\right)QC_h + \frac{D}{Q}C_0 \quad (11.14)$$

Suppose that a production facility operates 250 days per year; 115 days are idle due to weekends and holidays. Then we can write daily demand d in terms of annual demand D as follows:

$$d = \frac{D}{250}$$

Now let P denote the annual production for the product if it were produced every day. Then

$$P = 250p \quad \text{and} \quad p = \frac{P}{250}$$

Thus[5]

$$\frac{d}{p} = \frac{D/250}{P/250} = \frac{D}{P}$$

[5]The ratio $d/p = D/P$ regardless of the number of days of operation; 250 days was used here merely as an illustration.

Therefore we can write the total annual cost as follows:

$$\text{TC} = \frac{1}{2}\left(1 - \frac{D}{P}\right)QC_h + \frac{D}{Q}C_0 \qquad (11.15)$$

Equations (11.14) and (11.15) are equivalent. However, equation (11.15) may be used more frequently since an *annual* cost model tends to make the analyst think in terms of collecting *annual* demand D and *annual* production P data rather than daily rate data.

Finding the Economic Production Lot Size

Given the estimates of the inventory holding cost C_h, setup cost C_0, annual demand rate D, and annual production rate P, we could use a trial-and-error approach to compute the total annual cost for various production lot sizes Q. However, this is not necessary; we can use the minimum cost formula for Q^* that has been developed using differential calculus (see Appendix 11.2). The equation is as follows:

$$Q^* = \sqrt{\frac{2DC_0}{(1 - D/P)C_h}} \qquad (11.16)$$

An Example. Beauty Bar Soap is produced on a production line that has an annual capacity of 60,000 cases. The annual demand is estimated at 26,000 cases, with the demand rate essentially constant throughout the year. The cleaning, preparation, and setup of the production line cost approximately $135.00. The manufacturing cost per case is $4.50, and annual inventory holding cost is figured at a 24% rate. Thus $C_h = IC = 0.24(\$4.50) = \$1.08$. What is the recommended production lot size?
    Using equation (11.16) we have

$$Q^* = \sqrt{\frac{2(26,000)(135)}{(1 - 26,000/60,000)(1.08)}} = \sqrt{\frac{7,020,000}{0.612}} = 3387$$

The total annual cost using equation (11.15) and $Q^* = 3387$ is estimated to be $2073.
    Other relevant data include a 1-week lead time to schedule and set up a production run. Thus a 1-week demand of $26,000/52 = 500$ cases is the reorder point. The cycle time between production runs, using equation (11.7), is estimated to be $T = [(250)(3387)]/26,000$, or about 33 working days. Thus we should plan a production run of 3387 units about every 33 working days.
    Certainly the manager will want to review the model recommendations. Adjusting the recommended $Q^* = 3387$ to a slightly more practical figure and/or adding safety stock may be desirable.

11.3 AN INVENTORY MODEL WITH PLANNED SHORTAGES

In many inventory situations a shortage or stockout—a demand that cannot be supplied from inventory or production—is undesirable and should be avoided if at all possible. However, there are other cases in which it may be desirable—from an economic point of view—to plan for and allow shortages. In practice these types of situations are most commonly found where the value per unit of the inventory is very high and hence the inventory holding cost is high. An example of this type of situation is a new car dealer's inventory. It is not uncommon for a dealer not to have the specific car you want in stock. However, if you are willing to wait a few weeks, the dealer may be able to order a car for you.

The specific model developed in this section allows the type of shortage known as a *backorder*. In a backorder situation an assumption is made that when a customer places an order and discovers that the supplier is out of stock, the customer does not withdraw the order. Rather, the customer waits until the next shipment arrives, and then the order is filled. Frequently the waiting period in backordering situations will be relatively short and, by promising the customer top priority and immediate delivery when the goods become available, companies may be able to convince customers to wait for the order. In these cases the backorder assumption is valid. If for a particular product a firm finds that a shortage causes the customer to withdraw the order and a lost sale results, the backorder model would not be the appropriate inventory model.

Using the backorder assumption for shortages, we will develop an extension to the EOQ model presented in Section 11.1. The EOQ model assumptions of the goods arriving in inventory all at one time and a constant demand rate for the product will be used. If we let S indicate the amount of the shortage or the number of backorders that have accumulated when a new shipment of size Q is received, then the inventory system for the backorder case has the following characteristics:

1. With S backorders existing when a new shipment of size Q arrives, the S backorders will be shipped to the appropriate customers immediately and the remaining $Q - S$ units will be placed in inventory.
2. $Q - S$ will be the maximum inventory level.
3. The inventory cycle of T days will be divided into two distinct phases; t_1 days when inventory is on hand and orders are filled as they occur and t_2 days when there are stockouts and all orders are placed on backorder.

The inventory pattern for this model, where negative inventory represents the number of backorders, is shown in Figure 11.5.

With the inventory pattern now defined, we should be able to proceed with the basic step of all inventory models; namely, the development of a total cost expression. For the inventory model with backorders we will encounter the usual inventory holding costs and ordering costs. In addition, we will incur a backorder cost in terms of the labor and special delivery costs directly associated with the handling of the backorders. Another portion of the backorder cost can be expressed as a loss of goodwill with customers due to the fact that customers will have to wait for their orders. Since the *goodwill cost* depends upon how long the customer has to wait, it is customary to adopt the convention

FIGURE 11.5
Inventory Pattern for an Inventory Model with Backorders

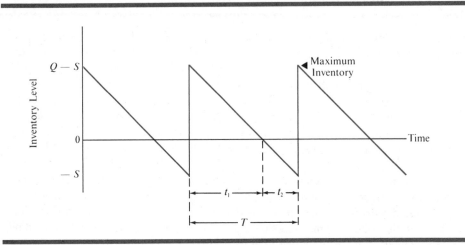

of expressing all backorder costs in terms of how much it costs to have a unit on backorder for a stated period of time. This method of costing backorders on a time basis is similar to the method we have used to compute the inventory holding cost.

Using this method for costing backorders, we can compute a total annual cost of backorders once the average backorder level and the backorder cost per unit per unit time are known.

Admittedly, the backorder cost rate (especially the goodwill cost) is difficult to determine in practice. However, noting that EOQ models are rather insensitive to the cost estimates (see Table 11.2), we should feel confident that reasonable estimates of the backorder cost will lead to a good approximation of the overall minimum cost inventory policy.

Let us begin the development of a total cost model by showing how to calculate the inventory holding costs. First we use a small hypothetical example to suggest a procedure for computing the average inventory level. If we have an average inventory of 2 units for 3 days and no inventory on the fourth day, what is the average inventory level over the 4-day period? It is

$$\frac{2 \text{ units (3 days)} + 0 \text{ units (1 day)}}{4 \text{ days}} = \frac{6}{4} = 1.5 \text{ units}$$

Refer to Figure 11.5. You can see that the above situation is exactly what happens in the backorder model. With a maximum inventory of $Q - S$ units the t_1 days we have inventory on hand will have an average inventory of $(Q - S)/2$. No inventory is carried for the t_2 days in which we experience backorders. Thus over the total cycle time of $T = t_1 + t_2$ days, we can compute the average inventory level as follows:

$$\text{Average inventory level} = \frac{\frac{1}{2}(Q - S) t_1 + 0 t_2}{t_1 + t_2} = \frac{\frac{1}{2}(Q - S) t_1}{T} \qquad (11.17)$$

Can we find other ways of expressing t_1 and T? Since we know that the maximum inventory is $Q - S$ and that d represents the constant daily demand, we have

$$t_1 = \frac{Q - S}{d} \text{ days} \tag{11.18}$$

That is, the maximum inventory level of $Q - S$ units will be used up in $(Q - S)/d$ days. Since Q units are ordered and shipped each cycle, we know the length of a cycle must be

$$T = \frac{Q}{d} \text{ days} \tag{11.19}$$

Using equations (11.18) and (11.19) with equation (11.17), we can write the following:

$$\text{Average inventory level} = \frac{\frac{1}{2}(Q - S)[(Q - S)/d]}{Q/d} = \frac{(Q - S)^2}{2Q} \tag{11.20}$$

Thus the average inventory level is expressed in terms of two inventory decisions, how much we order (Q) and the maximum number of backorders we will allow (S).

The formula for the annual number of orders placed under this model is identical to that for the EOQ model. With D representing the annual demand we have

$$\text{Annual number of orders} = \frac{D}{Q} \tag{11.21}$$

The next step is to develop an expression for the average backorder level. Since there is a maximum of S backorders, we can use the same logic that we used to establish average inventory to find the average number of backorders. We have an average number of backorders during the period t_2 of $\frac{1}{2}$ the maximum number of backorders or $\frac{1}{2} S$. Since we do not have any backorders during the t_1 days we have inventory, we can calculate the average backorder level in a manner similar to equation (11.17). Using this approach, we have

$$\text{Average backorder level} = \frac{0t_1 + (S/2)t_2}{T} = \frac{(S/2)t_2}{T} \tag{11.22}$$

Since we let the maximum number of backorders reach an amount S at a daily rate of d, the length of the backorder portion of the inventory cycle is

$$t_2 = \frac{S}{d} \tag{11.23}$$

Using equations (11.23) and (11.19) in equation (11.22), we have

$$\text{Average backorder level} = \frac{(S/2)(S/d)}{Q/d} = \frac{S^2}{2Q} \tag{11.24}$$

Let

$$C_h = \text{cost to maintain one unit in inventory for 1 year}$$
$$C_0 = \text{cost per order}$$
$$C_b = \text{cost to maintain one unit on backorder for 1 year}$$

The total annual cost expression (TC) for the inventory model with backorders becomes

$$TC = \frac{(Q - S)^2}{2Q} C_h + \frac{D}{Q} C_0 + \frac{S^2}{2Q} C_b \qquad (11.25)$$

Given the cost estimates C_h, C_0, and C_b and the annual demand D, we can determine the minimum cost values for the inventory decisions, Q and S. With two decision components a trial-and-error approach, while valid, becomes cumbersome. Using calculus, management scientists have established the following minimum cost formulas for the order quantity Q^* and the planned backorders S^* (see Appendix 11.3):

$$Q^* = \sqrt{\frac{2DC_0}{C_h}\left(\frac{C_h + C_b}{C_b}\right)} \qquad (11.26)$$

and

$$S^* = Q^*\left(\frac{C_h}{C_h + C_b}\right) \qquad (11.27)$$

An Example.   Suppose the Higley Radio Components Company has a product for which the assumptions of the inventory model with backorders are valid. Information obtained by the company is as follows:

$$D = 2000 \text{ units per year}$$
$$I = 20\% \text{ per year}$$
$$C = \$50 \text{ per unit}$$
$$C_h = IC = \$10 \text{ per unit per year}$$
$$C_0 = \$25 \text{ per order}$$

The company is considering the possibility of allowing some backorders to occur for the product. The annual unit backorder cost has been estimated to be approximately $30 per unit per year. Using equations (11.26) and (11.27), we have

$$Q^* = \sqrt{\frac{2(2000)(25)}{10}\left(\frac{10 + 30}{30}\right)} = \sqrt{10,000(^{40}\!/_{30})} = 115$$

and

$$S^* = 115\left(\frac{10}{10 + 30}\right) = 115(^{10}\!/_{40}) = 29$$

If this solution is implemented, the system will operate with the following properties:

$$\text{Maximum inventory} = Q - S = 115 - 29 = 86$$

$$\text{Cycle time} = T = \frac{Q}{D}(250) = 14.4 \text{ working days}$$

The total annual cost is

$$\text{Inventory holding cost} = \frac{(86)^2}{2(115)}(10) = \$322$$

$$\text{Ordering cost} = \frac{2000}{115}(25) = \$435$$

$$\text{Backorder cost} = \frac{(29)^2}{2(115)}(30) = \underline{\$110}$$

$$\text{Total cost} \qquad \$867$$

If the company had chosen to prohibit backorders and had adopted the regular EOQ model, the recommended inventory decision would have been

$$Q* = \sqrt{\frac{2DC_0}{C_h}} = \sqrt{10,000} = 100$$

This order quantity would have resulted in an inventory holding cost and ordering cost of $500 each or a total annual cost of $1000. Thus in this example, allowing back orders is projecting a $1000 − $867 = $133 or 13.3% savings in cost from the no-stockout EOQ model. The above comparison and conclusion are based on the assumption that the backorder model (no lost sales) with an annual cost per backordered unit of $30 is a valid model for the actual inventory situation. If the company has strong fears that stockouts might lead to lost sales, then the above savings might not be enough to warrant switching to an inventory policy that allowed for planned shortages.

Note that as the backordering cost C_b becomes large relative to the inventory holding cost C_h, the quantity $C_h/(C_h + C_b)$ in equation (11.27) will be relatively small, and thus $S*$ will also be small. In this case the backorder model and the regular EOQ model provide very similar results. Also note that as the holding costs ($C_h = IC$) become large, the number of backorders S becomes larger. This explains why many items that have a very high per-unit cost, C, are handled on a backorder basis.

11.4 QUANTITY DISCOUNTS FOR THE EOQ MODEL

Quantity discounts occur in numerous businesses and industries where suppliers provide an incentive for large purchase quantities by offering lower unit costs when items are purchased in larger lots or quantities. In this section we show how the EOQ model can be used when quantity discounts are offered.

Assume that we have a product where the basic EOQ model is applicable, but instead of a fixed unit cost, the supplier quotes the following discount schedule:

Discount Category	Order Size	Discount	Unit Cost
1	0 to 999	0%	$5.00
2	1000 to 2499	3%	$4.85
3	2500 and over	5%	$4.75

The 5% discount for the 2500-unit minimum order quantity looks tempting; however, realizing that higher order quantities result in higher inventory carrying costs, we should prepare a thorough cost analysis before making a final ordering and inventory policy recommendation.

Suppose the data and cost analysis show an inventory holding cost rate of 20% per year, ordering costs of $49 per order, and an annual demand of 5000 units; what order quantity should we select? The following three-step procedure shows the calculations necessary to make this decision. In our preliminary calculations we will use Q_1 to indicate the order quantity for discount category 1, Q_2 for discount category 2, and Q_3 for discount category 3.

Step 1   For each discount category, compute a Q^* using the EOQ formula for the unit cost associated with the discount category.

Recall that the EOQ model provides $Q^* = \sqrt{2DC_0/C_h}$. In this case for the three discount categories, we obtain,

$$Q_1^* = \sqrt{\frac{2(5000)49}{(0.20)(5.00)}} = 700$$

$$Q_2^* = \sqrt{\frac{2(5000)49}{(0.20)(4.85)}} = 711$$

$$Q_3^* = \sqrt{\frac{2(5000)49}{(0.20(4.75)}} = 718$$

Since the only differences in the EOQ formulas are slight differences in the inventory holding costs, the economic order quantities resulting from this step will be approximately the same. However, these order quantities will usually not all be of the size necessary to qualify for the discount price assumed. In the above case, both Q_2^* and Q_3^* are insufficient order quantities to obtain their assumed discounted costs of $4.85 and $4.75, respectively. For those order quantities for which the assumed price is incorrect, the following procedure must then be used.

Step 2 For those $Q*$'s that are too small to qualify for the assumed discount price, adjust the order quantity upward to the nearest order quantity which will allow the product to be purchased at the assumed price.

In our example this causes us to set

$$Q_2^* = 1000$$

and

$$Q_3^* = 2500$$

If a calculated $Q*$ for a given discount price is large enough to qualify for a bigger discount, that value of $Q*$ cannot lead to an optimal solution. While the reason may not be obvious, it does turn out to be a property of the EOQ quantity discount model. Problem 23 at the end of the chapter will ask you to show that this property is true.

In the previous inventory models considered we have ignored the annual purchase cost of the item because it was constant and never affected by the inventory-order policy decision. However, in the quantity discount model total annual purchase cost depends on the order quantity decision and the associated unit cost. Thus annual purchase cost (annual demand D × unit cost C) is included in the total cost model as shown below:

$$\text{TC} = \frac{Q}{2} C_h + \frac{D}{Q} C_0 + DC \qquad (11.28)$$

Using this total cost formula we can determine the optimal order quantity for the EOQ discount model in step 3 below.

Step 3 For each of the order quantities resulting from step 1 and step 2, compute the total annual cost using the unit price from the appropriate discount category and equation (11.28). The order quantity yielding the minimum total annual cost is the optimal order quantity.

The step 3 calculations for the example problem are summarized in Table 11.3. As you can see, a decision to order 1000 units at the 3% discount rate yields the minimum cost solution. While the 2500-unit order quantity would result in a 5% discount, its excessive inventory holding cost makes it the second best solution.

TABLE 11.3
Total Annual Cost Calculations for the EOQ Quantity Discount Model

Discount Category	Unit Cost	Order Quantity	Annual Inventory Cost	Annual Ordering Cost	Annual Purchase Cost	Total Annual Cost
1	$5.00	700	$ 350	$350	$25,000	$25,700
2	$4.85	1000	$ 485	$245	$24,250	$24,980
3	$4.75	2500	$1188	$ 98	$23,750	$25,036

11.5 ORDER QUANTITY–REORDER POINT MODELS WITH PROBABILISTIC DEMAND

In this section we consider the situation where the demand for the inventory item fluctuates and can only be expressed in probabilistic terms. Since the mathematical sophistication required for an exact formulation of a probabilistic inventory model is beyond the scope of this text, we will restrict the discussion to a probabilistic model where a heuristic procedure can be used to obtain good, workable inventory decisions. While the solution procedure can only be expected to provide approximations of the optimal inventory decisions, it has been found to yield very good decisions in many practical situations.

Let us consider the inventory problem of Dabco Industrial Lighting Distributors. Dabco purchases a special high-intensity light bulb for industrial lighting systems from a well-known light bulb manufacturer. Dabco would like a recommendation on how much to order and when to order so that a low-cost inventory policy can be realized. Pertinent facts are that ordering costs are $12 per order, one bulb costs $6, and Dabco uses a 20% annual holding cost rate for its inventory ($C_h = 0.20 \times 6 = \$1.20$). Dabco, which has over 1000 different customers, experiences a probabilistic demand in that the number of orders will vary considerably from day to day and week to week. While demand is not specifically known, historical sales data indicate that an annual demand of 8000 bulbs, while not exact, can be used as a good estimate of the anticipated annual volume.

The How-Much-to-Order Decision

Although we are in a probabilistic demand situation, we have an estimate of the expected annual volume of 8000 units. As an approximation of the best order quantity we can apply the EOQ model with the expected annual volume substituted for the annual demand D. In Dabco's case,

$$Q^* = \sqrt{\frac{2DC_0}{C_h}} = \sqrt{\frac{2(8000)(12)}{(1.20)}} = 400 \text{ units}$$

When we studied the sensitivity of the EOQ models, we learned that the total cost of operating an inventory system was relatively insensitive to order quantities that were in the neighborhood of Q^*. Using this knowledge, we expect 400 units per order to be a good approximation of the optimal order quantity. Even if annual demand were as low as 7000 units or as high as 9000 units, an order quantity of 400 units should be a relatively good low-cost order size. Thus, given our best estimate of annual demand at 8000 units, we will use $Q^* = 400$.

We have established the 400-unit order quantity by ignoring the fact that demand is probabilistic. Using $Q^* = 400$, Dabco can anticipate placing approximately $D/Q^* = 8000/400 = 20$ orders per year with an average of approximately $250/20 = 12.5$ working days between orders.

The When-to-Order Decision

We now want to establish a when-to-order decision rule or reorder point that will trigger the ordering process. Further pertinent data indicate that it takes a lead time of 1 week for Dabco to receive a new supply of light bulbs from the manufacturer. With an average weekly demand of 8000/52 weeks = 154 units, you might first suggest a 154-unit reorder point. However, it now becomes extremely important to consider the probability of demand. If 154 is the average weekly demand, and if the demands are symmetrically distributed about 154, then weekly demand will be more than 154 units roughtly 50% of the time.

When the demand during the 1-week lead time exceeds 154 units, Dabco will experience a shortage or stockout. Thus with a reorder point of 154 units approximately 50% of the time (10 of the 20 orders a year), Dabco will be short of bulbs before the new supply arrives. This shortage rate would most likely be viewed as unacceptable. In order to determine a reorder point with a reasonably low likelihood or probability of a stockout it is necessary to establish a probability distribution for the lead time demand and analyze stockout probabilities.

Using historical data and some judgment, the *lead time demand distribution* for Dabco's light bulbs is assumed to be a normal distribution with a mean of 154 units and a standard deviation of 25 units. This is shown in Figure 11.6. While the normal distribution of lead time demand is used in the Dabco problem, any demand probability distribution is acceptable. By collecting historical data on actual demands during the lead time period, an analyst should be able to determine if the normal distribution or some other probability distribution is the most realistic representation of the lead time demand distribution.

FIGURE 11.6
Distribution of Demand During the Lead Time for Dabco

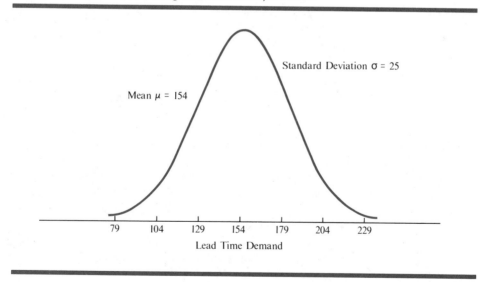

Given the lead time demand probability distribution, we can now determine how the reorder point *r* affects the probability of a stockout. Since stockouts occur whenever the demand during the lead time exceeds the reorder point, we can find the probability of a stockout by using the lead time demand distribution to compute the probability of demand exceeding *r*.

We could now approach the when-to-order problem by defining a cost per stockout and then attempting to include this cost in a total-cost equation. Possibly a more practical approach is to ask management to define an acceptable *service level*, where the service level refers to the average number of stockouts we are willing to allow per year. If demand for a product is probabilistic, a manager who will never tolerate a stockout is being somewhat unrealistic because attempting to avoid stockouts completely will require high reorder points, high inventory levels, and an associated high inventory holding cost.

Suppose in this case that Dabco management is willing to tolerate an average of one stockout per year. Since Dabco places 20 restocking orders per year, this implies management is willing to allow demand during lead time to exceed the reorder point one time in 20, or 5% of the time. This suggests that the reorder point r can be found by using the lead time demand distribution to find the value of r for which there is only a 5% chance of having a lead time demand exceeding it. This situation is shown graphically in Figure 11.7.

FIGURE 11.7
Reorder Point r that Allows a 5% Chance of Stockout for Dabco Light Bulbs

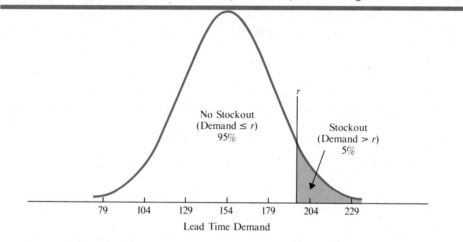

From the normal distribution tables in Appendix A, we see that an r value that is 1.645 standard deviations above the mean will allow stockouts during lead time 5% of the time. Therefore, for the assumed normal distribution for lead time demand with $\mu = 154$ and $\sigma = 25$, the reorder point r is determined by

$$r = 154 + 1.645(25) = 195$$

If a normal distribution is used for lead time demand, the general equation for r is

$$r = \mu + z\sigma \qquad (11.29)$$

where z is the number of standard deviations necessary to obtain the acceptable stockout probability.

Thus the recommended inventory decisions are to order 400 units whenever the inventory level reaches the reorder point of 195. Since the mean or expected demand during the lead time is 154 units, the $195 - 154 = 41$ units serve as a safety stock which absorbs higher-than-usual demand during the lead time. Roughly 95% of the time the 195 units will be able to satisfy demand during the lead time. The anticipated annual cost for this system is as follows:

Ordering cost	$(D/Q)C_0 = (8000/400)12$	$= \$240.00$
Holding cost—normal inventory	$(Q/2)C_h = (400/2)(1.20)$	$= \$240.00$
Holding cost—safety stock	$(41)C_h = 41(1.20)$	$= \underline{\$\ 49.20}$
		$\$529.20$

If Dabco could have assumed that a known, constant demand rate of 8000 units per year existed for the light bulbs, a $Q^* = 400$, $r = 154$, and total annual cost of $\$240 + \$240 = \$480$ would have been optimal. When demand is uncertain and can only be expressed in probabilistic terms, a larger total cost can be expected. The larger cost occurs in the form of larger inventory holding costs due to the fact that more inventory must be maintained in order to limit stockouts. For Dabco this additional inventory or safety stock was 41 units with an additional annual inventory holding cost of $49.20.

11.6 SINGLE-PERIOD INVENTORY MODELS

In the previous treatment of inventory problems we assumed that the inventory system operates continuously and that we will have many repeating cycles or periods. Furthermore, we assumed that the inventory may be carried for one or more repeat periods and that we will be placing repeat orders for the product in the future. The *single-period* inventory model refers to inventory situations in which *one* order is placed for the product; at the end of the period the product has either sold out or there is a surplus of unsold items which will be sold for a salvage value. The single-period models occur in situations involving seasonal or perishable items that cannot be carried in inventory and sold in future periods. Seasonal clothing (such as bathing suits, winter coats) are typically handled in a single-period manner. In these situations a buyer places one preseason order for each item and then experiences a stockout or holds a clearance sale on the surplus stock at the end of the season. No items are carried in inventory and sold the following year. Newspapers are another example of a product that is ordered one time and is either sold or not sold during the single period. While newspapers are ordered daily, they cannot be carried in inventory and sold in later periods. Thus newspaper orders may be treated as a sequence of single-period models; that is, each day or period is separate, and a single-period inventory decision must be made each period (day). Since we only order once for the period, the only inventory decision we must make is *how much* of the product to order at the start of the period. Because newspaper sales is an excellent example of a single-period situation, the single-period inventory problem is sometimes referred to as the *newsboy problem*.

Obviously, if the demand were known for a single-period inventory situation, the solution would be easy: we would simply order the amount we knew would be demanded. However, in most single-period models the exact demand is not known. In fact, forecasts may show that demand can have a wide variety of values. If we are going to analyze this type of inventory decision problem in a quantitative manner, we will need information about the probabilities associated with the various demand possibilities. Thus the single-period model is another type of probabilistic demand model.

Let us consider a single-period inventory model that could be used to make a how-much-to-order decision for the Johnson Shoe Company. The buyer for the Johnson Shoe Company has decided to order a shoe for men that has just been shown at a buyers' meeting in New York City. The shoe will be part of the company's spring–summer promotion and will be sold through nine retail stores in the Chicago area. Since the shoe is designed for spring and summer months, it cannot be expected to sell in the fall. Johnson plans to hold a special August clearance sale in an attempt to sell all shoes that have not been sold by July 31. The shoes cost $40 per pair and retail for $60 per pair. At the sale price of $30 per pair, it is expected that all surplus shoes can be sold during the August sale. If you were the buyer for the Johnson Shoe Company, how many pairs of the shoes would you order?

An obvious question at this time is, what are the possible levels of demand for the shoe? We will need this information in order to answer the question of how much to order. Let us suppose that the uniform probability distribution shown in Figure 11.8 can be used to describe the demand for the size 10D shoes. In particular, note that the range of demand is from 350 to 650 pairs of shoes with an average or expected demand of 500 pairs of shoes.

FIGURE 11.8
Uniform Probability Distribution of Demand for the Johnson Shoe Company Size 10D Shoes

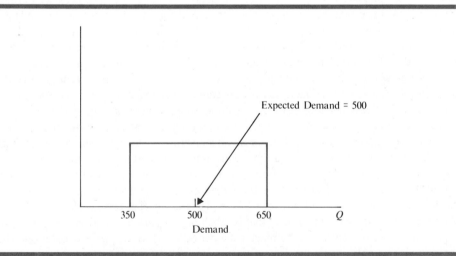

Let us show how the method of *incremental analysis* can be used to determine the optimal order quantity for a single-period inventory model. Incremental analysis addresses the how-much-to-order question by comparing the cost or loss of *ordering one additional unit* with the cost or loss of *not ordering one additional unit*. The costs involved are defined as follows:

c_o = the cost per unit of *overestimating* demand;
    this cost represents the loss of ordering one additional unit
    and finding that it cannot be sold.

c_u = the cost per unit of *underestimating* demand; this
    cost represents the opportunity loss of not ordering one additional
    unit and finding that it could have been sold.

In the Johnson Shoe Company example, the company will incur the cost of overestimating demand whenever it orders too much and has to sell the extra shoes during the August sale. Thus the cost per unit of overestimating demand is equal to the purchase cost per unit minus the August sales price per unit; that is; c_o = \$40 − \$30 = \$10. That is, Johnson will lose \$10 for each pair of shoes that it orders over the quantity demanded. The cost of underestimating demand is the lost profit (opportunity loss) due to the fact that a pair of shoes that could have been sold was not available in inventory. Thus the per-unit cost of underestimating demand is the difference between the regular selling price per unit and the purchase cost per unit; that is, c_u = \$60 − \$40 = \$20.

Since the exact level of demand for the size 10D shoes is unknown, we will have to consider the probability of demand and thus the probability of obtaining the above costs or losses. For example, let us assume that the Johnson Shoe Company wished to consider an order quantity equal to the average or expected demand for 500 pairs of shoes. In incremental analysis we will consider the possible losses associated with an order quantity of 501 (ordering one additional unit) and an order quantity of 500 (not ordering one additional unit). The order quantity alternatives and the possible losses are summarized below:

Order Quantity Alternatives	Loss Occurs If	Possible Loss	Probability Loss Occurs
Q = 501	Demand overestimated: The additional unit *cannot* be sold	c_o = \$10	P(demand $\leq$ 500)
Q = 500	Demand underestimated: An additional unit *could have* been sold	c_u = \$20	P(demand $>$ 500)

By looking at the demand probability distribution in Figure 11.8, we see that P(demand $\leq$ 500) = 0.50 and that P(demand $>$ 500) = 0.50. By multiplying the possible losses, c_o = \$10 and c_u = \$20, by the probability of obtaining the loss, we can compute the expected value of the loss, or simply the *expected loss* (EL), associated with the order quantity alternatives. Thus

$$\text{EL}(Q = 501) = c_o\, P(\text{demand} \leq 500) = \$10(0.50) = \$\ 5$$
$$\text{EL}(Q = 500) = c_u\, P(\text{demand} > 500) = \$20(0.50) = \$10$$

Based on the above expected losses, do you prefer an order quantity of 501 or an order quantity of 500 pairs of shoes? Since the expected loss is greater for $Q = 500$, and since we want to avoid this higher cost or loss, we should make $Q = 501$ the preferred decision. We could now consider incrementing the order quantity one additional unit to $Q = 502$ and repeating the above expected loss calculations.

While we could continue this unit-by-unit analysis, it would be very time consuming and cumbersome. We would have to evaluate $Q = 502$, $Q = 503$, $Q = 504$, and so on, until we found the value of Q where the expected loss of ordering one incremental unit is equal to the expected loss of not ordering one incremental unit; that is, the optimal order quantity Q^* occurs when the incremental analysis shows that

$$EL(Q^* + 1) = EL(Q^*) \tag{11.30}$$

When the above relationship holds, there is no economic advantage to increasing the order quantity by one additional unit. Using the logic we used to compute the expected losses for the order quantities of 501 and 500, the general expressions for $EL(Q^* + 1)$ and $EL(Q^*)$ can be written

$$EL(Q^* + 1) = c_o\, P(\text{demand} \le Q^*) \tag{11.31}$$

$$EL(Q^*) = c_u\, P(\text{demand} > Q^*) \tag{11.32}$$

Since we know from basic probability that

$$P(\text{demand} \le Q^*) + P(\text{demand} > Q^*) = 1 \tag{11.33}$$

we can write

$$P(\text{demand} > Q^*) = 1 - P(\text{demand} \le Q^*) \tag{11.34}$$

Using this expression, (11.32) can be rewritten as

$$EL(Q^*) = c_u\, [1 - P(\text{demand} \le Q^*)] \tag{11.35}$$

Expressions (11.31) and (11.35) can be used to show that $EL(Q^* + 1) = EL(Q^*)$ whenever

$$c_o\, P(\text{demand} \le Q^*) = c_u\, [1 - P(\text{demand} \le Q^*)] \tag{11.36}$$

Solving for $P(\text{demand} \le Q^*)$, we have

$$P(\text{demand} \le Q^*) = \frac{c_u}{c_u + c_o} \tag{11.37}$$

The above expression provides the general condition for the optimal order quantity Q^* in any single-period inventory model.

In the Johnson Shoe Company example, we found that $c_o = \$10$ and $c_u = \$20$. Thus (11.37) shows that the optimal order size for Johnson shoes must satisfy the following condition:

$$P(\text{demand} \le Q^*) = \frac{c_u}{c_u + c_o} = \frac{20}{20 + 10} = \frac{20}{30} = \frac{2}{3}$$

We can find the optimal order quantity Q^* by referring to the assumed probability distribution shown in Figure 11.8 and finding the value of Q that will provide P (demand $\leq Q^*$) = $\frac{2}{3}$. In order to do this, we note that in the uniform distribution the probability is evenly distributed over the range from 350 to 650 pairs of shoes. Thus we can satisfy the expression for Q^* by moving two-thirds of the way from 350 to 650. Since this is a range of $650 - 350 = 300$, we move 200 units from 350 toward 650. Doing so provides the optimal order quantity of 550 pairs of size 10D shoes.

In summary, the key to establishing an optimal order quantity for single-period inventory models is to identify the probability distribution that describes the demand for the item and the costs of overestimation and underestimation. Then, using the information for the cost of overestimation and underestimation, equation (11.37) can be used to find the location of Q^* in the probability distribution. Thus in the Johnson Shoe Company example, the condition that P (demand ≤ 550) = $\frac{2}{3}$ resulted in an optimal order quantity Q^* of 550 pairs of size 10D shoes.

We note that in equation (11.37) the value of $c_u/(c_u + c_o)$ will be equal to 0.50 whenever $c_u = c_o$; in this case, we select an order quantity corresponding to the median of the probability distribution of demand. With this choice, it is just as likely to have a stockout as a surplus. This makes sense since the costs are equal. Whenever $c_u < c_o$ equation (11.37) leads to the choice of an order quantity more likely to be less than demand; hence a higher risk of a stockout is present. However, for the Johnson Shoe example, $c_u > c_o$ and the optimal order quantity leads to a higher risk of a surplus. This can be seen from the fact that the order quantity is 50 pairs of shoes over the expected demand of 500 pairs of shoes. Thus, the optimal order quantity for Johnson has a probability of a stockout of $\frac{1}{3}$ and a probability of a surplus of $\frac{2}{3}$. This is what we should have expected since $c_u = 20$ is greater than $c_o = 10$.

As another example of a single-period inventory model, consider the situation faced by the Kremer Chemical Company, which has a contract with one of its customers to supply a unique liquid chemical product. Historically the customer places orders approximately every 6 months. Since an aging process of 2 months exists for the product, Kremer will have to make its production quantity decision before the customer places an order. Kremer's inventory problem is to determine the number of pounds of the chemical to produce in anticipation of the customer's order.

Kremer's manufacturing costs for the chemical are $15 per pound and the product sells at the fixed contract price of $20 per pound. If Kremer "underproduces," it will be unable to satisfy the customer's demand. When this condition occurs, Kremer has agreed to absorb the added cost of filling the order by purchasing a higher-quality substitute product from another chemical firm. The substitute product, including additional transportation expenses, will cost Kremer $24 per pound. If Kremer "overproduces," it will have more product in inventory than the customer requires. Because of the spoilage potential for the product, Kremer cannot store excess production until the customer's next order. As a result, Kremer reprocesses the excess production and sells the surplus for $5 per pound.

Based on previous experience with the customer's orders, Kremer has established the normal distribution shown in Figure 11.9 as the probability distribution that best describes the possible levels of demand the customer may request. Note that the normal distribution shows an average or expected demand of $\mu = 1000$ pounds with a standard deviation of $\sigma = 100$ pounds. Using Kremer's price and cost data as well as the probability distribution of demand shown in Figure 11.9, how much production should Kremer plan for in anticipation of the customer's order for the liquid chemical?

FIGURE 11.9
Normal Probability Distribution of Demand for Kremer Chemical Company

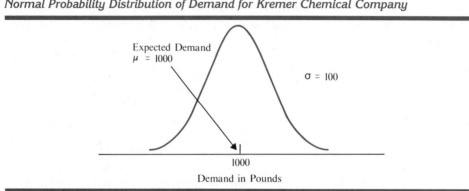

Let us begin by computing the cost of underestimation c_u and the cost of overesti-mation c_o as required for equation (11.37). First, if Kremer underproduces, it will have to purchase a substitute product at a higher cost per unit in order to satisfy the customer's demand for the product. Kremer sells the product to the customer for $20 per pound; however, purchasing the substitute product costs $24 per pound. As a result, Kremer incurs a cost of c_u = $24 − $20 = $4 for every pound of underestimated demand. If Kremer overestimates demand, the company incurs a cost of $15 per pound to manufacture the product and then sells the reprocessed excess product for $5 per pound. Thus, Kremer has a per-unit cost of c_o = $15 − $5 = $10 for overestimating demand.

Applying equation (11.37) indicates that the optimal order quantity must satisfy the following condition:

$$P(\text{demand} \le Q^*) = \frac{c_u}{c_u + c_o} = \frac{4}{4 + 10} = 0.29$$

Now we can use the normal probability distribution for demand as shown in Figure 11.10 to find the order quantity that satisfies the condition that P (demand $\le Q^*$) = 0.29. From Appendix A we see that 0.29 of the area in the left tail of the curve of the

FIGURE 11.10
Probability Distribution of Demand for Kremer Chemical Company Showing the Location of the Optimal Order Quantity Q*

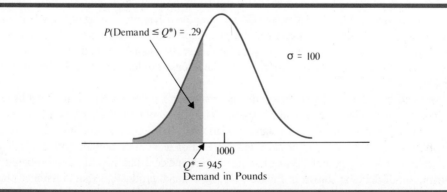

normal distribution occurs at $z = 0.55$ standard deviations *below* the mean. Since the mean or expected demand is given by $\mu = 1000$ and the standard deviation is $\sigma = 100$, we have

$$Q^* = \mu - 0.55\sigma$$
$$= 1000 - 0.55(100) = 945$$

Thus with the assumed normal probability distribution of demand the Kremer Chemical Company should produce 945 pounds of the chemical in anticipation of the customer's order. Note that in this case the cost of underestimation is less than the cost of overestimation. Thus Kremer is willing to risk a higher probability of underestimation and hence a higher probability of a stockout. In fact, Kremer's optimal order quantity has a 0.29 probability of having a surplus and a $1 - 0.29 = 0.71$ probability of a stockout.

In any probabilistic inventory model the assumption about the probability distribution of demand is critical and can affect the recommended inventory decision. Equation (11.37) which provides the critical probability value, $P(\text{demand} \le Q^*)$, can be applied to any demand probability distribution. Thus in using quantitative approaches to inventory decision problems with probabilistic demand we must exercise care in selecting the probability distribution that is the best approximation of reality.

11.7 MATERIAL REQUIREMENTS PLANNING

The inventory models we have discussed thus far have been found to be most appropriate for managing the inventories of finished goods. Finished goods are characterized as having *independent* demands which may be forecast. In this section we focus on the planning and controlling of manufacturing inventories such as raw materials, components, and subassemblies. The demand for these types of items is *dependent* on the amounts of finished goods that are scheduled to be produced and can be *calculated* from the forecasts and scheduled production of finished goods. A technique that can be used to manage dependent-demand inventories is called *material requirements planning*, MRP.

Dependent Demand and the MRP Concept

Let us consider a finished product with one component part in order to illustrate dependent demand and the MRP concept. The demand for the finished product consists of many independent demands from many customers. Since these demands occur somewhat randomly, the demand rate is often fairly constant and the assumptions of the production lot size model are reasonable. The inventory level for the finished product is shown at the top of Figure 11.11. Assume that the single component is purchased from an outside supplier. When production of the finished product is initiated (point *A* on the time axis), the component parts are withdrawn from inventory in order to meet the manufacturing needs. The inventory level of the component part is shown at the bottom of Figure 11.11. When the component inventory level falls below its reorder point, an order for the component is placed with the supplier. The shipment is received at point *B* and the component inventory is replenished. However, note that the component is not needed again until the next production run for the finished product which is scheduled to occur at point *C*. Clearly, the investment in the component inventory from points *B* to *C* is unnecessary. We can eliminate this unnecessary component inventory by "backing up" from point C according to the purchase lead time so that the components will arrive just at time C. This situation is illustrated in Figure 11.12. Note that the component inventory level and corresponding inventory investment is less in Figure 11.12 than it is in Figure 11.11.

FIGURE 11.11
Finished Product and Component Part Inventory Levels without an MRP System

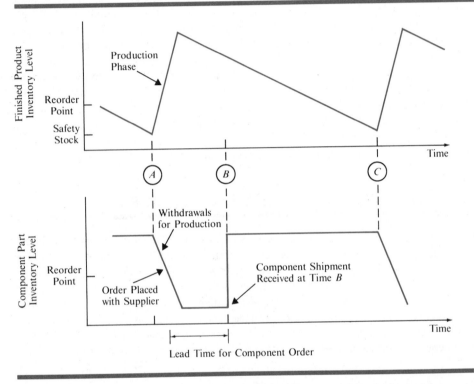

The philosophy of ordering component inventory depending upon the demand and production needs of other items is the approach followed by MRP. When operating properly, the MRP system will reduce inventory investment, improve work flow, reduce the shortage of materials and components, and help achieve more reliable delivery schedules.

Information System for MRP

What makes the MRP process difficult to implement is that many finished products consist of dozens or hundreds of parts, many of which are in turn dependent on other parts. Therefore, there must be accurate data and a reliable computer information system to perform the many calculations that will be required for MRP.

Material requirements planning calculations begin with the *master production schedule* which states the number of units of each finished product to be produced each time

FIGURE 11.12
Finished Product and Component Part Inventory Levels with an MRP System

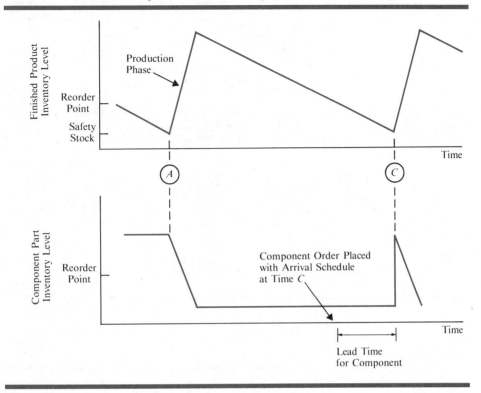

period. With the information in the master production schedule, we can begin to determine when the various components that make up the final products must be available. Thus the next step will be to identify the list of components that are required by the products. This information is available from the *bill of materials* (BOM).

The BOM is a structured parts list; however, it differs from an ordinary parts list in that it shows the hierarchical relationship between the finished product and its various components. An example of a BOM for the Spiecker Company is shown in Figure 11.13. This figure shows the bill of materials for a 14-inch snowblower. The finished product is shown at the top of the hierarchy (called level 0). It consists of one main housing assembly, one wheel assembly, one engine assembly, and one handle assembly. If we consider the BOM as a "family tree," then the 14-inch snowblower is the "parent" item for each of these assemblies. These assemblies, in turn, are parent items for all the components included in them. Thus the wheel assembly is the parent item of one blade assembly and two wheels. In general, items at level k are parent items for components at level $k + 1$. From the BOM we can determine exactly how many components are needed in order to produce the quantity of finished products stated in the master production schedule.

A schematic diagram of an MRP information system is given in Figure 11.14. Forecasts and orders are used to develop the master production schedule. The master production schedule, BOM, and current inventory files are the inputs needed to begin

FIGURE 11.13
Bill of Materials for the Spiecker 14-inch Snowblower

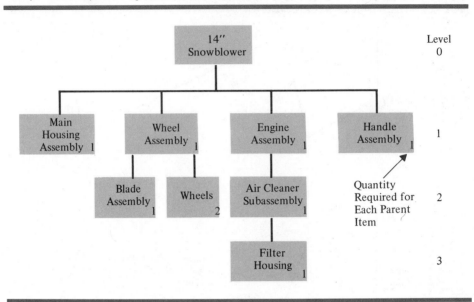

FIGURE 11.14
An MRP Computer System

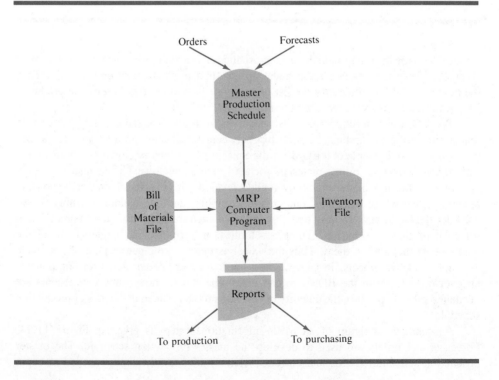

the MRP computations. The outputs from the MRP system are the requirements for each item in the BOM along with the dates each item is needed. This information is used to plan order releases for production and purchasing. In order to illustrate how these calculations are performed, let us consider an MRP system for the Spiecker snowblower example.

MRP Calculations

In MRP terminology, the time periods are called *buckets* and are usually 1 week in length. Small buckets, such as 1 week, are good for scheduling production over a short time horizon but may be too precise for long-range planning. Often, larger buckets are used as the planning horizon gets larger. However, for the Spiecker Manufacturing problem, we assume that all buckets are 1 week in length.

The master production schedule calls for the final assembly of 1250 units of the 14-inch snowblower during week 21 of the current planning period. The assembly lead time is 1 week; thus to meet this schedule, the four main assemblies in the bill of materials must be completed no later than the end of week 20. We now examine the production and inventory-control aspects for the engine assembly in detail, concentrating on how the MRP approach can be applied. Relevant data regarding the number of units in inventory and lead time are given in Table 11.4.

TABLE 11.4
Inventory On Hand and Lead Time for the Spiecker Manufacturing Example

Component	Units in Inventory	Lead Time (weeks)
Engine assembly	450	4
Air cleaner subassembly	250	1
Filter housing	500	2

Before the advent of MRP, the net requirement for each component was often found using the following formula:

$$\text{Net component requirement} = \left(\begin{array}{c}\text{number of components}\\\text{required to meet}\\\text{demand for}\\\text{finished good}\end{array}\right) - \left(\begin{array}{c}\text{number of}\\\text{components}\\\text{in inventory}\end{array}\right)$$

Thus the net requirements based on 1250 snowblowers are calculated as follows:

Components	Number of Components Required to Meet Demand for 1250 Snowblowers	−	Number in Inventory	=	Net Requirement
Engines	1250	−	450	=	800
Air cleaners	1250	−	250	=	1000
Filter housings	1250	−	500	=	750

However, note that this approach does not recognize the nature of dependent demand; for example, the number of filter housings required is dependent upon the number of air cleaners produced, and so on.

The approach to determining net requirements whenever a dependent demand situation exists is

$$\begin{pmatrix} \text{Net component} \\ \text{requirement} \end{pmatrix} = \begin{pmatrix} \text{gross component} \\ \text{requirement} \end{pmatrix} - \begin{pmatrix} \text{scheduled} \\ \text{receipts} \end{pmatrix} - \begin{pmatrix} \text{number of} \\ \text{components} \\ \text{in inventory} \end{pmatrix}$$

where the gross component requirement is the quantity of the component needed to support production at the next higher level of assembly. For example, the gross component requirement for the filter housing is the number of filter housings required to meet the net requirement for the air cleaner subassembly; the gross component requirement for the air cleaner subassembly is the number of air cleaners needed to meet the net requirement for the engine assembly; and so on. Let us see how these requirements can be computed for Spiecker Manufacturing. (We assume, for simplicity, that scheduled receipts are zero.)

Quantity of snowblowers to be produced:	1250
Gross requirements, engines:	1250
Less engines in inventory:	450
Net requirements, engines:	800 ← Engines
Gross requirements, air cleaners:	800
Less air cleaners in inventory:	250
Net requirements, air cleaners:	550 ← Air cleaners
Gross requirements, filter housings:	550
Less filter housings in inventory:	500
Net requirements, filter housings:	50 ← Filter housings

While the net requirements for engines under the MRP approach is still 800 units, note how MRP has used the dependent-demand information to show that fewer air cleaners and filter housings will be needed. In addition to considering dependent demand in the determination of net requirements for components, an MRP system also determines when the net requirements are needed. MRP handles this aspect of production and inventory control using the *time-phasing* concept. By starting with the time that the finished product must be completed, we can work backward in order to determine when an order for each component must be placed. For example, the time-phasing calculations for the Spiecker snowblower problem might appear as follows:

	Week
Complete order for engines:	20
Minus lead time for engines:	4
Place an order for engines:	16 ← Order engines
Complete order for air cleaners:	16
Minus lead time for air cleaners:	1
Place an order for air cleaners:	15 ← Order air cleaners
Complete order for filter housings:	15
Minus lead time for filter housings:	2
Place an order for filter housings:	13 ← Order filter housings

The components are scheduled so that they are made available only when required for the next higher level of assembly. Similar calculations can be made for all the other components of the snowblower, and if the bill of materials is exploded into detailed part requirements, a complete schedule for shop orders and purchase requisitions is available.

Until the development of large-scale computers, the sheer volume of calculations prohibited the implementation of an MRP system. For example, even in our small illustration, you can begin to appreciate the complexity involved in keeping track of the production and inventory status for every component. Fortunately, because of modern computer technology, we find that what was an unmanageable problem for earlier manual approaches can now be routinely handled by an MRP system.

Summary

In this chapter we have presented some of the approaches management scientists use when developing inventory models that will assist managers in establishing low-cost operating policies. We first considered cases where the demand for the product occurs at a rather stable or constant rate. In analyzing these inventory systems, total cost models were developed which include ordering costs, inventory holding costs, and, in some cases, backordering costs. Then minimum cost formulas for the order quantity Q were presented. A reorder point r can be established by considering the lead time demand for the item.

In addition, we discussed inventory decision models where a constant demand could not be assumed, and thus demand was described by a probability distribution. A critical issue with these probabilistic demand models is obtaining a probability distribution that most realistically approximates the actual demand distribution for the item. Solution procedures were presented for approximating the order quantity and reorder point decisions under probabilistic demand. In addition, solution procedures were presented for the single-period probabilistic inventory model.

We pointed out that the order point type of approaches referred to above are most applicable for controlling finished goods inventory. For manufacturing inventories, where dependent demand exists, methods such as MRP offer significant advantages.

With an increasing emphasis on lowering costs and improving productivity, the continued use of quantitative models for optimal inventory decisions, as well as the development of new methods of inventory management, can be expected. A recent development that evolved from the Japanese approach to material management and control is known as *just-in-time* (JIT). JIT is based on the goal of producing or delivering parts and material only when and where they are needed. It has been shown in practice that the JIT approach results in less inventory investment, reduces scrap, provides higher quality, and, in general, elicits improved productivity. Although a full discussion of JIT is beyond the scope of this text, further information can be found in a variety of texts dealing with modern techniques of production and operations management.

In closing this chapter we reemphasize that inventory and inventory systems can be an expensive phase of a firm's operation. It is of utmost economic importance for managers to be aware of the cost of inventory systems and to make the best possible operating policy decisions for the inventory system. Inventory decision models, as presented in this chapter, can help managers to develop good inventory policies.

Glossary

Inventory holding or inventory carrying cost   All costs associated with maintaining an inventory investment: cost of the capital investment in the inventory, insurance, taxes, warehouse overhead, and so on. This cost may be stated as a percentage of the inventory investment or a cost per unit.

Cost of capital   The cost a firm incurs, usually interest payments on borrowed funds or dividend payments on stocks, in order to obtain capital for investment. The cost of capital, which may be stated as an annual percentage rate, is part of the holding cost associated with maintaining inventory levels.

Economic order quantity (EOQ)   The order quantity that minimizes the total inventory costs in the most fundamental inventory model.

Constant demand rate   An assumption of many inventory models that states that the same number of units are taken from inventory in each period of time.

Ordering cost   The fixed cost (salaries, paper, transportation, and so on) associated with placing an order for an item.

Reorder point   The inventory level at which a new order should be placed.

Lead time   The time between the placing of an order and its receipt in the inventory system.

Lead time demand   The number of units demanded during the lead time period.

Cycle time   The length of time between the placing of two consecutive orders.

Safety stock   Inventory maintained in order to reduce the number of stockouts resulting from higher-than-expected demand during lead time.

Constant supply rate   The situation in which the inventory is built up at a constant rate over a period of time. This assumption applies to the production lot size model of this chapter.

Backorder   The receipt of an order for a product when there are no units on hand in inventory. These backorders become shortages, which are eventually satisfied when a new supply of the product becomes available.

Quantity discounts   Discounts or lower unit costs offered by the manufacturer when a customer purchases larger quantities of the product.

Goodwill cost   A cost associated with a backorder, a lost sale, or any form of stockout or unsatisfied demand. This cost may be used to reflect the loss of future profits due to the fact a customer experienced an unsatisfied demand.

Probabilistic demand   Situations in which demand for the inventory item is not known exactly and probabilities must be used to describe the demand alternatives for the product.

Lead time demand distribution   In probabilistic inventory models, this is the distribution of demand that occurs during the lead time period.

Service level   The average number of stockouts we are willing to allow per year.

Single-period inventory models   Inventory models in which it is assumed that only one order is placed for the product, and at the end of the period the item has either sold out or there is a surplus of unsold items that will be sold for a salvage value.

Material requirements planning (MRP)   A computerized inventory management system whose function is to schedule production and control the level of inventory for components with dependent demand.

Master production schedule   A statement of how many finished items are to be produced and when.

Bill of materials   A structured parts list that shows the manner in which the product is actually put together.

Dependent demand   The demand for one component depends upon the demand for

Time phasing   Adding the dimension of time to inventory status data in an MRP environment.

Problems

1. Suppose R&B Beverage Company has a soft-drink product that has a constant annnual demand rate of 3600 cases. A case of the soft drink costs R&B $3. If ordering costs are $20 and inventory holding costs are charged at 25%, what is the economic order quantity and cycle time in days for this product?

2. A general property of the EOQ inventory model is that total inventory holding and total ordering costs are equal or balanced at the optimal solution. Use the data in problem 1 to show that this result is observed for this problem. Use equations (11.1), (11.2), and (11.5) to show in general that total inventory holding costs and total ordering costs are equal whenever Q^* is used.

3. The XYZ Company purchases a component used in the manufacture of automobile generators directly from the supplier. XYZ's generator production operation, which is operated at a constant rate, will require 1000 components per month throughout the year (12,000 units annually). Assume ordering costs are $25 per order, unit cost is $2.50 per component, and annual inventory holding costs are charged at 20%, and answer the following inventory policy questions for XYZ:
    a. What is the EOQ for this component?
    b. What is the cycle time in months?
    c. What are the total annual inventory holding and ordering costs associated with your recommended EOQ?

4. Assuming 250 days of operation per year and a lead time of 5 days, what is the reorder point for the XYZ Company in problem 3?

5. Suppose that XYZ's management in problem 3 likes the operational efficiency of ordering in quantities of 1000 units and ordering once each month. How much more expensive would this policy be than your EOQ recommendation? Would you recommend in favor of the 1000-unit order quantity? Explain. What would the reorder point be if the 1000-unit quantity were acceptable?

6. Tele-Reco is a new specialty store that sells television sets, videotape recorders, video games, and other television-related products. A new Japanese-manufactured videotape recorder costs Tele-Reco $600 per unit. Tele-Reco's inventory carrying cost is figured at an annual rate of 22%. Ordering costs are estimated to be $70 per order.
    a. If demand for the new videotape recorder is expected to be constant with a rate of 20 units per month, what is the recommended order quantity for the video tape recorder?
    b. What is the estimated annual cost for inventory and ordering costs associated with this product?
    c. How many times will orders be placed per year, and what is the cycle time for this product?

7. A large distributor of oil-well drilling equipment has operated over the past 2 years with EOQ policies based on an annual inventory carrying charge of 22%. Under

the EOQ policy, a particular product has been ordered with a $Q^* = 80$. A recent evaluation of carrying costs shows that because of an increase in the interest rate associated with bank loans, the inventory carrying charge should be 27%.

a. What should be the new Q^* for the above product?

b. Develop a general expression showing how the economic order quantity changes when the inventory carrying cost is changed from I to I'.

8. Nation-Wide Bus Lines is proud of its 6-week bus driver training program that it conducts for all new Nation-Wide drivers. A 6-week training program costs Nation-Wide $22,000 for instructors, equipment, and so on, and is independent of the number of new drivers in the class as long as the class size remains less than or equal to 35. The Nation-Wide training program must provide the company with approximately five new fully trained drivers per month. After completing the training program, new drivers are paid $1600 per month but do not work until a full-time driver position is open. Nation-Wide views the $1600 per month paid to each idle new driver as a holding cost necessary to maintain a supply of newly trained drivers available for immediate service. Viewing new drivers as inventory-type units, how large should the training classes be in order to minimize Nation-Wide's total annual training and new driver idle-time costs? How many training classes should the company hold each year? What is the total annual cost associated with your recommendation?

9. Cress Electronic Products manufactures components used in the automotive industry. Cress purchases parts for use in its manufacturing operation from a variety of different suppliers. One particular supplier provides a part where the assumptions of the EOQ model are realistic. The annual demand is 5000 units. Ordering costs are $80 per order and inventory carrying costs are figured at an annual rate of 25%.

a. If the cost of the part is $20 per unit, what is the economic order quantity?

b. Assume 250 days of operation per year. If the lead time for an order is 12 days, what is the reorder point?

c. If the lead time for the part is 7 weeks (35 days), what is the reorder point?

d. What is the amount of inventory on hand when an order is placed?

10. All-Star Bat Manufacturing, Inc. supplies baseball bats to major and minor league baseball teams. After an initial order in January, demand over the 8-month baseball season is approximately constant at 1000 bats per month. Assuming that the bat production process can handle up to 4000 bats per month, the bat production setup costs are $150 per setup, the production cost is $10 per bat, and assuming that All-Star uses a 24% annual or 2% monthly inventory holding cost, what production lot size would you recommend to meet the demand during the baseball season? How often will the production process operate, and what is the length of a production run?

11. Assume a production line operates such that the production lot size model of Section 11.2 is applicable. Given $D = 6400$ units per year, $C_0 = \$100$, and $C_h = \$2$ per unit per year, compute the minimum cost production lot size for each of the following production rates:

a. 8000 units per year

b. 10,000 units per year

c. 32,000 units per year

d. 100,000 units per year

Compute the EOQ recommended lot size using equation (11.5). What two observations can you make about the relationship between the EOQ model and the production lot size model?

12. Assume you are reviewing the production lot size decision associated with a production operation where $P = 8000$ units per year, $D = 2000$ units per year, $C_0 = \$300$, and $C_h = \$1.60$ per unit per year. Also assume that current practice calls for production runs of 500 units every 3 months. Would you recommend changing the current production lot size? Why or why not? How much could be saved by converting to your production lot size recommendation?

13. Wilson Publishing Company produces books for the retail market. Demand for a current book is expected to occur at a constant annual rate of 7200 copies. The cost of one copy of the book is $14.50. Inventory holding costs are based on an 18% annual rate, and production setup costs are $150 per setup. The equipment the book is produced on has an annual production volume of 25,000 copies. Use the production lot size model to compute the following values:
    a. Minimum cost production lot size
    b. Number of production runs per year
    c. Cycle time (assuming 250 days of operation per year)
    d. Length of a production run
    e. Maximum inventory level
    f. Average inventory level
    g. Total annual cost

14. A well-known manufacturer of several brands of toothpaste uses the production lot size model to determine production quantities for its various products. The product known as Extra White is currently being produced in production lot sizes of 5000 units. The length of the production run for this quantity is 10 days. Because of a recent shortage of a particular raw material, the supplier of the material has announced a cost increase that will be passed along to the manufacturer of Extra White. Current estimates are that the new raw material cost will increase the manufacturing cost of the toothpaste products by 23% per unit. What will be the effect of this price increase on the production lot sizes for Extra White? What is the new length of the production run?

15. Suppose the XYZ Company of problem 3, with $D = 12,000$ units per year, $C_h = (2.50)(0.20) = \$0.50$, and $C_0 = \$25$, decided to operate with a backorder inventory policy. Backorder costs are estimated to be $5 per unit per year. Identify the following:
    a. Minimum cost order quantity
    b. Maximum number of backorders
    c. Maximum inventory level
    d. Cycle time
    e. Total annual cost

16. Assuming 250 days of operation per year and a lead time of 5 days, what is the reorder point for the XYZ Company in problem 15? Show the general formula for the reorder point for the EOQ model with backorders. In general, is the reorder point when backorders are allowed greater than or less than the reorder point when backorders are not allowed? Explain.

17. A manager of an inventory system believes inventory models are important decision-making aids. While he frequently uses the EOQ policy, he has never considered a

backorder model because he has always felt backorders were "bad" and should be avoided. However, with upper management's continued pressure for cost reduction, he has asked you to analyze the economics of a backordering policy for some products that he believes can possibly be backordered. For a specific product with $D = 800$ units per year, $C_0 = \$150$, $C_h = \$3$, and $C_b = \$20$, what is the economic difference in the EOQ and the planned backorder model? If the manager puts constraints that no more than 25% of the units can be backordered and that no customer will have to wait more than 3 weeks (21 days) for an order, should the backorder inventory policy be adopted?

18. If the lead time for new orders is 1 month for the inventory system discussed in problem 17, find the reorder point for both the EOQ and the planned backorder models.

19. The A&M Hobby Shop carries a line of radio-controlled model racing cars. Demand for the cars is assumed to be constant at a rate of 40 cars per month. The cars cost $60 each, and ordering costs are approximately $15 per order, regardless of the order size. Inventory carrying costs are 20% annually.

   a. Determine the economic order quantity and total annual cost under the assumption that no backorders are permitted.
   b. Using a $45 per unit per year backorder cost, determine the minimum cost inventory policy and total annual cost for the model racing cars?
   c. What is the maximum number of days a customer would have to wait for a backorder under the policy in part b? Assume the Hobby Shop is open for business 300 days per year.
   d. Would you recommend a no backorder or a backorder inventory policy for this product? Explain.
   e. If the lead time is 6 days, what is the reorder point in terms of on-hand inventory for both the no-backorder and backorder inventory policies?

20. Assume that the following quantity discount schedule is appropriate:

Order Size	Discount	Unit Cost
0 to 49	0%	$30.00
50 to 99	5%	$28.50
over 99	10%	$27.00

If annual demand is 120 units, ordering cost is $20 per order, and annual inventory carrying cost is 25%, what order quantity would you recommend?

21. Apply the EOQ model to the following quantity discount situation:

Discount Category	Order Size	Discount	Unit Cost
1	0 to 99	0%	$10.00
2	over 99	3%	$ 9.70

$D = 500$ units per year, $C_0 = \$40$, and an annual inventory holding cost of 20% are given. What order quantity do you recommend?

22. Keith Shoe Stores carries a basic black dress shoe for men that sells at an approximate constant rate of 500 pairs of shoes every 3 months. Keith's current buying policy is to order 500 pairs each time an order is placed. It costs Keith $30 to place an order. Inventory carrying costs have an annual rate of 20%. With the order quantity of 500, Keith obtains the shoes at the lowest possible unit cost of $28 per pair. Other quantity discounts offered by the manufacturer are as follows:

Order Quantity	Price Per Pair
0–99	$36
100–199	$32
200–299	$30
300 or more	$28

What is the minimum cost order quantity for the shoes? What are the annual savings of your inventory policy over the policy currently being used by Keith?

23. In the EOQ model with quantity discounts we stated that if the Q^* for a price category is larger than necessary to qualify for the category price, the category cannot be optimal. Use the two discount categories in problem 21 to show that this is true. That is, plot the total cost curves for the two categories and show that if the category 2 minimum cost Q is an acceptable solution, we do not have to consider category 1.

24. Floyd Distributors, Inc. provides a variety of auto parts to small local garages. Floyd purchases parts from manufacturers according to the EOQ model and then ships the parts from a regional warehouse direct to its customers. For a particular type of muffler, Floyd's EOQ analysis recommends orders with $Q^* = 25$ to satisfy an annual demand of 200 mufflers (average demand is approximately four units per week). Floyd has a 3-week lead time on all orders placed with the muffler supplier.
   a. What is the reorder point if Floyd assumes a constant demand of four units per week?
   b. Suppose an analysis of Floyd's muffler demand shows that the lead time demand follows a normal distribution with $\mu = 12$ and $\sigma = 2.5$. If Floyd's management can tolerate one stockout per year, what is the revised reorder point?
   c. What is the safety stock for part b? If $C_h = \$5$/unit/year, what is the extra cost due to the uncertainty of demand?

25. For Floyd Distributors in problem 24, we were given $Q^* = 25$, $D = 200$, $C_h = \$5$, and a normal lead time demand distribution with $\mu = 12$ and $\sigma = 2.5$.
   a. What is Floyd's reorder point if the firm is willing to tolerate two stockouts during the year?
   b. What is Floyd's reorder point if the firm wants to restrict the probability of a stockout on any one cycle to at most 1%?
   c. What are the safety stock levels and the annual safety stock costs for the reorder points found in parts a and b?

26. A firm with an annual demand of approximately 1000 units has C_0 = $25.50 and C_h = $8. The demand exhibits some variability such that the lead time demand follows a normal distribution with μ = 25 and σ = 5.
    a. What is the recommended order quantity?
    b. What are the reorder point and safety stock if the firm desires at most a 2% probability of stockout on any given order cycle?
    c. If a manager sets the reorder point at 30, what is the probability of a stockout on any given order cycle? How many times would you expect to stock-out during the year if this reorder point were used?

27. The B&S Novelty and Craft Shop in Bennington, Vt., sells a variety of quality handmade items to tourists. B&S will sell approximately 300 hand-carved miniature replicas of a colonial soldier each year, but the demand pattern during the year is uncertain. The replicas sell for $20 each, and B&S uses a 15% annual inventory holding cost rate. Ordering costs are $5 per order, and demand during the lead time follows a uniform distribution with the demand alternatives from six to 25 each having approximately the same probability of occurrence.
    a. What is the recommended order quantity?
    b. If B&S is willing to accept a stockout roughly twice a year, what reorder point would you recommend? What is the probability B&S will have a stockout in any one order cycle?
    c. What are the safety stock and annual safety stock costs for this product?

28. The J&B Card Shop sells calendars with different colonial pictures shown for each month. The once-a-year order for each year's calendar arrives in September. From past experience the September-to-July demand for the calendars can be approximated by a normal distribution with μ = 500 and σ = 120. The calendars cost $1.50 each, and J&B sells them for $3 each.

    a. If J&B throws out all unsold calendars at the end of July (that is, salvage value is zero), how many calendars should be ordered?
    b. If J&B reduces the calendar price to $1 at the end of July and can sell all surplus calendars at this price, how many calendars should be ordered?

29. The Gilbert Air-Conditioning Company is considering the purchase of a special shipment of portable air conditioners manufactured in Japan. Each unit will cost Gilbert $80 and it will be sold for $125. Gilbert does not want to carry surplus air conditioners over until the following year. Thus all supplies will be sold to a wholesaler who has agreed to take all surplus units for $50 per unit. The probability distribution for air conditioner demand is as follows:

Interval	Estimated Probability
0–9	0.30
10–19	0.35
20–29	0.20
30–39	0.10
40–49	0.05

What is the recommended order quantity for Gilbert?

30. Refer to problem 29. Suppose the air conditioner demand had been approximated by a normal distribution with $\mu = 20$ and $\sigma = 8$.
   a. What is the recommended order quantity under this assumed demand distribution?
   b. What is the probability Gilbert will sell all units it orders?

31. A popular newsstand in a large metropolitan area is attempting to determine how many copies of the Sunday paper it should purchase each week. Demand for the newspaper on Sundays can be approximated by a normal distribution with $\mu = 450$ and $\sigma = 100$. The newspaper costs the newsstand 35¢ a copy and sells for 50¢ a copy. The newsstand does not receive any value from surplus papers and thus absorbs a 100% loss on all unsold papers.
   a. How many copies of the Sunday paper should be purchased each week?
   b. What is the probability that the newsstand will have a stockout?
   c. The manager of the newsstand is concerned about the newsstand's image if the probability of stockout is high. The customers often purchase other items after coming to the newsstand for the Sunday paper. Frequent stockouts would cause customers to go to another newsstand. The manager agrees that a 50¢ loss of goodwill cost should be assigned to any stockout. What are the new recommended order quantity and the new probability of a stockout?

32. A perishable dairy product is ordered daily at a particular supermarket. The product, which costs $1.19 per unit, sells for $1.65 per unit. If units are unsold at the end of the day, the supplier takes them back at a rebate of $1 per unit. Assume that daily demand is approximately normally distributed with $\mu = 150$ and $\sigma = 30$.
   a. What is your recommended daily order quantity for the supermarket?
   b. What is the probability that the supermarket will sell all the units it orders?
   c. In problems such as these, why would the supplier offer a rebate as high as $1? For example, why not offer a nominal rebate of, say, 25¢ per unit? What happens to the supermarket order quantity as the rebate is reduced?

33. A retail outlet sells a seasonal product for $10 per unit. The cost of the product is $8 per unit. All units not sold during the regular season are sold for half the retail price in an end-of-season clearance sale. Assume that demand for the product is normally distributed with $\mu = 500$ and $\sigma = 100$.
   a. What is the recommended order quantity?
   b. What is the probability that at least some customers will ask to purchase the product after the outlet is sold out? That is, what is the probability of a stockout using your order quantity in part a?
   c. Suppose the owner's policy is that in order to keep customers happy and returning to the store later, stockouts should be avoided if at all possible. What is your recommended order quantity if you get the owner to agree to a 0.15 probability of stockout?
   d. Using your answer to part c, what is the goodwill cost you are assigning to a stockout? That is, how many dollars per unit is the owner implying he would pay to avoid a stockout?

34. The McCormick Hardware Store places one order for riding lawn mowers each February. The lawn mowers being purchased this year cost $300 and sell for $425. In the past McCormick has always been able to sell all surplus lawn mowers during the September "end-of-summer" sale. The clearance sale price for these lawn mowers will be $250. If the following probability distribution for demand is assumed, how many lawn mowers should McCormick order?

Demand	Probability
0	0.10
1	0.15
2	0.30
3	0.20
4	0.15
5	0.10

35. Consider the Spiecker Manufacturing example of Section 11.7. Determine the net requirements for the engine assembly, the air cleaner subassembly, and the filter housing if the number of units in inventory were 2000, 1500, and 1000, respectively. Assume that 5000 units of the 14-inch snowblower are required in week 21.

36. For the Spiecker Manufacturing example of Section 11.7, determine the effect on time phasing if lead times were 10 for the engine assembly, 3 for the air cleaner subassembly, and 5 for the filter housing.

37. C & D Lawn Products manufactures a rotary spreader for applying fertilizer. A portion of the bill of materials is shown below:

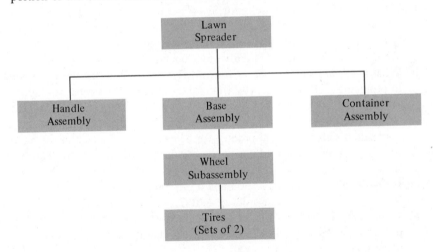

If 3000 lawn spreaders are needed to satisfy a customer's order, determine the net requirements for the base assembly, wheel subassembly, and tires (sets of two). Assume that 1000 base assemblies, 1500 wheel subassemblies, and 800 tires (sets of two) are currently in inventory.

38. In problem 37, assume that the lead time for the base assembly, wheel subassembly, and tires are 2 weeks, 4 weeks, and 5 weeks, respectively. If all components must be completed no later than week 15 of the current production period, determine when orders must be placed to meet the production schedule.

———— *Case Problem:* ————

A MAKE OR BUY ANALYSIS

Wagner Fabricating Company is reviewing the economic feasibility of manufacturing a part that it currently purchases from a supplier. Forecasted annual demand for the part is 3200 units. Wagner operates 250 days per year.

Wagner's financial analysts have established a cost of capital of 14% on the use of funds for investments within the company. In addition, over the past year $600,000 has been the average investment in the company's inventory. Accounting information shows that a total of $24,000 was spent on taxes and insurance related to the company's inventory. In addition, it has been estimated that $9000 was lost due to inventory shrinkage, which included damaged goods as well as pilferage. A remaining $15,000 was spent on warehouse overhead, including utility expenses for heating and lighting.

An analysis of the purchasing operation shows that approximately 2 hours are required to process and coordinate an order for the part regardless of the quantity ordered. Purchasing salaries average $28 per hour, including employee benefits. In addition, a detailed analysis of 125 orders showed that $2375 was spent on telephone, paper, and postage directly related to the ordering process.

A 1-week lead time is required to obtain the part from the supplier. An analysis of demand during the lead time shows that lead time demand is approximately normally distributed with a mean of 64 units and a standard deviation of 10 units. Service level guidelines indicate that one stockout per year is acceptable.

Currently the company has a contract to purchase the part from a supplier at a cost of $18 per unit. However, over the past few months, the company's production capacity has been expanded. As a result, excess capacity is now available in certain production departments and the company is considering the alternative of producing the parts itself.

Forecasted utilization of equipment shows that production capacity will be available for the part being considered. The production capacity is available at the rate of 1000 units per month, with up to 5 months of production time available. It is felt that with a 2-week lead time, schedules can be arranged so that the part can be produced whenever needed. The demand during the 2-week lead time is approximately normally distributed with a mean of 128 units and a standard deviation of 20 units. Production costs are expected to be $17 per part.

A concern of management is that setup costs will be significant. The total cost of labor and lost production time is estimated to be $50 per hour, and it will take a full 8-hour shift to set up the equipment for producing the part.

MANAGERIAL REPORT

Develop a report for management of Wagner Fabricating that will address the question of whether the company should continue to purchase the part from the supplier or should begin to produce the part itself. Include the following factors in your report:

1. An analysis of the inventory holding cost, including the appropriate annual inventory holding cost rate.
2. An analysis of ordering costs, including the appropriate cost per order from the supplier.
3. An analysis of setup costs for the production operation.
4. A development of the inventory policy for the following two alternatives:
   a. Ordering a fixed quantity Q from the supplier
   b. Ordering a fixed quantity Q from in-plant production
5. Include the following in the policies of 4(a) and 4(b) above:
   a. The quantity Q
   b. The number of order or production runs per year
   c. The cycle time
   d. The reorder point
   e. The amount of safety stock
   f. The expected maximum inventory level
   g. The average inventory level
   h. The total annual inventory holding cost
   i. The total annual ordering cost
   j. The total annual cost of the units purchased or manufactured
   k. The total annual cost of the purchase policy and the total annual cost of the production policy
6. Make a recommendation as to whether the company should purchase or manufacture the part. What is the saving associated with your recommendation as compared with the other alternative?

Appendix 11.1   Development of the Optimal Order Quantity (Q*) Formula for the EOQ Model

Given equation (11.3) as the general total annual cost formula for the EOQ model,

$$TC = \tfrac{1}{2} QC_h + \frac{D}{Q} C_0 \tag{11.3}$$

we can find the order quantity Q that minimizes the total cost by setting the derivative, dTC/dQ, equal to zero and solving for $Q*$.

$$\frac{dTC}{dQ} = \tfrac{1}{2} C_h - \frac{D}{Q^2} C_0 = 0$$

$$\tfrac{1}{2} C_h = \frac{D}{Q^2} C_0$$

$$C_h Q^2 = 2DC_0$$

$$Q^2 = \frac{2DC_0}{C_h}$$

Hence

$$Q* = \sqrt{\frac{2DC_0}{C_h}} \tag{11.5}$$

The second derivative is

$$\frac{d^2TC}{dQ^2} = \frac{2D}{Q^3} C_0$$

Since the value of the second derivative is greater than zero for D, C_0, and Q greater than zero, $Q*$ from equation (11.5) is in fact the minimum cost solution.

Appendix 11.2 Development of the Optimal Lot Size (Q*) for the Production Lot Size Model

Given equation (11.15) as the total annual cost formula for the production lot size model,

$$\text{TC} = \frac{1}{2}\left(1 - \frac{D}{P}\right)QC_h + \frac{D}{Q}C_0 \tag{11.15}$$

we can find the order quantity Q that minimizes the total cost by setting the derivative, $d\text{TC}/dQ$, equal to zero and solving for Q^*.

$$\frac{d\text{TC}}{dQ} = \frac{1}{2}\left(1 - \frac{D}{P}\right)C_h - \frac{D}{Q^2}C_0 = 0$$

Solving for Q^* we have

$$\frac{1}{2}\left(1 - \frac{D}{P}\right)C_h = \frac{D}{Q^2}C_0$$

$$\left(1 - \frac{D}{P}\right)C_hQ^2 = 2DC_0$$

$$Q^2 = \frac{2DC_0}{(1 - D/P)C_h}$$

Hence

$$Q^* = \sqrt{\frac{2DC_0}{(1 - D/P)C_h}} \tag{11.16}$$

The second derivative is

$$\frac{d^2\text{TC}}{dQ^2} = \frac{2DC_0}{Q^3}$$

Since the value of the second derivative is greater than zero for D, C_0, and Q greater than zero, Q^* from equation (11.16) is a minimum cost solution.

Appendix 11.3   Development of the Optimal Order Quantity (Q*) and Optimal Backorder (S*) Formulas for the Planned ————— Shortage Model —————

Given equation (11.25) as the total annual cost model for the planned shortage case,

$$\text{TC} = \frac{(Q - S)^2}{2Q} C_h + \frac{D}{Q} C_0 + \frac{S^2}{2Q} C_b \tag{11.25}$$

we have two inventory decision variables Q and S. To find the Q and S values that minimize equation (11.25) we must set the two partial derivatives $\partial TC/\partial Q$ and $\partial TC/\partial S$ equal to zero.

First, let us rewrite equation (11.25) as follows:

$$\text{TC} = \left(\frac{Q^2 - 2QS + S^2}{2Q}\right) C_h + \frac{D}{Q} C_0 + \frac{S^2}{2Q} C_b$$

$$= \frac{Q}{2} C_h - SC_h + \frac{C_h}{2Q} S^2 + \frac{DC_0}{Q} + \frac{C_b}{2Q} S^2$$

$$= \left(\frac{C_h + C_b}{2Q}\right) S^2 - SC_h + \frac{QC_h}{2} + \frac{DC_0}{Q}$$

Then, setting $\partial TC/\partial S = 0$, we get

$$\frac{\partial TC}{\partial S} = \left(\frac{C_h + C_b}{Q}\right) S - C_h = 0$$

Solving for S^*, we have

$$\left(\frac{C_h + C_b}{Q}\right) S = C_h$$

Thus

$$S^* = Q \left(\frac{C_h}{C_h + C_b}\right) \tag{11.27}$$

Setting $\partial TC/\partial Q = 0$, we get

$$\frac{\partial TC}{\partial Q} = \frac{-(C_h + C_b) S^2}{2Q^2} + \frac{C_h}{2} - \frac{DC_0}{Q^2} = 0$$

Substituting $S*$ of equation (11.27), we have

$$\frac{\partial \text{TC}}{\partial Q} = \frac{-(C_h + C_b)Q^2(C_h)^2/(C_h + C_b)^2}{2Q^2} + \frac{C_h}{2} - \frac{DC_0}{Q^2} = 0$$

Solve for $Q*$ as follows:

$$\frac{-(C_h)^2}{2(C_h + C_b)} + \frac{C_h}{2} = \frac{DC_0}{Q_2}$$

$$\frac{-(C_h)^2 + C_h(C_h + C_b)}{2(C_h + C_b)} = \frac{DC_0}{Q^2}$$

$$Q^2 = \frac{2(C_h + C_b)\, DC_0}{C_h C_b}$$

$$Q^2 = \frac{2C_h DC_0}{C_h C_b} + \frac{2C_b DC_0}{C_h C_b}$$

$$Q^2 = \frac{2DC_0}{C_h}\left(\frac{C_h}{C_b} + \frac{C_b}{C_{b\prime}}\right)$$

Hence

$$Q* = \sqrt{\frac{2DC_0}{C_h}\left(\frac{C_h + C_b}{C_b}\right)} \qquad (11.26)$$

The second-order conditions will show equations (11.26) and (11.27) to be the minimum cost solutions.

Management Science in Practice

INFORMATICS GENERAL CORPORATION*

Woodland Hills, California

Informatics General Corporation was formed in 1962 as a computer software company. Today it has offices located throughout the United States and in several foreign countries.

Informatics has concentrated its business activities in three areas:

1. Software products—selling computer software packages
2. Information processing—selling computer time-sharing services and turnkey systems
3. Professional services—providing consultants, computer programmers, and other trained personnel

The application that follows describes the use of an Informatics system known as DISTRIBUTION IV. This computerized system has been used for effective inventory management and merchandise distribution in several of Informatics' client companies.

AN INVENTORY MANAGEMENT APPLICATION

Medi-$ave Pharmacies, part of National Medical Enterprises, distributes prescription and over-the-counter merchandise to drugstores across the United States. The company was experiencing profitability problems stemming from a very rapid growth rate. The total number of distribution outlets had climbed to 86, and the company was handling more than 7000 items in its inventory.

To improve bottom-line profits, Medi-$ave attacked the problem of poorly controlled expansion by working toward resource concentration. The company moved away from small chain store distribution and began to develop a business base with leased pharmacy departments in major discount stores.

One of the key factors in making the resource concentration strategy successful was to meticulously control the flow of goods from inventory to drug outlets. To achieve tight inventory control, Medi-$ave installed the merchandise management reporting system called DISTRIBUTION IV. DISTRIBUTION IV is a computerized information system developed for the wholesale and retail distribution industry by Informatics General Corporation. With the DISTRIBUTION IV system, Medi-$ave

*The authors are indebted to Carol Hays of Informatics General Corporation for providing this application.

generates as many as 500 different reports, which provide all types of inventory status information. Many of these reports not only provide raw information, but also analyze it. For instance, DISTRIBUTION IV generates "picking" reports that give instructions to warehouse workers as each merchandise order is received. The picking report tells the worker exactly where to find the merchandise by aisle and bin location. "Screened" picking reports instruct the worker on how many items to draw from that location. For example, a report might list an order for five bottles of aspirin, show that only three bottles are in inventory, and then instruct the worker to pick all three bottles.

Medi-$ave also uses a billing system report that issues billings at the retail rate for each store. These billings come from store-by-store statements that show the number of items ordered and the number shipped, and they include a supply of retail price stickers.

An inventory management system issues reports on low stock, dead items, and items with excessive demand. These are examples of raw information reports that are analyzed by an inventory manager. The reports can be issued in any number of variations—by department, by age of inventory, by dollar amount in inventory— and the variation is selectable at any time.

Medi-$ave also analyzes its stock by velocity code. Velocity codes define the typical demand and movement of certain types of stock. For instance, an item coded "A" is ordered regularly and usually in large amounts, "B"-coded items have less movement than "A" items, and "C" items less movement then "B" items. Velocity code reports provide information on the amount of time each coded item remains in stock, helping to determine reorder rates.

The scientific buying module of DISTRIBUTION IV is an example of analytical reporting. Records on the history of activity levels for each item in inventory are analyzed and recommendations on purchases are made based on past demand. An objective of this scientific buying module is to make the inventory replenishment decisions in such a fashion that the contribution margin on inventory investment is maximized. What has evolved is a system known as "cycle time max." Under this system, 80–85% of the inventory replenishment orders are placed at a specified point in time. With such an ordering policy, larger orders are placed, resulting in quantity discounts and other concessions from suppliers.

The 15–20% of the inventory items that are not under the "cycle time max" system are handled by the scientific buying module on an exception basis. These items are generally the high-volume items that require standard order quantity and reorder level rules based on inventory carrying and ordering costs.

All of the reports provided by the DISTRIBUTION IV system have helped Medi-$ave to achieve tight controls on methods of inventory. Prescription merchandise is now shipped from the Medi-$ave warehouse in Baton Rouge, La., to all stores 5 days a week. Over-the-counter merchandise is shipped once every 2 weeks. Stores place their orders at prearranged times each day through direct order entry devices. At the same time, management information on store sales, number of prescriptions, purchases for the day, and bank deposits are also transmitted to the Medi-$ave headquarters.

With the new reporting system, Medi-$ave has been able to track the gross margin return on investment for every inventoried item and every vendor. Consequently, Medi-$ave has decided to concentrate on leased pharmacy departments of discount stores, minimizing activity with freestanding drugstores. In addition, the discount stores themselves stock health and beauty aids, allowing Medi-$ave to eliminate these items from its own inventory.

As a result of Medi-$ave's strategy, the total number of outlets was cut from 86 to 64. Inventory was reduced from 7000 items to 4500. These efforts have had positive effects on profit figures for Medi-$ave. Over the 5 years the company has conducted the program, profits have increased by 35.3%, and return on investment for the most recent year was up by 16.1%.

Sales per square foot are $286, as compared with the National Association of Chain Drug Stores (NACDS) reported national median of $158, and Medi-$ave now has a net pretax profit-to-sales ratio of 3.6% (versus the NACDS median of 2.3%).

The DISTRIBUTION IV merchandise management system was first introduced by Informatics in 1971. Today it is being used for the inventory control and management of over one million items.

Questions

1. What was the major problem of Medi-$ave pharmacies that led to the installation of DISTRIBUTION IV?

2. What is the purpose of the "picking" reports that are generated by the DISTRIBUTION IV system?

3. Describe the primary objective of the scientific buying module of DISTRIBUTION IV.

4. What are the major benefits Medi-$ave realized through the use of a merchandise management reporting system?

12

Computer Simulation

The management science techniques presented in the other chapters of this text emphasize the formulation and solution of a mathematical model of the system under study. Frequently, the "solution" process employs an analytical procedure that identifies an optimal solution for the model. Although this process of formulating and solving a mathematical model has been successfully applied in many practical situations, there are other systems that are so complex they cannot be modeled and solved in this manner. Computer simulation has proved to be a valuable management science tool in these instances.

As with all models, the purpose of a computer simulation model is to provide a representation of a real system. Great care is usually taken to ensure that the simulation model is descriptive of the real system. Then, through a series of computer runs, or experiments, we study the behavior of the simulation model. The operating characteristics of the simulation model are then used to make inferences about the operating characteristics of the real system. The more representative the simulation model is of the real system, the better the inferences will be.

The surveys of current uses of management science techniques referred to in Chapter 1 indicate that computer simulation is one of the most popular and frequently used problem-solving tools. Some of the reasons why computer simulation is so widely used are as follows:

1. Computer simulation can be used to obtain good solutions to problems that are too complex to be solved with procedures such as linear programming or inventory models.
2. The simulation approach is relatively easy to explain and understand. As a result management confidence is increased, and consequently acceptance of the technique is more easily obtained.
3. Computer manufacturers have developed extensive software packages which consist of specialized simulation programming languages, thus facilitating use by analysts.
4. Simulation is a very flexible technique that can be applied to a wide variety of situations. For example, the technique has been used to describe the behavior of production systems, financial systems, inventory systems, waiting-line systems, and so on.

In this chapter we will introduce the concepts and procedures of computer simulation by studying how the approach can be applied to a waiting-line system and an inventory system. Analytic techniques for these problems are presented in Chapters 11 and 13. The analytic techniques should be used when the mathematical model is not too complex and the underlying assumptions are satisfied. In other cases the simulation approach, as described in this chapter, is a viable alternative.

12.1   COUNTY BEVERAGE DRIVE-THRU

County Beverage Drive-Thru, Inc. is a company that is building a chain of beverage supply stores throughout an area in northern Illinois. The stores are designed to enable customers to pick up beverages, snacks, and party supplies without getting out of their cars. A typical store design is shown in Figure 12.1. A service lane runs through the middle of the store, and soft drinks, beer, and other supplies are stored at various locations along both sides of the service lane. When a customer drives into the store, the store clerk takes the order, fills the order, and collects the money. The customer remains in the car while receiving service. When additional customers arrive at the store, they wait in a line outside the store until the preceding customer's order is complete. Then the next customer in line drives into the store for service.

FIGURE 12.1
Layout of County Beverage Drive-Thru

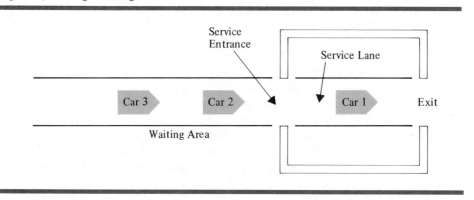

The County Beverage Drive-Thru operation is an example of a *waiting-line* or *queueing system*. This particular waiting-line configuration has one service lane and is therefore referred to as a *single-channel waiting line*. If we are willing to assume that the number of cars arriving at the store has a Poisson probability distribution and that the length of time that the customer is actually in the store (service time) has an exponential probability distribution, the mathematical models presented in the next chapter can be used to study this waiting-line system. However, for the County Beverage Drive-Thru we are not willing to make these assumptions; thus we will be using computer simulation to study the operation of the store.

The specific situation we will simulate is a new store that will be located near a major shopping center. Construction of the store will not begin for approximately 3 months. County Beverage's president has requested planning information on the projected operation of the store, including estimates of the number of customers served, profitability of the store, and the number of lost sales due to long waiting lines.

In modeling the system we will study the store's operation in terms of what happens during time periods of 3 minutes each. That is, we will count the number of customer arrivals, count the number of customers lost, and determine whether or not a customer is being serviced during each 3-minute interval. A simulation model that increments time in fixed intervals is referred to as a *fixed-time simulation model*.[1]

Based on a study of traffic flow, the company has estimated that the probability distribution of customer arrivals is as shown in Table 12.1. This probability distribution is believed to be representative of the number of arrivals during the peak business period occurring in the late afternoon and early evening. As the data show, there is a 0.19 probability of no customers arriving during a given 3-minute period, a 0.39 probability of one customer arriving during the same 3-minute period, and so on.

TABLE 12.1
Probability Distribution for the Number of Customers Arriving at the County Beverage Drive-Thru During a 3-Minute Period

Number of Customers Arriving	Probability
0	0.19
1	0.39
2	0.19
3	0.15
4	0.08
	1.00

Sales records from the company's other stores show that customers vary in terms of the size of the order placed. For three classes of order size (small, medium, and large), the probability for the various order sizes, the average time to fill the orders, and the average profit per order are shown in Table 12.2.

TABLE 12.2
Order Size Data for the County Beverage Drive-Thru

Order Size	Probability	Time to Fill Order	Average Profit
Small	0.39	3 minutes	$0.75
Medium	0.50	6 minutes	$1.50
Large	0.11	9 minutes	$3.00
	1.00		

---

[1] Simulation models that increment time based on the occurrence of the next event (time of next arrival, time of next service, and so on) are referred to as *next-event simulation models*. Next-event simulation models will not be discussed in detail in this text.

As an additional operating condition, experience with other company stores indicates that customers will wait for service only if there are less than four cars in the waiting line. If a customer arrives and there are already four cars in the waiting area, the customer will drive off. This failure to enter the waiting line is referred to as *balking* and results in a lost customer and a lost profit.

Simulation of Customer Arrivals

Before developing the complete simulation model, let us concentrate on simulating the number of customers that arrive at the store during any 3-minute period. In simulating the customer arrival process for County Beverage we will also be demonstrating how the probabilistic component of a real-world process or system is modeled.

The technique used to simulate customer arrivals is based on the use of random numbers. Almost everyone who has been exposed to simple random sampling and basic statistics is familiar with tables of random digits or random numbers.[2] We have included a table of random numbers in Appendix B. Twenty random numbers from the first line of this table are as follows:

63271   59986   71744   51102

The specific digit appearing in a given position is a random selection of the digits 0, 1, 2, . . . , 9, with each digit having an equal chance of selection. The grouping of the numbers in sets of five is simply for the convenience of making the table easier to read.

Suppose we select random numbers from our table in sets of two digits. There are 100 two-digit random numbers from 00 to 99, with each two-digit random number having a $1/100 = 0.01$ chance of occurring. While we could select two-digit random numbers from any part of the random number table, suppose we start by using the first row of random numbers from Appendix B. The first 10 two-digit random numbers are

63   27   15   99   86   71   74   45   11   02

Now let us see how we can simulate the number of customers arriving in a 3-minute period by associating a given number of arrivals with each of the 100 two-digit random numbers. For example, let us consider the possibility of no customers arriving during a 3-minute interval. The probability distribution in Table 12.1 shows this event to have a 0.19 probability. Since each two-digit random number has a 0.01 probability of occurrence, we can let 19 of the 100 possible two-digit random numbers correspond to no customers arriving. Any 19 numbers from 00 to 99 will do, but for convenience we associate the arrival of 0 customers with the first 19 two-digit numbers: 00, 01, 02, 03, . . . , 18. Thus any time one of these two-digit numbers is observed in a random selection, we will say that no customers arrived during that period. Since the numbers 00 to 18 include 19% of the possible two-digit random numbers, we expect the arrival of no customers for any given 3-minute interval to have a probability of 0.19.

Now consider the possibility of one customer arriving during a 3-minute period, an event that has a 0.39 probability of occurring (see Table 12.1). Letting 39 of the 100 two-digit numbers (such as 19, 20, 21, 22, . . . , 57) correspond to a simulated arrival

[2]See, for example, *A Million Random Digits with 100,000 Normal Deviates*, Rand Corporation, 1955.

of one customer will provide a 0.39 probability for one customer arrival. Continuing to assign the number of customers arriving to sets of two-digit numbers according to the probability distribution shown in Table 12.1 results in the sets of random numbers and customer arrival assignments shown in Table 12.3.

TABLE 12.3
Random-Number Assignments for the Number of Customers Arriving at the County Beverage Drive-Thru During a 3-Minute Time Period

Number of Customers	Associated Two-Digit Random Numbers	Interval Description	Probability
0	00, 01, . . . , 18	00 but less than 19	0.19
1	19, 20, . . . , 57	19 but less than 58	0.39
2	58, 59, . . . , 76	58 but less than 77	0.19
3	77, 78, . . . , 91	77 but less than 92	0.15
4	92, 93, . . . , 99	92 but less than 100	0.08

Using Table 12.3 and the two-digit random numbers in the first row of Appendix B (63, 27, 15, 99, 86, . . .), we can simulate the number of customers arriving during the 3-minute periods. The results for 10 such 3-minute periods, or ½ hour of store operation, are shown in Table 12.4. The first two-digit random number, 63, is in the interval 58 to 76; thus according to Table 12.3 this corresponds to two customers arriving during the first 3-minute period. The second random number, 27, is in the interval 19 to 57; thus the number of simulated customer arrivals during the second period is one, and so on.

TABLE 12.4
Simulated Customer Arrivals for Ten 3-Minute Periods at the County Beverage Drive-Thru

Period	Random Number	Simulated Customer Arrivals
1	63	2
2	27	1
3	15	0
4	99	4
5	86	3
6	71	2
7	74	2
8	45	1
9	11	0
10	02	0
	Total	15

By selecting a two-digit random number for each 3-minute period, we can simulate the number of customer arrivals during that period. In doing so, the simulated probability distribution for the number of customer arrivals is the same as the given probability distribution shown in Table 12.1. In this manner, the simulation of customer arrivals has the same characteristics as the specified distribution of customer arrivals. Simulations that use a random-number procedure to generate probabilistic inputs such as the number of customer arrivals are referred to as *Monte Carlo simulations*.

For any simulation model it is relatively easy to apply the above random-number procedure to simulate values of a random variable. First develop a table similar to Table 12.3 by associating an interval of random numbers with each possible value of the random variable. In doing so, be sure that the probability of selecting a random number from each interval is the same as the actual probability associated with the value of the random variable. Then each time a value of the random variable is needed, we simply select a new random number and use the corresponding interval of random numbers to find the value of the random variable.

Using a similar procedure, we see that the random-number intervals given in Table 12.5 can be used to simulate order sizes for customers stopping at the County Beverage Drive-Thru.

A Simulation Model for County Beverage Drive-Thru

Now that we know how to simulate the number of customers arriving and the customer order size, let us proceed with the development of the logic for the County Beverage simulation model. We will develop the model in a step-by-step manner. In doing so, we will carry out the necessary calculations to demonstrate how the simulation process works.

Whenever we need to generate a value for the number of customers arriving and/or the order size, we will use the random numbers from row 10 of Appendix B. Tables 12.3 and 12.5 will be used to determine the corresponding number of customer arrivals and the order sizes. For convenience, the first five two-digit random numbers from row 10 are reproduced here:

$$81 \qquad 62 \qquad 83 \qquad 61 \qquad 00$$

TABLE 12.5
Random-Number Assignments for the Order Size of Customers at the County Beverage Drive-Thru

Order Size	Associated Two-Digit Random Numbers	Interval Description	Probability
Small	00, 01, . . . , 38	00 but less than 39	0.39
Medium	39, 40, . . . , 88	39 but less than 89	0.50
Large	89, 90, . . . , 99	89 but less than 100	0.11

In developing the logic and mathematical relationships for the simulation model, we follow the logic and relationships of the actual operation as closely as possible. To demonstrate the simulation process, we begin with an idle or empty store and simulate what happens for each of the first three periods. Try to follow the logic of the model and see if you agree with the statements under the column labeled "Things that Happen."

Period 1 (see Figure 12.2)

Random Number	Things That Happen
81	Three cars arrive for service; thus the first car, identified as car 1, gets immediate service.
62	Car 1 places a medium order and hence will not finish service until the end of period 2 (6 minutes).
	Cars 2 and 3 still want service and consequently are in the waiting line.

FIGURE 12.2
Status of the Operation for the First 3-Minute Simulation Period

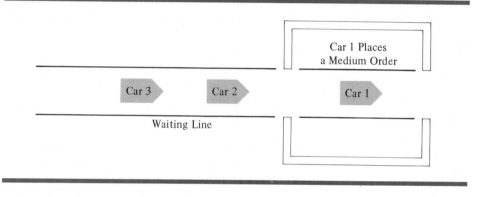

Period 2 (see Figure 12.3)

Random Number	Things That Happen
83	Three more cars, identified as cars 4, 5, and 6, arrive for service.
	The Drive-Thru is still busy serving the customer from period 1; thus a total of five cars (two waiting plus three new customers) are wanting service this period.
	Too many cars are attempting to get service; hence one customer (car 6) will be lost and four cars will remain in the waiting line.
	Car 1 completes service at the end of this period; a profit of $1.50 is recorded.

The flowchart of the simulation model we have been using is shown in Figure 12.5. Continue to use the random numbers from row 10 of Appendix B and see if you can conduct the simulation calculations for the first 10 periods of operation. Your simulation results should agree with those shown in Table 12.6.

FIGURE 12.3
Status of the Operation for the Second 3-Minute Simulation Period

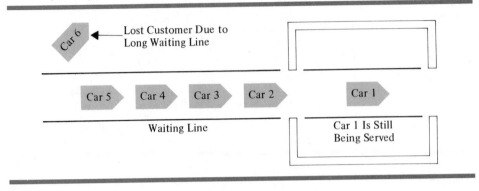

Period 3 (see Figure 12.4)

Random Number	Things That Happen
61	Two more cars, identified as cars 7 and 8, arrive for service.
	The service area is free at the beginning of the period, since the customer from period 1 (car 1) has completed service and left the Drive-Thru.
	One car from the waiting line (car 2) begins service, leaving five cars still wanting service; hence one customer (car 8) will be lost and four cars will remain in the waiting line.
00	The customer in car 2 places a small order; thus car 2 will finish service at the end of this period. Total profit as of the end of this period will be $1.50 (car 1) + $0.75 (car 2) = $2.25.

FIGURE 12.4
Status of the Operation for the Third 3-Minute Simulation Period

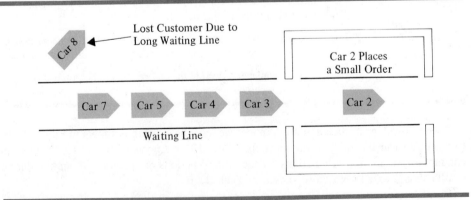

FIGURE 12.5
Flowchart of the County Beverage Drive-Thru Simulation Model

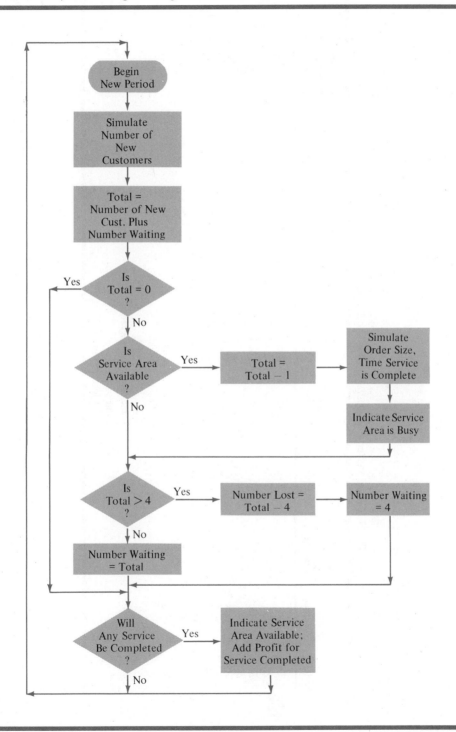

TABLE 12.6
Simulation Results from Ten 3-Minute Periods of Operation for the County Beverage Drive-Thru

Period	Random Number	Number of New Customers	Is Service Area Available?	Random Number	Order Size	Service Periods	Number of Lost Customers	Number Waiting	Was Service Completed This Period?	Profit
1	81	3	Yes	62	Medium	2	0	2	No	—
2	83	3	No	—	—	—	1	4	Yes	$1.50
3	61	2	Yes	00	Small	1	1	4	Yes	0.75
4	39	1	Yes	25	Small	1	0	4	Yes	0.75
5	45	1	Yes	68	Medium	2	0	4	No	—
6	35	1	No	—	—	—	1	4	Yes	1.50
7	37	1	Yes	63	Medium	2	0	4	No	—
8	60	2	No	—	—	—	2	4	Yes	1.50
9	24	1	Yes	21	Small	1	0	4	Yes	0.75
10	98	4	Yes	06	Small	1	3	4	Yes	0.75

Total customers served   7
Total profit $7.50
Total lost customers   8

At this point we have succeeded in simulating 10 periods, or a total of 30 minutes of operation. Although the results in Table 12.6 show evidence of long waiting lines and high lost customer rates (eight in the first ½ hour), a 30-minute simulation period is too short a time frame to draw general conclusions about the operation of the store. In order to take full advantage of the simulation procedure, we must continue to simulate the store's operation for many more time periods. But even for this relatively small simulation problem, continuing the hand simulation computations as we have been doing is unrealistic, if not practically impossible. Thus we will look to the computer to provide the computational assistance necessary to conduct the simulation process.

Computer Simulation: Generating Pseudorandom Numbers

If a computer procedure is going to be used to perform the simulation calculations, we will need a way for the computer to generate random numbers and values for the probabilistic components of the model. While the computer could be programmed to store random-number tables and then follow the procedure outlined previously, the computer storage space required would result in an inefficient use of computer resources. For this reason, computer simulations make use of mathematical formulas that generate numbers which, for all practical purposes, have the same properties as the numbers selected from random-number tables. These numbers are called *pseudorandom numbers*. In computer simulations pseudorandom numbers are used in exactly the same way as we used the random numbers selected from random-number tables in our hand simulation.

Most mathematical formulas designed to generate pseudorandom numbers produce numbers from 0 up to but not including 1. Thus we must consider a somewhat different approach in order to simulate the number of customer arrivals and the order size. We must now associate an interval of pseudorandom numbers with each number of arrivals so that the probability of generating a pseudorandom number in the interval will be equal to the probability of the corresponding number of arrivals. Table 12.7 shows how this would be done for the number of cars arriving at the County Beverage Drive-Thru. Note that Table 12.7 shows a pseudorandom number less than 0.19 corresponds to no arrivals, a pseudorandom number greater than or equal to 0.19 but less than 0.58 corresponds to one arrival, and so on. Table 12.8 provides the pseudorandom number intervals that can be used to simulate the order sizes for County Beverage customers.

TABLE 12.7
Pseudorandom-Number Intervals and the Associated Number of Customers Arriving at the County Beverage Drive-Thru

Interval of Pseudorandom Numbers	Simulated Customer Arrivals	Probability
0.00 but less than 0.19	0	0.19
0.19 but less than 0.58	1	0.39
0.58 but less than 0.77	2	0.19
0.77 but less than 0.92	3	0.15
0.92 but less than 1.00	4	0.08
		1.00

TABLE 12.8
Pseudorandom-Number Intervals and the Associated Order Sizes for County Beverage Customers

Interval of Pseudorandom Numbers	Simulated Order Size	Probability
0.00 but less than 0.39	Small	0.39
0.39 but less than 0.89	Medium	0.50
0.89 but less than 1.00	Large	0.11
		1.00

Computer Simulation: Computer Program and Results

A computer *simulator* is a computer program written to conduct simulation computations. In order to simulate the operation of the County Beverage Drive-Thru, we need to develop a computer program containing the logic shown in Figure 12.5. Such a program would perform the calculations and keep track of the simulation results in a form similar to that shown in Table 12.6. Figure 12.6 shows a computer program written in the BASIC language that will simulate the County Beverage operation. This particular program was developed for and run on an IBM Personal Computer. For relatively small simulation models, the use of the BASIC language and a microcomputer is a realistic approach to conducting a simulation of a particular system.

Results from the computer simulation are shown in Table 12.9. The store's operation was simulated for a total of 30 hours (600 time periods). Based on the simulation results, we are able to make the following observations about the behavior of the system:

1. 365 customers were serviced during the 30 hours of simulated operation. However, 575 cars (61.2%) were lost because of long waiting lines.
2. The average profit was $16.28 per hour or $1.34 per car serviced ($488.25/365 = $1.34).
3. The biggest problem with the store's operation appears to be the number of lost customers (an average of 19.17 per hour). An estimate of the average dollar loss per hour due to lost customers is 19.17 ($1.34 per car) = $25.69.

TABLE 12.9
Computer Simulation Results for 30 Hours of Operation

Item of Interest	Total	Percent	Hourly Average
Number served	365	38.8	12.17
Number lost	575	61.2	19.17
Profit	$488.25	—	$16.28

Recall for a moment that a primary objective of simulation is to describe the behavior of a real system. In the County Beverage Drive-Thru simulation this is exactly what we have done. We have not determined an optimal solution or decision for the store; we

FIGURE 12.6
BASIC Program (IBM Personal Computer) for Simulation of the County Beverage
Drive-Thru

```
10   RANDOMIZE
20   REM
30   REM THIS PROGRAM SIMULATES THE OPERATION
40   REM OF THE COUNTY BEVERAGE DRIVE-THRU
50   REM
60   HOUR=-1
70   WORK=0
80   WAITING=0
90   FINISH=0
100  TSERVD=0
110  TPROF=0
120  TLOST=0
130  TIME=0
140  IF FINISH>=20 THEN FINISH=FINISH-20
150  REM
160  REM SIMULATE THE NUMBER OF CARS ARRIVING IN A TIME PERIOD
170  REM
180  TIME=TIME+1
190  X=RND(1)
200  IF X<.19 THEN CAR=0
210  IF (X>=.19) and (X<.58) THEN CAR=1
220  IF (X>=.58) and (X<.77) THEN CAR=2
230  IF (X>=.77) and (X<.92) THEN CAR=3
240  IF (X>=.92) THEN CAR=4
250  TOTAL=WAITING+CAR
260  IF TOTAL=0 GOTO 500
270  IF WORK=1 GOTO 400
280  TOTAL=TOTAL-1
290  REM
300  REM SIMULATE THE ORDER SIZE OF THE NEXT CAR TO BE SERVICED
310  REM
320  X=RND(1)
330  IF X<.39 THEN LENGTH=1
340  IF (X>=.39) AND (X<.89) THEN LENGTH=2
350  IF (X>=.89) THEN LENGTH=3
360  FINISH=TIME+LENGTH-1
370  WORK=1
380  REM
390  REM CALCULATE THE NUMBER OF LOST CUSTOMERS AND NUMBER WAITING
400  REM
410  IF TOTAL>4 GOTO 440
420  WAITING=TOTAL
430  GOTO 500
440  LOST=TOTAL-4
450  WAITING=4
460  TLOST=TLOST+LOST
470  REM
480  REM RELEASE A CAR COMPLETING SERVICE AND RECORD THE PROFIT
490  REM
500  IF FINISH>TIME GOTO 180
510  IF LENGTH=1 THEN PROFIT=.75
520  IF LENGTH=2 THEN PROFIT=1.5
530  IF LENGTH=3 THEN PROFIT=3
540  TPROF=TPROF+PROFIT
550  TSERVD=TSERVD+1
560  WORK=0
570  REM
580  REM SIMULATION RUN OF 20 TIME PERIODS PER HOUR
590  REM
600  IF TIME<20 GOTO 180
610  HOUR=HOUR+1
```

Continued

FIGURE 12.6
Continued

```
620   IF HOUR=0 GOTO 100
630   REM
640   REM WRITE SUMMARY RESULTS OF SIMULATION RUN
650   REM
660   IF HOUR<30 GOTO 130
670   ASERVD=TSERVD/30
680   PSERVD=TSERVD/(TSERVD+TLOST)*100
690   ALOST=TLOST/30
700   PLOST=100-PSERVD
710   APROF=TPROF/30
720   PRINT
730   PRINT
740   PRINT TAB(8) "ITEM OF INTEREST" TAB(29) "TOTAL" TAB(41) "PERCENT"
TAB(53) "HOURLY AVERAGE"
750   PRINT
760   S$="SERVED"
770   L$="LOST"
780   P$="PROFIT"
790   PRINT USING "      \     \        ####       ###.#         ####.##"
;S$;TSERVD;PSERVD;ASERVD
800   PRINT
810   PRINT USING "      \     \        ####       ###.#         ####.##"
;L$;TLOST;PLOST;ALOST
820   PRINT
830   PRINT USING "      \     \        -$###.##                 -$##.#
#";P$;TPROF;APROF
840   END
```

have simply simulated what could happen in 30 hours of actual operation of the Drive-Thru. If the actual operation behaves as the simulation model indicates, County Beverage will have a significant waiting-line problem with a sizable lost profit.

12.2   COUNTY BEVERAGE DRIVE-THRU: ADDITIONAL SIMULATION RESULTS

The primary conclusion from the simulation results presented in Section 12.1 for the County Beverage operation is that the store cannot handle the amount of business that is anticipated. Undoubtedly, County Beverage management would like to explore alternative operating policies that might improve service and hence company profits. Certainly, the addition of a second store clerk should help the performance of the system. In addition, since construction of the building has not begun, management could consider a possible redesign of the store. Thus the following two operating policies and store layouts are being considered.

System A (see Figure 12.7)

Two clerks will operate the store during the peak business period. Two cars will be permitted into the store area for servicing at the same time. Bottlenecks may still occur because both cars must use the same lane. If the second car completes service before the first car, it will have to wait for the first car to complete service before it can leave the store. Also, if the first car finishes service first, it can leave the store, but a new customer cannot enter the store until the car in the second position has its order filled.

FIGURE 12.7
Proposed Design, System A, for the County Beverage Drive-Thru

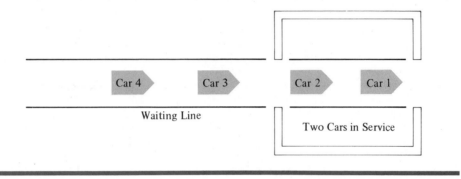

System B *(see Figure 12.8)*

Two clerks will operate the store during the peak period. The service lane of the store will be widened to permit two cars to be serviced simultaneously, with each car being permitted to leave the store as soon as it is finished. Waiting cars move into the store as soon as either lane opens up.

FIGURE 12.8
Proposed Design, System B, for the County Beverage Drive-Thru

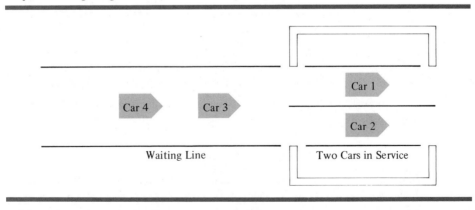

In order to help the company determine which system should be adopted, simulation models were developed for both systems. Tables 12.10 and 12.11 show the results of 30 hours of simulation for each system. These simulation results provide critical information to the individual responsible for the final design decision.

System *A* shows an average profit of $27.88 per hour, an increase of $11.60 per hour over the original one-lane, one-server system. However, 302 customers (32.8%) were lost because of long waiting lines. Although system *B* shows a higher average profit ($34.48) and a lower lost customer rate (15.9%), the advantage of system *B* may be offset by the added construction cost required to widen the service lane. The final decision may still take more study, but the simulation results provide important information for the decision maker. Perhaps a creative person could come up with an idea for modifying the single-service-lane operation to increase the number of cars served and still avoid the costly two-lane construction. If such an idea occurs, a simulation model could be developed to evaluate its effectiveness.

TABLE 12.10
Computer Simulation Results for 30 Hours of Operation at the County Beverage Drive-Thru Under System A

Item of Interest	Total	Percent	Hourly Average
Number served	618	67.2	20.60
Number lost	302	32.8	10.07
Profit	$836.25	—	$27.88

TABLE 12.11
Computer Simulation Results for 30 Hours of Operation at the County Beverage Drive-Thru Under System B

Item of Interest	Total	Percent	Hourly Average
Number served	785	84.1	26.17
Number lost	148	15.9	4.93
Profit	$1034.25	—	$34.48

12.3 SOME PRACTICAL CONSIDERATIONS

Let us now describe some other aspects of simulation that are encountered in almost every simulation study.

Selecting a Simulation Language

In developing the computer program or simulator, a decision must be made as to the computer language that will be used. General-purpose programming languages such as BASIC, FORTRAN, Pascal, and PL/1 can be used to develop the computer programs. However, as simulation applications and interest have increased, users as well as computer manufacturers have recognized that most computer simulations have many common features: values of random variables must be generated from probability distributions; tables are needed to keep track of simulation results; and so on. Thus special programming languages have been developed to enable analysts and programmers to describe more easily simulation models in computer form.

Some of the more common simulation languages in use today are GPSS, SIM-SCRIPT, DYNAMO, GASP, and SLAM. These special simulation languages frequently have automatic or built-in time indicators, simplified procedures for generating probabilistic components, and automatic collection and printout of statistical results. One programming statement of a simulation language often performs the computation and record keeping that would require several BASIC, FORTRAN, PASCAL, or PL/1 statements to duplicate. There are complete textbooks devoted to a discussion of the use of computer languages in simulation, and the interested reader can refer to one of the references listed at the end of this text.

Validation

An important step in any simulation study is the validation of the simulation model. Validation involves verifying that the simulation model accurately represents the real-world system it is designed to simulate. Models that do not adequately reflect the behavior of the real system cannot be expected to provide worthwhile information. Thus before implementing any simulation results the analyst must be sure that a thorough job of model validation has been done.

If the simulation model applies to a system currently in operation, the simulation results can be compared with the current and past behavior of the system in order to determine the validity of the model. The procedure usually followed is to run the simulation model using an actual set of past observations. In this way the output of the simulation model can be directly compared with the behavior of the actual system. Any major difference in the results is indicative of problems in the model.

Another approach to model validation is to have the overall model reviewed by people who are most familiar with the operation of the real system. This review is subjective in nature, with the appropriate individuals evaluating the reasonableness of the simulation model and the simulation results.

In addition, careful attention should also be paid to the programming of the simulation model. Even if the model is formulated correctly, improper programming of the model can lead to inaccurate results. Standard quality-control steps and good programming practice can be the best safeguards against this type of error.

A further check in the validation procedure is to compare the simulated distributions for the probabilistic components with the corresponding distributions in the real system. For example, in the County Beverage study, the probability distribution for the number of cars arriving in a three-minute period was considered known and was an important input for the simulation model. Recall that the simulation results shown in Table 12.9 were based on 30 hours of simulated operation. Since each hour has twenty three-minute periods, the total simulation contained 30(20) = 600 three-minute periods. Thus if the simulation model is correctly simulating the number of customers arriving at the store, the relative frequencies of the number of cars arriving should approximate the probability distribution for the real system as shown in Table 12.1.

Table 12.12 shows the relative frequencies for the number of customers that arrived during the 600 three-minute periods in the simulation run. A comparison of the simulated distribution and the actual probability distribution from Table 12.1 shows no major differences. Thus we conclude that the number of customer arrivals is being simulated

TABLE 12.12
Model-Validation Step Showing a Comparison of the Simulated Relative Frequencies and the Actual Probability Distribution for the Number of Customer Arrivals at the County Beverage Drive-Thru

Number of Customer Arrivals	Number of Simulated Periods Having This Number of Arrivals	Simulated Relative Frequencies	Actual Probabilities (See Table 12.1)
0	124	0.207	0.19
1	229	0.382	0.39
2	104	0.173	0.19
3	86	0.143	0.15
4	57	0.095	0.08
Totals	600	1.000	1.00

correctly.[3] A similar comparison of the actual and simulated distributions for the size of the customer orders resulted in the conclusion that the model was valid in terms of its simulation of this probabilistic component.

Start-Up Problems

Most simulation studies are concerned with the operation of a system during its normal, or *steady-state*, condition. In the County Beverage example the firm is interested in what happens during a "normal" hour of operation. Recall, however, that when we started the simulation calculations we assumed that no cars were waiting and that no cars were being served. Therefore data collected during the first part of the simulation can be expected to differ from the data collected during time intervals later in the simulation. The usual way to avoid start-up difficulties is to run the simulation model for a specified time period without collecting any data. The length of this start-up period must be sufficient for the system to have stabilized. Data are then collected on the system after it has reached a stable, or steady-state, condition. For the County Beverage simulation, the first hour of operation was considered a start-up period. The data for the 30 hours of simulation reported in Table 12.9 are the simulation results for hours 2 through 31.

Statistical Considerations

The results of any simulation run actually represent a sample. For example, the simulation results in Table 12.9 can be viewed as a sample of 30 hours of operation. Thus $16.28 is an estimate of the average hourly profit for the County Beverage operation. The important thing to keep in mind is that different values for average hourly profit would be observed if the simulation was run again using a different sequence of random numbers.

---

[3]Standard statistical procedures, such as the chi-square goodness-of-fit test, can be performed to test whether or not the results observed are representative of those expected. The use of such tests is described in most standard statistics texts. For example, see Anderson, D. R., D. J. Sweeney, and T. A. Williams, *Statistics for Business and Economics*, 3d ed. St. Paul, Minn., West Publishing Company, 1987.

To illustrate this, we ran two additional simulations each for 30 hours of operation. The results are as follows:

	Simulation 1	Simulation 2	Simulation 3
Number served	365	361	356
Number lost	575	558	622
Average hourly profit	$16.28	$16.13	$16.10

Although different results are obtained in each case, by running the simulations for long periods, most analysts are willing to use the values obtained from the original simulation run to estimate the true mean value of interest.

Determining the best statistical approach to estimating the value of some quantity (such as hourly profit) is not a simple problem. A complete study of this issue would require a background in the area of statistics referred to as experimental design. Consequently, the interested reader is referred to one of the more advanced texts in simulation listed at the end of the text.

12.4 AN INVENTORY SIMULATION MODEL

In this section we present a simulation model of an inventory system being operated by an auto supply company. While we are interested in understanding how the inventory system operates, we are also interested in making decisions concerning the reorder point and order quantity for a particular inventory item. By designing a set of experiments, we will simulate the operation of the inventory system for a variety of reorder point and order quantity alternatives. Upon completion of the experiments with the simulation model we should be able to select a good reorder point and order quantity for the item.

Art's Auto Supplies, Inc. is a specialty auto supplies store that carries over 1000 items in inventory. Although the store's manager has used inventory models to determine how-much-to-order and when-to-order for most of the products, the manager has become especially concerned about the inventory problem for a deluxe tool cabinet. Demand for the cabinets has been relatively low but subject to some variability. While on approximately one-half of the days the store is open for business no one orders a cabinet, about 1 day per month three or four orders occur. If variable demand were the only source of uncertainty, the store manager believes the order quantity and reorder point decisions could be based on an inventory model, perhaps similar to the inventory model discussed in Section 11.1. However, the tool cabinet inventory problem is further complicated by the fact that the lead time—the time between order placement and order arrival—also varies. Historically the length of the lead time has been anywhere between 1 and 5 days. These lead times have caused the store to run out of inventory on several occasions. Orders received during the out-of-stock period have caused lost sales. Thus given this situation, the store manager would like to establish order quantity and reorder point decisions that minimize total relevant inventory costs—that is, ordering, holding, and stockout or shortage costs.

After an analysis of delivery charges and other costs associated with each order, the store manager was able to estimate the order cost at $20 per order. An analysis of interest, insurance, and other inventory carrying costs led to an estimate for the holding cost of $0.10 per unit per day. Finally, the shortage cost was estimated to be $50 per unit. The total cost of the system is given by the sum of the ordering cost, the holding cost, and the shortage cost. The objective is to find the order quantity and reorder point combination that will result in the lowest possible total cost.

A first step in the simulation approach to this problem is to develop a model that can be used to simulate the total costs corresponding to a specific order size and reorder point. Then, using this model, the two decision variables can be varied systematically in order to determine what appears to be the lowest cost combination. Let us see what is involved in developing such a model to carry out a 1-day simulation of the inventory process.

Assume that a specific reorder point and order quantity have already been selected. We must begin each day of the simulation by checking whether any inventory that had been ordered has just arrived. If so, the current inventory on hand must be increased by the quantity of goods received. Note that this assumes that orders are received and inventory on hand is updated at the start of each day. If this assumption is not appropriate, a different model, perhaps calling for goods to be received at the end of the day, would have to be developed.

Next our simulator must generate a value for the daily demand from the appropriate probability distribution. If there is sufficient inventory on hand to meet the daily demand, the inventory on hand will be decreased by the amount of the daily demand. If, however, inventory on hand is not sufficient to satisfy all the demand, we will satisfy as much of the demand as possible. The inventory will then be zero, and a shortage cost will be computed for all unsatisfied demand. In using this procedure we are assuming that if a customer orders more cabinets than the store has in inventory, the customer will take what is available and shop elsewhere for the remainder of the order. With another auto supply store only two blocks away, the store manager is sure unsatisfied demand will result in lost sales, and a $50 goodwill cost for each shortage is appropriate.

After the daily order has been processed, the next step is to determine if the ending inventory has reached the reorder point and a new order should be placed. However, prior to placing a new order, we must check to see if the most recent order is outstanding and should be arriving shortly. If so, we do not place another order.[4] Otherwise an order is placed and the company incurs an ordering cost. If a new order is placed, a lead time must be randomly generated to reflect the time between the placement and the receipt of the goods.

Finally, an inventory holding cost, which is $0.10 for each unit in the daily ending inventory, is computed. The sum of the shortage costs, ordering costs, and inventory holding costs becomes the total daily cost for the simulation. Performing the above sequence of operations would complete one day of simulation. Figure 12.9 depicts this daily simulation process for the deluxe tool cabinet inventory operation.

The daily simulation process should be repeated for as many days as are necessary to obtain meaningful results. The output from the simulation will show the total cost involved in using one particular order quantity and reorder point combination. By simulating the inventory operation with different order quantity–reorder point combinations, we can compare total operating costs and select the apparent "best" order quantity and reorder point decisions for the deluxe tool cabinets.

---

[4]We are assuming that it will never be necessary to have two orders outstanding simultaneously. However, in other simulation models, having several orders outstanding may be an entirely appropriate assumption.

FIGURE 12.9
Flowchart of the Simulation of 1 Day of Operation for the Art's Auto Supplies Inventory System

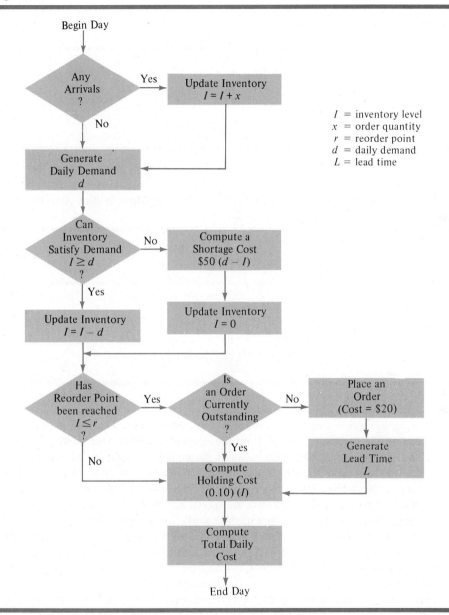

Suppose the store has a complete set of records showing the demand for the deluxe tool cabinets for the past year (300 days). Furthermore, suppose the records also show the number of days between placement and receipt of each order over the same period. Table 12.13 shows the frequency and relative frequency distributions for demand, and Table 12.14 shows the frequency and relative frequency distributions for lead time.

TABLE 12.13
Frequency and Relative Frequency Distributions for Demand in Art's Auto Supplies Problem

Demand (units)	Frequency (days)	Relative Frequency
0	150	0.50
1	75	0.25
2	45	0.15
3	15	0.05
4	15	0.05
	300	1.00

TABLE 12.14
Frequency and Relative Frequency Distributions for Lead Time in Art's Auto Supplies Problem

Lead Time (days)	Frequency (days)	Relative Frequency
1	6	0.20
2	3	0.10
3	12	0.40
4	6	0.20
5	3	0.10
	30	1.00

In order to carry out the simulation steps depicted in Figure 12.9, we must develop the procedure for generating values from the demand and lead time distributions. As before, we shall associate with each value of the random variable an interval of pseudorandom numbers such that the probability of generating a pseudorandom number in that interval is the same as the relative frequency of the associated demand and lead time. The intervals of pseudorandom numbers are shown in Tables 12.15 and 12.16.

To appreciate how the simulation method works for this problem, we will follow a 10-day simulation of the process. Let us assume that the store manager wants to determine the effect of using an order quantity of five units with a reorder point of three units. For purposes of starting the simulation, let us assume that we have a beginning inventory of five units at the start of day 1 of our 10-day simulation.

Refer to the flowchart in Figure 12.9. The first step is to check to see if any shipments have arrived. Since this is the first day of the simulation, we assume no arrivals, and generate the daily demand for day 1. Let us assume we use a computer to generate pseudorandom numbers between 0 and 0.999 · · · and that the first number generated is 0.093. From Table 12.15 we see that this pseudorandom number corresponds to a demand of 0 units. Note that we have no shortage costs to compute since the inventory on hand (five units) is greater than the reorder point (three units); and, we do not place an order. The holding costs for day 1 are computed to be ($0.10)5, or $0.50. With no shortages

TABLE 12.15
Pseudorandom Numbers and Associated Daily Demands for Art's Auto Supplies Problem

Daily Demand	Relative Frequency	Interval of Pseudorandom Numbers	Probability of Selecting a Pseudorandom Number in Interval
0	0.50	0.00 but less than 0.50	0.50
1	0.25	0.50 but less than 0.75	0.25
2	0.15	0.75 but less than 0.90	0.15
3	0.05	0.90 but less than 0.95	0.05
4	0.05	0.95 but less than 1.00	0.05
	1.00		1.00

TABLE 12.16
Pseudorandom Number Intervals and Associated Lead Times for Art's Auto Supplies Problem

Lead Time (days)	Relative Frequency	Interval of Pseudorandom Numbers	Probability of Selecting a Pseudorandom Number in Interval
1	0.20	0.00 but less than 0.20	0.20
2	0.10	0.20 but less than 0.30	0.10
3	0.40	0.30 but less than 0.70	0.40
4	0.20	0.70 but less than 0.90	0.20
5	0.10	0.90 but less than 1.00	0.10
	1.00		1.00

and no ordering, the total cost for day 1 is just the holding cost of $0.50. Continuing the simulation in this manner, we obtained the computer-generated results shown in Table 12.17.

At the start of day 4 the beginning inventory was four units. The random number selected to generate daily demand was 0.528; thus a daily demand of one unit was generated. As a result, the ending inventory dropped to three units and an order for five units was placed. Generating another random number, in this case 0.620, indicates (see Table 12.16) a lead time of 3 days, which means that the new order will be available on day 7. The day 4 costs are ($0.10)3 = $0.30 for the inventory holding cost and $20.00 for the ordering cost. Since there is no shortage cost, the total cost for the day is $20.30. The figures at the bottom of Table 12.17 provide the average holding cost, average ordering cost, average shortage cost, and average total cost for the 10-day simulation. Prior to drawing any firm conclusions based on these limited simulation results, we should run the simulation for many more days. Also we will want to test many other order quantity–reorder point combinations.

TABLE 12.17
Computer Simulation Results for 10 Days of Operation of Art's Auto Supplies with an
Order Quantity of Five and Reorder Point of Three

Day	Beg Inv	Units Rec'd	Rndm Num	Units Demd	End Inv	Rndm Num	Lead Time	Holding Cost $	Order Cost $	Short Cost $	Total Cost $
1	5	0	0.093	0	5			0.50	0.00	0.00	0.50
2	5	0	0.681	1	4			0.40	0.00	0.00	0.40
3	4	0	0.292	0	4			0.40	0.00	0.00	0.40
4	4	0	0.528	1	3	0.620	3	0.30	20.00	0.00	20.30
5	3	0	0.866	2	1			0.10	0.00	0.00	0.10
6	1	0	0.975	4	0			0.00	0.00	150.00	150.00
7	0	5	0.622	1	4			0.40	0.00	0.00	0.40
8	4	0	0.819	2	2	0.939	5	0.20	20.00	0.00	20.20
9	2	0	0.373	0	2			0.20	0.00	0.00	0.20
10	2	0	0.353	0	2			0.20	0.00	0.00	0.20
				Average cost for 10 simulated days				0.27	4.00	15.00	19.27

A computer programmer could develop a computer simulation program or simulator that would enable the store to explore a variety of order quantities and reorder points for a large number of simulated days. In Table 12.18 we present output from a simulator that was developed to solve inventory problems such as the auto supplies problem. In this simulator the decision maker has the option of selecting a variety of order quantities and reorder points. For purposes of illustration, the computer simulation output is shown for simulations with order quantities of from five units to 50 units in increments of five and for reorder points of from one to 10 in increments of one. A total of 1000 days is represented in the simulation of each order quantity–reorder point combination.

TABLE 12.18
Simulated Average Daily Cost for 1000 Days of Art's Auto Supplies Inventory Problem

Reorder Point	Order Quantity 5	10	15	20	25	30	35	40	45	50
1	14.35	8.30	6.58	5.20	5.35	4.16	3.30	4.42	3.98	5.22
2	11.51	5.93	5.46	3.92	3.91	3.44	2.96	3.69	3.62	3.71
3	9.34	5.64	3.37	3.01	3.03	2.84	3.96	3.29	2.90	3.07
4	6.90	4.12	3.47	2.78	3.14	2.79	3.29	3.25	3.37	3.42
5	5.41	3.31	2.85	2.42	2.61	3.24	3.25	2.93	3.18	3.22
6	4.72	2.75	2.69	2.60	2.39	2.74	2.93	3.06	3.13	3.34
7	4.72	2.85	2.52	2.60	2.76	2.71	3.06	2.99	3.02	3.28
8	5.50	2.89	2.66	2.50	2.62	2.75	2.99	3.05	3.33	3.56
9	4.36	3.11	2.62	2.62	2.66	2.77	3.05	3.18	3.34	3.49
10	4.68	3.05	2.75	2.72	2.80	2.85	3.18	3.28	3.31	3.72

We see that the results of this computer simulation indicate that the lowest cost solution occurs at an order quantity of 25 units and a reorder point of six units; in this case the resulting average total cost is $2.39 per day. After studying these results, the store manager might wish to explore other order quantities near the apparent ''best'' order quantity of 25. In Table 12.19 the results of varying the order quantity from 21 to 30 (in increments of one) and reorder points from four to eight are shown. The smallest simulated average total cost of $2.33 now occurs when the order quantity is 22 units and the reorder point is six units. Note, however, that in this second set of simulation experiments the previously best order quantity of 25 units and reorder point of six units has a total cost of $2.75 per day. Since different random numbers were used in the two simulations, different total costs are to be expected. The selection of the "best" order quantity and reorder point is now up to the analyst. What decisions would you make? While you might want to run more or longer simulations, the simulation data of Tables 12.18 and 12.19 indicate that good solutions apparently exist with order quantities around 20 to 25 units and reorder points around six or seven units. Thus while simulation has not guaranteed an optimal solution, it has enabled us to identify apparent low-cost or "near-optimal" decisions for the inventory problem. The final decision for an order quantity and reorder point will be based on the store manager's preference from among the good or "near-optimal" solutions.

TABLE 12.19
Simulated Average Daily Cost for 1000 Days of Art's Auto Supplies Inventory Problem

Reorder	Order Quantity									
Point	21	22	23	24	25	26	27	28	29	30
4	2.94	3.02	3.13	2.74	2.89	2.56	2.74	3.07	2.67	3.24
5	2.59	2.58	2.84	2.70	2.66	2.59	2.88	2.57	2.48	2.75
6	2.55	2.33	2.87	2.35	2.75	2.45	2.81	2.79	2.61	2.60
7	2.52	2.45	2.47	2.51	2.57	2.62	2.61	2.63	2.62	2.67
8	2.50	2.69	2.48	2.49	2.63	2.57	2.63	2.69	2.69	2.71

12.5 ADVANTAGES AND DISADVANTAGES OF COMPUTER SIMULATION

A primary advantage of computer simulation is that it is applicable in complex cases where analytical procedures cannot be employed. For example, the County Beverage waiting-line system and the Art's Auto Supply inventory system were sufficiently complex that the analytical approaches discussed in other chapters of this text do not apply. That is, the forms of the probability distributions involved do not satisfy the assumptions of the analytical models. In general, as the number of probabilistic components in the system becomes larger, the more likely it is that simulation will be the best approach.

Another advantage of the simulation approach is that the simulation model and simulator provide a convenient experimental laboratory. Once the computer program has been developed, it is usually relatively easy to experiment with the model. For example, if we wanted to know the effect of an increase in shortage cost on the recommended solution to our inventory problem, we could have simply changed the shortage cost input value and rerun the simulation. The effect of experimental changes in other inputs, such as the probability distributions of customer arrivals, lead time, and so on, could also be investigated.

Simulation is not without its disadvantages. One obvious disadvantage is that some-one must develop the computer program. For large simulation projects this is usually a substantial undertaking. Hence one should certainly not attempt to develop a simulation model unless the potential gains promise to outweigh the costs of model development. This disadvantage has been reduced with the development of computer simulation languages such as GPSS, SIMSCRIPT, and SLAM (available on microcomputers). The use of these languages often leads to considerable savings in time and money as the computer program or simulator is developed.

Another disadvantage of simulation is that it does not guarantee an optimal solution to a problem. One usually selects those values of the decision variables to test in the model that have a good chance of being near the optimal solution. However, since it is usually too costly to try all values of the decision variables, and since different simulation runs may provide different results, there is no guarantee that the best simulation solution found is the overall optimal solution. Nonetheless, the danger of obtaining bad solutions is slight if good judgment is exercised in developing and running the simulation model. The decision maker usually has a good idea of reasonable values to try for the decision variables, and it is usually possible to run the simulation long enough to identify the apparent best decisions.

Summary

In this chapter we have seen how two different problems could be analyzed and solved using computer simulation. Based on these two simulation models, we can make the following general observations about the simulation approach:

1. Simulation is most appropriate when the problem is too complex or difficult to solve using another quantitative technique.
2. A model must be developed to represent the various relationships existing in the problem situation.
3. A process involving random numbers must be used to generate values for the probabilistic components in the model.
4. A bookkeeping procedure must be developed to keep track of what is happening in the simulation process (see Table 12.6).
5. Because of the numerous calculations required in most simulations, a computer program or simulator is required.
6. The simulation process must be conducted for many days or periods in order to establish the long-run averages for the decision alternatives or other variables in the system.

Simulation should not be thought of as a technique for finding optimal solutions to problems. However, once a simulation model has been developed, a quantitative analyst may vary certain key design parameters and observe the effect on the output of the computer runs. Through a series of experiments with the simulation model good values may be selected for the key design parameters of the system. In the County Beverage problem, simulation experiments helped to identify the two-lane design as the one yielding the highest average hourly profit. In the simulation of Art's Auto Supply the simulation experiments helped identify an order quantity of 22 and a reorder level of six as a good low-cost inventory policy. Thus through these two examples we have shown how simulation experiments can be used to provide information on how to improve the performance of a system.

In both problems studied in this chapter, the probabilistic components resulted from discrete probability distributions; the random variables involved could take on only a finite number of values. In many situations probabilistic components are encountered that follow continuous distributions such as the normal or exponential probability distributions. The basic simulation approach we have developed in this chapter is still appropriate for these situations. The only difference concerns the method of generating random values from the appropriate continuous probability distributions.

Glossary

Simulation   A technique used to describe the behavior of a real-world system over time. Most often this technique employs a computer program to perform the simulation computations.

Monte Carlo simulation   Simulations that use a random-number procedure to create values for the probabilistic components.

Pseudorandom numbers   Computer-generated numbers developed from mathematical expressions that have the properties of random numbers.

Simulator   The computer program written to perform the simulation calculations.

Problems

Most of the problems in this section are designed to enable you to perform simulations with hand calculations. To keep the calculations reasonable, we will ask you to consider only a few decision alternatives and relatively short periods of simulation. While this should give you a good understanding of the simulation process, the simulation results will not be sufficient for you to make final conclusions or decisions about the problem situation. If you have access to a computer, we suggest that you develop a computer simulation model for some of the problems. Then, by using the model to test several decision alternatives over a much longer simulated period of time, you will be able to obtain the desired decision-making information.

1. A retail store has experienced the following historical daily demand for a particular product:

Sales (units)	Frequency (days)
0	4
1	6
2	14
3	12
4	7
5	5
6	2
Total	50

a. Develop a relative frequency distribution for the above data.

b. Use the random numbers from row 4 of Appendix B to simulate daily sales for a 10-day period.

2. A study was conducted in order to investigate the number of cars arriving at the drive-in window of Community Savings Bank. The following data were collected for 100 randomly selected 5-minute intervals.

Number of Arrivals	Number of Occurrences
0	12
1	24
2	37
3	19
4	8
Total	100

a. Develop a relative frequency distribution for the above data.

b. Use random numbers to simulate the number of customers that arrive between 9:00 A.M. and 9:15 A.M. on a given day.

3. Decca Industries has experienced the following weekly absenteeism frequency over the past 20 weeks:

Number of Employees Absent	Frequency
1	2
2	4
3	7
4	3
5	2
6	2
Total	20

a. Develop a relative frequency distribution for the above data.

b. Use random numbers to simulate weekly absenteeism for a 15-week period.

4. Given below are 50 weeks of historical sales data for cars sold by Domoy Motors, Inc., a new-car dealer in Newton, Ohio.

Number of Sales	Number of Weeks
0	2
1	5
2	8
3	22
4	10
5	3
Total	50

a. Develop the relative frequency distribution for these data.
b. Use a random-number procedure to simulate weekly automobile sales for a 12-week period.

5. Charlestown Electric Company is building a new generator for its Mount Washington plant. Even with good maintenance procedures, the generator will have periodic failures or breakdowns. Historical figures for similar generators indicate that the relative frequency of failures during a year is as follows:

Number of Failures	Relative Frequency
0	0.80
1	0.15
2	0.04
3	0.01

Assume that the useful lifetime of the generator is 25 years. Use simulation to estimate the number of breakdowns that will occur in the 25 years of operation. Is it common to have 5 or more consecutive years of operation without a failure?

6. Use row 15 of Appendix B to simulate 15 minutes of operation for the County Beverage Drive Thru application presented in Section 12.1. Show your simulation results in the format of Table 12.6.

7. A service technician for a major photocopier company is trained to service two models of copier: the X100 and the Y200. Approximately 60% of the technician's service calls are for the X100, and 40% are for the Y200. The service time distributions for the two models are as follows:

X100		Y200	
Time (minutes)	Relative Frequency	Time (minutes)	Relative Frequency
25	0.50	20	0.40
30	0.25	25	0.40
35	0.15	30	0.10
40	0.10	35	0.10

a. Show the random-number intervals that can be used to simulate the type of machine to be serviced and the length of the service time.
b. Simulate 20 service calls. What is the total service time the technician spends on the 20 calls?

8. Bushnell's Sand and Gravel (BSG) is a small firm that supplies sand, gravel, and topsoil to contractors and landscaping firms. BSG maintains an inventory of high-quality screened topsoil that is used to supply the weekly orders for two companies: Bath Landscaping Service and Pittsford Lawn Care, Inc. The problem BSG has is to determine how many cubic yards of screened topsoil to have in inventory at the beginning of each week in order to satisfy the needs of both of its customers. BSG

would like to select the lowest possible inventory level that would have a 0.95 probability of satisfying the combined weekly orders from both customers. The demand distributions for the two customers are as follows:

	Weekly Demand	Relative Frequency
Bath Landscaping	10	0.20
	15	0.35
	20	0.30
	25	0.10
	30	0.05
Pittsford Lawn Care	30	0.20
	40	0.40
	50	0.30
	60	0.10

Simulate 20 weeks of operation for beginning inventories of 70 and of 80 cubic yards. Based upon your limited simulation results, how many cubic yards should BSG maintain in inventory? Discuss what you would want to do in a full-scale simulation of this problem.

9. Paula Williams is currently completing the design for a drive-in movie theater to be located in Big Flats, N.Y. Paula has purchased the land and is now in the planning stages of determining the number of automobiles to accommodate. Each automobile location requires installing a speaker system at a total cost of $250 per location. Based upon her experience with the five other drive-ins she has been operating for the past 8 years, Paula estimates that the nightly attendance will range from 100 to 500 automobiles with the relative frequencies shown below:

Approximate Number of Automobiles	Relative Frequency
100	0.10
200	0.25
300	0.40
400	0.15
500	0.10

a. Simulate 20 days of attendance for capacities of 300, 400, and 500.
b. In the 20 days of simulated operation, how many daily demands of 300 would you have expected? Did you observe this many in your simulation? Should you have? Explain.
c. After considering personnel and other operating costs, the average profit is $1 per car. Using your 20 days of simulated data, what is the average nightly profit for the capacities of 300, 400, and 500? How many days of operation will it

take Paula to recover the speaker installation cost if all profits are allocated to this cost?

10. A door-to-door magazine salesperson has the following historical sales record. If the salesperson talks to the woman of the house, there is a 15% chance of making a sale. Furthermore, if the salesperson convinces the woman of the house to purchase some magazines, the relative frequency distribution for the number of the subscriptions ordered is as follows:

Number of Subscriptions	Relative Frequency
1	0.60
2	0.30
3	0.10

On the other hand, if the man of the house answers the door, the salesperson's chances of making a sale are 25%. In addition, the relative frequency distribution for the number of subscriptions ordered is as follows:

Number of Subscriptions	Relative Frequency
1	0.10
2	0.40
3	0.30
4	0.20

The salesperson has found that no one answers the door at about 30% of the houses contacted. However, of the people who do answer the door, 80% are women and 20% are men. The salesperson's profit is $2 for each subscription sold.

a. Prepare a simulation model flowchart (see Figure 12.5) for this problem. The output of the model should be the total profit the salesperson makes from calling upon N houses.

b. Simulate this problem and show the house-by-house results for 25 calls. What is the total profit projected for the 25 calls?

c. Based upon your results from part b, how many subscriptions should the salesperson expect to sell by calling on 100 houses per day? What is the salesperson's expected daily profit?

11. A project has four activities (A, B, C, and D) that must be completed sequentially in order to complete the project. The probability distribution for the time required to complete each of the activities is as follows:

Activity	Activity Times (weeks)	Probability
A	5	0.25
	6	0.30
	7	0.30
	8	0.15
B	3	0.20
	5	0.55
	7	0.25
C	10	0.10
	12	0.25
	14	0.40
	16	0.20
	18	0.05
D	8	0.60
	10	0.40

a. Use a random-number procedure to simulate the completion time for each activity. Sum the activity times to establish a completion time for the entire project.

b. Use the simulation procedure developed in part a to simulate 20 completions of this project. Show the distribution of completion times and estimate the probability that the project can be completed in 35 weeks or less.

12. A New York City corner newsstand orders 250 copies of the *New York Times* daily. Primarily due to weather conditions, the demand for newspapers varies from day to day. The probability distribution of the demand for newspapers is as follows:

Number of Newspapers	Probability
150	0.10
175	0.30
200	0.30
225	0.20
250	0.10

The newsstand makes a 15-cent profit on every paper sold, but it loses 10 cents on every paper unsold by the end of the day. Use 10 days of simulated results to determine whether the newsstand should order 200, 225, or 250 papers per day. What is the average daily profit that the newsstand can anticipate based on your recommendation?

13. For the Art's Auto Supplies problem in Section 12.4, develop a 10-day simulation when the following demand distribution is assumed:

Demand	Relative Frequency
0	0.25
1	0.50
2	0.15
3	0.05
4	0.05

Using an order quantity of five and a reorder point of three, show your results in the format of Table 12.17.

14. Bristol Bikes, Inc. would like to develop an order quantity and reorder point policy that would minimize the total costs associated with the company's inventory of exercise bikes. The relative frequency distribution for retail demand on a weekly basis is shown below:

Demand	Probability
0	0.20
1	0.50
2	0.10
3	0.10
4	0.05
5	0.05

The relative frequency distribution for lead time is as follows:

Lead Time (weeks)	Relative Frequency
1	0.10
2	0.25
3	0.60
4	0.05

The inventory holding costs are $1 per unit per week, the ordering cost is $20 per order, the shortage cost is $25 per unit, and the beginning inventory is seven units. Using an order quantity of 12 and a reorder point of five, simulate 10 weeks of operation of this inventory system.

15. Stollar's Bakery Shop would like to determine how many ,10-inch white cakes should be produced each day in order to maximize profits. The production costs are $2.50 per cake, and the selling price is $4.50. Any cakes that are not sold at the end of the day are sold for $1.50 to a local store that specializes in day-old goods. Assume that the bakery has available the following data showing the daily demand during the past month (20 days of operation):

Daily Demand	Frequency (number of days observed)
0	1
1	2
2	1
3	2
4	3
5	6
6	3
7	1
8	1
	Total 20

Develop a 10-day simulation for production sizes ranging from one to eight cakes per day. Use the following random numbers to generate daily demand:

48   12   77   24   32   43   96   03   62   77

What appears to be the best production size?

16. Domoy Motors, Inc. purchases a certain model automobile for $5778. In order to finance the purchase of cars of this model, Domoy must pay an 18% annual interest rate on borrowed capital. This interest rate amounts to approximately $20 per car per week. Orders for additional cars can be placed each week, but a minimum order size of five cars is required on any given order. It currently takes 3 weeks to receive a new shipment of cars after the order is placed. The cost of placing an order is $50. If Domoy runs out of cars in inventory, a shortage cost of $300 per car is incurred. Currently Domoy has 20 cars of this model in inventory. Historical data showing the weekly demand were given in problem 4.

a. Assuming an order quantity of 15 cars and a reorder point of 10 cars, perform a 12-week simulation of Domoy's operation. Use the first 12 two-digit random numbers from row 2 of Appendix B. Show your simulation results in the format of Table 12.17.

b. Write a computer program to simulate weekly sales at Domoy Motors. Use the program to determine the order policy that appears to minimize Domoy's overall costs.

17. A firm with a national chain of hotels and motels is interested in learning where individuals prefer to stay when on business trips. Three competing hotel and motel chains are included in the study. They are the Marimont Inn, the Harrison Inn, and the Hinton Hotel. The study found that where an individual stays on one trip is a good predictor of where the individual will stay the next trip. However, the study showed that there is also a tendency of individuals to switch from one chain to another. The probabilities of staying at each chain are shown below. For example, if an individual stayed at the Marimont Inn on one trip, there is a 0.70 probability of staying at the Marimont Inn the next trip, a 0.10 probability of staying at the Harrison Inn the next trip, and a 0.20 probability of staying at the Hinton Hotel the next trip. Similar probability values are shown for individuals staying at the Harrison Inn and Hinton Hotel on a particular trip.

Currently Staying at	Probability of Staying the Next Trip at		
	Marimont	Harrison	Hinton
Marimont	0.70	0.10	0.20
Harrison	0.20	0.60	0.20
Hinton	0.15	0.05	0.80

a. Show the random-number assignments that can be used to simulate the next visit for an individual currently staying at the Marimont, Harrison, and Hinton chains.

b. Develop a flowchart that describes the simulation process for simulating where an individual will stay during a series of business trips.

c. Assume an individual most recently stayed at the Marimont Inn. Simulate where the individual would stay on the next 50 business trips. What percentage of time will the person select each chain? Which appears to be the most popular chain?

d. Repeat the simulation in part c starting with an individual most recently staying at the Harrison Inn. Repeat part c again with the individual most recently staying at the Hinton Inn. Which is the most popular chain based on these simulation results?

18. Shown below is the probability distribution for the number of pins a bowler obtains on a first ball.

Number of Pins	Probability
6	0.02
7	0.08
8	0.20
9	0.30
10	0.40

The probability table showing the number of pins obtained on a second ball is as follows:

If Number of Pins on First Ball is	Number of Pins on Second Ball				
	0	1	2	3	4
6	0.01	0.03	0.20	0.26	0.50
7	0.04	0.10	0.36	0.50	
8	0.05	0.25	0.70		
9	0.15	0.85			

a. Using the above information, simulate a game of bowling. What is the bowler's score?

b. Develop a simulation program for this problem and simulate several games of bowling. What is an estimate of the bowler's average score?

19. Mount Washington Garage sells regular and unleaded gasoline. Pump 1, a self-service facility, is used by customers who want to pump their own gas. Pump 2, a full-service facility, is used by customers who are willing to pay a higher cost per gallon in order to have an attendant pump the gas, check the oil, and so on. Both pumps can service one car at a time. Based upon past data, the owner of the garage estimates that 70% of the customers select the self-service pump and 30% want full service. The arrival rate of cars for each minute of operation is given by the following probability distribution:

Number of Arrivals in 1 Minute of Operation	Probability
0	0.10
1	0.20
2	0.35
3	0.30
4	0.05
	1.00

The time to service a car, which depends upon whether the self-service or full-service facility is used, is given by the following probability distribution:

Self-Service Pump		Full-Service Pump	
Service Time (minutes)	Probability	Service Time (minutes)	Probability
2	0.10	3	0.20
3	0.20	4	0.30
4	0.60	5	0.35
5	0.10	6	0.10
	1.00	7	0.05
			1.00

Study the operation of the system for 10 minutes using simulation. As part of your analysis consider the following types of questions. What is the average number of cars waiting for service per minute at both facilities? What is the average amount of time a car must wait for service? Prepare a brief report for Mount Washington Garage that describes your analysis and any conclusions.

20. A medical consulting firm has been asked to determine the facilities required in the x-ray laboratory of a new hospital. In particular, the firm should provide recommendations on the number of x-ray units for the laboratory. How could computer simulation assist in reaching a good decision? What factors would you consider in a simulation model of this problem?

21. Consider a medium-sized community that currently has only one fire station. You have been hired by the city manager to assist in the determination of the best location

for a second fire station. What would be your objective for this problem? Explain how computer simulation might be used to evaluate alternative locations and help identify the best location.

22. A bus company is considering adding a new 10-stop route to its operation. The bus will be scheduled to complete the route once each hour. If the company has determined the approximate demand distribution for each location, discuss how simulation might be used to project the hourly profit associated with the new route. If the company can assign a regular bus or a more economical minibus to this route, discuss how simulation might help make this decision. Note that with the minibus the company's management is concerned about being unable to pick up customers if the bus is already carrying its maximum number of riders.

▬▬▬▬▬▬ *Case Problem:* ▬▬▬▬▬▬
MACHINE REPAIR

Jerry Masters, president of Pacific Plastics, Inc. (PPI), has become concerned with reports that downtime for PPI's plastic injection molding machines has been increasing. The downtime for a machine includes the time the machine must wait for a repair service technician to arrive after a breakdown plus the actual repair time. Currently PPI has three plastic injection molding machines, which are repaired by one service technician. However, because of an increase in business, PPI is considering the purchase of three additional machines. Jerry is concerned that with the additional machines the downtime problem will increase.

An analysis of historical data shows that the probability of each machine breaking down during 1 hour of operation is .10. In addition, the distribution of the repair time for a machine that breaks down is as follows:

Repair Time (hours)	Probability
1	0.20
2	0.35
3	0.25
4	0.15
5	0.05

The loss in revenue associated with a machine being down for 1 hour is $100. PPI pays its service technician $22 per hour and it is believed that additional service technicians can be hired at the same wage rate.

In reviewing the breakdown problem, Jerry decided that the best way to learn about the machine repair operation would be to simulate the performance of the system. In considering the potential use of simulation, Jerry indicated that PPI must deal with the two conflicting sources of cost: the cost of the service technician(s) and the cost of machine downtime. He indicated that PPI could minimize salaries by employing only one service technician. On the other hand, PPI could minimize the cost of machine downtime by hiring so many service technicians that a machine could be serviced immediately after a breakdown.

Jerry would like you to develop a simulation model of the machine repair operation and use it to determine how many service technicians PPI should employ in order to minimize its total cost. When developing the simulation model, you can assume that if a machine has a breakdown, the breakdown can be treated as occurring at the beginning of the hour of operation. Thus if a machine were to break down in hour 4 it would be considered to break down at the beginning of the hour. If one hour was spent waiting for a service technician and the length of time required to service the machine were 2 hours, the machine would be down during hours 4, 5 and 6 then be ready for operation at the beginning of hour 7. You can also assume that the probability of any machine breakdown is independent of the breakdown of any other machine, and that the service times are also independent of other service times.

MANAGERIAL REPORT

Prepare a report that discusses the general development of the simulation model, the conclusions that you plan to draw by using the model, and any recommendations that you have regarding the best decision for PPI. Include the following:

1. List the information the simulation model should generate so that the decision can be made about the desired number of service technicians.
2. Set up a flowchart of the machine repair operation for one machine and one service technician.
3. Use a random-number table and hand computations to demonstrate the simulation of the machine repair operation with three machines and one service technician. Use a table similar to Table 12.6 to summarize 10 hours of simulation results.
4. Develop a computer simulation model for the machine repair operation when PPI expands to six machines. Use your simulation results to make a recommendation about the number of service technicians PPI should employ.

Management Science in Practice
CHAMPION INTERNATIONAL CORPORATION*
New York, New York

Champion International Corporation is one of the largest forest products companies in the world, employing over 41,000 people in the United States, Canada, and Brazil. Champion manages over three million acres of timberlands in the United States. Its objective is to maximize the return of this timber base by converting trees into three basic product groups: (1) building materials, such as lumber and plywood; (2) white paper products, including printing and writing grades of white paper; (3) brown paper products, such as linerboard and corrugated containers. Given the highly competitive markets within the forest products industry, survival dictates that Champion must maintain its position as a low-cost producer of quality products. This requires an ambitious capital program to improve the timber base and to build additional modern, cost-effective timber conversion facilities.

MANAGEMENT SCIENCE FUNCTION

The management science function at Champion International Corporation is organizationally structured within the corporate planning department and operates as an internal consulting service within the company. Approximately 40% of the project activity is involved with facility and production planning, 30% with physical distribution, 20% with process improvement, and 10% with capital budgeting. The primary techniques used are mathematical programming (e.g., linear programming), simulation, and statistical analyses.

A SIMULATION APPLICATION

An integrated pulp and paper mill is a facility in which wood chips and chemicals are processed in order to produce paper products or dried pulp. To begin with, wood chips are cooked and bleached in the pulp mill; the resulting pulp is piped directly into storage tanks, as shown in Figure A12.1. From the storage tanks the pulp is sent to either the paper mill or a dryer. In the paper mill the pulp is routed to one or more paper machines, which produce the finished paper products. Al-

*The authors are indebted to Bill Griggs and Walter Foody of Champion International for providing this application.

FIGURE A12.1
The Champion Integrated Pulp and Paper Mill Facility

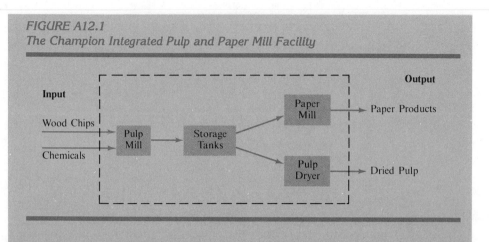

ternatively, the pulp is sent to a dryer, and the dried pulp is then sold to other paper mills that do not have the capability of producing their own pulp. The total system, referred to as an integrated pulp and paper mill, is a large facility costing several hundred million dollars.

One of Champion's major pulp and paper facilities consists of a pulp mill, three paper machines, and a dryer. As the facility developed, it was found that the pulp mill could produce more pulp than the combination of paper machines and the dryer could use. A study was undertaken to determine whether it would be worthwhile to invest in improvements that would increase the capacity of the dryer. One of the first questions to be answered in the study was: How much additional pulp could be produced and dried, given each possible capacity increase for the dryer?

A simple approach to this question is to look at average flows. For example, the pulp mill has a capacity of 940 tons[1] per day (TPD), the three paper machines together average 650 TPD of pulp use, and the dryer can handle 200 TPD. Based on average flows for each ton of increased dryer capacity, we can produce one more ton of pulp in the pulp mill. Note, however, that this is only true until the capacity of the dryer reaches 290 TPD, after which further improvements to the dryer will have no benefit.

The above analysis is inadequate because it ignores the day-to-day deviations from the average. That is, all of the equipment in the mill is subject to downtime and to variations in efficiency. For example, suppose that on one day the pulp mill is inoperable for more than the average length of time and on the same day the paper machines are experiencing less than the usual downtime. In this case there will be very little pulp available for the dryer, regardless of its capacity. This lack of pulp will not "average out" on days when the opposite conditions occur, since there will be far more pulp available than the pulp dryer can handle. Consequently, the pulp storage tanks will become full, and the pulp mill will have to shut down.

Based upon the above analysis, we can conclude that in order not to reduce the production on the paper machines the ratio of additional pulp production to the

---

[1] All numerical values have been modified to protect proprietary information.

increase in dryer capacity will be less than 1. Since the benefits of any investment in the dryer are directly proportional to this ratio, a simulation was undertaken in order to estimate this ratio as precisely as possible. The simulation model that was developed had the following components:

Pulp Mill   The pulp mill was assumed to have an average production rate of 1044 TPD when it is operating, with an average of 10% downtime. The actual downtime used in the model in each time period simulated was drawn randomly from a sample of actual downtimes experienced by the pulp mill over several months. Thus one day the pulp mill might be down 2% of the time, the next day 20%, etc.

Paper Machine   The rate of pulp flow to the paper machines in a time period is a function of the particular type of paper being made and the amount of downtime on the paper machines. In the simulation, the rate of pulp flow was input to the model based on a typical schedule of types of paper to be made. The downtime for each machine was drawn from a sample of actual downtimes.

Pulp Dryer   In each run of the model, downtime on the dryer was drawn from a sample of actual downtimes. The capacity of the dryer was set at different levels in different runs.

Storage Tanks   The connecting link between the pulp mill, the paper machines, and the dryer is the pulp storage tanks. In the model all pulp produced by the pulp mill is added to the inventory in these tanks. All pulp drawn by the dryer and paper machines is subtracted from this inventory. If the storage tanks are empty, the model must shut down the paper machines. If the tanks are full, the pulp mill must be shut down. The actual rate at which the dryer is operated at any moment must be set by the model (as it is in reality) to try to keep the storage tanks from becoming ''too empty or too full.''

RESULTS

A PL/1 computer program was developed to simulate the above process. The simulation program was run at various levels of dryer capacity. The simulation results showed that for every TPD of additional pulp capacity, approximately 0.8 TPD of additional pulp could actually be dried without reducing the production of the paper machines. This number was then used by management in comparing the costs and benefits of the capital investment necessary to increase the pulp dryer capacity. Note that if the ''average basis'' analysis had been used, the benefits of the project would have been overstated by 25%.

Questions

1. Briefly describe the function of an integrated pulp and paper facility.
2. What is the primary reason why Champion conducted a study of its integrated pulp and paper facility?

3. Why is an analysis of average flows inadequate in studying the current operation?
4. Describe how you might use a sample of actual downtimes for the pulp mill in order to simulate its operation.
5. What were the advantages of using a simulation model of the pulp and paper mill facility?

13

Waiting Line Models

Everyone has experienced waiting line situations such as a line of customers at a supermarket checkout counter, a line of customers at a teller window of a bank, or a line of cars at a traffic light. In these and many other situations, *waiting* time is undesirable for all parties concerned. For example, the customer in the supermarket checkout line can become very annoyed with excessive waiting times. In addition, the excessive waiting times, while indicative of the presence of many customers, are equally undesirable for the manager of the supermarket. The manager realizes that long waiting lines mean that customers are not being promptly serviced. Eventually these long waiting times may cause potential repeat customers to seek better service elsewhere, thus proving costly in terms of lost future sales.

If the manager of the supermarket is concerned about the existence of long waiting lines, one obvious solution would be to add more checkout counters. The added service capability should provide better service and correspondingly shorter customer waiting lines. However, additional supermarket checkout counters will lead to greater costs in terms of additional personnel, equipment, and space requirements. Thus the supermarket waiting line problem will require the manager to balance the benefits of better service with the added costs involved.

Quantitative models have been developed to help managers understand and make better decisions concerning the operation of waiting lines. In management science terminology, *queueing theory* involves the study of waiting lines, where the waiting line is referred to as the *queue*. Thus in the supermarket example, customers in the waiting line could have been referred to as the customers in the queue.

For a given waiting line system, waiting line models may be used to identify *operating characteristics*, such as

1.   The percentage of time or probability that the service facilities are idle
2.   The probability of a specific number of units (customers) in the system[1]
3.   The average number of units in the system
4.   The average time each unit spends in the system (waiting time plus service time)
5.   The average number of units in the waiting line

[1]The system includes the waiting line and the service facility.

6. The average time each unit spends in the waiting line
7. The percentage of time or probability that an arriving unit will have to wait

Managers who are provided with the above information will be better equipped to make decisions that balance desirable service levels with service costs.

In this chapter we will discuss how analytical and simulation models of waiting lines can assist in developing good decisions for waiting line problems. As an illustration of an application of a waiting line model, let us consider the problem Schips, Inc. is presently having with the truck dock at the company's Western Hills store.

13.1   THE SCHIPS, INC. TRUCK DOCK PROBLEM

Schips, Inc. is a large department store chain that has six branch stores located throughout the city. The company's Western Hills store, which was built some years ago, has recently been experiencing some problems in its receiving and shipping department because of the substantial growth in the branch's sales volume. Unfortunately, the store's truck dock was designed to handle only one truck at a time, and the branch's increased business volume has led to a bottleneck in the truck dock area. At times the branch manager has observed as many as five Schips trucks waiting to be loaded or unloaded. As a result, the manager would like to consider various alternatives for improving the operation of the truck dock and reducing the truck waiting times.

One alternative the manager is considering is to speed up the loading/unloading operation by installing a conveyor system at the truck dock. As another alternative, the manager is considering adding a second truck dock so that two trucks could be loaded and/or unloaded simultaneously.

What should the manager do in order to improve the operation of the truck dock? Obviously more information is needed before a course of action can be taken. While the alternatives being considered should reduce the truck waiting times, they may also increase the cost of operating the dock. Thus the manager will want to know how each alternative will affect both the waiting times and the cost of operating the dock before making a final decision. Let us see how a waiting line model of the truck dock operation can assist the manager in making this decision.

The Single-Channel Waiting Line

Schip's current receiving and shipping operation is an example of a *single-channel* waiting line. By this we mean that each truck entering the system must pass through *one* channel—the one truck dock—in order to complete the loading and/or unloading process. The trucks form a waiting line and wait for the truck dock to become available. A diagram of the Schips single-channel waiting line is shown in Figure 13.1

In order to develop a waiting line model for the truck dock operation, we will need to identify some important characteristics of the system: (1) the arrival distribution for the trucks; (2) the service time distribution for the truck loading and unloading operation; and (3) the waiting line or queue discipline for the trucks.

FIGURE 13.1
Diagram of Schips Single-Channel Truck Dock Waiting Line

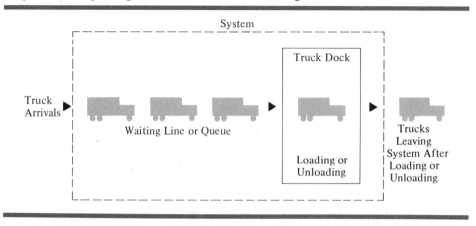

Arrival Distribution

Defining the arrival distribution for a waiting line involves determining how many units arrive and the pattern of arrivals over a given period of time. For example, in the Schips waiting line problem we will be interested in determining the number of trucks that arrive at the truck dock in a 1-hour period. Since the number of trucks arriving varies from hour to hour, we will need to define a probability distribution that describes the truck arrivals.

For many waiting lines, the arrivals occurring in a given period of time appear to have a *random pattern*; that is, each arrival is independent of other arrivals and we cannot predict when an arrival will occur. In such cases, management scientists have found that the *Poisson* probability distribution provides a good description of the arrival pattern.

Using the Poisson probability distribution[2], the probability of x arrivals in a specific time period is defined as follows:

$$P(x) = \frac{\lambda^x e^{-\lambda}}{x!} \qquad \text{for } x = 0, 1, 2, \dots \qquad (13.1)$$

where

x = number of arrivals in the time period
λ = average or expected number of arrivals for the time period
e = 2.71828

Values of $e^{-\lambda}$ are provided in Table 13.1

In the Schips loading dock problem, truck arrivals occur at an average rate of 3 trucks per hour ($\lambda = 3$). Thus we can use the following Poisson distribution to compute the probability of x truck arrivals in an hour:

$$P(x) = \frac{\lambda^x e^{-\lambda}}{x!} = \frac{3^x e^{-3}}{x!} \qquad (13.2)$$

[2]The term $x!$, referred to as *x factorial*, is defined as $x! = x(x - 1)(x - 2) \dots (2)(1)$. For example, $5! = (5)(4)(3)(2)(1) = 120$. For the special case of $x = 0$, $0! = 1$ by definition.

Table 13.1 can be used to verify that $e^{-3} = 0.0498$. Thus the probabilities for 0, 1, and 2 trucks arriving in an hour are as follows:

$$P(x = 0 \text{ trucks}) = \frac{3^0 e^{-3}}{0!} = e^{-3} = 0.0498$$

$$P(x = 1 \text{ truck}) = \frac{3^1 e^{-3}}{1!} = 3e^{-3} = 3(0.0498) = 0.1494$$

$$P(x = 2 \text{ trucks}) = \frac{3^2 e^{-3}}{2!} = \frac{9e^{-3}}{2} = \frac{9(0.0498)}{2} = 0.2241$$

Thus we see that the probability of no trucks arriving in a 1-hour period is 0.0498, the probability of exactly one truck arriving in a 1-hour period is 0.1494, and the probability of exactly two trucks arriving in a 1-hour period is 0.2241. Continuing the probability calculations for other values of x will provide additional probability information about the number of truck arrivals during a 1-hour period. Figure 13.2 shows a graphical summary of the arrival probabilities for Schips trucks based on the assumption of a Poisson arrival distribution.

In the analysis that follows, we will use the Poisson distribution to describe the truck arrivals for Schips. You will see that the assumption of a Poisson arrival distribution will help simplify the analysis of the waiting line problem. In practice you would want to record the actual number of arrivals per time period for several days or weeks and compare the frequency distribution of the observed number of arrivals to the Poisson distribution to see if the Poisson distribution is a good approximation of the arrival distribution for the trucks.

FIGURE 13.2
Poisson Distribution of Truck Arrivals for Schips

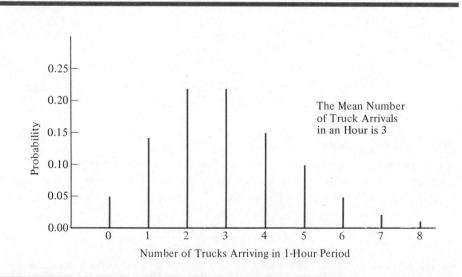

TABLE 13.1
Values of $e^{-\lambda}$

λ	$e^{-\lambda}$	λ	$e^{-\lambda}$
0.0	1.0000	3.3	0.0369
0.1	0.9048	3.4	0.0334
0.2	0.8187	3.5	0.0302
0.3	0.7408	3.6	0.0273
0.4	0.6703	3.7	0.0247
0.5	0.6065	3.8	0.0224
0.6	0.5488	3.9	0.0202
0.7	0.4966	4.0	0.0183
0.8	0.4493	4.1	0.0166
0.9	0.4066	4.2	0.0150
1.0	0.3679	4.3	0.0136
1.1	0.3329	4.4	0.0123
1.2	0.3012	4.5	0.0111
1.3	0.2725	4.6	0.0101
1.4	0.2466	4.7	0.0091
1.5	0.2231	4.8	0.0082
1.6	0.2019	4.9	0.0074
1.7	0.1827	5.0	0.0067
1.8	0.1653	5.1	0.0061
1.9	0.1496	5.2	0.0055
2.0	0.1353	5.3	0.0050
2.1	0.1225	5.4	0.0045
2.2	0.1108	5.5	0.0041
2.3	0.1003	5.6	0.0037
2.4	0.0907	5.7	0.0033
2.5	0.0821	5.8	0.0030
2.6	0.0743	5.9	0.0027
2.7	0.0672	6.0	0.0025
2.8	0.0608	7.0	0.0009
2.9	0.0550	8.0	0.000335
3.0	0.0498	9.0	0.000123
3.1	0.0450	10.0	0.000045
3.2	0.0408		

Service Time Distribution

A service time probability distribution is needed to describe how long it takes to load or unload (that is, service) a truck once the loading or unloading operation begins. Since the trucks carry different quantities of different items, the loading and unloading service times will vary from truck to truck. Management scientists have found that the *exponential* probability distribution often provides a good description of a service time distribution.

With an exponential service time distribution, *the probability of a service being completed within a specific period of time, t,* is given by

$$P(\text{service time} \leq t) = 1 - e^{-\mu t} \qquad (13.3)$$

where

μ = average or expected number of units that the service facility can service per unit of time

Suppose that after collecting data on loading and unloading times for Schips trucks, we find that when working continuously the truck dock can service an average of four trucks per hour. Then using $\mu = 4$, the probability of a service being completed within t hours [see equation (13.3)] is as follows:

$$P(\text{service time} \leq t) = 1 - e^{-4t}$$

Using this equation and values from Table 13.1, we can compute the probability that a truck is loaded and/or unloaded (serviced) within any specified time t. For example,

$P(\text{service time} \leq 0.1 \text{ hours}) = 1 - e^{-4(0.1)} = 1 - e^{-0.4} = 1 - 0.6703 = 0.3297$
$P(\text{service time} \leq 0.3 \text{ hours}) = 1 - e^{-4(0.3)} = 1 - e^{-1.2} = 1 - 0.3012 = 0.6988$
$P(\text{service time} \leq 0.5 \text{ hours}) = 1 - e^{-4(0.5)} = 1 - e^{-2.0} = 1 - 0.1353 = 0.8647$

Thus using the exponential distribution we would expect 32.97% of the trucks to be serviced in $t = 0.1$ hour or less (6 minutes), 69.88% in $t = 0.3$ hour or less (18 minutes), and 86.47% in $t = 0.5$ hour or less (30 minutes). Figure 13.3 shows graphically the probability that t hours or less will be required to service a Schips truck.

In the analysis of a specific waiting line you will want to collect data on actual service times to see if the exponential distribution assumption is appropriate. For the Schips problem we will assume that it has already been determined that the exponential distribution is the most appropriate representation of the service times.

FIGURE 13.3
Probability that a Schips Truck Will Be Serviced Within t Hours

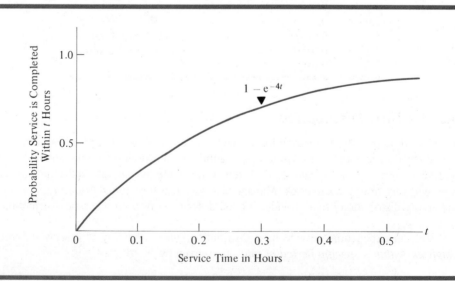

Queue Discipline

In describing a waiting line, we must define the manner in which the waiting units are ordered for service. For the Schips, Inc. problem, and in general for most customer-oriented waiting lines, the waiting units are ordered on a *first-come first-served* basis, which is referred to as a FCFS queue discipline. When people wait in line for an elevator, it is usually the last one in line who is the first one serviced (that is, first to leave the elevator). Other types of queue disciplines assign priorities to the waiting units and service the unit with the highest priority first. We will restrict our attention to waiting lines with a FCFS queue discipline.

13.2   THE SINGLE-CHANNEL WAITING LINE MODEL WITH POISSON ARRIVALS AND EXPONENTIAL SERVICE TIMES

The waiting line model presented in this section can be applied to waiting lines where the following assumptions or conditions exist:

1. The waiting line has a single channel
2. The pattern of arrivals follows a Poisson probability distribution
3. The service times follow an exponential probability distribution
4. The queue discipline is first-come–first-served (FCFS)

Since we have assumed that the above conditions are applicable to the Schips problem, we will show how this waiting line model can be used to analyze the truck dock operation.

The quantitative methodology used in the development of most waiting line models is rather complex. However, our purpose in this chapter is not to provide a theoretical development. Rather we restrict our presentation to showing how the operating characteristics of a waiting line model can be determined and how this information can be applied to problems such as the one encountered at Schips, Inc.

Let us begin by reviewing the following notation:

$$\lambda = \text{expected number of arrivals per time period (mean arrival rate)}$$

$$\mu = \text{expected number of services possible per time period (mean service rate)}$$

For the Schips problem we have already concluded that $\lambda = 3$ trucks per hour and $\mu = 4$ trucks per hour.

Using the assumptions of Poisson arrivals and exponential service times, management scientists have developed the following expressions, which define the operating characteristics of a single-channel waiting line:[3]

---

[3]These equations apply to the *steady-state* operation of a waiting line, which occurs after a start-up or transient period.

1. The probability that the service facility is idle (that is, the probability of 0 units in the system):

$$P_0 = \left(1 - \frac{\lambda}{\mu}\right) \tag{13.4}$$

2. The probability of n units in the system:

$$P_n = \left(\frac{\lambda}{\mu}\right)^n P_0 \tag{13.5}$$

3. The average number of units waiting for service:

$$L_q = \frac{\lambda^2}{\mu(\mu - \lambda)} \tag{13.6}$$

4. The average number of units in the system:

$$L = L_q + \frac{\lambda}{\mu} \tag{13.7}$$

5. The average time a unit spends waiting for service:

$$W_q = \frac{L_q}{\lambda} \tag{13.8}$$

6. The average time a unit spends in the system (waiting time plus service time):

$$W = W_q + \frac{1}{\mu} \tag{13.9}$$

7. The probability that an arriving unit has to wait for service:

$$P_w = \frac{\lambda}{\mu} \tag{13.10}$$

The values of the mean arrival rate λ and the mean service rate μ are clearly important components in the above formulas. From equation (13.10) we see that the ratio of these two values, λ/μ, is simply the probability that an arriving unit has to wait because the server is busy. Thus λ/μ is often referred to as the *utilization factor* for the waiting line.

The formulas for determining the operating characteristics of a single-channel waiting line presented in equations (13.4) to (13.10) are applicable only when the utilization factor $\lambda/\mu < 1$. This condition occurs when the mean service rate μ is greater than the mean arrival rate λ, and hence the service rate is sufficient to process or service all arrivals.

Returning to the Schips truck dock problem, we see that with $\lambda = 3$ trucks per hour, $\mu = 4$ trucks per hour, and $\lambda/\mu = \frac{3}{4}$, we can use equations (13.4) to (13.10) to determine the operating characteristics of the loading dock operation. This is done as follows:

$$P_0 = \left(1 - \frac{\lambda}{\mu}\right) = \left(1 - \frac{3}{4}\right) = 0.25$$

$$L_q = \frac{\lambda^2}{\mu(\mu - \lambda)} = \frac{3^2}{4(4 - 3)} = 2.25 \text{ trucks}$$

$$L = L_q + \frac{\lambda}{\mu} = 2.25 + \frac{3}{4} = 3 \text{ trucks}$$

$$W_q = \frac{L_q}{\lambda} = \frac{2.25}{3} = 0.75 \text{ hours per truck}$$

$$W = W_q + \frac{1}{\mu} = 0.75 + \frac{1}{4} = 1 \text{ hour per truck}$$

$$P_w = \frac{\lambda}{\mu} = \frac{3}{4} = 0.75$$

By looking at the above data for the waiting line, we can learn several important things about the operation of the truck dock. In particular, the fact that trucks wait an average of $W_q = 0.75$ hours or 45 minutes before being loaded or unloaded appears excessive and undesirable. In addition, the facts that the average number of trucks waiting for service is $L_q = 2.25$ trucks and that 75% of the arriving trucks ($P_w = 0.75$) have to wait for service are indicators that something should be done to improve the efficiency of the truck dock operation.

Before we continue with the Schips truck dock problem, let us review how the use of the single-channel waiting line model has contributed to our understanding of the truck dock operation. We began the discussion of the Schips problem by pointing out that the branch manager had become aware of the fact that an increase in business volume was leading to a bottleneck in the truck dock area. However, the manager did not have detailed information readily available concerning operating characteristics, such as the average number of trucks waiting for service, the average time trucks wait for service, the percent of arriving trucks that have to wait for service, and so on. Thus the contribution of the single-channel waiting line model is that if the assumptions are satisfied, formulas are available for computing a variety of operating characteristics for the system. In the case of Poisson arrivals and exponential service times, the formulas are based upon the mean arrival rate, λ, and the mean service rate, μ.

In general, waiting line models provide descriptive information about the operating characteristics of the waiting line system. If a manager or decision maker wishes to implement changes in the design of a waiting line, a waiting line model and its formulas can be used to predict the operating characteristics that will result from the changed design. In this sense, waiting line models provide important and helpful information that assists the decision maker in designing waiting line systems.

Improving the Service Rate for the Schips Truck Dock

Assume that after reviewing the operating characteristics provided by the waiting line model, the branch manager has concluded that improvements in the truck dock operation are necessary. While the manager cannot change the arrival rate of $\lambda = 3$ trucks per hour, it may be possible to make changes in the system that will enable the truck dock to service an average of more than four trucks per hour. The value of the waiting line model is that if the manager can identify an alternative design that will increase the service rate to $\mu = 6$ trucks per hour, the waiting line model with $\lambda = 3$ and $\mu = 6$ can be used to identify the operating characteristics of the new system. In this way the manager can determine how an improved service rate will affect the performance of the waiting line system.

Let us assume that in an effort to improve the operation of the truck dock the branch manager is considering the use of a conveyor system to speed up the loading/unloading process. Table 13.2 was prepared to help the manager better understand the potential benefits of improving the service rate. In particular, note that as the mean service rate increases, the average waiting time per truck, the average number of trucks waiting, and the probability of an arriving truck having to wait all improve. For example, if installing the conveyor system will increase the service rate to $\mu = 6$ trucks per hour, Table 13.2 shows that the average time a truck spends in the system can be reduced from 1 hour to 0.33 hour, or 20 minutes. In addition, we see that the percentage of trucks having to wait for service would be reduced from 75% to 50%.

TABLE 13.2
Waiting Line System Characteristics for the Schips Truck Dock Problem

Mean Service Rate μ, Trucks Per Hour	4	6	8	10
Probability that the dock is idle, P_0	0.25	0.5	0.625	0.7
Average number of trucks waiting, L_q	2.25	0.5	0.225	0.129
Average number of trucks in system, L	3	1	0.6	0.429
Average time a truck spends waiting, W_q, hours	0.75	0.167	0.075	0.043
Average time a truck spends in system, W, hours	1	0.33	0.2	0.143
Probability that an arriving truck has to wait for service, P_w	0.75	0.5	0.375	0.3

In evaluating a specific proposal for a conveyor system, the manager can use the projected service rate μ and the information in Table 13.2 to determine what improvements can be anticipated in the truck dock operation. The added cost of any proposed change can be compared with the corresponding benefits to help the manager determine whether or not the specific proposal is worthwhile.

13.3 THE MULTIPLE-CHANNEL WAITING LINE MODEL WITH POISSON ARRIVALS AND EXPONENTIAL SERVICE TIMES

A logical extension of the single-channel waiting line is the *multiple-channel waiting line*. By multiple-channel waiting lines we mean that two or more channels or service locations are present. Although items arriving for service wait in a single waiting line, they may move to the first available channel to be serviced. The Schips truck dock problem involved a single channel. However, a multiple-channel waiting line model could be applied if the branch manager implemented an expansion of the dock area such that two trucks could be loaded and/or unloaded simultaneously. The trucks arriving for service would form a waiting line and wait for either of the two service areas or channels to become available. A diagram of the Schips two-channel waiting line system is shown in Figure 13.4

In this section we present formulas that can be used to compute various operating characteristics for a multiple-channel waiting line. The model we will use can be applied to situations where the following assumptions are met:

1. The waiting line has two or more identical channels.
2. The arrivals are Poisson with a mean arrival rate of λ.
3. The service times have an exponential distribution.

FIGURE 13.4
Diagram of Schips Two-Channel Truck Dock Waiting Line

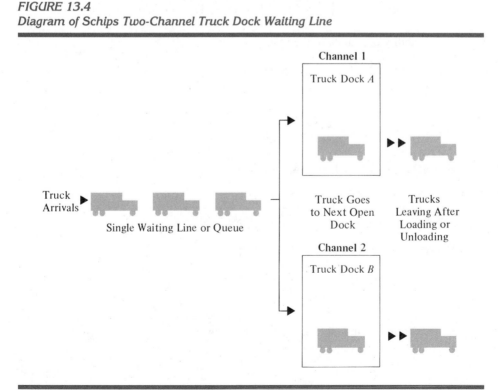

4. The mean service rate μ is the same for each channel.
5. The arrivals wait in a single waiting line and then move to the first open channel for service.
6. The queue discipline is a first-come–first-served (FCFS) discipline.

Using these assumptions, management scientists have developed formulas for determining the operating characteristics of the multiple-channel waiting line.
Let

$$k = \text{number of channels}$$
$$\lambda = \text{mean arrival rate for the system}$$
$$\mu = \text{mean service rate for } each \text{ channel}$$

The following equations apply to multiple-channel waiting lines for which the overall mean service rate, $k\mu$, is greater than the mean arrival rate, λ; in such cases, the service rate is sufficient to process or service all arrivals.

1. The probability that all k service channels are idle (that is, the probability of zero units in the system):

$$P_0 = \frac{1}{\left[\sum_{n=0}^{k-1} \frac{(\lambda/\mu)^n}{n!}\right] + \frac{(\lambda/\mu)^k}{(k-1)!}\frac{\mu}{k\mu - \lambda}} \qquad (13.11)$$

2. The probability of n units in the system:

$$P_n = \frac{(\lambda/\mu)^n}{k!\,k^{n-k}}P_0 \qquad \text{for } n > k \qquad (13.12)$$

$$P_n = \frac{(\lambda/\mu)^n}{n!}P_0 \qquad \text{for } 0 \leq n \leq k \qquad (13.13)$$

3. The average number of units waiting for service:

$$L_q = \frac{(\lambda/\mu)^k \lambda \mu}{(k-1)!(k\mu - \lambda)^2}P_0 \qquad (13.14)$$

4. The average number of units in the system:

$$L = L_q + \frac{\lambda}{\mu} \qquad (13.15)$$

5. The average time a unit spends waiting for service:

$$W_q = \frac{L_q}{\lambda} \qquad (13.16)$$

6. The average time a unit spends in the system (waiting time + service time):

$$W = W_q + \frac{1}{\mu} \qquad (13.17)$$

7. The probability that an arriving unit has to wait for service:

$$P_w = \frac{1}{k!} \left(\frac{\lambda}{\mu}\right)^k \frac{k\mu}{k\mu - \lambda} P_0 \qquad (13.18)$$

While the equations describing the operating characteristics of a multiple-channel waiting line with Poisson arrivals and exponential service times are somewhat more complex than the single-channel equations, they provide the same information and are used exactly as we used the results from the single-channel model. To simplify the use of equations (13.11)–(13.18), Table 13.3 shows values of P_0 for selected values of λ/μ; note that the values provided correspond to cases for which $k\mu > \lambda$ and hence the service rate is sufficient to service all arrivals.

As an illustration of the multiple-channel waiting line model, let us return to the Schips truck dock problem. Suppose the manager wishes to consider the desirability of expanding the loading dock area to provide space to load and/or unload two trucks simultaneously. If this were done, Schips would have a two-channel waiting line. What are the operating characteristics of this two-channel system.

We can answer this question by applying equations (13.11) to (13.18) specifically for the two-channel ($k = 2$) waiting line. Using $\lambda = 3$ trucks per hour and $\mu = 4$ trucks per hour for each channel, we have the following operating characteristics:

$$P_0 = 0.4545 \qquad \text{(From Table 13.3 for } \lambda/\mu = .75 \text{ and } k = 2)$$

$$L_q = \frac{(\frac{3}{4})^2 3(4)}{(1)!(8 - 3)^2} (0.4545) = 0.123 \text{ truck}$$

$$L = 0.123 + \frac{3}{4} = 0.873 \text{ truck}$$

$$W_q = \frac{0.123}{3} = 0.041 \text{ hour}$$

$$W = 0.041 + \frac{1}{4} = 0.291 \text{ hour}$$

$$P_w = \frac{1}{2!} \left(\frac{3}{4}\right)^2 \frac{2(4)}{(2(4) - 3)} (0.4545) = 0.2045$$

Shown below are some of the operating characteristics of the two-channel truck dock operation as compared with the single-channel system discussed in Section 13.2.

1. The average time a truck is at the dock (waiting time plus service time) is reduced from 1 hour to $W = 0.291$ hour, or 17.46 minutes).
2. The average length of the waiting line is reduced from 2.25 trucks to $L_q = 0.123$ truck.
3. The average time a truck waits for service is reduced from 45 minutes to $W_q = 0.041$ hour, or 2.46 minutes.

TABLE 13.3
Values of P_0 for Multiple-Channel Waiting Lines with Poisson Arrivals and Exponential Service Times

Ratio λ/μ	Number of Channels (k)			
	2	3	4	5
0.15	0.8605	0.8607	0.8607	0.8607
0.20	0.8182	0.8187	0.8187	0.8187
0.25	0.7778	0.7788	0.7788	0.7788
0.30	0.7391	0.7407	0.7408	0.7408
0.35	0.7021	0.7046	0.7047	0.7047
0.40	0.6667	0.6701	0.6703	0.6703
0.45	0.6327	0.6373	0.6376	0.6376
0.50	0.6000	0.6061	0.6065	0.6065
0.55	0.5686	0.5763	0.5769	0.5769
0.60	0.5385	0.5479	0.5487	0.5488
0.65	0.5094	0.5209	0.5219	0.5220
0.70	0.4815	0.4952	0.4965	0.4966
0.75	0.4545	0.4706	0.4722	0.4724
0.80	0.4286	0.4472	0.4491	0.4493
0.85	0.4035	0.4248	0.4271	0.4274
0.90	0.3793	0.4035	0.4062	0.4065
0.95	0.3559	0.3831	0.3863	0.3867
1.00	0.3333	0.3636	0.3673	0.3678
1.20	0.2500	0.2941	0.3002	0.3011
1.40	0.1765	0.2360	0.2449	0.2463
1.60	0.1111	0.1872	0.1993	0.2014
1.80	0.0526	0.1460	0.1616	0.1646
2.00		0.1111	0.1304	0.1343
2.20		0.0815	0.1046	0.1094
2.40		0.0562	0.0831	0.0889
2.60		0.0345	0.0651	0.0721
2.80		0.0160	0.0521	0.0581
3.00			0.0377	0.0466
3.20			0.0273	0.0372
3.40			0.0186	0.0293
3.60			0.0113	0.0228
3.80			0.0051	0.0174
4.00				0.0130
4.20				0.0093
4.40				0.0063
4.60				0.0038
4.80				0.0017

4. The percentage of trucks having to wait for service is reduced from 75% to $P_w = 0.2045$ or 20.45%.

The advantages are clear. The two-channel system will greatly improve the operating characteristics of the waiting line. However, before implementing the two-dock system, the manager will undoubtedly want to consider the economic aspects of such a change.

13.4 ECONOMIC ANALYSIS OF WAITING LINES

As we have shown, waiting line models can be used to determine operating characteristics of a waiting line system. In the economic analysis of waiting lines we will seek to use the information provided by the waiting line model to develop a cost model for the waiting line under study. Then we will use the cost model to help the manager balance the cost of waiting for service with the cost of providing the service.

In developing a cost model for the Schips truck dock problem, we will want to consider the cost of waiting for the trucks, both in the waiting line and while being serviced at the dock, and the cost of the truck dock service. We can develop a mathematical model that will enable us to compare the costs of Schips single-channel and two-channel truck dock operations as follows:

Let

$$c_1 = \text{hourly cost for each truck}$$
$$L = \text{average number of trucks in the system}$$
$$c_2 = \text{hourly cost for each channel}$$
$$k = \text{number of channels}$$

Then

$$\text{Total truck cost/hour} = c_1 L$$
$$\text{Total channel cost/hour} = c_2 k$$
$$\text{Total cost per hour} = c_1 L + c_2 k \tag{13.19}$$

By evaluating the above total cost model for the one- and two-channel systems, we will be able to obtain cost information helpful in making the decision regarding the truck dock operation. For example, suppose that the Schips trucks are operated at a cost of $c_1 = \$25$ per hour and that the dock cost is $c_2 = \$30$ per hour for each channel in operation. Table 13.4 summarizes the costs associated with the Schips truck dock alternatives. These cost projections tell us that the hourly costs will be reduced by $105 - 81.83 = \$23.17$ per hour in changing to the two-channel system. This is a 22% reduction in costs resulting from an improved truck dock operation. Assuming an annual operation of 40 hours per week for 52 weeks a year, this hourly saving results in a total savings of $(40)(52)(\$23.17) = \$48,193.60$ per year. Although the manager must now consider the cost of expanding the operation to the two-channel system, the projected savings of $48,193.60 per year makes the two-channel operation an attractive alternative.

TABLE 13.4
Total Hourly Cost Summary for the Schips Truck Dock Problem

System	Average Number of Trucks in System	Total Truck Cost/Hour	Number of Channels	Total Channel Cost/Hour	Total Cost/Hour
Single-channel	3.00	($25)3.00 = $75	1	($30)1 = $30	$105.00
Two-channel	0.873	($25)0.873 = $21.83	2	($30)2 = $60	$ 81.83

As a final comment concerning the use of economic analysis in waiting line situations, we note that in the Schips truck dock problem the expenses associated with both the customer (trucks) and the server (docks) are being paid by the company. In cases such as this, where the customer and the server have common interests, balancing the cost of offering the service with the cost of waiting for the service is generally not too difficult. However, in many other waiting line situations the customer and server do not share common interests. For example, in a supermarket customers generally prefer more check-out counters than fewer checkout counters because this will shorten the time they have to wait. The fact that the cost of providing more checkout counters might be very expensive is usually of little concern to the customer. On the other hand, from the point of view of the supermarket, it may be very difficult to assign a monetary value to the cost of customer waiting time. Thus whenever the customer and the server do not share common interests, it may be difficult to estimate the cost of waiting. In such cases the decision maker may wish to specify a desired service goal such as a reasonable average waiting time, a reasonable probability of waiting a specified length of time, and so on. The results of the waiting line model may then be used to determine the system design that will achieve the desired service goal.

13.5 OTHER WAITING LINE MODELS

In this chapter you have been exposed to single-channel and multiple-channel waiting lines with Poisson arrivals and exponential service times. However, many variations of these specific systems exist in actual waiting line situations. Management scientists have analyzed a wide variety of possible waiting lines and developed general expressions for average customer waiting time, average number of customers in the system, percent of the time servers are idle, and other operating characteristics of the system. Specifically, models are available covering some of the following types of waiting line situations:

1. Arrivals other than Poisson
2. Service times other than exponential
3. Arrivals in bulk quantities rather than one at a time
4. Limited or finite waiting lines, called *truncated queues*
5. Mean arrival and mean service rates that vary with the number of the units waiting for service
6. Queue disciplines other than first-come-first-served
7. Sequential waiting lines, where units pass through a fixed sequence or series of servers

D. G. Kendall suggested a special notation for classifying waiting line models. The Kendall system is a shorthand notation for identifying the waiting line model being considered. While the Kendall notation cannot completely describe all waiting line configurations, it has been adopted as a common method for classifying the arrival distribution, service time distribution, and number of parallel servers in a waiting line system. The three-symbol Kendall notation is as follows:

_____ / _____ / _____

	code indicating	
code indicating	service time	number of
arrival distribution	distribution	parallel servers

With M being the code for both the Poisson arrival distribution and also the exponential service time distribution, the single-channel waiting line discussed in Section 13.2 is the $M/M/1$ waiting line model. The two-channel system of Section 13.3 is an example of the $M/M/2$ model. Several other arrival and service time distributions are possible and are denoted by other code letters.

With many models of waiting lines available, a decision maker with a specific waiting line problem should attempt to identify a model that closely approximates the specific problem; that is, the decision maker should attempt to identify a model with an arrival distribution, service time distribution, number of servers, queue discipline, and so on that closely approximates the actual situation. Even with the numerous waiting line models in existence, many practical waiting line problems are so complex that management scientists have been unable to develop the analytical expressions necessary to determine the operating characteristics. If the decision maker is unable to find an analytical model applicable to the specific waiting line, a computer simulation model of the problem may be used to develop the necessary operating characteristics.

13.6 SIMULATION OF WAITING LINES

Computer simulation models offer an attractive alternative to the use of mathematical models when studying the behavior and operating characteristics of waiting lines. In Chapter 12 we saw how a simulation model could be used to study the waiting line situation at the County Beverage Drive-Thru. The attractiveness of computer simulation models rests primarily with their versatility. Although we pointed out that mathematical models have been developed for waiting line situations that differ from the Poisson-exponential systems described in this chapter, the complexity and diversity of waiting lines often prohibits an analyst from finding an existing model that fits the specific situation being studied. Even when models that appear to be good approximations of the problem can be identified, the mathematics of the models are often so complex that many practitioners are unable to determine whether the models are applicable or not. Thus a computer simulation model of a waiting line problem offers another approach to studying waiting line situations.

Let us consider a deviation from the assumptions which enabled us to utilize existing mathematical models for the Schips truck dock waiting line. One key assumption was that the service times in the Schips problem were essentially random *and* independent of all other conditions. This enabled us to use the same exponential distribution and mean service rate for all trucks. Let us suppose that the Schips truck dock crew does not work independently of the number of trucks waiting to be serviced. That is, suppose that management has observed that as the length of the waiting line increases, the rate at which the dock crew loads and unloads also increases. Thus our previous assumption that service times are always exponentially distributed with a mean service rate of four trucks per hour would not reflect the actual situation. Hence, while the decision maker might still elect to use the Poisson-exponential model as a rough approximation, it may be desirable to develop a computer simulation model that attempts to account for the varying work rates of the crew.

Also recall that the waiting line models in this chapter employ a first-come–first-served queue discipline. Suppose the branch manager wanted to evaluate the policy of having delivery trucks loaded before unloading incoming shipments from the central warehouse. How would the waiting times and operating costs be affected by this policy? We cannot answer this question with a waiting line model that assumes a first-come–first-served queue discipline. However, a computer simulation model could be used to test this new priority policy.

Finally, suppose that we collected actual arrival and service time data for the Schips trucks for a 2-week period and found that arrivals did not follow a Poisson distribution and the service times did not follow an exponential distribution. We might try to identify the general distributions that these data follow and attempt to identify an existing waiting line model based on these distributions. However, if an existing model cannot be found or if the arrivals and/or service times do not follow any recognizable probability distribution, we could input the observed relative frequency data for the arrival and service times into a simulation model and use computer simulation to generate the operating characteristics of the truck dock.

Although we have mentioned only a few specific changes in the characteristics of the Schips waiting line problem, it should be apparent that many other possibilities could be considered. Again, this is where computer simulation starts to become especially attractive as a solution procedure. Instead of using an existing waiting line model that is perhaps a poor approximation of the waiting line being studied, we develop a computer simulation model that more closely reflects the true characteristics of the waiting line.

Summary

Waiting line problems occur in a variety of practical situations in which customers or other units may wait for a service. Waiting line models have been developed that provide information regarding waiting times, idle time, number of units waiting, and other operating characteristics of a waiting line. This information, along with cost data, may be used to balance the benefits of improved service with the cost necessary to improve the service.

In this chapter we have presented models for single-channel and multiple-channel waiting lines with Poisson arrivals and exponential service times. In addition, we pointed out that models exist that are applicable in a variety of other waiting line situations. However, a computer simulation model of the waiting line is recommended if the assumptions of existing waiting line models do not closely approximate the specific problem under study.

Glossary

Queueing theory A term for the body of knowledge dealing with waiting lines.
Queue A waiting line.
Single-channel line A waiting line with only one service facility.

Multiple-channel line   A waiting line with two or more parallel identical service facilities.

Mean arrival rate   The expected number of customers or units arriving or entering the system in a given period of time.

Poisson distribution   A probability distribution used to describe the random arrival pattern for some waiting lines.

Mean service rate   The expected number of customers or units that can be serviced by one server in a given period of time.

Exponential distribution   A probability distribution used to describe the pattern of service times for some waiting lines.

Problems

The following waiting line problems are all based upon the assumptions of Poisson arrivals and exponential service times:

1. The demand for access to a time-sharing computer occurs at a mean rate of three requests for service per 5-minute period.
    a. What is the probability that no one will attempt to use the system in a given 5-minute period?
    b. What is the probability of exactly one request? Exactly two requests?
    c. What is the probability the computer facility will have three or more requests in a 5-minute period?

2. Computer programs require an average of 10 minutes of computer time.
    a. What is the mean service rate in programs per hour?
    b. What percentage of the programs will be completed in 5 minutes or less ($t \leq$ 0.083 hour)?
    c. What percentage require 10 minutes or less?
    d. What percentage of the computer programs will require *more than* 30 minutes to complete?

3. Phone calls come into the dispatcher's office at the Madeira Cab Company at the rate of five calls per 15-minute interval. Answer the following questions:
    a. What is the probability of three calls during a 15-minute interval?
    b.. What is the probability of three calls during a 6-minute interval?
    c. What is the probability of five calls during a 3-minute interval?

4. The reference desk of a large library receives requests for assistance at a mean rate of 10 requests per hour. Assuming that the reference desk has a mean service rate of 12 requests per hour, consider the following questions:
    a. What is the utilization factor for the reference desk?
    b. What is the probability that the reference desk is idle?
    c. What is the average number of requests that will be waiting in the queue?
    d. What is the average waiting time plus service time for a request for assistance?

5. Trucks using a single-channel loading dock have a mean arrival rate of 12 per day. The loading/unloading rate is 18 per day.
    a. What is the probability of one truck in the system?
    b. What is the probability the dock will be idle?

c. What is the probability that at least one truck will be waiting (that is, the probability of two or more trucks in the system)?

d. What is the probability a new arrival will have to wait?

6. A mail-order nursery specializes in European beech trees. New orders, which are processed by a single shipping clerk, have a mean arrival rate of 30 per week and a mean service rate of 40 per week. Assume a week consists of 5 working days.

a. What is the average time in days an order spends in the queue waiting for the clerk to begin service?

b. What is the average time in days an order spends in the system?

7. For the Schips single-channel waiting line, assume the mean arrival rate is four trucks per hour and the mean service rate for the channel is five trucks per hour.

a. What is the probability the dock channel will be idle?

b. What is the average number of trucks in the queue?

c. What is the average number of trucks in the system?

d. What is the average time a truck spends in the queue waiting for service?

e. What is the average time a truck spends in the system?

f. What is the probability an arriving truck will have to wait?

g. What is the probability that at least one unit will be waiting?

h. Does this waiting line provide more or less service than the original Schips dock operation (see Table 13.2)?

8. Marty's Barber Shop has one barber. Customers arrive at a rate of 2.2 per hour, and haircuts are given at an average rate of five customers per hour.

a. What is the probability that the barber is idle?

b. What is the probability that one customer is receiving a haircut and no one is waiting?

c. What is the probability that one customer is receiving a haircut and one customer is waiting?

d. What is the probability that one customer is receiving a haircut and two customers are waiting?

e. What is the probability that more than two customers are waiting?

f. What is the average customer waiting time?

9. Trosper Tire Company has decided to hire a new mechanic to handle all tire changes for customers ordering a new set of tires. Two mechanics are available for the job. One mechanic has limited experience and can be hired for $7 per hour. It is expected that this mechanic can service an average of three customers per hour. A mechanic with several years of experience is also being considered for the job. This mechanic can service an average of four customers per hour, but must be paid $10 per hour. Assume that customers arrive at the Trosper garage at the rate of two per hour.

a. Compute waiting line operating characteristics for each mechanic.

b. If the company assigns a customer waiting cost of $15 per hour, which mechanic provides the lower operating cost?

10. Agan Interior Design provides home and office decorating assistance for its customers. In normal operation an average of 2.5 customers arrive per hour. One design consultant is available to answer customer questions and make product recommendations. The consultant averages 10 minutes with each customer.

a. Compute operating characteristics for the customer waiting line.

b. Service goals dictate that an arriving customer should not wait more than an average of five minutes. Is this goal being met? What action do you recommend?

c. If the consultant can reduce the average time spent per customer to 8 minutes, will the service goal be met?

11. Pete's Market is a small local grocery store with only one checkout counter. Assume that shoppers arrive at the checkout lane at an average rate of 15 customers per hour and that the average order takes 3 minutes to ring up and bag. What information would you develop for Pete to aid him in analyzing his current operation? If Pete does not want the average waiting time in the queue to exceed 5 minutes, what would you tell Pete about his current system?

12. In problem 11 we analyzed the checkout waiting line for Pete's Market. After reviewing our analysis, Pete felt it would be desirable to hire a full-time person to assist in the checkout operation. Pete believed that if the new employee assisted the checkout cashier, average service time could be reduced to 2 minutes. However, Pete was also considering installing a second checkout lane, which could be operated by the new person. This second alternative would provide a two-channel system with the average service time of 3 minutes for each server. Should Pete use the new employee to assist on the current checkout counter or operate a second counter? Justify your recommendation.

13. Keuka Park Savings and Loan currently has one drive-in teller window. The arrival of cars occurs at a mean rate of 10 cars per hour. The mean service rate is 12 cars per hour.
a. What is the probability the service facility will be idle?
b. If you were to drive up to the facility, what is the expected number of cars you would see waiting and being serviced?
c. What is the probability that at least one car will be waiting to be serviced?
d. What is the average time in the queue waiting for service?
e. As a potential customer of the system, would you be satisfied with the above waiting line characteristics? How do you think management could go about assessing the feelings of its customers with respect to the operation of the current system?

14. In order to improve the service to the customer, Keuka Park Savings and Loan wants to investigate the effect of a second drive-in teller window. Assume a mean arrival rate of 10 cars per hour. In addition assume a mean service rate of 12 cars per hour for each drive-in window. What effect would the addition of a new teller window have upon the system? Does this system appear acceptable?

15. Fore and Aft Marina is a newly planned marina that is to be located on the Ohio River near Madison, Ind. Assume that Fore and Aft decides to build one docking facility and that a mean arrival rate of five boats per hour and a mean service rate of 10 boats per hour are expected. Consider the following questions:
a. What is the probability that the boat dock will be idle?
b. What is the average number of boats that will be waiting in the queue for service?
c. What is the average time a boat will spend waiting for service? What is the average time a boat will spend at the dock?
d. If you were the management of Fore and Aft Marina would you be satisfied with the service level your system would be providing?

16. Management of the Fore and Aft Marina project in problem 15 wants to investigate the possibility of adding a second dock. Assume a mean arrival rate of five boats per hour for the marina and a mean service rate of 10 boats per hour for each channel.

a. What is the probability that a boat that stops for fuel will have to wait?

b. What is the average waiting time a boat will spend in the queue?

c. What is the probability the system is idle?

d. Would you consider this good service? Is it too good?

17. The City Beverage Drive-Thru is considering a two-channel system. Cars arrive at the beverage store at the mean rate of six per hour. The service rate for each channel is 10 per hour.

a. What is the probability of an empty system?

b. What is the probability that an arriving car will have to wait?

18. Consider a two-channel waiting line with a mean arrival rate for the system of 50 per hour and a mean service rate of 75 per hour for each channel.

a. What is the probability of an empty system?

b. What is the probability that an arrival will have to wait?

c. Would the answers to parts a and b change if the mean arrival rate for the system were two per hour and the mean service rate were three per hour for each channel? Why?

19. For a two-channel waiting line with a mean arrival rate of 15 per hour and a mean service rate of 10 per hour per channel, determine the probability that an arrival has to wait. What is the probability of waiting if the system is expanded to three channels?

20. Big Al's Quickie Car Wash has two wash areas with a mean rate of 15 cars per hour. Cars arrive at the car wash at the rate of 10 cars per hour on the average, join the waiting line, and select the next open wash area when it becomes available.

a. What is the probability a wash area will be empty?

b. What is the probability that a customer who arrives at the car wash will have to wait?

c. As a customer of Big Al's Quickie Car Wash, do you think the service of the system favors the customer? If you were Al, what would your attitude be relative to this service level?

21. Refer to the Agan Interior Design situation in problem 10. Agan would like to evaluate two alternatives:

(1) Use one consultant with an average service time of 8 minutes per customer.

(2) Expand to two consultants, each of whom has an average service time of 10 minutes per customer.

If the consultants are paid $16 per hour and the customer waiting time is valued at $25 per hour for waiting time prior to service, should Agan expand to the two design consultant system? Explain.

22. A fast-food franchise is currently operating a drive-up window. Orders are placed at an intercom station at the back of the parking lot. After placing an order the customer pulls up and waits in line at the drive-up window until the cars in front have been served. By hiring a second person to help take and fill orders, management is hoping to improve customer service.

   With one person filling orders the average service time for a drive-up customer is 2 minutes; with a second person working, the average service time can be reduced to 1 minute, 15 seconds. Note that the drive-up window operation with two people is still a single-channel waiting line. However, with the addition of the second person, the average service time can be decreased. Cars arrive at the rate of 24 per hour.

a. Determine the average waiting time in the queue when only one person is working the drive-up window.

b. With only one person working the drive-up window what percentage of time will that person not be occupied serving customers?

c. Determine the average waiting time when two people are working at the drive-up window.

d. With two persons working the drive-up window, what percentage of time will no one be occupied serving drive-up customers?

e. Would you recommend hiring a second person to work the drive-up window? Justify your answer.

23. Refer to problem 22. Space is available to install a second drive-up window adjacent to the first. Management is considering adding such a window. One person will be assigned to serve customers at each window.

a. Determine the average customer waiting time for this two-channel system.

b. What percentage of the time will only one window be idle?

c. What percentage of the time will both windows be idle?

d. Which design would you recommend for providing service at the drive-up window? One attendant at one window? Two attendants at one window? Two attendants and two windows with one attendant at each window?

24. All-National Insurance handles customer telephone claims at its central office. Between the hours of 10:00 A.M. and noon, telephone calls arrive at the rate of 12 per hour. One or more agents are assigned to the telephone claim service, depending upon the anticipated call volume. Each agent can process an average of eight telephone claims per hour. If all agents are busy when a telephone call arrives, the customer receives a recorded message that says an agent will be available shortly. Waiting calls are answered in the order in which they are received. Company guidelines are that on average the calling customers should not have to wait more than 1 minute before an agent becomes available.

a. How many agents are needed between the hours of 10:00 A.M. and noon?

b. Determine the waiting line characteristics for the system you recommended in part a.

25. In Sections 13.3 and 13.4 we determined the operating characteristics and prepared an economic analysis of the Schips problem using a two-channel waiting line. Our waiting line model assumed that each channel operated with a mean service rate of four trucks per hour. Suppose that in actual operation of the truck dock the four trucks per hour service rate per channel is appropriate when two trucks are being loaded/unloaded simultaneously. However, when only one truck is in the dock area, all dock workers are assigned to it. Thus when only one truck is present, the service rate is temporarily increased. The formulas presented in Section 13.3 are not applicable to this new situation since the service rate varies depending upon the situation. This is a case in which a simulation model of the waiting line would be helpful.

a. Discuss in a step-by-step fashion how you would develop a simulation model to determine the operating characteristics for this waiting line system.

b. What type of output would you like to have as a result of the simulation?

c. Do you anticipate that the cost model would show this approach to be better or worse than the two-channel system considered in Section 13.3? Explain.

—————————— *Case Problem:* ——————————

AIRLINE RESERVATIONS

Regional Airlines is establishing a new phone system for handling flight reservations. During the 10:00 A.M. to 11:00 A.M. time period, past data show that calls to the ticket agents occur at an average rate of one call every 3.75 minutes. In addition, service time data indicate that an average of 3 minutes will be required to process a call. If a customer calls and the ticket agents are busy, a recorded message tells the customer that the call is being held in the order received and that a ticket agent will be available shortly; the customer will be asked to wait until an agent is free.

Regional Airline's management feels that offering an efficient telephone reservation system is an important part of establishing an image as a service-oriented carrier and, if properly implemented, the system will increase business. However, management also is aware of the fact that a busy or overloaded system with long waiting times may result in negative customer reaction to the point that Regional might even lose business. The cost per hour for a ticket reservation agent is $20. Thus management wants to provide good service, but does not want to overstaff the telephone reservation operation with more agents than are necessary.

At a planning meeting, Regional's management team agreed that an acceptable service goal is to immediately answer and process at least 85% of the incoming calls. During the planning meeting, Regional's vice-president of administration pointed out that the historical data show that the average service rate by the agent is faster than the average arrival rate of the telephone calls. His conclusion is that one agent should be able to handle the telephone reservations and still have some idle time. The vice-president of marketing disagreed and felt the company should use at least two agents.

MANAGERIAL REPORT

Prepare a report for Regional Airlines, analyzing the telephone reservation operation. Include the following information in your report:

1. A detailed analysis of the operating characteristics of the reservation system with one ticket agent as proposed by the vice-president of administration.
2. A detailed analysis of the operating characteristics of the ticket reservation system based upon your recommendation regarding the number of reservation agents Regional should use.
3. The telephone arrival data presented above are for the 10:00 A.M. to 11:00 A.M time period; however, the arrival rate of incoming calls is expected to change from hour to hour. Describe how your waiting line analysis could be used to develop a ticket agent staffing plan that would enable the company to provide different levels of staffing for the ticket reservation system at different times during the day. Indicate the information that you would need to develop this staffing plan.

Management Science in Practice

GOODYEAR TIRE & RUBBER COMPANY*
Akron, Ohio

The Goodyear Tire & Rubber Company had its beginning in an old converted strawboard factory in 1898. Its first product was bicycle tires. Since 1926 it has been the world's largest rubber company and one of the nation's leading industrial corporations.

Although tires are Goodyear's biggest single product line, the company has become a highly diversified corporate enterprise. The company's product line has changed from the original bicycle tires, carriage tires, and horseshoe pads to tires of all types, chemicals, industrial rubber products, defense products, packaging films, foam cushioning, shoe soles and heels, flooring and counter tops, metal rims and wheels, aircraft brakes and wheels, aerospace products, and atomic energy.

Goodyear has more than 129 production facilities—about half in the United States, half overseas—and approximately 155,000 employees. Its sales and distribution operations cover virtually all areas of the free world. Corporate headquarters are in Akron, Ohio.

Familiar to millions of people are the company airships, named the *Enterprise*, *Columbia*, and *America*, which are stationed in the United States, and the *Europa*, which is stationed in Europe. These airships are made by Goodyear Aerospace Corporation, a subsidiary of The Goodyear Tire & Rubber Company.

MANAGEMENT SCIENCE AT GOODYEAR

Goodyear has many departments that make use of management science applications. Most analyses are performed by one of the computer programming departments under the guidance of a user (client) department. These computer programming departments are involved in a variety of applications from routine data collection and systems maintenance to queueing analysis. For example, one department is responsible for maintaining a system that gathers records of orders and sales; another department is responsible for forecasting and assisting production schedulers; and a third department is responsible for quality control. The waiting line (queueing) application discussed in the remainder of this presentation was the responsibility of yet another department. Many of the applications performed by the departments are interrelated, and one department will often use data generated by another department.

*The authors are indebted to Dr. Walt Fenske of The Goodyear Tire & Rubber Company for providing this application.

A WAITING LINE APPLICATION

The application discussed involves a system for dispatching maintenance personnel to fix machines. Under the then current manual system, whenever a machine needed repair a production supervisor used a phone intercom system to call an individual referred to as a dispatcher. The dispatcher recorded the information provided by the production supervisor on cards. Then, whenever maintenance personnel called the dispatcher to request a new assignment, the information on these cards was used by the dispatcher to tell the maintenance personnel which machine should be repaired.

Due primarily to a need to develop a computerized data base that could be analyzed to improve the maintenance function, Goodyear decided to replace the manual system with a computer-controlled system. In the computer-controlled system the dispatcher function is performed by a person called a coordinator. The function of the coordinator is to enter service information when received into the computer using a remote computer terminal. The need for more information to be entered causes the coordinator's task to be more time consuming than the dispatcher's function in the old system. However, the computer-controlled system offers many potential advantages in other areas because of the wide variety of information entered by the coordinator.

A waiting line model was used in designing the computer-controlled system. The problem to be solved was to determine how many coordinators (and consequently, remote computer terminals) were needed. If there are not enough coordinators, production supervisors and maintenance personnel will have difficulty reaching a coordinator. If the computer system is to be a success, people trying to reach the coordinator should not have long waits. However, if there are too many coordinators, excessive coordinator and computer terminal expenses will be incurred. Some of the questions that had to be answered were the following:

1. What percentage of the time will the coordinator be busy?
2. What is the maximum number of people waiting to reach the coordinator?
3. What is the average time spent waiting to reach the coordinator?
4. How many calls does the coordinator receive?
5. How many callers have to wait longer than 4 minutes to reach the coordinator?
6. How many callers do not have to wait to reach the coordinator?

These questions suggest that the design of the new system may be aided by use of a waiting line model. In a waiting line model of this situation, the coordinators are the servers, and the people waiting to talk to the coordinators constitute the waiting line. Thus if one coordinator is used, the model is a single-channel waiting line model. Otherwise it is a multiple-channel waiting line model.

The complexity of the proposed computer system can best be understood by considering the four types of arrivals that must be handled. The first type of arrival is a call received from a production supervisor stating that a machine needs repair. At this time a *work order is initiated*. The second type of arrival is a call from a maintenance person stating that the repair work is being started; this is referred to as placing the *work order in process*. The third type of arrival, referred to as *completing a work order*, is a call from a maintenance person stating that the repair work has been completed. The fourth type of arrival is any other type of call. Note that each work order generates three calls to the coordinator.

For this problem the arrivals were known to differ from the Poisson distribution. In addition, there were a number of other complicating factors that precluded the use of the waiting line models introduced in this chapter. However, a simulation model of the system, built on many of the basic waiting line principles in this chapter, was implemented. The General Purpose Simulation System (GPSS) was the programming language used for the simulation model.

Computer simulation runs were performed for a system with one coordinator and a system with two coordinators. In the one-coordinator system the simulation runs showed the coordinator would be busy about 69% of the time and that the average waiting time to reach the coordinator would be 4.9 minutes. The average waiting time for the one-coordinator system was considered to be much too high.

For the two-coordinator system the simulation results indicated that each coordinator would be busy approximately 35% of the time. However, the average waiting time to reach a coordinator dropped to 42 seconds. In fact, it was found that a call would get through immediately about 90% of the time. Since management believed that these times were reasonable, the system was designed to have two coordinators and two remote computer terminals.

Questions

1. What is the primary reason that Goodyear decided to replace the manual system with a computer-controlled system?
2. What factors in this application led to the use of a simulation model rather than an analytical model of the waiting line?

14

Decision Analysis

Decision analysis can be used to determine optimal strategies when a decision maker is faced with several decision alternatives and an uncertain or risk-filled pattern of future events. For example, a manufacturer of a new style or line of seasonal clothing would like to manufacture large quantities of the product if consumer acceptance and consequently demand for the product are going to be high. However, the manufacturer would like to produce much smaller quantities if consumer acceptance and demand for the product are going to be low. Unfortunately, the seasonal clothing items require the manufacturer to make a production quantity decision before the demand is actually known. The actual consumer acceptance of the new product will not be determined until the items have been placed in the stores and the buyers have had the opportunity to purchase them. The selection of the best production volume decision from among several production volume alternatives when the decision maker is faced with the uncertainty of future demand is a problem suited for decision analysis.

We begin our study of decision analysis by considering problems in which there are reasonably few decision alternatives and possible future events. The concepts of a payoff table and a decision tree are introduced to provide a structure for this type of decision situation and to illustrate the fundamentals involved in decision analysis. Our discussion is then extended to show how additional information obtained through experimentation can be combined with the decision maker's preliminary information in order to develop an optimal decision strategy.

14.1 STRUCTURING THE DECISION PROBLEM

In order to illustrate the decision analysis approach, let us consider the case of Political Systems, Inc. (PSI), a newly formed computer service firm specializing in information services such as surveys and data analysis for individuals running for political office.

PSI is in the final stages of selecting a computer system for its Midwest branch located in Chicago. While the firm has decided on a computer manufacturer, it is currently attempting to determine the size of the computer system that would be the most economical to lease. We will use decision analysis to help PSI make its computer leasing decision.

The first step in the decision analysis approach to a given problem is to identify the alternatives considered by the decision maker. For PSI, the final decision will be to lease one of three computer systems, which differ in size and capacity. The three decision alternatives, denoted d_1, d_2, and d_3, are as follows:

$$d_1 = \text{lease the large computer system}$$
$$d_2 = \text{lease the medium-sized computer system}$$
$$d_3 = \text{lease the small computer system}$$

Obviously, the selection of the *best* decision alternative will depend upon what PSI management foresees as the possible market acceptance of the service and consequently the possible demand or load on the PSI computer system. Often the future events associated with a decision situation are uncertain. That is, while a decision maker may have an idea of the variety of possible future events, the decision maker will often be unsure as to which particular event will occur. Thus the second step in a decision analysis approach is to identify the future events that might occur. These future events, which are not under the control of the decision maker, are referred to as the *states of nature*. It is assumed that the list of possible states of nature includes everything that can happen and that the individual states of nature do not overlap; that is, the states of nature are defined so that one and only one of the listed states of nature will occur.

When asked about the states of nature for the PSI decision problem, management viewed the possible acceptance of the PSI service as an either-or situation. That is, management believed that the firm's overall level of acceptance in the market place would be one of two possibilities: high acceptance or low acceptance. Thus the PSI states of nature, denoted s_1 and s_2, are as follows:

$$s_1 = \text{high customer acceptance of PSI services}$$
$$s_2 = \text{low customer acceptance of PSI services}$$

Given the three decision alternatives and the two states of nature, which computer system should PSI lease? In order to answer this question, we will need information on the profit associated with each combination of a decision alternative and a state of nature. For example, what profit would PSI experience if the firm decided to lease the large computer system d_1 and market acceptance was high s_1? What profit would PSI experience if the firm decided to lease the large computer system d_1 and market acceptance was low s_2? And so on.

Payoff Tables

In decision analysis terminology, we refer to the outcome resulting from making a certain decision and the occurrence of a particular state of nature as the *payoff*. Using the best information available, management has estimated the payoffs or profits for the PSI computer leasing problem. These estimates are presented in Table 14.1. A table of this form

TABLE 14.1
Payoff Table for the PSI Computer Leasing Problem

| | | States of Nature | |
| | | High Acceptance | Low Acceptance |
Decision Alternatives		s_1	s_2
Lease a large system	d_1	200,000	−20,000
Lease a medium-sized system	d_2	150,000	20,000
Lease a small system	d_3	100,000	60,000

Profit or
payoff in $

is referred to as a *payoff table*. In general, entries in a payoff table can be stated in terms
of profits, costs, or any other measure of output that may be appropriate for the particular
situation being analyzed. The notation we will use for the entries in the payoff table is
$V(d_i, s_j)$, which denotes the payoff associated with decision alternative d_i and state of
nature s_j. Using this notation we see that $V(d_3, s_1) = \$100,000$.

Decision Trees

A *decision tree* provides a graphical representation of the decision-making process. Figure
14.1 shows a decision tree for the PSI computer leasing problem. Note that the tree shows
the natural or logical progression that will occur. First the firm must make its decision
(d_1, d_2, or d_3); then, once the decision is implemented, the state of nature (s_1 or s_2) will
occur. The number at each end point of the tree represents the payoff associated with a
particular chain of events. For example, the topmost payoff of 200,000 arises whenever
management makes the decision to purchase a large system (d_1) and market acceptance
turns out to be high (s_1). The next lower terminal point of −20,000 is reached when
management has made the decision to lease the large system (d_1) and the true state of

FIGURE 14.1
Decision Tree for the PSI Problem

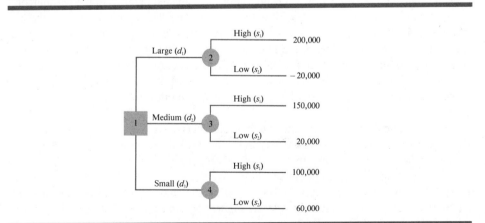

nature turns out to be a low degree of market acceptance (s_2). Thus we see that each possible sequence of events for the PSI problem is represented in the decision tree.

Using the general terminology associated with decision trees, we will refer to the intersection or junction points of the tree as *nodes* and the arcs or connectors between the nodes as *branches*. Figure 14.1 shows the PSI decision tree with the nodes numbered 1 to 4. When the branches *leaving* a given node are decision branches, we refer to the node as a *decision node*. Decision nodes are denoted by squares. Similarly, when the branches leaving a given node are state-of-nature branches, we refer to the node as a *state-of-nature node*. State-of-nature nodes are denoted by circles. Using this node-labeling procedure, node 1 is a decision node, whereas nodes 2, 3, and 4 are state-of-nature nodes.

The identification of the decision alternatives, the states of nature, and the determination of the payoff associated with each decision alternative and state of nature combination are the first three steps in the decision analysis process. The question we now turn to is the following: How can the decision maker best utilize the information presented in the payoff table or the decision tree to arrive at a decision? As we shall see, there are several decision criteria that may be used.

14.2   DECISION MAKING WITHOUT PROBABILITIES

In this section we consider decision-making criteria that do not require knowledge of the probabilities of the states of nature. These criteria are appropriate in situations where the decision maker has very little confidence in the ability to assess the probabilities of the various states of nature, or where it is desirable to consider best- and worst-case analyses that do not require state-of-nature probabilities. Because different criteria sometimes lead to different decision recommendations, it is important for the decision maker to understand the criteria available and then select the specific criterion, which, according to the decision maker's judgment, is the most appropriate.

An Optimistic Approach: The Maximax Decision Criterion

The maximax decision criterion uses an optimistic or best-case approach when evaluating each decision alternative; that is, each alternative is evaluated in terms of the *best* outcome that can occur. The decision alternative that is recommended is the one that has the best of the best possible outcomes. For a problem in which the output measure is profit, as it is in the PSI leasing problem, the maximax decision criterion would lead the decision maker to *maximize* the *maximum* possible profit that could be obtained; hence the name *maximax* decision criterion. For problems in which the output measure is cost, this criterion identifies the alternative that will minimize the minimum possible cost that could be obtained.

To illustrate the use of the maximax decision criterion we will show how this criterion could be used to develop a recommendation for the PSI leasing problem. First the decision maker would determine the maximum payoff possible for each of the decision alternatives; then the decision maker would select the decision that provides the overall maximum profit. Note that this procedure is just a systematic way of identifying the decision alternative that can potentially provide the highest possible profit. Table 14.2 illustrates this process for the PSI problem.

TABLE 14.2
PSI Maximum Payoff ($) for Each Decision Alternative

Decision Alternatives		Maximum Payoff		
Large system	d_1	200,000	⟵	Maximum of the
Medium system	d_2	150,000		maximum payoff
Small system	d_3	100,000		values

Since $200,000, corresponding to d_1, yields the maximum of the maximum payoffs, the decision to lease a large system is the recommended maximax decision alternative. The maximax decision criterion reflects an optimistic point of view because it simply recommends the decision alternative that provides the possibility of obtaining the best of all payoffs, $200,000.

A Conservative Approach: The Maximin Decision Criterion

The maximin decision criterion uses a conservative approach when comparing decision alternatives; that is, each alternative is evaluated in terms of the *worst* outcome that can occur. The decision alternative recommended is the one that has the best of the worst possible outcomes. For a problem in which the output measure is profit, as it is in the PSI leasing problem, the maximin decision criterion would lead the decision maker to *maximize* the *minimum* possible profit that could be obtained; hence the name *maximin* decision criterion. For problems in which the output measure is cost, this criterion identifies the alternative that will minimize the maximum possible cost that could be obtained.

To illustrate the use of the maximin decision criterion we will show how the criterion could be used to develop a recommendation for the PSI leasing problem. First the decision maker would list the minimum payoff for each of the decision alternatives; then, using this list, the decision maker would select the decision that has the maximum payoff. Table 14.3 illustrates this process for the PSI problem.

TABLE 14.3
PSI Minimum Payoff ($) for Each Decision Alternative

Decision Alternatives		Minimum Payoff		
Large system	d_1	−20,000		Maximum of the
Medium system	d_2	20,000		minimum payoff
Small system	d_3	60,000	⟵	values

Since $60,000, corresponding to d_3, yields the maximum of the minimum payoffs, the decision alternative to lease a small system is recommended as the maximin decision. This decision criterion is considered conservative because it concentrates on the worst possible payoffs and then recommends the decision alternative that avoids the possibility of extremely "bad" payoffs. In using the maximin criterion PSI is guaranteed a profit of at least $60,000. While PSI may still make more, it *cannot* make less than the maximin value of $60,000.

Minimax Regret Decision Criterion

Minimax regret is another decision criterion that is available for decision making without probabilities. This criterion is neither purely optimistic or purely conservative in its approach to selecting a preferred decision alternative. Let us illustrate the minimax regret criterion by showing how it can be used to select a decision alternative for the PSI leasing problem.

Suppose we make the decision to lease the small system d_3 and afterwards learn that market acceptance of the PSI service is high s_1. Table 14.1 shows the resulting profit to be $100,000. However, now that we know state of nature s_1 has occurred, we see that the large system decision d_1 yielding a profit of $200,000 would have been the optimal decision. The difference between the optimal payoff ($200,000) and the payoff experienced ($100,000) is referred to as the *opportunity loss* or *regret* associated with the d_3 decision when state s_1 occurs ($200,000 − $100,000 = $100,000). If we had made decision d_2 and state of nature s_1 had occurred, the opportunity loss or regret for this decision and state of nature would have been $200,000 − $150,000 = $50,000.

In maximization problems the general expression for opportunity loss or regret is given by

$$R(d_i, s_j) = V^*(s_j) - V(d_i, s_j) \tag{14.1}$$

where

$R(d_i, s_j)$ = regret associated with decision alternative d_i and state of nature s_j

$V^*(s_j)$ = best payoff value[1] under state of nature s_j

$V(d_i, s_j)$ = payoff associated with decision alternative d_i and state of nature s_j

Using (14.1) and the payoffs in Table 14.1, we can compute the regret associated with all combinations of decision alternatives d_i and states of nature s_j. We simply replace each entry in the payoff table with the value found by subtracting the entry from the largest entry in its column. Table 14.4 shows the regret, or opportunity loss, table for the PSI problem.

TABLE 14.4
Regret or Opportunity Loss ($) for the PSI Problem

		States of Nature	
Decision Alternatives		High Acceptance s_1	Low Acceptance s_2
Large system	d_1	0	80,000
Medium system	d_2	50,000	40,000
Small system	d_3	100,000	0

The next step in applying the minimax regret criterion requires the decision analyst to identify the maximum regret for each decision alternative. These data are shown in

[1]In cost minimization problems $V^*(s_j)$ will be the smallest entry in column j. Thus for minimization problems, equation (14.1) must be changed to $R(d_i, s_j) = V(d_i, s_j) - V^*(s_j)$.

Table 14.5. The final decision is made by selecting the alternative corresponding to the *mini*mum of the *maxi*mum *regret* values; hence the name *minimax regret*. For the PSI problem, the decision to lease a medium-sized computer system, with a corresponding regret of $50,000, is the recommended minimax regret decision.

TABLE 14.5
PSI Maximum Regret or Opportunity Loss ($) for Each Decision Alternative

Decision Alternatives		Maximum Regret or Opportunity Loss		
Large system	d_1	80,000		
Medium system	d_2	50,000	⟵———————	Minimum of the
Small system	d_3	100,000		maximum regret

Note that the three decision criteria discussed in this section have provided different recommendations. This is not in itself bad. It simply reflects the difference in decision-making philosophies that underlie the various criteria. Ultimately, the decision maker will have to choose the most appropriate criterion and then make the final decision accordingly. The major criticism of the criteria discussed in this section is that they do not consider any information about the probabilities of the various states of nature. In the next section we discuss criteria that utilize probability information in selecting a decision alternative.

14.3 DECISION MAKING WITH PROBABILITIES

In many decision making situations, it is possible to obtain probability estimates for each of the possible states of nature. When such probabilities are available and when payoffs are measured in terms of monetary value, the decision criterion of *expected monetary value* can be used to identify the best decision alternative. Let us first define the expected monetary value criterion and then show how it can be used for the PSI decision problem.

Let

$$N = \text{the number of possible states of nature}$$
$$P(s_j) = \text{the probability of state of nature } j$$
$$j = 1, 2, \ldots N$$

Since one and only one of the N states of nature can occur, the associated probabilities must satisfy the following two conditions:

$$P(s_j) \geq 0 \quad \text{for all states of nature } j \qquad (14.2)$$

$$\sum_{j=1}^{N} P(s_j) = P(s_1) + P(s_2) + \cdots + P(s_N) = 1 \qquad (14.3)$$

The expected monetary value (EMV) of a decision alternative d_i is given by

$$\text{EMV}(d_i) = \sum_{j=1}^{N} P(s_j)V(d_i, s_j) \tag{14.4}$$

In words, the expected monetary value of a decision alternative is the sum of weighted payoffs for the alternative. The weight for a payoff is the probability of the associated state of nature and therefore the probability that the payoff occurs. Let us now return to the PSI problem to see how the expected monetary value criterion can be applied.

Suppose that PSI management believes that the high acceptance state of nature, while very desirable, has only a 0.3 probability of occurrence, while the low acceptance state of nature has a 0.7 probability. Thus $P(s_1) = 0.3$ and $P(s_2) = 0.7$. Using the payoff values $V(d_i, s_j)$ shown in Table 14.1 and equation (14.4), expected monetary values for the three decision alternatives can be calculated:

$$\text{EMV}(d_1) = 0.3(200,000) + 0.7(-20,000) = \$46,000$$
$$\text{EMV}(d_2) = 0.3(150,000) + 0.7(\ \ 20,000) = \$59,000$$
$$\text{EMV}(d_3) = 0.3(100,000) + 0.7(\ \ 60,000) = \$72,000$$

Thus according to the expected monetary value criterion the small system decision d_3 with the highest expected monetary value of $72,000 is the recommended decision.

Note, however, that if the probabilities of the states of nature change, a different decision alternative might be selected. For example, if $P(s_1) = 0.6$ and $P(s_2) = 0.4$, we find the following expected monetary values:

$$\text{EMV}(d_1) = 0.6(200,000) + 0.4(-20,000) = \$112,000$$
$$\text{EMV}(d_2) = 0.6(150,000) + 0.4(\ \ 20,000) = \$\ 98,000$$
$$\text{EMV}(d_3) = 0.6(100,000) + 0.4(\ \ 60,000) = \$\ 84,000$$

We now see that, with these probabilities, decision alternative d_1 with an expected monetary value of $112,000 is the recommended decision.

The calculations required to identify the decision alternative with the best expected monetary value can be conveniently carried out on a decision tree. To demonstrate this, Figure 14.2 shows the decision tree for the PSI problem with state-of-nature branch probabilities. We will now use the branch probabilities and the expected monetary value criterion to arrive at the optimal decision for PSI.

Working backward through the decision tree, we first compute the expected monetary value at each state-of-nature mode. That is, at each state-of-nature node we weigh each possible payoff by its chance of occurrence. By doing this we obtain the expected monetary values for nodes 2, 3, and 4 as shown in Figure 14.3.

Since the decision maker controls the branch leaving decision node 1 and since we are trying to maximize expected profits, the best decision branch at node 1 is d_3. Thus the decision tree analysis leads us to recommend d_3 with an expected monetary value of $72,000. Note that this is the same recommendation that was obtained using the expected monetary value criterion in conjunction with the payoff table.

We have seen how decision trees can be used to analyze decisions with state-of-nature probabilities. While other decision problems may be substantially more complex

FIGURE 14.2
PSI Decision Tree with State-of-Nature Branch Probabilities

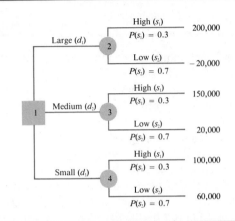

FIGURE 14.3
Applying the Expected Monetary Value Criterion Using Decision Trees

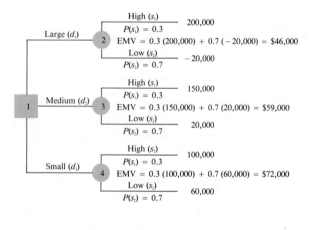

than the PSI problem, if there are a reasonable number of decision alternatives and states of nature, the decision tree approach outlined in this section can be used. First, the analyst must draw a decision tree consisting of decision and state-of-nature nodes and branches that describe the sequential nature of the problem. Assuming the expected monetary value criterion is to be used, the next step is to determine the probabilities for each of the state-of-nature branches and compute the expected monetary value at each state-of-nature node. The decision branch leading to the state-of-nature node with the best expected monetary value is then selected. The decision alternative associated with this branch is the best decision using the expected monetary value criterion.

14.4   EXPECTED VALUE OF PERFECT INFORMATION

Suppose that PSI had the opportunity to conduct a market research study which would evaluate consumer needs for the PSI service. Such a study could help by improving the current probability assessments for the states of nature. However, if the cost of obtaining the market research information exceeds its value, PSI should not conduct the market research study.

To determine the maximum possible value that PSI should pay for additional information, let us suppose that PSI could obtain perfect information regarding the states of nature; that is, we will assume that PSI could determine with certainty which state of nature will occur. To make use of perfect information we need to develop a decision strategy for PSI to follow. As we will show, a decision strategy is simply a policy or decision rule that is to be followed by the decision maker. In computing the expected value of perfect information, the decision strategy is a rule that specifies which decision alternative should be selected given each state of nature.

To help determine the optimal decision strategy for PSI we have reproduced PSI's payoff table as Table 14.6. We see that if state of nature s_1 occurs, then the best decision alternative is d_1 with a profit of \$200,000. Similarly, if state of nature s_2 occurs, then the best decision alternative is d_3 with a profit of \$60,000. Thus the optimal decision strategy the company should follow if perfect information were available can be stated as follows:

Optimal Decision Strategy with Perfect Information

If s_1 occurs, then select d_1.

If s_2 occurs, then select d_3.

What is the expected monetary value for this decision strategy? Since $P(s_1) = 0.3$ and $P(s_2) = 0.7$, we see that there is a 0.3 probability that PSI will make \$200,000 and a 0.7 probability PSI will make \$60,000. Thus the expected monetary value of the decision strategy that uses perfect information is

$$(0.3)(\$200,000) + (0.7)(\$60,000) = \$102,000$$

TABLE 14.6
Payoff Table for the PSI Problem

		States of Nature	
		High Acceptance	Low Acceptance
Decision Alternatives		s_1	s_2
Large system	d_1	200,000	−20,000
Medium system	d_2	150,000	20,000
Small system	d_3	100,000	60,000

Recall that when perfect information was not available, the expected monetary value criterion resulted in recommending decision alternative d_3 with an expected monetary value of $72,000. Since $72,000 is the expected monetary value without perfect information and $102,000 is the expected monetary value with perfect information, $102,000 − $72,000 = $30,000 represents the expected value of perfect information (EVPI); that is,

$$\text{EVPI} = \$102,000 - \$72,000 = \$30,000$$

In other words, $30,000 represents the additional expected monetary value that can be obtained if perfect information were available about the states of nature. Figure 14.4 provides a summary of the computation of the EVPI for the PSI problem.

FIGURE 14.4
The Expected Value of Perfect Information

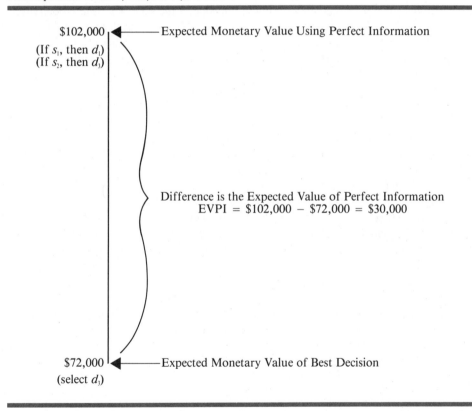

Generally speaking, we would not expect a market research study to provide ''perfect'' information, but the information provided might be worth a good portion of the $30,000. In any case, PSI's management knows it should never pay more than $30,000 for any information, no matter how good. Provided the market survey cost is reasonably small—say $5000 to $10,000—it appears economically desirable for PSI to consider the market research study.

14.5 DECISION ANALSYSIS WITH SAMPLE INFORMATION

In applying the expected monetary value criterion, we have seen how probability information about the states of nature affects the expected value calculations and thus the decision recommendation. Frequently decision makers have preliminary or prior probability estimates for the states of nature that are initially the best probability values available. However, in order to make the best possible decision, the decision maker may want to seek additional information about the states of nature. This new information can be used to revise or update the prior probabilities so that the final decision is based upon more accurate probability estimates for the states of nature.

The seeking of additional information is most often accomplished through experiments designed to provide sample information or more current data about the states of nature. Raw material sampling, product testing, and test market research are examples of experiments that may enable a revision or updating of the state-of-nature probabilities. In the following discussion we will reconsider the PSI computer leasing problem and show how sample information can be used to revise the state-of-nature probabilities. We will then show how the revised probabilities can be used to develop an optimal decision strategy for PSI.

Recall that management had assigned a probability of $P(s_1) = 0.3$ to state of nature s_1 and a probability of $P(s_2) = 0.7$ to state of nature s_2. At this point we will refer to these initial probability estimates, $P(s_1)$ and $P(s_2)$, as the *prior* probabilities for the states of nature. Using these prior probabilities we found that the decision to lease the small system d_3 was optimal, yielding an expected monetary value of $72,000. Recall also that we showed that the expected value of new information about the states of nature could potentially be worth as much as EVPI = $30,000.

Suppose that PSI decides to consider hiring a market research firm to study the potential acceptance of the PSI service. The market research study will provide new information that can be combined with the prior probabilities through a Bayesian procedure to obtain updated or revised probability estimates for the states of nature. These revised probabilities are called *posterior* probabilities. The process of revising probabilities is depicted in Figure 14.5.

We usually refer to the new information obtained through research or experimentation as an *indicator*. Since in many cases the experiment conducted to obtain the additional information will consist of taking a statistical sample, the new information is also often referred to as *sample information*.

Using the indicator terminology, we can denote the outcomes of the PSI marketing research study as follows:

FIGURE 14.5
Probability Revision Based on New Information

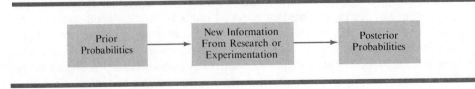

I_1 = favorable market research report (i.e., in the market research study the individuals contacted generally express considerable interest in PSI's services)

I_2 = unfavorable market research report (i.e., in the market research study the individuals contacted generally express little interest in PSI's services)

Given one of these possible indicators, our objective is to provide improved estimates of the probabilities of the various states of nature. The end result of the Bayesian revision process depicted in Figure 14.5 is a set of posterior probabilities of the form $P(s_j|I_k)$, where $P(s_j|I_k)$ represents the conditional probability that state of nature s_j will occur given that the outcome of the market research study was indicator I_k.

To make effective use of this indicator information, we must know something about the probability relationships between the indicators and the states of nature. For example, in the PSI problem, given that the state of nature ultimately turns out to be high customer acceptance, what is the probability that the market research study will result in a favorable report? In this case we are asking about the conditional probability of indicator I_1 given state of nature s_1, written $P(I_1|s_1)$. In order to carry out the analysis, we will need conditional probability relationships for all indicators given all states of nature, i.e., $P(I_1|s_1)$, $P(I_1|s_2)$, $P(I_2|s_1)$, and $P(I_2|s_2)$. Historical relative frequency data and/or subjective probability estimates are usually the primary source for these conditional probability values.

In the PSI case the past record of the marketing research company on similar studies has led to the following estimates of the relevant conditional probabilities:

	Market Research Report	
States of Nature	Favorable I_1	Unfavorable I_2
High acceptance s_1	$P(I_1|s_1) = 0.8$	$P(I_2|s_1) = 0.2$
Low acceptance s_2	$P(I_1|s_2) = 0.1$	$P(I_2|s_2) = 0.9$

Note that these probability estimates indicate that a great degree of confidence can be placed in the market research report. When the true state of nature is s_1, the market research report will be favorable 80% of the time and unfavorable only 20%. When the true state is s_2, the report will make the correct indication 90% of the time. Now let us see how this additional information can be incorporated into the decision-making process.

14.6 DEVELOPING A DECISION STRATEGY

A decision strategy is a policy or decision rule that is to be followed by the decision maker. In the PSI case, with the market research study, a decision strategy is a rule that recommends a particular decision based upon whether the market research report is favorable or unfavorable. We will employ a decision tree analysis to find the optimal decision strategy for PSI.

Figure 14.6 shows the decision tree for the PSI computer leasing problem provided a market research study is conducted. Note that as you move from left to right the tree shows the natural or logical order that will occur in the decision-making process. First,

FIGURE 14.6
The PSI Decision Tree Incorporating the Results of the Market Research Study

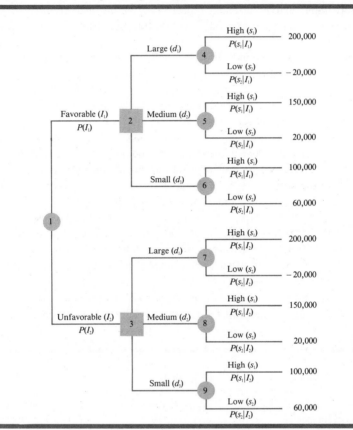

the firm will obtain the market research report indicator (I_1 or I_2); then a decision (d_1, d_2, or d_3) will be made; finally, the state of nature (s_1 or s_2) will occur. The decision and the state of nature combine to provide the final profit or payoff.

Using decision tree terminology, we have now introduced an *indicator node*, node 1, and *indicator branches*, I_1 and I_2. Since the branches emanating from indicator nodes are not under the control of the decision maker but are determined by chance, these nodes are depicted by a circle just like the state-of-nature nodes. We see that nodes 2 and 3 are decision nodes, while nodes 4, 5, 6, 7, 8, and 9 are state-of-nature nodes. For decision nodes the decision maker must select the specific branch d_1, d_2, or d_3 that will be taken. Selecting the best decision branch is equivalent to making the best decision. However, since the indicator and state-of-nature branches are not controlled by the decision maker, the specific branch leaving an indicator or a state-of-nature node will depend upon the probability associated with the branch. Thus before we can carry out an analysis of the decision tree and develop a decision strategy, we must compute the probability of each indicator branch $P(I_k)$ and the probability of each state-of-nature branch. Note from the decision tree that the state-of-nature branches occur *after* the indicator branches. Thus when we attempt to compute state-of-nature branch probabilities, we will need to consider which indicator was previously observed. That is, we will express state-of-nature probabilities in terms of the probability of state of nature s_j *given* indicator I_k was observed. Thus all state-of-nature probabilities will be expressed in a $P(s_j|I_k)$ form.

Computing Branch Probabilities

The prior probabilities for the states of nature in the PSI problem were given as $P(s_1) = 0.3$ and $P(s_2) = 0.7$. In Section 14.5 we identified the relationship between the market research indicator and states of nature with the conditional probabilities

$$P(I_1|s_1) = 0.8 \quad P(I_2|s_1) = 0.2$$
$$P(I_1|s_2) = 0.1 \quad P(I_2|s_2) = 0.9$$

In order to develop a decision strategy utilizing the decision tree in Figure 14.6, we need indicator branch probabilities $P(I_k)$ and state-of-nature branch probabilities $P(s_j|I_k)$. The problem now facing us is determining how to use the given prior probability estimates $P(s_j)$ and conditional probability estimates $P(I_k|s_j)$ to calculate the branch probabilities $P(I_k)$ and $P(s_j|I_k)$. In this section we will show how the Bayesian revision process referred to in Figure 14.5 can be used to calculate the branch probabilities $P(I_k)$ and $P(s_j|I_k)$.

In order to see how this Bayesian procedure is applied and at the same time understand why the procedure works, let us look closely at the calculation of the indicator branch probability, $P(I_1)$, for the PSI market research study. First, note that there are only two ways in which the outcome I_1 can occur.

1. The market research report is favorable (I_1) *and* the state of nature turns out to be high acceptance (s_1), written ($I_1 \cap s_1$).
2. The market research report is favorable (I_1) *and* the state of nature turns out to be low acceptance (s_2), written ($I_1 \cap s_2$).

The probabilities of these two outcomes are written $P(I_1 \cap s_1)$ and $P(I_1 \cap s_2)$, respectively. We can now add these two probabilities to obtain the following branch probability:

$$P(I_1) = P(I_1 \cap s_1) + P(I_1 \cap s_2) \tag{14.6}$$

The multiplication law of probability provides the following formulas for $P(I_1 \cap s_1)$ and $P(I_1 \cap s_2)$

$$P(I_1 \cap s_1) = P(I_1|s_1) P(s_1) \tag{14.7}$$
$$P(I_1 \cap s_2) = P(I_1|s_2) P(s_2) \tag{14.8}$$

Finally, substituting the above expressions for $P(I_1 \cap s_1)$ and $P(I_1 \cap s_2)$ in (14.6) we obtain

$$P(I_1) = P(I_1|s_1) P(s_1) + P(I_1|s_2) P(s_2) \tag{14.9}$$

Generalizing the above expression for any indicator branch probability, $P(I_k)$, and N states of nature, $s_1, s_2, \ldots s_N$, we have

$$P(I_k) = P(I_k|s_1)P(s_1) + P(I_k|s_2)P(s_2) + \cdots + P(I_k|s_N)P(s_N)$$

or

$$P(I_k) = \sum_{j=1}^{N} P(I_k|s_j)P(s_j) \qquad (14.10)$$

Returning to the PSI problem with two prior probabilities $P(s_1) = 0.3$ and $P(s_2) = 0.7$ and the conditional probabilities $P(I_1|s_1) = 0.8, P(I_1|s_2) = 0.1, P(I_2|s_1) = 0.2$, and $P(I_2|s_2) = 0.9$, we can use (14.10) to compute the two indicator branch probabilities. These calculations are as follows:

$$P(I_1) = P(I_1|s_1)P(s_1) + P(I_1|s_2)P(s_2)$$
$$= (0.8)(0.3) + (0.1)(0.7) = 0.31$$

and

$$P(I_2) = P(I_2|s_1)P(s_1) + P(I_2|s_2)P(s_2)$$
$$= (0.2)(0.3) + (0.9)(0.7) = 0.69$$

The above probabilities indicate that the probability of a favorable market research report I_1 is 0.31 and the probability of an unfavorable market research report I_2 is 0.69.

Now that we know the indicator branch probabilities, let us show how the Bayesian process enables us to compute the revised, or posterior, state-of-nature branch probabilities $P(s_j|I_k)$. Let us illustrate this procedure by considering the state-of-nature branch probability $P(s_1|I_1)$, the probability the market acceptance is high (s_1) given the market research report is favorable (I_1). The fundamental conditional probability relationship as presented in texts dealing with probability and statistics can be written

$$P(s_1|I_1) = \frac{P(I_1 \cap s_1)}{P(I_1)} \qquad (14.11)$$

Using (14.7) for $P(I_1 \cap s_1)$, we have

$$P(s_1|I_1) = \frac{P(I_1|s_1)P(s_1)}{P(I_1)} \qquad (14.12)$$

With known probabilities $P(I_1|s_1) = 0.8, P(s_1) = 0.3$ and $P(I_1) = 0.31$, the revised state-of-nature probability, $P(s_1|I_1)$ becomes

$$P(s_1|I_1) = \frac{(0.8)(0.3)}{0.31} = \frac{0.24}{0.31} = 0.7742$$

Recall that the prior probability of a high market acceptance was $P(s_1) = 0.3$. The above probability information now tells us that if the market research indicator is favorable, the

probability of a high market acceptance should be revised to $P(s_1|I_1) = 0.7742$.
Generalizing (14.12) for any state of nature s_j and any indicator I_k provides

$$P(s_j|I_k) = \frac{P(I_k|s_j)P(s_j)}{P(I_k)} \qquad (14.13)$$

Thus, we can use (14.13) to compute the revised or posterior state-of-nature branch probabilities. For example, the revised probability of low market acceptance, s_2, given the market research indicator is favorable, I_1, becomes

$$P(s_2|I_1) = \frac{P(I_1|s_2)P(s_2)}{P(I_1)} = \frac{(0.1)(0.7)}{0.31} = \frac{0.07}{0.31} = 0.2258$$

Similar calculations for an unfavorable market research indicator, I_2, will provide the revised state-of-nature branch probabilities $P(s_1|I_2) = 0.0870$ and $P(s_2|I_2) = 0.9130$. Figure 14.7 shows the PSI decision tree after all indicator and all revised state-of-nature branch probabilities have been computed.

FIGURE 14.7
The PSI Decision Tree with Branch Probabilities

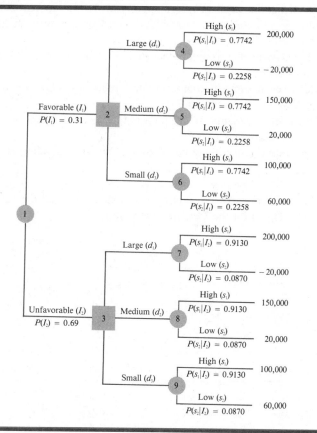

Although the above procedure can be used to compute branch probabilities, the calculations can become quite cumbersome as the problem size grows larger. Thus in order to assist in applying Bayes' rule to compute branch probabilities, we present a tabular procedure that will make it easier to carry out the computations, especially for large decision analysis problems.

Computing Branch Probabilities: A Tabular Procedure

The procedure used for computing the probabilities of the indicator and state-of-nature branches can be carried out by utilizing the following tabular approach. First, for each indicator I_k we form a table consisting of the following five column headings:

Column 1: States of nature s_j
Column 2: Prior probabilities $P(s_j)$
Column 3: Conditional probabilities $P(I_k|s_j)$
Column 4: Joint probabilities $P(I_k \cap s_j)$
Column 5: Posterior probabilities $P(s_j|I_k)$

Then the following procedure can be utilized to calculate $P(I_k)$ and the $P(s_j|I_k)$ values.

Step 1 In column 1 list the states of nature appropriate to the problem being analyzed.
Step 2 In column 2 enter the prior probability corresponding to each state of nature listed in column 1.
Step 3 In column 3 write the appropriate value of $P(I_k|s_j)$ for each state of nature specified in column 1.
Step 4 To compute each entry in column 4, multiply each entry in column 2 by the corresponding entry in column 3.
Step 5 Add the entries in column 4. The sum is the value of $P(I_k)$. For convenience, write the sum below column 4.
Step 6 To compute each entry in column 5 divide the corresponding entry in column 4 by $P(I_k)$.

We will now illustrate the above procedure to compute $P(I_1)$ and the revised state-of-nature probabilities $P(s_j|I_1)$ for the PSI, Inc. problem.

Steps 1, 2, and 3:

s_j	$P(s_j)$	$P(I_1|s_j)$	$P(I_1 \cap s_j)$	$P(s_j|I_1)$
s_1	0.3	0.8		
s_2	0.7	0.1		

Steps 4 and 5:

s_j	$P(s_j)$	$P(I_1|s_j)$	$P(I_1 \cap s_j)$	$P(s_j|I_1)$
s_1	0.3	0.8	0.24	
s_2	0.7	0.1	0.07	

$$P(I_1) = 0.31$$

Step 6:

s_j	$P(s_j)$	$P(I_1\|s_j)$	$P(I_1 \cap s_j)$	$P(s_j\|I_1)$
s_1	0.3	0.8	0.24	$0.24/0.31 = 0.7742$
s_2	0.7	0.1	$\underline{0.07}$	$0.07/0.31 = 0.2258$
			$P(I_1) = 0.31$	

Note that $P(I_1)$, $P(s_1\|I_1)$, and $P(s_2\|I_1)$ are exactly the same as we calculated by applying equations (14.10) and (14.13) directly. The above tabular computations could be repeated in order to compute $P(I_2)$ and the revised state-of-nature probabilities $P(s_j\|I_2)$.

An Optimal Decision Strategy

Regardless of the approach used to compute the branch probabilities, we can now use the branch probabilities and the expected monetary value criterion to arrive at the optimal decision for PSI. Working *backward* through the decision tree, we first compute the expected monetary value at each state-of-nature node. That is, at each state-of-nature node the possible payoffs are weighted by their chance of occurrence. Thus the expected monetary values for nodes 4 through 9 are computed as follows:

$$\text{EMV(node 4)} = (0.7742)(200,000) + (0.2258)(-20,000) = 150,324$$

$$\text{EMV(node 5)} = (0.7742)(150,000) + (0.2258)(\ \ 20,000) = 120,646$$

$$\text{EMV(node 6)} = (0.7742)(100,000) + (0.2258)(\ \ 60,000) = \ \ 90,968$$

$$\text{EMV(node 7)} = (0.0870)(200,000) + (0.9130)(-20,000) = \ \ \ \ -860$$

$$\text{EMV(node 8)} = (0.0870)(150,000) + (0.9130)(\ \ 20,000) = \ \ 31,310$$

$$\text{EMV(node 9)} = (0.0870)(100,000) + (0.9130)(\ \ 60,000) = \ \ 63,480$$

Figure 14.8 shows the above calculations directly on the decision tree. Since the decision maker controls the branch leaving a decision node, and since we are trying to maximize expected profits, the optimal decision at node 2 is d_1. Thus since d_1 leads to an expected value of \$150,324, we say EMV(node 2) = \$150,324 if the optimal decision of d_1 is made.

A similar analysis of decision node 3 shows that the optimal decision branch at this node is d_3. Thus EMV(node 3) becomes \$63,480 provided the optimal decision of d_3 is made.

As a final step, we can continue working backward to the indicator node and establish its expected value. We see that since node 1 has probability branches, we cannot select the best branch. Rather we must compute the expected value over all possible branches. Thus we have

$$\text{EMV(node 1)} = (0.31)\,\text{EMV(node 2)} + (0.69)\,\text{EMV(node 3)}$$

$$= (0.31)(\$150,324) + (0.69)(\$63,480) = \$90,402$$

FIGURE 14.8
Developing a Decision Strategy for the PSI Problem

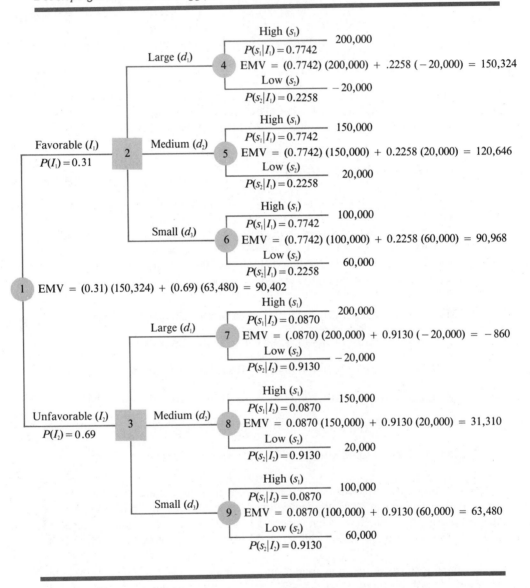

The value of \$90,402 is viewed as the expected value of the optimal decision strategy when the market research study is used or the expected monetary value using sample information (i.e., that provided by the market research report).

Note that the final decision has not yet been determined. We will need to know the results of the market research study before deciding to lease a large system (d_1) or a small system (d_3). The results of the decision analysis at this point, however, have provided us with the following optimal *decision strategy* if the market research study is conducted.

Decision Strategy	
If	*Then*
Report favorable (I_1)	Lease large system (d_1)
Report unfavorable (I_2)	Lease small system (d_3)

Thus we have seen how the decision tree approach can be used to develop optimal decision strategies when sample information is available. While other decision analysis problems may not be as simple as the PSI problem, the approach we have outlined is still applicable. First draw a decision tree consisting of indicator, decision, and state-of-nature nodes and branches such that the tree describes the specific decision-making process. Posterior probability calculations must be made in order to establish indicator and state-of-nature branch probabilities. Then by working backward through the tree, computing expected values at state-of-nature and indicator nodes, and selecting the best decision branch at decision nodes, the analyst can determine an optimal decision strategy and the associated expected value for the problem.

14.7 EXPECTED VALUE OF SAMPLE INFORMATION

In the PSI problem, management now has a decision strategy of leasing the large computer system if the market research report is favorable and leasing the small computer system if the market research report is unfavorable. Since the additional information provided by the market research firm will result in an added cost for PSI in terms of the fee paid to the research firm, PSI management may question the value of this market research information.

The value of sample information is often measured by calculating what is referred to as the *expected value of sample information* (EVSI). For maximization problems[2]

$$\text{EVSI} = \begin{bmatrix} \text{expected value of the} \\ \text{optimal decision } with \\ \text{sample information} \end{bmatrix} - \begin{bmatrix} \text{expected value of the} \\ \text{optimal decision } without \\ \text{sample information} \end{bmatrix} \quad (14.14)$$

For PSI the market research information is considered the "sample" information. The decision tree calculations indicated that the expected value of the optimal decision with the market research information was $90,402, while the expected value of the optimal decision without the market research information was $72,000. Using equation (14.14), the expected value of the market research report is

$$\text{EVSI} = \$90,402 - \$72,000 = \$18,402$$

Thus PSI should be willing to pay up to $18,402 for the market research information.

[2]In minimization problems the expected value with sample information will be less than or equal to the expected value without sample information. Thus in minimization problems,

$$\text{EVSI} = \begin{bmatrix} \text{expected value of the} \\ \text{optimal decision } without \\ \text{sample information} \end{bmatrix} - \begin{bmatrix} \text{expected value of the} \\ \text{optimal decision } with \\ \text{sample information} \end{bmatrix}$$

Efficiency of Sample Information

In Section 14.4 we saw that the expected value of perfect information (EVPI) for the PSI problem is $30,000. While we never expected the market research report to obtain perfect information, we can use an *efficiency* measure to express the value of the report. With perfect information having an efficiency rating of 100%, the efficiency rating E for sample information is computed as follows:

$$E = \frac{\text{EVSI}}{\text{EVPI}} \times 100$$

For our PSI example,

$$E = \frac{18,402}{30,000} \times 100 = 61\%$$

In other words, the information from the market research firm is 61% as "efficient" as perfect information.

Low efficiency ratings for information might lead the decision maker to look for other types of information. On the other hand, high efficiency ratings indicate that the information is almost as good as perfect information, and additional sources of information should not be worthwhile.

14.8   OTHER TOPICS IN DECISION ANALYSIS

In the discussion of decision analysis, we have only considered decision situations where the states of nature are finite and can be listed. The next step would be to consider situations where the states of nature were so numerous that it would be impractical, if not impossible, to treat the states of nature as a discrete random variable consisting of a finite number of values. For example, let us suppose that we were attempting to price a new product and were concerned with the potential sales volume we might experience at different prices. We might think of the states of nature as being all possible sales volumes from 0 to 200,000 units. Although there are a finite number of states of nature, no units sold, one unit sold, and so on, we recognize that attempting to deal with this large number of possible states of nature is extremely impractical. The solution procedure that is used in such circumstances is to treat the state of nature as a continuous random variable. For example, perhaps a reasonable approximation of the state of nature (that is, sales volume) is that sales are normally distributed with a mean of 100,000 units and a standard deviation of 25,000 units. Although decision analysis techniques have been developed to handle such situations, we shall not attempt to present these procedures in this chapter.

Another area of decision analysis is concerned with alternative measures of the payoffs. In our PSI example we used profit in dollars as the measure of the payoff. Then the expected *monetary* value criterion was used to select the best decision. While decision analysis applications are often based on expected monetary value, there are other measures of payoff that could be used. In Chapter 15 we introduce another measure of payoff known as utility.

Summary

In this chapter we have introduced the decision analysis approach to decision making. We have discussed in detail the decision analysis procedures designed to solve problems with a limited number of decision alternatives and a finite list of possible states of nature. The goal of the decision analysis approach was to identify the best decision alternative given an uncertain or risk-filled pattern of future events (that is, states of nature).

We discussed the decision criteria of maximax, maximin, and minimax regret for solving problems of decision making without probabilities. We then discussed the use of the expected monetary value criterion for solving problems of decision making with probabilities. We also showed how additional information about the states of nature can be used to revise or update the probability estimates and develop an optimal decision strategy for the problem. The notions of expected value of sample information, expected value of perfect information, and efficiency were used to evaluate the contribution of the additional information.

Glossary

States of nature The uncontrollable future events that can affect the outcome of a decision.

Payoff The outcome measure such as profit, cost, etc. Each combination of a decision alternative and a state of nature has an associated payoff.

Payoff table A tabular representation of the payoffs for a decision problem.

Maximin A maximization decision criterion that seeks to maximize the minimum payoff.

Maximax A maximization decision criterion that seeks to maximize the maximum payoff.

Opportunity loss or regret The amount of loss (lower profit or higher cost) due to not making the best decision for each state of nature.

Minimax regret A maximization or minimization decision criterion that seeks to minimize the maximum regret.

Expected monetary value A decision criterion that weighs the monetary payoff for each decision alternative by its probability of occurrence.

Decision tree A graphical representation of the decision-making situation from decision to state-of-nature to payoff.

Nodes The intersection or junction points of the decision tree.

Branches Lines or arcs connecting nodes of the decision tree.

Expected value of perfect information (EVPI) The expected value of information that would tell the decision maker exactly which state of nature was going to occur (that is, perfect information).

Indicators Information about the states of nature obtained by experimentation. An indicator may be the result of a sample.

Prior probabilities The probabilities of the states of nature prior to obtaining experimental information.

Posterior (revised) probabilities The probabilities of the states of nature after using Bayes' theorem to adjust the prior probabilities based upon given indicator information.

Bayesian revision The process of adjusting prior probabilities to create the posterior probabilities based upon information obtained by experimentation.

Expected value of sample information (EVSI)   The difference between the expected value of an optimal strategy based on new information and the "best" expected value without any new information. It is a measure of the economic value of new information.

Efficiency   The ratio of EVSI to EVPI; perfect information is 100% efficient.

Problems

1. Suppose that a decision maker faced with four decision alternatives and four states of nature develops the following profit payoff table:

		States of Nature			
		s_1	s_2	s_3	s_4
Decisions	d_1	14	9	10	5
	d_2	11	10	8	7
	d_3	9	10	10	11
	d_4	8	10	11	13

a. If the decision maker knows nothing about the chances or probability of occurrence of the four states of nature, what is the recommended decision using the maximax, maximin, and minimax regret criteria?

b. Which decision criterion do you prefer? Explain. Is it important for the decision maker to establish the most appropriate decision criterion before analyzing the problem? Explain.

c. Assume the payoff table in problem 1 provides *cost* rather than profit payoffs. What is the recommended decision using the optimistic, conservative, and minimax regret decision criteria?

2. Suppose that the decision maker in problem 1 obtains information that enables the following probability estimates to be made: $P(s_1) = 0.5$, $P(s_2) = 0.2$, $P(s_3) = 0.2$, $P(s_4) = 0.1$.

a. Use the expected monetary value criterion to determine the optimal decision.

b. Now assume the entries in the payoff table are costs and use the expected monetary value criterion to determine the minimum cost solution.

3. Southland Corporation's decision to produce a new line of recreational products has resulted in the need to construct either a small plant or a large plant. The decision as to which plant size to select depends upon how the marketplace reacts to the new product line. In order to conduct an analysis, marketing management has decided to view the possible long-run demand as either low, medium, or high. The following payoff table shows the projected profit in millions of dollars.

		Long-Run Demand		
		Low	Medium	High
Decision	Small plant	150	200	200
	Large plant	50	200	500

a. Construct a decision tree for this problem and determine the recommended decision using the maximax, maximin, and minimax regret decision criteria.

b. Assume that the best estimate of the probability of a low long-run demand is 0.20, a medium long-run demand is 0.15, and a high long-run demand is 0.65. What is the recommended decision using the expected monetary value criterion?

4. Hale's TV Productions is considering producing a pilot for a comedy series for a major TV network. While the network may reject the pilot and the series, it may also purchase the program for 1 or 2 years. Hale may decide to produce the pilot or transfer the rights for the series to a competitor for $100,000. Hale's profits are summarized in the following payoff table:

		States of Nature		
		Reject	1 Year	2 Years
Produce pilot	d_1	− 100	50	150
Sell to competitor	d_2	100	100	100

Profit in $\$ \times 10^3$

If the probability estimates for the states of nature are $P(\text{reject}) = 0.2$, $P(1 \text{ year}) = 0.3$, $P(2 \text{ years}) = 0.5$, what should the company do? What is the maximum Hale should be willing to pay for inside information on what the network will do?

5. McHuffter Condominiums, Inc. of Pensacola, Fla., recently purchased land near the Gulf of Mexico and is attempting to determine the size of the condominium development it should build. Three sizes of developments are being considered: small d_1, medium d_2, and large d_3. At the same time an uncertain economy makes it difficult to ascertain the demand for the new condominiums. McHuffter's management realizes that a large development followed by a low demand could be very costly to the company. However, if McHuffter makes a conservative small development decision and then finds a high demand, the firm's profits will be lower than they might have been. With the three levels of demand—low, medium, and high—McHuffter's management has prepared the following payoff table:

			Demand	
		Low	Medium	High
	Small	400	400	400
Decision	Medium	100	600	600
	Large	− 300	300	900

Profit in $\$ \times 10^3$

a. If nothing is known about the demand probabilities, what are the decision recommendations under the maximin, maximax, and minimax regret criteria?
b. If $P(\text{low}) = 0.20$, $P(\text{medium}) = 0.35$, and $P(\text{high}) = 0.45$, what decision is recommended under the expected monetary value criterion?
c. What is the expected value of perfect information?

6. Construct a decision tree for the McHuffter Condominiums problem (problem 5). What is the expected value at each state-of-nature node? What is the optimal decision?

7. Martin's Service Station is considering investing in a heavy-duty snowplow this fall. Martin has analyzed the situation carefully and feels this would be a very profitable investment if the snowfall is heavy. A small profit could still be made if the snowfall is moderate, but Martin would lose money if snowfall is light. Specifically, Martin forecasts a profit of $7000 if snowfall is heavy and $2000 if it is moderate, and a $9000 loss if it is light. Based on the weather bureau's long-range forecast Martin estimates $P(\text{heavy snowfall}) = 0.4$, $P(\text{moderate snowfall}) = 0.3$, and $P(\text{light snowfall}) = 0.3$.
   a. Prepare a decision tree for Martin's problem.
   b. Using the expected monetary value criterion, would you recommend that Martin invest in the snowplow?

8. Refer again to the investment problem faced by Martin's Service Station (problem 7). Martin can purchase a blade to attach to his service truck that can also be used to plow driveways and parking lots. Since this truck must also be available to start cars, etc., Martin will not be able to generate as much revenue plowing snow if he elects this alternative. But he will keep his loss smaller if there is light snowfall. Under this alternative Martin forecasts a profit of $3500 if snowfall is heavy and $1000 if it is moderate, and a $1500 loss if snowfall is light.
   a. Prepare a new decision tree showing all three alternatives.
   b. Using the expected monetary value criterion, what is the optimal decision?
   c. What is the expected value of perfect information?

9. The Gorman Manufacturing Company must decide whether it should purchase a component part from a supplier or manufacture the component at its Milan, Mich., plant. If demand is high, it would be to Gorman's advantage to manufacture the component. However, if demand is low, Gorman's unit manufacturing cost will be high due to underutilization of equipment. The projected profit in thousands of dollars for Gorman's make or buy decision is shown below:

| | Demand | | |
	Low	Medium	High
Manufacture component	−20	40	100
Purchase component	10	45	70

The states of nature have the following probabilities: $P(\text{low demand}) = 0.35$, $P(\text{medium demand}) = 0.35$, and $P(\text{high demand}) = 0.30$.
   a. Use a decision tree to recommend a decision.
   b. Use EVPI to determine whether Gorman should attempt to obtain a better estimate of demand.

10. In order to save on gasoline expenses, Rona and Jerry agreed to form a car pool for traveling to and from work. After limiting the travel routes to two alternatives, Rona and Jerry could not agree on the best way to travel to work. Jerry preferred the expressway, since it was usually the fastest; however, Rona pointed out that traffic jams on the expressway sometimes led to long delays. Rona preferred the somewhat longer, but more consistent, Queen City Avenue. While Jerry still preferred the expressway, he agreed with Rona that they should take Queen City Avenue if the expressway had a traffic jam. Unfortunately they do not know the state of

the expressway ahead of time. The following payoff table provides the one-way time estimates for traveling to or from work:

		States of Nature	
		Expressway Open s_1	Expressway Jammed s_2
Expressway	d_1	25	45
Queen City Avenue	d_2	30	30

Travel time in minutes

After driving to work on the expressway for 1 month (20 days), they found the expressway jammed three times. Assuming that these days are representative of future days, should they continue to use the expressway for traveling to work? Explain. Would it make sense not to adopt the expected value criterion for this particular problem? Explain.

11. In problem 10, suppose that Rona and Jerry wished to determine the best way to return home in the evenings. In 20 days of traveling home on the expressway they found the expressway jammed six times. Using the travel time table shown in problem 10, what route would you recommend they take on their way home in the evening? If they had perfect information about the traffic condition of the expressway, what would be their savings in terms of expected travel time?

12. A firm produces a perishable food product at a cost of $10 per case. The product sells for $15 per case. For planning purposes the company is considering possible demands of 100, 200, or 300 cases. If the demand is less than production, the excess production is lost. If demand is more than production, the firm, in an attempt to maintain a good service image, will satisfy the excess demand with a special production run at a cost of $18 per case. The product, however, always sells at $15 per case.

a. Set up the payoff table for this problem.
b. If $P(100) = 0.2$, $P(200) = 0.2$ and $P(300) = 0.6$, should the company produce 100, 200, or 300 cases?
c. What is the EVPI?

13. The Kremer Chemical Company has a contract with one of its customers to supply a unique liquid chemical product that will be used by the customer in the manufacture of a lubricant for airplane engines. Because of the chemical process used by the Kremer Company, batch sizes for the liquid chemical product must be 1000 pounds. The customer has agreed to adjust manufacturing to the full batch quantities and will order either one, two, or three batches every 6 months. Since an aging process of 2 months exists for the product, Kremer will have to make its production (how much to make) decision before its customer places an order. Thus Kremer can list the product demand alternatives of 1000, 2000, or 3000 pounds, but the exact demand is unknown.

Kremer's manufacturing costs are $15 per pound, and the product sells at the fixed contract price of $20 per pound. If the customer orders more than Kremer has produced, Kremer has agreed to absorb the added cost of filling the order by purchasing a higher quality substitute product from another chemical firm. The substitute product, including transportation expenses, will cost Kremer $24 per pound. Since the product cannot be stored more than 4 months without spoilage, Kremer cannot inventory excess production until the customer's next 6-month order. Therefore if the customer's current order is less than Kremer has produced, the excess production will be reprocessed and is valued at $5 per pound.

The inventory decision in this problem is how much should Kremer produce given the above costs and the possible demands of 1000, 2000, or 3000 pounds? Based on historical data and an analysis of the customer's future demands, Kremer has assessed the following probability distribution for demand.

Demand	Probability
1000	0.3
2000	0.5
3000	0.2
Total	1.0

a. Develop a payoff table for the Kremer problem.
b. How many batches should Kremer produce every 6 months?
c. How much of a discount should Kremer be willing to allow the customer for specifying in advance exactly how many batches will be purchased?

14. A quality control procedure involves 100% inspection of parts received from a supplier. Historical records show the following defective rates have been observed.

Percent Defective	Probability
0	0.15
1	0.25
2	0.40
3	0.20

The cost for the quality control 100% inspection is $250 for each shipment of 500 parts. If the shipment is not 100% inspected, defective parts will cause rework problems later in the production process. The rework cost is $25 for each defective part.

a. Complete the following payoff table, where the entries represent the total cost of inspection and reworking:

	Percent Defective			
	0	1	2	3
100% Inspection	$250	$250	$250	$250
No Inspection				

b. The plant manager is considering eliminating the inspection process in order to save the $250 inspection cost per shipment. Do you support this action? Use EMV to justify your answer.

c. Show the decision tree for this problem.

15. Milford Trucking, located in Chicago, has requests to haul two shipments, one to St. Louis and one to Detroit. Because of a scheduling problem, Milford will only be able to select one of these assignments. The St. Louis customer has guaranteed a return shipment, but the Detroit customer has not. Thus if Milford accepts the Detroit shipment and cannot find a Detroit-to-Chicago return shipment, the truck will return to Chicago empty. The payoff table showing profit is as follows:

		Return Shipment from Detroit s_1	No Return Shipment from Detroit s_2
St. Louis	d_1	2000	2000
Detroit	d_2	2500	1000

a. If the probability of a Detroit return shipment is 0.4, what should Milford do?

b. What is the expected value of information that would tell Milford whether or not Detroit had a return shipment?

16. Suppose you are given a decision situation with three possible states of nature: s_1, s_2, and s_3. The prior probabilities are $P(s_1) = 0.2$, $P(s_2) = 0.5$, and $P(s_3) = 0.3$. Indicator information I is obtained and it is known that $P(I|s_1) = 0.1$, $P(I|s_2) = 0.05$, and $P(I|s_3) = 0.2$. Compute the revised or posterior probabilities: $P(s_1|I)$, $P(s_2|I)$, and $P(s_3|I)$.

17. The payoff table showing profit for a decision problem with two states of nature and three decision alternatives is presented below:

	s_1	s_2
d_1	15	10
d_2	10	12
d_3	8	20

The prior probabilities for s_1 and s_2 are $P(s_1) = 0.8$ and $P(s_2) = 0.2$

a. Using only the prior probabilities and the expected monetary value criterion, find the optimal decision.

b. Find the EVPI.

c. Suppose some indicator information I is obtained with $P(I|s_1) = 0.2$ and $P(I|s_2) = 0.75$. Find the posterior probabilities $P(s_1|I)$ and $P(s_2|I)$. Recommend a decision alternative based on these probabilities.

18. Consider the following decision tree representation of a decision theory problem with two indicators, two decision alternatives, and two states of nature:

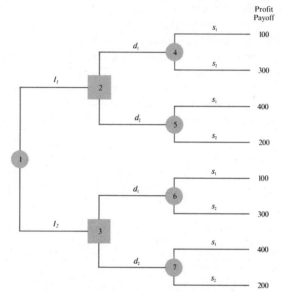

Assume the following probability information is given:

$$P(s_1) = 0.4 \qquad P(I_1|s_1) = 0.8 \qquad P(I_2|s_1) = 0.2$$
$$P(s_2) = 0.6 \qquad P(I_1|s_2) = 0.4 \qquad P(I_2|s_2) = 0.6$$

a. What are the values for $P(I_1)$ and $P(I_2)$?

b. What are the values of $P(s_1|I_1)$, $P(s_2|I_1)$, $P(s_1|I_2)$, and $P(s_2|I_2)$?

c. Use the decision tree approach and determine the optimal decision strategy. What is the expected value of your solution?

19. The payoff table for problem 18 is as follows:

	s_1	s_2
d_1	100	300
d_2	400	200

a. What is your decision without the indicator information?

b. What is the expected value of the indicator or sample information EVSI?

c. What is the expected value of perfect information EVPI?

d. What is the efficiency of the indicator information?

20. The payoff table for Hale's TV Productions (problem 4) is as follows:

		States of Nature		
		s_1	s_2	s_3
Produce pilot	d_1	-100	50	150
Sell to competitor	d_2	100	100	100
Probability of states of nature		0.2	0.3	0.5

For a consulting fee of $2500 an agency will review the plans for the comedy series and indicate the overall chances of a favorable network reaction to the series. If the special agency review results in a favorable (I_1) or an unfavorable (I_2) evaluation, what should Hale's decision strategy be? Assume Hale believes the following conditional probabilities are realistic appraisals of the agency's evaluation accuracy:

$$P(I_1|s_1) = 0.3 \qquad P(I_2|s_1) = 0.7$$

$$P(I_1|s_2) = 0.6 \qquad P(I_2|s_2) = 0.4$$

$$P(I_1|s_3) = 0.9 \qquad P(I_2|s_3) = 0.1$$

a. Show the decision tree for this problem.
b. What is the recommended decision strategy and the expected value, assuming the agency information is obtained?
c. What is the EVSI? Is the $2500 consulting fee worth the information? What is the maximum Hale should be willing to pay for the consulting information?

21. McHuffter Condominiums (problem 5) is conducting a survey that will help evaluate the demand for the new condominium development. McHuffter's payoff table (profit) is as follows:

			States of Nature		
			Low	Medium	High
			s_1	s_2	s_3
Decision	Small	d_1	400	400	400
	Medium	d_2	100	600	600
	Large	d_3	-300	300	900
Probability of states of nature			0.20	0.35	0.45

The survey will result in three indicators of demand [weak (I_1), average (I_2), or strong (I_3)], where the conditional probabilities are as follows:

	$P(I_k|s_k)$		
	I_1	I_2	I_3
s_1	0.6	0.3	0.1
s_2	0.4	0.4	0.2
s_3	0.1	0.4	0.5

a. What is McHuffter's optimal strategy?
b. What is the value of the survey information?
c. What are the EVPI and the efficiency of the survey information?

22. The payoff table for Martin's Service Station (problems 7 and 8) is as follows:

		Snowfall		
		Heavy s_1	Moderate s_2	Light s_3
Purchase snowplow	d_1	7000	2000	-9000
Do not invest	d_2	0	0	0
Purchase snowplow with blade	d_3	3500	1000	-1500
Probabilities of states of nature		0.4	0.3	0.3

Suppose Martin decides to wait to check the September temperature pattern before making a final decision. Estimates of the probabilities associated with an unseasonably cold September (I) are as follows: $P(I|s_1) = 0.30$; $P(I|s_2) = 0.20$; $P(I|s_3) = 0.05$. If Martin observes an unseasonably cold September, what is the recommended decision? If Martin does not observe an unseasonably cold September, what is the recommended decision?

23. A food processor considers daily production runs of 100, 200, or 300 cases. Possible demands for the product are 100, 200, or 300 cases. The payoff table is as follows:

			Demand (cases)		
			100 s_1	200 s_2	300 s_3
	d_2	100	500	200	-100
Production	d_2	200	-400	800	700
	d_3	300	-1000	-200	1600

a. If $P(s_1) = 0.20$, $P(s_2) = 0.20$, and $P(s_3) = 0.60$, what is your recommended production quantity?

b. On some days the firm receives phone calls for advance orders and on some days it does not. Let I_1 = advance orders are received and I_2 = no advance orders are received. If $P(I_2|s_1) = 0.80$, $P(I_2|s_2) = 0.40$, and $P(I_2|s_3) = 0.10$, what is your recommended production quantity for days the company does not receive any advance orders?

24. The Gorman Manufacturing Company (problem 9) has the following payoff table for a make-or-buy decision:

		Demand		
		Low s_1	Medium s_2	High s_3
Manufacture component	d_1	-20	40	100
Purchase component	d_2	10	45	70
Probabilities		0.35	0.35	0.30

A test market study of the potential demand for the product is expected to report either a favorable (I_1) or unfavorable (I_2) condition. The relevant conditional probabilities are as follows:

$$P(I_1|s_1) = 0.10 \quad P(I_2|s_1) = 0.90$$
$$P(I_1|s_2) = 0.40 \quad P(I_2|s_2) = 0.60$$
$$P(I_1|s_3) = 0.60 \quad P(I_2|s_3) = 0.40$$

a. What is the probability the market research report will be favorable?
b. What is Gorman's optimal decision strategy?
c. What is the expected value of the market research information?
d. What is the efficiency of the information?

25. The traveling time to work for Rona and Jerry has the following time payoff table (problem 10):

		States of Nature for Expressway	
		Open	Jammed
		s_1	s_2
Expressway	d_1	25	45
Queen City Avenue	d_2	30	30
Probability of states of nature		0.85	0.15

After a period of time Rona and Jerry noted that the weather seemed to affect the traffic conditions on the expressway. They identified three weather conditions (indicators) with the following conditional probabilities:

I_1 = clear

I_2 = overcast

I_3 = rain

$P(I_1|s_1) = 0.8 \quad P(I_2|s_1) = 0.2 \quad P(I_3|s_1) = 0$
$P(I_1|s_2) = 0.1 \quad P(I_2|s_2) = 0.3 \quad P(I_3|s_2) = 0.6$

a. Show the decision tree for the problem of traveling to work.
b. What is the optimal decision strategy and the expected travel time?
c. What is the efficiency of the weather information?

26. The research and development manager for Beck Company is trying to decide whether or not to fund a project to develop a new lubricant. It is assumed the project will be a major technical success, a minor technical success, or a failure. The company has estimated that the value of a major technical success is $150,000, since the lubricant can be used in a number of products the company is making. If the project is a minor technical success, its value is $10,000, since Beck feels the knowledge gained will benefit some other ongoing projects. If the project is a failure, it will cost the company $100,000.

Based on the opinion of the scientists involved and the manager's own subjective assessment, the assigned prior probabilities are as follows:

$$P(\text{major success}) = 0.15$$
$$P(\text{minor success}) = 0.45$$
$$P(\text{failure}) = 0.40$$

  a. Using the expected monetary value criterion, should the project be funded?

  b. Suppose that a group of expert scientists from a research institute could be hired as consultants to study the project and make a recommendation. If this study will cost $30,000, should the Beck Company consider hiring the consultants?

27. Consider again the problem faced by the R&D manager of Beck Company (problem 26). Suppose an experiment can be conducted to shed some light on the technical feasibility of the project. There are three possible outcomes for the experiment:

I_1 = prototype lubricant works well at all temperatures

I_2 = prototype lubricant works well only at temperatures above 10°F

I_3 = prototype lubricant does not work well at any temperature

Suppose that we can determine the following conditional probabilities:

$$P(I_1|\text{major success}) = 0.70$$
$$P(I_1|\text{minor success}) = 0.10$$
$$P(I_1|\text{failure}) = 0.10$$

$$P(I_2|\text{major success}) = 0.25$$
$$P(I_2|\text{minor success}) = 0.70$$
$$P(I_2|\text{failure}) = 0.30$$

$$P(I_3|\text{major success}) = 0.05$$
$$P(I_3|\text{minor success}) = 0.20$$
$$P(I_3|\text{failure}) = 0.60$$

  a. Assuming the experiment is conducted and the prototype lubricant works well at all temperatures, should the project be funded?

  b. Assuming the experiment is conducted and the prototype lubricant works well only at temperatures above 10°F, should the project be funded?

  c. Develop a decision strategy that Beck's R&D manager can use to recommend a funding decision based on the outcome of the experiment.

  d. Find the EVSI for the experiment. How efficient is the information in the experiment?

28. The payoff table for the Kremer Chemical Company (problem 13) is as follows:

Production Quantity		Demand 1,000 s_1	2,000 s_2	3,000 s_3
1000	d_1	5,000	1,000	3,000
2000	d_2	$-5,000$	10,000	6,000
3000	d_3	$-15,000$	0	15,000
Probabilities		0.30	0.50	0.20

Kremer has identified a pattern in the demand for the product based on the customer's previous order quantity. Let

$$I_1 = \text{customer's last order was 1000 pounds}$$
$$I_2 = \text{customer's last order was 2000 pounds}$$
$$I_3 = \text{customer's last order was 3000 pounds}$$

The conditional probabilities are as follows:

$$P(I_1|s_1) = 0.10 \quad P(I_2|s_1) = 0.40 \quad P(I_3|s_1) = 0.50$$
$$P(I_1|s_2) = 0.22 \quad P(I_2|s_2) = 0.68 \quad P(I_3|s_2) = 0.10$$
$$P(I_1|s_3) = 0.80 \quad P(I_2|s_3) = 0.20 \quad P(I_3|s_3) = 0.00$$

a. Develop an optimal decision strategy for Kremer.
b. What is the EVSI?
c. What is the efficiency of the information for the most recent order?

29. Milford Trucking Company (problem 15) has the following payoff table:

		Return Shipment from Detroit s_1	No Return Shipment from Detroit s_2
St. Louis	d_1	2000	2000
Detroit	d_2	2500	1000
Probabilities		0.40	0.60

a. Milford can phone a Detroit truck dispatch center and determine if the general Detroit shipping activity is busy (I_1) or slow (I_2). If the report is busy, the chances of obtaining a return shipment will increase. Suppose the following conditional probabilities are given:

$$P(I_1|s_1) = 0.6 \quad P(I_2|s_1) = 0.4$$
$$P(I_1|s_2) = 0.3 \quad P(I_2|s_2) = 0.7$$

What should Milford do?

b. If the Detroit report is busy (I_1), what is the probability that Milford obtains a return shipment if it makes the trip to Detroit?

c. What is the efficiency of the phone information?

30. The quality control inspection process (problem 14) has the following payoff table:

		Percent Defective			
		0	1	2	3
		s_1	s_2	s_3	s_4
100% Inspection	d_1	250	250	250	250
No inspection	d_2	0	125	250	375
Probabilities		0.15	0.25	0.40	0.20

Suppose a sample of five parts is selected from the shipment and one defect is found.

a. Let I = one defect in a sample of five. Use the binomial probability distribution to compute $P(I|s_1)$, $P(I|s_2)$, $P(I|s_3)$, and $P(I|s_4)$, where the state of nature identifies the value for p.

b. If I occurs, what are the revised probabilities for the states of nature?

c. Should the entire shipment be 100% inspected whenever one defect is found in a sample of size five?

d. What is the cost saving associated with the sample information?

—————— *Case Problem:* ——————

PROPERTY PURCHASE STRATEGY

Glenn Foreman, president of Oceanview Development Corporation, is considering submitting a bid to purchase property that will be sold by sealed bid at a county tax foreclosure. Glenn's initial judgment is to submit a bid of $5 million. From past experience Glenn estimates that a bid of $5 million will have a 0.20 probability of being the highest bid and securing the property for Oceanview. The current date is June 1. Sealed bids for the property must be submitted by August 15. The winning bid will be announced on September 1.

If Oceanview submits the highest bid and obtains the property, the firm plans to build and sell a complex of luxury condominiums. However, a complicating factor is that the property is currently zoned for single-family residences only. Glenn feels that a referendum could be placed on the voting ballot in time for the November election. Passage of the referendum would change the zoning of the property and permit the construction of the condominiums.

The sealed bid procedure requires the bid to be submitted with a certified check for 10% of the amount bid. If the bid is rejected, the deposit is refunded. If the bid is accepted, the deposit is the down payment for the property. However, if the bid is accepted and the bidder does not follow through with the purchase and meet the remainder of the financial obligation within 6 months, the deposit will be forfeited. In this case the county will offer the property to the next highest bidder.

In order to determine whether or not to submit the $5 million bid, Glenn has done some preliminary analysis. This preliminary work provides an estimate of the probability that the referendum for a zoning change will be approved and estimates of the revenues and costs that will be incurred if the condominiums are built. The data obtained are shown below:

Probability the Request for Zoning Change Passes
$$P(\text{passes}) = 0.3$$

Cost and Revenue Estimates

Revenue from condominium sales $15,000,000
Expenses
        Property $5,000,000
        Construction expenses 8,000,000

If Oceanview obtains the property and the zoning change is not approved in November, Glenn feels that the best option would be for the firm not to complete the purchase of the property. In this case Oceanview would forfeit the 10% deposit that accompanied the bid.

Because the likelihood of the zoning referendum being approved is such an important factor in the decision process, Glenn has suggested that the firm hire a market research service to conduct a survey of voters. The survey would provide a better estimate of the likelihood that the referendum for a zoning change would be approved. The market research firm that Oceanview Development has worked with in the past has agreed to do the study for $15,000. The results of the study will be available August 1 so that Oceanview will have this information before the August 15 bid deadline. The results of the survey will either be a prediction that the zoning change will be approved or a prediction that the zoning change will not be approved. After a consideration of the record of the market research service in previous studies conducted for Oceanview, Glenn has developed the following probability estimates concerning the accuracy of the market research information.

$$P(I_1|s_1) = 0.9$$

and

$$P(I_1|s_2) = 0.2$$

where

I_1 = prediction that the zoning change will be approved
I_2 = prediction that the zoning change will not be approved
s_1 = the zoning change is approved by the voters
s_2 = the zoning change is not approved by the voters

MANAGERIAL REPORT

Perform an analysis of the problem facing the Ocean Development Corporation and prepare a report that summarizes your findings and recommendations. Include information on an analysis of the following:

1. A decision tree that shows the logical sequence of the decision problem.
2. A recommendation regarding what Oceanview should do if the market research information is not available.
3. A decision strategy that Oceanview should follow if the market research is conducted.
4. A recommendation as to whether Oceanview should employ the market research firm. What is the value of the information provided by the market research firm?

Include a copy of the details of your analysis in the appendix to your report.

Management Science in Practice
OHIO EDISON COMPANY*
Akron, Ohio

Ohio Edison Company is an investor-owned electric utility headquartered in northeastern Ohio. Ohio Edison and a Pennsylvania subsidiary provide electrical service to over two million people. Most of this electricity is generated by coal-fired power plants. In order to meet evolving air quality standards, Ohio Edison embarked on a program to replace existing pollution control equipment on most of its generating plants with more efficient equipment. The combination of this program to upgrade air quality control equipment with the continuing need to construct new generating plants to meet future power requirements has resulted in a large capital investment program.

Management science activities at Ohio Edison are distributed throughout the company rather than centralized in a management science department. This activity is more or less evenly divided among the following areas: fossil and nuclear fuel planning, environmental studies, capacity planning, large equipment evaluation, and corporate planning. Applications include decision analysis, optimal ordering strategies, computer modeling, and simulation.

A DECISION ANALYSIS APPLICATION

The flue gas emitted by coal-fired power plants contains small ash particles and sulfur dioxide (SO_2). Federal and state regulatory agencies have established emission limits for both particulates and sulfur dioxide. Recently, Ohio Edison developed a plan to comply with new air quality standards at one of its largest power plants. This plant consists of seven coal-fired units and constitutes about one-third of the generating capacity of Ohio Edison and the subsidiary company. Most of these units had been constructed in the 1960s. Although all the units had initially been constructed with equipment to control particulate emissions, that equipment was not capable of meeting new particulate emission requirements.

A decision had already been made to burn low sulfur coal in four of the smaller units (units 1 to 4) at the plant in order to meet SO_2 emission standards. Fabric filters were to be installed on these units to control particulate emissions. Fabric filters, also known as baghouses, use thousands of fabric bags to filter out the particulates; they function in much the same way as a household vacuum cleaner.

It was considered likely, although not certain, that the three larger units (units 5 to 7) at this plant would burn medium to high sulfur coal. A method of controlling particulate emissions at these units had not yet been selected. Preliminary studies had narrowed the particulate control equipment choice to a decision between fabric

*The authors are indebted to Thomas J. Madden and M. S. Hyrnick of Ohio Edison Company, Akron, Ohio, for providing this application.

filters and electrostatic precipitators (which remove particulates suspended in the flue gas as charged particles by passing the flue gas through a strong electric field). This decision was affected by a number of uncertainties, including the following:

Uncertainty in the way some air quality laws and regulations might be interpreted. Certain interpretations could require that either low sulfur coal or high sulfur Ohio coal (or neither) be burned in units 5 to 7.

Potential future changes in air quality laws and regulations.

An overall plant reliability improvement program was underway at this plant.

The outcome of this program would affect the operating costs of whichever pollution control technology was installed in these units.

Construction costs of the equipment were uncertain, particularly since limited space at the plant site made it necessary to install the equipment on a massive bridge deck over a four-lane highway immediately adjacent to the power plant.

The costs associated with replacing the electrical power required to operate the particulate control equipment were uncertain.

Various uncertain factors, including potential accidents and chronic operating problems which could increase the costs of operating the generating units, were identified. The degree to which each of these factors affected operating costs varied with the choice of technology and with the sulfur content of the coal.

DECISION ANALYSIS

The decision to be made involved a choice between two types of particulate control equipment (fabric filters or electrostatic precipitators) for units 5 to 7. Because of the complexity of the problem, the high degree of uncertainty associated with factors affecting the decision, and the importance (due to potential reliability and cost impact on Ohio Edison) of the choice, decision analysis was used in the selection process.

The decision measure used to evaluate the outcomes of the particulate technology decision analysis was the annual revenue requirements for the three large units over their remaining lifetime. Revenue requirements are the monies that would have to be collected from the utility customers in order to recover costs that are a result of the decision. They include not only direct costs but also the cost of capital and return on investment.

A decision tree was constructed to represent the particulate control decision, its uncertainties and costs. A simplified version of this decision tree is shown in Figure A14.1. The decision and state-of-nature nodes are indicated. Note that to conserve space a type of shorthand notation is used. The coal sulfur content state-of-nature node should actually be located at the end of each branch of the capital cost state-of-nature node, as the dotted lines indicate. Each of the indicated state-of-nature nodes actually represents several probabilistic cost models or submodels.

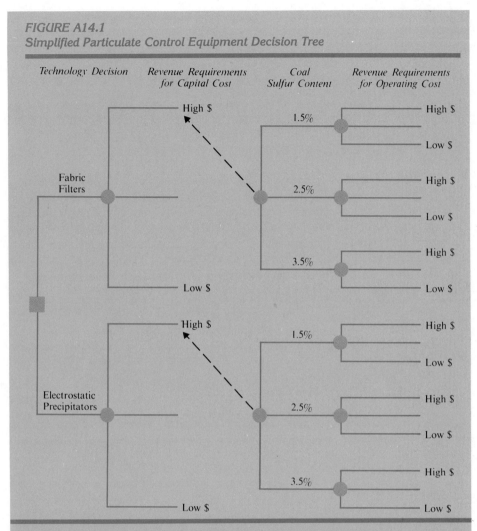

FIGURE A14.1
Simplified Particulate Control Equipment Decision Tree

The total revenue requirements calculated are the sum of the revenue requirements for capital and operating costs. Costs associated with these models were obtained from engineering calculations or estimates. Probabilities were obtained from existing data or the subjective assessments of knowledgeable persons.

RESULTS

A decision tree similar to that shown in Figure A14.1 was used to generate cumulative probability distributions for the annual revenue requirements outcomes calculated for each of the two particulate control alternatives. Careful study of these results led to the following conclusions:

The expected value of annual revenue requirements for the electrostatic precipitator technology was approximately $1 million lower than that for the fabric filters.

The fabric filter alternative had a higher "upside risk"—that is, a higher probability of high revenue requirements—than did the precipitator alternative.

The precipitator technology had nearly an 80% probability of having lower annual revenue requirements than the fabric filters.

Although the capital cost of the fabric filter equipment (the cost of installing the equipment) was lower than for the precipitator, this was more than offset by the higher operating costs associated with the fabric filter.

These results led Ohio Edison to select the electrostatic precipitator technology for the generating units in question. Had the decision analysis not been performed, the particulate control decision might have been based chiefly on capital cost, a decision measure that would have favored the fabric filter equipment. Decision analysis offers a means for effectively analyzing the uncertainties involved in a decision. Because of this, it is felt that the use of decision analysis methodology in this application resulted in a decision that yielded both lower expected revenue requirements and lower risk.

Questions

1. Why was decision analysis used in the selection of particulate control equipment for units 5, 6, and 7?
2. List the decision alternatives for the decision analysis problem developed by Ohio Edison.
3. What were the benefits of using decision analysis in this application?

15

Utility and Decision Making

In the previous chapter we expressed the payoffs in terms of monetary values. When probability information was available about the states of nature, we recommended using the expected monetary value decision criterion. Indeed, in many business decision-making situations, expected monetary value is an excellent criterion. However, there are situations in which the expected monetary value criterion may not lead to the most desirable decision alternative.

By the most desirable decision alternative, we mean the one that is preferred by the decision maker, taking into account not only the expected monetary value but also many other factors, such as the possibility of making a very large profit and/or the ability to incur a very large loss. Examples of situations in which expected monetary value may not lead to the selection of the most preferred alternative are numerous. One such example is the decision made by most people to buy insurance. Clearly the decision to buy insurance for a house does not provide a higher expected monetary value than not buying such insurance. Otherwise insurance companies could not pay expenses and make a profit. Similarly, many people buy tickets to state lotteries even though the expected monetary value of such a decision is negative.

Should we conclude that persons or businesses that buy insurance or participate in lotteries do so because they are unable to determine which decision alternative leads to the highest expected monetary value? On the contrary, we take the view that in these cases, monetary value is not the sole measure of the true worth of the outcome to the decision maker.

We will see that in cases where expected monetary value does not lead to the most preferred decision alternative, expressing the value (or worth) of an outcome in terms of its *utility* will permit the use of *expected utility* as the most desirable decision criterion.

15.1 THE MEANING OF UTILITY

Utility is a measure of the total worth of a particular outcome and reflects the decision maker's attitude toward a collection of factors such as profit, loss, and risk. Researchers have found that as long as the monetary value of payoffs stay within a range that is considered reasonable to the decision maker, expected monetary value is a good decision criterion. However, when the payoffs or losses become extreme, most decision makers are not satisfied with the expected monetary value criterion.

As an example of a case where utility can help in selecting the best decision alternative, let us consider the problem faced by Swofford, Inc., a relatively small real estate investment firm located in Atlanta, Ga. Swofford currently has two investment opportunities, which require approximately the same cash outlay. The cash requirements necessary prohibit Swofford from making more than one investment at this time. Consequently there are three possible decision alternatives that may be considered.

The three decision alternatives, denoted by d_1, d_2, and d_3, are as follows:

$$d_1 = \text{make investment } A$$
$$d_2 = \text{make investment } B$$
$$d_3 = \text{do not invest}$$

The monetary payoffs associated with the investment opportunities depend largely upon what happens to the real estate market during the next 6 months. Either real estate prices will go up, remain stable, or go down. Thus the Swofford states of nature, denoted by s_1, s_2, and s_3, are as follows:

$$s_1 = \text{real estate prices go up}$$
$$s_2 = \text{real estate prices remain stable}$$
$$s_3 = \text{real estate prices go down}$$

Using the best information available, Swofford has estimated the profits or payoffs associated with each decision alternative and state-of-nature combination. The resulting payoff table is shown in Table 15.1.

TABLE 15.1
Payoff Table for Swofford, Inc.

		States of Nature		
		Prices Up s_1	Prices Stable s_2	Prices Down s_3
Decision Alternatives	Investment A, d_1	$30,000	$20,000	− $50,000
	Investment B, d_2	$50,000	− $20,000	− $30,000
	Do not invest, d_3	0	0	0

The best estimate of the probability that prices will go up is 0.30; the best estimate of the probability that prices will remain stable is 0.50; and the best estimate of the probability that real estate prices will go down is 0.20. Thus the expected monetary values for the three decision alternatives are

$$\text{EMV}(d_1) = 0.3(30,000) + 0.5(20,000) + 0.2(-50,000) = 9000$$
$$\text{EMV}(d_2) = 0.3(50,000) + 0.5(-20,000) + 0.2(-30,000) = -1000$$
$$\text{EMV}(d_3) = 0.3(0) + 0.5(0) + 0.2(0) = 0$$

Using the expected monetary value criterion, the optimal decision is to select investment A with an expected monetary value of $9000. Is this really the best decision alternative? Let us consider some other relevant factors that relate to Swofford's capability for absorbing the loss of $50,000 if investment A is made and prices actually go down.

It turns out that Swofford's current financial position is very weak. This was partly reflected in Swofford's ability to undertake at most one investment at the current time. More importantly, however, the firm's president feels that if the next investment results in substantial losses, Swofford's future will be in jeopardy. Although the expected monetary value criterion leads to a recommendation for d_1, do you think this is the decision the firm's president would prefer? Unless the president is a gambler, we suspect d_2 or d_3 would be selected in order to avoid the possibility of incurring a $50,000 loss. In fact, it is reasonable to believe that if a loss as great as even $30,000 could drive Swofford out of business, the president would select d_3, feeling that both investment A and investment B are too risky for Swofford's current financial position.

The way we can resolve Swofford's dilemma is to first determine Swofford's utility for the various monetary outcomes. Recall that the utility of any outcome is the total worth of that outcome taking into account the risks and payoffs involved. If the utilities for the various outcomes are correctly assessed, then the decision alternative with the highest expected utility is the most preferred or best alternative. In the next section we will see how to determine the utility of the monetary outcomes in such a fashion that the alternative with the highest expected utility is most preferred.

15.2 DEVELOPING UTILITIES FOR MONETARY PAYOFFS

The procedure we shall use to establish utility values for the payoffs in Swofford's problem requires that we first assign a utility value to the best and worst possible payoffs in the decision situation. Any values will work as long as the utility assigned to the best payoff is greater than the utility assigned to the worst payoff. In this case, $50,000 is the best payoff and −$50,000 is the worst. Suppose then that we arbitrarily make the following assignments to these two payoffs:

$$\text{Utility of } -\$50,000 = U(-50,000) = 0$$
$$\text{Utility of } \quad \$50,000 = U(50,000) \quad = 10$$

Now let us see how we can determine the utility associated with every other payoff.

Consider the process of establishing the utility of a payoff of $30,000. First we ask Swofford's president to state a preference between a guaranteed $30,000 payoff and the opportunity to engage in the following *lottery*, or bet:

Lottery: Swofford's obtains a payoff of $50,000 with probability p
and a payoff of −$50,000 with probability $(1 - p)$.

Obviously, if p is very close to 1, Swofford's president would prefer the lottery to the certain payoff of $30,000, since the firm would virtually guarantee itself a payoff of $50,000. On the other hand, if p is very close to 0, Swofford's president would clearly prefer the guarantee of $30,000. In any event, as p changes continuously from 0 to 1, the preference for the guaranteed payoff of $30,000 will change at some point into a preference for the lottery. At this value of p, Swofford's president would have no greater preference for the guaranteed payoff of $30,000 than for the lottery. For example, let us assume that when $p = 0.95$, Swofford's president is indifferent between the certain payoff of $30,000 and the lottery. Given this value of p, we can compute the utility of a $30,000 payoff as follows:

$$U(30,000) = pU(50,000) + (1 - p)U(-50,000)$$
$$= 0.95(10) + (0.05)(0)$$
$$= 9.5$$

Obviously, if we had started with a different assignment of utilities for a payoff of $50,000 and $-$50,000, we would have ended up with a different utility for $30,000. For example, if we had started with an assignment of 100 for $50,000 and 10 for $-$50,000, the utility of a $30,000 payoff would be

$$U(30,000) = 0.95(100) + 0.05(10)$$
$$= 95 + 0.5$$
$$= 95.5$$

Hence we must conclude that the utility assigned to each payoff is not unique but merely depends upon the initial choice of utilities for the best and worst payoffs. We will discuss this further at the end of this section. For now, however, we will continue to use a value of 10 for the utility of $50,000 and 0 for the utility of $-$50,000.

Before computing the utility for the other payoffs, let us consider the significance of Swofford's president assigning a utility of 9.5 to a payoff of $30,000. Clearly, when $p = 0.95$, the expected monetary value of the lottery is

$$EMV(\text{lottery}) = 0.95(\$50,000) + 0.05(-\$50,000)$$
$$= \$47,500 - \$2,500$$
$$= \$45,000$$

We see that although the expected monetary value of the lottery when $p = 0.95$ is $45,000, Swofford's president would just as soon take a guaranteed payoff of $30,000. Thus Swofford's president is taking a conservative, or risk-avoiding, viewpoint. The president would rather have $30,000 for certain than risk anything greater than a 5% chance of incurring a loss of $50,000. One can view the difference between the EMV of $45,000 and the $30,000 amount for certain as the risk premium Swofford's would be willing to pay to avoid the 5% chance of losing $50,000. Thus in this case expected monetary value is not a true measure of the president's actual preference.

To compute the utility associated with a payoff of $-$20,000, we must ask Swofford's president to state a preference between a guaranteed $-$20,000 payoff and the opportunity to engage in the following lottery.

> Lottery: Swofford's obtains a payoff of $50,000 with probability p
> and a payoff of $-$50,000 with probability $(1 - p)$.

Note that this is exactly the same lottery we used to establish the utility of a payoff of $30,000. In fact, this will be the lottery used to establish the utility for any monetary value in the Swofford payoff table. Using this lottery, then, we must ask Swofford's president to state the value of p that would make the president indifferent between a guaranteed payoff of $-\$20,000$ and the lottery. For example, we might begin by asking the president to choose between a certain loss of $\$20,000$ and the lottery with a payoff of $\$50,000$ with probability $p = 0.90$ and a payoff of $-\$50,000$ with probability $(1 - p)$ $= 0.10$. What answer do you think we would get? Surely, with this high probability of obtaining a payoff of $\$50,000$, the president would elect the lottery. Next we might ask if $p = 0.85$ would result in indifference between the loss of $\$20,000$ for certain and the lottery. Again the president might tell us that the lottery would be preferred. Suppose we continue in this fashion until we get up to $p = 0.55$, where we find that with this value of p, the president is indifferent between the payoff of $-\$20,000$ and the lottery. That is, for any value of p less than 0.55, the president would rather take a loss of $\$20,000$ for certain than risk the potential loss of $\$50,000$ with the lottery, and for any value of p above 0.55, the president would elect the lottery. Thus the utility assigned to a payoff of $-\$20,000$ is

$$
\begin{aligned}
U(-\$20,000) &= pU(50,000) + (1 - p)U(-\$50,000) \\
&= 0.55(10) + 0.45(0) \\
&= 5.5
\end{aligned}
$$

Again let us examine the significance of this assignment as compared with the expected monetary value criterion. When $p = 0.55$, the expected monetary value of the lottery is

$$
\begin{aligned}
\text{EMV(lottery)} &= 0.55(\$50,000) + 0.45(-\$50,000) \\
&= \$27,500 - \$22,500 \\
&= \$5000
\end{aligned}
$$

Thus Swofford's president would just as soon absorb a loss of $\$20,000$ for certain as take the lottery, even though the expected monetary value of the lottery is $\$5000$. Once again we see the conservative, or risk-avoiding, point of view of Swofford's president.

In the above two examples where we computed the utility for a specific monetary payoff, M, we first found the probability p where the decision maker was indifferent between a guaranteed payoff of M and a lottery with a payoff of $\$50,000$ with probability p and $-\$50,000$ with probability $(1 - p)$. The utility of M was then computed as

$$
\begin{aligned}
U(M) &= pU(\$50,000) + (1 - p)U(-\$50,000) \\
&= p(10) + (1 - p)0 \\
&= 10p
\end{aligned}
$$

Using the above procedure, utility values for the rest of the payoffs in Swoffords's problem were developed. The results are presented in Table 15.2.

Now that we have determined the utility value of each of the possible monetary values, we can write the original payoff table in terms of utility values. Table 15.3 shows the utility for the various outcomes in the Swofford problem. The notation we will use for the entries in the utility table is $U(d_i, s_j)$, which denotes the utility associated with decision alternative d_i and state of nature s_j. Using this notation, we see that $U(d_2, s_3)$ $= 4.0$.

TABLE 15.2
Utility of Monetary Payoffs for the Swofford, Inc. Problem

Monetary Value	Indifference Value of p	Utility Value
$50,000	Does not apply	10.0
30,000	0.95	9.5
20,000	0.90	9.0
0	0.75	7.5
−20,000	0.55	5.5
−30,000	0.40	4.0
−50,000	Does not apply	0

TABLE 15.3
Utility Table for Swofford, Inc.

		States of Nature		
		Prices Up s_1	Prices Stable s_2	Prices Down s_3
Decision Alternatives	Investment A, d_1	9.5	9.0	0
	Investment B, d_2	10.0	5.5	4.0
	Do not invest, d_3	7.5	7.5	7.5

The Expected Utility Criterion

We can now apply the *expected utility criterion* (EU) to select an optimal decision alternative for Swofford, Inc. The expected utility criterion requires the analyst to compute the expected utility for each decision alternative and then select the alternative yielding the best expected utility. If there are N possible states of nature, the expected utility of a decision alternative d_i is given by

$$EU(d_i) = \sum_{j=1}^{N} P(s_j)U(d_i, s_j) \qquad (15.1)$$

The expected utility for each of the decision alternatives in the Swofford problem is computed next.

$$EU(d_1) = 0.3(9.5) + 0.5(9.0) + 0.2(0) \quad = 7.35$$
$$EU(d_2) = 0.3(10) \; + 0.5(5.5) + 0.2(4.0) = 6.55$$
$$EU(d_3) = 0.3(7.5) + 0.5(7.5) + 0.2(7.5) = 7.5$$

We see that the optimal decision using the expected utility criterion is d_3, do not invest. The ranking of alternatives according to the president's utility assignments is as follows:

Ranking of Decision Alternatives	Expected Utility	Expected Monetary Value
Do not invest	7.50	0
Investment A	7.35	9000
Investment B	6.55	−1000

Note that whereas investment *A* had the highest expected monetary value of $9000, the analysis indicates that Swofford should decline this investment. The rationale behind not selecting investment *A* is that the 0.20 probability of a $50,000 loss was considered to involve a very serious risk by Swofford's president. The seriousness of this risk and its associated impact on the company were not adequately reflected when the expected monetary value criterion was employed. It was necessary to assess the utility for each payoff in order to adequately take this risk into account.

In the Swofford problem we have been using a utility of 10 for the largest possible payoff and 0 for the smallest. Since the choice of values could have been anything, we might have chosen 1 for the utility of the largest payoff and 0 for the utility of the smallest. Had we made this choice, the utility for any monetary value *M* would have been the value of *p* at which the decision maker was indifferent between a payoff of *M* for certain and a lottery in which the best payoff is obtained with probability *p* and the worst payoff is obtained with probability $(1 - p)$. Thus the utility for any monetary value would have been equal to the probability of earning the highest payoff. Often this choice is made because of the ease in computation. We chose not to do so to emphasize the distinction between the utility values and the indifference probabilities for the lottery.

15.3 SUMMARY OF STEPS FOR DETERMINING THE UTILITY OF MONEY

Before considering other aspects of utility, let us summarize the steps involved in determining the utility for money and using it within the decision analysis framework. The steps outlined below state in general terms the procedure used to solve the Swofford, Inc. investment problem. The steps are as follows:

Step 1. Develop a payoff table using monetary values.

Step 2. Identify the best and worst payoff values in the table and assign each a utility value with *U*(best payoff) > *U*(worst payoff).

Step 3. For every other monetary value *M* in the original payoff table, perform steps a through c below in order to determine its utility value.
   a. Define the following lottery: The best payoff is obtained with probability *p* and the worst payoff is obtained with probability $(1 - p)$.
   b. Determine the value of *p* such that the decision maker is indifferent between a payoff of *M* for certain and the lottery defined in step a.
   c. Calculate the utility of *M* as follows: $U(M) = pU(\text{best payoff}) + (1 - p)U(\text{worst payoff})$.

Step 4. Convert the payoff table from monetary values to the calculated utility values.

Step 5. Apply the expected utility criterion to the utility table and select the decision alternative with the highest expected utility.

15.4 RISK AVOIDERS VERSUS RISK TAKERS

The financial position of Swofford, Inc. was such that the firm's president evaluated investment opportunities from a conservative, or risk-avoiding, point of view. However, if the firm had had a surplus of cash and a very stable future, we might have found Swofford's president looking for investment alternatives which, although perhaps risky, contained a potential for substantial profit. If the president had behaved in this manner, the president would have been classified as a *risk taker*. In this section we analyze the decision problem faced by Swofford from the point of view of a decision maker who would be classified as a risk taker. We then compare the conservative, or risk-avoiding, point of view of Swofford's president with the behavior of a decision maker who is a risk taker.

Given the decision problem faced by Swofford, Inc. and using the general procedure for developing utilities as discussed in Section 15.3, a risk taker might express the utility for the various payoffs as shown in Table 15.4. As before, we have taken $U(50,000)$ = 10 and $U(-50,000) = 0$. Note carefully the difference in behavior reflected in Table 15.4 and Table 15.2. That is, in determining the value of p at which the decision maker is indifferent between a payoff of M for certain and a lottery in which $50,000 is obtained with probability p and $-$50,000 with probability $(1 - p)$, the risk taker is willing to accept a greater risk of incurring a loss of $50,000 in order to gain the opportunity to realize a profit of $50,000.

TABLE 15.4
Revised Utility Values for the Swofford, Inc. Problem Assuming a Risk Taker

Monetary Value	Indifference Value of p	Utility Value
$50,000	Does not apply	10.0
30,000	0.50	5.0
20,000	0.40	4.0
0	0.25	2.5
−20,000	0.15	1.5
−30,000	0.10	1.0
−50,000	Does not apply	0

To help develop the utility table for the risk taker, we have reproduced the Swofford, Inc. payoff table in Table 15.5. Using these payoffs and the risk taker's utility values given in Table 15.4, we can write the risk taker's utility table as shown in Table 15.6.

TABLE 15.5
Payoff Table for Swofford, Inc. Problem

		States of Nature		
		Prices Up s_1	Prices Stable s_2	Prices Down s_3
Decision Alternatives	Investment A, d_1	$30,000	$20,000	−$50,000
	Investment B, d_2	$50,000	−$20,000	−$30,000
	Do not invest, d_3	0	0	0

TABLE 15.6
Utility Table of a Risk Taker for the Swofford, Inc. Problem

		States of Nature		
		Prices Up s_1	Prices Stable s_2	Prices Down s_3
Decision Alternatives	Investment A, d_1	5.0	4.0	0
	Investment B, d_2	10.0	1.5	1.0
	Do not invest, d_3	2.5	2.5	2.5

Using the state of nature probabilities $P(s_1) = 0.3$, $P(s_2) = 0.5$ and $P(s_3) = 0.2$, the expected utility calculations now show

$$EU(d_1) = 0.3(5) + 0.5(4.0) + 0.2(0) = 3.5$$
$$EU(d_2) = 0.3(10) + 0.5(1.5) + 0.2(1.0) = 3.95$$
$$EU(d_3) = 0.3(2.5) + 0.5(2.5) + 0.2(2.5) = 2.5$$

What is the recommended decision? Perhaps somewhat to your surprise, the analysis recommends investment B, with the highest expected utility of 3.95. Recall that this investment has a −$1000 expected monetary value; why is it now the recommended decision? Remember that the decision maker in this revised problem is a risk taker with high utilities associated with large profits. Thus although the expected profit of investment B is negative, utility analysis has shown that this decision maker is enough of a risk taker to prefer investment B and its potential for the $50,000 profit.

Using the expected utility values the order of preference of the decision alternatives for the risk taker and the associated expected monetary values are as follows:

Ranking of Decision Alternatives	Expected Utility	Expected Monetary Value
Investment B	3.95	−$1000
Investment A	3.50	$9000
Do not invest	2.50	0

When we compare the above utility analysis for a risk taker with the more conservative, *risk avoider* preferences of the president of Swofford, Inc., we see, even with the same decision problem, how different attitudes toward risk can lead to different recommended decisions. The utility values established by Swofford's president indicated that the firm should not invest at this time, whereas the utilities established by the risk taker showed a preference for investment *B*. Note that both of these decisions differ from the best expected monetary value decision, which was investment *A*.

We can obtain another perspective of the difference between behaviors of a risk avoider and a risk taker by developing a graph that depicts the relationship between monetary value and utility. The horizontal axis of the graph will be used to represent monetary values, and the vertical axis will represent the utility associated with each monetary value. Now, consider the data in Table 15.2, with a utility value corresponding to each monetary value for the original Swofford, Inc. problem. These values can be plotted on a graph such as in Figure 15.1, and a curve can be drawn through the observed points. The resulting curve is the *utility function for money* for Swofford's president. Recall that these points reflected the conservative or risk-avoiding nature of Swofford's president. Hence we refer to the curve in Figure 15.1 as a utility function for a risk avoider. Using the data in Table 15.4, developed for a risk taker, we can plot these points on a graph such as in Figure 15.2. The resulting curve depicts the utility function for a risk taker.

FIGURE 15.1
Utility Function for Money for the Risk Avoider

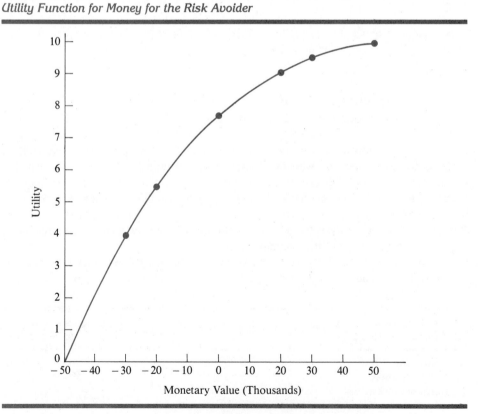

FIGURE 15.2
Utility Function for Money for the Risk Taker

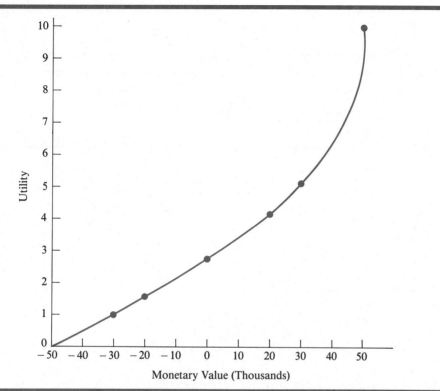

By looking at the utility functions of Figures 15.1 and 15.2, we can begin to generalize about the utility functions for risk avoiders and risk takers. Although the exact shape of the utility function will vary from one decision maker to another, we can see the general shape of these two classifications of utility functions. The utility function for the risk avoider class shows a diminishing marginal return for money. For example, the increase in utility going from a monetary value of −$30,000 to $0 is 7.5 − 4.0 = 3.5, whereas the increase in utility in going from $0 to $30,000 is only 9.5 − 7.5 = 2.0. On the other hand, the utility function for a risk taker shows an increasing marginal return for money. For example, in Figure 15.2, we see that the increase in utility in going from −$30,000 to $0 is 2.5 − 1.0 = 1.5, whereas the increase in utility in going from $0 to $30,000 is 5.0 − 2.5 = 2.5. Note also that in either case the utility function is always increasing. That is, more money leads to more utility. This is a property possessed by all utility functions.

We concluded above that the utility function for a risk avoider shows a diminishing marginal return for money and that the utility function for a risk taker shows an increasing marginal return. When the marginal return for money is neither decreasing nor increasing but remains constant, the corresponding utility function describes the behavior of a decision maker who is neutral to risk. The following characteristics are associated with a *risk-neutral decision maker*.

1. The utility function can be drawn as a straight line connecting the "best" and the "worst" points.
2. The expected utility criterion and the expected monetary value criterion result in the same action.

Figure 15.3 depicts the utility function of a risk-neutral decision maker using the Swofford, Inc. problem data. For comparison purposes, we also show the utility functions for the cases where the decision maker is either a risk taker or a risk avoider.

FIGURE 15.3
Utility Functions for Risk Avoider, Risk Taker, and Risk-Neutral

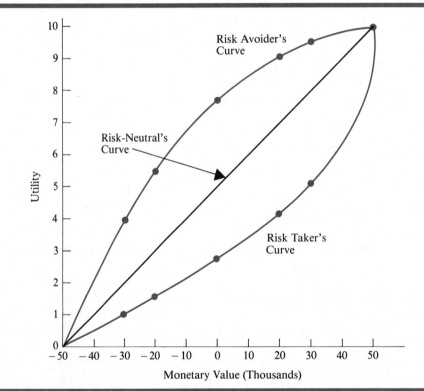

15.5 EXPECTED MONETARY VALUE VERSUS EXPECTED UTILITY AS A DECISION-MAKING CRITERION

In many decision-making problems, expected monetary value and expected utility will lead to identical recommendations. In fact, this will always be true if the decision maker is neutral to risk. In general, if the decision maker is almost risk-neutral over the range of payoffs (from lowest to highest) for a particular decision problem, the expected monetary value criterion is a good one. The trick lies in recognizing the range of monetary values over which a decision maker's utility function is risk-neutral.

It is generally agreed that when the payoffs for a particular decision-making problem fall into a reasonable range—the best is not too good and the worst is not too bad—decision makers tend to express preferences in agreement with the expected monetary value criterion. Thus as a general guideline we suggest asking the decision maker to consider the best and worst possible payoffs for a problem and assess their reasonableness. If the decision maker believes they are in the reasonable range, the expected monetary value criterion can be used. However, if the payoffs appear unreasonably large or unreasonably small (for example, a huge loss) and if the decision maker feels monetary values do not adequately reflect her or his true preferences for the payoffs, a utility analysis of the problem should be considered.

Unfortunately the determination of the appropriate utilities is not a trivial task. As we have seen, measuring utility requires a degree of subjectivity on the part of the decision maker, and different decision makers will have different utility functions. This aspect of utility often causes decision makers to feel uncomfortable about using the utility criterion in decision making. However, if we encounter a decision situation in which we are convinced monetary value is not necessarily the primary measure of performance and if we agree that a quantitative analysis of the decision problem is desirable, then some form of utility analysis should be performed.

———— *Summary* ————

In this chapter we have suggested that expected utility should be used as a criterion in many decision situations in which the expected monetary value criterion would lead to unacceptable decisions. Unlike monetary value, utility is a measure of the total worth of an outcome resulting from the choice of a decision alternative and the occurrence of a state of nature. As such, utility takes into account the decision maker's attitude toward the profit, loss, and risk associated with an outcome. In our examples we have seen how the use of utility analysis can lead to decision recommendations that differ from those that would be selected under the expected monetary value criterion.

While admittedly a decision maker's utility can be difficult to measure, we have offered a step-by-step procedure that can be used to determine a decision maker's utility for money. Using the decision maker's evaluation of a lottery involving only the best and worst payoffs, the procedure provides a method whereby each entry in the payoff table can be converted to a utility value. Then the expected utility criterion can be used to select the best decision alternative.

Even with utility as a measure of worth, we saw how the analysis for a conservative, or risk-avoiding, decision maker could lead to different decision recommendations than for a risk taker. In cases where the decision maker is risk-neutral, however, we saw that the recommendations using the expected utility criterion are identical to the recommendations using the expected monetary value criterion.

———— *Glossary* ————

Utility   A measure of the total worth of an outcome reflecting a decision maker's attitude toward considerations such as profit, loss, and intangibles such as risk.

Lottery   A hypothetical investment alternative with a probability p of obtaining the best possible payoff and a probability of $(1 - p)$ of obtaining the worst possible payoff in a payoff table.

Expected utility criterion   A decision criterion that requires the analyst to compute the expected utility for each decision alternative and then select the alternative yielding the highest expected utility.

Risk taker   A decision maker who tends to prefer decisions that, although risky, have a possibility for a high or extremely good payoff.

Risk avoider   A decision maker who tends to avoid decisions that have the risk of a low or extremely bad payoff.

Utility function for money   A curve that depicts the relationship between monetary value and utility.

Risk-neutral decision maker   A decision maker who is neutral to risk. For this decision maker the expected monetary value criterion yields results identical to those obtained with the expected utility criterion.

Problems

1. A firm has three investment alternatives. The payoff table and associated probabilities are as follows:

		Economic Conditions			
		Up	Stable	Down	
Investment	d_1	100	25	0	
	d_2	75	50	25 ← Thousands of Dollars
	d_3	50	50	50	
Probabilities		.40	.30	.30	

a. Using the EMV criterion, which decision is preferred?
b. For the lottery having a payoff of $100,000 with probability p and $0 with probability $(1 - p)$, two decision makers expressed the following indifference probabilities:

	Indifference Probability (p)	
Profit	Decision Maker A	Decision Maker B
75,000	0.80	0.60
50,000	0.60	0.30
25,000	0.30	0.15

Find the most preferred decision for each decision maker using the expected utility criterion.
c. Why don't decision makers A and B select the same decision alternative?

2. Alexander Industries is considering purchasing an insurance policy for its new office building in St. Louis, MO. The policy has an annual cost of $10,000. If minor fire damage occurs to the office building, a cost of $100,000 is anticipated, while a

major or total destruction carries a cost of $200,000. The payoff table, including the state-of-nature probabilities, is as follows:

			Damage		
			s_1 None	s_2 Minor	s_3 Major
Decision	Purchase insurance	d_1	10,000	10,000	10,000
Alternatives	Do not purchase insurance	d_2	0	100,000	200,000
	Probabilities		0.96	0.03	0.01

(last column arrow: ← Cost)

a. Using the expected monetary criterion, what decision do you recommend?
b. What lottery would you use to assess utilities? (Note that since the data are costs, the best payoff is $0.)
c. Assume we found the following indifference probabilities for the lottery defined in part b:

Cost	Indifference Probability
10,000	$p = 0.99$
100,000	$p = 0.60$

What decision would you recommend?
d. Do you favor using the expected monetary value or expected utility criterion for this decision problem? Why?

3. In a certain state lottery, a lottery ticket costs $2. In terms of the decision to purchase or not to purchase a lottery ticket, suppose the following payoff table applies:

			Outcomes	
			s_1 Win	s_2 Lose
Decision	Purchase lottery ticket	d_1	300,000	−2
Alternatives	Do not purchase lottery ticket	d_2	0	0

a. If a realistic estimate of the chances of winning are one in 250,000, use the expected monetary value criterion to recommend a decision.
b. If a particular decision maker assigns an indifference probability of 0.000001 to the $0 payoff, would this individual purchase a lottery ticket? Use the expected utility criterion to justify your answer.

4. There are two different routes for traveling between two cities. Route A normally takes 60 minutes, while route B normally takes 45 minutes. If traffic problems are encountered on route A, the travel time increases to 70 minutes, while traffic problems on route B increase travel time to 90 minutes. The probability of the delay is 0.20 for route A and 0.30 for route B.
a. Using the expected value criterion, what is the recommended route?

    b. If utilities are to be assigned to the travel times, what is the appropriate lottery? Note that the smaller times should reflect higher utilities.

    c. Using the lottery of part b, assume that the decision maker expresses indifference probabilities of

$$p = 0.80 \quad \text{for 60 minutes}$$
$$p = 0.60 \quad \text{for 70 minutes}$$

What route should this decision maker select? Is the decision maker a risk taker or a risk avoider?

5. Three decision makers have assessed utilities for the following decision problem:

		States of Nature			
		s_1	s_2	s_3	
Decision	d_1	20	50	−20	
Alternatives	d_2	80	100	−100	← Payoff in dollars

The indifference probabilities are as follows:

Payoffs	Indifference Probabilties (p)		
	Decision Maker A	Decision Maker B	Decision Maker C
100	1.00	1.00	1.00
80	0.95	0.70	0.90
50	0.90	0.60	0.75
20	0.70	0.45	0.60
−20	0.50	0.25	0.40
−100	0.00	0.00	0.00

    a. Plot the utility function for money for the three decision makers.

    b. Classify each decision maker as a risk avoider, a risk taker, or risk-neutral.

    c. For the payoff of 20, what is the premium the risk avoider will pay to avoid risk? What is the premium the risk taker will pay to have the opportunity of the high payoff?

6. In problem 5, if $P(s_1) = 0.25$, $P(s_2) = 0.50$, and $P(s_3) = 0.25$, find a recommended decision for each of the three decision makers. Note that for the same decision problem, different utilities can lead to different decisions.

7. Suppose that the point spread for a particular sporting event is 10 points and that with this spread you are convinced you would have a 0.60 probability of winning a bet on your team. However, the local bookie will only accept a $1000 bet. Assuming such bets are legal, would you bet on your team? (Disregard any commission charged by the bookie.) Remember that *you* must pay losses out of your own pocket. Your payoff table is as follows:

			States of Nature	
			s_1 *You Win*	s_2 *You Lose*
Decision	Bet	d_1	1000	−1000
Alternatives	Don't bet	d_2	0	0

   a. What decision does EMV recommend?

   b. What is *your* indifference probability for the $0 payoff? (While this is not easy, be as realistic as possible. Remember, this is required if we are to do an analysis that reflects your attitude toward risk.)

   c. What decision would you make based on the expected utility criterion? In this case are you a risk taker or risk avoider?

   d. Would other individuals assess the same utility values you do? Explain.

   e. If your decision in part c was to place the bet, repeat the analysis assuming a minimum bet of $10,000.

8. A Las Vegas roulette wheel has 38 different numerical values. If an individual bets on one number and wins, the payoff is 35 to one.

   a. Show a payoff table for a $10 bet on one number using decision alternatives of bet and do not bet.

   b. What is the EMV decision?

   c. Do the Las Vegas casinos want risk-taking or risk-avoiding customers? Explain.

   d. What range of utility values would a decision maker have to assign to the $0 payoff in order to have expected utility justify his or her decision to place the $10 bet?

9. A new product has the following profit projections and associated probabilities:

Profit	Probability
$150,000	0.10
$100,000	0.25
$ 50,000	0.20
0	0.15
−$ 50,000	0.20
−$100,000	0.10

   a. Use the EMV criterion to make the decision of whether to market the new product.

   b. Because of the high dollar values involved, especially the possibility of a $100,000 loss, the marketing vice-president has expressed some concern about the use of the EMV criterion. As a consequence, if a utility analysis is performed, what is the appropriate lottery?

   c. Assume that the following indifference probabilities are assigned:

Profit	Indifference Probability (p)
100,000	0.95
50,000	0.70
0	0.50
−50,000	0.25

Do the utilities reflect the behavior of a risk taker or a risk avoider?

   d. Use the expected utility criterion to make a recommended decision.

   e. Should the decision maker feel comfortable with the final decision recommended by the analysis?

10. A television network has been receiving low ratings for its programs. Currently, management is considering two alternatives for the Monday night 8:00 P.M.–9:00 P.M. time slot: a Western program with a well-known star or a musical variety program with a relatively unknown husband and wife team. The percentages of viewing audience estimates depend on the degree of program acceptance. The relevant data are as follows:

Program Acceptance	Percentage of Viewing Audience	
	Western	Musical Variety
High	30%	40%
Moderate	25%	20%
Poor	20%	15%

The probabilities associated with program acceptance levels are as follows:

Program Acceptance	Probability	
	Western	Musical Variety
High	0.30	0.30
Moderate	0.60	0.40
Poor	0.10	0.30

a. Using the expected value criterion, which program should the network choose?
b. Assuming a utility analysis is desired, what is the appropriate lottery?
c. Using the appropriate lottery in part b, assume that the network's program manager has assigned the following indifference probabilities:

Percentage of Audience	Indifference Probability (p)
30%	0.40
25%	0.30
20%	0.10

Using utility measures, which program would you recommend? Is the manager in this problem a risk taker or a risk avoider?

16

Forecasting

A critical aspect of managing any organization is planning for the future. Indeed, the long-run success of an organization is closely related to how well management is able to foresee the future and develop appropriate strategies. Good judgment, intuition, and an awareness of the state of the economy may give a manager a rough idea or "feeling" of what is likely to happen in the future. However, it is often difficult to convert this "feeling" into hard data such as next quarter's sales volume or next year's raw-material cost per unit. The purpose of this chapter is to introduce several methods that can help predict many future aspects of a business operation.

Let us suppose for a moment that we have been asked to provide quarterly estimates of the sales volume for a particular product during the coming 1-year period. Production schedules, raw-material purchasing plans, inventory policies, and sales quotas will all be affected by the quarterly estimates we provide. Consequently, poor estimates may result in poor planning and hence result in increased costs for the firm. How should we go about providing the quarterly sales volume estimates?

We will certainly want to review the actual sales data for the product in past periods. Suppose that we have actual sales data for each quarter over the past 3 years. From these historical data we can identify the general level of sales and determine whether or not there is any trend such as an increase or decrease in sales volume over time. A further review of the data might reveal a seasonal pattern, such as peak sales occurring in the third quarter of each year and sales volume bottoming out during the first quarter. By reviewing historical data over time we are in a better position to understand the pattern of past sales and hence better able to predict future sales for the product.

The historical sales data referred to form what is called a *time series*. Specifically, a time series is a set of observations measured at successive points in time or over successive periods of time. In this chapter we will introduce several procedures that can be used to analyze time series data. The objective of this analysis will be to provide good *forecasts* or predictions of future values of the time series.

Forecasting methods can be classified as quantitative or qualitative. Quantitative forecasting methods are based on an analysis of historical data concerning a time series and possibly other related time series. If the historical data used are restricted to past values of the series that we are trying to forecast, the forecasting procedure is called a time series method. In this chapter we discuss three time series methods: smoothing (moving averages and exponential smoothing), trend projection, and trend projection adjusted for seasonal influences. If the historical data used in a quantitative forecasting method involve other time series that are believed to be related to the time series we are trying to forecast, we say that we are using a causal method. We discuss the use of regression analysis as a causal forecasting method. Qualitative forecasting methods generally utilize the judgment of experts to make forecasts. An advantage of these procedures is that they can be applied in situations where no historical data are available. We discuss some of these approaches in Section 16.5. Figure 16.1 provides an overview of the different types of forecasting methods.

FIGURE 16.1
An Overview of Forecasting Methods

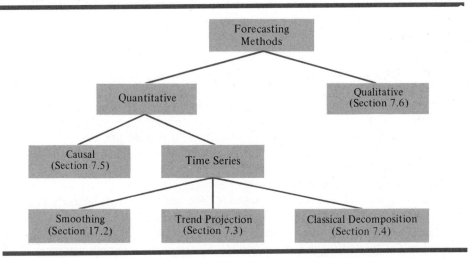

16.1 THE COMPONENTS OF A TIME SERIES

In order to explain the pattern or behavior of the data in a time series it is often helpful to think of the time series as consisting of several components. The usual assumption is that four separate components—trend, cyclical, seasonal, and irregular—combine to make the time series take on specific values. Let us look more closely at each of these components of a time series.

Trend Component

In time series analysis the measurements may be taken every hour, day, week, month, or year or at any other regular interval.[1] Although time series data generally exhibit random fluctuations, the time series may still show gradual shifts or movements to

---

[1] We restrict our attention here to time series where the values of the series are recorded at equal intervals. Treatment of cases where the observations are not made at equal intervals is beyond the scope of this text.

relatively higher or lower values over a longer period of time. This gradual shifting of the time series, which is usually due to long-term factors such as changes in the population, changes in demographic characteristics of the population, changes in technology, and changes in consumer preferences, is referred to as the *trend* in the time series.

For example, a manufacturer of photographic equipment may see substantial month-to-month variability in the number of cameras sold. However, in reviewing the sales over the past 10 to 15 years this manufacturer may find a gradual increase in the annual sales volume. Suppose that the sales volume was approximately 1800 cameras per month in 1975, 2200 cameras per month in 1980, and 2600 cameras per month in 1985. While actual month-to-month sales volumes may vary substantially, this gradual growth in sales over time shows an upward trend for the time series. Figure 16.2 shows a straight line that may be a good approximation of the trend in the sales data. While the trend for camera sales appears to be linear and increasing over time, sometimes the trend in a time series is better described by other patterns.

FIGURE 16.2
Linear Trend of Camera Sales

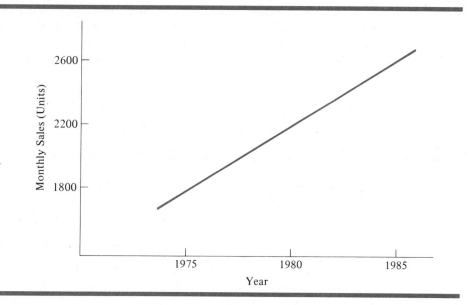

Figure 16.3 shows some other possible time series trend patterns. In (a) we see a nonlinear trend. This curve describes a time series showing very little growth initially, followed by a period of rapid growth, and then a leveling off. This might be a good approximation to sales for a product from introduction through a growth period and into a period of market saturation. The linear decreasing trend in (b) is useful for time series displaying a steady decrease over time. The horizontal line in (c) is used for a time series that does not show any consistent increase or decrease over time. It is actually the case of no trend.

FIGURE 16.3
Examples of Some Possible Time Series Trend Patterns

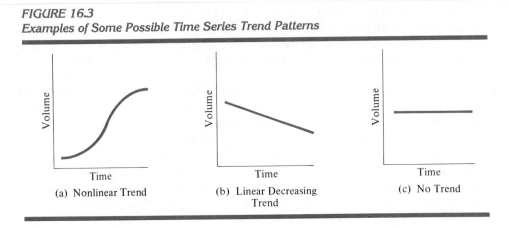

(a) Nonlinear Trend   (b) Linear Decreasing Trend   (c) No Trend

Cyclical Component

While a time series may exhibit a gradual shifting or trend pattern over long periods of time, we cannot expect all future values of the time series to be exactly on the trend line. In fact, time series often show alternating sequences of points below and above the trend line. Any regular pattern of sequences of points above and below the trend line is attributable to the cyclical component of the time series. Figure 16.4 shows the graph of a time series with an obvious cyclical component. The observations are taken at intervals 1 year apart.

FIGURE 16.4
Trend and Cyclical Components of a Time Series
Data Points Are 1 Year Apart

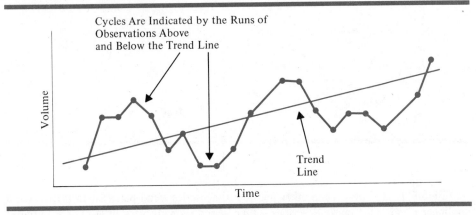

Many time series exhibit cyclical behavior with regular runs of observations below and above the trend line. The general belief is that this component of the time series represents multiyear cyclical movements in the economy. For example, periods of moderate inflation followed by periods of rapid inflation can lead to many time series that alternate below and above a generally increasing trend line (e.g., housing costs). Many time series in the late 1970s displayed this type of behavior.

Seasonal Component

While the trend and cyclical components of a time series are identified by analyzing multiyear movements in historical data, many time series show a regular pattern of variability within 1-year periods. For example, a manufacturer of swimming pools expects low sales activity in the fall and winter months, with peak sales occurring in the spring and summer months. Manufacturers of snow removal equipment and heavy clothing, however, expect just the opposite yearly pattern. It should not be surprising that the component of the time series that represents the variability in the data due to seasonal influences is called the seasonal component. While we generally think of seasonal movement in a time series as occurring within 1 year, the seasonal component can also be used to represent any repeating pattern that is less than 1 year in duration. For example, daily traffic volume data show within-the-day "seasonal" behavior, with peak levels during rush hours, moderate flow during the rest of the day and early evening, and light flow from midnight to early morning.

Irregular Component

The irregular component of the time series is the residual or "catchall" factor that accounts for the deviation of the actual time series value from what we would expect if the trend, cyclical, and seasonal components completely explained the time series. It accounts for the random variability in the time series. The irregular component is caused by the short-term, unanticipated, and nonrecurring factors that affect the time series. Since this component accounts for the random variability in the time series, it is unpredictable. We cannot attempt to predict its impact on the time series in advance.

16.2 FORECASTING USING SMOOTHING METHODS

In this section we discuss forecasting techniques that are appropriate for a fairly stable time series, one that exhibits no significant trend, cyclical, or seasonal effects. In such situations the objective of the forecasting method is to "smooth out" the irregular component of the time series through some type of averaging process. We begin with a consideration of the method known as moving averages.

Moving Averages

The *moving averages* method consists of computing an average of the *most recent n* data values in the time series. This average is then used as the forecast for the next period. Mathematically, the moving average calculation is made as follows:

$$\text{Moving average} = \frac{\Sigma \text{ (most recent } n \text{ data values)}}{n} \tag{16.1}$$

The term "moving" average is based on the fact that as a new observation becomes available for the time series, it replaces the oldest observation in equation (16.1), and a new average is computed. As a result the average will change or "move" as new observations become available.

To illustrate the moving averages method, consider the 12 weeks of data presented in Table 16.1 and Figure 16.5. These data show the number of gallons of gasoline sold by a gasoline distributor in Bennington, Vt., over the past 12 weeks.

TABLE 16.1
Gasoline Sales Time Series

Week	Sales (1000s of Gallons)
1	17
2	21
3	19
4	23
5	18
6	16
7	20
8	18
9	22
10	20
11	15
12	22

FIGURE 16.5
Graph of Gasoline Sales Time Series

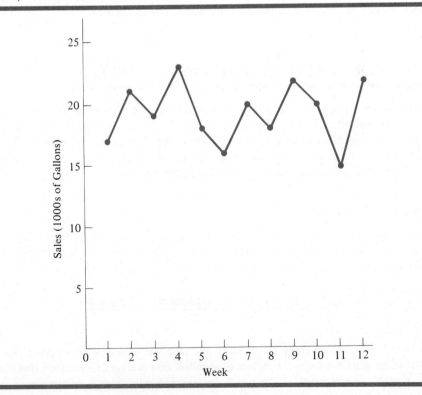

In order to use moving averages to forecast the gasoline sales time series, we must first select the number of data values to be included in the moving average. As an example, let us compute forecasts based upon a 3-week moving average. The moving average calculation for the first 3 weeks of the gasoline sales time series is as follows:

$$\text{Moving average (weeks 1-3)} = \frac{17 + 21 + 19}{3} = 19$$

This moving average value is then used as the forecast for week 4. Since the actual value observed in week 4 is 23, we see that the forecast error in week 4 is $23 - 19 = 4$. In general, the error associated with any forecast is the difference between the observed value of the time series and the forecast value.

The calculation for the second 3-week moving average is shown below:

$$\text{Moving average (weeks 2-4)} = \frac{21 + 19 + 23}{3} = 21$$

This moving average provides a forecast for week 5 of 21. The error associated with this forecast is $18 - 21 = -3$. Thus we see that the forecast error can be positive or negative depending upon whether the forecast is too low or too high.

A complete summary of the 3-week moving average calculations for the gasoline sales time series is shown in Table 16.2 and Figure 16.6.

TABLE 16.2
Summary of 3-Week Moving Average Calculations

Week	Time Series Value	Moving Average Forecast	Forecast Error	(Error)^2
1	17			
2	21			
3	19			
4	23	19	4	16
5	18	21	-3	9
6	16	20	-4	16
7	20	19	1	1
8	18	18	0	0
9	22	18	4	16
10	20	20	0	0
11	15	20	-5	25
12	22	19	3	9
			Totals 0	92

An important consideration in using any forecasting method is the accuracy of the forecast. Clearly, we would like the forecast errors to be small. The last two columns of Table 16.2, which contain the forecast errors and the forecast errors squared, can be used to develop measures of accuracy.

FIGURE 16.6
Graph of Gasoline Sales Time Series and 3-Week Moving Average Forecasts

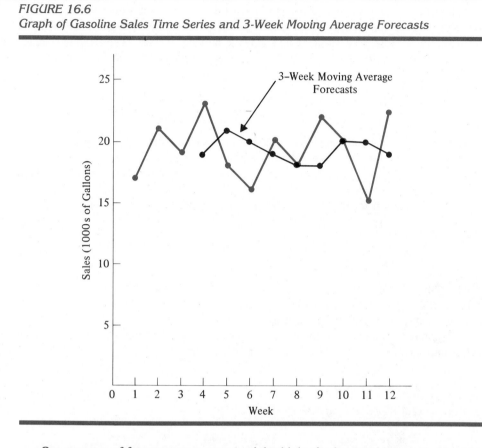

One measure of forecast accuracy you might think of using would be to simply sum the forecast errors over time. The problem with this measure is that if the errors are random (as they should be if our choice of forecasting method is appropriate), some errors will be positive and some errors will be negative, resulting in a sum near zero regardless of the size of the individual errors. Referring to Table 16.2, we see that the sum of forecast errors for the gasoline sales time series is zero. This difficulty can be avoided by either squaring or taking the absolute value of each of the individual forecast errors.

For the gasoline sales time series we can use the last column of Table 16.2 to compute the average of the sum of the squared errors. Doing so we obtain

$$\text{Average of the sum of squared errors} = \frac{92}{9} = 10.22$$

This average of the sum of squared errors is commonly referred to as the *mean squared error* (MSE). The mean squared error is an often used measure of the accuracy of a forecasting method.

Another commonly used measure of forecast accuracy is the *mean absolute deviation* (MAD). This measure is simply the average of the sum of the absolute deviations for all the forecast errors. Using the errors in Table 16.2, we obtain

$$\text{Mean absolute deviation (MAD)} = \frac{4 + 3 + 4 + 1 + 0 + 4 + 0 + 5 + 3}{9}$$

$$= 2.67$$

One major difference between MSE and MAD is that the MSE measure is influenced much more by large forecast errors than by small errors (since for the MSE measure the errors are squared). The selection of the best measure of forecasting accuracy is not a simple matter. Forecasting experts often disagree as to which measure should be used. In this chapter we will use the MSE measure.

As we indicated previously, in order to use the moving averages method we must first select the number of data values to be included in the moving average. It should not be too surprising that, for a particular time series, different length moving averages will differ in their ability to accurately forecast the time series. One possible approach to choosing the proper length is to use "trial and error" to identify the length that minimizes the MSE measure of forecast accuracy. Then, if we are willing to assume that the length which is best for the past will also be best for the future, we would forecast the next value in the time series using the number of data values that minimized the MSE for the historical time series. Problem 1 at the end of the chapter will ask you to consider 4-week and 5-week moving averages for the gasoline sales data. A comparison of the mean square error for each will indicate the number of weeks of data you may want to include in the moving average calculation.

Weighted Moving Averages

In the moving averages method each observation in the moving average calculation receives the same weight. One possible variation, known as *weighted moving averages*, involves selecting different weights for each data value and then computing a weighted mean as the forecast. In most cases the most recent observation receives the most weight, and the weight decreases for older data values. For example, using the gasoline sales time series, let us illustrate the computation of a weighted 3-week moving average, where the most recent observation receives a weight three times as great as that given the oldest observation, and the next oldest observation receives a weight twice as great as the oldest. The weighted moving average forecast for week 4 would be computed as follows:

$$\begin{aligned}
\text{Weighted moving} \\
\text{average forecast} \\
\text{for week 4} \quad &= \tfrac{3}{6}(19) + \tfrac{2}{6}(21) + \tfrac{1}{6}(17) \\
&= 19.33
\end{aligned}$$

Note that for the weighted moving average the sum of the weights is equal to one. This was also true for the simple moving average, where each weight was $\frac{1}{3}$. However, recall that the simple or unweighted moving average provided a forecast of 19. Problem 2 at the end of the chapter asks you to calculate the remaining values for the 3-week weighted moving average and compare the forecast accuracy with what we have obtained for the unweighted moving average.

Exponential Smoothing

Exponential smoothing is a forecasting technique that uses a smoothed value of the time series in one period to forecast the value of the time series in the next period. The basic exponential smoothing model is as follows:

$$F_{t+1} = \alpha Y_t + (1 - \alpha)F_t \qquad (16.2)$$

where

$$F_{t+1} = \text{forecast of the time series for period } t + 1$$
$$Y_t = \text{actual value of the time series in period } t$$
$$F_t = \text{forecast of the time series for period } t$$
$$\alpha = \text{smoothing constant } (0 \le \alpha \le 1)$$

Using equation (16.2), the forecast for any period is a weighted average of the previous actual values for the time series. To see this, let us suppose that we have three periods of data, Y_1, Y_2, and Y_3. Then the forecast for period 4 becomes

$$F_4 = \alpha Y_3 + (1 - \alpha)F_3$$

The forecast value for period 4 is clearly a weighted average of Y_3 and F_3, with weights of α and $1 - \alpha$, respectively. But from equation (16.2) we also know

$$F_3 = \alpha Y_2 + (1 - \alpha)F_2$$
$$F_2 = \alpha Y_1 + (1 - \alpha)F_1$$

Since there are no previous data values for the time series, the first forecast value is taken to be equal to Y_1. That is, $F_1 = Y_1$. Using this value for F_1, F_2 is written

$$F_2 = \alpha Y_1 + (1 - \alpha)Y_1 = Y_1$$

Substituting $F_2 = Y_1$ in the expression for F_3, we have

$$F_3 = \alpha Y_2 + (1 - \alpha)Y_1$$

Finally, substituting this expression for F_3 in the above expression for F_4, we obtain

$$F_4 = \alpha Y_3 + (1 - \alpha)[\alpha Y_2 + (1 - \alpha)Y_1]$$
$$= \alpha Y_3 + \alpha(1 - \alpha)Y_2 + (1 - \alpha)^2 Y_1$$

Hence we see that F_4 is a weighted average of the first three time series values. The sum of the coefficients or weights for Y_1, Y_2, and Y_3 will always equal 1. A similar argument can be made to show that any forecast F_{t+1} is a weighted average of the previous t time series values.

An advantage of exponential smoothing is that it is a simple procedure and requires very little historical data for its use. Once the smoothing constant α has been selected, only two pieces of information are required in order to compute the forecast for the next period. Referring to equation (16.2), we see that with a given α we can compute the forecast for period $t + 1$ simply by knowing the actual and forecast time series values for period t; that is, Y_t and F_t.

As an illustration of the exponential smoothing model, consider the gasoline sales time series presented previously in Table 16.1 and Figure 16.5. With no forecast available for period 1 we begin our calculations by letting F_1 equal the actual value of the time series in period 1. That is, with $Y_1 = 17$, we will set $F_1 = 17$ simply to get the exponential smoothing computations started. Using a smoothing constant of $\alpha = 0.2$, the forecast for period 2 becomes

$$F_2 = 0.2Y_1 + (1 - 0.2)F_1 = 0.2(17) + 0.8(17) = 17$$

Referring to the time series data in Table 16.1, we find an actual time series value in period 2 of $Y_2 = 21$. Thus period 2 has a forecast error of $21 - 17 = 4$.

Continuing with the exponential smoothing computations provides the following forecast for period 3:

$$F_3 = 0.2Y_2 + 0.8F_2 = 0.2(21) + 0.8(17) = 17.8$$

Once the actual time series value in period 3, $Y_3 = 19$, is known, we can generate a forecast for period 4 as follows:

$$F_4 = 0.2Y_3 + 0.8F_3 = 0.2(19) + 0.8(17.8) = 18.04$$

As stated previously, we note that each forecast is obtained from a simple calculation using the actual and forecast time series value from the previous period.

By continuing the exponential smoothing calculations we are able to determine the weekly forecast values and the corresponding weekly forecast errors, as shown in Table 16.3. For week 12, we have $Y_{12} = 22$ and $F_{12} = 18.48$. Can you use this information to generate a forecast for week 13 before the actual value of week 13 becomes known? Using the exponential smoothing model, we have

$$F_{13} = 0.2Y_{12} + 0.8F_{12} = 0.2(22) + 0.8(18.48) = 19.18$$

Thus the exponential smoothing forecast of the amount sold in week 13 is 19.18, or 19,180 gallons of gasoline. With this forecast the firm can make plans and decisions accordingly. The accuracy of the forecast will not be known until the firm conducts its business through week 13. However, the exponential smoothing model has provided a good forecast for the unknown 13th week gasoline sales volume. Figure 16.7 shows the plot of the actual and the forecast time series values. Note in particular how the forecasts "smooth out" the irregular fluctuations in the time series.

TABLE 16.3
Summary of the Exponential Smoothing Forecasts and Forecast Errors for Gasoline
Sales with Smoothing Constant $\alpha = 0.2$

Week t	Time Series Value Y_t	Exponential Smoothing Forecast F_t	Forecast Error $Y_t - F_t$
1	17	17.00	*
2	21	17.00	4.00
3	19	17.80	1.20
4	23	18.04	4.96
5	18	19.03	−1.03
6	16	18.83	−2.83
7	20	18.26	1.74
8	18	18.61	−0.61
9	22	18.49	3.51
10	20	19.19	0.81
11	15	19.35	−4.35
12	22	18.48	3.52

*Forecast error for week 1 is not considered because F_1 was set equal to Y_1 in order to begin the smoothing computations.

In the preceding smoothing calculations we used a smoothing constant of $\alpha = 0.2$, although any value of α between 0 and 1 is acceptable. However, some values will yield better forecasts than others. Some insight into choosing a good value for α can be obtained by rewriting the basic exponential smoothing model as follows:

$$F_{t+1} = \alpha Y_t + (1 - \alpha)F_t$$
$$F_{t+1} = \alpha Y_t + F_t - \alpha F_t$$
$$F_{t+1} = \underset{\substack{\uparrow \\ \text{Forecast} \\ \text{in period } t}}{F_t} + \underset{\substack{\uparrow \\ \text{Forecast error} \\ \text{in period } t}}{\alpha(Y_t - F_t)} \tag{16.3}$$

Thus we see that the new forecast F_{t+1} is equal to the previous forecast F_t plus an adjustment, which is α times the most recent forecast error, $Y_t - F_t$. That is, the forecast in period $t + 1$ is obtained by adjusting the forecast in period t by a fraction of the forecast error. If the time series is very volatile and contains substantial random variability, a small value of the smoothing constant is preferred. The reason for this choice is that since much of the forecast error is due to random variability, we do not want to overreact and adjust the forecasts too quickly. For a fairly stable time series with relatively little random variability, larger values of the smoothing constant have the advantage of quickly adjusting the forecasts when forecasting errors occur and therefore allowing the forecast to react faster to changing conditions.

The criterion that we shall use to determine a desirable value for the smoothing constant α is the same as the criterion we proposed earlier for determining the number

FIGURE 16.7
Graph of Actual and Forecast Gasoline Sales Time Series with Smoothing Constant
$\alpha = 0.2$

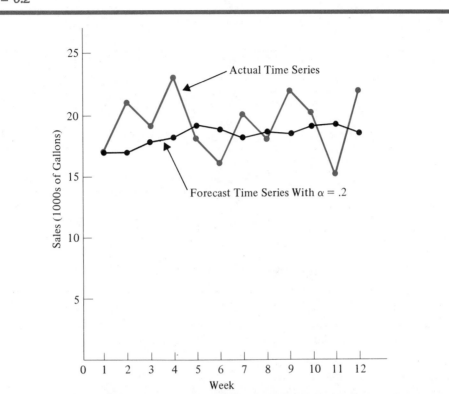

of periods of data to include in the moving averages calculation. That is, we choose the value of α that minimizes the mean square error (MSE).

A summary of the mean square error calculations for the exponential smoothing forecast of gasoline sales with $\alpha = 0.2$ is shown in Table 16.4. Note that there is one less squared error term than the number of time periods. This is because we had no past values with which to make a forecast for period 1. As a result we set $F_1 = Y_1$, and do not obtain a squared error in period 1.

Would a different value of α have provided better results in terms of a lower MSE value? Perhaps the most straightforward way to answer this question is simply to try another value for α. We will then compare its mean square error with the MSE value of 8.98 obtained by using a value of 0.2 for the smoothing constant.

The exponential smoothing results with $\alpha = 0.3$ are shown in Table 16.5. With MSE = 9.35, we see that for the current data set a smoothing constant of $\alpha = 0.3$ results in less forecast accuracy than a smoothing constant of $\alpha = 0.2$. Thus we would be inclined to prefer the original smoothing constant of 0.2. With a trial-and-error calculation with other values of α a ''good'' value for the smoothing constant can be found. This value can be used in the exponential smoothing model to provide forecasts for the future. At a later date, after a number of new time series observations have been obtained,

TABLE 16.4
Mean Square Error Computations for Forecasting Gasoline Sales with $\alpha = 0.2$

Week t	Time Series Value Y_t	Forecast F_t	Forecast Error $Y_t - F_t$	Squared Error $(Y_t - F_t)^2$
1	17	17.00	—	—
2	21	17.00	4.00	16.00
3	19	17.80	1.20	1.44
4	23	18.04	4.96	24.60
5	18	19.03	−1.03	1.06
6	16	18.83	−2.83	8.01
7	20	18.26	1.74	3.03
8	18	18.61	−0.61	0.37
9	22	18.49	3.51	12.32
10	20	19.19	0.81	0.66
11	15	19.35	−4.35	18.92
12	22	18.48	3.52	12.39
			Total	98.80

$$\text{Mean Square Error (MSE)} = \frac{98.80}{11} = 8.98$$

it is good practice to analyze the newly collected time series data to see if the smoothing constant should be revised to provide better forecasting results.

TABLE 16.5
Mean Square Error Computations for Forecasting Gasoline Sales with $\alpha = 0.3$

Week t	Time Series Value Y_t	Forecast F_t	Forecast Error $Y_t - F_t$	Squared Error $(Y_t - F_t)^2$
1	17	17.00	—	—
2	21	17.00	4.00	16.00
3	19	18.20	0.80	0.64
4	23	18.44	4.56	20.79
5	18	19.81	−1.81	3.28
6	16	19.27	−3.27	10.69
7	20	18.29	1.71	2.92
8	18	18.80	−0.80	0.64
9	22	18.56	3.44	11.83
10	20	19.59	0.41	0.17
11	15	19.71	−4.71	22.18
12	22	18.30	3.70	13.69
			Total	102.83

$$\text{Mean square error (MSE)} = \frac{102.83}{11} = 9.35$$

16.3 FORECASTING A TIME SERIES USING TREND PROJECTION

In this section we will see how to forecast the values of a time series that exhibits a long-term linear trend. Specifically, let us consider the time series data for bicycle sales of a particular manufacturer over the past 10 years, as shown in Table 16.6 and Figure 16.8. Note that 21,600 bicycles were sold in year 1, 22,900 were sold in year 2, and so on; in year 10, the most recent year, 31,400 bicycles were sold. Although the graph in Figure 16.8 shows some up-and-down movement over the past 10 years, the time series seems to have an overall increasing or upward trend in the number of bicycles sold.

FIGURE 16.8
Graph of the Bicycle Sales Time Series

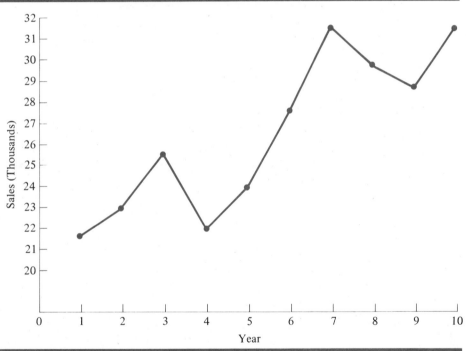

We do not want the trend component of a time series to follow each and every "up" and "down" movement. Rather, the trend component should reflect the gradual shifting—in this case, growth—of the time series values. After we view the time series data in Table 16.6 and the graph in Figure 16.8, we might agree that a linear trend as shown in Figure 16.9 has the potential of providing a reasonable description of the long-run movement in the series. Thus we can now concentrate on finding the linear function that best approximates the trend.

TABLE 16.6
Bicycle Sales Data

Year t	Sales in Thousands Y_t
1	21.6
2	22.9
3	25.5
4	21.9
5	23.9
6	27.5
7	31.5
8	29.7
9	28.6
10	31.4

For a linear trend the estimated sales volume expressed as a function of time can be written as

$$T_t = b_0 + b_1 t \qquad (16.4)$$

FIGURE 16.9
Trend Represented by a Linear Function for Bicycle Sales

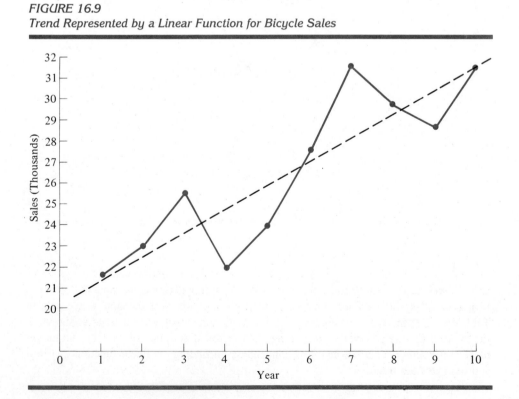

where

$$T_t = \text{trend value for bicycle sales in period } t$$
$$b_0 = \text{intercept of the trend line}$$
$$b_1 = \text{slope of the trend line}$$
$$t = \text{time in years}$$

In the linear trend relationship in equation (16.4) we will let $t = 1$ for the time of the first observation in the time series, $t = 2$ for the time of the second observation, and so on.

The approach most often used to determine the linear function that best approximates the trend is based upon a procedure referred to as the least-squares method. The least-squares method identifies the values of b_0 and b_1 that minimize the sum of squared forecast errors. That is, the objective is to determine the values of b_0 and b_1 that minimize

$$\sum_{t=1}^{n} (Y_t - T_t)^2 \tag{16.5}$$

where

$$Y_t = \text{actual value of the time series in period } t$$
$$T_t = \text{forecast value (based upon trend) of the time series in period } t$$
$$n = \text{number of periods}$$

The least-squares method, which is also used for the statistical technique known as regression analysis, is described in most elementary books on statistics. Shown below are the formulas that can be used to compute the value of b_0 and the value of b_1 using this approach:

$$b_1 = \frac{\sum tY_t - (\sum t \sum Y_t)/n}{\sum t^2 - (\sum t)^2/n} \tag{16.6}$$

$$b_0 = \overline{Y} - b_1 \overline{t} \tag{16.7}$$

where

$$\overline{Y} = \text{average value of the time series; that is, } \overline{Y} = \frac{\sum Y_t}{n}$$

$$\overline{t} = \text{average value of } t; \text{ that is, } \overline{t} = \frac{\sum t}{n}$$

The above summations are for values of t from 1 through n. Using the above relationships for b_0 and b_1 and the bicycle sales data of Table 16.6, we have the following calculations:

t	Y_t	tY_t	t^2
1	21.6	21.6	1
2	22.9	45.8	4
3	25.5	76.5	9
4	21.9	87.6	16
5	23.9	119.5	25
6	27.5	165.0	36
7	31.5	220.5	49
8	29.7	237.6	64
9	28.6	257.4	81
10	31.4	314.0	100
Totals 55	264.5	1545.5	385

$$\bar{t} = \frac{55}{10} = 5.5 \text{ years}$$

$$\bar{Y} = \frac{264.5}{10} = 26.45 \text{ thousands}$$

$$b_1 = \frac{1545.5 - (55)(264.5)/10}{385 - (55)^2/10} = \frac{90.75}{82.5} = 1.10$$

$$b_0 = 26.45 - 1.10(5.5) = 20.4$$

Therefore

$$T_t = 20.4 + 1.1t \tag{16.8}$$

is the expression for the linear trend component of the bicycle sales time series.

Trend Projections

The slope of 1.1 indicates that over the past 10 years the firm has experienced an average growth in sales of around 1100 units per year. If we assume that the past 10-year trend in sales is a good indicator of the future, then equation (16.8) can be used to project the trend component of the time series. For example, substituting $t = 11$ into equation (16.8) yields next year's trend projection, T_{11}:

$$T_{11} = 20.4 + 1.1(11) = 32.5$$

Thus, using the trend component only, we would forecast sales of 32,500 bicycles next year.

The use of a linear function to model the trend is common. However, as we discussed earlier, sometimes time series exhibit a nonlinear trend. Figure 16.10 shows two common nonlinear trend functions. More advanced texts discuss in detail how to solve for the trend component when a nonlinear function is used and how to decide when to use such a function. For our purposes it is sufficient to note that the analyst should choose the function that provides the best fit to the data.

FIGURE 16.10
Some Possible Functional Forms for Nonlinear Trend Patterns

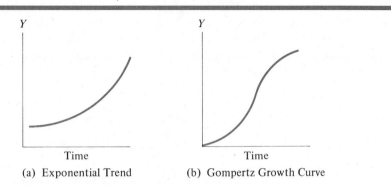

(a) Exponential Trend   (b) Gompertz Growth Curve

16.4 FORECASTING A TIME SERIES WITH TREND AND SEASONAL COMPONENTS

In the previous section we showed how to forecast a time series that had a trend component. In this section, we expand our discussion by showing how to forecast a time series that has both trend and seasonal components. The approach we will take is first to remove the seasonal effect or seasonal component from the time series. This step is referred to as *deseasonalizing* the time series. After deseasonalizing, the time series will have only a trend component. As a result we can use the least-squares method described in the previous section to identify the trend component of the time series. Then, using a trend projection calculation, we will be able to forecast the trend component of the time series in future periods. The final step in developing the forecast will be to incorporate the seasonal component by using a seasonal factor to adjust the trend projection. In this manner we will be able to identify the trend and seasonal components and consider both in forecasting the time series.

In addition to a trend component (T) and seasonal component (S), we will assume that the time series also has an irregular component (I). The irregular component accounts for any random effects in the time series that cannot be explained by the trend and seasonal components. Using T_t, S_t, and I_t to identify the trend, seasonal, and irregular components at time t, we will assume that the actual time series value, denoted by Y_t, can be described by the following *multiplicative model*:

$$Y_t = T_t \times S_t \times I_t \tag{16.9}$$

In this model T_t is the trend measured in units of the item being forecast. However, the S_t and I_t components are measured in relative terms, with values above 1.00 indicating effects above the normal or average level. Values below 1.00 indicate below-average levels for each component. In order to illustrate the use of (16.9) to model a time series, suppose that we have a trend projection of 540 units. In addition, suppose that $S_t = 1.10$ shows a seasonal effect 10% above average and $I_t = 0.98$ shows an irregular effect 2%

below average. Using these values in (16.9), the time series value would be $Y_t =$ 540(1.10)(0.98) = 582.

In this section we will illustrate the use of the multiplicative model with trend, seasonal, and irregular components by working with the quarterly data presented in Table 16.7 and Figure 16.11. These data show the television set sales (in thousands of units) for a particular manufacturer over the past 4 years. We begin by showing how to identify the seasonal component of the time series.

TABLE 16.7
Quarterly Data for Television Set
Sales

Year	Quarter	Sales (1000s)
1	1	4.8
	2	4.1
	3	6.0
	4	6.5
2	1	5.8
	2	5.2
	3	6.8
	4	7.4
3	1	6.0
	2	5.6
	3	7.5
	4	7.8
4	1	6.3
	2	5.9
	3	8.0
	4	8.4

Calculating the Seasonal Indexes

By referring to Figure 16.11 we can begin to identify a seasonal pattern for the television set sales. Specifically, we observe that sales are lowest in the second quarter of each year, followed by higher sales levels in quarters 3 and 4. The computational procedure used to identify each quarter's seasonal influence begins with the use of moving averages to isolate the seasonal and irregular components, S_t and I_t.

With moving averages, we will use 1 year of data in each calculation. Since we are working with a quarterly series, we will use four data values in each moving average. The moving average calculation for the first four quarters of the television set sales data is as follows:

$$\text{First moving average} = \frac{4.8 + 4.1 + 6.0 + 6.5}{4} = \frac{21.4}{4} = 5.35$$

Note that the moving average calculation for the first four quarters yields the average quarterly sales over the first year of the time series. Continuing the moving average

FIGURE 16.11
Graph of Quarterly Television Set Sales Time Series

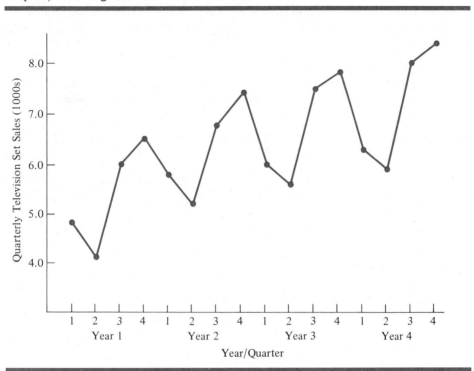

calculation, we next add the 5.8 value for the first quarter of year 2 and drop the 4.8 for the first quarter of year 1. Thus the second moving average is

$$\text{Second moving average} = \frac{4.1 + 6.0 + 6.5 + 5.8}{4} = \frac{22.4}{4} = 5.6$$

Similarly, the third moving average calculation is $(6.0 + 6.5 + 5.8 + 5.2)/4 = 5.875$.

Before we proceed with the moving average calculations for the entire time series, let us return to the first moving average calculation, which resulted in a value of 5.35. The 5.35 value represents an average quarterly sales volume (across all seasons) for year 1. As we look back at the calculation of the 5.35 value, perhaps it makes sense to associate 5.35 with the "middle" quarter of the moving average group. However, note that some difficulty in identifying the middle quarter is encountered; with 4 quarters in the moving average, there is no middle quarter. The 5.35 value corresponds to the end of quarter 2 and the beginning of quarter 3. Similarly, if we go to the next moving average value of 5.60, the middle corresponds to the end of quarter 3 and the beginning of quarter 4.

Recall that the reason for computing moving averages is to isolate the combined seasonal irregular components. However, the moving average values we have computed do not correspond directly to the original quarters of the time series. We can resolve this difficulty by using the midpoints between successive moving average values. For example, since 5.35 corresponds to the beginning of quarter 3 and 5.60 corresponds to the end of quarter 3, we will use $(5.35 + 5.60)/2 = 5.475$ as the moving average value for quarter 3. Similarly, we associate a moving average value of $(5.60 + 5.875)/2 = 5.738$ with quarter 4. What results is called a centered moving average. A complete summary of the centered moving average calculations for the television set sales data is shown in Table 16.8.

TABLE 16.8
Centered Moving Average Calculations for the Television Set Sales Time Series

Year	Quarter	Sales (1000s)	Four-Quarter Moving Average	Centered Moving Average
1	1	4.8		
	2	4.1		
			5.350	
	3	6.0		5.475
			5.600	
	4	6.5		5.738
			5.875	
2	1	5.8		5.975
			6.075	
	2	5.2		6.188
			6.300	
	3	6.8		6.325
			6.350	
	4	7.4		6.400
			6.450	
3	1	6.0		6.538
			6.625	
	2	5.6		6.675
			6.725	
	3	7.5		6.763
			6.800	
	4	7.8		6.838
			6.875	
4	1	6.3		6.938
			7.000	
	2	5.9		7.075
			7.150	
	3	8.0		
	4	8.4		

Let us pause for a moment to consider what the moving averages in Table 16.8 tell us about this time series. A plot of the actual time series values and the corresponding centered moving average is shown in Figure 16.12. Note particularly how the centered moving average values tend to "smooth out" the fluctuations in the time series. Since the moving average values are for four quarters of data, they do not include the fluctuations due to seasonal influences. Each point in the centered moving average represents what the value of the time series would be if there were no seasonal or irregular influence.

By dividing each time series observation by the corresponding centered moving average value we can identify the seasonal-irregular effect in the time series. For example, the third-quarter of year 1 shows $6.0/5.475 = 1.096$ as the combined seasonal-irregular component. The resulting seasonal-irregular values for the entire time series values are summarized in Table 16.9.

Consider the third quarter. The results from years 1, 2, and 3 show third-quarter values of 1.096, 1.075, and 1.109, respectively. Thus in all cases the seasonal-irregular component appears to have an above average influence in the third quarter. Since the year-to-year fluctuations in the seasonal-irregular component can be attributed primarily to the irregular component, we can average the computed values to eliminate the irregular influence and obtain an estimate of the third-quarter seasonal influence:

$$\text{Seasonal effect of third quarter} = \frac{1.096 + 1.075 + 1.109}{3} = 1.09$$

FIGURE 16.12

Graph of Quarterly Television Set Sales Time Series and Centered Moving Average

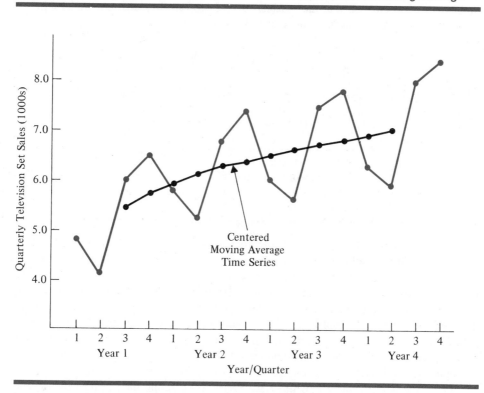

TABLE 16.9

Seasonal-Irregular Factors for the Television Set Sales Time Series

Year	Quarter	Sales (1000s)	Centered Moving Average	Seasonal-Irregular Component
1	1	4.8		
	2	4.1		
	3	6.0	5.475	1.096
	4	6.5	5.738	1.133
2	1	5.8	5.975	0.971
	2	5.2	6.188	0.840
	3	6.8	6.325	1.075
	4	7.4	6.400	1.156
3	1	6.0	6.538	0.918
	2	5.6	6.675	0.839
	3	7.5	6.763	1.109
	4	7.8	6.838	1.141
4	1	6.3	6.938	0.908
	2	5.9	7.075	0.834
	3	8.0		
	4	8.4		

We refer to 1.09 as the *seasonal index* for the third quarter. In Table 16.10 we summarize the calculations involved in computing the seasonal indexes for the television set sales time series. Thus we see that the seasonal indexes for all four quarters are as follows: quarter 1, 0.93; quarter 2, 0.84; quarter 3, 1.09; and quarter 4, 1.14.

TABLE 16.10
Seasonal Index Calculations for the Television Set Sales Time
Series

Quarter	Seasonal-Irregular Component Values $(S_t I_t)$	Seasonal Index (S_t)
1	0.971, 0.918, 0.908	0.93
2	0.840, 0.839, 0.834	0.84
3	1.096, 1.075, 1.109	1.09
4	1.133, 1.156, 1.141	1.14

Interpretation of the values in Table 16.10 provides some observations about the "seasonal" component in television set sales. The best sales quarter is the fourth quarter, with sales averaging 14% above the average quarterly level. The worst, or slowest, sales quarter is the second quarter, with its seasonal index of 0.84, showing the sales average 16% below the average quarterly sales. The seasonal component corresponds nicely to the intuitive expectation that television viewing interest and thus television purchase patterns tend to peak in the fourth quarter, with its coming winter season and fewer outdoor activities. The low second-quarter sales reflect the reduced television interest resulting from the spring and presummer activities of the potential customers.

One final adjustment is sometimes necessary in obtaining the seasonal index. The multiplicative model requires that the average seasonal index equal 1.00; that is, the sum of the four seasonal indexes in Table 16.10 must equal 4.00. This is necessary if the seasonal effects are to even out over the year, as they must. The average of the seasonal indexes in our example is equal to 1.00, and hence this type of adjustment is not necessary. In other cases a slight adjustment may be necessary. The adjustment can be made by simply multiplying each seasonal index by the number of seasons divided by the sum of the unadjusted seasonal indexes. For example, for quarterly data we would multiply each seasonal index by 4/(sum of the unadjusted seasonal indexes). Some of the problems at the end of the chapter will require this adjustment in order to obtain the appropriate seasonal factors.

Deseasonalizing the Time Series

Often the purpose of finding seasonal indexes is to remove the seasonal effects from a time series. This process is referred to as *deseasonalizing the time series*. Economic time series adjusted for seasonal variations (deseasonalized time series) are often reported in publications such as the *Survey of Current Business* and the *Wall Street Journal*. Using the notation of the multiplicative model, we have

$$Y_t = T_t \times S_t \times I_t$$

By dividing each time series observation by the corresponding seasonal index we have removed the effect of season from the time series. The deseasonalized time series for television set sales is summarized in Table 16.11. A graph of the deseasonalized television set sales time series is shown in Figure 16.13.

TABLE 16.11
Deseasonalized Time Series for Television Set Sales

Year	Quarter	Sales (1000s) (Y_t)	Seasonal Index (S_t)	Deseasonalized Sales $(Y_t/S_t = T_tI_t)$
1	1	4.8	0.93	5.16
	2	4.1	0.84	4.88
	3	6.0	1.09	5.50
	4	6.5	1.14	5.70
2	1	5.8	0.93	6.24
	2	5.2	0.84	6.19
	3	6.8	1.09	6.24
	4	7.4	1.14	6.49
3	1	6.0	0.93	6.45
	2	5.6	0.84	6.67
	3	7.5	1.09	6.88
	4	7.8	1.14	6.84
4	1	6.3	0.93	6.77
	2	5.9	0.84	7.02
	3	8.0	1.09	7.34
	4	8.4	1.14	7.37

FIGURE 16.13
Deseasonalized Television Set Sales Time Series

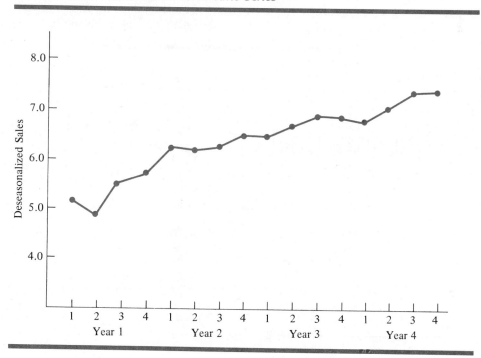

Using the Deseasonalized Time Series to Identify Trend

Looking at Figure 16.13, we see that while the graph shows some up-and-down movement over the past 16 quarters, the time series seems to have an upward linear trend. Now to identify this trend, we can use the same procedure we introduced for identifying trend when forecasting with annual data; in this case, since we have deseasonalized the data, quarterly sales values can be used. Thus for a linear trend the estimated sales volume expressed as a function of time can be written

$$T_t = b_0 + b_1 t$$

where

T_t = trend value for television set sales in period t

b_0 = intercept of the trend line

b_1 = slope of the trend line

As before, we will let $t = 1$ for the time of the first observation on the time series data, $t = 2$ for the time of the second observation, and so on. Thus for the deseasonalized television set sales time series $t = 1$ corresponds to the first deseasonalized quarterly sales value and $t = 16$ corresponds to the most recent deseasonalized quarterly sales value. The formulas for computing the value of b_0 and the value of b_1 are shown again

$$b_1 = \frac{\Sigma\, tY_t - (\Sigma\, t\, \Sigma\, Y_t)/n}{\Sigma\, t^2 - (\Sigma\, t)^2/n}$$

$$b_0 = \bar{Y} - b_1 \bar{t}$$

Note, however, that Y_t now refers to the deseasonalized time series value at time t and not the actual value of the time series. Using the given relationships for b_0 and b_1 and the deseasonalized sales data of Table 16.11, we have the following calculations:

t	Y_t (Deseasonalized)	tY_t	t^2
1	5.16	5.16	1
2	4.88	9.76	4
3	5.50	16.50	9
4	5.70	22.80	16
5	6.24	31.20	25
6	6.19	37.14	36
7	6.24	43.68	49
8	6.49	51.92	64
9	6.45	58.05	81
10	6.67	66.70	100
11	6.88	75.68	121
12	6.84	82.08	144
13	6.77	88.01	169
14	7.02	98.28	196
15	7.34	110.10	225
16	7.37	117.92	256
Totals 136	101.74	914.98	1496

$$\bar{t} = \frac{136}{16} = 8.5$$

$$\overline{Y} = \frac{101.74}{16} = 6.359$$

$$b_1 = \frac{914.98 - (136)(101.74)/16}{1496 - (136)^2/16} = \frac{50.19}{340} = 0.148$$

$$b_0 = 6.359 - 0.148(8.5) = 5.101$$

Therefore,

$$T_t = 5.101 + 0.148t$$

is the expression for the linear trend component of the time series.

The slope of 0.148 indicates that over the past 16 quarters, the firm has experienced an average deseasonalized growth in sales of around 148 sets per quarter. If we assume that the past 16-quarter trend in sales data is a reasonably good indicator of the future, then this equation can be used to project the trend component of the time series for future quarters. For example, substituting $t = 17$ into the equation yields next quarter's trend projection, T_{17}:

$$T_{17} = 5.101 + 0.148(17) = 7.617$$

Using the trend component only, we would forecast sales of 7617 television sets for the next quarter. In a similar fashion, if we were to use the trend component only, we would forecast sales of 7765, 7913, and 8061 television sets in quarters 18, 19, and 20, respectively.

Seasonal Adjustments

Now that we have a forecast of sales for each of the next four quarters based upon trend, we must adjust these forecasts to account for the effect of season. For example, since the seasonal index for the first quarter is 0.93, the forecast for the first quarter of year 5 can be obtained by multiplying the forecast based upon trend ($T_{17} = 7617$) times the seasonal index (0.93). Thus the forecast for the next quarter is 7617(0.93) = 7084. Table 16.12 shows the quarterly forecast for quarters 17, 18, 19, and 20. The quarterly forecasts show the high volume fourth quarter with a 9190 unit forecast, while the low volume second quarter has a 6523-unit forecast.

TABLE 16.12
Quarter-by-Quarter Short-Range Forecasts for the Television Set Sales Time Series

Year	Quarter	Trend Forecast	Seasonal Index (see Table 16.10)	Quarterly Forecast
5	1	7617	0.93	(7617)(0.93) = 7084
	2	7765	0.84	(7765)(0.84) = 6523
	3	7913	1.09	(7913)(1.09) = 8625
	4	8061	1.14	(8061)(1.14) = 9190

Models Based on Monthly Data

The television set sales example provided in this section used quarterly data to illustrate the computation of seasonal indexes with relatively few computations. Many businesses use monthly rather than quarterly forecasts. In such cases the procedures introduced in this section can be applied with minor modifications. First, a 12-month moving average replaces the four-quarter moving average; second, 12 monthly seasonal indexes, rather than four quarterly seasonal indexes, will need to be computed. Other than these changes, the computational and forecasting procedures are identical. Problem 18 at the end of the chapter asks you to develop monthly seasonal indexes for a situation requiring monthly forecasts.

Cyclical Component

Mathematically the multiplicative model of (16.9) can be expanded to include a cyclical component as follows:

$$Y_t = T_t \times C_t \times S_t \times I_t \tag{16.10}$$

Just as with the seasonal component, the cyclical component is expressed as a percent of trend. As mentioned in Section 16.1, this component is attributable to multiyear cycles in the time series. It is analogous to the seasonal component, but over a longer period of time. However, because of the length of time involved and the varying length of cycles, it is often difficult to obtain enough relevant data to estimate the cyclical component. We leave further discussion of the cyclical component to texts on forecasting methods.

16.5   FORECASTING USING REGRESSION MODELS

Regression analysis is a statistical technique that can be used to develop forecasts based upon the relationship between two or more variables. In regression notation and terminology, we let y indicate the *dependent* or *response* variable. This is the variable whose value we wish to forecast. The forecast of y will be based on one or more *independent* or *predictor* variables denoted by $x_1, x_2, \ldots, x_n$. If we can obtain a sample of data for all variables involved, regression analysis will provide an equation that can be used to forecast the value of y given the values of $x_1, x_2, \ldots, x_n$. In this section we restrict our attention to regression models involving one independent variable.

To demonstrate the use of regression analysis in forecasting, let us consider the sales forecasting problem faced by Armand's Pizza, Inc. Armand's Pizza, Inc. is a chain of Italian-food restaurants located in a five-state area. One of the most successful locations for Armand's has been near college campuses. Prior to opening a new restaurant Armand's management requires a forecast of the yearly sales revenues. Such an estimate is used in planning the appropriate restaurant capacity, making initial staffing decisions, and deciding whether the potential revenue justifies the cost of operation. Since no past data are available on sales at a new store, Armand's cannot use time series data to develop the forecast.

Armand's management believes that annual sales revenue is related to the size of the student population on the nearby campus. On an intuitive basis, management believes that restaurants located near large campuses generate more revenue than those located near small campuses. If a relationship can be established between sales revenue and the size of the campus population, Armand's can use the size of the campus population to predict revenues for the new restaurant. To evaluate the relationship between annual sales y and student population x, Armand's collected data from a sample of 10 of its restaurants located near college campuses. These data are summarized in Table 16.13. For example, we see that restaurant 1, with $y = 58$ and $x = 2$, had \$58,000 in sales revenue and was located near a campus with 2000 students.

TABLE 16.13

Data on Student Population and Annual Sales for 10 Armand's Restaurants

Restaurant	y = Annual Sales ($1000s)	x = Student Population (1000s)
1	58	2
2	105	6
3	88	8
4	118	8
5	117	12
6	137	16
7	157	20
8	169	20
9	149	22
10	202	26

Figure 16.14 shows graphically the data presented in Table 16.13. The size of the student population is shown on the horizontal axis, with annual sales on the vertical axis. A graph such as this is known as a *scatter diagram*. The usual practice is to plot the independent variable on the horizontal axis and the dependent variable on the vertical axis. The advantage of a scatter diagram is that it provides an overview of the data and enables us to draw preliminary conclusions about a possible relationship between the variables.

What preliminary conclusions can we draw from Figure 16.14? It appears that low sales volumes are associated with small student populations and higher sales volumes are associated with larger student populations. It also appears that the relationship between the two variables can be approximated by a straight line. In Figure 16.15 we have drawn a straight line through the data that appear to provide a good linear approximation of the relationship between the variables. However, observe that the relationship is not perfect. Indeed, few if any of the data items fall exactly on the line. However, if we can develop the mathematical expression for this line, we may be able to use it to predict or forecast the value of y corresponding to each possible value of x. We will refer to the resulting equation of the line as the *estimated regression equation*.

FIGURE 16.14
Scatter Diagram of Annual Sales versus Student Population

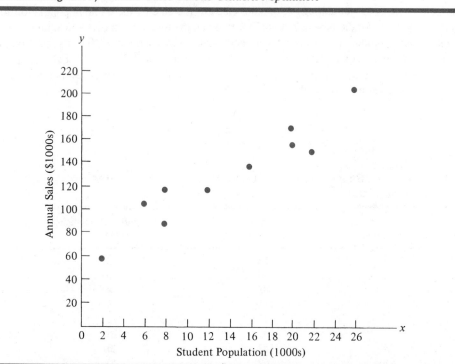

Using the least squares method of estimation, we can develop the following estimated regression equation:

$$\hat{y} = b_0 + b_1 x \qquad (16.11)$$

where

$\hat{y}$ = estimated value of the dependent variable (sales revenue $)
b_0 = intercept of the estimated regression equation
b_1 = slope of the estimated regression equation
x = value of the independent variable (student population)

Using the sample data, the intercept b_0 and slope b_1 can be computed using the following expression

$$b_1 = \frac{\sum x_i y_i - (\sum x_i \sum y_i)/n}{\sum x_i^2 - (\sum x_i)^2/n} \qquad (16.12)$$

$$b_0 = \bar{y} - b_1 \bar{x} \qquad (16.13)$$

FIGURE 16.15
Straight-Line Approximation

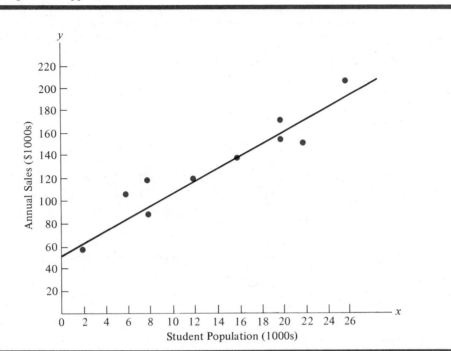

where

x_i = value of the independent variable for the ith observation

y_i = value of the dependent variable for the ith observation

$\bar{x}$ = mean value for the independent variable

$\bar{y}$ = mean value for the dependent variable

n = total number of observations

Some of the calculations necessary to develop the least squares estimated regression equation for the Armand's Pizza problem are shown in Table 16.14. In our example there are 10 restaurants or observations; hence $n = 10$. Using (16.12) and (16.13), we can now compute the slope and intercept of the estimated regression equation for Armand's Restaurants. The calculation of the slope b_1 proceeds as follows:

$$b_1 = \frac{\Sigma x_i y_i - (\Sigma x_i \Sigma y_i)/n}{\Sigma x_i^2 - (\Sigma x_i)^2/n}$$

$$= \frac{21{,}040 - (140)(1300)/10}{2528 - (140)^2/10}$$

$$= \frac{2840}{568}$$

$$= 5$$

TABLE 16.14
Calculations Necessary to Develop the Least Squares
Estimated Regression Equation for Armand's Pizza

Restaurant (i)	y_i	x_i	$x_i y_i$	x_i^2
1	58	2	116	4
2	105	6	630	36
3	88	8	704	64
4	118	8	944	64
5	117	12	1,404	144
6	137	16	2,192	256
7	157	20	3,140	400
8	169	20	3,380	400
9	149	22	3,278	484
10	202	26	5,252	676
Totals	1300	140	21,040	2528
	Σy_i	Σx_i	$\Sigma x_i y_i$	Σx_i^2

The calculation of the y intercept b_0 is as follows:

$$\bar{x} = \frac{\Sigma x_i}{n} = \frac{140}{10} = 14$$

$$\bar{y} = \frac{\Sigma y_i}{n} = \frac{1300}{10} = 130$$

$$b_0 = \bar{y} - b_1\bar{x}$$
$$= 130 - 5(14)$$
$$= 60$$

Thus the estimated regression equation found by using the method of least squares is

$$\hat{y} = 60 + 5x$$

In Figure 16.16 we show the graph of this equation.

The slope of the estimated regression equation ($b_1 = 5$) is positive, implying that as student population increases, annual sales increase. In fact we can conclude (since sales are measured in $1000s and student population in 1000s) that an increase in the student population of 1000 is associated with an increase of $5000 in expected annual sales; that is, sales are expected to increase by $5.00 per student.

If we believe that the least squares estimated regression equation adequately describes the relationship between x and y, then it would seem reasonable to use the estimated regression equation to forecast the value of y for a given value of x. For example, if we

FIGURE 16.16
FIGURE 16.16
Graph of the Estimated Regression Equation for Armand's Pizza: $\hat{y} = 60 + 5x$

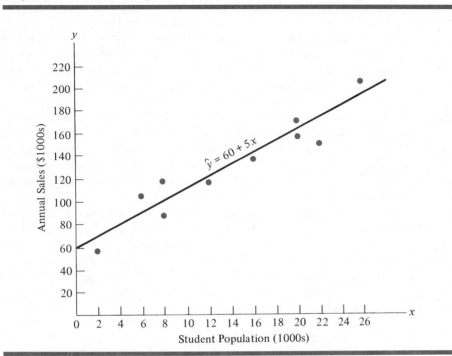

wanted to forecast annual sales for a new restaurant location near a campus with 16,000 students we would compute

$$\hat{y} = 60 + 5(16)$$
$$= 140$$

Hence we would forecast sales of $140,000 per year.

16.6 QUALITATIVE APPROACHES TO FORECASTING

In the previous sections we have discussed several types of quantitative forecasting methods. Since each of these techniques requires historical data on the variable of interest, in situations where no historical data are available these techniques cannot be applied. Furthermore, even when historical data are available a significant change in environmental conditions affecting the time series may make the use of past data questionable in predicting future values of the time series. For example, a government-imposed gas rationing program would cause one to question the validity of a gas sales forecast based on past data. Qualitative forecasting techniques offer an alternative in these, and other, cases.

One of the most commonly used qualitative forecasting methods is the *Delphi approach*. This technique, originally developed by a research group at the Rand Corporation, attempts to obtain forecasts through ''group consensus.'' In the usual application of this technique, the members of a panel of experts—all of whom are physically separated from and unknown to each other—are asked to respond to a series of questionnaires. The responses from the first questionnaire are tabulated and used to prepare a second questionnaire, which contains information and opinions of the whole group. Each respondent is then asked to reconsider and possibly revise his or her previous response in light of the group information that has been provided. This basic process continues until the coordinator feels that some degree of consensus has been reached. Note that the goal of the Delphi approach is not to produce a single answer as output but to produce instead a relatively narrow spread of opinions within which the ''majority'' of experts concur.

The qualitative procedure referred to as *scenario writing* consists of developing a conceptual scenario of the future based upon a well defined set of assumptions. Thus by starting with a different set of assumptions many different future scenarios can be presented. The job of the decision maker is to decide which scenario is most likely to occur in the future and then to make decisions accordingly.

Subjective or intuitive qualitative approaches are based upon the ability of the human mind to process a variety of information that is, in most cases, difficult to quantify. These techniques are often used in group work, wherein a committee or panel seeks to develop new ideas or solve complex problems through a series of ''brainstorming sessions.'' In such sessions individuals are freed from the usual group restrictions of peer pressure and criticism, since any idea or opinion can be presented without regard to its relevancy and, even more importantly, without fear of criticism.

Summary

The purpose of this chapter has been to provide an introduction to the basic methods of time series analysis and forecasting. First we showed that in order to explain the behavior of a time series, it is often helpful to think of the time series as consisting of four separate components: trend, cyclical, seasonal, and irregular. By isolating these components and measuring their apparent effect, it is possible to forecast future values of the time series.

We discussed how smoothing methods can be used to forecast a time series that exhibits no significant trend, seasonal, or cyclical effect. The moving averages approach consists of computing an average of past data values and then using this average as the forecast for the next period. The exponential smoothing method is a more preferred technique that uses a weighted average of past time series values to compute a forecast.

When the time series exhibits only a long-term trend, we showed how regression analysis could be used to make trend projections. When both trend and seasonal influences are significant, we showed how a multiplicative model could be used to isolate the effects of the two factors and prepare better forecasts. Finally, regression analysis was described as a procedure for developing so-called causal forecasting methods. A causal forecasting method is one that relates the time series value (dependent variable) to other independent variables that are believed to explain (cause) the time series behavior.

Qualitative forecasting methods were discussed as approaches that could be used when little or no historical data were available. These methods are also considered most appropriate when the past pattern of the time series is not expected to continue into the future.

It is important to realize that time series analysis and forecasting is a major field in its own right. In this chapter we have just scratched the surface of the field of time series and forecasting methodology.

Glossary

Time series A set of observations measured at successive points in time or over successive periods of time.

Forecast A projection or prediction of future values of a time series.

Multiplicative time series model A model that assumes that the separate components can be multiplied together to identify the time series value. When the components of trend, seasonal, and irregular are assumed present, we obtain $Y_t = T_t \times S_t \times I_t$.

Trend The long-run shift or movement in the time series observable over several periods of time.

Cyclical component The component of the time series model that results in periodic above-trend and below-trend behavior of the time series lasting more than 1 year.

Seasonal component The component of the time series model that shows a periodic pattern over 1 year or less.

Irregular component The component of the time series model that reflects the random variation of the actual time series values beyond what can be explained by the trend, cyclical, and seasonal components.

Moving averages A method of forecasting or smoothing a time series by averaging each successive group of data points.

Weighted moving averages A method of forecasting or smoothing a time series by computing a weighted average of past data values. The sum of the weights must equal one.

Exponential smoothing A forecasting technique that uses a weighted average of past time series values in order to arrive at smoothed time series values which can be used as forecasts.

Smoothing constant A parameter of the exponential-smoothing model that provides the weight given to the most recent time series value in the calculation of the forecast value.

Mean square error (MSE) One approach to measuring the accuracy of a forecasting model. This measure is the average of the sum of the squared difference between the forecast values and the actual time series values.

Mean absolute deviation (MAD) A measure of forecast accuracy. MAD is the average of the sum of the absolute value of the forecast errors.

Deseasonalized time series A time series that has had the effect of season removed by dividing each original time series observation by the corresponding seasonal index.

Causal forecasting methods Forecasting methods that relate a time series value to other variables that are believed to explain or cause its behavior. Regression analysis is a commonly used causal forecasting method.

Delphi approach A qualitative forecasting method that obtains forecasts through "group consensus."

Scenario writing A qualitative forecasting method that consists of developing a conceptual scenario of the future based upon a well-defined set of assumptions.

Problems

1. Refer to the gasoline sales time series data in Table 16.1.
   a. Compute 4- and 5-week moving averages for the time series.
   b. Compute the mean square error (MSE) for the 4- and 5-week moving average forecasts.

    c. What appears to be the best number of weeks of past data to use in the moving average computation? Remember that the MSE for the 3-week moving average is 10.22.

2. Refer again to the gasoline sales time series data in Table 16.1.

    a. Using a weight of $\frac{1}{2}$ for the most recent observation, $\frac{1}{3}$ for the second most recent, and $\frac{1}{6}$ for the third most recent, compute a 3-week weighted moving average for the time series.

    b. Compute the mean square error for the weighted moving average in part a. Do you prefer this weighted moving average to the unweighted moving average? Remember that the MSE for the unweighted moving average is 10.22.

    c. Suppose you are allowed to choose any weights as long as they sum to one. Could you always find a set of weights that would make the MSE smaller for a weighted moving average than an unweighted moving average? Why or why not?

3. Use the gasoline sales time series data from Table 16.1 to show the exponential smoothing forecasts using $\alpha = 0.1$. Using the mean square error criterion, would you prefer a smoothing constant of $\alpha = 0.1$ or $\alpha = 0.2$ for the gasoline sales time series?

4. Using a smoothing constant of $\alpha = 0.2$ equation (16.2) shows that the forecast for the 13th week of the gasoline sales data from Table 16.1 is given by $F_{13} = 0.2Y_{12} + 0.8F_{12}$. However, the forecast for week 12 is given by $F_{12} = 0.2Y_{11} + 0.8Y_{11}$. Thus we could combine these two results to show that the forecast for the 13th week can be written

$$F_{13} = 0.2Y_{12} + 0.8(0.2Y_{11} + 0.8F_{11}) = 0.2Y_{12} + 0.16Y_{11} + 0.64F_{11}$$

    a. Making use of the fact that $F_{11} = 0.2Y_{10} + 0.8F_{10}$ (and similarly for F_{10} and F_9), continue to expand the expression for F_{13} until it is written in terms of the past data values Y_{12}, Y_{11}, Y_{10}, Y_9, Y_8, and the forecast for period 8.

    b. Refer to the coefficients or weights for the past data Y_{12}, Y_{11}, Y_{10}, Y_9, and Y_8; what observation do you make about how exponential smoothing weights past data values in arriving at new forecasts? Compare this weighting pattern with the weighting pattern of the moving averages method.

5. The following time series shows the sales of a particular product over the past 12 months:

Month	Sales
1	105
2	135
3	120
4	105
5	90
6	120
7	145
8	140
9	100
10	80
11	100
12	110

Use $\alpha = 0.3$ to compute the exponential smoothing values for the time series.

6. Analyze the forecasting errors for the time series in problem 5 by using a smoothing constant of 0.5. Does a smoothing constant of 0.3 or 0.5 appear to provide the better forecasts?

7. The number of component parts used in a production process each week in the last 10 weeks showed the following:

Week	Parts	Week	Parts
1	200	6	210
2	350	7	280
3	250	8	350
4	360	9	290
5	250	10	320

Use a smoothing constant of 0.25 and develop the exponential smoothing values for this time series. Indicate your forecast for next week.

8. A chain of grocery stores experienced the following weekly demand (cases) for a particular brand of automatic-dishwasher detergent:

Week	Demand
1	22
2	18
3	23
4	21
5	17
6	24
7	20
8	19
9	18
10	21

Use exponential smoothing with $\alpha = 0.2$ in order to develop a forecast for week 11.

9. United Dairies, Inc. supplies milk to several independent grocers throughout Dade County in Florida. Management of United Dairies would like to develop a forecast of the number of half-gallons of milk sold per week. Sales data for the past 12 weeks are as follows:

Week	Sales (units)
1	2750
2	3100
3	3250
4	2800
5	2900
6	3050
7	3300
8	3100
9	2950
10	3000
11	3200
12	3150

Use the above 12 weeks of data and exponential smoothing with $\alpha = 0.4$ to develop a forecast of demand for the 13th week.

10. Average attendance figures at home football games for a major university show the following 7-year pattern:

Year	Attendance
1	28,000
2	30,000
3	31,500
4	30,400
5	30,500
6	32,200
7	30,800

Develop the trend expression shown in equation (16.4) for this time series.

11. Automobile sales at B. J. Scott Motors, Inc. provided the following 10-year time series:

Year	Sales
1	400
2	390
3	320
4	340
5	270
6	260
7	300
8	320
9	340
10	370

Plot the time series and comment on the appropriateness of a linear trend. What type of functional form do you believe would be most appropriate for the trend pattern of this time series?

12. The president of a small manufacturing firm has been concerned about the continual growth in manufacturing costs over the past several years. Shown below is a time series of the cost per unit for the firm's leading product over the past 8 years:

Year	Cost/Unit ($)
1	20.00
2	24.50
3	28.20
4	27.50
5	26.60
6	30.00
7	31.00
8	36.00

a. Show a graph of this time series. Does a linear trend appear to exist?
b. Develop a linear trend expression for the above time series. What is the average cost increase that the firm has been realizing per year?

13. The enrollment data for a state college for the past 6 years are shown below:

Year	Enrollment
1	20,500
2	20,200
3	19,500
4	19,000
5	19,100
6	18,800

Develop a linear trend expression and comment on what is happening to enrollment at this institution.

14. Canton Supplies, Inc. is a service firm that employs approximately 100 individuals. Because of the necessity of meeting monthly cash obligations, management of Canton Supplies would like to develop a forecast of monthly cash requirements. Due to a recent change in operating policy, only the past 7 months of data were considered to be relevant. Use the historical data shown below to develop a forecast of cash requirements for each of the next 2 months.

Month	1	2	3	4	5	6	7
Cash Required ($1000)	205	212	218	224	230	240	246

15. The Costello Music Company has been in business for 5 years. During this time the sale of electric organs has grown from 12 units in the first year to 76 units in the most recent year. Fred Costello, the firm's owner, would like to develop a forecast of organ sales for the coming year. The historical data are shown below:

Year	1	2	3	4	5
Sales	12	28	34	50	76

a. Show a graph of this time series. Does a linear trend appear to exist?
b. Develop a linear trend expression for the above time series. What is the average increase in sales that the firm has been realizing per year?

16. Hudson Marine has been an authorized dealer for C&D marine radios for the past 7 years. The number of radios sold each year is shown below:

Year	1	2	3	4	5	6	7
Number Sold	35	50	75	90	105	110	130

a. Show a graph of this time series. Does a linear trend appear to exist?
b. Develop a linear trend for the above time series.
c. Use the linear trend developed in part b and prepare a forecast for annual sales in year 8.

17. The quarterly sales data for a college textbook over the past 3 years are as follows:

	Year 1	Year 2	Year 3
Quarter 1	1690	1800	1850
Quarter 2	940	900	1100
Quarter 3	2625	2900	2930
Quarter 4	2500	2360	2615

a. Show the four-quarter moving average values for this time series. Plot both the original time series and the moving averages on the same graph.
b. Compute seasonal indexes for the four quarters.
c. When does the textbook publisher experience the largest seasonal effect? Does this appear reasonable? Explain.

18. Identify the monthly seasonal indexes for the following 3 years of expenses for a six-unit apartment house in souhern Florida. Use a 12-month moving average calculation.

Month	Year 1	Year 2	Year 3
January	170	180	195
February	180	205	210
March	205	215	230
April	230	245	280
May	240	265	290
June	315	330	390
July	360	400	420
August	290	335	330
September	240	260	290
October	240	270	295
November	230	255	280
December	195	220	250

19. Refer to the Hudson Marine problem presented in problem 16. Suppose that the quarterly sales values for the 7 years of historical data are as follows:

	Quarter 1	Quarter 2	Quarter 3	Quarter 4	Total Sales
Year 1	6	15	10	4	35
Year 2	10	18	15	7	50
Year 3	14	26	23	12	75
Year 4	19	28	25	18	90
Year 5	22	34	28	21	105
Year 6	24	36	30	20	110
Year 7	28	40	35	27	130

a. Show the four-quarter moving average values for this time series. Plot both the original time series and the moving average series on the same graph.

b. Compute the seasonal indexes for the four quarters.

c. When does Hudson Marine experience the largest seasonal effect? Does this seem reasonable? Explain.

20. Consider the Costello Music Company problem presented in problem 15. The quarterly sales data are shown below:

	Quarter 1	Quarter 2	Quarter 3	Quarter 4	Total Yearly Sales
Year 1	4	2	1	5	12
Year 2	6	4	4	14	28
Year 3	10	3	5	16	34
Year 4	12	9	7	22	50
Year 5	18	10	13	35	76

a. Compute the seasonal indexes for the four quarters.

b. When does Costello Music experience the largest seasonal effect? Does this appear reasonable? Explain.

21. Refer to the Hudson Marine data presented in problem 19.

a. Deseasonalize the data and use the deseasonalized time series to identify the trend.

b. Use the results of part a to develop a quarterly forecast for next year based upon trend.

c. Use the seasonal indexes developed in problem 19 to adjust the forecasts developed in part b to account for the effect of season.

22. Consider the Costello Music Company time series presented in problem 20.

a. Deseasonalize the data and use the deseasonalized time series to identify the trend.

b. Use the results of part a to develop a quarterly forecast for next year based upon trend.

c. Use the seasonal indexes developed in problem 20 to adjust the forecasts developed in part b to account for the effect of season.

23. Eddie's Restaurants collected the following data on the relationship between advertising and sales at a sample of five restaurants:

Advertising Expenditures ($1000s)	Sales ($1000s)
1.0	19.0
4.0	44.0
6.0	40.0
10.0	52.0
14.0	53.0

a. Let x equal advertising expenditures ($1000s) and y equal sales ($1000s). Use the method of least squares to develop a straight line approximation to the relationship between the two variables.

b. Use the equation developed in part a to forecast sales for an advertising expenditure of $8000.

24. The management of a chain of fast-food restaurants would like to investigate the relationship between the daily sales volume of a company restaurant and the number of competitor restaurants within a 1-mile radius of the firm's restaurant. The following data have been collected:

Number of Competitors within 1 Mile	Sales ($)
1	3600
1	3300
2	3100
3	2900
3	2700
4	2500
5	2300
5	2000

a. Develop the least squares estimated regression equation that relates daily sales volume to the number of competitor restaurants within a 1-mile radius.

b. Use the estimated regression equation developed in part a to forecast the daily sales volume for a particular company restaurant that has four competitors within a 1-mile radius.

25. In a manufacturing process the assembly line speed (feet/minute) was thought to affect the number of defective parts found during the inspection process. To test this theory, management devised a situation where the same batch of parts was inspected visually at a variety of line speeds. The following data were collected:

Line Speed	Number of Defective Parts Found
20	21
20	19
40	15
30	16
60	14
40	17

a. Develop the estimated regression equation that relates line speed to the number of defective parts found.

b. Use the equation developed in part a to forecast the number of defective parts found for a line speed of 50 feet per minute.

——— *Case Problem* ———

FORECASTING SALES

The Vintage Restaurant is located on Captiva Island, a resort community located near Fort Meyers, Fla. The restaurant, which is owned and operated by Karen Payne, has just completed its third year of operation. During this period of time, Karen has sought to establish a reputation for the restaurant as a high-quality dining establishment that specializes in fresh seafood. The efforts made by Karen and her staff have proved successful and her restaurant has become one of the best and fastest growing restaurants on the island.

Karen has concluded that in order to plan better for the growth of the restaurant in the future, it is necessary to develop a system that will enable her to forecast food and beverage sales by month for up to 1 year in advance. Karen has available data on the total food and beverage sales that were realized during the previous 3 years of operation. These data are provided below:

Food and Beverage Sales for the Vintage Restaurant ($1000s)

Month	First Year	Second Year	Third Year
January	242	263	282
February	235	238	255
March	232	247	265
April	178	193	205
May	184	193	210
June	140	149	160
July	145	157	166
August	152	161	174
September	110	122	126
October	130	130	148
November	152	167	173
December	206	230	235

MANAGERIAL REPORT

Perform an analysis of the sales data for the Vintage Restaurant. Prepare a report for Karen that summarizes your findings, forecasts, and recommendations. Include information on the following:

1. A graph of the time series.
2. An analysis of the seasonality of the data. Include the seasonal indexes for each month and comment on the high seasonal and low seasonal sales months. Do the seasonal indexes make intuitive sense? Discuss.
3. Forecast sales for January through December of the fourth year.

4. Assume the January sales for the fourth year turned out to be $295,000. What was your forecast error? If this is a large error, Karen may be puzzled as to why there is such a difference between your forecast and the actual sales value. What can you do to resolve her uncertainty in the forecasting procedure?

5. Develop recommendations as to when the system that you have developed should be updated to account for new sales data that will occur.

6. Include any detailed calculations of your analysis in the appendix of your report.

Management Science in Practice
THE CINCINNATI GAS & ELECTRIC COMPANY*
Cincinnati, Ohio

The Cincinnati Gas Light and Coke Company was chartered by the State of Ohio on April 3, 1837. Under this charter the company manufactured gas by distillation of coal and sold it for lighting purposes. During the last quarter of the 19th century the company successfully marketed gas for lighting, heating, and cooking and as fuel for gas engines.

In 1901 the Cincinnati Gas Light and Coke Company and the Cincinnati Electric Light Company merged to form The Cincinnati Gas & Electric Company (CG&E). This new company was able to shift from manufactured gas to natural gas and adopt the rapidly emerging technologies in generating and distributing electricity. CG&E operated as a subsidiary of the Columbia Gas Electric Company from 1909 until 1944.

Today CG&E is a privately owned public utility serving approximately 370,000 gas customers and 600,000 electric customers. The company's service area covers approximately 3000 square miles in and around the Greater Cincinnati area.

FORECASTING AT CG&E

As in any modern company, forecasting at CG&E is an integral part of operating and managing the business. Depending upon the decision to be made, the forecasting techniques used range from judgment and graphical trend projections to sophisticated multiple regression models.

Forecasting in the utility industry offers some unique perspectives as compared to other industries. Since there are no finished-goods or in-process inventories of electricity, this product must be generated to meet the instantaneous requirements of the customers. Electrical shortages are not just lost sales, but "brownouts" or "blackouts." This situation places an unusual burden on the utility forecaster. On the positive side, the demand for energy and the sale of energy is more predictable than for many other products. Also, unlike the situation in a multiproduct firm, a great amount of forecasting effort and expertise can be concentrated on the two products: gas and electricity.

*The authors are indebted to Dr. Richard Evans, The Cincinnati Gas & Electric Company, Cincinnati, Ohio, for providing this application.

FORECASTING ELECTRIC ENERGY AND PEAK LOADS

The two types of forecasts discussed in this section are the long-range forecasts of electric peak load and electric energy. The largest observed electric demand for any given period, such as an hour, a day, a month, or a year, is defined as the peak load. The cumulative amount of energy generated and used over the period of an hour is referred to as electric energy.

Until the mid-1970s the seasonal pattern of both electric energy and electric peak load were very regular; the time series for both of these exhibited a fairly steady exponential growth. Business cycles had little noticeable effect on either. Perhaps the most serious shift in the behavior of these time series came from the increasing installation of air conditioning units in the Greater Cincinnati area. This fact caused an accelerated growth in the trend component and also in the relative magnitude of the summer peaks. Nevertheless, the two time series were very regular and generally quite predictable.

Trend projection was the most popular method used to forecast electric energy and electric peak load. The forecast accuracy was quite acceptable and even enviable when compared to forecast errors experienced in other industries.

A NEW ERA IN FORECASTING

In the mid-1970s a variety of actions by the government, the off-and-on energy shortages, and price signals to the consumer began to affect the consumption of electric energy. As a result the behavior of the peak load and electric energy time series became more and more unpredictable. Hence a simple trend projection forecasting model was no longer adequate. As a result a special forecasting model—reffered to as an econometric model—was developed by CG&E to better account for the behavior of these time series.

The purpose of the econometric model is to forecast the annual energy consumption by residential, commercial, and industrial classes of service. These forecasts are then used to develop forecasts of summer and winter peak loads. First energy consumption in the industrial and commercial classes is forecast. For an assumed level of economic activity, the projection of electric energy is made along with a forecast of employment in the area. The employment forecast is converted to a forecast of adult population through the use of unemployment rates and labor force participation rates. Household forecasts are then developed through the use of demographic statistics on the average number of persons per household. The resulting forecast of households is used as an indicator of residential customers.

At this point a comparison is made with the demographic projections for the area population. The differences between the residential customers forecast and the population forecast are reconciled to produce the final forecast of residential customers. This forecast becomes the principal independent variable in forecasting residential electric energy.

Summer and winter peak loads are then forecast by applying class peak contribution factors to the energy forecasts. The contributions that each class makes toward the peak are summed to establish the peak forecast.

A number of economic and demographic time series are used in the construction of the above econometric model. Simply speaking, the entire forecasting system is a compilation of several statistically verified multiple regression equations.

IMPACT AND VALUE OF THE FORECASTS

The forecast of the annual electric peak load guides the timing decisions for constructing future generating units. The financial impact of these decisions is great. For example, the last generating unit built by the company cost nearly $600 million and the interest rate on a recent first mortgage bond was 16%. At this rate, annual interest costs would be nearly $100 million. Obviously, a timing decision which leads to having the unit available no sooner than necessary is crucial.

The energy forecasts are important in other ways also. For example, purchases of coal and nuclear fuel for the generating units are based on the forecast levels of energy needed. The revenue from the electric operations of the company is determined from forecasted sales, which in turn enters into the planning of rate changes and external financing. These planning and decision-making processes are among the most important management activities in the company. It is imperative that the decision makers have the best forecast information available to assist them in arriving at these decisions.

Questions

1. Describe some of the unique perspectives associated with forecasting in the utility industry as compared with other industries.
2. Until the mid-1970s what type of forecasting procedure was used by CG&E? What necessitated a change?
3. Briefly describe CG&E's current approach to forecasting.
4. What are the benefits of accurate forecasts for CG&E?

17

Markov Processes

Markov process models are useful in studying the evolution of certain systems over repeated trials. These repeated trials are often successive time periods where the state or outcome of the system in any particular time period cannot be determined with certainty. Rather, a set of transition probabilities is used to describe the manner in which the system makes transitions from one period to the next. Hence we talk about the probability of the system being in a particular state at a given time period.

Markov processes have been used to describe the probability that a machine that is functioning in one period will continue to function or will break down in the next period. They have also been used to describe the probability that a consumer purchasing brand *A* in one period will purchase brand *B* in the next period. In this chapter we will study a marketing application of Markov process models that involves an analysis of the store-switching behavior of supermarket customers. As a second illustration of Markov process models, we will consider an accounting application that is concerned with the transitioning of accounts receivable dollars to different aging categories.

Since an in-depth treatment of Markov processes is beyond the scope of this text, our analysis in both illustrations will be restricted to Markov processes in which there are a finite number of states, the transition probabilities remain constant over time, and the probability of being in a particular state at any one time period depends only upon the state of the process in the immediately preceding period. Such Markov processes are often referred to as Markov chains with stationary transition probabilities.

17.1 MARKET SHARE ANALYSIS

Suppose that we are interested in analyzing the market share and customer loyalty for Murphy's Foodliner and Ashley's Supermarket, the only two grocery stores in a small town. We focus our attention on the sequence of shopping trips of one customer. We assume that the customer makes one shopping trip each week and that the customer will select either Murphy's Foodliner or Ashley's Supermarket, but not both, on each weekly trip.

Using the terminology of Markov processes, we refer to the weekly time periods or shopping trips as the *trials of the process*. Thus at each trial the customer will shop at either Murphy's Foodliner or Ashley's Supermarket. The particular store selected in a given week is referred to as the *state of the system* in that time period. Since the customer has two shopping alternatives at each trial, we say the system has two states. Since the number of states is finite, we can list and identify each state in detail. The two possible states are

State 1   The customer shops at Murphy's Foodliner
State 2   The customer shops at Ashley's Supermarket

If we say the system is in state 1 at trial 3, we are simply saying that the customer shops at Murphy's during the third weekly shopping period.

As we continue the shopping trip process into the future, we cannot say for certain where the customer will shop during a given week or trial. In fact, we realize that during any given week, the customer may be either a Murphy's customer or an Ashley's customer. However, using a Markov process model we will be able to compute the probability that the customer shops at each store during any time period. For example, we may find there is a 0.6 probability that the customer will shop at Ashley's during a particular week and a 0.4 probability that the customer will shop at Murphy's.

In order to determine the probabilities of the various states occurring at successive trials of the Markov process, we need information on the probability that a customer remains with the same store or switches to the competing store as the process continues from trial to trial or week to week.

Suppose as part of a market research study we collect data from 100 shoppers over a 10-week period. Suppose further that these data show each customer's weekly shopping-trip pattern in terms of the sequence of visits to Murphy's and Ashley's. In order to develop a Markov process model for the sequence of weekly shopping trips, we need to express the probability of selecting each store (state) in a given time period solely in terms of the store (state) that was selected during the previous time period. In reviewing the data, suppose we find that out of all customers who shopped at Murphy's in a given week, 90% shopped at Murphy's the following week while 10% switched to Ashley's. Suppose that similar data for the customers who shopped at Ashley's in a given week show that 80% shopped at Ashley's the following week while 20% switched to Murphy's. Probabilities based on these data are shown in Table 17.1. Since these are the probabilities that a customer moves, or makes a transition, from a state in a given period to a state in the following period, these probabilities are given the special name of *transition probabilities*.

An important property of the table of transition probabilities is that the sum of the entries in each row is 1; this indicates that each row of the table provides a probability distribution. For example, a customer who shops at Murphy's one week must shop at either Murphy's or Ashley's the next week. The entries in row 1 give the probabilities associated with each of these events. The 0.9 and 0.8 probabilities in Table 17.1 can be interpreted as measures of store loyalty in that they indicate the probability of a repeat visit to the same store. Similarly, the 0.1 and 0.2 probabilities are measures of the store-switching characteristics of customers.

It is important to realize that in developing a Markov process model for the problem, we are assuming that the transition probabilities will be the same for any customer and

TABLE 17.1
Transition Probabilities for Murphy's and Ashley's Grocery Stores

| | | Next Weekly Shopping Period | |
		Murphy's Foodliner	Ashley's Supermarket
Current Weekly Shopping Period	Murphy's Foodliner	0.9	0.1
	Ashley's Supermarket	0.2	0.8

that the transition probabilities will not change over time; that is, at any point in time, the transition probabilities can be used to assess the probability a customer will shop at Murphy's or Ashley's in the next period, given we know where the customer is shopping during the current time period.

Note that the table of transition probabilities, Table 17.1, has one row and one column for each state of the system. We will use the symbol p_{ij} to represent the individual transition probabilities and the symbol P to represent the matrix (table) of transition probabilities; that is,

p_{ij} = probability of making a transition from state i in a given time period to state j in the next time period

For the supermarket problem we have

$$P = \begin{bmatrix} p_{11} & p_{12} \\ p_{21} & p_{22} \end{bmatrix} = \begin{bmatrix} 0.9 & 0.1 \\ 0.2 & 0.8 \end{bmatrix}$$

Using the matrix of transition probabilities, we can now determine the probability that a customer will be a Murphy's or an Ashley's customer at some time period in the future. Let us begin by assuming that we have a customer whose last weekly shopping trip was to Murphy's. What is the probability that this customer will shop at Murphy's on the next weekly shopping trip, time period 1? In other words, what is the probability that the system will be in state 1 after the first transition? The matrix of transition probabilities indicates that this probability is $p_{11} = 0.9$.

Now let us consider the state of the system in period 2. A useful way of depicting what can happen on the second weekly shopping trip is to draw a tree diagram of the possible outcomes (see Figure 17.1). Using this tree diagram, we see that the probability that the customer shops at Murphy's during both the first and second weeks is (0.9)(0.9) = 0.81. Also, note that the probability of the customer switching to Ashley's on the first trip and then switching back to Murphy's on the second trip is (0.1)(0.2) = 0.02. Since these are the only two ways that the customer can be in state 1 (shopping at Murphy's) during the second period, the probability of the system being in state 1 during the second period is 0.81 + 0.02 = 0.83. Similarly, the probability of the system being in state 2 during the second period of the process is 0.09 + 0.08 = 0.17.

FIGURE 17.1
Tree Diagram Depicting Two Weekly Shopping Trips of a Customer Who Shopped Last at Murphy's

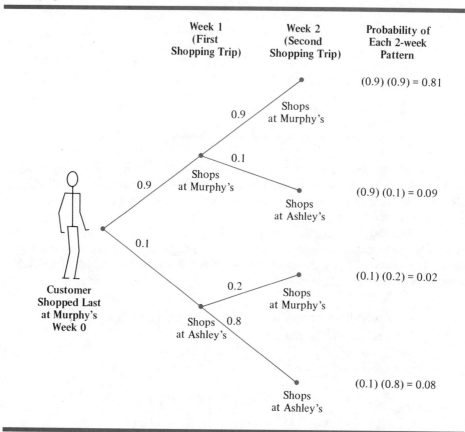

| | Week 1 (First Shopping Trip) | Week 2 (Second Shopping Trip) | Probability of Each 2-week Pattern |

As desirable as the tree diagram approach may be from an intuitive point of view, this approach becomes very cumbersome when we want to extend the analysis three, four, and so on, periods into the future. Fortunately, there is an easier way to calculate the probabilities of the system being in state 1 or state 2 for any subsequent period. First, we introduce notation that will allow us to represent the probability of the system being in state 1 or state 2 for any given period of time. Let

$$\pi_i(n) = \text{probability that the system is in state } i \text{ at the } n\text{th period}$$

Index denotes the state

Denotes the time period or number of transitions

For example, $\pi_1(1)$ would represent the probability of the system being in state 1 in period 1 (that is, after 1 transition), while $\pi_2(1)$ denotes the probability of the system being in state 2 after one transition. Since $\pi_i(n)$ is the probability that the system is in state i at period n, this probability is referred to as a *state probability*.

$\pi_1(0)$ and $\pi_2(0)$ will denote the probability of the system being in state 1 or state 2 at some initial or starting time period. Period or week 0 represents the most recent time period, when we are beginning the analysis of a Markov process. If we set $\pi_1(0) = 1$ and $\pi_2(0) = 0$, we are saying that as an initial condition the customer shopped last week at Murphy's; whereas if we set $\pi_1(0) = 0$ and $\pi_2(0) = 1$, we would be starting the system with a customer who shopped last week at Ashley's. In the tree diagram of Figure 17.1 we considered the situation where the customer shopped last at Murphy's. Thus

$$[\pi_1(0) \quad \pi_2(0)] = [1 \quad 0]$$

is a vector that represents the initial state probabilities of our system. In general we use the notation

$$\Pi(n) = [\pi_1(n) \quad \pi_2(n)]$$

to denote the vector of state probabilities for the system at period n. In our example $\Pi(1)$ is a vector representing the state probabilities for the first week, $\Pi(2)$ is a vector representing the state probabilities for the second week, and so on.

Using this notation, we can find the state probabilities for period $n + 1$ by simply multiplying the known state probabilities for period n by the transition probability matrix. Using the vector of state probabilities and the matrix of transition probabilities, the multiplication[1] can be expressed as follows:

$$\Pi(\text{next period}) = \Pi(\text{current period})P$$

or

$$\Pi(n + 1) = \Pi(n)P \tag{17.1}$$

Beginning with the system in state 1 at period 0, we have $\Pi(0) = [1 \quad 0]$. We can compute the state probabilities for period 1 as follows:

$$\Pi(1) = \Pi(0)P$$

or

$$[\pi_1(1) \quad \pi_2(1)] = [\pi_1(0) \quad \pi_2(0)]\begin{bmatrix} p_{11} & p_{12} \\ p_{21} & p_{22} \end{bmatrix}$$

$$= [1 \quad 0]\begin{bmatrix} 0.9 & 0.1 \\ 0.2 & 0.8 \end{bmatrix}$$

$$= [0.9 \quad 0.1]$$

[1] Appendix E provides the step-by-step procedure for vector and matrix multiplication.

The state probabilities $\pi_1(1) = 0.9$ and $\pi_2(1) = 0.1$ are the probabilities that a customer shops at Murphy's or Ashley's during week 1, given that he or she shopped at Murphy's during week 0.

Using equation (17.1), we can compute the state probabilities for the second week as follows:

$$\Pi(2) = \Pi(1)P$$

or

$$[\pi_1(2) \quad \pi_2(2)] = [\pi_1(1) \quad \pi_2(1)] \begin{bmatrix} p_{11} & p_{12} \\ p_{21} & p_{22} \end{bmatrix}$$

$$= [0.9 \quad 0.1] \begin{bmatrix} 0.9 & 0.1 \\ 0.2 & 0.8 \end{bmatrix}$$

$$= [0.83 \quad 0.17]$$

We see that the probability of shopping at Murphy's during the second week is 0.83, while the probability of shopping at Ashley's during this time period is 0.17. These same results were previously obtained using the tree diagram of Figure 17.1. By continuing to apply equation (17.1), we can easily compute the state probabilities for any future time period; that is,

$$\Pi(3) \quad = \Pi(2)P$$
$$\Pi(4) \quad = \Pi(3)P$$
$$\vdots \qquad \qquad \vdots$$
$$\Pi(n + 1) = \Pi(n)P$$

Table 17.2 shows the result of carrying out these calculations for a number of periods in the future.

The vectors $\Pi(1)$, $\Pi(2)$, $\Pi(3)$, . . . contain the probabilities that a customer who started out as a Murphy customer will be in state 1 or state 2 in the first period, the second period, the third period, and so on. In Table 17.2 we see that after a large number of periods these probabilities do not change much from one period to the next. In fact, the probability of the system being in state 1 or state 2 is approaching $\frac{2}{3}$ and $\frac{1}{3}$ after a large number of shopping periods.

If we had started with 1000 Murphy customers—that is, 1000 consumers who last shopped at Murphy's—our analysis indicates that during the fifth subsequent weekly shopping period 723 would be customers of Murphy's and 277 would be customers of Ashley's. Moreover, after a large number of shopping periods, approximately 667 would be customers of Murphy's and 333 customers of Ashley's.

Now let us repeat the analysis, but this time we will begin the process with a customer who shopped last at Ashley's. Thus

$$\Pi(0) = [\pi_1(0) \quad \pi_2(0)] = [0 \quad 1]$$

TABLE 17.2
Probabilities of States for Future Periods Beginning Initially with a Murphy's Customer, $\Pi(0) = [1 \quad 0]$

State Probability		Period (n)									
	0	1	2	3	4	5	6	7	8	9	10
$\pi_1(n)$	1	0.9	0.83	0.781	0.747	0.723	0.706	0.694	0.686	0.680	0.676
$\pi_2(n)$	0	0.1	0.17	0.219	0.253	0.277	0.294	0.306	0.314	0.320	0.324

Using equation (17.1), the probability of the system being in state 1 or state 2 in period 1 is given by

$$\Pi(1) = \Pi(0)P$$

or

$$[\pi_1(1) \quad \pi_2(1)] = [\pi_1(0) \quad \pi_2(0)] \begin{bmatrix} p_{11} & p_{12} \\ p_{12} & p_{22} \end{bmatrix}$$

$$= [0 \quad 1] \begin{bmatrix} 0.9 & 0.1 \\ 0.2 & 0.8 \end{bmatrix}$$

$$= [0.2 \quad 0.8]$$

Proceeding as before we can calculate subsequent state probabilities. Doing so, we obtain the results shown in Table 17.3.

In the fifth shopping period the probability that the customer will be shopping at Murphy's is 0.555 and the probability that the customer will be shopping at Ashley's is 0.445. After a large number of shopping periods the probability of the system being in state 1 approaches $2/3$ and the probability of it being in state 2 approaches $1/3$. These are the same as the probabilities obtained after a large number of transitions when the system started in state 1. Thus we see that the probability of the system being in a particular state after a large number of periods is independent of the beginning state of the system. The probabilities that we approach after a large number of transitions are referred to as *steady-state probabilities*. We shall denote the steady-state probability for state 1 with the symbol π_1 and the steady-state probability for state 2 with the symbol π_2. We simply omit the period designation from $\pi_i(n)$, since it is no longer necessary.

Thus if we have 1000 customers in the system, the Markov process model tells us that in the long run, with steady-state probabilities $\pi_1 = 2/3$ and $\pi_2 = 1/3$, approximately two-thirds, or 667 customers, would be Murphy's, while approximately one-third, or 333 customers, would be Ashley's. These steady-state probabilities can be interpreted as the market shares for the two stores.

The analysis of Tables 17.2 and 17.3 indicates that as n gets larger, the difference between the state probabilities for the nth shopping period and the $(n + 1)$th period becomes increasingly smaller. This leads us to the conclusion that as n gets extremely large, the state probabilities at the $(n + 1)$th period are equal to those at the nth period. This observation provides the basis for a simple method for computing the steady-state probabilities without having to actually carry out a large number of calculations.

In general we know from equation (17.1) that

$$[\pi_1(n + 1) \quad \pi_2(n + 1)] = [\pi_1(n) \quad \pi_2(n)] \begin{bmatrix} p_{11} & p_{12} \\ p_{21} & p_{22} \end{bmatrix}$$

Since for sufficiently large n the difference between $\Pi(n + 1)$ and $\Pi(n)$ is negligible, we see that in the steady state $\pi_1(n + 1) = \pi_1(n) = \pi_1$ and $\pi_2(n + 1) = \pi_2(n) = \pi_2$. Thus we have

TABLE 17.3
Probabilities of States for Future Periods Beginning Initially with an Ashley's Customer, $\Pi(0) = [0 \quad 1]$

State Probability		0	1	2	3	4	Period (n) 5	6	7	8	9	10
$\pi_1(n)$	0	0	0.2	0.34	0.438	0.507	0.555	0.589	0.612	0.628	0.640	0.648
$\pi_2(n)$	1	1	0.8	0.66	0.562	0.493	0.445	0.411	0.388	0.372	0.360	0.352

$$[\pi_1 \quad \pi_2] = [\pi_1 \quad \pi_2] \begin{bmatrix} p_{11} & p_{12} \\ p_{21} & p_{22} \end{bmatrix}$$

$$= [\pi_1 \quad \pi_2] \begin{bmatrix} 0.9 & 0.1 \\ 0.2 & 0.8 \end{bmatrix}$$

After carrying out the above multiplications we obtain

$$\pi_1 = 0.9\pi_1 + 0.2\pi_2 \tag{17.2}$$

and

$$\pi_2 = 0.1\pi_1 + 0.8\pi_2 \tag{17.3}$$

However, we also know that

$$\pi_1 + \pi_2 = 1 \tag{17.4}$$

since the sum of the probabilities must equal 1.

Using equation (17.4) to solve for π_2 and substituting the result in equation (17.2), we obtain

$$\pi_1 = 0.9\pi_1 + 0.2(1 - \pi_1)$$
$$\pi_1 = 0.9\pi_1 + 0.2 - 0.2\pi_1$$
$$\pi_1 - 0.7\pi_1 = 0.2$$
$$0.3\pi_1 = 0.2$$
$$\pi_1 = \tfrac{2}{3}$$

Then using equation (17.4), we can conclude that $\pi_2 = 1 - \pi_1 = \tfrac{1}{3}$.

Thus we see that using the simultaneous equations given by equations (17.2) and (17.4) allows us to solve for the steady-state probabilities directly. You can check for yourself that we could have obtained the same result using equations (17.3) and (17.4).[2] In our example these steady-state probabilities represent the share of the market each store would receive in the long run regardless of its initial market share.

This market share information is often quite valuable in decision-making situations. For example, suppose Ashley's Supermarket is contemplating an advertising campaign to attract more of Murphy's customers to its store. Let us suppose further that Ashley's believes this promotional strategy will increase the probability of a Murphy's customer switching to Ashley's from 0.10 to 0.15. The new transition probabilities that would result are given in Table 17.4.

---

[2]Even though equations (17.2) and (17.3) provide two equations and two unknowns, we must include equation (17.4) when solving for π_1 and π_2 to ensure that the sum of steady-state probabilities will equal 1.

TABLE 17.4
New Transition Probabilities for Murphy's and Ashley's Grocery Stores

		Next Weekly Shopping Period	
		Murphy's Foodliner	*Ashley's Supermarket*
Current Weekly Shopping Period	*Murphy's Foodliner*	0.85	0.15
	Ashley's Supermarket	0.20	0.80

Given the new transition probabilities, we can solve for the new steady-state probabilities or market shares as we did before, using equations (17.2) and (17.4). Thus we obtain

$$\pi_1 = 0.85\pi_1 + 0.20\pi_2$$

Substituting $\pi_2 = 1 - \pi_1$ from equation (17.4), we have

$$\pi_1 = 0.85\pi_1 + 0.20(1 - \pi_1)$$
$$\pi_1 = 0.85\pi_1 + 0.20 - 0.20\pi_1$$
$$\pi_1 - 0.65\pi_1 = 0.20$$
$$0.35\pi_1 = 0.20$$
$$\pi_1 = \frac{4}{7} = 0.57$$

and

$$\pi_2 = 1 - 0.57 = 0.43$$

Thus we see that the proposed promotional strategy will lead to approximately a 10% increase in Ashley's market share. Suppose that the total market consists of 6000 customers per week. The new promotional strategy will approximately increase the number of customers doing their weekly shopping at Ashley's from 2000 to 2580. If the average weekly profit per customer is $10, the proposed promotional strategy can be expected to increase Ashley's profits by $5800 per week. Clearly, then, if the cost of the promotional campaign is less than $5800 per week, Ashley should seriously consider such a strategy.

This is but one illustration of how a Markov analysis of a firm's market share can be useful in a decision-making situation. Suppose that instead of trying to attract customers away from Murphy's Foodliner, Ashley's directed a promotional effort at increasing the loyalty of its own customers. In this case p_{22} would increase and p_{21} would decrease. Once we knew the amount of the change, we could calculate new steady-state probabilities and compute the impact on profits.

17.2 ACCOUNTS RECEIVABLE ANALYSIS

Another area in which Markov processes have produced useful results involves the estimation of the allowance for doubtful accounts. This allowance is an estimate of the amount of accounts receivable that will ultimately prove to be uncollectable (that is, bad debts).

Let us begin our analysis by considering the accounts receivable for Heidman's Department Store. Heidman's has two aging categories for its accounts receivable: (1) accounts that are classified as 0 to 30 days old and (2) accounts that are classified as 31 to 90 days old. If any portion of an account balance exceeds 90 days, that portion is written off as a bad debt. Heidman's follows the procedure of aging the total balance in any customer's account according to the oldest unpaid bill. For example, suppose one customer's account balance on September 30 is as follows:

Date of Purchase	Amount Charged
August 15	$25
September 18	10
September 28	50
Total	$85

An aging of accounts receivable on September 30 would assign the total balance of $85 to the 31–90-day-old category because the oldest unpaid bill of August 15 is 46 days old. Let us assume that one week later, October 7, the customer pays the August 15 bill of $25. The remaining total balance of $60 would now be placed in the 0–30-day aging category, since the oldest unpaid amount, corresponding to the September 18 purchase, is less than 31 days old. This method of aging accounts receivable is called the *total balance method*, since the total account balance is placed in the age category corresponding to the oldest unpaid amount.

Note that under the total balance method of aging accounts receivable, dollars appearing in a 31–90-day age category at one point in time may appear in a 0–30-day age category at a later point in time. In the above example this was true for $60 of September billings, which shifted from a 31–90-day to a 0–30-day aging category after the August bill had been paid.

Let us assume that on December 31 Heidman's shows a total of $3000 in its accounts receivable and that the firm's management would like an estimate of how much of the $3000 will eventually be collected and how much will eventually result in bad debts. The estimated amount of bad debts will appear as an allowance for doubtful accounts in the year-ending financial statements.

Let us see how we can view the accounts receivable operation as a Markov process. First, concentrate on what happens to *one* dollar currently in accounts receivable. As the firm continues to operate into the future, we can consider each week as a trial of a Markov process with a dollar existing in one of the following states of the system:

State 1 Paid category
State 2 Bad debt category
State 3 0–30-day age category
State 4 31–90-day age category

Thus we can track the week-by-week status of one dollar by using a Markov analysis to identify the state of the system at a particular week or time period in the future.

Using a Markov process model with the above states, we define our transition probabilities as follows:

$$p_{ij} = \text{probability of a dollar in state } i \text{ in one week moving to}$$
$$\text{state } j \text{ in the next week}$$

Based on historical transitions of accounts receivable dollars, the following transition matrix, P, has been developed for Heidman's Department Store:

$$P = \begin{bmatrix} p_{11} & p_{12} & p_{13} & p_{14} \\ p_{21} & p_{22} & p_{23} & p_{24} \\ p_{31} & p_{32} & p_{33} & p_{34} \\ p_{41} & p_{42} & p_{43} & p_{44} \end{bmatrix} = \begin{bmatrix} 1 & 0 & 0 & 0 \\ 0 & 1 & 0 & 0 \\ 0.4 & 0 & 0.3 & 0.3 \\ 0.4 & 0.2 & 0.3 & 0.1 \end{bmatrix}$$

From the transition matrix we see that the probability of a dollar in the 0–30-day age category (state 3) moving to the paid category (state 1) in the next period is 0.4. Also we see that there is a 0.3 probability that this dollar will remain in the 0–30-day category (state 3) one week later, while there is a 0.3 probability that it will be in the 31–90-day category (state 4) one week later. Note that a dollar in a 0–30-day account cannot make the transition to a bad debt (state 2) in one week.

An important property of the Markov process model for Heidman's accounts receivable is the presence of *absorbing states*. Note that once a dollar makes a transition to state 1, the paid state, the probability of making a transition to any other state is zero. Similarly, once a dollar is in state 2, the bad debt state, the probability of a transition to any other state is zero. Thus once a dollar reaches state 1 or state 2, the system will remain in this state indefinitely. This leads us to conclude that all accounts receivable dollars will eventually be absorbed into either the paid or the bad debt state, and hence the name *absorbing state*.

When a Markov process has absorbing states present, we do not compute steady-state probabilities in the context of the previous section because the process will eventually end up in one of the absorbing states. However, we may be interested in knowing the probability that the dollar will end up in each of the absorbing states. To determine these probabilities, we need to develop the notion of a fundamental matrix.

The Fundamental Matrix and Associated Calculations

In the following discussion we present the appropriate formulas for determining the probability that a dollar starting in state 3 or 4 will end up in each of the absorbing states. The underlying concept in the analysis involves the notion of a *fundamental matrix*. We begin the development of this concept by partitioning the matrix of transition probabilities into four parts; that is, we let

$$P = \left[\begin{array}{cc|cc} 1 & 0 & 0 & 0 \\ 0 & 1 & 0 & 0 \\ \hline 0.4 & 0 & 0.3 & 0.3 \\ 0.4 & 0.2 & 0.3 & 0.1 \end{array} \right] = \left[\begin{array}{c|c} I & O \\ \hline R & Q \end{array} \right]$$

where

$$I = \begin{bmatrix} 1 & 0 \\ 0 & 1 \end{bmatrix} \qquad O = \begin{bmatrix} 0 & 0 \\ 0 & 0 \end{bmatrix}$$

$$R = \begin{bmatrix} 0.4 & 0 \\ 0.4 & 0.2 \end{bmatrix} \qquad Q = \begin{bmatrix} 0.3 & 0.3 \\ 0.3 & 0.1 \end{bmatrix}$$

A matrix N, called a *fundamental matrix*, can be calculated using the following formula:

$$N = (I - Q)^{-1} \tag{17.5}$$

The superscript -1 is used to indicate the inverse of the matrix $(I - Q)$. In Appendix E we present formulas for finding the inverse of a matrix with two rows and two columns. In the current problem,

$$I - Q = \begin{bmatrix} 1 & 0 \\ 0 & 1 \end{bmatrix} - \begin{bmatrix} 0.3 & 0.3 \\ 0.3 & 0.1 \end{bmatrix}$$

$$= \begin{bmatrix} 0.7 & -0.3 \\ -0.3 & 0.9 \end{bmatrix}$$

and (see Appendix E)

$$N = (I - Q)^{-1} = \begin{bmatrix} 1.67 & 0.56 \\ 0.56 & 1.30 \end{bmatrix}$$

If we multiply the fundamental matrix N times the R portion of the P matrix, we obtain the probabilities that accounts receivable dollars initially in states 3 or 4 will eventually reach each of the absorbing states. The multiplication of N times R for the Heidman's Department Store problem is shown below (see Appendix E for the steps of this matrix multiplication):

$$NR = \begin{bmatrix} 1.67 & 0.56 \\ 0.56 & 1.30 \end{bmatrix} \begin{bmatrix} 0.4 & 0 \\ 0.4 & 0.2 \end{bmatrix} = \begin{bmatrix} 0.89 & 0.11 \\ 0.74 & 0.26 \end{bmatrix}$$

The first row of the product NR is the probability that a dollar in the 0–30 age category will end up in each of the absorbing states. Thus we see that there is a 0.89 probability that a dollar in the 0–30-day-old category will eventually be paid and a 0.11 probability that it will become a bad debt. Similarly, the second row tells us the probabilities associated with a dollar in the 31–90-day category; that is, a dollar in the 31–90-day category has a 0.74 probability of eventually being paid and a 0.26 probability of proving to be uncollectible. Using this information we can predict the amount of money that will be paid and the amount that will be lost as bad debts.

Establishing the Allowance for Doubtful Accounts

Let B represent a two-element vector that contains the current accounts receivable balances in the 0–30-day and the 31–90-day age categories; that is,

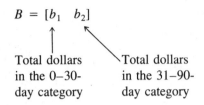

$$B = [b_1 \quad b_2]$$

Total dollars
in the 0–30-
day category

Total dollars
in the 31–90-
day category

Suppose that the December 31 balance of accounts receivable for Heidman's shows $1000 in the 0–30-day category (state 3) and $2000 in the 31–90-day category (state 4).

$$B = [1000 \quad 2000]$$

We can multiply B times NR to determine how much of the $3000 will be collected and how much will be lost. In our example,

$$BNR = [1000 \quad 2000] \begin{bmatrix} 0.89 & 0.11 \\ 0.74 & 0.26 \end{bmatrix}$$
$$= [2370 \quad 630]$$

Thus we see that $2370 of the accounts receivable balances will be collected and $630 will have to be written off as a bad debt expense. Based on this analysis, the accounting department of the company would set up an allowance for doubtful accounts of $630.

The matrix multiplication of BNR is simply a convenient way of computing the eventual collections and bad debts of the accounts receivable. Recall that the NR matrix showed a 0.89 probability of collecting dollars in the 0–30-day category and a 0.74 probability of collecting dollars in the 31–90-day category. Thus as was shown by the BNR calculation, we expect to collect a total of $0.89(1000) + 0.74(2000) = 890 + 1480 = \$2370$.

Suppose that on the basis of the previous analysis Heidman's would like to investigate the possibility of reducing the amount of bad debts. Recall that our analysis indicated that a 0.11 probability or 11% of the dollars in the 0–30-day age category and 26% of the amount in the 31–90-day age category will prove to be uncollectible. Let us assume that Heidman's is considering instituting a new credit policy involving a discount for prompt payment.

Management believes that the policy under consideration will increase the probability of a transition from the 0–30-day age category to the paid category and decrease the probability of a transition from the 0–30-day to the 31–90-day age category. Let us assume that a careful study of the effects of this new policy leads management to conclude that the following transition matrix would be applicable:

$$P = \begin{bmatrix} 1 & 0 & 0 & 0 \\ 0 & 1 & 0 & 0 \\ 0.6 & 0 & 0.3 & 0.1 \\ 0.4 & 0.2 & 0.3 & 0.1 \end{bmatrix}$$

We see that the probability of a dollar in the 0–30-day age category making a transition to the paid category in the next period has increased to 0.6 and that the probability of a dollar in the 0–30-day age category making a transition to the 31–90-day category has decreased to 0.1. To determine the effect of these changes on bad debt expense we must calculate N, NR, and BNR. We begin by using equation (17.5) to calculate the fundamental matrix N:

$$
N = (I - Q)^{-1} = \left\{ \begin{bmatrix} 1 & 0 \\ 0 & 1 \end{bmatrix} - \begin{bmatrix} 0.3 & 0.1 \\ 0.3 & 0.1 \end{bmatrix} \right\}^{-1}
$$

$$
= \begin{bmatrix} 0.7 & -0.1 \\ -0.3 & 0.9 \end{bmatrix}^{-1}
$$

$$
= \begin{bmatrix} 1.5 & 0.17 \\ 0.5 & 1.17 \end{bmatrix}
$$

By multiplying N times R we obtain the new probabilities that the dollars in each age category will end up in the two absorbing states:

$$
NR = \begin{bmatrix} 1.5 & 0.17 \\ 0.5 & 1.17 \end{bmatrix} \begin{bmatrix} 0.6 & 0 \\ 0.4 & 0.2 \end{bmatrix}
$$

$$
= \begin{bmatrix} 0.97 & 0.03 \\ 0.77 & 0.23 \end{bmatrix}
$$

We see that with the new credit policy we would expect only 3% of the funds in the 0–30-day age category and 23% of the funds in the 31–90-day age category to prove to be uncollectible. If, as before, we assume that there is a current balance of $1000 in the 0–30-day age category and $2000 in the 31–90-day age category, we can calculate the total amount of accounts receivable that will end up in the two absorbing states by multiplying B times NR. We obtain

$$
BNR = \begin{bmatrix} 1000 & 2000 \end{bmatrix} \begin{bmatrix} 0.97 & 0.03 \\ 0.77 & 0.23 \end{bmatrix}
$$

$$
= \begin{bmatrix} 2510 & 490 \end{bmatrix}
$$

Under the previous credit policy we found the bad debt expense to be $630. Thus a savings of $630 − 490 = $140 could be expected as a result of the new credit policy. Given our total accounts receivable balance of $3000, this is a 4.7% reduction in bad debt expense. After considering the costs involved, management can evaluate the economics of adopting the new credit policy. If the cost, including discounts, is less than 4.7% of the accounts receivable balance, we would expect the new policy to lead to increased profits for Heidman's Department Store.

Summary

In this chapter we have presented Markov process models as well as examples of their application. We saw that a Markov analysis could provide helpful decision-making information about a process or situation that involved a sequence of repeated trials with a number of possible outcomes or states on each trial. A primary objective of our analysis was obtaining information about the probability of each state occurring a certain number of transitions or time periods in the future.

A market share analysis showed the computational procedure for determining the steady-state probabilities that could be interpreted as market shares for two competing supermarkets. In an accounts receivable application of Markov processes we introduced the notion of absorbing states. The two absorbing states were the bad debt and paid categories, and we showed how to determine the percentage of accounts receivable balances that would be absorbed in each of these states.

Glossary

Trials of the process The events that trigger transitions of the system from one state to another. In many applications successive time periods represent the trials of the process.
State of the system The condition of the system at any particular trial or time period.
Transition probability Given the system is in state i during one period, the transition probability p_{ij} is the probability that the system will be in state j during the next period.
State probability The probability the system will be in any particular state. [$\pi_i(n)$ is the probability that the system will be in state i during period n.]
Steady-state probability The probability that the system will be in any particular state after a large number of transitions. Once steady state has been reached, the state probabilities do not change from period to period.
Absorbing state A state is said to be absorbing if the probability of making a transition out of that state is zero. Thus once the system has made a transition into an absorbing state, it will remain there forever.
Fundamental matrix A matrix necessary for the computation of probabilities associated with absorbing states of a Markov process.

Problems

1. In the market share analysis of Section 17.1 suppose that we are considering the Markov process associated with the shopping trips of one customer but we do not know where the cutomer shopped during the last week. Thus we might make the assumption that there is a 0.5 probability that the customer shopped at Murphy's and a 0.5 probability that the customer shopped at Ashley's at time period 0; that is, $\pi_1(0) = 0.5$ and $\pi_2(0) = 0.5$. Given these initial state probabilities, develop a table similar to Table 17.2 showing the probability of each state in future periods. What do you observe about the long-run probabilities of each state?
2. Management of the New Fangled Softdrink Company believes that the probability of a customer purchasing Red-Rot Pop and the company's major competition, Super Cola, is based on the customer's most recent purchase. Suppose the following transition matrix is appropriate:

		To	
		Red-Rot Pop	Super Cola
From	Red-Rot Pop	0.9	0.1
	Super Cola	0.1	0.9

a. Show the two-period tree diagram for one customer who last purchased Red-Rot Pop. What is the probability that this customer purchases Red-Rot Pop on the second purchase?

b. What is the long-run market share for each of these two products?

c. A major advertising campaign is being planned to increase the probability of attracting Super Cola customers. Management believes that the new campaign will result in the probability of a customer switching from Super Cola to Red-Rot Pop increasing to 0.15. What is the projected effect of the advertising campaign on the market shares?

3. The computer center at Rockbottom University has been experiencing substantial periods of computer downtime. Let us assume that the trials of an associated Markov process are defined to be 1-hour periods and that the probability of the system being in a running state or a down state is based upon the state of the system in the previous period. Historical data show the following transition probabilities:

		To	
		Running	Down
From	Running	0.90	0.10
	Down	0.30	0.70

a. If the system is initially running, what is the probability of the system being down in the next hour of operation?

b. What are the steady-state probabilities of the system being in the running state and in the down state?

4. In problem 3 one cause of the downtime problem was traced to a specific piece of computer hardware. Management believes that switching to a different hardware component will result in the following transition probability matrix:

		To	
		Running	Down
From	Running	0.95	0.05
	Down	0.60	0.40

a. What are the steady-state probabilities of the system being in the running and down states?

b. If the cost of the system being down for any period is estimated to be $500 (including lost profits for time down and maintenance), what is the breakeven cost for the new hardware component on a time-period basis?

5. A major traffic problem in the greater Cincinnati area involves traffic attempting to cross the Ohio River from Cincinnati to Kentucky using Interstate I-75. Let us assume that the probability of no traffic delay in one period, given no traffic delay in the preceding period, is 0.85 and that the probability of finding a traffic delay in one period, given a delay in the preceding period, is 0.75. Traffic will be classified as having either a delay or a no-delay state, and a time period will be considered to be 30 minutes.

a. Assuming you are a motorist entering the traffic system and receive a radio report of a traffic delay, what is the probability that for the next 60 minutes (two time periods) the system will be in the delay state? Note that this is the probability of being in the delay state for two consecutive periods. A tree diagram should be helpful.

b. What is the probability that in the long run the traffic will not be in the delayed state?

c. An important assumption of the Markov process models presented in this chapter has been the constant or stationary transition probabilities as the system operates in the future. Do you believe this assumption is appropriate in the above traffic problem? Explain.

6. The purchase patterns of two brands of toothpaste can be expressed as a Markov process with the following transition probabilities:

		To	
		Special B	MDA
From	Special B	0.90	0.10
	MDA	0.05	0.95

a. Which brand appears to have the most loyal customers? Explain.

b. What are the projected market shares for the two brands?

7. Suppose that in problem 6 a new toothpaste brand enters the market such that the following transition probabilities exist:

		To		
		Special B	MDA	T-White
From	Special B	0.80	0.10	0.10
	MDA	0.05	0.75	0.20
	T-White	0.40	0.30	0.30

What are the new long-run market shares? Which brand will suffer most from the introduction of the new brand of toothpaste? Note that solving for the steady-state probabilities for this problem requires the solution of three equations and three unknowns.

8. Given the following transition matrix with states 1 and 2 as absorbing states, what is the probability that units in state 3 and state 4 end up in each of the absorbing states?

$$P = \begin{bmatrix} 1 & 0 & 0 & 0 \\ 0 & 1 & 0 & 0 \\ 0.2 & 0.1 & 0.4 & 0.3 \\ 0.2 & 0.2 & 0.1 & 0.5 \end{bmatrix}$$

9. In the Heidman's Department Store problem of Section 17.2, suppose the following transition matrix is appropriate:

$$P = \begin{bmatrix} 1 & 0 & 0 & 0 \\ 0 & 1 & 0 & 0 \\ 0.5 & 0 & 0.25 & 0.25 \\ 0.5 & 0.2 & 0.05 & 0.25 \end{bmatrix}$$

If Heidman's has $4000 in the 0–30-day age category and $5000 in the 31–90-day age category, what is your estimate of the amount of bad debts the company will experience?

10. The KLM Christmas Tree Farm owns a plot of land with 5000 evergreen trees. Each year KLM allows retailers of Christmas trees to select and cut trees for sale to individual customers. KLM protects small trees (usually less than 4 feet tall) so that they will grow and be available for sale in future years. Currently 1500 trees are classified as protected trees, while the remaining 3500 are available for cutting. However, even though a tree is available for cutting in a given year, it may not be selected for cutting until future years. While most trees not cut in a given year live until the next year, some trees die during the year and are lost.

   In viewing the KLM Christmas trees operation as a Markov process with yearly time periods, we define the following four states:

   State 1   Cut and sold
   State 2   Lost to disease
   State 3   Too small for cutting
   State 4   Available for cutting but not cut and sold

   The following transition matrix is appropriate:

$$P = \begin{bmatrix} 1 & 0 & 0 & 0 \\ 0 & 1 & 0 & 0 \\ 0.1 & 0.2 & 0.5 & 0.2 \\ 0.4 & 0.1 & 0 & 0.5 \end{bmatrix}$$

   How many of the farm's 5000 trees will be sold eventually and how many will be lost?

Management Science in Practice
U.S. GENERAL ACCOUNTING OFFICE*
Washington, D.C.

The U.S. General Accounting Office (GAO) is an independent, nonpolitical audit organization in the Legislative branch of the federal government. GAO was created by the Budget and Accounting Act of 1921 and has three basic purposes:

To assist Congress, its committees, and its members carry out their legislative and oversight responsibilities, consistent with its role as an independent, nonpolitical agency.

To audit and evaluate the programs, activities, and financial operations of federal departments and agencies, and to make recommendations toward more efficient and effective operations.

To carry out financial control and other functions with respect to federal government programs and operations including accounting, legal, and claims settlement work.

GAO evaluators, the main occupation in GAO, determine the effectiveness of existing or proposed federal programs and the efficiency, economy, legality, and effectiveness with which federal agencies carry out their responsibilities. These evaluations culminate in reports to the Congress and to the heads of federal departments and agencies. Such reports typically include recommendations to Congress concerning the need for enabling or remedial legislation and suggestions to agencies concerning the need for changes in programs or operations to improve their economy, efficiency, and effectiveness.

GAO evaluators analyze policies and practices, and the use of resources within and among federal programs; identify problem areas and deficiencies in meeting program goals; develop and analyze alternative solutions to problems of program execution; and develop and recommend changes to enable the programs to better conform to Congressional goals and legislative intent. To effectively carry out their duties evaluators must be proficient in interviewing, data processing, records review, legislative research, management science, and statistical analysis techniques.

IMPACT OF SERVICES ON THE WELL-BEING OF OLDER PEOPLE

GAO evaluators obtained data from a random sample of noninstitutionalized persons aged 65 and older living in Cleveland, Ohio. The health conditions of the sampled

*The authors are indebted to Bill Ammann, U.S. General Accounting Office, Washington, D.C., for providing this application.

individuals in the 65- to 69-year-old groups were defined by the following three states:

Best.   Individual able to perform 13 identified activities of daily living without help.
Next best.   Individual able to perform the same 13 activities but required help for at least one activity.
Worst.   Individual unable to perform the same 13 activities even with help.

Using a 2-year period of time, GAO evaluators developed estimates of the year-to-year transition probabilities for individuals in the 65- to 69-year-old group. These estimates were then used to develop a transition probability matrix such as that shown in Table A17.1. Note that a death state has been added as an absorbing state.

TABLE A17.1
Transition Probability Matrix for the Health Condition of Individuals 65 to 69 Years Old

		Following Year Condition			
		Best	Next Best	Worst	Death
Current Year Condition	Best	p_{11}	p_{12}	p_{13}	p_{14}
	Next Best	p_{21}	p_{22}	p_{23}	p_{24}
	Worst	p_{31}	p_{32}	p_{33}	p_{34}
	Death	0	0	0	1

Using the transition probabilities, a Markov process analysis can be used to determine the state probabilities for any number of periods (years) into the future. To verify the appropriateness of the Markov process model, GAO evaluators used the transition probabilities to determine the state probabilities for the 65- to 69-year-old age group 5 years into the future. The resulting state probabilities were compared with the health states of individuals in a known 70- to 74-year-old age group. There was no statistically significant difference between the probabilities provided by the model and the actual state probabilities of the 70- to 74-year-old group.

ESTIMATING THE LIKELY EFFECTS OF HEALTH CARE PROGRAMS

The individuals in the original study were subdivided into two groups: those receiving all appropriate health care and those not receiving all appropriate health care. For the purpose of the study, a person was classified as receiving all appropriate health care if the person was taking medication and/or treatment for each illness present and if the person was receiving the help necessary to perform each of the 13 specific activities of daily living that could not be performed without help. As a result, GAO evaluators developed two matrices of transition probabilities: one for individuals receiving all appropriate health care and one for individuals not receiving all appropriate health care.

For any individuals not receiving all appropriate help, the kind of additional help needed was determined and the cost of that help was estimated. Then those persons were artificially aged over time using the transition probabilities in order to establish the likely benefits in terms of improved health states for the individuals. Over a 20-year period of time, there was shown to be a net savings for the health care program provided all other factors remained equal. That is, the increased cost to provide sufficient appropriate help to all persons was eventually offset by individuals either improving their health state or by not spending as much time in a worse state. Although benefits of health care are often proclaimed theoretically, the Markov process model provided evidence that indicated benefits would be achieved with the health care program.

This type of Markov analysis was also conducted for economic, social, and life view status as well as for the health status. In some instances, the Markov model showed that additional help and/or programs did not result in net savings over time.

Questions

1. Suppose the transition probabilities in Table A17.1 were as follows:

$$\begin{bmatrix} 0.80 & 0.10 & 0.06 & 0.04 \\ 0.05 & 0.75 & 0.15 & 0.05 \\ 0.00 & 0.05 & 0.75 & 0.20 \\ 0 & 0 & 0 & 1 \end{bmatrix}$$

Assume a particular city has 1000 individuals in the best state, 2000 in the next best state, and 500 in the worst state. Estimate how many of each of these individuals will be in each state 2 years from now.

2. How might health care programs affect the matrix of transition probabilities in (1) above? What effect would you expect to see in the distribution of individuals across the four states 2 years from now?

18

Dynamic Programming

Dynamic programming is an approach to problem solving that permits decomposing one large mathematical model that may be very difficult to solve into a number of smaller problems that are usually much easier to solve. Moreover, the dynamic programming approach allows us to break up a large problem in such a fashion that once all the smaller problems have been solved, we are left with an optimal solution to the large problem. We shall see that each of the smaller problems created is identified with a *stage* of the dynamic programming solution procedure. As a consequence, the technique has been applied to many decision problems that are multistage in nature. Often the multiple stages are created by the fact that a sequence of decisions must be made over time. For example, a problem of determining an optimal decision over a 1-year time horizon might be broken into 12 smaller stages, where each stage requires an optimal decision over a 1-month time horizon. In most cases each of these smaller problems cannot be considered to be completely independent of the others, and this is where the dynamic programming approach is helpful. Let us begin by discovering how to solve a shortest-route problem using a dynamic programming approach.

18.1 A SHORTEST-ROUTE PROBLEM

In Chapter 9 we studied a labeling algorithm for solving the shortest-route problem. Let us now illustrate the dynamic programming approach by using it to solve a shortest-route problem. Consider the network presented in Figure 18.1. Assuming that the numbers above each arc denote the direct distance in miles between two nodes, find the shortest route from node 1 to node 10.

Before attempting to solve this problem, let us note an important characteristic of shortest-route problems. This characteristic is actually a restatement of Richard Bellman's famous *principle of optimality* as it applies to the shortest-route problem[1]:

---

[1]See Dreyfus, S., *Dynamic Programming and the Calculus of Variations*. New York, Academic Press, 1965.

FIGURE 18.1
Network for the Shortest-Route Problem

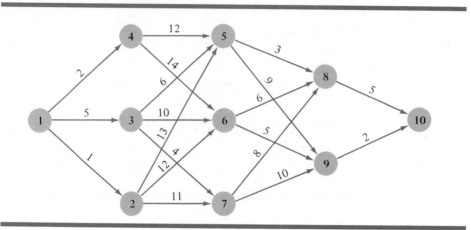

The Principle of Optimality.

If a particular node is on the optimal route, then the shortest path from that node to the end is also on the optimal route.

The dynamic programming approach to this problem essentially involves treating each node as if it were on the optimal route and making calculations accordingly. In doing so we work backward; that is, we start at the terminal node, node 10, and work backward, calculating the shortest route from each node to node 10 until we reach the origin, node 1. Then we will have solved the original problem of finding the shortest route from node 1 to node 10.

As we stated in the introduction to this chapter, the dynamic programming approach decomposes the original problem into a number of smaller problems that are much easier to solve. In the shortest-route problem for the network in Figure 18.1 the smaller problems that we will create define a four-stage dynamic programming problem. The first stage begins with nodes that are exactly one arc away from the destination and ends at the destination node. Note from Figure 18.1 that only nodes 8 and 9 are exactly one arc away from node 10. The second stage begins with all nodes that are exactly two arcs away from the destination and ends with all nodes that are exactly one arc away. Hence in dynamic programming terminology nodes 5, 6, and 7 would be considered the input nodes for stage 2 and nodes 8 and 9 would be considered output nodes for stage 2. The output nodes for stage 2 are the input nodes for stage 1. The input nodes for our third-stage problem are those that are exactly three arcs away from the destination, that is, nodes 2, 3, and 4. The output nodes, all of which are one arc closer to the destination, are nodes 5, 6, and 7. Finally, the input to stage 4 is node 1 and the output nodes are 2, 3, and 4. The decision problem we shall want to solve at each stage is to determine which arc it is best to travel over in moving from each particular input node to an output node. Let us consider the stage 1 problem.

We arbitrarily begin the stage 1 calculations with node 9. Since there is only one way to travel from node 9 to node 10, this is obviously the shortest route and requires us to travel a distance of 2 miles. Similarly there is only one path from node 8 to node 10. The shortest route from node 8 to the end is thus the length of that route, or 5 miles. The stage 1 decision problem is solved. For each input node we have identified an optimal decision, that is, the best arc to travel over to reach the output node. The stage 1 results are summarized below.

Stage 1

Input Nodes	Arc Decision	Shortest Distance to Node 10 (miles)
8	8–10	5
9	9–10	2

To begin the solution to the stage 2 problem, we move to node 7. (We could have selected node 5 or 6; the order of the nodes selected at any stage is arbitrary.) There are two arcs that leave node 7 and are connected to input nodes for stage 1. These are arc 7–8, which has a length of 8, and arc 7–9, which has a length of 10. If we select arc 7–8, we will have a distance from node 7 to node 10 that is 8 (that is, the length of arc 7–8) plus the shortest distance to node 10 from node 8. Thus the decision to select arc 7–8 has a total associated distance of 8 + 5 = 13. With a distance of 10 for arc 7–9 and stage 1 results showing a distance of 2 from node 9 to node 10, the decision to select arc 7–9 has an associated distance of 10 + 2 = 12. Thus given we are at node 7, we should select arc 7–9, since it is on the path that will reach node 10 in the shortest distance (12 miles). By performing similar calculations for nodes 5 and 6, we can generate the following stage 2 results:

Stage 2

Input Nodes	Arc Decision	Output Nodes	Shortest Distance to Node 10 (miles)
5	5–8	8	8
6	6–9	9	7
7	7–9	9	12

In Figure 18.2 the number in the square by each node considered so far indicates the length of the shortest route from that node to the end. We have completed the solution to our first two subproblems (stages 1 and 2). We now know the shortest route from nodes 5, 6, and 7 to node 10.

To begin our third stage, let us start with node 2. To find the shortest route from node 2 to node 10, we must make three calculations because we have three arcs that connect node 2 to stage 2 input nodes. If we select arc 2–7 and then follow the shortest route to the end, we will travel 11 + 12 = 23 miles. Similarly, selecting arc 2–6 requires

FIGURE 18.2

Intermediate Solution to the Shortest-Route Problem Using Dynamic Programming

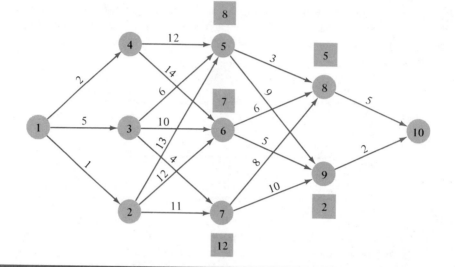

12 + 7 = 19 miles, and selecting arc 2–5 requires 13 + 8 = 21 miles. Thus the shortest route from node 2 to node 10 is 19 miles, which indicates that arc 2–6 is the best decision, given that we are at node 2. Similarly, we find that the shortest route from node 3 to node 10 is given by min {4 + 12, 10 + 7, 6 + 8} = 14; the shortest route from node 4 to node 10 is given by min {14 + 7, 12 + 8} = 20. This completes our stage 3 calculations. The results are summarized below:

Stage 3

Input Nodes	Arc Decision	Output Nodes	Shortest Distance to Node 10 (miles)
2	2–6	6	19
3	3–5	5	14
4	4–5	5	20

In solving the stage 4 subproblem we find that the shortest route from node 1 to node 10 is given by min {1 + 19, 5 + 14, 2 + 20} = 19. Thus the optimal decision at stage 4 is to select arc 1–3. By moving through the network from stage 4 to stage 3 to stage 2 to stage 1, we can identify the best decision at each stage and therefore the shortest route from node 1 to node 10. This is as follows:

Stage	Arc Decision
4	1–3
3	3–5
2	5–8
1	8–10

Thus the shortest route is through nodes 1–3–5–8–10 with a distance of 5 + 6 + 3 + 5 = 19 miles.

Note how the calculations at each successive stage made use of the calculations at prior stages. This characteristic is an important part of the dynamic programming procedure. Figure 18.3 illustrates the final network calculations. Note that we have now determined the shortest route from every node to node 10.

FIGURE 18.3
Final Solution to the Shortest-Route Problem Using Dynamic Programming

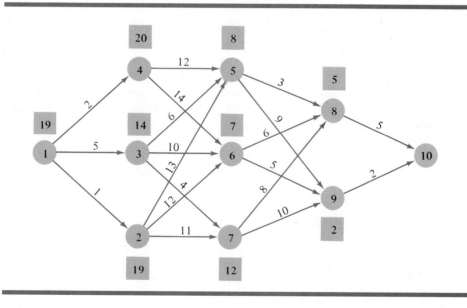

The dynamic programming approach, while enumerating or evaluating several paths at each stage, did not require us to enumerate all possible paths from node 1 to node 10. Returning to our stage 4 calculations, we considered three alternatives for leaving node 1. The complete route associated with each of these alternatives is presented below.

Arc Alternatives at Node 1	Complete Path to Node 10	Distance (miles)	
1–2	1–2–6–9–10	20	
1–3	1–3–5–8–10	19 ←————————— Selected as
1–4	1–4–5–8–10	22	best

However, when you realize that there are a total of 16 alternate routes from node 1 to node 10, you can see that dynamic programming has provided substantial computational savings over a total enumeration of all possible solutions.

The fact that we did not have to evaluate all the paths at each stage as we moved backward from node 10 to node 1 is illustrative of the power of dynamic programming. Using dynamic programming, we need only make a small fraction of the number of calculations that would be required using total enumeration. If our example network had been larger, the savings would have been even greater.

18.2   DYNAMIC PROGRAMMING NOTATION

Perhaps one of the most difficult aspects of learning how to apply dynamic programming involves understanding the notation used to develop the approach. The notation we will use is the same as that used by Nemhauser[2] and is fairly standard.

The *stages* of a dynamic programming solution procedure are formed by decomposing the original problem of interest into a number of subproblems. Associated with each subproblem is a stage in the dynamic programming solution procedure. For example, the shortest-route problem introduced in the preceding section was solved using a four-stage dynamic programming solution procedure. We had a four-stage procedure because we decomposed the original problem into the following four subproblems:

1. **Stage 1 Problem:**   Where should we go from nodes 8 and 9 so that we will reach node 10 along the shortest route?
2. **Stage 2 Problem:**   Using the results of stage 1, where should we go from nodes 5, 6, and 7 so that we will reach node 10 along the shortest route?
3. **Stage 3 Problem:**   Using the results of stage 2, where should we go from nodes 2, 3, and 4 so that we will reach node 10 along the shortest route?
4. **Stage 4 Problem:**   Using the results of stage 3, where should we go from node 1 so that we will reach node 10 along the shortest route?

Let us look closely at what occurs at the stage 2 problem. Consider the following representation of this stage.

[2]See Nemhauser, G. L., *Introduction to Dynamic Programming*. New York, Wiley, 1966.

	Decision Problem	
Input	For a given input, which arc should we select to reach stage 1?	**Output**
→		→
(a location in the network, node 5, 6, or 7)	*Decision Criterion* Shortest distance to destination (arc value plus shortest distance from output node to destination)	(a location in the network, node 8 or 9)

Using dynamic programming notation, we define

x_2 = input to stage 2. x_2 represents our location in the network at the beginning of stage 2 (node 5, 6, or 7). Note that the input to stage 2 is the output of stage 3.

d_2 = decision variable at stage 2. This represents the arc selected to move to stage 1.

x_1 = output for stage 2. This will be the node we reach (node 8 or 9) after considering the input x_2 and the decision d_2. This will also be the input to stage 1.

Using this notation the stage 2 problem can be partially represented as follows:

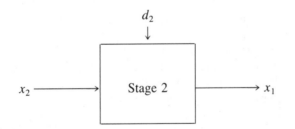

Recall that in the dynamic programming approach to the shortest-route problem we worked backward through the stages, beginning at node 10. When we reached stage 2 we did not know x_2 because the stage 3 problem had not yet been solved. The approach used was to consider *all* alternatives for the input x_2. Then we determined the best decision d_2 for each of the inputs x_2. Later, when we moved forward through the system to recover the optimal sequence of decisions, we saw that the stage 3 decision provided a specific x_2, node 5, and from our previous analysis we knew the best decision (d_2) to make as we continued on to stage 1.

Let us consider a general dynamic programming problem with N stages and adopt the following general notation:

$$x_n = \text{input to stage } n \text{ (output from stage } n + 1)$$
$$d_n = \text{decision at stage } n$$

The general N-stage problem is decomposed as follows:

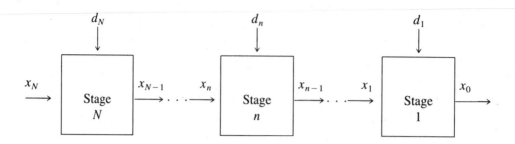

The four-stage shortest-route problem can be represented as follows:

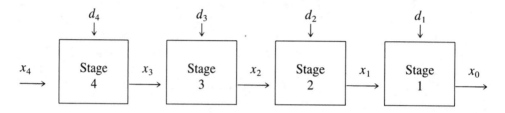

The values of the input and output variables x_4, x_3, x_2, x_1, and x_0 are important because they couple the four subproblems together. At any stage we will ultimately need to know the input x_n in order to make the best decision d_n. These x_n variables can be thought of as defining the *state* or condition of the system as we move from stage to stage. Accordingly, these variables are referred to as the *state variables* of the problem. In our shortest-route problem, the state variables represented our location in the network at each stage (that is, a particular node).

At stage 2 of the shortest-route problem we considered the input x_2 and made the decision d_2 that would provide the shortest distance to the destination. The output x_1 was based upon a combination of the input and the decision; that is, x_1 was a function of x_2 and d_2. In dynamic programming notation we could write

$$x_1 = t_2(x_2, d_2)$$

where $t_2(x_2, d_2)$ is the function at stage 2 that determines the stage 2 output.

Since $t_2(x_2, d_2)$ is the function that "transforms" the input to the stage into the output, this function is referred to as the *stage transformation function*. The general expression for this function is

$$x_{n-1} = t_n(x_n, d_n) \tag{18.1}$$

The mathematical form of the stage transformation function is dependent upon the particular dynamic programming problem. In our shortest-route problem, the transformation function was based upon a tabular type of calculation. For example, Table 18.1 shows the stage transformation function $t_2(x_2, d_2)$ for stage 2. The possible values of d_2 are the arcs selected in the body of the table.

Each stage also has a return associated with it. In our shortest-route problem the return was the arc distance traveled in moving from an input node to an output node. For example, if node 7 were the input state for stage 2 and we selected arc 7–9 as d_2,

TABLE 18.1
Table Showing Output Node Corresponding to
Each Input Node and Decision, $x_1 = t_2(x_2, d_2)$

	x_1	Output State	
	x_2	8	9
	5	5–8	5–9
Input State	6	6–8	6–9
	7	7–8	7–9

the return for that stage would be the arc length, 10 miles. The return at a stage, which may be thought of as the payoff or value for a stage, is represented by the general notation $r_n(x_n, d_n)$.

Using the stage transformation function and the *return function*, our shortest-route problem can be shown as follows.

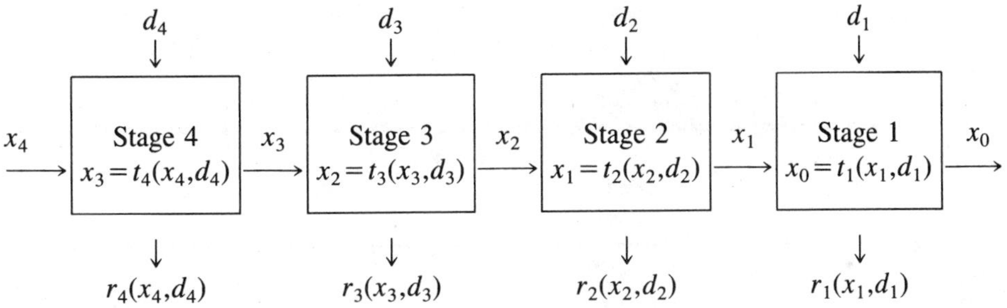

If we view a system or a process as consisting of N stages, we can represent a dynamic programming formulation schematically as follows:

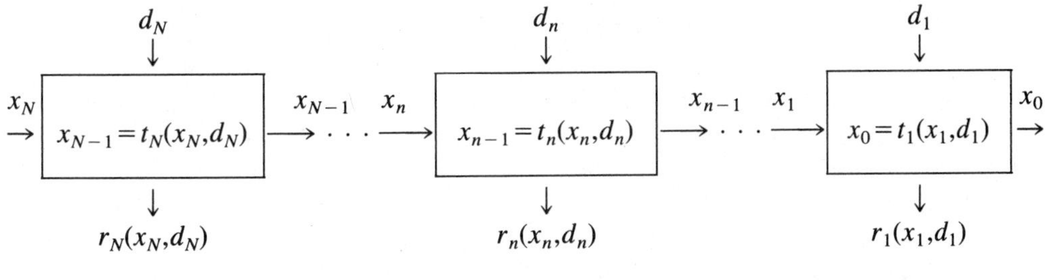

Each of the squares in the diagram represents a stage in the process. As indicated, there are two inputs to each stage: the state variable and the decision variable. There are also two outputs: a new value for the state variable and a return for the stage. The new value for the state variable is determined as a function of the inputs using $t_n(x_n, d_n)$. The value of the return for a stage is also determined as a function of the inputs using $r_n(x_n, d_n)$.

In addition we will use the notation $f_n(x_n)$ to represent the optimal total return from stage n and all remaining stages, given an input of x_n to stage n. For example, in our shortest-route problem $f_2(x_2)$ represents the optimal total return (that is, the minimum distance) from stage 2 and all remaining stages, given an input of x_2 to stage 2. Thus we see from Figure 18.3 that $f_2(x_2 = \text{node } 5) = 8$, $f_2(x_2 = \text{node } 6) = 7$, and $f_2(x_2 = \text{node } 7) = 12$. These are just the values in the squares at nodes 5, 6, and 7. Let us now turn to a well-known dynamic programming problem and use the notation just developed.

18.3 THE KNAPSACK PROBLEM

The knapsack problem is often encountered in dynamic programming applications. The basic idea is that there are N different types of items that can be put into a knapsack. Each item has a certain weight associated with it as well as a value. The problem is to determine how many units of each item to place in the knapsack in order to maximize the total value. A constraint is placed on the maximum weight permissible.

Consider a manager of a manufacturing operation who must make a biweekly selection of jobs to process during the following 2-week period. A list of the jobs waiting to be processed at the beginning of the current week is presented in Table 18.2. The estimated time required for completion and the value rating associated with each category of job are also shown in the table.

TABLE 18.2
Job Data for the Manufacturing Operation

Job	Number of Jobs To Be Processed	Estimated Completion Time per Job (days)	Value Rating
Category 1	4	1	2
Category 2	3	3	8
Category 3	2	4	11
Category 4	2	7	20

The value rating assigned to each job is a subjective score assigned by the supervisor. A scale from 1 to 20 is used to measure the value of each job, where 1 represents jobs of the least value, and 20 represents jobs of most value. The value of a job depends upon such things as expected profit, length of time the job has been waiting to be processed, priority, and so on. In this situation we would like to make a selection of jobs to process during the next 2 weeks such that all the jobs selected can be processed within 10 days and that the total value of the jobs selected is maximized. In knapsack problem terminology we are in essence selecting the best jobs for our 2-week knapsack, where the knapsack has a capacity equal to the 10-day production capacity. Let us formulate and solve this problem using a dynamic programming solution procedure.

This problem can be formulated as a dynamic programming problem involving four stages. At stage 1 we must decide how many jobs from category 1 to process, at stage 2 we must decide how many jobs from category 2 to process, and so on. Thus we let d_n denote the number of jobs in category n selected (that is, the decision variable at stage n). The state variable x_n is defined as the number of days of processing time remaining when we reach stage n.

Thus with a 2-week production period, $x_4 = 10$ represents the total number of days that are available for processing jobs. The stage transformation functions are then defined so that

$$Stage\ 4: \quad x_3 = t_4(x_4, d_4) = x_4 - 7d_4$$
$$Stage\ 3: \quad x_2 = t_3(x_3, d_3) = x_3 - 4d_3$$
$$Stage\ 2: \quad x_1 = t_2(x_2, d_2) = x_2 - 3d_2$$
$$Stage\ 1: \quad x_0 = t_1(x_1, d_1) = x_1 - 1d_1$$

The return at each stage is based on the value rating of the jobs and the number of jobs selected at each stage. The return functions are as follows:

$$Stage\ 4: \quad r_4(x_4, d_4) = 20d_4$$
$$Stage\ 3: \quad r_3(x_3, d_3) = 11d_3$$
$$Stage\ 2: \quad r_2(x_2, d_2) = 8d_2$$
$$Stage\ 1: \quad r_1(x_1, d_1) = 2d_1$$

Figure 18.4 shows a schematic representation of the problem.

FIGURE 18.4
Schematic Presentation of the Dynamic Programming Formulation of the Manufacturing Problem

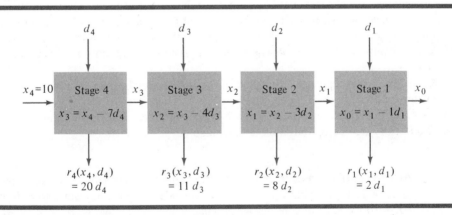

As with the shortest-route problem in Section 18.1, we will apply a backward solution procedure; that is, we will begin by considering the stage 1 decision. A restatement of the principle of optimality can be made in terms of this problem. That is, regardless of whatever decisions have been made at previous stages, if our decision at stage n is to be part of an optimal overall strategy, the decision made at stage n must necessarily be optimal for all remaining stages.

Let us set up a table that will help us calculate the optimal decisions for stage 1.

Stage 1   Note that the input to stage 1, x_1, which is the number of days of processing time available at stage 1, is unknown because we have not yet identified the decisions at the previous stages. Therefore in our analysis at stage 1 we will have to consider all possible values of x_1 and identify the best decision d_1 for each case; $f_1(x_1)$ will be the total return after decision d_1 is made. The possible values of x_1 and the associated d_1 and $f_1(x_1)$ values are as follows:

x_1	d_1^*	$f_1(x_1)$
0	0	0
1	1	2
2	2	4
3	3	6
4	4	8
5	4	8
6	4	8
7	4	8
8	4	8
9	4	8
10	4	8

The d_1^* column gives the optimal values of d_1 corresponding to a particular value of x_1, where x_1 can range from 0 to 10. The specific value of x_1 will depend upon how much processing time has been used by the jobs in the other categories selected in stages 2, 3, and 4. Since each stage 1 job requires 1 day of processing time and has a positive return of 2 per job, we always select as many jobs at this stage as possible. The number of category 1 jobs selected will depend upon the processing time available but cannot exceed 4.

Recall that $f_1(x_1)$ represents the value of the optimal total return from stage 1 and all remaining stages, given an input of x_1 to stage 1. Therefore $f_1(x_1) = 2x_1$ for values of $x_1 \le 4$. Thus the optimization of stage 1 is accomplished. Let us now move on to stage 2 and carry out the optimization at that stage.

Stage 2   Again we will use a table to help identify the optimal decision. Since the input to stage 2, x_2, is unknown, we have to consider all possible values from 0 to 10. Also we have to consider all possible values of d_2 (that is, 0, 1, 2, or 3). The entries under the heading $r_2(x_2, d_2) + f_1(x_1)$ represent the total return that will be forthcoming from the final two stages, given the input of x_2 and the decision of d_2. For example, if stage 2 were entered with $x_2 = 7$ days of processing time remaining, and if a decision were made to select two jobs from category 2, that is, $d_2 = 2$, the total return for stages 1 and 2 would be 18.

The return for stage 2 would be $r_2(x_2, d_2) = 8d_2 = 8(2) = 16$, and with $x_2 = 7$ and $d_2 = 2$, we would have $x_1 = x_2 - 3d_2 = 7 - 6 = 1$. From the previous table we see that the optimal return from stage 1 with $x_1 = 1$ is $f_1(1) = 2$. Thus the total return corresponding to $x_2 = 7$, $d_2 = 2$ is given by $r_2(7, 2) + f_1(1) = 16 + 2 = 18$. Similarly, with $x_2 = 5$, and $d_2 = 1$, we get $r_2(5, 1) + f_1(2) = 8 + 4 = 12$. Note that some combinations of x_2 and

x_2 \ d_2	$r_2(x_2,d_2) + f_1(x_1)$				d_2^*	$f_2(x_2)$	$x_1 = t_2(x_2,d_2^*)$ $= x_2 - 3d_2^*$
	0	1	2	3			
0	⓪	–	–	–	0	0	0
1	②	–	–	–	0	2	1
2	④	–	–	–	0	4	2
3	6	⑧	–	–	1	8	0
4	8	⑩	–	–	1	10	1
5	8	⑫	–	–	1	12	2
6	8	14	⑯	–	2	16	0
7	8	16	⑱	–	2	18	1
8	8	16	⑳	–	2	20	2
9	8	16	22	㉔	3	24	0
10	8	16	24	㉖	3	26	1

d_2 are not feasible. For example with $x_2 = 2$ days, $d_2 = 1$ is infeasible because category 2 jobs each require 3 days to process. The infeasible solutions are indicated by a dash.

After all the total returns in the rectangle have been calculated, we can determine an optimal decision at this stage for each possible value of the input or state variable x_2. For example, if $x_2 = 9$ there are four possible values we can select for d_2: 0, 1, 2, or 3. Clearly $d_3 = 3$ with a value of 24 yields the maximum total return for the last two stages. Therefore we record this value in the d_2^* column. For additional emphasis we circle the element inside the rectangle corresponding to the optimal return. The optimal total return, given that we are in state $x_2 = 9$ and must pass through two more stages, is thus 24, and we record this value in the $f_2(x_2)$ column. Given that we enter stage 2 with $x_2 = 9$ and make the optimal decision $d_2^* = 3$, we will enter stage 1 with $x_1 = t_2(9, 3) = x_2 - 3d_2 = 9 - 3(3) = 0$. This value is recorded in the last column in our table. We can now go on to stage 3.

Stage 3 The table we construct here is much the same as for stage 2. The entries under the heading $r_3(x_3, d_3) + f_2(x_2)$ represent the total return over stages 3, 2, and 1 for all possible inputs x_3 and all possible decisions d_3.

x_3 \ d_3	$r_3(x_3, d_3) + f_2(x_2)$			d_3^*	$f_3(x_3)$	$x_2 = t_3(x_3, d_3^*)$ $= x_3 - 4d_3^*$
	0	1	2			
0	⓪	–	–	0	0	0
1	②	–	–	0	2	1
2	④	–	–	0	4	2
3	⑧	–	–	0	8	3
4	10	⑪	–	1	11	0
5	12	⑬	–	1	13	1
6	⑯	15	–	0	16	6
7	18	⑲	–	1	19	3
8	20	21	㉒	2	22	0
9	㉔	23	㉔	0,2	24	9,1
10	26	㉗	26	1	27	6

There are some features of interest in this table that were not present at stage
2. We note that if the state variable $x_3 = 9$, then there are two decisions that
will lead to an optimal total return from stages 1, 2, and 3; that is, we may
elect to process no jobs from category 3, in which case we will obtain no return
from stage 3 but will enter stage 2 with $x_2 = 9$. Since $f_2(9) = 24$, the selection
of $d_3 = 0$ would result in a total return of 24. However, a selection of $d_3 =$
2 also leads to a total return of 24. We obtain a return of $11(d_3) = 11(2) =$
22 for stage 3 and a return of 2 for the remaining two stages, since $x_2 = 1$.
To show that there are alternate optimal solutions at this stage we have placed
two entries in the d_3^* and $x_2 = t_3(x_3, d_3^*)$ columns. The other entries in this
table are calculated in the same manner as at stage 2. Let us now move on to
the last stage.

Stage 4 Since we know that there are 10 days available in the planning period, the
input to stage 4 is $x_4 = 10$. Thus we have to consider only one row in the
table, corresponding to stage 4.

x_4 \ d_4	$r_4(x_4,d_4) + f_3(x_3)$ 0	1	d_4^*	$f_4(x_4)$	$x_3 = t_4(x_4,d_4^*)$ $= 10 - 7d_4^*$
10	27	(28)	1	28	3

The optimal decision, given $x_4 = 10$, is $d_4^* = 1$.
We have completed the dynamic programming solution of this problem. In order to
identify the overall optimal solution, we must now trace back through the tables beginning
at stage 4. The optimal decision at stage 4 is $d_4^* = 1$. Thus $x_3 = 10 - 7d_4^* = 3$, and
we enter stage 3 with 3 days available for processing. With $x_3 = 3$ we see that the best
decision at stage 3 is $d_3^* = 0$. Thus we enter stage 2 with $x_2 = 3$. The optimal decision
at stage 2 with $x_2 = 3$ is $d_2^* = 1$, resulting in $x_1 = 0$. Finally the decision at stage 1
must be $d_1^* = 0$. The optimal strategy for our manufacturing operation is then as follows:

Decision	Return
$d_1^* = 0$	0
$d_2^* = 1$	8
$d_3^* = 0$	0
$d_4^* = 1$	20
Total return	28

We should schedule one job from category 2 and one job from category 4 for processing
over the next 10-day planning period.

Another advantage of the dynamic programming approach can now be illustrated. Suppose that we wanted to schedule the jobs to be processed over an 8-day period only. We can solve this new problem simply by making a recalculation at stage 4. The new stage 4 table would appear as follows:

d_4 x_4	$1_4(x_4,d_4) + f_5(x_3)$		d_4^*	$f_4(x_4)$	$x_3 = t_4(x_4,d_4^*)$ $= 8 - 7d_4^*$
	0	1			
8	㉒	㉒	0,1	22	8,1

Actually, we are testing the sensitivity of our optimal solution to a small change in the total number of days available for processing. We have here the case of alternate optimal solutions. One solution can be found by setting $d_4^* = 0$ and tracing through the tables. Doing so, we obtain the following:

Decision	Return
$d_1^* = 0$	0
$d_2^* = 0$	0
$d_3^* = 2$	22
$d_4^* = 0$	0
Total return	22

A second optimal solution can be found by setting $d_4^* = 1$ and tracing back through the tables. Doing so, we obtain another solution (which has exactly the same total return):

Decision	Return
$d_1^* = 1$	2
$d_2^* = 0$	0
$d_3^* = 0$	0
$d_4^* = 1$	20
Total return	22

From the shortest-route and the knapsack examples you should start to become familiar with the basic stage-by-stage solution procedure of dynamic programming. In the next section we see how dynamic programming can be used to solve a production and inventory control problem.

18.4   A PRODUCTION AND INVENTORY CONTROL PROBLEM

In the chapter covering inventory decision models, we commented on problems where the demand was considered known but fluctuated from period to period. The dynamic programming approach developed in this section makes solving this type of production and inventory control problem possible.

Suppose that we have developed forecasts of the demand for a particular product over a certain number of periods and that we would like to decide upon a production quantity for each of the periods so that demand can be satisfied at a minimum cost. There are two costs to be considered: production costs and inventory holding costs. We will assume that one production setup will be made each period, thus setup costs will be constant. As a result, setup costs are not considered in the analysis.

We will allow the production and inventory holding costs to vary across periods. This makes our model more flexible since it also allows for the possibility of using different facilities for production and storage in different periods. Production and storage capacity constraints, which may vary across periods, will be included in the model. Let us adopt the following notation:

N = number of periods (stages in our dynamic programming formulation)

D_n = demand during stage n; $n = 1, 2, \ldots, N$

x_n = a state variable representing the amount of inventory on hand at the beginning of stage n; $n = 1, 2, \ldots, N$

d_n = decision variable for stage n; the production quantity for the corresponding period; $n = 1, 2, \ldots, N$

P_n = production capacity in stage n; $n = 1, 2, \ldots, N$

W_n = storage capacity at the end of stage n; $n = 1, 2, \ldots, N$

C_n = production cost per unit in stage n; $n = 1, 2, \ldots, N$

H_n = holding cost per unit of ending inventory for stage n; $n = 1, 2, \ldots, N$

We will develop the dynamic programming solution for a problem covering 3 months of operation. The data for our problem are presented in Table 18.3.

TABLE 18.3
Data for the Production and Inventory Control Problem

Month	Demand	Production Capacity	Storage Capacity	Production Cost per Unit	Holding Cost per Unit
January	2	3	2	$175	$30
February	3	2	3	150	30
March	3	3	2	200	40

The beginning inventory for January is one unit.

We can think of each month in our problem as a stage in a dynamic programming formulation. Figure 18.5 shows a schematic representation of such a formulation. Note that the beginning inventory in January is one unit.

FIGURE 18.5
Schematic Representation of the Production and Inventory Control Problem as a Three-Stage Dynamic Programming Problem

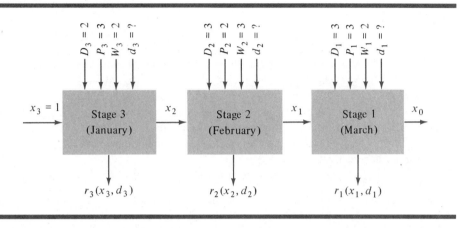

In Figure 18.5 we have numbered the periods backward; that is, stage 1 corresponds to March, stage 2 corresponds to February, and stage 3 corresponds to January. The stage transformation functions take the form of ending inventory = beginning inventory + production − demand. Thus we have

$$x_3 = 1$$
$$x_2 = x_3 + d_3 - D_3 = x_3 + d_3 - 2$$
$$x_1 = x_2 + d_2 - D_2 = x_2 + d_2 - 3$$
$$x_0 = x_1 + d_1 - D_1 = x_1 + d_1 - 3$$

The return functions for each stage represent the sum of production and inventory holding costs for the month. For example, in stage 1 (March), $r_1(x_1, d_1) = 200d_1 + 40(x_1 + d_1 - 3)$ represents the total production and holding costs for the period. The production costs are \$200 per unit and the holding costs are \$40 per unit of ending inventory. The other return functions are

$$r_2(x_2, d_2) = 150d_2 + 30(x_2 + d_2 - 3) \quad \text{Stage 2—February}$$

$$r_3(x_3, d_3) = 175d_3 + 30(x_3 + d_3 - 2) \quad \text{Stage 3—January}$$

This problem is particularly interesting because there are three constraints that must be satisfied at each stage as we perform the optimization procedure. Two are fairly straightforward, while the third is a little tricky. The first constraint is that the ending inventory must be less than or equal to the warehouse capacity. Mathematically we have

$$x_n + d_n - D_n \le W_n$$

or

$$x_n + d_n \le W_n + D_n \tag{18.2}$$

The second constraint is that the production level in each period may not exceed the production capacity. Mathematically we have

$$d_n \leq P_n \tag{18.3}$$

The most difficult constraint to handle is the requirement that beginning inventory plus production must exceed demand for each period. The difficulty with this constraint becomes clear if we study stage 2. The demand for this period is 3, but the production capacity is 2. Therefore we must require that the beginning inventory x_2 be greater than or equal to 1. In general, for each stage this means we must have a constraint that requires beginning inventory plus production to be greater than or equal to demand. Mathematically this constraint can be written as

$$x_n + d_n \geq D_n \tag{18.4}$$

Let us now begin the stagewise solution procedure. At each stage we want to minimize $r_n(x_n, d_n) + f_{n-1}(x_{n-1})$ subject to the constraints given by equations (18.2), (18.3), and (18.4).

Stage 1   The stage 1 problem is as follows:

$$\min \quad r_1(x_1, d_1) = 200d_1 + 40(x_1 + d_1 - 3)$$

s.t.

$$x_1 + d_1 \leq 5 \quad \text{Warehouse constraint}$$
$$d_1 \leq 3 \quad \text{Production constraint}$$
$$x_1 + d_1 \geq 3 \quad \text{Satisfy demand constraint}$$

Combining terms in the objective function, we can rewrite the problem:

$$\min \quad r_1(x_1, d_1) = 240d_1 + 40x_1 - 120$$

s.t.

$$x_1 + d_1 \leq 5$$
$$d_1 \leq 3$$
$$x_1 + d_1 \geq 3$$

Following the tabular approach we adopted in Section 18.3, we will consider all possible inputs to stage 1 (x_1) and make the corresponding minimum cost decision. Since we are attempting to minimize cost, we will want the decision variable d_1 to be as small as possible and still satisfy the demand constraint. Thus the table for stage 1 is as follows:

x_1	d_1^*		$f_1(x_1) = r_1(x_1, d_1^*)$ $240d_1 + 40x_1 - 120$
0	3 ←		600
1	2		400
2	1	Production	200
3	0	capacity of 3 for stage 1 limits d_1	0

Warehouse
capacity of 3
from stage 2
limits value of x_1

Demand constraint: $x_1 + d_1 \geq 3$

Now let us proceed to stage 2.

Stage 2

$$\min \quad r_2(x_2, d_2) + f_1(x_1) = 150d_2 + 30(x_2 + d_2 - 3) + f_1(x_1)$$
$$= 180d_2 + 30x_2 - 90 + f_1(x_1)$$

s.t.

$$x_2 + d_2 \leq 6$$
$$d_2 \leq 2$$
$$x_2 + d_2 \geq 3$$

The stage 2 calculations are summarized in the table below:

	d_2	$r_2(x_2, d_2) + f_1(x_1)$			Production capacity of 2 for stage 2		
x_2		0	1	2 ←	d_2^*	$f_2(x_2)$	$x_1 = x_2 + d_2^* - 3$
0		–	–	–	–	M	–
1		–	–	900	2	900	0
2		–	750	730	2	730	1

Warehouse
capacity of 2
from stage 3

Check demand constraint $x_2 + d_2 \geq 3$ for
each x_2, d_2 combination
(–indicates an infeasible solution)

The detailed calculations for $r_2(x_2, d_2) + f_1(x_1)$ when $x_2 = 1$ and $d_2 = 2$ are as follows:

$$r_2(1, 2) + f_1(0) = 180(2) + 30(1) - 90 + 600 = 900$$

For $r_2(x_2, d_2) + f_1(x_1)$ when $x_2 = 2$ and $d_2 = 1$, we have

$$r_2(2, 1) + f_1(0) = 180(1) + 30(2) - 90 + 600 = 750$$

For $x_2 = 2$ and $d_2 = 2$, we have

$$r_2(2, 2) + f_1(1) = 180(2) + 30(2) - 90 + 400 = 730$$

Note that an arbitrarily high cost M is assigned to the $f_2(x_2)$ column for $x_2 = 0$. Since an input of 0 to stage 2 does not provide a feasible solution, the M cost associated with the $x_2 = 0$ input will prevent $x_2 = 0$ from occurring in the optimal solution.

Stage 3

$$\min \quad r_3(x_3, d_3) + f_2(x_2) = 175d_3 + 30(x_3 + d_3 - 2) + f_2(x_2)$$
$$= 205d_3 + 30x_3 - 60 + f_2(x_2)$$

s.t.

$$x_3 + d_3 \le 4$$
$$d_3 \le 3$$
$$x_3 + d_3 \ge 2$$

With $x_3 = 1$ already defined by the beginning inventory level, the table for stage 3 becomes

x_3 $\diagdown$ d_3	$r_3(x_3, d_3) + f_2(x_2)$ 0	1	2	3	d_3^*	$f_3(x_3)$	$x_2 = x_3 + d_3^* - 2$
1	–	M	(1280)	1315	2	1280	1

Production capacity of 3 at stage 3

Thus we find that the total cost associated with the optimal production and inventory policy is \$1280. To find the optimal decisions and inventory levels for each period, we may trace back through each stage and identify x_n and d_n^* as we go. Table 18.4 summarizes the optimal production and inventory policy.

TABLE 18.4
Optimal Production and Inventory Control Policy

Month	Beginning Inventory	Production	Production Cost	Ending Inventory	Holding Cost	Total Monthly Cost
January	1	2	\$ 350	1	\$30	\$ 380
February	1	2	300	0	0	300
March	0	3	600	0	0	600
Totals			\$1250		\$30	\$1280

Summary

Dynamic programming is an attractive approach to problem solving when it is possible to break a large problem up into smaller multiple stages. The solution procedure then proceeds recursively, solving one of the smaller problems at each stage. Dynamic programming is not a specific algorithm, but rather an approach to problem solving. Thus the recursive optimization may be carried out differently for different problems. While we have used a tabular approach to determine optimal decisions at each stage, other dynamic programming problems might use linear programming, branch and bound, calculus, and other methods to solve the subproblems. In any case it is almost always easier to solve a series of smaller problems than one large one. This is how the dynamic programming approach obtains its power.

Glossary

Dynamic programming   An approach to problem solving that permits decomposing one large mathematical model that may be very difficult to solve into a number of smaller problems that are usually easier to solve.

Principle of optimality   Regardless of the decisions that have been made at the previous stages, if the decision made at stage n is to be part of an overall optimal solution, the decision made at stage n must be optimal for all remaining stages.

Stages   When a large problem is deomposed into a number of smaller problems, the dynamic programming solution approach creates a stage to correspond to each of the subproblems.

State variables x_n and x_{n-1}   An input state variable x_n and an output state variable x_{n-1} together define the condition of the process at the beginning and end of stage n.

Decision variable d_n   A variable representing the possible decisions that can be made at stage n.

Stage transformation function $t_n(x_n, d_n)$ The rule or equation that relates the output state variable x_{n-1} for stage n to the input state variable x_n and the decision variable d_n.

Return function $r_n(x_n, d_n)$ A value (such as profit or loss) associated with making decision d_n at stage n for a specific value of the input state variable x_n.

Knapsack problem N items, each of which has a different weight and value, are to be placed into a knapsack with limited weight capacity so as to maximize the total value of the items placed in the knapsack.

Problems

1. In Section 18.1 we solved a shortest-route problem using dynamic programming. Find the optimal solution to this problem by total enumeration; that is, list all possible routes from the origin, node 1, to the destination, node 10, and pick the one with the smallest value. Explain why the dynamic programming approach results in fewer computations for this problem.

2. Consider the following network. The numbers above each arc represent the distance between the connected nodes.

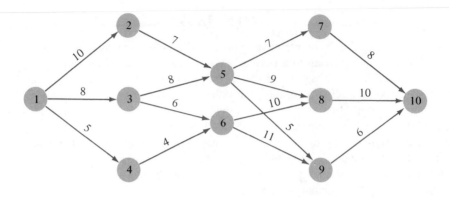

a. Find the shortest route from node 1 to node 10 using dynamic programming.
b. What is the shortest route from node 4 to node 10?
c. Enumerate all possible routes from node 1 to node 10. Explain how dynamic programming has reduced the number of computations below required by total enumeration.

3. A firm has just hired eight new employees and would like to determine how to allocate the new employees to four activities. The firm has prepared the table below, which gives the estimated profit for each activity as a function of the number of new employees allocated to it:

	Number of New Employees								
Activities	0	1	2	3	4	5	6	7	8
1	22	30	37	44	49	54	58	60	61
2	30	40	48	55	59	62	64	66	67
3	46	52	56	59	62	65	67	68	69
4	5	22	36	48	52	55	58	60	61

a. Use dynamic programming to determine the optimal allocation of new employees to the activities.
b. Suppose there were only six new employees hired. Which activities would you assign to these six employees?

4. A sawmill receives logs in 20-foot lengths, cuts them to smaller lengths, and then sells these smaller lengths to a number of manufacturing companies. The lengths the company has orders for are

$$l_1 = 3 \text{ ft}$$
$$l_2 = 7 \text{ ft}$$
$$l_3 = 11 \text{ ft}$$
$$l_4 = 16 \text{ ft}$$

The sawmill currently has an inventory of 2000 logs in 20-foot lengths and would like to select a cutting pattern that will maximize the profit made on this inventory. Assuming the sawmill has sufficient orders available, its problem becomes one of determining the cutting pattern that will maximize profits. The per-unit profit for each of the smaller lengths is as follows:

Length (feet)	Profit ($)
3	1
7	3
11	5
16	8

Any cutting pattern is permissible as long as

$$3d_1 + 7d_2 + 11d_3 + 16d_4 \leq 20$$

where d_i is the number of pieces of length l_i cut, $i = 1, 2, 3, 4$.
a. Set up a dynamic programming model of this problem and solve it. What are your decision variables? What is your state variable?
b. Explain briefly how this model can be extended to find the best cutting pattern in cases where the overall length l can be cut into N lengths, $l_1, l_2, \ldots, l_N$.

5. A large manufacturing company has a very-well-developed management training program. Each trainee is expected to complete a four-phase program, but there are a number of different assignments each trainee can be given at each phase of the training program. The assignments available and the estimated completion times in months at each phase of the program are shown below:

Phase I	Phase II	Phase III	Phase IV
A—13	E—3	H—12	L—10
B—10	F—6	I—6	M—5
C—20	G—5	J—7	N—13
D—17		K—10	

Assignments made at subsequent phases depend upon the previous assignment. For example, a trainee who completes assignment A at phase I may only go on to assignments F or G at phase II. That is, there is a precedence relationship for each assignment as shown below:

Assignment	Feasible Succeeding Assignments
A	F, G
B	F
C	G
D	E, G
E	H, I, J, K
F	H, K
G	J, K
H	L, M
I	L, M
J	M, N
K	N
L	Finish
M	Finish
N	Finish

a. The company would like to determine the sequence of assignments that will minimize the time in the training program. Formulate and solve this as a dynamic programming problem. (*Hint*: Develop a network representation of the problem where each node represents completion of an activity.)

b. If a trainee has just completed assignment *C* and would like to complete the remainder of the training program in the shortest possible time, which assignment should be chosen next?

6. Crazy Robin, the owner of a small chain of Robin Hood Sporting Goods stores in Des Moines and Cedar Rapids, Iowa, has just purchased a new supply of top-line golf balls. Because she was willing to purchase the entire amount of a production overrun, Robin was able to buy the golf balls at one-half the usual price.

   Three of Robin's stores do a good business in the sale of golf equipment and supplies and, as a result, Robin has decided to retail the balls at these three stores. Thus Robin is faced with the problem of determining how many dozen balls to allocate to each store. The following estimates show the expected profit from allocating 100, 200, 300, 400, or 500 dozen to each store:

| | Number of Dozens of Golf Balls | | | | |
	100	200	300	400	500
Store 1	$600	$1100	$1550	$1700	$1800
Store 2	500	1200	1700	2000	2100
Store 3	550	1100	1500	1850	1950

Assuming the lots cannot be broken into any sizes smaller than 100 dozen each, how many dozen golf balls should Crazy Robin send to each store?

7. The Max X. Posure Advertising Agency is conducting a 10-day advertising campaign for a local department store. The agency has determined that the most effective campaign would possibly include placing ads in four media: daily newspaper, Sunday newspaper, radio, and television. A total of $8000 has been made available for this campaign, and the agency would like to distribute this in $1000 increments across the media in such a fashion that an advertising exposure index is maximized. Research that has been conducted by the agency permits the following estimates to be made of the exposure per each $1000 expenditure in each of the media.

Media	Thousands of Dollars Spent							
	1	2	3	4	5	6	7	8
Daily newspaper	24	37	46	59	72	80	82	82
Sunday newspaper	15	55	70	75	90	95	95	95
Radio	20	30	45	55	60	62	63	63
Television	20	40	55	65	70	70	70	70

    a. How much should the agency spend on each medium in order to maximize the department store's exposure?

    b. How would your answer change if only $6000 were budgeted?

    c. How would your answers in parts a and b change if television was not considered as one of the media?

8. Suppose that we have a three-stage process where the yield for each stage is a function of the decision made. In mathematical notation we may state our problem as follows:

$$\max \quad r_1(d_1) + r_2(d_2) + r_3(d_3)$$
$$\text{s.t.}$$
$$d_1 + d_2 + d_3 \leq 1000$$

The possible values the decision variables may take on at each stage and the corresponding returns are presented in tabular form below:

Stage 1		Stage 2		Stage 3	
d_1	$r_1(d_1)$	d_2	$r_2(d_2)$	d_3	$r_3(d_3)$
0	0	100	120	100	175
100	110	300	400	500	700
200	300	500	650		
300	400	600	700		
400	425	800	975		

    a. Use total enumeration to list all feasible sequences of decisions for this problem. Which one is optimal [that is, maximizes $r_1(d_1) + r_2(d_2) + r_3(d_3)$]?

    b. Use dynamic programming to solve this problem.

9. Recall the production and inventory control problem of Section 18.4. Mills Manufacturing Company has just such a production and inventory control problem for an armature the company manufactures as a component for a generator. The available data for the next 3-month planning period are presented below:

Month	Demand	Production Capacity	Warehouse Capacity	Production Cost per Unit	Holding Cost per Unit
1	20	30	40	$2.00	$0.30
2	30	20	30	1.50	0.30
3	30	30	20	2.00	0.20

Using the dynamic programming approach outlined in Section 18.4 find the optimal production quantities and inventory levels in each period for the Mills Manufacturing Company. Assume there is a beginning inventory of 10 units on hand at the beginning of month 1 and that production runs are completed in multiples of 10 units (that is, 10, 20, or 30 units).

10. A chemical processing plant is considering introducing a new product on the market. However, before making a final decision, management has requested you to provide estimates of profits associated with different process designs. The general flow process is represented below.

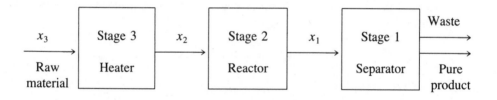

Raw material is fed into a heater at the rate of 4500 pounds per week. The heated material is then routed to a reactor where a portion of the raw material is converted to pure product. A separator then withdraws the finished product for sale. The unconverted material is discarded as waste.

Profit considerations are to be based on a 2-year payback period on investments; that is, all capital expenditures must be recovered in 2 years (100 weeks). All calculations will be based on weekly operations. Raw material costs are expected to stay fixed at $1 per pound, and it has been forecast that the finished product will sell for $6 per pound.

It is your responsibility to determine the process design that will yield maximum profit per week. You and your co-workers have collected the following preliminary data.

At stage 3 one heater with an initial cost of $12,000 is being considered. Two temperatures, 700°F and 800°F, are feasible. The operating costs for the heater depend directly on the temperature to be attained. These costs are as follows:

Operating Costs at Stage 3

		Decisions at Stage 3	
Input x_3	4500 lb	$280/week	$380/week

The output from stage 3, x_2, which is also the input to stage 2, may be expressed as 4500 pounds of raw material heated to either 700°F or 800°F. One of the decisions you must make is to what temperature the raw material should be heated.

For stage 2, a reactor, which can operate with either of two catalysts, $C1$ or $C2$, is to be used. The initial cost of this reactor is $50,000. The operating costs of this reactor are independent of the input x_2 and depend only upon the catalyst selected. The costs of the catalysts are included in the operating costs. The output will be expressed in pounds of converted (or pure) material. The percent of material converted depends on the incoming temperature and the catalyst used. The tables below summarize the pertinent information. Thus a second decision you must make is to specify which catalyst should be used.

Percent Conversion

		Decisions at Stage 2	
		$C1$	$C2$
x_2	(4500 lb, 700°F)	20%	40%
	(4500 lb, 800°F)	40%	60%

Operating Costs

Decision at Stage 2	
$C1$	$C2$
$450/week	$650/week

One of two separators, $S1$ or $S2$, will be purchased for stage 1. $S1$ has an initial cost of $20,000 and a weekly operating cost of $0.10 per pound of pure product to be separated. Comparatively, $S2$ has an initial cost of $5000 and a weekly operating cost of $0.20 per pound of pure product to be separated. Included in these operating costs is the expense of discarding the unconverted raw material as waste.

Develop a dynamic programming model for this problem. What is your recommendation for best temperature for the heater? Best catalyst to use with the reactor? Best separator to purchase? What is the maximum weekly profit?

Management Science in Practice

THE UNITED STATES ENVIRONMENTAL PROTECTION AGENCY*

Washington, D.C.

The United States Environmental Protection Agency (EPA) is an independent agency of the executive branch of the federal government. Fifteen components of five executive departments and independent agencies were consolidated to form EPA on December 2, 1970, under Reorganization Plan No. 3 by then President Richard M. Nixon. Today, EPA administers comprehensive environmental protection laws related to:

Water pollution control, water quality and drinking water
Air pollution and radiation
Pesticides and toxic substances
Solid and hazardous waste including emergency spill response and superfund site
    remediation

Program offices for each of these media support the Administrator through policy development, standards and criteria development, and support and evaluation of regional activities. The 10 regional offices implement and enforce standards, conduct monitoring and surveillance programs, and provide technical and financial assistance to state and local governments.

Functional activities at EPA headquarters, which transcend all media, include planning and management, enforcement, and research and development. Quantitative analysis techniques are used extensively in the experimental design of research studies, providing quality assurance of monitoring surveys and enforcement actions, as well as environmental modeling and simulation studies to evaluate the cost-effectiveness of alternative environmental policies, regulations, and control technologies.

EPA's Office of Research and Development serves as the primary source of scientific and technical support to the Agency's operating programs and regional offices by conducting in-house and extramural research at 14 locations throughout the country. Research activities focus upon analytical methods development and quality assurance, environmental processes and effects research, health effects research, and environmental engineering. Environmental modeling is conducted for

*The authors are indebted to John Convery, Environmental Protection Agency, for providing this application.

all media at many of these research locations. ORD maintains a Center for Water Quality Modeling at its laboratory in Athens, Ga. The following dynamic programming application was developed by the Municipal Environmental Research Laboratory in Cincinnati, Ohio, as part of an effort to evaluate the usefulness of seasonal discharge permits in reducing the cost of wastewater treatment while maintaining water quality.

WATER QUALITY MANAGEMENT PROGRAM

The Environmental Protection Agency administers programs designed to maintain acceptable water quality conditions for rivers and streams throughout the United States. In order to guard against polluted rivers and streams, the government requires companies to obtain a discharge permit from federal or state authorities before any form of pollutants can be discharged into a body of water. These permits specifically notify each discharger as to the amount of legally dischargeable waste that can be placed in the river or stream. The discharge limits are determined by ensuring that water quality criteria are met even in unusually dry seasons when the river or stream has a critically low-flow condition. Most often this low-flow condition is based on the lowest flow recorded over the past 10 years. By ensuring that water quality is maintained under the low-flow conditions, there is a high degree of reliability that the water quality criteria can be maintained throughout the year.

At different seasons of the year, water will flow at different rates in the various rivers and streams. With these seasonal flow variations, seasonal discharge permits can be issued which allow different discharge limits at the different times of the year. As a result, companies can take advantage of higher stream flow rates to reduce treatment requirements and to lower the discharge treatment costs. A goal of the EPA is to establish seasonal discharge limits that enable lower treatment costs while maintaining water quality standards at a prescribed level of reliability.

A DYNAMIC PROGRAMMING MODEL FOR SEASONAL DISCHARGE LIMITS

A dynamic programming model has been formulated for establishing the allowable waste discharge load during the various seasons of the year. The periods or stages of the model correspond to different seasons considered during the year; there is a separate stage for each season. The return function at each stage is the cost of the waste treatment for waste discharged during the stage, or season. The decision variable at each stage is the design streamflow for the body of water receiving the waste. Once the design streamflow has been established, an allowable waste discharge and its associated treatment cost can be determined. The design streamflow decisions at each stage interact to determine the overall reliability that the annual water quality conditions will be maintained. In this regard, the decision variable choice at any one stage, or period, is affected by the decision variable choices at the other stages.

The probability that there will be no water quality violations over the entire year is the product of the seasonal probabilities of no violations. To maintain reliability standards the probability of no violation during the year must exceed a certain value. Suppose we let $P_j(q_j)$ represent the probability of no violation during season j when the design streamflow is q_j. Then the probability of no water quality violation over the entire year is given by

$$\prod_{j=1}^{N} P_j(q_j) = \text{probability of no violation}$$

where N is the number of seasons during the year.

The reliability requirement is satisfied when this probability is sufficiently high. Suppose α is the minimal acceptable probability. The water quality constraint is then

$$\prod_{j=1}^{N} P_j(q_j) \geq \alpha$$

By taking the logarithm of both sides, this constraint can be written as

$$\sum_{j=1}^{N} \log P_j(q_j) \leq \log \alpha$$

The state variable at stage j is then defined to be

$$s_j = \sum_{k=1}^{j} P_k(q_k)$$

The design streamflows (the decision variables) are chosen to minimize treatment cost subject to requirements that the allowable waste discharge is within given limits and in such a fashion that the state variable will ensure sufficient reliability of no water quality violations.

The solution to the model provides the design streamflows for each seasonal period. These streamflows combine with the water quality criterion to establish the seasonal waste discharge load. With the return function measuring treatment cost, the model obtains the minimum treatment cost solution that will maintain the EPA water quality standards.

Questions

1. Suppose there are four seasons and the probabilities of a water quality violation in each season are 0.01, 0.05, 0.02, and 0.01, respectively. What is the probability that there will be no water quality violation over the entire year?
2. Let P_i = the probability of no water quality violation in season i. Suppose there are three seasons. Write a constraint specifying that the minimal acceptable probability of no violation over the three seasons is 0.90.

19

Calculus-Based Solution Procedures

In this chapter we consider mathematical models where the functions or mathematical relationships involved are not all linear. For example, in formulating a profit or cost function for a specific problem we may find that a linear function is inappropriate and that a curve or a nonlinear function is necessary. Recall that in our analysis of inventory models (see Section 11.1) we developed the following nonlinear function to show how total inventory cost could be expressed in terms of the order quantity Q:

$$\text{TC} = \frac{Q}{2} C_h + \frac{D}{Q} C_0$$

The graph of the total cost curve for an economic order quantity inventory model is shown in Figure 19.1.

In determining the optimal values of the decision variables in nonlinear models, we will find calculus-based solution procedures quite valuable. In this chapter we show how differential calculus can be used to find maximum and minimum values for such models. We begin by using differential calculus to analyze nonlinear objective functions having only one decision variable. Then we discuss the procedures for handling nonlinear functions with two or more decision variables. Finally, we show how calculus-based solution procedures can be used to solve nonlinear models that have constraints.

This is the only chapter in this book where a working knowledge of calculus, specifically differential calculus, is a prerequisite. However, the reader with no calculus background may still find this chapter useful in terms of learning about nonlinear models and the role that calculus-based solution procedures play in analyzing these models.

19.1 MODELS WITH ONE DECISION VARIABLE

The Macon Psychiatric Institute, a nonprofit organization, is interested in redesigning its mental health care delivery system in order to maximize the number of people who can benefit from its services. Based on some recent studies, the institute has learned that the

731

FIGURE 19.1
Total Cost Curve for the Economic Order Quantity Inventory Model

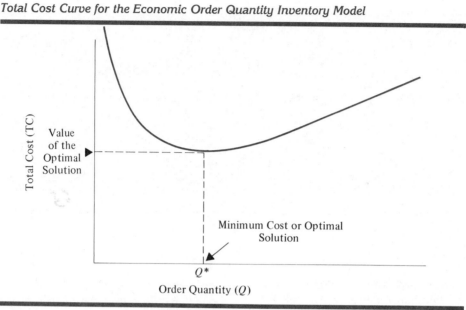

average treatment time per patient is a function of the number of patients the clinic is treating simultaneously. With more patients simultaneously receiving treatment, the patients remain in residence longer; that is, with more patients in the system, the clinic's staff becomes overloaded and the patient's time in residence at the clinic increases. If the institute reduces the number of patients simultaneously being treated, the patients can receive more personal attention, and thus the treatment time can be shortened. The institute's problem can be stated in terms of how many active or in-residence patients should be maintained by the clinic so that the total number of patients treated per year is maximized.

Based on patient records and recovery time estimates by the clinic's staff members, the following mathematical relationship can be used to describe how the number of in-residence patients affects the patient treatment or recovery time:

$$T = \frac{45}{180 - P} \qquad (19.1)$$

where

T = average patient treatment time in years
P = number of in-residence patients

This relationship is believed to be valid as long as the number of in-residence patients P remains between 45 and 135.

Using equation (19.1), we see that if the clinic operates with $P = 135$ patients, then $T = 45/(180 - 135) = 1$ year (that is, on the average a patient receives 1 year of treatment before being released). However, if the clinic reduces its number of in-residence patients to 60, then the average recovery period can be shortened to $T = 45/(180 - 60)$ = 0.375 year, or 4.5 months. The relationship between the number of in-residence patients and the average treatment time is shown in Figure 19.2.

FIGURE 19.2
Average Treatment Time T as a Function of the Number of In-Residence Patients P

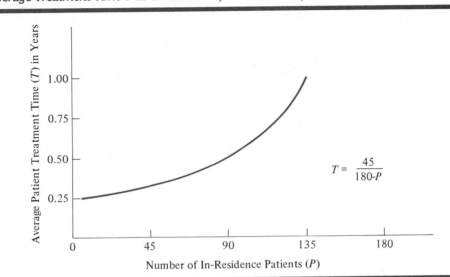

The institute wants to maximize the total number of people treated per year. Since T is the average treatment time per patient and since the clinic treats P patients *simultaneously*, the total number of patients treated per year is given by

$$N = \frac{1}{T}P = \frac{P}{T} \tag{19.2}$$

For $P = 135$ we saw earlier that $T = 1$ year; thus $N = P/T = {}^{135}/_1 = 135$ patients per year. However, for $P = 60$, $T = 0.375$ and $N = 60/0.375 = 160$ patients per year. Therefore reducing the number of active patients to 60 does improve the effectiveness of the clinic; more patients can be treated over a specified time period. However, the question of what is the optimal number of in-residence patients still needs to be answered.

Since T is a function of P [equation (19.1)], we can substitute into equation (19.2) and write the mathematical model for the problem as a function of the one variable, P:

$$N = \frac{P}{T} = \frac{P}{45/(180 - P)} = \frac{(180 - P)P}{45} = 4P - {}^{1}/_{45}P^2 \tag{19.3}$$

We are interested in maximizing the number of patients treated per year N. Thus the above model provides a nonlinear objective function for a maximization problem with one decision variable, P, and our problem becomes

$$\max N = 4P - {}^{1}/_{45}P^2 \tag{19.4}$$

With only one decision variable we can observe how the number of patients treated per year varies for different P values by drawing a graph of the relationship. This graph, shown in Figure 19.3, indicates that the maximum value of the objective function is 180, corresponding to an in-residence patient volume of 90. Since sketching the graph of a function may be time consuming, and since the determination of the optimal solution is dependent upon the accuracy of the graph, we will usually want to use a differential calculus procedure for solving such a problem.

FIGURE 19.3
Number of Patients Treated per Year as a Function of the Number of Patients in Residence

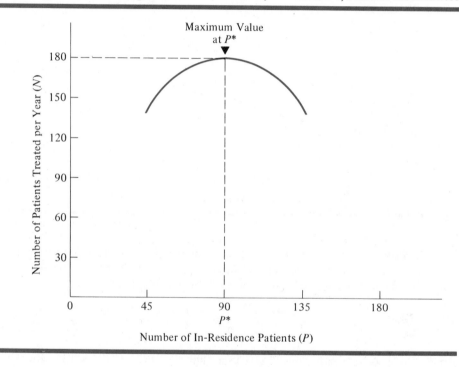

Recall from calculus that the first derivative of an unconstrained function must be equal to zero at a *local maximum* or *local minimum*. The reason for this is that the first derivative is the slope of the line tangent to the curve, and the slope of the tangent line is zero at any local maximum or local minimum value of the function. In the Macon Psychiatric Institute problem we see that the function relating the number of patients treated per year to the number of in-residence patients has one local maximum (Figure 19.3). Many functions, however, possess a number of local maxima and/or minima. For example, consider the graph of the function depicted in Figure 19.4, which has two local maxima and one local minimum. At each of the local maxima and at the local minimum the first derivatives, and hence the slope of the tangent lines, are equal to zero. Rule 1 below summarizes the above discussion in the form of a *necessary condition* for determining all the local maxima or minima of an unconstrained function of one variable:

FIGURE 19.4
Graph of a Function f(x) Having Two Local Maxima and One Local Minimum

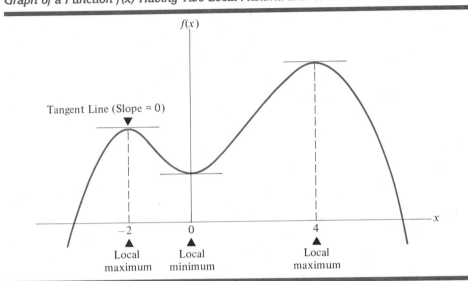

Tangent Line (Slope = 0)

Local maximum   Local minimum   Local maximum

Rule 1 (Necessary Condition).

The first derivative of an unconstrained function of one variable must equal zero at its local maximum or local minimum points.

Let us now calculate the first derivative for the institute's problem[1]:

$$\text{First derivative} = \frac{dN}{dP} = 4 - \frac{2}{45}P$$

Setting the first derivative equal to zero and solving, we obtain

$$\frac{dN}{dP} = 4 - \frac{2}{45}P = 0$$

$$\frac{2}{45}P = 4$$

$$P^* = \frac{(4)(45)}{2} = 90$$

Thus we see that $P^* = 90$ is the value of P that sets the first derivative equal to zero. Figure 19.5 shows that the slope of the line tangent to the curve at this local maximum point is in fact zero.

---

[1]A short table of derivative formulas is provided in Appendix D.

FIGURE 19.5
Maximum is at Value of P where Derivative = 0

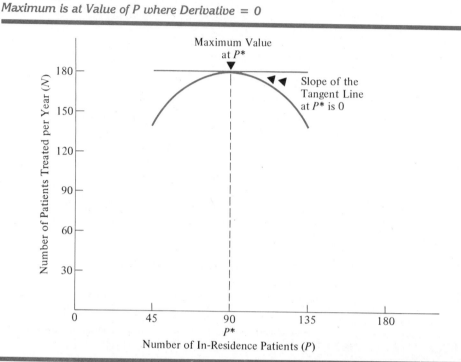

Unfortunately, while it is a necessary condition that the first derivative equal zero at a local maximum point, this is not sufficient to guarantee that we have in fact located a local maximum. Actually, a point where the first derivative equals zero could be a local maximum, a local minimum, or an inflection point. Thus a second derivative test is needed to determine whether or not we have a local maximum. Rule 2 provides such a test and establishes a *sufficient condition* that guarantees that we have reached a local maximum (or a local minimum) solution.

Rule 2 (Sufficient Condition).

If rule 1 is satisfied at a point, and
a. If the second derivative[2] *is greater than* zero, then the point is a local *minimum*.
b. If the second derivative is *less than* zero, then the point is a local *maximum*.

Let us apply this second derivative test to the Macon Psychiatric Institute problem. The second derivative is given by

$$\text{Second derivative} = \frac{d^2N}{dP^2} = -\,{}^2\!/_{45} < 0$$

[2]The second derivative is found simply by applying the differentiation rule to the first derivative function.

Since the second derivative is less than zero, rule 2 tells us that $P^* = 90$ does indeed yield a local maximum of the objective function for our problem.

We call a point a *global maximum* if it yields the highest value for the function. Similarly, we call a point a *global minimum* if it yields the lowest value. In this case it is easy to verify that the local maximum, $P^* = 90$, is also a global maximum. Since the function has only one point at which rule 1 is satisfied, and since rule 2 says that this point is a local maximum, this local maximum must be the global maximum.

Assuming that the relationships we used in developing the mathematical model are accurate reflections of reality, the institute should admit 90 patients and maintain this many patients in residence all the time. This will maximize the number of patients the institute can treat per year at 180.

The problem we have just described illustrates how calculus can assist in finding the optimum for an unconstrained function of one variable. However, in some situations we will find that it is of interest to consider finding the optimal value for a function over a specified interval. This situation may come about because of constraints placed on the decision maker or because the function of interest is defined only over a specified interval, and as a result we choose to limit ourselves to finding the best value for the function over that interval. In problems of this type the optimal solution could occur at the endpoints of the interval as well as at points where rules 1 and 2 hold.

As an illustration of this type of situation, suppose we are trying to find the maximum of the function $f(x) = x^3 - 3x^2$ over the interval $-1 \le x \le 4$. A graph of the function over this interval is shown in Figure 19.6.

FIGURE 19.6
Graph of the Function $f(x) = x^3 - 3x^2$

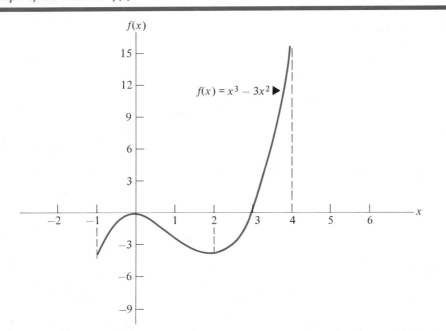

Clearly, the global maximum of the function over this interval occurs at $x = 4$. However, rule 1 is not satisfied at this point because the first derivative (the slope of the tangent line) is not equal to zero. When we are constrained to a specific interval in our search for the optimum of a function of one variable, we must extend our solution procedure beyond just checking points that satisfy rules 1 and 2. The general procedure for finding the global maximum or minimum of a function of one variable is as follows:

Step 1   Find all the points that satisfy rules 1 and 2. These are candidates for yielding the optimal solution to the problem.

Step 2   If the solution is restricted to a specified interval, evaluate the function at the endpoints of the interval.

Step 3   Compare the values of the function at all the points found in steps 1 and 2. The largest of these is the global maximum solution; the smallest is the global minimum solution.

Let us apply this procedure to the function in Figure 19.6. Following step 1 we first find all the points at which the first derivative equals zero:

$$\frac{df(x)}{dx} = 3x^2 - 6x = 0$$

Therefore

$$x(3x - 6) = 0$$

and we see that both $x = 0$ and $x = 2$ satisfy rule 1. Checking rule 2, we find

$$\frac{d^2f(x)}{dx^2} = 6x - 6$$

At $x = 0$,

$$\frac{d^2f(0)}{dx^2} = -6 < 0$$

and we have a local maximum of the function at $x = 0$. The value of the function at $x = 0$ is $f(0) = 0^3 - 3(0)^2 = 0$. Looking back to Figure 19.6 we see that this is indeed a local maximum and the slope of the tangent line is equal to zero at this point. At $x = 2$,

$$\frac{d^2f(2)}{dx^2} = 6(2) - 6 = 6 > 0$$

Therefore by rule 2 we have a local minimum at $x = 2$. The value of the function at $x = 2$ is $f(2) = (2)^3 - 3(2)^2 = -4$.

Proceeding to step 2 we evaluate the function at both of its endpoints:

$$f(-1) = (-1)^3 - 3(-1)^2 = -4$$
$$f(4) = (4)^3 - 3(4)^2 = 16$$

At step 3 we compare the values at the points found in steps 1 and 2. The largest value occurs at $x = 4$ and yields a global maximum value of 16 over the specified interval. The smallest value occurs at both $x = -1$ and $x = 2$; that is, there is a tie for global minimum, and we say that both $x = -1$ and $x = 2$ are global minima. The minimum value is -4. Note that one of these candidates was found in step 1 and the other in step 2 of our solution procedure. Figure 19.6 illustrates graphically the conclusions we have reached.

Let us return for a moment to the Macon Psychiatric Institute problem. The objective function for this problem was believed to be applicable only over the interval $45 \leq P \leq 135$. It may be reasonable to assume that this means the institute will not consider letting the number of in-residence patients fall below 45 or exceed 135. If this were the case then, why did we not need to check the endpoints of this interval in our search for a maximum? The reason is that there was only one point ($P* = 90$) that satisfied rule 1, and it was a local maximum. Since $P*$ is a local maximum, the value of the function decreases as we move away from it, and since no other points satisfy rule 1, we know that the function does not turn up again anywhere. Therefore no other point could yield a higher value than $P* = 90$. Nevertheless, the three-step procedure we have specified for maximizing or minimizing a function of one variable would have led to the same conclusion. The value of the function is smaller at $P = 45$ and $P = 135$ than at the maximum, $P* = 90$.

Before concluding this section, let us consider another numerical example to make sure that we know how to apply steps 1, 2, and 3.

Example. Suppose we want to minimize the function

$$f(x) = x^3 - 6x^2 + 50 \tag{19.5}$$

over the interval $0 \leq x \leq 5$.

Step 1 Setting the first derivative equal to zero, we find

$$\frac{df(x)}{dx} = 3x^2 - 12x = 0$$

or

$$x(3x - 12) = 0$$

This provides two possible values for x: either $x = 0$ or $3x - 12 = 0$ and $x = 4$. That is, $x = 0$ and $x = 4$ both set the first derivative equal to zero, satisfying rule 1. To see if either of these yields a local minimum, we must calculate the second derivative:

$$\frac{d^2f(x)}{dx^2} = 6x - 12$$

At $x = 0$ we have

$$\frac{d^2f(0)}{dx^2} = 6(0) - 12 = -12 < 0$$

Therefore by rule 2, $x = 0$ yields a local maximum for $f(x)$. At $x = 4$ we have

$$\frac{d^2f(4)}{dx^2} = 6(4) - 12 = 12 > 0$$

Therefore by rule 2, $x = 4$ yields a local minimum for $f(x)$. The graph of $f(x)$ [equation (19.5)] is shown in Figure 19.7. Again note that the slopes of the lines tangent to the curve at these local minimum and local maximum points are both zero.

FIGURE 19.7
Graph of the Function $f(x) = x^3 - 6x^2 + 50$

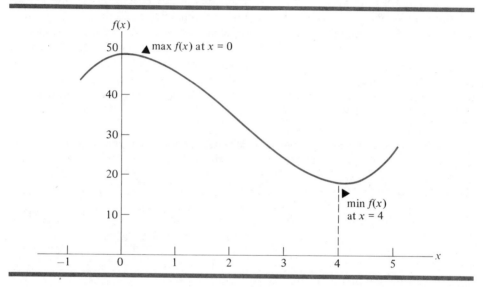

Step 2   Evaluating the function at the endpoints, we obtain

$$f(0) = 50$$
$$f(5) = 25$$

Step 3   Since we are searching for a minimum and $f(4) = 18 < f(5) = 25$, we conclude that $x^* = 4$ is the global minimum solution. We note also in this example that the local maximum found in step 1 corresponded to one of the endpoints. This is purely a coincidence where the first derivative of the function happens to be zero at an endpoint of the interval.

19.2   UNCONSTRAINED MODELS WITH MORE THAN ONE DECISION VARIABLE

As we have seen in the previous section and elsewhere in the text, there are a number of problem situations for which we can develop mathematical models involving only one decision variable. However, there are perhaps even more decision-making situations in which the decision maker must select the best values for two or more decision variables. In this section we discuss a problem that leads to the formulation of a nonlinear mathematical model involving two decision variables. Then we show how first and second derivative tests similar to rules 1 and 2 can be developed for finding the local maximum and local minimum values of unconstrained functions of two variables. We do not attempt to extend the analysis to the case where each of the variables is restricted to an interval. This case is inherently more difficult than the situation for one variable, and its analysis would take us too far afield for an introductory text of this nature.[3] For completeness, we will discuss the extension to unconstrained models involving several decision variables.

In order to see how a mathematical model involving two decision variables might arise, let us suppose that Lawn King, Inc. manufactures two styles of lawn mower. One is a riding mower, and the other is a standard walking power mower. Lawn King is interested in establishing a pricing policy for the two mowers that will maximize the total profit for the product line. Sales for these two products are not independent. Over time, Lawn King has observed that an increase in the price of the riding mower is usually accompanied by a decrease in the number of riding mowers sold and an increase in the number of walking mowers sold. Similarly, increases in the price of the walking mower have been accompanied by a decrease in sales of the walking mower and an increase in sales of the riding mower. Economists would say that the two types of lawn mower are *substitutable products*. Because these two products are substitutable, we should expect that an appropriate mathematical model for maximizing total profit would involve the simultaneous consideration of prices for both products.

Suppose that after a study of the relationships between sales prices and quantities sold, Lawn King has established the following expressions:

$$q_1 = 95 - 2p_1 + 0.7p_2 \tag{19.6}$$
$$q_2 = 188 + 0.3p_1 - 0.5p_2 \tag{19.7}$$

where

q_1 = number of walking mowers sold in thousands
q_2 = number of riding mowers sold in thousands
p_1 = price of walking mower in dollars
p_2 = price of riding mower in dollars

Further information, prepared by the accounting department, is available on the total cost of producing each type of mower:

$$c_1 = 100 + 90q_1 \tag{19.8}$$
$$c_2 = 50 + 250q_2 \tag{19.9}$$

---

[3]The analysis of this case essentially involves treating each endpoint as a separate constraint. For a discussion, see Gottfried, B. S., and J. Weisman, *Introduction to Optimization Theory*. Englewood Cliffs, N.J., Prentice-Hall, 1973.

where

c_1 = total cost of producing q_1 walking mowers in thousands of dollars

c_2 = total cost of producing q_2 riding mowers in thousands of dollars

Note that the production costs are in thousands of dollars and the number of lawn mowers are being measured in thousands of units. The fixed cost of producing walking mowers (the part that is independent of the number of units produced) is thus $100,000, and the variable cost is $90,000 per 1000 walking mowers, or $90 per mower. Similarly, the fixed cost of production for riding mowers is $50,000, and the variable cost is $250,000 per 1000 mowers, or $250 per mower.

We would like to develop a mathematical model of the relationship between the controllable inputs p_1 and p_2 and the output we would like to maximize, gross profit (GP). The appropriate relationship is established as follows:

$$GP = \text{total revenue} - \text{total cost}$$
$$= (p_1 q_1 + p_2 q_2) - (c_1 + c_2) \tag{19.10}$$

We can use equations (19.6) through (19.9) to eliminate q_1 and q_2 from the model, permitting us to write a mathematical model that is a function of only the two decision variables p_1 and p_2. Using equations (19.6) and (19.7) to substitute into equations (19.8) and (19.9), we obtain (in thousands of dollars)

$$c_1 = 100 + 90(95 - 2p_1 + 0.7p_2)$$
$$= 8650 - 180p_1 + 63p_2$$

and

$$c_2 = 50 + 250(188 + 0.3p_1 - 0.5p_2)$$
$$= 47,050 + 75p_1 - 125p_2$$

Substituting these two expressions along with equations (19.6) and (19.7) into the gross profit expression (19.10) allows us to write the gross profit model as a function of p_1 and p_2 only:

$$GP = p_1(95 - 2p_1 + 0.7p_2) + p_2(188 + 0.3p_1 - 0.5p_2)$$
$$- (8650 - 180p_1 + 63p_2) - (47,050 + 75p_1 - 125p_2)$$

After multiplying and collecting terms we obtain

$$GP = -2p_1^2 - 0.5p_2^2 + p_1 p_2 + 200p_1 + 250p_2 - 55,700 \tag{19.11}$$

This is the function we would like to maximize. The gross profit in this model is represented by an unconstrained nonlinear function of two variables. The rules for finding the local maximum and/or local minimum of functions of two variables are similar to the ones we developed in the previous section for functions of one variable. There is a first derivative test that serves as a necessary condition that must be satisfied by any local maximum or local minimum point. In addition, there is a second derivative test that can be applied to determine whether a point satisfying the necessary condition is a local maximum, a local minimum, or neither. This second derivative test is referred to as a sufficient condition. The first derivative test is stated as rule 3:

Rule 3 (Necessary Condition).

Both partial derivatives of an unconstrained function of two variables must equal zero at any local maximum or local minimum point.

Let us apply the first derivative test to the gross profit function (19.11) in our Lawn King problem. Recall from calculus that when taking the partial derivative of a function of more than one variable, we treat all the variables except the one we are taking the partial derivative with respect to as if they were constants. Taking the two partial derivatives of the gross profit function yields

$$\frac{\partial GP}{\partial p_1} = -4p_1 + p_2 + 200 \qquad (19.12)$$

and

$$\frac{\partial GP}{\partial p_2} = -p_2 + p_1 + 250 \qquad (19.13)$$

Following rule 3 and setting both partial derivatives equal to zero, we obtain a system of two simultaneous equations in the two variables p_1 and p_2:

$$-4p_1 + p_2 + 200 = 0 \qquad (19.14)$$
$$p_1 - p_2 + 250 = 0 \qquad (19.15)$$

Adding equations (19.14) and (19.15) yields

$$-3p_1 + 450 = 0$$

Thus we have

$$3p_1 = 450$$

or

$$p_1 = 150$$

Substituting $p_1 = 150$ into equation (19.15) yields

$$p_2 = 400$$

Hence the point $p_1 = 150$ and $p_2 = 400$ satisfies the necessary condition given by rule 3. Since $p_1 = 150$ and $p_2 = 400$ are the only values of p_1 and p_2 satisfying the necessary condition, we know that if this point is a local maximum, it must also be global maximum for our function. Just as in the single-variable case, when there is only one point satisfying the necessary condition, the function cannot have more than one local maximum or local minimum. In order to ensure that we have found a local maximum, and not perhaps a local minimum, a second derivative test is necessary.

The second derivative test requires that we know the values of all the second partial derivatives of the function. There are four second partial derivatives for a function of two variables; each of the two first partial derivatives has two partial derivatives itself. Let us calculate the second partial derivatives for our Lawn King problem.

In order to calculate the partial derivative of GP, first with respect to p_1 and then again with respect to p_1, we simply take the partial derivative of equation (19.12) with respect to p_1. Thus

$$\frac{\partial^2 \text{GP}}{\partial p_1^2} = -4$$

The notation $\partial^2 \text{GP}/\partial p_1^2$ is used to indicate that the partial derivative of GP was taken first with respect to p_1 and then again with respect to p_1.

To calculate the second partial derivative denoted by $\partial^2 \text{GP}/\partial p_2 \partial p_1$ we first take the partial derivative of GP with respect to p_1 and then again with respect to p_2. Thus we can compute this partial derivative by taking the partial derivative of equation (19.12) with respect to p_2. Doing so, we obtain

$$\frac{\partial^2 \text{GP}}{\partial p_2 \partial p_1} = 1$$

Similarly, the notation $\partial^2 \text{GP}/\partial p_1 \partial p_2$ is used to indicate that the partial derivative of GP was taken first with respect to p_2 and then with respect to p_1. Taking the partial derivative of equation (19.13) with respect to p_1, we obtain this second partial derivative:

$$\frac{\partial^2 \text{GP}}{\partial p_1 \partial p_2} = 1$$

Finally, the notation $\partial^2 \text{GP}/\partial p_2^2$ is used to indicate that the partial derivative of GP was taken first with respect to p_2 and then again with respect to p_2. Hence we obtain this second partial derivative by taking the partial derivative of equation (19.13) with respect to p_2:

$$\frac{\partial^2 \text{GP}}{\partial p_2^2} = -1$$

We can make one observation as a result of calculating these second partial derivatives. In our Lawn King problem the *mixed partials* (that is, with respect to one variable, then the other) are equal. This is true except for certain rare cases. We shall not be interested in such cases and thus will assume that the second mixed partials are always equal. Rule 4 can now be stated as supplying sufficient conditions for a point (x_1, x_2) to give a local maximum, a local minimum, or a saddle point of an unconstrained function $f(x_1, x_2)$ of two variables:

Rule 4 (Sufficient Condition).

If rule 3 is satisfied at the point (x_1, x_2) and

   a. If

$$\frac{\partial^2 f}{\partial x_1^2} > 0$$

and

$$\left(\frac{\partial^2 f}{\partial x_1^2}\right)\left(\frac{\partial^2 f}{\partial x_2^2}\right) - \left(\frac{\partial^2 f}{\partial x_1 \partial x_2}\right)^2 > 0$$

then the point is a local *minimum*.

   b. If

$$\frac{\partial^2 f}{\partial x_1^2} < 0$$

and

$$\left(\frac{\partial^2 f}{\partial x_1^2}\right)\left(\frac{\partial^2 f}{\partial x_2^2}\right) - \left(\frac{\partial^2 f}{\partial x_1 \partial x_2}\right)^2 > 0$$

then the point is a local *maximum*.

   c. If

$$\left(\frac{\partial^2 f}{\partial x_1^2}\right)\left(\frac{\partial^2 f}{\partial x_2^2}\right) - \left(\frac{\partial^2 f}{\partial x_1 \partial x_2}\right)^2 < 0$$

then the point is a *saddle point*, which is neither a local maximum nor a local minimum.

Condition (c) of rule 4 referring to a saddle point means that the point we have found attains a maximum with respect to one of the variables but a minimum with respect to the other. Hence the function indeed looks like a saddle at that point, and the solution is neither a local maximum nor a local minimum value of the function.

Cases in which

$$\left(\frac{\partial^2 f}{\partial x_1^2}\right)\left(\frac{\partial^2 f}{\partial x_2^2}\right) - \left(\frac{\partial^2 f}{\partial x_1 \partial x_2}\right)^2 = 0$$

have not been mentioned. In this situation the point could actually be a local minimum or a local maximum, but further analysis would be necessary to establish that fact. However, that further analysis is beyond the scope of this text.

Let us now apply rule 4 to our Lawn King problem to see if we have found a local maximum. We have

$$\frac{\partial^2 GP}{\partial p_1^2} = -4 < 0$$

and

$$\left(\frac{\partial^2 GP}{\partial p_1^2}\right)\left(\frac{\partial^2 GP}{\partial p_2^2}\right) - \left(\frac{\partial^2 GP}{\partial p_1 \partial p_2}\right)^2 = (-4)(-1) - (1)^2 = 3 > 0$$

Therefore case (b) of rule 4 applies and we have indeed found a local maximum, which from our previous discussion we know to be a global maximum.

Our analysis of the Lawn King problem is now complete. We have determined that a pricing policy of $150 for the walking mower and $400 for the riding mower will maximize the company's gross profit. Using equation (19.11), the gross profit the company can anticipate if it employs this pricing policy is

$$GP = -2(150)^2 - 0.5(400)^2 + (150)(400) + 200(150) + 250(400) - 55,700 = 9300$$

Since the model measures gross profit in thousands of dollars, Lawn King can anticipate a gross profit of $9,300,000 with this pricing policy. Of course, there are a number of other expenses that must yet be subtracted before we can determine the company's net profit.

At a price of $150 for the walking mower and $400 for the riding mower, we can now determine the number of mowers that will be sold by using equations (19.6) and (19.7). The number of walking mowers sold, q_1, is

$$q_1 = 95 - 2p_1 + 0.7p_2$$
$$= 95 - 2(150) + 0.7(400)$$
$$= 75 \text{ (thousand)}$$

The number of riding mowers sold, q_2, is

$$q_2 = 188 + 0.3p_1 - 0.5p_2$$
$$= 188 + 0.3(150) - 0.5(400)$$
$$= 33 \text{ (thousand)}$$

Thus if Lawn King produces 75,000 walking mowers at a price of $150 each and 33,000 riding mowers at a price of $400 each, the company will maximize gross profit at an anticipated level of $9,300,000. Note that the applicability of these results depends critically upon the confidence management has in the relationships established between sales prices and quantities sold and costs and quantities sold. That is, if management believes equations (19.6) to (19.9) are accurate representations of the true relationships between these factors, then the information developed using our calculus-based solution procedures can be valuable input to the decision-making process.

In our discussion of the Lawn King problem we concluded that the local maximum point $p_1 = 150$ and $p_2 = 400$ was also the global maximum, since $p_1 = 150$ and $p_2 = 400$ were the only values satisfying the necessary condition given by rule 3. Let us now discuss in general how we can determine the global optimal solution for any unconstrained function of two variables. We will state the procedure for a maximization problem in order to simplify the exposition. The modifications necessary to solve minimization problems should be apparent.

Step 1   Find all local maxima by applying rules 3 and 4.
Step 2   Select the largest of the local maxima as the global maximum (maxima).[4]

Note that a function can have more than one global maximum. Such situations are analogous to the case of alternate optima in a linear program.

To make sure that we understand the concepts involved in optimizing unconstrained mathematical models with two decision variables, let us consider the following numerical example:

Example.   Suppose we want to find all the minimum and maximum points of the function below:

$$f(x_1, x_2) = 5x_1^2 + 10x_2^2 + 10x_1x_2 - 22x_1 - 26x_2 + 25 \qquad (19.16)$$

Applying rule 3, we must set the partial derivatives with respect to x_1 and x_2 equal to zero and then solve the resulting equations for x_1 and x_2:

$$\frac{\partial f}{\partial x_1} = 10x_1 + 10x_2 - 22 = 0$$

$$\frac{\partial f}{\partial x_2} = 20x_2 + 10x_1 - 26 = 0$$

Solving these equations, we obtain the solution $x_1 = \frac{9}{5}$, $x_2 = \frac{2}{5}$. To see if this is a local maximum or a local minimum, we must calculate the second partial derivatives and apply rule 4. Calculating the second partial derivatives, we get

$$\frac{\partial^2 f}{\partial x_1^2} = 10 \qquad \frac{\partial^2 f}{\partial x_2^2} = 20 \qquad \frac{\partial^2 f}{\partial x_1 \partial x_2} = 10$$

Since

$$\frac{\partial^2 f}{\partial x_1^2} = 10 > 0$$

---

[4]For those unconstrained functions that go to infinity, a global maximum does not exist. Hence in such cases steps 1 and 2 will not yield a global maximum. However, such functions could never be realistic models of real-world optimization problems, and consequently we avoid a digression into such considerations in this text.

and

$$\left(\frac{\partial^2 f}{\partial x_1^2}\right)\left(\frac{\partial^2 f}{\partial x_2^2}\right) - \left(\frac{\partial^2 f}{\partial x_1 \partial x_2}\right)^2 = (10)(20) - (10)^2 = 100 > 0$$

case (a) of rule 4 applies, and the point $x_1 = \frac{9}{5}$, $x_2 = \frac{2}{5}$ yields a local minimum value for the function. Since this is the only point at which rule 3 applies, we can further conclude that this local minimum is the global minimum.

Let us pause for a moment to reflect on what we have learned in this section. Just as for unconstrained functions of a single variable, there is a first and second derivative test that must be applied in order to determine if a point is a local maximum or local minimum. The first derivative test, which must be satisfied by both local maximum and local minimum points, is called a necessary condition and is stated in rule 3. The second derivative test, just as with functions of a single variable, allows us to distinguish between a local maximum point, a local minimum point, and a point that may be neither a local maximum nor a local minimum. This is called a sufficient condition and is stated in rule 4.

We would like to comment, before closing this section, that for unconstrained functions of more than two variables, the first and second derivative tests are given by extensions of rules 3 and 4. For an unconstrained function of n variables, $f(x_1, x_2, \ldots, x_n)$, the first derivative test for a local maximum or local minimum requires that all n of the partial derivatives equal zero. Since it is a simple extension of rule 3, we state it here as rule 5:

Rule 5 (Necessary Condition).

All n partial derivatives of an unconstrained function of n variables, $f(x_1, x_2, \ldots, x_n)$, must equal zero at any local maximum or local minimum point.

For an unconstrained function of n variables, the second derivative test requires that all the second partial derivatives be calculated. Although this test is similar to rule 4, a simple statement of the test requires that we construct a matrix of second partial derivatives and perform some tests on the matrix. The tests require a knowledge of determinants of matrices which is not a prerequisite for the text. Thus we omit an extension of rule 4 to a second derivative test for functions of n variables. This extension is discussed in a number of more advanced texts on mathematical programming.[5]

19.3   MODELS WITH EQUALITY CONSTRAINTS: LAGRANGE MULTIPLIERS

In this section we discuss a problem that leads to the formulation of a nonlinear mathematical model involving two decision variables and one constraint. After we have seen

[5]A good discussion of these tests is contained in Luenberger, D. G., *Introduction to Linear and Nonlinear Programming*. Reading, Mass., Addison-Wesley, 1973.

how such a problem might arise, we present a solution procedure which once again involves a calculus-based first and second derivative test.

Green Lawns, Inc. provides a lawn fertilizer and weed control service. The company provides four treatments of fertilizer and weed control chemical to its subscribers each year. Green Lawns is adding a special aeration treatment as a low-cost extra service option, which it hopes will help attract new customers. Management is planning to promote this new service in two media: radio and direct-mail advertising. A budget of $2000 is to be used on this promotional campaign over the next quarter. Based on past experience in promoting its other services, Green Lawns has been able to obtain an estimate of the relationship between sales and the amount spent on promotion in these two media:

$$s = -2x_1^2 - 10x_2^2 - 8x_1x_2 + 18x_1 + 34x_2 \qquad (19.17)$$

where

$$s = \text{total sales in thousands of dollars}$$
$$x_1 = \text{thousands of dollars spent on radio advertising}$$
$$x_2 = \text{thousands of dollars spent on direct-mail promotion}$$

Green Lawns would like to develop a promotional strategy that will lead to maximum sales subject to the restriction provided by the promotional budget. Recognizing that the promotional budget is $2000, we may state Green Lawn's problem as the following constrained optimization problem:

$$\max \quad -2x_1^2 - 10x_2^2 - 8x_1x_2 + 18x_1 + 34x_2$$
$$\text{s.t.}$$
$$x_1 + x_2 = 2 \qquad (19.18)$$

We note that the constraint is written as $x_1 + x_2 = 2$ because x_1 and x_2 are being measured in thousands of dollars. Also, the objective function calls for the maximization of sales in thousands of dollars.

In general, all problems involving the minimization or maximization of a function of two variables subject to an equality constraint can be written as follows:

$$\min \text{ or } \max \quad f(x_1, x_2)$$
$$\text{s.t.}$$
$$g(x_1, x_2) = b \qquad (19.19)$$

The approach we shall follow to solve the above class of problems is first to introduce a new variable, called a *Lagrange multiplier*, and use this new variable to combine the constraint and objective function together into a single function. The new single function we shall form is called a *Lagrangian function* and is written below, where λ denotes the Lagrange multiplier:

$$\text{Lagrangian function} = L(x_1, x_2, \lambda) = f(x_1, x_2) + \lambda[g(x_1, x_2) - b] \qquad (19.20)$$

The first derivative test that every local minimum or local maximum point of a constrained problem must satisfy[6] is stated in rule 6:

Rule 6 (Necessary Condition).

For a function of two variables, x_1 and x_2, subject to one constraint to have a local minimum or a local maximum at a point, the partial derivatives of the Lagrangian function with respect to x_1, x_2, and λ must all equal zero at that point.

Thus once we have set up the Lagrangian function, this first derivative test for a constrained problem turns out to be very similar to the first derivative test for unconstrained functions. Let us now apply this test to the problem faced by Green Lawns, Inc.

Introducing a Lagrange multiplier as indicated by equations (19.19) and (19.20), we obtain the following Lagrangian function:

$$
\begin{aligned}
L(x_1, x_2, \lambda) = &-2x_1^2 - 10x_2^2 - 8x_1 x_2 + 18x_1 + 34x_2 \\
&+ \lambda(x_1 + x_2 - 2)
\end{aligned} \tag{19.21}
$$

Following rule 6, we first determine the partial derivatives with respect to x_1, x_2, and λ, and then set them equal to zero:

$$
\frac{\partial L}{\partial x_1} = -4x_1 - 8x_2 + 18 + \lambda = 0 \tag{19.22}
$$

$$
\frac{\partial L}{\partial x_2} = -20x_2 - 8x_1 + 34 + \lambda = 0 \tag{19.23}
$$

$$
\frac{\partial L}{\partial x_3} = x_1 + x_2 - 2 = 0 \tag{19.24}
$$

We are left with three equations in three unknowns: x_1, x_2, and λ. Solving these will give us a point satisfying rule 6 and thus a candidate for a maximum solution of the Green Lawns problem. Subtracting equation (19.22) from equation (19.23) allows us to form a new equation not including λ:

$$
-4x_1 - 12x_2 + 16 = 0 \tag{19.25}
$$

Multiplying equation (19.24) by 4 and adding to equation (19.25) yields

$$
-8x_2 + 8 = 0
$$

Hence

$$
x_2 = 1
$$

---

[6]There are certain examples that can be constructed for which the maximum or minimum does not satisfy rule 6, but these are exceptions that rarely occur in practice. Thus we shall not be concerned with them.

Substituting $x_2 = 1$ into equation (19.24), we find that $x_1 = 1$. As a consequence, from equations (19.22) and (19.23) we find that $\lambda = -6$. Thus the necessary condition of rule 1 is satisfied with

$$x_1^* = 1$$
$$x_2^* = 1$$
$$\lambda^* = -6$$

Since there is only one solution satisfying rule 6, we know that if it is a local maximum it is also a global maximum. It remains to be seen if this point truly yields a local maximum solution for the Green Lawns problem. We must develop a second derivative rule in order to make that determination. Rule 7 provides such a test and thus gives sufficient conditions for a local maximum or local minimum point.

Rule 7 (Sufficient Condition).

If rule 6 is satisfied at a point $(x_1^*, x_2^*, \lambda^*)$, apply conditions (a) and (b) of rule 4 to the Lagrangian function with λ fixed at a value of λ^* in order to determine if the point (x_1^*, x_2^*) is a local maximum or a local minimum.

Rule 7 says first to fix λ at the value necessary to satisfy rule 6. Then the Lagrangian function is expressed as a function of the two variables x_1 and x_2 with λ fixed at the value λ^*. Conditions (a) and (b) of rule 4 may be applied to this new function in order to determine if we have a local maximum or a local minimum.[7]

Let us apply rule 7 to our Green Lawns problem to see if the solution we have found is a local maximum.

The Lagrangian function [equation (19.21)] with λ fixed at $\lambda^* = -6$ is

$$L(x_1, x_2, \lambda = -6) = -2x_1^2 - 10x_2^2 - 8x_1x_2 + 18x_1 + 34x_2$$
$$- 6(x_1 + x_2 - 2)$$

We need to find the second partial derivatives of this function with respect to x_1 and x_2 to determine if the $x_1^* = 1$ and $x_2^* = 1$ solution yields a maximum. Taking the first partial derivatives with respect to x_1 and x_2, we obtain the same result we could have obtained by substituting $\lambda = -6$ into equation (19.22) and (19.23):

$$\frac{\partial L}{\partial x_1} = -4x_1 - 8x_2 + 18 - 6 = -4x_1 - 8x_2 + 12$$

$$\frac{\partial L}{\partial x_2} = -20x_2 - 8x_1 + 34 - 6 = -20x_2 - 8x_1 + 28$$

[7]Condition (c) of rule 4 is not used for equality constrained problems, since a saddle point of the Lagrangian function need not correspond to a saddle point of the equality constrained problem we want to solve.

The second partial derivatives of this function with respect to x_1 and x_2 are

$$\frac{\partial^2 L}{\partial x_1^2} = -4 \qquad \frac{\partial^2 L}{\partial x_2^2} = -20 \qquad \frac{\partial^2 L}{\partial x_1 \partial x_2} = -8$$

To see if the Lagrangian function with λ fixed at $\lambda^* = -6$ has an unconstrained minimum at $x_1^* = 1$ and $x_2^* = 1$, we apply the second derivative test developed in rule 4 for unconstrained functions of two variables:

$$\frac{\partial^2 L}{\partial x_1^2} = -4 < 0$$

$$\left(\frac{\partial^2 L}{\partial x_1^2}\right)\left(\frac{\partial^2 L}{\partial x_2^2}\right) - \left(\frac{\partial^2 L}{\partial x_1 \partial x_2}\right)^2 = (-4)(-20) - (-8)^2 = 16 > 0$$

Case (b) of rule 4 applies, and the point $x_1^* = 1$, $x_2^* = 1$ is an unconstrained maximum of the Lagrangian function with $\lambda = -6$. Thus we see that $x_1^* = 1$ and $x_2^* = 1$ is the optimal solution to the Green Lawns problem. The company should invest $1000 in radio advertising and $1000 in direct-mail promotion. To determine the expected sales volume from this strategy we must evaluate the objective function, equation (19.17), with $x_1 = 1$ and $x_2 = 1$. Doing so, we obtain

$$\text{Sales} = -2(1)^2 - 10(1)^2 - 8(1)(1) + 18(1) + 34(1) = 32$$

Thus the expected sales volume resulting from this promotional strategy is $32,000.

The following numerical example provides another illustration of the use of the Lagrange multiplier method for solving equality constrained optimization problems:

Example.   Suppose we have the following constrained optimization problem:

$$\min \quad x_1^2 + 2x_2^2 - 8x_1 - 12x_2 + 34$$
$$\text{s.t.}$$
$$x_1 + 2x_2 = 4$$

Setting up the Lagrangian function for this problem, we obtain

$$L(x_1, x_2, \lambda) = x_1^2 + 2x_2^2 - 8x_1 - 12x_2 + 34 + \lambda(x_1 + 2x_2 - 4) \qquad (19.26)$$

Applying rule 6 we set the partial derivatives of this Lagrangian function with respect to x_1, x_2, and λ equal to zero:

$$\frac{\partial L}{\partial x_1} = 2x_1 - 8 + \lambda = 0$$

$$\frac{\partial L}{\partial x_2} = 4x_2 - 12 + 2\lambda = 0$$

$$\frac{\partial L}{\partial \lambda} = x_1 + 2x_2 - 4 = 0$$

Solving the resulting three equations for the three unknowns, we obtain

$$x_1^* = 2 \quad x_2^* = 1 \quad \lambda^* = 4$$

Once again, there is only one solution satisfying rule 6. Thus if it is a local maximum or minimum, it must also be a global maximum or minimum.

We must now apply rule 7 to see if this is a local maximum or a minimum point. Setting $\lambda^* = 4$ in equation (19.26), the second partial derivatives of the Lagrangian function with respect to x_1 and x_2 are

$$\frac{\partial^2 L}{\partial x_1^2} = 2 \quad \frac{\partial^2 L}{\partial x_2^2} = 4 \quad \frac{\partial^2 L}{\partial x_1 \partial x_2} = 0$$

Checking conditions (a) and (b) of the test procedures for rule 4, we have

$$\frac{\partial^2 L}{\partial x_1^2} = 2 > 0$$

and

$$\left(\frac{\partial^2 L}{\partial x_1^2}\right)\left(\frac{\partial^2 L}{\partial x_2^2}\right) - \left(\frac{\partial^2 L}{\partial x_1 \partial x_2}\right)^2 = (2)(4) - (0)^2 = 8 > 0$$

Thus we have a local minimum of the Lagrangian function with λ fixed at 4, and in light of our previous discussion we have found a global minimum at $x_1 = 2$ and $x_2 = 1$.

The Green Lawns, Inc. problem and the above problem are examples of models having a nonlinear objective function and a linear equality constraint. In applying rules 6 and 7, we were able to develop the necessary and sufficient condition test relatively easily. However, for problems where the equality constraint is also nonlinear, you will find that the solution computations become somewhat more difficult. Problems 12 and 14 at the end of this chapter ask you to use rules 6 and 7 to solve a problem with a nonlinear objective function and a nonlinear equality constraint.

To complete our discussion, we mention briefly how rule 6 can be extended to supply a necessary condition for minimizing or maximizing a function of n variables subject to m equality constraints. This extended problem may be stated in the following form:

$$\text{min or max} \quad f(x_1, x_2, \ldots, x_n)$$
$$\text{s.t.}$$
$$g_1(x_1, x_2, \ldots, x_n) = b_1$$
$$g_2(x_1, x_2, \ldots, x_n) = b_2$$
$$\vdots \qquad\qquad \vdots$$
$$g_m(x_1, x_2, \ldots, x_n) = b_m \qquad\qquad (19.27)$$

A Lagrangian function, combining the objective function and all the constraints into one function, can be formulated by introducing a separate Lagrange multiplier for each constraint:

$$
\begin{aligned}
L(x_1, x_2, &\ldots, x_n, \lambda_1, \lambda_2, \ldots, \lambda_m) \\
&= f(x_1, x_2, \ldots, x_n) + \lambda_1[g_1(x_1, x_2, \ldots, x_n) - b_1] \\
&\quad + \lambda_2[g_2(x_1, x_2, \ldots, x_n) - b_2] + \cdots \\
&\quad + \lambda_m[g_m(x_1, x_2, \ldots, x_n) - b_m]
\end{aligned}
\tag{19.28}
$$

The extension of rule 6 to this problem can now be stated in terms of this new Lagrangian function:

Rule 8 (Necessary Condition).

For a function of n variables, $f(x_1, x_2, \ldots, x_n)$, subject to m constraints to have a local minimum or a local maximum at a point, the partial derivatives of the Lagrangian function with respect to $x_1, x_2, \ldots, x_n$ and $\lambda_1, \lambda_2, \ldots, \lambda_m$ must all equal zero at that point.

The second derivative test for this problem is a natural extension to rule 7; that is, we would check for a local maximum or a local minimum of the Lagrangian function with $\lambda_1, \lambda_2, \ldots, \lambda_m$ fixed at the values found when applying rule 8. This would require that we have a second derivative test for an unconstrained function of n variables. A matrix of second partial derivatives provides the basis for this test; however, as we stated earlier, the methodology is beyond the scope of this text.

Before concluding this section, we comment briefly on its similarity to the previous two sections. Once again we had a first derivative test that any local maximum or local minimum point had to satisfy. Then we had a second derivative test that could be used to determine if a point satisfying the first derivative test was indeed a local maximum or a local minimum. The only conceptual difference in solving these constrained problems was that we had to formulate a Lagrangian function and then perform the first and second derivative tests on that function. Only conditions (a) and (b) of the second derivative test were applicable for constrained problems.

19.4 INTERPRETATION OF THE LAGRANGE MULTIPLIER

In the previous section we saw that it was necessary to introduce an additional variable called a Lagrange multiplier in order to solve constrained problems. This variable was used in setting up the Lagrangian function. In meeting the necessary condition (rule 6), we actually found a value for the Lagrange multiplier. The value of this Lagrange multiplier can often be used to provide valuable managerial information about the sensitivity of an optimal solution to changes in resource levels.

In order to be more specific, let us reconsider the Green Lawns problem, which is restated below:

$$\max \quad -2x_1^2 - 10x_2^2 - 8x_1x_2 + 18x_1 + 34x_2$$

$$\text{s.t.}$$

$$x_1 + x_2 = 2$$

Here, x_1 represents the amount spent on radio advertising and x_2 the amount spent on direct-mail promotion. The constraint indicates that $2000 is to be used for the promotional campaign and that it is to be divided between the two media, x_1 and x_2. In the previous section we saw that the optimal allocation was to divide the budget equally between the two media: $x_1 = 1$ and $x_2 = 1$. Management might wonder what the effect on sales would be if a different amount, say $1000 or $3000, were budgeted for the promotional campaign. The value of the Lagrange multiplier provides an estimate of that effect. Let us see how.

Recall that the general model with two decision variables and one equality constraint was written as

$$\min \text{ or } \max \quad f(x_1, x_2)$$

$$\text{s.t.}$$

$$g(x_1, x_2) = b$$

The interpretation of the Lagrange multiplier for this problem is stated as property 1.

Property 1 (Interpretation of the Lagrange Multiplier).

The value of the Lagrange multiplier associated with the general model above is the negative of the rate of change of the objective function with respect to a change in b. More formally, it is the negative of the partial derivative of $f(x_1, x_2)$ with respect to b; that is, $\lambda = -\partial f/\partial b$ or

$$\frac{\partial f}{\partial b} = -\lambda \tag{19.29}$$

The optimal solution to the Green Lawns problem has

$$x_1^* = 1 \qquad x_2^* = 1 \qquad \lambda^* = -6$$

Since $\lambda^* = -6$, property 1 indicates that with $\partial f/\partial b = -\lambda = -(-6) = 6$, the objective function should increase by approximately 6 if b is increased by 1. For example, if the budget is increased from $2000 to $3000 in the Green Lawns problem, the objective function should increase by approximately $6000. Let us change the budget to $3000 and see what happens.

After increasing the budget to $3000 the Green Lawns problem can be written as follows:

$$\max \quad -2x_1^2 - 10x_2^2 - 8x_1x_2 + 18x_1 + 34x_2$$
$$\text{s.t.} \tag{19.30}$$
$$x_1 + x_2 = 3$$

Formulating the Lagrangian function and setting the partial derivatives equal to zero yields

$$L(x_1, x_2, \lambda) = -2x_1^2 - 10x_2^2 - 8x_1x_2 + 18x_1 + 34x_2 \tag{19.31}$$
$$+ \lambda(x_1 + x_2 - 3)$$

and

$$\frac{\partial L}{\partial x_1} = -4x_1 - 8x_2 + 18 + \lambda = 0$$

$$\frac{\partial L}{\partial x_2} = -20x_2 - 8x_1 + 34 + \lambda = 0$$

$$\frac{\partial L}{\partial \lambda} = x_1 + x_2 - 3 = 0$$

Solving these three equations simultaneously for x_1, x_2, and λ yields

$$x_1^* = 2.5 \quad x_2^* = 0.5 \quad \lambda^* = -4$$

To check to see if we have a maximum we must determine the second partial derivatives of the Lagrangian with λ fixed at $\lambda^* = -4$. Using equation (19.31) with $\lambda = -4$, these second partial derivatives are

$$\frac{\partial^2 L}{\partial x_1^2} = -4 \quad \frac{\partial^2 L}{\partial x_2^2} = -20 \quad \frac{\partial^2 L}{\partial x_1 \partial x_2} = -8$$

Applying rule 4, we see that $x_1^* = 2.5$ and $x_2^* = 0.5$ does indeed yield an unconstrained maximum of the Lagrangian with λ fixed at $\lambda^* = -4$. According to rule 7 we have found the maximum for this new problem.

Now we would like to see how close the $6000 increase in the objective function predicted by $\lambda^* = -6$ comes to the true increase. The value of the objective function for $x_1^* = 2.5$ and $x_2^* = 0.5$ is

$$f(x_1, x_2) = \text{sales} = -2(2.5)^2 - 10(0.5)^2 - 8(2.5)(0.5)$$
$$+ 18(2.5) + 34(0.5) = 37$$

The maximum value of sales given a budget of $3000 is thus $37,000. Since the maximum value for a budget of $2000 was found previously to be $32,000, the increase in sales is $5000 and not the $6000 the value of the Lagrange multiplier predicted. We should not be too surprised at this. What we are observing is the law of diminishing returns in action. As the amount of resources available increases (advertising budget in this case), the per-unit increase in the objective function decreases. Note that the value we obtained for the Lagrange multiplier when the budget was increased to $3000 was $\lambda^* = -4$. This would lead us to predict that sales would increase by another $4000 if the budget were further increased to $4000. The rate of return per unit increase in the budget has decreased from 6 to 4 as the budget has increased from 2 to 3.

Also, we should note that the Lagrange multiplier value associated with a budget of $3000, $\lambda^* = -4$, would lead us to predict that sales would decrease by $4000 if the budget were decreased to $2000. The actual change, as we now know, is $5000. Thus if we used the Lagrange multiplier associated with $b = 2000$, $\lambda^* = -6$, to predict the change in sales associated with a $1000 change in the budget, we would overestimate the change. On the other hand, if we used the Lagrange multiplier associated with $b = 3000$, $\lambda^* = -4$, to predict the change in sales associated with changing the budget from $3000 to $2000, we would underestimate the change. The actual change, $5000, is halfway between.

The reason the Lagrange multiplier only provides an estimate of the change in the objective function and not the exact change is that it is a partial derivative of the objective function with respect to b. Thus for different values of b we get different values for the Lagrange multiplier. The estimate provided by λ^* will be very good as long as the change in b is small, but will be increasingly poor as the change in b gets larger.

In Table 19.1 we show the maximum sales levels for budget amounts varying between $1000 and $3000 in increments of $200 together with the maximum sales levels we would have predicted by using the property of the Lagrange multiplier.

TABLE 19.1
Maximum Sales Levels for Varying Budgets Compared with Estimates Based on the Lagrange Multiplier of $\lambda = -6$ for the Green Lawns Problem

Budget	Actual Maximum Sales $f(x_1^*, x_2^*)$	Estimated Maximum Sales $\lambda^* = -6$	Difference
$1000	$25,000	$26,000	-1000
1200	26,560	27,200	$-$ 640
1400	28,040	28,400	$-$ 360
1600	29,440	29,600	$-$ 160
1800	30,760	30,800	$-$ 40
2000	32,000	32,000	0
2200	33,160	33,200	$-$ 40
2400	34,240	34,400	$-$ 160
2600	35,240	35,600	$-$ 360
2800	36,160	36,800	$-$ 640
3000	37,000	38,000	-1000

Table 19.1 verifies that the estimates based on the Lagrange multiplier are good as long as the change in b is not large. For a $200 change in the budget, the estimate based on the Lagrange multiplier is pretty good. There is only a $40 error in the sales estimate. Of course, as we get further away from a budget of $2000, the predictions continue to get worse. We can also see the effect of diminishing returns with respect to the advertising

budget from studying the table. When the budget is set at $1000, a $200 increase causes an increase in sales of $1560. When the budget is set at $2800, a $200 increase causes an increase in sales of only $840.

From a managerial point of view we see that the value of the Lagrange multiplier can provide important information. It is an indication of the sensitivity of the optimal solution to changes in resource levels. In most real-world problems these resource levels are not some sacred number that cannot be changed. For example, in the Green Lawns situation management has initially budgeted $2000 for an advertising campaign. If the quantitative analyst can show the manager that an increase in the advertising budget of $1 can be expected to increase sales by $6, then the manager may want to consider expanding the budget. Of course, whether or not the manager chooses to expand it will depend on a number of other considerations as well. Can funds be freed from other uses for the campaign? How much confidence do we have that our model is representative of the real relationship between advertising in the two media and sales? Also, since the $6 increase in sales will cost us $1 of advertising, is the remaining $5 enough to offset all the other costs associated with the increased sales? Regardless of how this sensitivity information is eventually used by the manager, it is important to know what it means and that it can be made available as a by-product of the model solution.

The Lagrange multiplier analysis can be extended to problems with more variables and more constraints. However, because of the additional complexity involved, we leave a discussion of this extension to more advanced texts on mathematical programming.

19.5   MODELS INVOLVING INEQUALITY CONSTRAINTS

In this section we study problems that lead to nonlinear mathematical models involving two decision variables and one inequality constraint. We will find that this type of problem can be solved using the approaches we have already learned in the previous sections of this chapter.

Suppose that instead of stating that a budget of $2000 had to be spent on an advertising campaign for the aeration service, management of Green Lawns, Inc. had stated that the amount spent had to be less than or equal to the $2000 budget. This is actually a more realistic interpretation of the budget constraint. Certainly if more sales could be realized by spending less on advertising, the company would be willing to do so. Given this less-than-or-equal-to interpretation of the constraint, the Green Lawns model would involve two decision variables and one inequality constraint as shown below.

$$\max \quad -2x_1^2 - 10x_2^2 - 8x_1x_2 + 18x_1 + 34x_2$$
$$\text{s.t.}$$
$$x_1 + x_2 \leq 2$$

In solving this problem we recognize that there are actually two possibilities with respect to the constraint. The first is that the constraint $x_1 + x_2 \leq 2$ will be binding at the optimal solution. In this case we could assume that the constraint has the form $x_1 + x_2 = 2$ and solve just as we did in Section 19.3 for problems with equality constraints. The second possibility is that at the optimal solution the constraint is not binding, that is, $x_1^* + x_2^* < 2$. In this case we could simply ignore the constraint and solve as we did in Section 19.2 for unconstrained problems. The recognition that these are the only two possibilities is what motivates the solution procedure we are about to present.

We state the solution procedure for a maximization problem in order to simplify the exposition. The modifications necessary to solve minimization problems should be apparent.

Step 1 Assume the constraint is not binding and apply the procedures of Section 19.2 to find the global maximum of the function, if it exists. (Functions that go to infinity do not have a global maximum.) If this global maximum satisfies the constraint, stop. This is the global maximum for the inequality constrained problem. If not, the constraint may be binding at the optimum. Record the value of any local maximum that satisfies the inequality constraint and go on to step 2.

Step 2 Assume the constraint is binding and apply the procedures of Section 19.3 to find all the local maxima of the resulting equality constrained problem. Compare these values with any feasible local maxima found in step 1. The largest of these is the global maximum.

Let us apply this solution procedure to our new version of the Green Lawns problem. Applying step 1 and ignoring the constraint $x_1 + x_2 \leq 2$ would lead us to solve the unconstrained problem

$$\max \quad -2x_1^2 - 10x_2^2 - 8x_1x_2 + 18x_1 + 34x_2$$

Applying rule 3, we set the partial derivatives of the objective function equal to zero:

$$\frac{\partial f}{\partial x_1} = -4x_1 - 8x_2 + 18 = 0$$

$$\frac{\partial f}{\partial x_2} = -20x_2 - 8x_1 + 34 = 0$$

Solving these two equations simultaneously, we obtain $x_1^* = 5\frac{1}{2}$ and $x_2^* = -\frac{1}{2}$. Before checking the second derivatives for a local maximum or minimum, however, let us see if these values for x_1 and x_2 satisfy our constraint. Clearly, $x_1^* + x_2^* = 5\frac{1}{2} - \frac{1}{2} = 5$ is not less than or equal to 2, and therefore even if this solution did yield the global maximum to our unconstrained problem (which it does, by the way), it could not be optimal since it does not satisfy the inequality constraint. There are no other local maxima to record the values of; therefore we go on to step 2 and solve the following equality constrained optimization problem:

$$\max \quad -2x_1^2 - 10x_2^2 - 8x_1x_2 + 18x_1 + 34x_2$$
$$\text{s.t.}$$
$$x_1 + x_2 = 2$$

The global maximum for this problem was found in Section 19.3 and is given by $x_1 = 1$ and $x_2 = 1$. Since there are no feasible local maxima from step 1, the optimal solution to our constrained optimization problem is also $x_1 = 1$, $x_2 = 1$, with an expected sales volume of \$32,000.

Let us now look at another example involving a minimization problem:

Example.   Suppose we want to solve the following problem:

$$\min \quad f(x_1, x_2) = x_1^2 - 10x_1 + x_2^2 - 10x_2$$
$$\text{s.t.}$$
$$x_1 + 2x_2 \leq 20$$

Step 1 of the solution procedure says to ignore the constraint and solve the resulting unconstrained optimization problem. Applying rule 3, we set the partial derivatives of the objective function equal to zero:

$$\frac{\partial f}{\partial x_1} = 2x_1 - 10 = 0$$

$$\frac{\partial f}{\partial x_2} = 2x_2 - 10 = 0$$

Solving these two equations, we obtain $x_1^* = 5$ and $x_2^* = 5$. Since this point satisfies the constraint, we must check to see if it is a local minimum. Applying the second derivative test of rule 4, we obtain

$$\frac{\partial^2 f}{\partial x_1^2} = 2 > 0$$

and

$$\left(\frac{\partial^2 f}{\partial x_1^2}\right)\left(\frac{\partial^2 f}{\partial x_2^2}\right) - \left(\frac{\partial^2 f}{\partial x_2 \partial x_1}\right)^2 = (2)(2) - 0^2 = 4 > 0$$

Therefore the point $x_1 = 5$, $x_2 = 5$ yields a local minimum for our function. Further, since no other values of x_1, x_2 satisfy rule 3, we can conclude that $x_1 = 5$, $x_2 = 5$ yields a global minimum for our unconstrained function. Thus it is unnecessary to go on to step 2, since no point on the constraint boundary could possibly be better than the global minimum. We can therefore conclude that $x_1 = 5$, $x_2 = 5$ is the global minimum for our inequality constrained problem.

We have seen how the solution procedure of this section can be applied both in the case where the constraint is satisfied as an equality at the optimum and when it is satisfied as a strict inequality. Unfortunately the solution procedure we have outlined here cannot be extended to problems with more than one inequality constraint nor to problems with both equality and inequality constraints. We will comment briefly on what to do in such cases.

In some applications the appropriate mathematical model may have a mixture of equality and inequality constraints. In these kinds of mathematical models, the solution approach invariably requires a computerized mathematical programming algorithm. There are many research papers and a number of mathematical programming textbooks devoted to these computerized algorithms. The approach taken by all these algorithms is iterative in nature. Initially a starting point, which is a guess at the optimal solution, is picked and then an improved solution is determined by the computer algorithm. Another improvement is made, and so on, until eventually the optimal solution is reached. The details of these solution algorithms are beyond the scope of this text.

Summary

The kinds of problems discussed in this chapter have been examples of decision-making situations in which the appropriate mathematical model of the problem involved nonlinear relationships. When these decision-making situations arise, the linear programming procedures of Chapters 2 through 6 are not applicable, and calculus-based procedures must be employed.

For both unconstrained and constrained problems we saw that a first and a second derivative test were required. In the unconstrained single-variable case these tests were made on the first and second derivatives of the objective function. In the unconstrained two-variable case these tests were made on the first and second partial derivatives of the objective function. Equality constrained problems with two decision variables and one constraint were solved by first introducing a new variable called a Lagrange multiplier. A Lagrangian function was then formed by combining the objective function and constraint into one function. Tests on the first and second partial derivatives of the Lagrangian function were then developed to find the optimal solution. The Lagrange multiplier was found to provide valuable managerial information about the sensitivity of the optimal solution to changes in the value of the right-hand side of the constraint (the resource level).

Glossary

Necessary conditions   Conditions, usually requiring first derivatives to be equal to zero, that must be satisfied at an optimal solution. They do not guarantee an optimal solution.

Sufficient conditions   Conditions, usually involving the sign of second derivatives, that determine whether a solution meeting the necessary conditions is a maximum solution, a minimum solution, or no solution.

Saddle point   A condition that occurs in models with more than one decision variable when one variable reaches its maximum value and another reaches its minimum value at the same point.

Lagrange multiplier   A new variable added to a constrained nonlinear model in order to obtain a solution. In sensitivity analysis this variable tells us what effect a change in the level of resources will have on the objective function.

Lagrangian function   The function formed by using the Lagrange multiplier to combine the objective function and the constraint(s) into one function. For example, the constrained problem

$$\min \quad f(x_1, x_2)$$
$$\text{s.t.}$$
$$g(x_1, x_2) = b$$

has the following Lagrangian function:

$$L(x_1, x_2, \lambda) = f(x_1, x_2) + \lambda[g(x_1, x_2) - b]$$

where λ is the Lagrange multiplier.

Local maximum (minimum)   A point that gives at least as high (low) a value of the objective function as any nearby point.

Global maximum (minimum)   The point, or points, at which a function takes on its greatest (lowest) value.

Problems

1. a. Maximize the function

$$f(x) = 12x - 6x^2 - 30$$

   b. Maximize the above function over the interval

$$0 \leq x \leq 10$$

   c. Maximize the above function over the interval

$$2 \leq x \leq 10$$

2. a. Find the minimum of the function

$$f(x) = 3x^3 - 20x^2 + 60$$

   b. Find the minimum of the above function over the interval

$$0 \leq x \leq 4$$

3. A large grocery chain is interested in determining the best size for a new store that is being built at a particular site. The chain has made an extensive study of the sector in which the new store will be located. Based on such factors as sector population, weekly per capita food expenditures, and competition, the grocery chain has developed the following model that relates sales (in thousands of dollars) to the size of the store x (in units of 10,000 square feet):

$$\text{Sales} = 100x - 10x^2 - 150$$

   Determine the size of the store that will maximize sales. What are the maximum sales corresponding to the store size?

4. The manufacturer of King's Chunk Style Peanut Butter has determined that sales in any particular store are related to the amount of shelf space devoted to the peanut butter and the amount of traffic through the store. A detailed analysis led to the

following equation relating the square feet on shelves and the number of store customers per week to the total weekly sales in dollars:

$$\text{Sales} = -20x^2 - 50C^2 - 60Cx + 220x - 340C + 610$$

where

$$x = \text{square feet of shelf space}$$
$$C = \text{thousands of customers}$$

King uses the above formula to determine the optimal amount of shelf space for its product in any particular store. Suppose a particular store averages a thousand customers per week. How many square feet of shelf space would be required to maximize sales?

5. Suppose that the total cost (TC) of producing x pounds of a certain cleaning fluid is given by

$$\text{TC} = \tfrac{4}{3}x^4 - 3x^3 + 2x^2 + 5x$$

Write the mathematical expression for the cost per pound. If x must be at least 0.3, what batch size will lead to the minimum cost per pound?

6. A certain product sells for \$5 per unit. The total cost C of producing and selling this product is given by

$$C(x) = x^2 - 15x + 20$$

   a. What is the fixed cost of production? That is, what portion of the cost is independent of the number of units produced?

   b. Develop a mathematical model that shows total profit as a function of the number of units produced.

   c. What level of production will maximize profit?

7. The cost per batch of a certain production process is related to the setting of two control instruments. Suppose the total cost per batch is given by

$$f(x_1, x_2) = 4x_1^2 + 2x_2^2 + 4x_1x_2 - 8x_1 - 6x_2 + 35$$

Determine the settings for the two instruments that will minimize this cost.

8. Consider the function $f(x_1, x_2) = 2x_1^4 - 12x_1^2 + 2x_1^2x_2 + x_2^2 - 4x_2 + 20$. Determine whether the points below yield local minima, local maxima, saddle points, or none of these.

$$\left(\begin{matrix} x_1 = 0 \\ x_2 = 2 \end{matrix}\right) \left(\begin{matrix} x_1 = +2 \\ x_2 = -2 \end{matrix}\right) \left(\begin{matrix} x_1 = -2 \\ x_2 = -2 \end{matrix}\right)$$

9. The prices for two products, denoted by p_1 and p_2, are related to the quantities sold of the two products, x_1 and x_2, by the expressions

$$x_1 = 32 - 2p_1$$
$$x_2 = 22 - p_2$$

Further, the total cost (TC) of producing and selling the product is related to the quantities sold by the function

$$TC(x_1, x_2) = \tfrac{1}{2}x_1^2 + 2x_1x_2 + x_2^2 + 73$$

a. Develop a mathematical model that shows profit as a function of the quantities produced.
b. Determine the prices and quantities that maximize profit.

10. A shoe store has determined that its earnings $E(x_1, x_2)$, in thousands of dollars, can be approximated by a function of x_1, its investment in inventory in thousands of dollars, and x_2, its expenditure on advertising in thousands of dollars:

$$E(x_1, x_2) = -3x_1^2 + 2x_1x_2 - 6x_2^2 + 30x_1 + 24x_2 - 86$$

Find the maximum earnings, along with the amount of advertising expenditure and inventory investment that yields this maximum.

11. Consider the problem

$$\min \quad x_1^2 - 14x_1 + x_2^2 - 16x_2 + 113$$
$$\text{s.t.}$$
$$2x_1 + 3x_2 = 12$$

a. Find the minimum solution to this problem.
b. How much would you expect the value of the solution to change if the right-hand side of the constraint were increased from 12 to 13?

12. Consider the problem

$$\max \quad -x_1^2 - 4x_1x_2 + 20x_1 - 5x_2^2 + 82x_2 - 397$$
$$\text{s.t.}$$
$$2x_1^2 - 16x_1 + 9x_2^2 - 18x_2 + 5 = 0$$

Determine whether or not the point $x_1 = 4$, $x_2 = 3$ provides an optimal solution.

13. Heller Manufacturing has two production facilities that manufacture baseball gloves. Production costs at the two facilities differ because of varying labor rates, local property taxes, type of equipment, capacity, and so on. The Dayton plant has weekly production costs that can be expressed as a function of the number of gloves produced:

$$TC_1(x_1) = x_1^2 - x_1 + 5$$

where x_1 is the weekly production volume in thousands of units and $TC_1(x_1)$ is the cost in thousands of dollars. The Hamilton plant's weekly production costs are given by

$$TC_2(x_2) = x_2^2 + 2x_2 + 3$$

where x_2 is the weekly production volume in thousands of units and $TC_2(x_2)$ is the cost, in thousands of dollars. Heller Manufacturing would like to produce 8000 gloves per week at the lowest possible cost.

a. Formulate a mathematical model that can be used to determine the number of gloves to produce each week at each facility.

b. Find the solution to your mathematical model to determine the optimal number of gloves to produce at each facility.

14. Solve the problem

$$\min \quad x_1^2 + 2x_2^2 - 8x_1 - 12x_2 + 34$$
$$\text{s.t.}$$
$$x_1^2 + 2x_2^2 = 5$$

15. Consider the problem

$$\min \quad 2x_1^2 - 20x_1 + 2x_1x_2 + x_2^2 - 14x_2 + 58$$
$$\text{s.t.}$$
$$x_1 + 4x_2 \le 8$$

a. Find the minimum solution to this problem.

b. If the right-hand side of the constraint is increased from 8 to 9, how much do you expect the objective function to change?

16. Jingle Bells, Inc. has received a rush order for as many of two types of Christmas bells as can be produced and shipped during a 2-week period. Preliminary analysis by Jingle Bells indicates that the profit on this order is related to the number of each type of bell manufactured by the following function:

$$P = -x_1^2 - x_2^2 + 12x_1 + 10x_2 + 61$$

where

$$P = \text{profit in thousands of dollars}$$
$$x_1 = \text{number of units of type 1 bells in thousands}$$
$$x_2 = \text{number of units of type 2 bells in thousands}$$

Because of other commitments over the next two weeks, Jingle Bells has available only 60 hours in the shipping and packaging department to get the order out. It is estimated that every 1000 units of type 1 bells will require 20 hours in the shipping and packaging department and every 1000 units of type 2 bells will require 30 hours. Given the above information, how many of each type of bell should Jingle Bells produce in order to maximize profit?

17. Through regression analysis a firm has learned that total profit P as a function of the number of units of two products manufactured is given by the following function:

$$P = -x_1^2 - 4x_2^2 + 6x_1 + 16x_2 + 500$$

where

$$x_1 = \text{thousands of units of product 1}$$
$$x_2 = \text{thousands of units of product 2}$$

The number of units of each product that can be produced in the next planning period is constrained by the fact that there are only 12,000 pounds of an ingredient that is used in the production of both products available. Both products required two pounds of the ingredient per unit produced.

a. Develop a mathematical model that can be used to determine how many units of each product to manufacture in the next planning period.

b. Solve the mathematical model to determine how many units of x_1 and x_2 should be produced in order to maximize profit.

c. How much would you expect profit to increase if one extra pound of the scarce ingredient became available?

Management Science in Practice

U.S. DEPARTMENT OF AGRICULTURE FOREST SERVICE*
Washington, D.C.

The U.S. Department of Agriculture Forest Service is responsible for the management of the nation's forest resources. The Forest Engineering group at the Intermountain Forest and Range Experiment Station located in Montana is concerned with the application of engineering and management science principles to the harvesting of timberlands. This group conducts and contracts for studies related to the utilization of harvesting equipment, the modeling of cable yarding (timber collection) systems, the modeling of helicopter or other aerial yarding systems, the designing of statistically valid models for experimental forests, and the developing of a variety of forest harvesting methods. A concern of many of these studies is the productivity and cost of the harvesting method. Ultimately, the primary objective of all these studies is to determine the ''best'' methods for harvesting timber under a variety of conditions.

A HELICOPTER YARDING APPLICATION

Over the years the best and most accessible timber has tended to be harvested first. As a result, much of the currently available timber lies in relatively inaccessible regions of the forests where traditional harvesting methods cannot be used. This has created a need for new harvesting techniques. One recent development has been to use helicopters to remove felled trees from inaccessible regions.

A major problem with using helicopters in the harvesting process is the high cost of the helicopter operation. When helicopters are used, the usual harvesting procedure is to mark felled trees where they lie for inclusion in a helicopter load (called a turn). This approach has proved somewhat unsatisfactory due to the added cost of helicopter time to collect and prepare the load for removal. Also, problems with helicopter underloading (wasted capacity) and overloading (aborted loads) have occurred too often. If helicopters are to be used, high utilization of helicopter capacity is essential to maintain the highest possible levels of productivity and the lowest possible costs.

A study was proposed for exploring the feasibility and cost effectiveness of harvesting methods that would prebunch felled trees into unit loads for helicopter transport. Preliminary tests indicated that unit loads could be assembled with the

*The authors are indebted to Dr. William R. Taylor and Dr. Christopher B. Lofgren, consultants to the USDA Forest Service, for providing this application.

aid of a radio-controlled winch. The winch is anchored to a tree in the "bunching" area. In order to collect the felled trees for the unit loads, a cable from the winch is hooked to the felled trees. The winch then pulls the trees onto a deck where the unit loads can be assembled. Once the feasibility of this method was established, it became important to develop strategies that would provide the best productivity and cost advantages. A mathematical model was developed to identify the optimal movement and locations of the radio-controlled winch so that the total costs associated with preparing the loads in a given cutting area could be minimized.

Once a section of the forest, called a cutting unit, is identified for harvesting, the problem is to subdivide the cutting unit into smaller sections called bunching units. Figure A19.1 shows a cutting unit that has been subdivided into nine bunching units. The numerical sequence shows how the winch is moved from one bunching unit to the next.

FIGURE A19.1
A Cutting Unit Subdivided into Nine Bunching Units

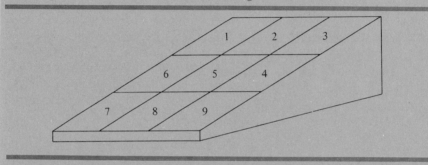

The total time to harvest a cutting unit is dependent upon specification of the bunching units. As the size of the bunching unit is increased, the idle time due to the setup of the winch is reduced because there are fewer bunching units and fewer winch setups necessary. However, as the size of the bunching unit is increased, the production time per tree increases because the average distance froi ɣ the felled trees to the winch is greater. Thus, optimal sizing of the bunching units requires a balance of the setup time for the winch with the production time for the trees. The effect of larger bunching areas (greater distance between anchor trees for the winch) on setup, production, and total time is shown in Figure A19.2. Ideally, we would like to find the bunching unit configuration that minimizes the total time to harvest the cutting unit.

The mathematical formulation of the problem involved two decision variables and seven constraints. The decision variables are as follows:

$$x_1 = \text{length of the bunching unit}$$
$$x_2 = \text{width of the bunching unit}$$

The objective function expresses the total time of production (bunching the trees) and the total time of the winch moves and setups in terms of the two decision variables. Four of the seven constraints represent upper and lower bounds on the acceptable length and width of the bunching units. A fifth constraint restricts the

FIGURE A19.2
Tradeoff Between Setup Time and Production Time

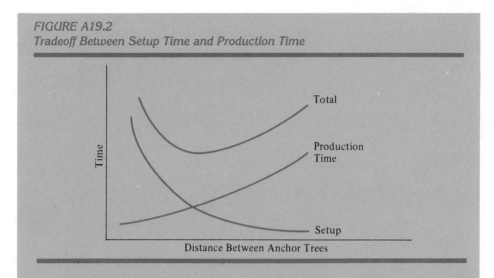

size of the bunching unit so that the winch cable can reach all areas of the unit. A sixth and seventh constraint place upper and lower bounds on the load weight.

Because of the complex nature of the objective function and constraints, it is not possible to simply form the Lagrangian function and take the derivatives in order to solve for the optimal values of x_1 and x_2. The solution procedure used is a computer algorithm that systematically identifies all the local optimal solutions to the problem. The local optimal solution that requires the minimum total time is selected as the optimal solution. The model provided excellent guidelines for increasing the productivity of the prebunching operation.

Questions

1. What factor necessitated the consideration of using helicopters in the harvesting process?
2. What was the objective of the mathematical model developed in this application?
3. What type of solution procedure was used? Why?

Epilogue: Management Science and Decision Support Systems

The purpose of this epilogue is to explore the interaction between management science and decision support systems. As you will see, decision support systems (DSSs) frequently make use of the models developed in this text. As a result, the development of such systems generally requires the joint efforts of management scientists and information systems specialists. We begin by providing a brief overview of DSSs.

DECISION SUPPORT SYSTEMS: AN OVERVIEW

A decision support system is a computer-based information system designed to provide support to a decision process. According to Donovan, "Traditional intuitive methods of decision making are no longer adequate to deal with the complex problems faced by the modern policymaker. Thus systems must be developed to provide the information and analysis necessary for the decisions to be made. These systems are called decision support systems."[1] Alter[2] states that the principal tenets of the decision support systems approach are as follows:

These systems can be designed specifically to facilitate decision processes (as opposed to making clerical transaction processing more efficient).

These systems should support rather than automate decision making.

These systems should be able to respond quickly to the changing needs of decision makers.

Alter points out that the focus of decision support systems is on improving individual effectiveness by improving personal efficiency, expediting problem solving, and improving organizational communications.

[1]Donovan, J. J., "Database System Approach to Management Decision Support." *ACM Transactions on Database Systems*, Vol. 1, No. 4, December 1976, pp. 344–369.
[2]Alter, Steven, *Decision Support Systems: Current Practice and Continuing Challenges*. Reading, Mass., Addison-Wesley, 1980.

Most decision support systems contain four basic subsystems. These subsystems are as follows:

1. Interactive capability that enables the user to communicate directly with the system

2. A data manager that makes it possible to extract necessary information from both internal and external data bases

3. A modeling subsystem that permits the user to interact with management science models by inputting parameters and tailoring situations to specific decision-making needs

4. An output generator with graphics capability that provides the user with the capability to ask "what if" questions and obtain output in easily interpretable form

A Classification of Decision Support Systems

The classification schemes that have been proposed for decision support systems parallel previous efforts from studies of decision making in general. The following are illustrative of the possible classifications:

1. By functional area (we could refer to a DSS for marketing, a DSS for finance, and so on)

2. By level of management involvement (for example, a DSS for strategic planning, a DSS for operational control, and so on)

3. Type of problem—does the DSS support highly structured problems (as in simple inventory control systems) or unstructured types of problems (as in where to locate a new warehouse or plant?)

4. Type of computer system (a large on-line, real-time system versus a network of small minicomputers or microprocessors)

5. Orientation of the system (is the DSS data oriented or model oriented?)

6. Type of decision-making situation (individual, or personal, versus group)

It is not surprising, then, that decision support systems take on a variety of forms. In some cases the DSS will contain a mathematical model that provides a decision maker with recommended courses of action—for example, a large-scale linear programming system designed to be used as a decision aid for production scheduling. In other cases the decision support system may involve a sophisticated computer hardware/software system that simply provides easy and rapid access to decision-making information contained in the data base.

Many of the applications ("Management Science in Practice") provided at the end of selected chapters of this text describe systems that can be called decision support systems. For example, the Optimal Decision Systems application at the end of Chapter 7 involves a DSS for scheduling a fleet of trucks. To better understand the concept of DSS, let us consider some of the details associated with that system and another one designed for portfolio management.

A DSS for Truck Fleet Scheduling

The scheduling process developed by Optimal Decision Systems begins with the DSS generating a schedule and displaying it on a cathode-ray tube (CRT). The schedule presented on the CRT shows the complete assignment of all drivers to all loads (at the various plants) for the day's operation. The dispatcher (system user) reviews this solution and then makes modifications to the daily model, based on a variety of factors. High priority loads that have been assigned to common carriers may be reassigned to company trucks. Loads may be switched to accommodate driver preferences. The dispatcher tries to balance driver workloads; if a driver has a difficult assignment one day, the dispatcher tries not to give that driver a heavy load the next day. The dispatcher might also, after consulting the plants, assign different pickup times in hopes of improving the schedule.

The DSS employs a network flow model (see Chapter 7) to optimize the schedules. After the dispatcher has modified the network model to accommodate the above considerations, a new solution is generated by the DSS. The new solution is displayed on the CRT, and the dispatcher reviews it to see if any further modifications are necessary. When the dispatcher is satisfied, the process is terminated and the schedule implemented. Experience with the DSS has shown that usually two or three iterations are required before the dispatcher is satisfied with the schedule. Figure E.1 depicts the use of this decision support system by the dispatcher.

FIGURE E.1
Decision Support System for Truck Fleet Scheduling

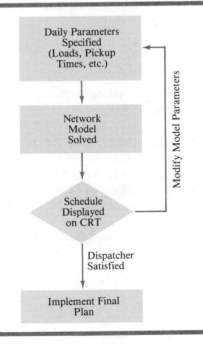

A DSS for Portfolio Management

Keen and Scott Morton[3] describe a DSS to assist portfolio managers. The system is called Portfolio Management System (PMS) and was initially designed by T. P. Gerrity.[4] PMS is a decision support system designed for use by investment managers in the trust departments of banks. It is an interactive system that is designed to provide decision-making support for managing portfolios.

A command language is provided with PMS to assist portfolio managers in interacting with the system. Some of the capabilities of the DSS are as follows:

1. The user can request a display of the contents of a portfolio.
2. Portfolio values and other information, such as price–earnings ratios, etc., can be requested.
3. Graphs and figures can be constructed.
4. Portfolios satisfying certain conditions can be identified.
5. Hypothetical portfolios can be created and evaluated.

The PMS is an example of a DSS for an unstructured problem. No recommended solutions (such as with the DSS for truck fleet scheduling) are presented. It is designed to help with the portfolio management process, but there are no specific criteria. Indeed, a variety of uses have been found for the system with different managers selecting different uses. Some found the system an aid in making cash management decisions, while others found it most helpful in providing a variety of information for interacting with customers.

Weak versus Strong DSS Designs

Moore and Chang[5] describe a weak versus strong dimension for DSS design in terms of how much influence the system exerts on the decision process of the user:

A stronger design is appropriate when it is desired for the DSS to exercise a "stronger" influence on the decision-making process.

A weak design is appropriate when considerable discretion over the choice of a decision is to be left with the manager/user.

Clearly the DSS for truck fleet scheduling has the characteristics of a strong design. The dispatcher is required to choose from among solutions satisfying a minimum cost criterion. Of course, the dispatcher does have some latitude for interacting and rerunning the model. The DSS for portfolio management, PMS, is at the weak end of the spectrum. Information is provided to support the manager's decision process, but the system does not suggest solutions to the user.

Decision support systems that make use of management science models tend to fall on the stronger end of this design dimension. While such systems do not replace the

[3]Keen, Peter G. W., and Michael S. Scott Morton, *Decision Support Systems: An Organizational Perspective.* Reading, Mass., Addison-Wesley, 1978.
[4]Gerrity, T. P., Jr., "The Design of Man-Machine Decision Systems: An Application to Portfolio Management." *Sloan Management Review*, Vol. 12, No. 2, 1971, pp. 59–75.
[5]Moore, Jeffrey H., and Michael G. Chang, "Design of Decision Support Systems." *Data Base*, September/November 1980, pp. 8–14.

judgment of the decision maker, they do force more structure on the problem by the introduction of performance criteria. This is, of course, good if it is desired to influence the decision process so that better decisions can be made. On the other hand, one would prefer a weaker design in cases where performance criteria are not clear and problem definition is vague. All that we can hope for is to provide better support for the decision maker and rely on that person's judgment to develop alternatives and select solutions. Figure E.2 shows the interaction between problem structure and use of management science models on the weak–strong design dimension. Several additional examples of decision support systems currently in use are shown in Table E.1.

FIGURE E.2
Interaction Between Use of Management Science Models and Problem Structure on Weak–Strong Design Dimension

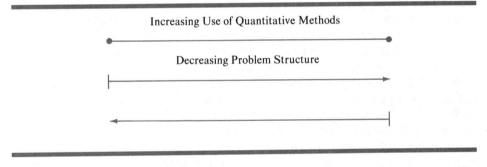

The Impact of Personal Computers

The rapid expansion of the use of personal computers in business has resulted in an increasing number of personal computer-based decision support systems. This is especially true for decision support systems designed to support personal decision making; that is, decision-making situations for which a single decision maker has the responsibility and the authority to make and implement the decision.

TABLE E.1
Examples of Current Decision Support Systems

Organization	Nature of Decision Support System
Goodyear Tire & Rubber Co.	Scheduling maintenance personnel
Equitable Life Assurance	Assisting underwriters in calculating renewal rates on group life insurance policies
American Airlines	Analyzing performance trends from historical data
Kroger	Retail store performance model
Xerox	System for evaluating service technicians
Marathon Oil Company	Market planning model

For example, consider a situation in which the branch managers of a large bank have the authority to make personal loans of up to $100,000 based upon an analysis of the loan application and an interview with the loan applicant. It might be difficult for one branch manager to convince his/her superiors to invest in the development of a decision support system that could support a particular branch manager in deciding whether or not to make a loan. However, if the individual had access to a personal computer, and either he/she or someone else on his/her staff had some programming experience, a custom-designed system could be developed for a modest investment in time and money.

Decision support systems that are designed to support the needs of primarily one decision maker, that are limited in scope, and that were developed to be put into use as quickly as possible are often referred to as *ad hoc* or quick-hit DSSs. For example, a system developed to support the decision needs of one of the branch managers in making loan decisions would be classified as an *ad hoc* DSS. The primary reason why many organizations are beginning to encourage and support the development of *ad hoc* DSSs is that they have found that such systems have a higher success rate than larger systems designed for more general use. This is attributable to the fact that it is substantially more difficult to develop a system that will satisfy the needs of many different decision makers than it is to develop a system to meet the needs of just one decision maker.

Lucas[6] describes a situation involving a major service company with offices in the United States and Europe. To help the vice-chairman of the board of directors determine the possible effect of an employee stock ownership plan, the information systems manager wrote a BASIC program consisting of about 40 lines of code; the program showed the impact of the stock ownership plan over a period of 30 years. When the results were presented to the executive committee, the plan was adopted.

Sullivan and Secrest[7] describe the development of another *ad hoc* decision support system; it was designed to aid production planning at the Dairyman's Cooperative Creamery Association in Tulare, Calif. The system uses an interactive user-friendly linear programming model coded in BASIC and designed to run on a CompuPro microcomputer. The system was developed for a total cost, including hardware and design, of less than $15,000. This system is typical of many of the personal computer-based DSSs that utilize management science techniques such as linear programming.

Many *ad hoc* decision support systems are designed and developed by the user. Thus the availability of software packages that provide easy-to-use interactive capability has increased the use of personal computers in developing decision support systems.

In an article in the *Wall Street Journal*,[8] William Bulkeley describes a feed-mixing system developed by Agricultural Software Consultants, Inc., in Kingsville, Texas. The system asks the farmer or feed mill operator to enter costs and nutritional requirements and then uses a linear programming blending model to develop the optimal product mix. In another application a nursing administrator at Grant Hospital of Chicago used "What's Best!," a linear programming tool developed for personal computers by General Optimization, Inc., to develop monthly schedules for 300 nurses; the estimated cost savings were approximately $80,000 per month.

[6]Lucas, H. C., Jr., *Implementation: The Key to Successful Information Systems*. New York, Columbia University Press, 1981.

[7]Sullivan, Robert S., and Stephen C. Secrest, "A Simple Optimization DSS for Production Planning at Dairyman's Cooperative Creamery Association." *Interfaces*, Vol. 15, No. 5, pp. 46–53.

[8]Bulkeley, William M., "The Right Mix: New Software Makes the Choice Much Easier." *The Wall Street Journal*, March 27, 1987.

Expert Choice (EC) is another commercial software package that offers decision support capabilities on a personal computer. EC, marketed by Decision Support Software, provides a user-friendly environment for implementing the analytic hierarchy process (AHP) on a microcomputer. This process, developed by Thomas L. Saaty, is designed to assist decision makers in solving complex problems involving multiple criteria. The AHP requires the decision maker to make judgments about the relative importance of each of the criteria and then to specify a preference for each decision alternative relative to each criterion. The output of the AHP is a prioritized ranking indicating the overall preference for each of the decision alternatives.

The development of decision support tools such as those described indicates a bright and exciting future for the role of personal computers in the design, development, and implementation of decision support systems.

Expert Systems

An expert system is a computer program that consists of detailed knowledge in a particular subject area. An expert system can be thought of as a computer program that acts as a consultant for decision making.[9] The knowledge base contained in the system is usually represented in the form of IF . . . THEN . . . rules. Along with a database and an inference mechanism, the system in theory captures the knowledge and expertise of one or more experts.

Expert systems represent a direct application of research in the field of artificial intelligence. Proponents of expert systems argue that they can help a decision maker solve complex problems that previously required a human expert. Although there is some controversy in the field of decision support systems as to whether an expert system is really a DSS, there is no doubt that the expert systems that have been developed are capable of simulating the reasoning process of human experts, can apply rules of thumb that are based upon experience, and can recommend the best course of action from a list of alternatives.

Some of the typical applications of expert systems have been in medical diagnosis, credit analysis and approval, insurance policy and rate selection, automobile and computer repair, circuit design and layout, and weather forecasting. One of the leading developers of expert system software is Texas Instruments. Through the Personal Consultant Series, it offers a family of software tools that enable the user to custom-design expert-system applications.

Decision support systems that combine expert-system capabilities with management science models, such as those discussed in this text, offer very exciting potential for those individuals concerned with improving the decision-making process.

Management Science in Decision Support Systems

The purpose of this text is to provide students with a sound conceptual understanding of the role that management science plays in the decision-making process—specifically, that portion of management science dealing with quantitative approaches to decision making. As you have seen, the emphasis has been on management science models and

---

[9]Fordyce, K., P. Norden, and G. Sullivan, "Review of Expert Systems for the Management Science Practitioner." *Interfaces*, Vol. 17, No. 2, pp. 64–77.

how they can be used to contribute to the decision-making process. In this regard, the most important purpose of management science is to support managerial decision making by improving the quality of the information made available to an organization's managers. Thus to a great extent the reason for using management science models and the objective of decision support systems are the same.

Summary

Not all decision support systems make use of the mathematical models of management science. But many DSSs are based heavily on the mathematical models and solution procedures developed by management scientists. The DSS for truck fleet scheduling makes extensive use of management science models (network models). The same is true of the decision support system described in "Management Science in Practice" at the end of Chapter 8; it makes use of a mixed integer programming model to assign customer orders to sources of supply. DSSs that do make use of mathematical models are the ones with a stronger design in the sense of Moore and Chang. Thus we can expect them to have a significant influence on the user's decision process.

Decision support systems are showing promise of being a vehicle for integrating the efforts of management scientists and information system specialists. The potential exists for decision support systems to have a major impact on future managerial decision processes. We are enthusiastic about this potential and anticipate a larger combined role for management science and decision support systems in the organizations of the future.

APPENDIXES

APPENDIX A. AREAS FOR THE STANDARD NORMAL DISTRIBUTION

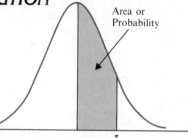

Area or Probability

Entries in the table give the area under the curve between the mean and z standard deviations above the mean. For example, for $z = 1.25$ the area under the curve between the mean and z is 0.3944.

z	0.00	0.01	0.02	0.03	0.04	0.05	0.06	0.07	0.08	0.09
0.0	0.0000	0.0040	0.0080	0.0120	0.0160	0.0199	0.0239	0.0279	0.0319	0.0359
0.1	0.0398	0.0438	0.0478	0.0517	0.0557	0.0596	0.0636	0.0675	0.0714	0.0753
0.2	0.0793	0.0832	0.0871	0.0910	0.0948	0.0987	0.1026	0.1064	0.1103	0.1141
0.3	0.1179	0.1217	0.1255	0.1293	0.1331	0.1368	0.1406	0.1443	0.1480	0.1517
0.4	0.1554	0.1591	0.1628	0.1664	0.1700	0.1736	0.1772	0.1808	0.1844	0.1879
0.5	0.1915	0.1950	0.1985	0.2019	0.2054	0.2088	0.2123	0.2157	0.2190	0.2224
0.6	0.2257	0.2291	0.2324	0.2357	0.2389	0.2422	0.2454	0.2486	0.2518	0.2549
0.7	0.2580	0.2612	0.2642	0.2673	0.2704	0.2734	0.2764	0.2794	0.2823	0.2852
0.8	0.2881	0.2910	0.2939	0.2967	0.2995	0.3023	0.3051	0.3078	0.3106	0.3133
0.9	0.3159	0.3186	0.3212	0.3238	0.3264	0.3289	0.3315	0.3340	0.3365	0.3389
1.0	0.3413	0.3438	0.3461	0.3485	0.3508	0.3531	0.3554	0.3577	0.3599	0.3621
1.1	0.3643	0.3665	0.3686	0.3708	0.3729	0.3749	0.3770	0.3790	0.3810	0.3830
1.2	0.3849	0.3869	0.3888	0.3907	0.3925	0.3944	0.3962	0.3980	0.3997	0.4015
1.3	0.4032	0.4049	0.4066	0.4082	0.4099	0.4115	0.4131	0.4147	0.4162	0.4177
1.4	0.4192	0.4207	0.4222	0.4236	0.4251	0.4265	0.4279	0.4292	0.4306	0.4319
1.5	0.4332	0.4345	0.4357	0.4370	0.4382	0.4394	0.4406	0.4418	0.4429	0.4441
1.6	0.4452	0.4463	0.4474	0.4484	0.4495	0.4505	0.4515	0.4525	0.4535	0.4545
1.7	0.4554	0.4564	0.4573	0.4582	0.4591	0.4599	0.4608	0.4616	0.4625	0.4633
1.8	0.4641	0.4649	0.4656	0.4664	0.4671	0.4678	0.4686	0.4693	0.4699	0.4706
1.9	0.4713	0.4719	0.4726	0.4732	0.4738	0.4744	0.4750	0.4756	0.4761	0.4767
2.0	0.4772	0.4778	0.4783	0.4788	0.4793	0.4798	0.4803	0.4808	0.4812	0.4817
2.1	0.4821	0.4826	0.4830	0.4834	0.4838	0.4842	0.4846	0.4850	0.4854	0.4857
2.2	0.4861	0.4864	0.4868	0.4871	0.4875	0.4878	0.4881	0.4884	0.4887	0.4890
2.3	0.4893	0.4896	0.4898	0.4901	0.4904	0.4906	0.4909	0.4911	0.4913	0.4916
2.4	0.4918	0.4920	0.4922	0.4925	0.4927	0.4929	0.4931	0.4932	0.4934	0.4936
2.5	0.4938	0.4940	0.4941	0.4943	0.4945	0.4946	0.4948	0.4949	0.4951	0.4952
2.6	0.4953	0.4955	0.4956	0.4957	0.4959	0.4960	0.4961	0.4962	0.4963	0.4964
2.7	0.4965	0.4966	0.4967	0.4968	0.4969	0.4970	0.4971	0.4972	0.4973	0.4974
2.8	0.4974	0.4975	0.4976	0.4977	0.4977	0.4978	0.4979	0.4979	0.4980	0.4981
2.9	0.4981	0.4982	0.4982	0.4983	0.4984	0.4984	0.4985	0.4985	0.4986	0.4986
3.0	0.4986	0.4987	0.4987	0.4988	0.4988	0.4989	0.4989	0.4989	0.4990	0.4990

APPENDIX B. RANDOM DIGITS

63271	59986	71744	51102	15141	80714	58683	93108	13554	79945
88547	09896	95436	79115	08303	01041	20030	63754	08459	28364
55957	57243	83865	09911	19761	66535	40102	26646	60147	15702
46276	87453	44790	67122	45573	84358	21625	16999	13385	22782
55363	07449	34835	15290	76616	67191	12777	21861	68689	03263
69393	92785	49902	58447	42048	30378	87618	26933	40640	16281
13186	29431	88190	04588	38733	81290	89541	70290	40113	08243
17726	28652	56836	78351	47327	18518	92222	55201	27340	10493
36520	64465	05550	30157	82242	29520	69753	72602	23756	54935
81628	36100	39254	56835	37636	02421	98063	89641	64953	99337
84649	38968	75215	75498	49539	74240	03466	49292	36401	45525
63291	11618	12613	75055	43915	26488	41116	64531	56827	30825
70502	53225	03655	05915	37140	57051	48393	91322	25653	06543
06426	24771	59935	49801	11082	66762	94477	02494	88215	27191
20711	55609	29430	70165	45406	78484	31639	52009	18873	96927
41990	70538	77191	25860	55204	73417	83920	69468	74972	38712
72452	36618	76298	26678	89334	33938	95567	29380	75906	91807
37042	40318	57099	10528	09925	89773	41335	96244	29002	46453
53766	52875	15987	46962	67342	77592	57651	95508	80033	69828
90585	58955	53122	16025	84299	53310	67380	84249	25348	04332
32001	96293	37203	64516	51530	37069	40261	61374	05815	06714
62606	64324	46354	72157	67248	20135	49804	09226	64419	29457
10078	28073	85389	50324	14500	15562	64165	06125	71353	77669
91561	46145	24177	15294	10061	98124	75732	00815	83452	97355
13091	98112	53959	79607	52244	63303	10413	63839	74762	50289
73864	83014	72457	22682	03033	61714	88173	90835	00634	85169
66668	25467	48894	51043	02365	91726	09365	63167	95264	45643
84745	41042	29493	01836	09044	51926	43630	63470	76508	14194
48068	26805	94595	47907	13357	38412	33318	26098	82782	42851
54310	96175	97594	88616	42035	38093	36745	56702	40644	83514
14877	33095	10924	58013	61439	21882	42059	24177	58739	60170
78295	23179	02771	43464	59061	71411	05697	67194	30495	21157
67524	02865	39593	54278	04237	92441	26602	63835	38032	94770
58268	57219	68124	73455	83236	08710	04284	55005	84171	42596
97158	28672	50685	01181	24262	19427	52106	34308	73685	74246
04230	16831	69085	30802	65559	09205	71829	06489	85650	38707
94879	56606	30401	02602	57658	70091	54986	41394	60437	03195
71446	15232	66715	26385	91518	70566	02888	79941	39684	54315
32886	05644	79316	09819	00813	88407	17461	73925	53037	91904
62048	33711	25290	21526	02223	75947	66466	06232	10913	75336

This table is reproduced with permission from The Rand Corporation, *A Million Random Digits*, The Free Press, New York, 1955 and 1983.

APPENDIX C. VALUES OF $e^{-\lambda}$

λ	$e^{-\lambda}$	λ	$e^{-\lambda}$
0.0	1.0000	3.3	0.0369
0.1	0.9048	3.4	0.0334
0.2	0.8187	3.5	0.0302
0.3	0.7408	3.6	0.0273
0.4	0.6703	3.7	0.0247
0.5	0.6065	3.8	0.0224
0.6	0.5488	3.9	0.0202
0.7	0.4966	4.0	0.0183
0.8	0.4493	4.1	0.0166
0.9	0.4066	4.2	0.0150
1.0	0.3679	4.3	0.0136
1.1	0.3329	4.4	0.0123
1.2	0.3012	4.5	0.0111
1.3	0.2725	4.6	0.0101
1.4	0.2466	4.7	0.0091
1.5	0.2231	4.8	0.0082
1.6	0.2019	4.9	0.0074
1.7	0.1827	5.0	0.0067
1.8	0.1653	5.1	0.0061
1.9	0.1496	5.2	0.0055
2.0	0.1353	5.3	0.0050
2.1	0.1225	5.4	0.0045
2.2	0.1108	5.5	0.0041
2.3	0.1003	5.6	0.0037
2.4	0.0907	5.7	0.0033
2.5	0.0821	5.8	0.0030
2.6	0.0743	5.9	0.0027
2.7	0.0672	6.0	0.0025
2.8	0.0608	7.0	0.0009
2.9	0.0550	8.0	0.000335
3.0	0.0498	9.0	0.000123
3.1	0.0450	10.0	0.000045
3.2	0.0408		

APPENDIX D.   A SHORT TABLE OF DERIVATIVES

1. $\dfrac{d(c)}{dx} = 0$ (where c is a constant)

2. $\dfrac{d(xn)}{dx} = nx^{n-1}$

3. $\dfrac{d(cu)}{dx} = c\,\dfrac{du}{dx}$

4. $\dfrac{d(u + v)}{dx} = \dfrac{du}{dx} + \dfrac{dv}{dx}$

5. $\dfrac{d(uv)}{dx} = u\,\dfrac{dv}{dx} + v\,\dfrac{du}{dx}$

6. $\dfrac{d(un)}{dx} = nu^{n-1}\,\dfrac{du}{dx}$

7. $\dfrac{d\left(\dfrac{u}{v}\right)}{dx} = \dfrac{v\,\dfrac{du}{dx} - u\,\dfrac{dv}{dx}}{v^2}$

8. $\dfrac{d(\ln x)}{dx} = \dfrac{1}{x}$

9. $\dfrac{d(e^x)}{dx} = e^x$

10. $\dfrac{d(\ln u)}{dx} = \left(\dfrac{1}{u}\right)\dfrac{du}{dx}$

11. $\dfrac{d(e^u)}{dx} = e^u\,\dfrac{du}{dx}$

APPENDIX E.   MATRIX NOTATION AND OPERATIONS

Matrix Notation

We define a matrix to be a rectangular array of numbers. For example, the following array of numbers is a matrix D:

$$D = \begin{bmatrix} 1 & 3 & 2 \\ 0 & 4 & 5 \end{bmatrix}$$

The matrix D is said to consist of six elements, where each element of D is a number. In order to identify a particular element of a matrix, we have to specify its precise location. To do this, we introduce the notion of rows and columns.

All elements across some horizontal line in a matrix are said to be in a row of the matrix. For example, elements 1, 3, and 2 in the matrix D are in the first row of D, and elements 0, 4, and 5 are in the second row of D. Thus we see that D is a matrix that has two rows. By convention, we always refer to the top row as row 1, the second row from the top as row 2, and so on.

All elements along some vertical line are said to belong to a column of the matrix. Elements 1 and 0 in the matrix D are elements in the first column of D, elements 3 and 4 are elements of the second column, and elements 2 and 5 are elements of the third column. Thus we see that the matrix D has three columns. By convention, we always refer to the leftmost column as column 1, the next column to the right as column 2, and so on.

An easy way to identify a particular element in a matrix is to specify its row and column position. For example, the element in row 1 and column 2 of the matrix D is the number 3. This is written as

$$d_{12} = 3$$

In general we use the following notation to refer to specific elements of the matrix D:

$$d_{ij} = \text{element located in the } i\text{th row and } j\text{th column of } D$$

We always use capital letters for the names of matrices and the corresponding lowercase versions of the same letter with two subscripts to denote the elements.

The *size* of a matrix is defined to be the number of rows and columns in the matrix and is written as the number of rows $\times$ the number of columns. Thus the size of the matrix D above is 2×3.

Frequently we will encounter matrices that have only one row or one column. For example,

$$G = \begin{bmatrix} 6 \\ 4 \\ 2 \\ 3 \end{bmatrix}$$

784

is a matrix that has only one column. Whenever we have a matrix that has only one column like G, we call the matrix a column vector. In a similar manner, any matrix that has only one row is called a row vector. Using our previous notation for elements of a matrix, we could refer to specific elements in G by writing g_{ij}. However, since G has only one column, the column position is unimportant, and we need only specify the row the element of interest is in. That is, instead of referring to elements in a vector using g_{ij}, we specify only one subscript, which denotes the position of the element in the vector. For example,

$$g_1 = 6 \quad g_2 = 4 \quad g_3 = 2 \quad g_4 = 3$$

Matrix Operations

Matrix Transpose

Given any matrix, we can form the transpose of the matrix by making the rows in the original matrix the columns in the tranpose matrix, and by making the columns in the original matrix the rows in the transpose matrix. For example, if we take the transpose of the matrix

$$D = \begin{bmatrix} 1 & 3 & 2 \\ 0 & 4 & 5 \end{bmatrix}$$

we get

$$D^t = \begin{bmatrix} 1 & 0 \\ 3 & 4 \\ 2 & 5 \end{bmatrix}$$

Note that we use the superscript t to denote the tranpose of a matrix.

Matrix Multiplication

We will demonstrate how to perform two types of matrix multiplication: (1) how to multiply two vectors, and (2) how to multiply a matrix times a matrix.

The product of a row vector of size $1 \times n$ times a column vector of size $n \times 1$ is the number obtained by multiplying the first element in the row vector times the first element in the column vector, the second element in the row vector times the second element in the column vector, and continuing on through the last element in the row vector times the last element in the column vector, and then summing the products. Suppose, for example, that we wanted to multiply the row vector H times the column vector G, where

$$H = \begin{bmatrix} 2 & 1 & 5 & 0 \end{bmatrix} \quad \text{and} \quad G = \begin{bmatrix} 6 \\ 4 \\ 2 \\ 3 \end{bmatrix}$$

The product HG is given by

$$HG = 2(6) + 1(4) + 5(2) + 0(3) = 26$$

The product of a matrix of size $p \times n$ and a matrix of size $n \times m$ is a new matrix of size $p \times m$. The element in the ith row and jth column of the new matrix is given by the vector product of the ith row of the $p \times n$ matrix times the jth column of the $n \times m$ matrix. Suppose, for example, that we want to multiply D times A, where

$$D = \begin{bmatrix} 1 & 3 & 2 \\ 0 & 4 & 5 \end{bmatrix} \quad A = \begin{bmatrix} 1 & 3 & 5 \\ 2 & 0 & 4 \\ 1 & 5 & 2 \end{bmatrix}$$

Let us denote by $C = DA$ the product of D times A. The element in row 1 and column 1 of C is given by the vector product of the first row of D times the first column of A. Thus we get

$$c_{11} = \begin{bmatrix} 1 & 3 & 2 \end{bmatrix} \begin{bmatrix} 1 \\ 2 \\ 1 \end{bmatrix} = 1(1) + 3(2) + 2(1) = 9$$

The element in row 2 and column 1 of C is given by the vector product of the second row of D times the first column of A. Thus we get

$$c_{21} = \begin{bmatrix} 0 & 4 & 5 \end{bmatrix} \begin{bmatrix} 1 \\ 2 \\ 1 \end{bmatrix} = 0(1) + 4(2) + 5(1) = 13$$

Calculating the remaining elements of C in a similar fashion, we obtain

$$C = \begin{bmatrix} 9 & 13 & 21 \\ 13 & 25 & 26 \end{bmatrix}$$

Clearly the product of a matrix and a vector is just a special case of multiplying a matrix times a matrix. For example, the product of a matrix of size $m \times n$ and a vector of size $n \times 1$ is a new vector of size $m \times 1$. The element in the ith position of the new vector is given by the vector product of the ith row of the $m \times n$ matrix times the $n \times 1$ column vector. Suppose, for example, that we want to multiply D times K, where

$$D = \begin{bmatrix} 1 & 3 & 2 \\ 0 & 4 & 5 \end{bmatrix} \quad K = \begin{bmatrix} 1 \\ 4 \\ 2 \end{bmatrix}$$

The first element of DK is given by the vector product of the first row of D times K. Thus we get

$$\begin{bmatrix} 1 & 3 & 2 \end{bmatrix} \begin{bmatrix} 1 \\ 4 \\ 2 \end{bmatrix} = 1(1) + 3(4) + 2(2) = 17$$

The second element of DK is given by the vector product of the second row of D and K. Thus we get

$$[0 \quad 4 \quad 5] \begin{bmatrix} 1 \\ 4 \\ 2 \end{bmatrix} = 0(1) + 4(4) + 5(2) = 26$$

Hence we see that the product of the matrix D times the vector K is given by

$$DK = \begin{bmatrix} 1 & 3 & 2 \\ 0 & 4 & 5 \end{bmatrix} \begin{bmatrix} 1 \\ 4 \\ 2 \end{bmatrix} = \begin{bmatrix} 17 \\ 26 \end{bmatrix}$$

Can any two matrices be multiplied? The answer is no. In order to multiply two matrices, the number of the columns in the first matrix must equal the number of rows in the second. If this property is satisfied, the matrices are said to conform for multiplication. Thus in our example D and K could be multiplied because D had three columns and K had three rows.

Matrix Inverse

The inverse, denoted by A^{-1}, of any square matrix A consisting of two rows and two columns is computed as follows:

$$A = \begin{bmatrix} a_{11} & a_{12} \\ a_{21} & a_{22} \end{bmatrix}$$

$$A^{-1} = \begin{bmatrix} a_{22}/d & -a_{12}/d \\ -a_{21}/d & a_{11}/d \end{bmatrix}$$

where $d = a_{11}a_{22} - a_{21}a_{12}$ is the determinant of the 2×2 matrix A. For example, if

$$A = \begin{bmatrix} 0.7 & -0.3 \\ -0.3 & 0.9 \end{bmatrix}$$

then

$$d = (0.7)(0.9) - (-0.3)(-0.3) = 0.54$$

and

$$A^{-1} = \begin{bmatrix} 0.9/0.54 & 0.3/0.54 \\ 0.3/0.54 & 0.7/0.54 \end{bmatrix} = \begin{bmatrix} 1.67 & 0.56 \\ 0.56 & 1.30 \end{bmatrix}$$

REFERENCES AND BIBLIOGRAPHY

THE ROLE AND NATURE OF MANAGEMENT SCIENCE (CHAPTER 1)

Churchman, C. W., R. L. Ackoff, and E. L. Arnoff, *Introduction to Operations Research*. New York, John Wiley & Sons, 1957.

Forgionne, G. A., "Corporate Management Science Activities: An Update." *Interfaces*, Vol. 13, No. 3, pp. 20–23, 1983.

Gaither, N., "The Adoption of Operations Research Techniques by Manufacturing Organizations." *Decision Sciences*, Vol. 6, No. 4, 1975, pp. 797–813.

Grayson, C. J., Jr., "Management Science and Business Practice," *Harvard Business Review*. Vol. 51, 1973, pp. 41–48.

Hillier, F., and G. J. Lieberman, *Introduction to Operations Research*. 4th ed., San Francisco, Holden-Day, 1986.

Ledbetter, W. and J. Cox, "Are OR Techniques Being Used?" *Industrial Engineering*, Vol. 9, 1977, pp. 19–21.

Radnor, M., and R. D. Neal, "The Progress of Management Science Activities in Large U.S. Industrial Corporations." *Operations Research* 21 (1973): 427–450.

Shannon, R. E., S. S. Long, and B. P. Buckles, "Operations Research Methodologies in Industrial Engineering: A Survey." *AIIE Transactions*, Vol. 12, No. 4, 1980, pp. 364–367.

Thomas, G., and J. DaCosta, "A Sample Survey of Corporate Operations Research." *Interfaces*, August 1979.

Thomas G., and M. Mitchell, "OR in the U.S. Marine Corps: A Characterization." *Interfaces*, June 1983.

LINEAR PROGRAMMING, GOAL PROGRAMMING, TRANSPORTATION, ASSIGNMENT AND TRANSSHIPMENT PROBLEMS (CHAPTERS 2 TO 7)

Anderson, D. R., D. J. Sweeney, and T. A. Williams, *Linear Programming for Decision Making*. St. Paul, West Publishing, 1974.

Bazarra, M. S., and J. J. Jarvis, *Linear Programming and Network Flows*. New York, John Wiley & Sons, 1977.

Bradley, S. P., A. C. Hax, and T. L. Magnanti, *Applied Mathematical Programming*. Reading, Mass., Addison-Wesley, 1977.

Charnes, A., and W. W. Cooper, *Management Models and Industrial Applications of Linear Programming*. New York, John Wiley & Sons, 1961.

Charnes, A., W. W. Cooper, J. K. DeVoe, D. B. Learner, and W. Remecke, "A Goal Programming Model for Media Planning." *Management Science*, Vol. 14, No. 8, April 1968, pp. B423–B430.

Daellenbach, Hans G., and J. Bell, *User's Guide to Linear Programming*. Englewood Cliffs, N.J., Prentice-Hall, 1970.

Dantzig, G. B., *Linear Programming and Extensions*. Princeton, N.J., Princeton University Press, 1963.

Gass, S., *Linear Programming*, 4th ed. New York, McGraw-Hill, 1975.

Hillier, F., and G. J. Lieberman, *Introduction to Operations Research*, 4th ed. San Francisco, Holden-Day, 1986.

Hooker, J. N., "Karmarkar's Linear Programming Algorithm." *Interfaces*, Vol. 16, No. 4, pp. 75–90, 1986.

Ijiri, Y., *Management Goals and Accounting for Control*. Chicago, Rand-McNally, 1965.

Lee, S. M., *Goal Programming for Decision Analysis*. Philadelphia, Auerbach, 1972.

Phillips, D. T., A. Ravindran, and J. J. Solberg, *Operations Research: Principles and Practice*, 2nd ed. New York, John Wiley & Sons, 1987.

Schrage, L., *Linear, Integer, and Quadratic Programming with LINDO*. Palo Alto, Calif., Scientific Press, 1986.

Schrage, L., *User's Manual for Linear, Integer, and Quadratic Programming with LINDO*. Redwood City, Calif., Scientific Press, 1987.

Wagner, H., *Principles of Operations Research with Applications to Managerial Decisions*, 2nd ed. Englewood Cliffs, N.J., Prentice-Hall, 1975.

INTEGER LINEAR PROGRAMMING (CHAPTER 8)

Garfinkel, R. S., and G. L. Nemhauser, *Integer Programming*. New York, John Wiley & Sons, 1972.

Plane, D. R., and C. McMillan, *Discrete Optimization*. Englewood Cliffs, N.J., Prentice-Hall, 1971.

Salkin, H. M., *Integer Programming*. Reading, Mass., Addison-Wesley, 1975.

Zionts, Stanley, *Linear and Integer Programming*. Englewood Cliffs, N.J., Prentice-Hall, 1974.

NETWORK MODELS (CHAPTER 9)

Bazarra, M. S., and J. J. Jarvis, *Linear Programming and Network Flows*. New York, John Wiley & Sons, 1977.

Glover, F., and D. Klingman, "Network Application in Industry and Government." *AIIE Transactions*, December 1977.

Ford, L. R., and D. R. Fulkerson, *Flows and Networks*. Princeton, N.J., Princeton University Press, 1962.

Jensen, P., and J. W. Barnes, *Network Flow Programming*. New York, John Wiley & Sons, 1980.

Minieka, Edward, *Optimization Algorithms for Networks and Graphs*. New York, Marcel Dekker, 1978.

PERT/CPM (CHAPTER 10)

Evarts, H. F., *Introduction to PERT*. Boston, Allyn & Bacon, 1964.

Moder, J. J., and C. R. Phillips, *Project Management with CPM and PERT*, 2nd ed. New York, Van Nostrand, 1970.

Wagner, H., *Principles of Operations Research with Applications to Managerial Decisions*, 2nd ed. Englewood Cliffs, N.J., Prentice-Hall, 1975.

Wiest, J., and F. Levy, *Management Guide to PERT-CPM*, 2nd ed. Englewood Cliffs, N.J., Prentice-Hall, 1977.

INVENTORY MODELS (CHAPTER 11)

Buffa, E. S., and W. Taubert, *Production-Inventory Systems: Planning and Control*, 3rd ed. Homewood, Ill., Richard D. Irwin, 1979.

Davis, E. W., *Case Studies in Material Requirements Planning*. Washington, D.C., APICS, 1978.

Greene, J. H., *Production and Inventory Control Handbook*. New York, McGraw-Hill, 1970.

Hadley, G., and T. M. Whitin, *Analysis of Inventory Systems*. Englewood Cliffs, N.J., Prentice-Hall, 1963.

Hillier, F., and G. J. Lieberman, *Introduction to Operations Research*, 4th ed. San Francisco, Holden-Day, 1986.

Naddor, E., *Inventory Systems*. New York, John Wiley & Sons, 1966.

Orlicky, J., *Material Requirements Planning*. New York, McGraw-Hill, 1975.

Plossl, G. W., *Manufacturing Control: The Last Frontier for Profits*. Reston, Va., Reston, 1973.

Starr, M., and D. Miller, *Inventory Control: Theory and Practice*. Englewood Cliffs, N.J., Prentice-Hall, 1962.

Stockton, R. S., *Basic Inventory Systems: Concepts and Analysis*. Boston, Allyn & Bacon, 1965.

Wagner, H., *Principles of Operations Research with Applications to Managerial Decisions*, 2nd ed. Englewood Cliffs, N.J., Prentice-Hall, 1975.

Wight, O. W., *Production and Inventory Management in the Computer Age*. Boston, Cahners Books, 1974.

COMPUTER SIMULATION (CHAPTER 12)

Christy, D. P., and H. J. Watson, "The Application of Simulation: A Survey of Industry Practice." *Interfaces*, October 1983.
Emshoff, J. R., and R. L. Sisson, *Design and Use of Computer Simulation Models*. New York, Macmillan, 1970.
Fishman, George S., *Principles of Discrete Event Simulation*. New York, John Wiley & Sons, 1978.
Greenberg, S., *GPSS Primer*. New York, John Wiley & Sons, 1972.
Maisel, H., and G. Gnugnoli, *Simulation of Discrete Stochastic Systems*. Chicago, SRA, 1972.
Naylor, T. H., *Computer Simulation Experiments with Models of Economic Systems*. New York, John Wiley & Sons, 1971.
Naylor, T. H., J. L. Balintfy, D. S. Burdick, and K. Chu, *Computer Simulation Techniques*. New York, John Wiley & Sons, 1968.
Schmidt, J. W., and R. E. Taylor, *Simulation and Analysis of Industrial Systems*. Homewood, Ill., Richard D. Irwin, 1970.
Schriber, T. J., *Simulation Using GPSS*. New York, John Wiley & Sons, 1974.

WAITING LINES (CHAPTER 13)

Bhat, U. N., *Elements of Applied Stochastic Processes*. New York, John Wiley & Sons, 1972.
Cooper, R. B., *Introduction to Queueing Theory*. New York, Macmillan, 1972.
Cox, D. R., and W. L. Smith, *Queues*. New York, John Wiley & Sons, 1965.
Gross, D., and C. M. Harris, *Fundamentals of Queueing Theory*. New York, John Wiley & Sons, 1974.
Hillier, F. and G. J. Lieberman, *Introduction to Operations Research*, 4th ed. San Francisco, Holden-Day, 1986
Newell, G. F., *Applications of Queueing Theory*. London, Chapman & Hall, Ltd., 1971.

DECISION ANALYSIS (CHAPTERS 14 AND 15)

Bunn, D., *Applied Decision Analysis*. New York, McGraw-Hill, 1984.
Chernoff, H., and L. E. Moses, *Elementary Decision Theory*. New York, John Wiley & Sons, 1959.
Keeney, R. L., and H. Raiffa, *Decisions with Multiple Objectives: Preferences and Value Trade Offs*, New York, John Wiley & Sons, Inc., 1976.
Raiffa, H., *Decision Analysis*. Reading, Mass., Addison-Wesley, 1968.
Schlaifer, R., *Analysis of Decisions under Uncertainty*. New York, McGraw-Hill, 1969.
Winkler, R. L., *An Introduction to Bayesian Inference and Decision*. New York, Holt, Rinehart & Winston, 1972.
Winkler, R. L., and W. L. Hays, *Statistics: Probability, Inference and Decision*, 2nd ed. New York, Holt, Rinehart & Winston, 1975.

FORECASTING (CHAPTER 16)

Bowerman, B. L., and R. T. O'Connell, *Forecasting and Time Series*. North Scituate, Mass., Duxbury Press, 1979.
Box, G. E. P., and G. M. Jenkins, *Time Series Analysis: Forecasting and Control*, rev. ed. San Francisco, Holden-Day, 1976.
Gilchrist, W. G., *Statistical Forecasting*. New York, John Wiley & Sons, 1976.
Hanke, J. E., and A. G. Reitsch, *Business Forecasting*, 2nd ed. Boston, Allyn & Bacon, 1986.
Makridakis, S., S. C. Wheelwright, and Victor E. McGee, *Forecasting: Methods and Applications*, 2nd ed. New York, John Wiley & Sons, 1983.
Nelson, C. R., *Applied Time Series Analysis*. San Francisco, Holden-Day, 1973.
Thomopoulos, N. T., *Applied Forecasting Methods*. Englewood Cliffs, N.J., Prentice-Hall, 1980.
Wheelwright, S. C., and S. Makridakis, *Forecasting Models for Management*, 4th ed. New York, John Wiley & Sons, 1985.

MARKOV PROCESSES (CHAPTER 17)

Derman, C., *Finite State Markovian Decision Processes*. New York, Academic Press, 1970.
Howard, R. A., *Dynamic Programming and Markov Processes*. Cambridge, Mass., M.I.T. Press, 1960.
Kemeny, J. G., and J. L. Snell, *Finite Markov Chains*. Englewood Cliffs, N.J., Prentice-Hall, 1960.
Phillips, D. T., A. Ravindran, and J. J. Solberg, *Operations Research: Principles and Practice*. New York, John Wiley & Sons, 1976.
Ross, S. M., *Applied Probability Models with Optimization Applications*. San Francisco, Holden-Day, 1970.

DYNAMIC PROGRAMMING (CHAPTER 18)

Bellman, R., *Dynamic Programming*. Princeton, N.J., Princeton University Press, 1957.
Dreyfus, S., *Dynamic Programming and the Calculus of Variations*. New York, Academic Press, 1965.
Dreyfus, S., and A. M. Law, *The Art and Theory of Dynamic Programming*. New York, Academic Press, 1977.
Hillier, F., and G. J. Lieberman, *Introduction to Operations Research*, 4th ed. San Francisco, Holden-Day, 1986.
Nemhauser, G. L., *Introduction to Dynamic Programming*. New York, John Wiley & Sons, 1967.

CALCULUS-BASED SOLUTION PROCEDURE (CHAPTER 19)

Beightler, C. S., D. T. Phillips, and D. Wilde, *Foundations of Optimization*, 2nd ed. Englewood Cliffs, N.J., Prentice-Hall, 1979.
Cooper, L., and D. Steinberg, *Introduction to Methods of Optimization*. Philadelphia, W. B. Saunders, 1970.
Gottfried, B. S., and J. Weisman, *Introduction to Optimization Theory*. Englewood Cliffs, N.J., Prentice-Hall, 1973.
Himmelblau, D. M., *Applied Nonlinear Programming*. New York, McGraw-Hill, 1972.
Luenberger, D. G., *Introduction to Linear and Nonlinear Programming*. Reading, Mass., Addison-Wesley, 1973.

MANAGEMENT SCIENCE AND DECISION SUPPORT SYSTEMS (EPILOGUE)

Alter, Steven, *Decision Support Systems: Current Practice and Continuing Challenges*. Reading, Mass., Addison-Wesley, 1980.
Blanning, R. W., "What is Happening in DSS?" *Interfaces*, October 1983.
Davis, Gordon B., *Management Information Systems: Conceptual Foundations, Structure and Development*. New York, McGraw-Hill, 1974.
Donovan, J. J., "Database System Approach to Management Decision Support." *ACM Transactions on Database Systems*, Vol. 1, No. 4, December 1976, pp. 344–369.
Fordyce, K., P. Norden, and G. Sullivan, "Review of Expert Systems for the Management Science Practitioner." *Interfaces*, Vol. 17, No. 2, pp. 64–77, 1987.
Gerrity, T. P., Jr., "The Design of Man-Machine Decision Systems: An Application to Portfolio Management." *Sloan Management Review*, Vol. 12, No. 2, 1971, pp. 59–75.
Hicks, James O., *Management Information Systems: A User Perspective*, 2nd ed. St. Paul, Mn, West Publishing Company, 1987.
Keen, Peter G. W., and Scott Morton, Michael S., *Decision Support Systems: An Organizational Perspective*. Reading, Mass., Addison-Wesley, 1978.
McLeod, R., *Management Information Systems*. Chicago, Science Research Associates, Inc.,
Mann, R. I., and H. J. Watson, "A Contingency Model for User Involvement in DSS Development." *MIS Quarterly*, March 1984.

Moore, Jeffery H., and Chang, Michael G., "Design of Decision Support Systems." *Data Base*, September/November 1980, pp. 8–14.

Scott, Jim, "The Management Science Opportunity: A Systems Development Viewpoint," presentation at the Society for Management Information Systems Annual Conference in Washington, D.C., September 1978.

Waterman, Donald A., *A Guide to Expert Systems*, Reading, Mass., Addison-Wesley, 1986.

Watson, H. J., and M. Hill, "Decision Support Systems or What Didn't Happen with MIS." *Interfaces*, October 1983.

ANSWERS TO EVEN-NUMBERED PROBLEMS

CHAPTER 1

2. Methodological developments based on research advances in computer technology
4. The problem is large, complex, important, new, and repetitive
6. Iconic—scale model of a new building
   Analog—barometer
   Mathematical—inventory cost equation
8. a. max $\quad 10x + 5y$
   s.t.
   $$5x + 2y \leq 40$$
   $$x \geq 0,\, y \geq 0$$
   b. Controllable inputs: x and y
   Uncontrollable inputs: profit, labor hours per units, and total labor hours available
   d. $x = 0,\, y = 20$, profit $= \$100$
10. For $a = 3$, $x = 13\frac{1}{3}$ and profit $= \$133$
    For $a = 4$, $x = 10$ and profit $= \$100$
    For $a = 5$, $x = 8$ and profit $= \$80$
    For $a = 6$, $x = 6\frac{2}{3}$ and profit $= \$67$
12. A deterministic model with $d =$ distance, $m =$ miles per gallon, and $c =$ cost per gallon, where Total Cost $= (2d/m)c$
14. Quicker to formulate, easier to solve and/or more easily understood
16. a. max $6x + 4y$
    b. $50x + 30y \leq 80,000$
    $\quad 50x \qquad\quad \leq 50,000$
    $\qquad\quad 30y \leq 45,000$

CHAPTER 2

6. $x_1 = 100$, $x_2 = 50$, $z = 750$
10. $x_1 = \frac{12}{7}$, $x_2 = \frac{15}{7}$, $z = \frac{69}{7}$
12. a. $x_1 = 2$, $x_2 = 2$, $z = 10$
    b. Yes, constraint 2
14. a. $x_1 = 300$, $x_2 = 420$, $z = 10,560$
    b. $x_1 = 708$, $x_2 = \quad 0$, $z = 14,160$
    c. $x_1 = 540$, $x_2 = 252$, $z = \quad 7668$

16. a. $x_1 = 500, x_2 = 150$
   b. $3700
   c. C & S   725 Hrs.
        F   300 Hrs.
        P & S   100 Hrs.
   d. C & S   175 Hrs.
        F   0 Hrs.
        P & S   0 Hrs.

18. a. $x_1 = 687\frac{1}{2}, x_2 = 500, z = 3562.50$
   b. Yes; $x_1 = 500, x_2 = 800, z = 3900$

20. $x_1 = 800, x_2 = 1200, z = 8400$

22.

Extreme Pt	z	
$x_1 = 250, x_2 = 100$	800	$s_1 = 125, s_2 = 0, s_3 = 0$
$x_1 = 125, x_2 = 225$	925	$s_1 = 0, s_2 = 0, s_3 = 125$
$x_1 = 125, x_2 = 350$	1300	$s_1 = 0, s_2 = 125, s_3 = 0$

24. $x_1 = 12, x_2 = 3, z = 63$

26. $x_1 = 12.14, x_2 = 3.86, z = \$0.60/\text{can}$
   Surplus for protein $= 2.55$

28. a. max $1x_1 + 1.5x_2 + 0s_1 + 0s_2 + 0s_3 + 0s_4$
        s.t.

$$
\begin{aligned}
1x_1 + 1x_2 + 1s_1 + &= 150 \,(\text{Dough}) \\
\tfrac{1}{4}x_1 + \tfrac{1}{2}x_2 + 1s_2 &= 50 \,(\text{Topping}) \\
1x_1 - 1s_3 &= 50 \,(\text{Regular}) \\
1x_2 - 1s_4 &= 25 \,(\text{Delux}) \\
x_1, x_2, s_1, s_2, s_3, s_4 &\geq 0
\end{aligned}
$$

   b. $s_1 = 0, s_2 = 0, s_3 = 50, s_4 = 25$
   c. Dough and topping are the binding constraints

30. a. max $100x_1 + 200x_2$
        s.t.

$$
\begin{aligned}
1x_1 + 1x_2 &\leq 500 \\
1x_1 &\leq 200 \\
2x_1 + 6x_2 &\leq 1200 \\
x_1, x_2 &\geq 0
\end{aligned}
$$

   b. Add a slack variable to each constraint with $s_1 =$ unused land, $s_2 =$ amount below soybean limit, and $s_3 =$ unused planting time
   c. $x_1 = 200, x_2 = 133\frac{1}{3}, z = 23{,}333$
   d. $x_1 = 0, x_2 = 0$
        $x_1 = 200, x_2 = 0$
        $x_1 = 200, x_2 = 133\frac{1}{3}$
        $x_1 = 0, x_2 = 200$
   e. Labor hours

32. a. $x_1 = 0, x_2 = 0$
        $x_1 = 35, x_2 = 0$
        $x_1 = 25, x_2 = 20$
        $x_1 = 18.75, x_2 = 25$
        $x_1 = 0, x_2 = 25$
   b. Yes; $x_1 = 18.75, x_2 = 25, z = 2250$
   c. Alternate optimal solutions: $x_1 = 25, x_2 = 20$ and $x_1 = 18.75, x_2 = 25$

34. b. $x_1 = 5$, $x_2 = 1$ and $x_1 = 2$, $x_2 = 4$
  c. $x_1 = 2$, $x_2 = 4$, $z = 10$
36.   Add a slack variable to each constraint.
      max $5x_1 + 2x_2 + 8x_3 + 0s_1 + 0s_2 + 0s_3$
38. b. $x_1 = {}^{20}\!/_3$, $x_2 = {}^{8}\!/_3$, $z = 30{}^{2}\!/_3$
  c. $s_1 = {}^{28}\!/_3$, $s_2 = 0$, $s_3 = 0$
40.   Infeasibility
42. a. $x_1 = {}^{30}\!/_{16}$, $x_2 = {}^{30}\!/_{16}$, $z = {}^{60}\!/_{16}$
  b. $x_1 = 0$, $x_2 = 3$, $z = 6$
  c. $1x_1 + {}^{5}\!/_3 x_2$
44.   Alternate optimal solutions: $x_1 = 125$, $x_2 = 225$ and $x_1 = 250$, $x_2 = 100$
46. a.   Infeasibility
  b.   Alternate optimal solutions: $x_1 = 500$, $x_2 = 150$ and $x_1 = 0$, $x_2 = 400$
  c.   All three constraints removed

CHAPTER 3

2.   Shadow price $= 44.44$
4. a.   Constraint 1 : 1.5, Constraint 2 : 0
  b.   Same as shadow prices
6. a.   Constraint 1 : .333, Constraint 2 : .333, Constraint 3 : 0
  b.   Constraint 1 : $-.333$, Constraint 2 : $-.333$, Constraint 3 : 0
8. a.   Optimal solution: $x_1 = 9$, $x_2 = 4$
  b.   Constraint 2 : 0, Constraint 3 : .0769
10. a. $x_1 = 0$, $x_2 = 10$
  b.   Same as for problem 7: $x_1 = 7$, $x_2 = 7$
12. a. $4 \le c_1 \le 12.0012$ $3.333 \le c_2 \le 10$
  c.
Min RHS	Max RHS
725.0038	∞
133.320	399.9999
75.00	134.9982
  d.   560.012
14. a.   more than $7.00
  b.   more than $3.50
  c.   None
16. a. $x_1 = 30$, $x_2 = 25$ minimum production cost $= \$55.00$
  b. $.5 \le c_1 < \infty$ $0.0 \le c_2 \le 2$
  c. $-.50, -.50, 0.00$
  d. $.50, .50, 0.00$
  e.   Increase by 2.50
  f.
Min RHS	Max RHS
70.0	∞
0.0	40.0
$-\infty$	25.0
18. a. $-\infty < c_1 \le 4.05$ $5.923 \le c_2 \le 9.00$
        $2.00 \le c_3 \le 12.00$ $-\infty < c_4 \le 4.50$
  b.   Accumulated percent change $= 78.57$.   100% rule indicates no change

c.
Min RHS	Max RHS
133.333	800.00
275.00	∞
137.50	825.00

d. Yes

20. a. $1.33 \leq c_1 \leq 15.54$ $14.32 \leq c_2 < \infty$
$13.50 \leq c_3 \leq 180.00$

b. Same

c. Accumulated percent change $= 83.00$. 100% rule indicates no change

22. a. Yes

b. -2.0

c. Alternate optimal solutions

d. Produce college ball

24. a. max $.20x_1 + .10x_2 + .06x_3$
s.t.

$$.10x_1 + .05x_2 + .01x_3 \leq 15000$$
$$x_1 \geq 30000$$
$$x_2 \geq 30000$$
$$x_3 \geq 60000$$
$$x_1 + x_2 + x_3 \leq 300000$$
$$x_1, x_2, x_3 \geq 0$$

b. $x_1 = 120000$ $x_2 = 30000$ $x_3 = 150000$

c. $.15 \leq c_1 \leq .60$ $-\infty \leq c_2 \leq .1222$ $.02 \leq c_3 \leq .20$

CHAPTER 4

2. a.
Advertisement	Number	Budget Allocation
television	4	$ 8,000
radio	14	4,200
newspaper	10	6,000
		$18,200

Audience $= 1,052,000$

b. Approximately 5,100

4. a. $x_1 = 77.89$, $x_2 = 63.16$, $z = \$3,284.21$

b. Dept. A $15.79, Dept. B $47.37

c. $x_1 = 87.21$, $x_2 = 65.12$, $z = \$3,341.34$
Dept. A 10 hours, Dept. B 3.2 hours

6. a. $x_1 = 500$, $x_2 = 300$, $x_3 = 200$, $z = \$550$

b. $0.55

c. Aroma 75, Taste 84.4

d. $0.60

8.   50 units of product 1
0 units of product 2
300 hours dept. A, 600 hours dept. B

10.
	Modern Line	Old Line	
1	500	0	
2	300	400	Cost $= \$3850$

12.

	Mfr.	Purchase
Base	3750	1250
Cartridge	5000	0
Handle	3750	1250

Cost = $11,875

  b. Depts. A and B; add only to A
  c. Only 25 hours can be used

14. x_i = number of 10-inch rolls processed by cutting alternative i
  a. $x_1 = 0$, $x_2 = 125$, $x_3 = 500$, $x_4 = 1500$, $x_5 = 0$, $x_6 = 0$, $x_7 = 0$; 2125 rolls with waste of 750 inches
  b. 2500 rolls with no waste; however, $1\frac{1}{2}$ inch size is overproduced by 3000 units

16. a. 5 super, 2 regular, and 3 econotankers
      Total cost $583,000; monthly operating cost $4650
  b. Order all supertankers

18. $x_1 = 48$, $x_2 = 96$, $z = 456$
  Assembler times: 480, 480 and 456

20. a. Marginal = .06; average = .079; diminishing marginal returns have set in
  b. Exposure is not as great for TV as it is for the other media

22. $x_1 = 5$, $x_2 = 7$, $d_1^+ = 4$, $e^- = 2$, $d_3^- = 1$, $e_3^+ = 5$, $z = 12$

CHAPTER 5

2. $x_1 = 5$, $x_2 = 1$, $x_3 = 4$
4. c. basic variables s_1, s_2, s_3;
         nonbasis variables x_1, x_2, x_3; yes
  d. 0
  e. x_3 enters and s_2 leaves
  f. 30; 750
  g. $x_1 = 10$, $x_3 = 30$, $s_1 = 20$, $z = 800$
8. a. $x_1 = 540$, $x_2 = 252$
  b. $7668
  c. 630, 480, 708, 117
  d. $s_1 = 0$, $s_2 = 120$, $s_3 = 0$, $s_4 = 18$
10. $x_2 = 650$, $s_1 = 690$, $s_3 = 310$, $z = 3250$
12. 35
14. b. No, any $c_j - z_j > 0$ will work
16. x_1 = number of units of product A; x_2 = number of units of product B;
       x_3 = number of units of product C; $x_1 = 0$, $x_2 = 0$, $x_3 = 33\frac{1}{3}$, $z = 500$
18. x_1 = Gal. Heid. Sweet, x_2 = Gal. Heid. Reg, x_3 = Gal Deut.
  a. $x_1 = 0$, $x_2 = 50$, $x_3 = 75$, $z = 210$
  c. Grade B grapes and hours
22. $x_2 = 2$, $x_3 = \frac{1}{2}$, $x_1 = 9$, $z = 41.5$
24. $x_1 = 20$ Gal., $x_2 = 30$ Gal., $x_3 = 33$ Gal;
       $x_1 = 0$, $x_2 = 0$, $x_3 = 2400$, $z = 480$

26.

	Incentive	Temptation	
John	480	0	
Brenda	0	480	
Red	0	800	$z = 46,400$

28. $x_1 = 203.5$, $x_2 = 285.2$, $x_3 = 20$, $z = 4,269,565$
30. Alternate optimal solutions
$x_1 = 4$, $x_2 = 4$ and $x_1 = 8$, $x_2 = 0$; $z = 24$
32. Alternate optimal solutions
$x_1 = 4$, $x_2 = 0$, $x_3 = 0$ and $x_1 = 0$, $x_2 = 0$, $x_3 = 8$; $z = 8$
34. Infeasible

CHAPTER 6

2. a. $12 \le b_2 < \infty$
  b. $233\frac{1}{3} \le b_3 \le 400$
  c. 104
4. a. $0 \le b_1 \le 12$ $2 \le b_2 \le 6$ $4.5 \le b_3 < \infty$
  b. $1\frac{7}{8}$
  c. $7\frac{1}{2}$
  d. 0
6. a. $495.6 \le b_1 \le 682.36$
  b. $480 \le b_2 < \infty$
  c. $580 \le b_3 \le 900$
  d. $117 \le b_4 < \infty$
  e. Cutting and dyeing, Finishing
8. a. 131.25
  b. No decrease
  c. 262.5
10. a. $24 \le c_1 \le 60$ $20 \le c_2 \le 50$
  b. No change in solution. Profit reduced to $1350
  c. $33.33
  d. Pay up to $44.44 per ton for material 3
12. a. $x_3 = 15$ $x_4 = 8\frac{1}{3}$
  b. $2 \le c_3 < \infty$
  c. New solution $x_1 = 10$, $x_4 = 8\frac{1}{3}$
  d. $-\infty < c_2 \le 4\frac{1}{2}$
  e. No effect
14. b. $u_1 = \frac{3}{10}$ $u_2 = 0$ $u_3 = \frac{54}{30}$
  c. Machines A and C at capacity. Machine C has priority
16. Dual because of fewer constraints
20. c. $u_1 = \frac{1}{2}$ $u_2 = 0$ $u_3 = \frac{1}{2}$
  d. Reduce cost by $.50
24. a. Extreme point 1 : $x_1 = 0$, $x_2 = 6$ value = 0
     Extreme point 2 : $x_1 = 5$, $x_2 = 0$ value = 15
     Extreme point 3 : $x_1 = 4$, $x_2 = 2$ value = 16
  b. $u_1 = \frac{1}{3}$, $u_2 = \frac{4}{3}$

c. $u_1 = 3$, $u_2 = 0$ value = 24
$u_1 = \frac{1}{3}$, $u_2 = \frac{4}{3}$ value = 16
$u_1 = 0$, $u_2 = 2$ value = 20
d.   Values of dual extreme points $\geq$ values of primal extreme points
e.   No

CHAPTER 7

2. b.   Change to maximize objective function
c. $P_1 - W_2$: 300 $P_2 - W_1$: 100 $P_2 - W_2$: 100
$P_2 - W_3$: 300 $P_3 - W_1$: 100
4. b.   Detroit - Atlanta   100
St. Louis - Atlanta   100
St. Louis - Houston   200
Denver - Boston   300
Total cost: $3900
c.   Add $x_{11} = 100$
d.   Delete x_{31} and x_{22}
6. a. $O_1 - D_1$: 150 $O_1 - D_2$: 100 $O_2 - D_2$: 100
$O_2 - D_3$: 50 $O_3 - D_3$: 100
b. $O_1 - D_1$: 150 $O_1 - D_2$: 50 $O_1 - D_3$: 50
$O_2 - D_2$: 150 $O_3 - D_3$: 100
c. $O_1 - D_1$: 50 $O_1 - D_2$: 50 $O_1 - D_3$: 150
$O_2 - D_2$: 150 $O_3 - D_1$: 100
8.   Clifton Springs - D_2 4000
Clifton Springs - D_4 1000
Danville - D_1 2000
Danville - D_4 1000
Customer 2 is 1000 short
Customer 3 is 3000 short
10. a.   Product A: 300 on I, 1200 on II, 500 on III
Product B: 500 on III
Product C: 1200 on I
b.   Yes   Product A: 1500 on I, 500 on III
Product B: 500 on III
Product C: 1200 on II
Recommend second solution—only one changeover
12.   Jackson - B   Ellis - A   Smith - C
14.   Bostock - Southwest
Miller - Northwest
16.   Toy—2   Auto Parts—4
Housewares—3   Record—1
18.   1—B   2—C
3—A   4—D   Total time = 74 hours
20.   Minimum value = 12
22.   1—D   2—C   3—B   4—A

24. b. $P_1 - W : 400 \quad\quad P_2 - W : 350$
$\quad\quad P_2 - R_2 : 250 \quad\quad W - R_1 : 750$
$\quad$ c. $P_1 - W : 400 \quad\quad P_2 - W : 100$
$\quad\quad P_2 - R_1 : 250 \quad\quad P_2 - R_2 : 250$
$\quad\quad\quad\quad W - R_1 : 500$

26. c. $O_1 - T_1 : 400 \quad\quad O_2 - T_1 : 450$
$\quad\quad O_3 - T_2 : 350 \quad\quad T_1 - D_2 : 500$
$\quad\quad T_1 - D_3 : 300 \quad\quad T_1 - D_4 : 50$
$\quad\quad T_2 - D_1 : 200 \quad\quad T_2 - D_4 : 150$

CHAPTER 8

2. b. $x_1 = 1.43, x_2 = 4.29$; its value is 41.47
$\quad\quad x_1 = 1, x_2 = 4$; its value is 37
$\quad$ c. $x_1 = 0, x_2 = 5$; its value is 40

4. a. $x_1 = 3, x_2 = 0$; its value is 30
$\quad\quad$ Lower bound $= 30$, upper bound is 36.7 (actually an upper bound of 36)
$\quad$ b. $x_1 = 3, x_2 = 2$; its value is 30
$\quad$ c. LP relaxation: $x_1 = 0, x_2 = 5.71$; its value is 34.26
$\quad\quad$ Rounding down: $x_1 = 0, x_2 = 5$ with value 30
$\quad\quad$ Upper bound $= 34.26$, lower bound $= 30$
$\quad\quad$ Optimal integer: $x_1 = 0, x_2 = 5$; its value is 30

6. b. $x_1 = 1.96, x_2 = 5.48$; its value is 7.44
$\quad\quad$ Upper bound $= 7.44$, lower bound $= 6.96$
$\quad$ c. $x_1 = 1.29, x_2 = 6$; its value is 7.29

8. $x_1 = x_2 = x_3 = 1$ and $x_4 = 0$ with a value of $140,000

10. $x_1 = 0, x_2 = 2, x_3 = 6\frac{2}{3}$

14. a. $x_1 + x_3 + x_5 + x_6 = 2$
$\quad$ b. $x_3 - x_5 = 0$
$\quad$ c. $x_1 + x_4 = 1$
$\quad$ d. $x_4 \le x_1 \quad\quad x_4 \le x_3$
$\quad$ e. $x_4 \le x_1 \quad\quad x_4 \le x_3 \quad\quad x_4 \ge x_1 + x_3 - 1$

16. b.&c. $y_9 = 6, y_{10} = 2, y_{12} = 6, y_1 = 1$, and $y_3 = 6$; all other variables are 0
$\quad$ d. $x_9 = 1, x_{11} = 4, y_9 = 5, y_{12} = 5, y_3 = 2$; all other variables equal zero

CHAPTER 9

2.

Node	Shortest Route from Node 7
1	7–6–5–3–1
2	7–4–2
3	7–6–5–3
4	7–4
5	7–6–5
6	7–6

4. 1–4–5–6–8

6.

Node	Shortest Route from Node C
1	C–1
2	C–2
3	C–3
4	C–4
5	C–3–5
6	C–3–6
7	C–3–8–7
8	C–3–8
9	C–4–10–9
10	C–4–10

8. 1–2–8–10–11 or
1–4–3–7–6–9–11;
value = 15

10. length = 38

12. 1–2, 2–5, 5–6, 6–3, 6–8, 3–4, 8–7; length = 29

14. 28 miles

16. 11,000 vehicles per hour

18. a.   10 hours; 10,000 gallons per hour

20. 23; 5

CHAPTER 10

2. b.

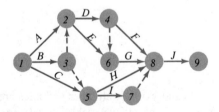

4. a.   A–D–G
   b.   Expected time: 15 months

6. a.   A–D–F–H
   b.   22 weeks
   c.   No
   d.   Yes, 2 weeks
   e.   ES = 3; LS = 4; EF = 10; LF = 11

8. b.   B–C–E–F–H
   d.   Yes; 49 weeks

10. a.

Activity	A	B	C	D	E	F
Expected time	5	9	8	8.83	7.17	6
Variance	.11	.11	.44	.25	.25	.11

   b.   23.83; .47

12. a. A–D–H–I
   b. 25.66 days
   c. .2578
14. a. A–D–F–G
   b. 1.5 days
   c. 29.5; 2.36
   d. .6255
16. a.
Path	A–D–G–J	A–C–F–J	B–H–I–J
Expected time	16	13	10
Variance	3.92	2.03	1.27

   b.
Path	A–D–G–J	A–C–F–J	B–H–I–J
Probability	.9783	1.0000	1.0000

18. c. A–B–C–G–H–I
   d. .0968; Definitely start prior to February 1
20. b. $y_A = 0$, $y_B = 1$, $y_C = 0$, $y_D = 2$, $y_E = 1$, $y_F = 1$, $y_G = 1$, $y_H = 0$
   additional cost = $2,427
   c. Critical path is B–D–E–F–H
22. Selected parts of the model:
   Obj. Function: min $600y_A + 700y_B + 400y_C + 400y_D + 500y_E + 400y_F + 500y_G$
   Node 5: $x_5 \geq x_4 + 2 - y_F$
   or $-x_4 + x_5 + y_F \geq 2$
   Activity F: $y_F \leq 1$
   Overall completion: $x_6 \leq 12$
   The total model has 15 constraints
24. a.

   d.
Crash	Weeks	Cost
A	2	$ 40,000
B	2	$ 30,000
C	1	$ 20,000
D	1	$ 10,000
E	1	$ 12,500
		$112,500

   f. $112,500

26.
Activity	Cost/Week
A	15
B	8
C	1
D	20
E	2

F	1
G	20
H	5
I	2
J	1

28. b. 6% overrun; followup desired on activity D
30. Corrective action desired:
Activity E—one week behind
Activity F—$3000 cost overrun

CHAPTER 11

4. 240
6. a. 16
   b. $2106
   c. 15/year, every 3–4 weeks
8. 12; 5/year; $225,200
10. $Q^* = 1414$ bats, $T = 1.414$ months, and $t = .3535$ months; hence, a full two-week or 10-day production period is perhaps desirable. In this case ($t = 10$), $Q = 1333$ and $T = 1.333$ months.
12. a. 1789   b. 1333   c. 894   d. 827
14. 4500, 9 days
16. 136
18. 67, 27
20. $Q = 100$
22. 300; $480
24. a. 12
   b. 15
   c. 3; $15
26. a. 80
   b. 35; 10
   c. .1587; 2
28. a. 500
   b. 580
30. a. 22
   b. .40
32. a. 166
   b. .292
34. 3
36. Order engines: 10
   Order air cleaners: 7
   Order filter housings: 2
38. Order base: 13
   Order wheel: 9
   Order tires: 4

CHAPTER 12

2. a. $0 - 0.12, 1 - 0.24, 2 - 0.37, 3 - 0.19, 4 - 0.08$
4. a. $0 - 0.04, 1 - 0.10, 2 - 0.16, 3 - 0.44, 4 - 0.20, 5 - 0.06$
6. Number served = 3, total profit = \$3.75, average profit = \$1.25, number lost = 0
12. Preferred order size is 200
16. Average costs: holding − 190.00, order − 12.50, shortage − 0, total − 202.50

CHAPTER 13

2. a. 6/hour
   b. 39.35%
   c. 63.21%
   d. 4.98%
4. a. 0.833
   b. 0.167
   c. ½ hour
   d. 4.167
6. a. ½ day
   b. ⅜ day
   c. Yes
8. a. .56   b. .2464   c. .1084
   d. .0477   e. .0375   f. .35
10. b. No; speed up service or hire an additional consultant
   c. W_q = .0667 hours = 4 minutes; service goal is met
12. Use the one-channel, two-person system
14. P_0 = 0.4118; L = 1.01; W_q = 1.08 min; it appears acceptable
16. a. $\frac{1}{10}$
   b. 24 seconds
   c. $\frac{6}{10}$
   d. Excellent
18. a. ½   b. ⅙   c. No
20. a. .50   b. .167
22. a. 7.998 minutes   b. 16.67%   c. 1.25 minutes   d. 50%
24. a. 4

CHAPTER 14

2. a. d_1 b. d_4
4. Sell the rights; EVPI = 25
6. d_2
8. b. Purchase blade attachment

   c. Same as (b)

   d. 2150

10. Expected value criterion—d_1; however, d_2 may be preferred

12. b. d_3

   c. EVPI = \$600

14. b. d_2–EMV(d_2) = 206.25

16. $P(s_1|I) = 0.19$, $P(s_2|I) = 0.24$, $P(s_3|I) = 0.57$

18. a. $P(I_1) = 0.56$, $P(I_2) = 0.44$

   b. 0.57, 0.43, 0.18, 0.82

   c. If I_1–d_2, if I_2–d_1, EMV = 292

20. b. If I_1–d_1, if I_2–d_2, EMV = \$101.5

   c. EVSI = \$1500, sell for \$100,000

22. If I–d_1, if $\bar{I}$–d_3

24. a. 0.355

   b. If favorable—d_1, if unfavorable—d_2

   c. \$3710

   d. 41.2%

26. a. Do not fund

   b. Do not hire the consultants

28. a. I_1–d_3, I_2–d_2, I_3–d_1

   b. 1054

   c. 22%

30. a. $P(I|s_1) = 0.0000$, $P(I|s_2) = 0.048$, $P(I|s_3) = 0.092$, $P(I|s_4) = 0.133$

   b. 0.000, 0.159, 0.488, 0.353

   c. 100% inspect

CHAPTER 15

2. a. No insurance; EMV(d_2) = 5000

   b. Lottery: \$0 and \$200,000

   c. Insurance; EU(d_1) = 9.9

4. a. Route B; EV(B) = 58.5

   b. Lottery: 45 and 90

   c. Route A: EV(A) = 7.6

6. Decision maker A—d_1; EU(d_1) = 7.5

Decision maker B—d_2; EU(d_2) = 6.75

Decision maker C—d_2; EU(d_2) = 7.25

8. a.

		s_1 Win	s_2 Lose	
Bet	d_1	350	−10	P(win) = 1/38
Don't bet	d_2	0	0	P(lose) = 37/38

   b. Don't bet; EMV(d_1) = −\$.53, EMV(d_2) = \$0

   c. .26

10. a. Western; EV(Western) = 26%

   b. Lottery: 15% and 40%

   c. Musical; EU(musical) = 3.4 (risk taker)

CHAPTER 16

2. a. Selected forecasts: week 4, 19.33; week 9, 18.33; week 12, 17.83
   b. MSE = 11.49
4. a. $F_{13} = .2Y_{12} + .16Y_{11} + .128Y_{10} + .1024Y_9 + .08192Y_8 + .32768F_8$
   b. The weights sum to 1 and decrease as we use more remote data values; moving averages weights the data values equally
6. Selected forecasts: month 5, 112.5, month 10, 116.95, month 12, 99.24; MSE = 540.54 for $\alpha = .5$, MSE = 510.28 for $\alpha = .3$; $\alpha = .3$ provides better forecasts
8. 20.26
10. $T_t = 28{,}800 + 421t$
12. a. Linear trend appears to exist
    b. $T_t = 19.99 + 1.77t$; average cost increase is $1.77
14. $T_t = 197.71 + 6.82t$; $T_8 = 252.27$ and $T_9 = 259.09$
16. a. Yes
    b. $T_t = 22.86 + 15.54t$
    c. $T_8 = 147.18$
18. Selected seasonal factors: month 4, .966; month 8, 1.225; month 12, .787
20. a. Selected seasonal factors: quarter 2, .6138; quarter 4, 1.6163
    b. Largest effect in quarter 4
22. a. $T_t = -.345 + .995t$
    b. 20.55, 21.55, 22.54, 23.54
    c. 26.10, 13.15, 11.27, 38.13
24. a. $\hat{y} = 3766.67 - 322.22x$
    b. 2477.79

CHAPTER 17

2. b. $\pi_1 = 0.5$, $\pi_2 = 0.5$
   c. $\pi_1 = 0.6$, $\pi_2 = 0.4$
4. a. $\pi_1 = 0.92$, $\pi_2 = 0.08$
   b. $85
6. a. MDA
   b. $\pi_1 = \frac{1}{3}$, $\pi_2 = \frac{2}{3}$
8. 3 − 1 (0.59), 4 − 1 (0.52)
10. 1420 will be lost

CHAPTER 18

2. a. 1 − 4 − 6 − 9 − 10
   b. 4 − 6 − 9 − 10
4. a. Set up a stage for each possible length of the log
   b. Create a stage for every length
6. 200 − 3,200 − 2,100 − 1 ($2900)
8. a. $d_1 = 200$, $d_2 = 300$, $d_3 = 500$
   b. Same as part a
10. 800°F catalyst C_2, separator S_1, weekly profit = $4470

CHAPTER 19

2. a. $40/9$
   b. 4
4. 4 ($540)
6. a. $20
   b. $-x^2 + 20x - 20$
   c. 10
8. $x_1 = 0, x_2 = 2$ is a saddle point
   $x_1 = 2, x_2 = -2$ is a local minimum
   $x_1 = -2, x_2 = -2$ is a local minimum
10. $x_1 = 6, x_2 = 3$ ($40,000 earnings)
12. Provides maximum solution

14. $x_1 = \dfrac{4}{\sqrt{34/5}}, x_2 = \dfrac{3}{\sqrt{34/5}}$ (minimum)

   $x_1 = \dfrac{-4}{\sqrt{34/5}}, x_2 = \dfrac{-3}{\sqrt{34/5}}$ (maximum)

16. $x_1 = 36/13, x_2 = 2/13$

INDEX

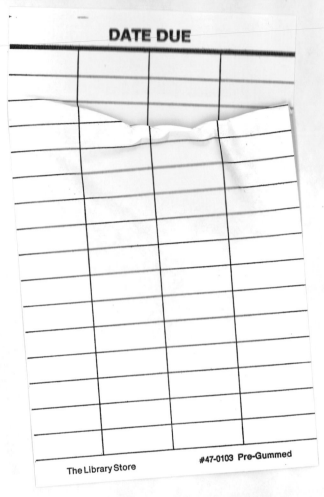

DATE DUE